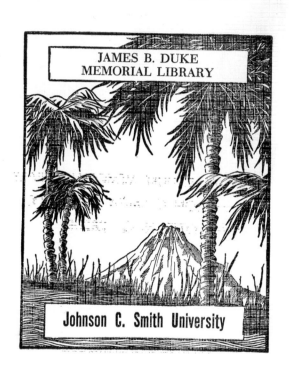

Compiler
Design
Theory

Compiler Design Theory

PHILIP M. LEWIS II
DANIEL J. ROSENKRANTZ
RICHARD E. STEARNS
General Electric Company

 ADDISON-WESLEY PUBLISHING COMPANY
Reading, Massachusetts · Menlo Park, California
London · Amsterdam · Don Mills, Ontario · Sydney

Second printing, May 1976

Copyright © 1976 by Addison-Wesley Publishing Company, Inc. Philippines copyright 1976 by Addison-Wesley Publishing Company, Inc.

ISBN 0-201-14455-7
ABCDEFGHIJ-HA-79876

To our wives — Carole   *and our children — Betsy*
                        Charlotte   *Chris*
                        Rhoda   *Holly*
                                                          Jody
                                                            Mike
                                                            Patty
                                                            Sherry

THE SYSTEMS PROGRAMMING SERIES

*The Program Development Process Part I—The Individual Programmer	Joel D. Aron
The Program Development Process Part II—The Programming Team	Joel D. Aron
*The Design and Structure of Programming Languages	John E. Nicholls
Mathematical Background of Programming	Frank Beckman
Structured Programming	Harlan D. Mills Richard C. Linger
The Environment for Systems Programs	Frederic G. Withington George Gardner

*An Introduction to Database Systems	C. J. Date
Interactive Computer Graphics	Andries Van Dam
*Sorting and Sort Systems	Harold Lorin
*Compiler Design Theory	Philip M. Lewis Daniel J. Rosenkrantz Richard E. Stearns

*Recursive Programming Techniques	William Burge
Conceptual Structures: Information Processing in Mind and Machines	John F. Sowa

IBM EDITORIAL BOARD

Foreword

The field of systems programming primarily grew out of the efforts of many programmers and managers whose creative energy went into producing practical, utilitarian systems programs needed by the rapidly growing computer industry. Programming was practiced as an art where each programmer invented his own solutions to problems with little guidance beyond that provided by his immediate associates. In 1968, the late Ascher Opler, then at IBM, recognized that it was necessary to bring programming knowledge together in a form that would be accessible to all systems programmers. Surveying the state of the art, he decided that enough useful material existed to justify a significant codification effort. On his recommendation, IBM decided to sponsor The Systems Programming Series as a long term project to collect, organize, and publish those principles and techniques that would have lasting value throughout the industry.

The Series consists of an open-ended collection of text-reference books. The contents of each book represent the individual author's view of the subject area and do not necessarily reflect the views of the IBM Corporation. Each is organized for course use but is detailed enough for reference. Further, the Series is organized in three levels: broad introductory material in the foundation volumes, more specialized material in the software volumes, and very specialized theory in the computer science volumes. As such, the Series meets the needs of the novice, the experienced programmer, and the computer scientist.

Taken together, the Series is a record of the state of the art in systems programming that can form the technological base for the systems programming discipline.

The Editorial Board

Preface

This book is intended to be a text for a one- or two-semester course in compiler design at the senior or first-year-graduate level. It covers the basic mathematical theory underlying the design of compilers and other language processors and shows how to use that theory in practical design situations.

The applicable mathematical concepts come from automata and formal language theory. We have developed these concepts in a rigorous but non-formal style to make them understandable to a wide range of readers, including those who are not mathematically oriented. We believe that automata and formal language concepts constitute an excellent basis both for teaching compiler design and for designing real compilers. We ourselves have designed two commercial compilers based on this theory.

In our selection and presentation of material we emphasize "translation," in contrast to just "parsing." The formal concept of a syntax-directed attributed translation is used to specify the input-output performance of various language processors.

Another concept we emphasize is that of an "automaton." We use such automata as finite-state machines and pushdown machines as basic building blocks for compilers. We emphasize synthesis procedures for designing an automaton to perform a specified translation.

The material in this book constitutes an essentially complete design theory for the lexical and syntax portions of a compiler. The use of attributed translations allows us to include in the syntax-box design a good deal of what is often characterized as "code generation" or "semantics." The book also includes additional material on code generation and a brief survey of code optimization.

The subject of run-time implementation is not discussed. Although this topic is of considerable importance in deciding what code a compiler should generate, we believe it is not a part of "compiler design theory" but rather a separate subject that should be treated in a course dealing specifically with programming language structures.

Because the automata theory in this text has been selected for its relevance to compiler design, certain basic automata-theory concepts have been bypassed; consequently, this book cannot be used as the exclusive text in an automata theory course. However, students who have taken a course using this book should find a subsequent course in automata-theory greatly simplified. Conversely, some training in basic automata theory permits students to cover the material in this book more rapidly; thus the text can be used either prior to or after taking an introductory course in automata theory.

Compiler Design Theory is completely self-contained and assumes only the familiarity with programming languages and the mathematical sophistication commonly found in juniors or seniors.

After an introductory chapter, Chapters 2, 3, and 4 cover finite-state machines and other topics relevant to lexical processing. Chapters 5 and 6 introduce pushdown machines and context-free grammars.

If students have had an introductory course in automata theory, much of the material in Chapters 2 through 6 can be omitted and the remainder covered very rapidly emphasizing the applications to compilers. In any case, Sections 2.7 through 2.11 can be omitted.

Chapter 7 introduces the ideas of translations and attributed translations; this material should be mastered before progressing.

Chapters 8, 9, and 10 cover top-down processing while Chapters 11, 12, and 13 deal with bottom-up processing. These portions of the book are independent and the instructor can elect to cover either or both of them. In any case, Sections 8.7, 10.5, 12.6, and 13.6 can be omitted.

To demonstrate the theoretical concepts in a "real" design situation, the book includes the design of a compiler for a subset of BASIC. The language was selected to be sufficiently complex to illustrate the concepts presented in the book and to have a trivial run-time implementation (since, as we have said, we believe the implementation of language features to be a separate subject). However the language has a variety of syntactic and semantic features including a syntactically recursive control structure (a FOR loop). In Chapter 4, we design a lexical box for the compiler and in Chapters 10 and 12 we design syntax boxes that operate top-down and bottom-up, respectively. In Chapter 14 we design a code generator. Either this design or some extension of it can be implemented in a laboratory portion of the course.

Chapter 15 contains a brief survey of code optimization.

The book also contains three appendices: Appendix A is a language manual for MINI-BASIC; Appendix B discusses those aspects of mathematical relations needed for various test and design procedures; Appendix C presents several methods for transforming a given programming-language grammar into one of the special forms presented in the text.

The material in this book has been taught for several years in one-semester first-year graduate courses at Rensselaer Polytechnic Institute in Troy, N.Y. and at the State University of New York at Albany. It has also been taught as a one-semester undergraduate elective at Union College in Schenectady, N.Y. We would like to thank the students at these institutions whose occasional bewildered looks have motivated us to do several rewrites of the material.

We would like to express our appreciation to the following people who read early versions of the manuscript and made helpful comments: John Hutchison, Michael Hammer, Stephen Morse, John Johnston, Donna Phillips, Daniel Berry, Alyce Orne, Gary Fisher, Walter Stone, James Roberts, and Robert Blean.

We are also grateful to the management of the General Electric Research and Development Center and especially to Richard L. Shuey and James L. Lawson who established the free and stimulating environment in which our work was done and provided the time and opportunity to write this book.

Schenectady, N.Y.   P.M.L.
December 1975   D.J.R.
                           R.E.S.

Contents

CHAPTER 3
IMPLEMENTING FINITE STATE MACHINES

CHAPTER 4
MINI-BASIC LEXICAL BOX

CHAPTER 5
PUSHDOWN MACHINES

CHAPTER 6
CONTEXT-FREE GRAMMARS

CHAPTER 7
SYNTAX-DIRECTED PROCESSING

CHAPTER 8
TOP-DOWN PROCESSING

CHAPTER 9
TOP-DOWN PROCESSING OF ATTRIBUTED GRAMMARS

CHAPTER 14
A CODE GENERATOR FOR THE MINI-BASIC COMPILER

CHAPTER 15
A SURVEY OF OBJECT CODE OPTIMIZATION

APPENDIX A
MINI-BASIC LANGUAGE MANUAL

APPENDIX B
RELATIONS

APPENDIX C
GRAMMATICAL TRANSFORMATIONS

1
Introduction

1.1 LANGUAGE PROCESSORS

There is a natural communication gap between man and machine. Computer hardware operates at a very atomic level in terms of bits and registers, whereas people tend to express themselves in terms of natural languages such as English or in mathematical notation. This communication gap is usually bridged by means of an artificial language which allows the human to express himself with a well-defined set of words, sentences, and formulas that can be "understood" by a computer. To achieve this communication, the human is supplied with a user manual which explains the constructs and meanings allowed by the language, and the computer is supplied with software by which it can take a stream of bits representing the commands or programs written in the language by the human and translate this input into the internal bit patterns required to carry out the human's intent.

Existing computer languages vary widely in complexity, including, for example:

the instruction set of a particular computer, the machine language, which is interpreted by the hardware or micro-programs of the machine itself;

assembly languages, the "low-level" languages that largely mirror the instruction set of a particular computer;

control-card and command languages that are used to communicate with an operating system;

"high-level" languages, such as FORTRAN, PL/I, LISP, etc., which have a complicated structure and do not depend on the instruction set or operating system of any particular machine.

1

We use the term "language processor" to describe the computer programs that enable the computer to "understand" the commands and inputs supplied by the human. Broadly speaking, there are two types of such language-processing programs: interpreters and translators.

An *interpreter* is a program that accepts as input a program written in a computer language called the *source language* and performs the computations implied by the program.

A *translator* is a program that accepts as input a program written in a *source language* and produces as output another version of that program written in another language called the *object language*. Usually the object language is the machine language of some computer, in which case the program can be immediately executed on that computer. Translators are rather arbitrarily divided into *assemblers* and *compilers* which translate low-level and high-level languages, respectively.

The common mathematical foundation of all language processing is the theory of automata and formal languages. Since the main concern of this book is the design of compilers, we present those portions of this theory that are most relevant to compiler design and show practical methods whereby this mathematics may be applied. Although the theory is presented in the context of compilers, it can be used in the design of any language processor.

1.2   A NAIVE COMPILER MODEL

The job of a compiler is to translate the bit patterns that represent a program written in some computer language into a sequence of machine instructions that carry out the programmer's intent. This task is sufficiently complex that understanding or designing a compiler as a single entity is both difficult and cumbersome. Therefore, it is desirable to consider the compilation process as an interconnection of smaller processes whose tasks can be more easily described.

The selection of these subprocesses for any particular compiler may depend on the details of the language being processed and, in any case, can best be done when taking available design theory into account. Hence, we do not want to endorse a specific set of subprocesses. On the other hand, it is impossible to describe a compiler design theory without having some ideas as to a possible internal organization of a compiler. Therefore, in order to establish a frame of reference, we introduce a rather naive but specific model.

In this model, the compiling job is done by a serial connection of three boxes which we call the *lexical box,* the *syntax box,* and the *code generator.* These three boxes have access to a common set of tables where long-term or

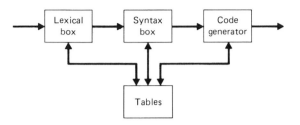

Figure 1.1

global information about the program may be entered. One such table, for example, is the *symbol table,* in which information about each variable or identifier is accumulated. The connection of these boxes and tables is shown in Fig. 1.1. We now describe the boxes in more detail.

Lexical box　The input to a compiler is a bit pattern representing a string of characters. The lexical box is concerned with breaking up the string of characters into the words they represent. For example, the character string might be:

$$IFB1 = 13GOTO4$$

The lexical box would discern the fact that this character string represents the word IF followed by variable B1 followed by an equality operator followed by the number 13 followed by the word GOTO followed by the label 4. Thus, the twelve input characters are transformed into six new entities. These entities are often called *tokens* and this is the name we use.

　　Each token consists of two parts, a *class* part and a *value* part. The class part denotes that the token is in one of a finite set of classes and indicates the nature of the information included in the value part. Returning to our example, the variable B1 might be of class "variable" and have a value which is a pointer to the symbol table entry for B1. This symbol table pointer is, in effect, the internal name of variable B1. The token 13 might be of class "constant," and the value might be the bit pattern for 13. The equal sign might be of class "operator," and the value might indicate which operator. The token IF might be of class "IF" and require no value information.

　　If we regard the symbol table as a dictionary, then the lexical processing is somewhat analogous to grouping the letters into words and finding their locations in the dictionary. Thus, the name "lexical" is appropriate for this box.

Syntax box　The syntax box is concerned with translating the sequence of tokens constructed by the lexical box into another sequence that more closely reflects the order in which the programmer intends the operations in the program to be performed. For example, if a FORTRAN programmer writes

$$A + B * C$$

he intends that the numbers represented by B and C be multiplied together and that the number represented by A be added to that result. A suitable translation for the above expression might be

$$\text{MULT}(B, C, R1) \ \text{ADD}(A, R1, R2)$$

where MULT($B, C, R1$) is interpreted to mean "multiply B and C and call the result $R1$" and ADD($A, R1, R2$) is interpreted to mean "add A and $R1$ and call the result $R2$". Thus, the five tokens supplied from the lexical box have been transformed into two new entities which describe the same intent. These new entities are called *atoms* and form the output of the syntax box. The important accomplishment is that the sequence of atoms reflects the order in which things are to be carried out. The programmer has written the plus operator ahead of the multiply operator, but the syntax box must put the multiplication first.

Again we assume that each atom consists of a class part and a value part. Thus, MULT($B, C, R1$) might be of class "MULT" and have a value part consisting of three pointers pointing to table entries for B, C, and $R1$, respectively. Within the compiler, the atom would be represented by an integer denoting "MULT" and the three pointers denoting the value part.

To carry out its transformation, the syntax box must account for the structure of the language in a way that is analogous to the grammatical considerations required for natural language translations. The translation of the sample expression might be compared with the translation of English (where verbs usually appear in the middle of a sentence) into German (where verbs frequently appear at the end). Thus, the name "syntax box" is appropriate for this box.

Code generator The code generator is concerned with expanding the atoms constructed by the syntax box into a sequence of computer instructions that carries out the same intent. The exact expansion may depend on the table entries referenced by the atoms and by the anticipated state of the computer when the code is actually executed. In the case of an atom like MULT($B, C, R1$), the expansion might depend on the type of the operands B and C, the location of the operands, and the contents of the computer registers. Integer operands would require integer multiplication, floating-point operands would require floating-point operations, and mixed operands would require additional type-conversion instructions. In some computers, a register would have to be made available to calculate the product.

In order to produce efficient code, it is frequently desirable that the code generator carry out a sophisticated analysis of the run-time contents of the various machine registers in order to avoid reloading information already available and to select the most favorable registers in which to store variables, partial results, and miscellaneous transient information. The particular choice of register-management scheme must depend to a large degree on the machine for which the code is being generated, as the number and capabilities of the registers vary greatly from machine to machine.

Compiler subactivities which are related to the "meaning" of the symbols are sometimes classified as *semantic processing*. For example, the semantics of an identifier may include its type and, if it is an array, its dimensions. One kind of semantic processing includes filling in the symbol table with the properties of the individual identifiers as they become known. Another kind of semantic processing includes the activities that depend on data types. For example, we suggested that a code generator might be concerned with the selection of fixed- or floating-point instructions for the expansion of the MULT(B, C, $R1$) atom. As this decision depends on the types of the operands, it could be called a semantic decision. In some compilers, certain semantic activities are carried out in a separate *semantic box* inserted between the syntax box and the code generator.

Compiler subactivities which are strictly speaking unnecessary, but which enable one to achieve better object programs, are often referred to as *optimization*. For some compilers, the optimization plans are so ambitious that an optimization box is inserted between the syntax box (or the semantic box if there is one) and the code generator. For example, an optimization box would probably be desirable if one wanted to take computations that occur inside a loop, but whose results never change during the execution of the loop, and do these computations once before entering the loop. The effect of an optimization box is often a rearrangement of the atoms.

Altogether, we have discussed five kinds of compiler subactivities, namely lexical processing, syntax processing, semantic processing, optimization, and code generation. These five concepts form a useful and perhaps indispensable set of heuristics for thinking about and organizing a compiler design. Nevertheless, these classifications should not be taken too seriously because:

1. the classification of some subactivities is open to debate;
2. the subactivities should be carried out where most convenient and not in a "box" which is named with a particular classification;
3. the lexical and syntactic conventions followed internally by the compiler may be somewhat different than those given in the human-oriented programming manual, although the overall effect must, of course, be what the human expects.

1.3 PASSES AND BOXES

Our discussion of the naive compiler model of Fig. 1.1 did not describe the way control is passed between the three boxes. Consider for example the interface between the lexical box and the syntax box. At least two types of interfaces could be designed.

In one type of interface, each time a token is produced by the lexical box, control is passed to the syntax box to process that token. Control is returned to the lexical box when the next token is needed.

In the second type of interface, the lexical box produces the entire token sequence before control is passed to the syntax box. In this case the lexical box is said to be a separate pass.

The naive compiler model could be organized into passes in four distinct ways. If the model is organized as a one-pass compiler, control is bounced back and forth among the boxes, as tokens and atoms are requested and produced. If it is organized as a three-pass compiler, the lexical box would prepare a complete file of lexical tokens which would then be used by the syntax box to produce a complete file of atoms which would then be used by the code generator to produce machine code. There are also two possible two-pass organizations. In one, the lexical and syntax boxes act together as a single pass to produce a complete file of atoms for the code generator. In the other, the syntax box and code generator are treated as a single pass.

In general, the more boxes a compiler has, the more possibilities exist for factoring the design into passes. An organization into passes may introduce some extra overhead because each interface between passes requires that an entire sequence of output symbols be saved. However, there are often compelling reasons for using the pass concept. Among these reasons are:

Logic of the language

Sometimes, the source language itself implies that a compiler must contain at least two passes. This occurs whenever a portion of the compiler requires information about later parts of the program. For example, if declarations about an identifier or variable could appear after it is used, it might be impossible for code to be generated before some processing was done on the entire input program. In this case, the code generator would require a separate pass.

Code optimization

Sometimes better object code can be produced if the code generator has information about the entire program. For example, some optimization methods require a knowledge of all the places in the program where variables are used and can have their value changed. Therefore, a complete pass of the program is required before optimization can begin.

Memory considerations

Frequently, multipass compilers use less storage space than single-pass compilers since the code for each pass can reuse the storage occupied by the code for the previous pass.

Each pass of a compiler can be designed as a single box or an interconnection of boxes. A box, for the purposes of our design theory, is simply a portion of the compiler that is conceived and designed as an entity.

Since boxes are the fundamental design entity, we will be mainly concerned with the specification and design of boxes. Whether a box is to be a pass or a portion of a pass is not of particular concern to the design theory. For example, the job of the lexical box is to produce tokens and can be discussed independently of whether these tokens are put into an intermediate file or sent immediately to the syntax box.

1.4   THE RUN-TIME IMPLEMENTATION

Usually the compiler design problem is specified to the compiler designer in a rather incomplete manner. The source language itself is frequently specified fairly precisely using a language manual of some type, but the details of the output the compiler is to produce are often not specified at all. The designer is only told that the output must correspond to the "meaning" of the language and must satisfy certain requirements as to execution speed or memory.

Therefore, the first step in the design is to plan what the output of the compiler should be. This involves deciding what data structures and control mechanisms will exist at execution time to implement the various features of the language; for example, how arrays will be laid out in memory and accessed, how procedures will be called, and, if recursive procedures are allowed, how the recursion will be handled. The set of these data structures and control mechanisms is called the *run-time implementation* of the language.

Specifying the run-time implementation is an important part of the overall compiler-design problem. However, this subject is not within the scope of this book as our emphasis is on the translation problem itself. We assume that both the input and the desired output are known and that we are concerned with how to perform the translation.

1.5   MATHEMATICAL TRANSLATION MODELS

The design theory presented in this book is based on a mathematical theory of language translation and translators. The compiler itself is a translator, as are each of the three boxes of the naive compiler model. However, the translators dealt with by the theory are not necessarily the boxes of the naive model. Instead, they are "machines" or "automata" that perform the basic operations required for translation but are simple enough that they can be studied in great theoretical detail. These automata are the "building blocks" of our design theory in the sense that we intend to design compilers as an interconnection of these basic machines.

The design theory consists of two parts:

1. the mathematical study of these machines including:
    a) their capabilities as language translators,
    b) their synthesis, given the translations they are to perform;
2. the application of this theory to compiler design including:
    a) expressing the design of the compiler (or a box of a compiler) as an interconnection of these machine models,
    b) implementing or simulating these models as a computer program.

The mathematical discipline that deals with machine models of this type is called automata theory. In fact, there is a hierarchy of automata theory models appropriate for the design of compilers. These models generally exhibit a tradeoff between their capabilities as translators and the efficiency in time and space of their implementation via computer programs. Thus, it behooves the designer to select the simplest machine that can perform a given job.

The material in this book is organized so that the simpler machine models are presented first. Even these very simple models are adequate in practice to solve a great many language-processing problems.

1.6   THE MINI-BASIC COMPILER

The primary emphasis of this book is on those aspects of automata theory that are useful in compiler design. In order to demonstrate this usefulness and show how the theory can be applied in a practical situation, we carry out the design of a compiler as we go along through the book.

The language for which the compiler is designed is a subset of the BASIC language, which we call MINI-BASIC (Manifestly-Imaginatively-Named-Illustrative-BASIC). A manual for MINI-BASIC is given in Appendix A. Although the language is probably too simple to be commercially acceptable, the design of the compiler illustrates many of the problems and solutions that do arise in practical compiler design.

The MINI-BASIC compiler is a one-pass compiler based on the naive three-box model of Section 1.2, and consists of a lexical box, a syntax box, and a code generator. Each box is assumed to be an independent entity. First the lexical box processes a symbol from the input string. When finished, it can either get another symbol from the input string or produce some output symbols that have the effect of waking up the syntax box. Similarly, when the syntax box is finished with these symbols, it can either ask the lexical box for a new input or produce some output symbols for the code generator. The code generator then processes these symbols producing the final output of the compiler and can then ask the syntax box for a new input.

The design of the lexical box is given in Chapter 4, and syntax boxes are designed in Chapters 10 and 12. The design of the code generator is presented in Chapter 14.

2
Finite-State Machines

2.1 INTRODUCTION

Since automata theory is the basis of the compiler-design theory presented in this book, we begin our studies with what is perhaps the most fundamental automata-theory concept — the *finite-state machine*. By a "machine" we do not of course refer to a real machine but to a mathematical model, whose properties and behavior we can study, and which we can simulate with a computer program. The finite-state machine is the simplest of the automata theory models and serves as the control device for all the other automata theory machines.

In addition to being basic to automata theory, finite-state machines are also directly useful in a number of compiler design situations because:

1. Finite-state machines have the capacity of performing (at least to a first approximation) a number of the easier compiling tasks. In particular, the design of the lexical box can almost always be based on a finite-state machine.

2. Since the simulation of a finite-state machine by a computer requires only a small number of operations to process an individual input symbol, it operates rapidly.

3. The simulation of a finite-state machine requires a fixed amount of memory storage which simplifies memory-management problems.

4. A number of theorems and algorithms exist which enable one to construct and simplify finite-state machines for various purposes.

The term "finite-state machine" is actually used in a number of different ways, depending on the intended applications. A variety of formal definitions may be found in automata literature. The commonality of these definitions is that they model computing devices that have a fixed and finite amount of memory and read sequences made up from a finite set of input symbols. The principle differences in the definitions concern what the machines do in the way of output. We begin our study in the next section with a finite-state machine whose only "output" is an indication as to whether or not a given input sequence is "acceptable." An acceptable sequence may be thought of as "well formed" or "syntactically correct"; for example, a sequence that is supposed to denote a numeric constant would not be well formed if it contained two decimal points.

2.2   FINITE-STATE RECOGNIZERS

A finite-state recognizer is a model of a finite-state device that discriminates between well-formed or "acceptable" input sequences and those input sequences that are not acceptable. Although this is a purely mathematical concept definable in terms of sets, sequences, and functions, it is best understood in the imagery of a computing machine.

An example of a recognition problem is determining whether a sequence of 1's and 0's has odd parity (i.e., if the number of 1's in the sequence is odd). A finite-state machine to solve this problem would therefore "accept" all sequences with an odd number of ones and "reject" those sequences with an even number of ones. Such a machine is called a "parity checker." We will design such a parity checker during the subsequent discussions as we develop the terminology for describing finite-state recognizers.

The input to a finite-state recognizer is a sequence of symbols from a finite set. This finite set is called the *input alphabet* of the machine and represents the set of symbols the machine is prepared to process. The sequences the machine accepts as well as those it rejects are all made up of symbols from the input set only. Any symbols not in the input set cannot be applied as input to the machine. For the parity checker, the input set consists of two symbols, 0 and 1.

We imagine that the finite-state machine is presented with an input sequence one symbol at a time. The capacity of the machine to retain information about the earlier symbols in the input sequence is represented by a finite set of states. Using this imagery, all the machine can remember about the past is that the past inputs caused the machine to enter some given state. The state thus represents the machine's memory about the past.

The parity checker will be designed so as to remember whether some initial sequence had odd or even parity. To this end, we let the state set of our parity checker have two states and give these states the suggestive names ODD and EVEN.

One of these states is designated to be the *starting state,* and the machine is assumed to be in that state when it begins its operation. The parity checker has EVEN as its starting state, since initially zero 1's have been encountered and zero is an even number.

When an input symbol is read in, the machine changes its state in a way that depends only on the current state and input symbol. This change of state is called a *transition.* It may happen that the new state is the same as the old state.

The operation of a machine is described mathematically by a function δ, called the transition function, which gives the new state s_{new} in terms of the current state s_{old} and the current input symbol x. Symbolically, this relation is written

$$\delta(s_{old}, x) = s_{new}$$

For the parity checker, we let

$$\delta(EVEN, 0) = EVEN$$
$$\delta(EVEN, 1) = ODD$$
$$\delta(ODD, 0) = ODD$$
$$\delta(ODD, 1) = EVEN$$

This is the function dictated by our interpretation that EVEN and ODD represent even and odd parity, respectively. The transition function reflects the fact that the parity changes if and only if the new input symbol is a 1.

Some of the states of a machine are designated as *accepting states.* If a sequence causes a machine started in the starting state to end up in an accepting state, then we say that the input sequence is *accepted* by the machine. If the last state entered is not an accepting state, we say that the sequence is *rejected.* The parity checker has one accepting state, namely ODD.

Summarizing the above paragraphs in a single sentence, we can define a finite-state recognizer by the following statement.

A finite state machine is described by:

1. a finite set of input symbols,

2. a finite set of states,

3. a transition function δ which assigns a new state to every combination of state and input,

4. a state designated as the starting state, and

5. a subset of the states designated as accepting states.

A machine transition from state s_{old} to state s_{new} while reading input symbol x may be described pictorially by

$$s_{old} \xrightarrow{\ x\ } s_{new}$$

For instance, for the parity checker we can write

$$\text{ODD} \xrightarrow{\ 1\ } \text{EVEN}$$

This same notation can be used to picture a sequence of transitions. For example,

$$\text{EVEN} \xrightarrow{\ 1\ } \text{ODD} \xrightarrow{\ 1\ } \text{EVEN} \xrightarrow{\ 0\ } \text{EVEN} \xrightarrow{\ 1\ } \text{ODD}$$

shows the effect of applying the input sequence 1101 to the machine in state EVEN. The first 1 changes state EVEN into state ODD because $\delta(\text{EVEN}, 1)$ = ODD. The next 1 changes state ODD to state EVEN. The 0 leaves the machine in state EVEN. The final 1 changes the state to ODD. Since EVEN is the starting state and ODD is an accepting state, the sequence 1101 is accepted by the machine.

The input sequence 101 is rejected by the machine because it causes the machine to go from the starting state into a final state that is not an accepting state. Symbolically,

$$\text{EVEN} \xrightarrow{\ 1\ } \text{ODD} \xrightarrow{\ 0\ } \text{ODD} \xrightarrow{\ 1\ } \text{EVEN}$$

Sometimes we want to discuss the entire set of sequences recognized by a particular finite-state recognizer. For example, the set recognized by the parity checker consists of those sequences of 1's and 0's containing an odd number of 1's. Such sets are commonly referred to as "regular sets."

A *regular set* is a set of sequences that can be recognized by a finite-state recognizer.

The set of sequences of 1's and 0's containing an odd number of 1's is thus an example of a regular set.

2.3   THE TRANSITION TABLE

One convenient way of representing a specific finite-state machine is by the use of a *transition* table such as the one shown in Fig. 2.1 for the parity checker. The information in the transition table is laid out according to the following conventions:

1. Columns are labeled with input symbols.

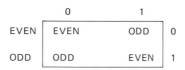

Figure 2.1

2. Rows are labeled with state symbols.
3. Table entries show the new state corresponding to the input column and state row.
4. The first row is labeled with the starting state.
5. The rows corresponding to accepting states are marked on the right with a one and rows corresponding to rejecting states are marked with a zero.

Thus we see that the transition table in Fig. 2.1 represents the machine with:

input set $= \{0, 1\}$
state set $= \{$EVEN, ODD$\}$
transitions $\delta($EVEN, 0$) =$ EVEN, etc.
starting state $=$ EVEN
accepting states $= \{$ODD$\}$

A second machine is illustrated in Fig. 2.2. Here we see that input sequence $xyzz$ is accepted by the machine because

$$1 \xrightarrow{x} 1 \xrightarrow{y} 3 \xrightarrow{z} 4 \xrightarrow{z} 3$$

and 3 is an accepting state, whereas zyx is rejected because

$$1 \xrightarrow{z} 4 \xrightarrow{y} 3 \xrightarrow{x} 2$$

and 2 is a rejecting state.

	x	y	z	
1	1	3	4	1
2	2	1	3	0
3	2	4	4	1
4	3	3	3	0

input set $= \{x, y, z\}$
state set $= \{1, 2, 3, 4\}$
transitions $\delta(1, x) = 1$, $\delta(1, y) = 3$, etc.
starting state $= 1$
accepting states $= \{1, 3\}$

Figure 2.2

2.4   EXITS AND ENDMARKERS

The finite-state recognizer provides a basis for recognizing sequences within a compiler. One way to use such a recognizer is to place it under the control of some master program which determines when the input sequence is over and then checks the state of the recognizer to see if the sequence is acceptable. However, in many compiler-design applications, we want the recognizer to take a more active role and be more like the master program. We expect the recognizer to know when its job is completed and exit accordingly. In these applications the type of transition table we discussed previously is no longer adequate and some small but essential adjustments must be made.

Consider the machine of Fig. 2.3. It accepts the set of all sequences written in input alphabet $\{a, b\}$ such that the symbol b either never appears or appears in pairs. For example, it accepts such sequences as *abb, abba, aaa, abbbbabb,* and *bba;* but not the sequences *baa, abbb,* or *abbab.* State 1 "remembers" that the input sequence processed so far is acceptable. State 2 is entered when the input sequence is an acceptable sequence followed by an extra b that needs matching. State E is entered when the input sequence is permanently deformed by an unmatched b followed by an a. State E might therefore be called an "error state" which remembers an error has been detected.

Now suppose we are asked to design a program or "compiler" which is to take a sequence or "program" written in the alphabet $\{a, b\}$ and exit to a routine "YES" if the sequence is in the set defined by the machine of Fig. 2.3 or exit to a routine "NO" if the sequence is not in this set. We would, of course, like to have our compiler imitate the finite-state machine in some straightforward manner, because this is what we mean when we claim that the finite-state machine is the basis of a design theory. However, it is apparent that the machine model of Fig. 2.3 does not capture the concept of an input sequence being "over." For example, after seeing the symbols *abb,* should the compiler exit to "YES" because the inputs processed so far form a sequence in the set, or should it wait to see if there are any more symbols? If

	a	b	
1	1	2	1
2	E	1	0
E	E	E	0

Figure 2.3

the *abb* is, in fact, followed by the symbols *ba,* the machine should exit to routine "NO" for the total sequence *abbba.*

In practice, a compiler can get around this problem by using end of file information supplied by the computer system on which it is implemented. Thus, in a batch environment, the program *abb* might be punched on cards and presented to the compiler surrounded by control cards so that the listing might look as follows:

$BEGIN

a

b

b

$END

When input files are supplied in a time-sharing environment, an end-of-file marker is provided by the operating system. If the input is on a single punched card, then the end can be detected from the fact that the card is limited to 80 characters.

Thus in these compiling situations we must assume that the input is presented to our machines with an endmarker. We use the symbol "⊣" as the endmarker. The input sequence *abb* will be presented to the machine as

$$abb \dashv$$

Thus the machine of Fig. 2.3 must be altered to process the additional symbol ⊣. A machine to do this is shown in Fig. 2.4(a). Here the symbol "YES" is a short-hand to indicate that the job is completed and that the machine should exit to routine "YES". No new state is called for, as the machine's job is then finished.

The use of an endmarker makes it necessary to distinguish between the alphabet of the language being processed and the input alphabet of the machine doing the processing. In the example under consideration, the lan-

	a	b	⊣
1	1	2	YES
2	E	1	NO
E	E	E	NO

(a)

	a	b	⊣
1	1	2	YES
2	NO	1	NO

(b)

Figure 2.4

guage alphabet is still $\{a, b\}$ and the language is described without reference to an endmarker. The input alphabet of the machine that *recognizes* the language (Fig. 2.3) is also $\{a, b\}$, but the input alphabet of the machine that *processes* the language (Fig. 2.4a) is $\{a, b, \dashv\}$.

The method we used to obtain our processing machine from the recognizing machine is very straightforward. We simply added a column labeled with the endmarker and entered a "YES" for rows corresponding to accepting states and a "NO" for those rows corresponding to rejecting states. Obviously, any recognizer can be reformulated into a processing machine by this same technique. It is therefore evident that any techniques for designing finite-state recognizers are potentially useful for designing processors.

Up to this point, we have been looking at finite-state processors as if they were forced to scan an entire input sequence. In practice, many of the finite-state processors used in compilers finish their job before the entire sequence is read and terminate their activity without reading an endmarker. Stated in terms of programming, there may be some routines in the compiler which have exits prior to a complete scan of their input sequence.

For example, we may want to design the machine so that as soon as it detects an error in the input sequence it transfers control to some external error processing routine. This routine may then abort the whole process, or it may reset the state and resume processing in the hope of detecting further errors.

Returning to Fig. 2.4(a), we recall that if state E is ever entered, then the input sequence will be rejected. Therefore the first transition into state E represents the fact that an error has been "detected." If we decide we are going to abort the processing as soon as an error is detected, then we replace each transition to E in the transition table by the exit routine "NO." The result is Fig. 2.4(b). State E has been deleted from the machine because the elimination of transitions to the state means that it can never be reached from the starting state. The original purpose of state E was simply to finish reading the input sequence after an error is detected; this need vanished when we decided to exit on detecting an error.

In general, we allow any entry in the transition table of a finite-state processor to be an exit instead of a transition. This aspect of sequence processing will be called *detection*. The machine *detects* some situation before its input is over and terminates its own operation.

Detection can occur for acceptable sequences as well as for errors. Consider, for example, the problem of recognizing all sequences of 1's and 0's that contain two consecutive 1's anywhere within the sequence. The recognizer for this problem is shown in Fig. 2.5(a) where state C is the state entered when the sequence 11 is detected. If we wish to have a recognizer that uses exit "YES" as soon as two 1's are detected then the transition to C

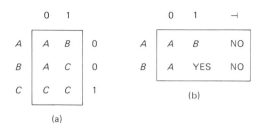

Figure 2.5

must be replaced by "YES". The recognizer of Fig. 2.5(a) thus becomes the processor of Fig. 2.5(b). State C does not appear in the processor because all transitions to it have been eliminated.

2.5   DESIGN EXAMPLE

In order to show automata techniques on a realistic example, we now design a machine to recognize what can follow the word INTEGER in a FOR-TRAN specification statement. Examples of such statements are:

$$\text{INTEGER A}$$
$$\text{INTEGER X, I(3)}$$
$$\text{INTEGER C(3, J, 4), B}$$

We assume that there is no limit on the number of subscripts allowed, although most FORTRAN compilers and standards place some limit on the number. Our input alphabet consists of the five symbols

$$v \; c \; , \; (\;)$$

where v is the token for an arbitrary variable and c is the token for an arbitrary integer constant (see Section 1.2). We assume that these tokens are produced by some other machine.

We design the machine according to a heuristic technique that we call "labeling symbols." The first step in this design is to write out one or more sample sequences in the set and then to label the symbols. If we perceive, using our intuitive knowledge of the sequences, that there are two symbols such that the set of sequences which can follow the first symbol is the same as the set that can follow the second, then the two symbols are given the same label. These labels represent a heuristic concept we call a "usage." These usages will later become the states of the finite-state recognizer.

Applying this step to the present example, we have written a sequence in Fig. 2.6 and labeled the symbols with the numbers 2 through 8. Number 1

INTEGER   A (3 , J , 4) , B

1 2 3 4 5 6 5 4 7 8 2

Figure 2.6

has been reserved for later use as a starting state and is written before the start of the sequence on the figure to help us visualize the transitions when we get around to constructing the transition table.

Notice that two commas have been labeled with a 5. This is because the sequence

4) , B

which is the continuation after the second comma could also be used after the first comma to form an acceptable sequence, namely:

INTEGER A(3, 4), B

In general, these two commas allow the same continuations and thus represent the same "usage." On the other hand, the comma labeled with an 8 is a different usage. For example, if its continuation was placed after an occurrence of usage 5, the resulting sequence:

INTEGER A(3, B

would not be an acceptable sequence.

Similarly, the two integers are both labeled with a 4 since they permit the same continuations.

Our usages may be described verbally as follows:

2 — name of variable to be made INTEGER;
3 — left parenthesis;
4 — integer giving a dimension;
5 — comma separating dimensions;
6 — variable giving an adjustable dimension;
7 — right parenthesis;
8 — comma separating items to be made integer.

We are confident that the symbols in any other acceptable sequence can be matched with one of these usages, so we do not try any other sequences in our search for usages.

Having identified the usages, the plan for constructing a recognizer is described by the following outline.

1. Introduce a starting state and an error state.

2. Introduce a state for each usage.

3. Create a transition from one state to another if the corresponding usages can follow each other.

4. Complete the transition table with transitions to the error state.

5. Mark states as accepting if the corresponding usages can end an acceptable sequence.

Applying the first step to our example, we introduce starting state 1 and error state *E*. Applying the second step, we introduce states 2 through 8 corresponding to the usages uncovered in our initial analysis.

Next we apply step 3 to obtain the required transitions. We see that the first symbol in any sequence must be a variable of usage 2 and so we create a transition from the starting state 1 to state 2 under the input symbol *v*. This entry may be seen in the transition table in Fig. 2.7, which shows the final outcome of our construction. Usage 2 can be followed by either usage 3 (as in Fig. 2.6) or usage 8 (as in INTEGER A, B). Thus, we enter transitions from 2 to 3 and 2 to 8 under the appropriate input. Upon completion of this analysis, we fill in the remaining table entries with transitions to state *E*.

Finally, we apply step 5. We see that an acceptable sequence can end with either usage 2 or usage 7 and no others and hence states 2 and 7 become accepting states and the construction is completed.

One objection to this technique is that the resulting machine might not be the best possible machine in the sense that there may be another machine with fewer states that defines the same set. In fact, we will see later that the machine of Fig. 2.7 is *not* best. This objection is overcome in Section 2.11

	v	*c*	,	(	)	
1	2	*E*	*E*	*E*	*E*	0
2	*E*	*E*	8	3	*E*	1
3	6	4	*E*	*E*	*E*	0
4	*E*	*E*	5	*E*	7	0
5	6	4	*E*	*E*	*E*	0
6	*E*	*E*	5	*E*	7	0
7	*E*	*E*	8	*E*	*E*	1
8	2	*E*	*E*	*E*	*E*	0
E	*E*	*E*	*E*	*E*	*E*	0

Figure 2.7

where we give an algorithm for reducing a given finite-state machine to a best finite-state machine.

A more serious objection is that the technique apparently breaks down when some usage can be followed by two different usages of the same input symbol. This objection is overcome in Section 2.13 where we show how to put two or more transitions in a single transition table entry and then convert that table into a new transition table with the required one transition per entry.

Thus the creative part of designing a machine is identifying the usages and transitions. One can then use the present methods, together with the procedures described later, to automatically transform this information into a best finite-state recognizer. In Chapter 6 we give an alternative method of specifying a regular set of sequences and show how this new description can be used to automatically derive a corresponding finite-state machine without any need to identify usages.

2.6   THE NULL SEQUENCE

Thus far we have tacitly assumed that the reader has a good intuitive concept of a sequence. For the most part, this assumption is justifiable and it is difficult to explain the concept of a sequence in simpler terms. We could for example say that a sequence is one of the following:

1. a succession of symbols,
2. a string of symbols,
3. a concatenation of symbols.

However, these are all essentially alternative ways of saying that a sequence is a sequence. Thus it is best to assume that the reader has seen enough sequences to know what they are.

The one possible flaw in this assumption is that many people do not appreciate that it makes good sense to talk about a zero-length sequence. This zero-length sequence, called the *null sequence,* comes up frequently in automata theory considerations and is actually of considerable practical importance. In order to develop a familiarity with this sequence, we now relate the null sequence to the concepts introduced so far.

First, consider the null sequence as a computer program. If we were to surround the null sequence with control cards and submit it to a computer for compilation, the complete listing might look as follows:

$BEGIN

$END

If we want one of the processing machines of Section 2.4 to process the null sequence, then we add the endmarker to the end of the null sequence thereby obtaining the sequence:

$$\dashv$$

which we use as input to the processing machine. The processing machine would then accept the sequence if the transition-table entry for the starting state and endmarker was "YES" and reject it if it were "NO".

If we consider the finite-state recognizers of Section 2.2, then it is obviously true that:

> A finite state recognizer accepts the null sequence if and only if its starting state is an accepting state.

Stating this in terms of transitions, the null sequence applied to the starting state (or any other state) causes no transitions at all; so its effect is to leave the state unchanged. Thus the null sequence applied to the starting state causes the recognizer to end in the starting state and its acceptability is thus determined by the starting state. Stated in terms of transition sequences, the transition sequence for the null sequence applied to any state s is:

$$s$$

Therefore when the first state in this sequence (s) is the starting state and the last state in this sequence (s) is an accepting state, then the null sequence is accepted.

The null sequence frequently arises in the description of programming languages. For example one of the possible ALGOL 60 statements is the "dummy statement" which is just the null sequence.

The one disconcerting property of the null sequence is that it is very difficult to display in a printed text. We have displayed the null sequence between two control cards and we have displayed the null sequence followed by an endmarker, but it cannot be directly displayed in a sentence because its effect on the sentence is invisible. We get around this problem by letting the symbol ϵ represent the null sequence. Symbolically, ϵ is defined by the following equation:

$$\epsilon =$$

It is so useful to have a symbol representing the null sequence that we reserve the symbol ϵ for this purpose throughout the remainder of this book. This same convention is used in large segments of the automata theory literature, although λ has also been used for this purpose.

The null *sequence* ϵ is sometimes confused with the null *set*, although a sequence and a set are two different concepts. The null or empty set is the set

Fig. 2.8 (a) Recognizer for { }; (b) Recognizer for {ε}

without any elements, sometimes represented in the literature by the symbols φ or ∅. To clarify this difference we contrast the empty set { } with the set {ε}. The empty set of course contains no elements whereas the set {ε} contains one element, namely the sequence ε. In Fig. 2.8(a), we show a machine over alphabet {a, b} which recognizes the set { }. The machine over this same alphabet which accepts the set {ε} is shown in Fig. 2.8(b). These machines are clearly different. Note that the symbol ε does not appear as an input to the machine for {ε}. The symbol ε is used for descriptive purposes and is not itself an input symbol of this machine. If we had said "let γ = abba," one would not expect us to add γ to the input set of this machine and by analogy, one should not expect the symbol ε to be added to the input set just because we have said "let ε = ".

Another misconception is that the null sequence corresponds to a blank character. However, the formula 1ε0 represents the sequence 10 and not the sequence 1 0. Since the null sequence contains no characters, its length is zero. However the sequence consisting of a single blank has a length of 1.

2.7   STATE EQUIVALENCE

For any given finite-state recognizer, there are an infinite number of other finite-state machines that recognize the same set of sequences. When one designs a finite-state recognizer for a given problem, it is natural to consider the possibility that some other recognizer for the same set might have a simpler specification and might require less computer memory to implement as a computer program. In this and in the next four sections we develop theory that applies to this question. One result of this theory is that for each recognition problem there exists a single machine with properties that are very similar to the ideas of "having the simplest specification" and "requiring least computer memory to implement." Furthermore, we show how this new machine can be obtained from any given original machine. Specifically, the goal of Sections 2.7 through 2.11 is to establish the following fact:

> For any given finite-state recognizer, one can find a unique finite-state recognizer which recognizes the same set of sequences and

which has fewer states than any other finite-state recognizer for that set.

The use of the word "unique" in the above statement requires some clarification. Given any machine, a new machine with the same number of states can be obtained simply by giving each state a new name. However, the state names have nothing to do with the sequences recognized or with the implementation of the machine as a computer program. Thus, for practical purposes, machines that are the same except for state names can be thought of as being the "same" machine. The word "unique" is understood in this context as meaning "unique except for state names." This unique machine will be called the *minimal* machine.

As we develop the theory, it will become evident that the minimal machine for a given recognition problem is actually a reduced version of the larger machines that solve the problem. The exact nature of this reduction will be described later. The point is that the minimal machine is actually a compact version of the larger machines and is not merely an alternative machine that happens to have fewer states. This fact strengthens the case for considering the minimal machine as a prime candidate for implementation. In Chapter 3, where we study in detail several methods for implementing finite-state machines as computer programs, the importance of the minimal machine will become even more evident.

The first step in our development of a theory of state minimization and state reduction is to introduce the concept of *equivalent states.* Informally, two states are equivalent if they will give the same response to all possible continuations of the input sequence. This concept applies both to states in the same machine and states in different machines. In the case of finite-state recognizers, whose purpose is to accept sequences, state equivalence may be stated more exactly as follows:

> State s in finite-state recognizer M is *equivalent* to state t in finite state recognizer N if and only if machine M starting in state s will accept exactly the same sequences as machine N starting in state t.

If two states s and t in the same machine are equivalent, then the machine can be simplified by replacing all transition table references to these states by some new name and then dropping one of the two rows corresponding to s and t. In the machine at Fig. 2.9(a) for example, it is obvious that states 4 and 5 serve the same purpose since they are both accepting states, both go into state 2 under input a and both go into state 3 under input b. We, therefore, decide that 4 and 5 will be combined into a single state which we choose to call state X. We replace each occurrence of the names 4 and 5 in the state table by the name X thereby obtaining the table of Fig.

	a	b	
1	1	4	0
2	3	5	1
3	5	1	0
4	2	3	1
5	2	3	1

(a)

	a	b	
1	1	X	0
2	3	X	1
3	X	1	0
X	2	3	1
X	2	3	1

(b)

	a	b	
1	1	X	0
2	3	X	1
3	X	1	0
X	2	3	1

(c)

Figure 2.9

2.9(b). This leaves us with two rows labeled X; we drop one of them to obtain the simplified state table of Fig. 2.9(c).

Usually, the equivalence is less obvious than in this example and we must resort to the equivalence test in the next section to decide the issue.

A second reason for testing state equivalence is to decide if two machines do the same thing, i.e., whether or not they accept the same set of sequences. This is done simply by testing to see if the starting state of one machine is equivalent to the starting state of the other. If this is true, then by the definition of state equivalence, both machines accept and reject the same sequences. Thus, the concept of *state equivalence* leads us to a concept of *machine equivalence,* namely:

Machines M and N are said to be equivalent if and only if their starting states are equivalent.

If two states are not equivalent, then any sequence which causes one state to make a transition into an accepting state and the other state to go into a rejecting state is called a *distinguishing sequence for the two states.* In Fig. 2.10, states a and x are not equivalent because 101 is a distinguishing sequence. Symbolically,

$$a \xrightarrow{1} c \xrightarrow{0} b \xrightarrow{1} c$$
$$x \xrightarrow{1} y \xrightarrow{0} z \xrightarrow{1} z$$

and state c is accepting while state z is not. Since a and x are the starting states of their respective machines, we have also shown that the two machines of Fig. 2.10 are not equivalent. We see that

Two states are equivalent if and only if they have no distinguishing sequence.

We note that the concept of state equivalence is an equivalence relation in the mathematical sense; the relation is *reflexive* (each state is equivalent to itself), *symmetric* (*s* equivalent to *t* implies *t* equivalent to *s*), and *transitive* (if *s* and *t* are equivalent and *t* and *u* are equivalent, then *s* and *u* are equivalent).

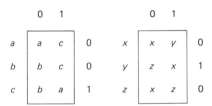

Figure 2.10

2.8 TESTING TWO STATES FOR EQUIVALENCE

We assume throughout this section that we are discussing machines that have a common input set. We develop a test for state equivalence based on the following fact:

Two states *s* and *t* are equivalent if and only if the following two conditions are fulfilled:
1. **compatibility condition** — States *s* and *t* must either both be accepting or both be rejecting
2. **propagation condition** — For all input symbols, states *s* and *t* must go into equivalent states

We now show that these two conditions are satisfied if and only if *s* and *t* have no distinguishing sequence.

First observe that if either condition is violated the two states have a distinguishing sequence. If the compatibility condition is violated, then the null sequence is a distinguishing sequence. If the propagation condition is violated, then an input symbol *x* causes *s* and *t* to go into nonequivalent states. Therefore *x* followed by the distinguishing sequence for the new states is a distinguishing sequence for *s* and *t*.

Now observe that if *s* and *t* have a distinguishing sequence, then at least one of these conditions must be violated. If the distinguishing sequence is the null sequence (of length zero) then the compatibility condition is violated. If the length of the distinguishing sequence is greater than zero, then its first

	y	z	
0	0	3	0
1	2	5	0
2	2	7	0
3	6	7	0
4	1	6	1
5	6	5	0
6	6	3	1
7	6	3	0

Figure 2.11

symbol will take s and t into a pair of states that are not equivalent because they can be distinguished by the remainder of the distinguishing sequence.

Thus we see that these conditions are both satisfied if the two states are equivalent and at least one condition is not satisfied if they are not equivalent.

Conditions 1 and 2 can be incorporated into a general equivalence test for any pair of states. The test is probably best understood as being a test for nonequivalence and may be looked upon as a search for a distinguishing sequence. We illustrate the test with the machine of Fig. 2.11 before we state the testing rules in general terms. As a bookkeeping device, we construct a new kind of table which we call the *state-equivalence table*.

First we test the states 0 and 7 of Fig. 2.11 for equivalence. The state-equivalence table for this test will have one column for each input, namely one column for input y and one for input z. Rows will be added during the course of the test. Initially we have one row labeled with the pair of states to be tested, namely the pair 0, 7. The result is Fig. 2.12(a).

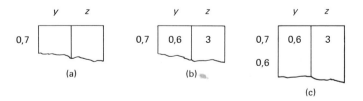

Figure 2.12

Our first hope for demonstrating the nonequivalence of states 0 and 7 is to show that the compatibility condition fails. Unfortunately, the compatibility condition is satisfied since both are rejecting states. Thus, the hope for nonequivalence is that the propagation condition fails. To investigate this possibility, we compute the effect of each input symbol on the state pair and write the result in the corresponding table entry. Since states 0 and 7 go into states 0 and 6, respectively, under input y, we write 0, 6 in the table under input y. Since states 0 and 7 both go into state 3 under input z, we write a 3 in the z column. We now have Fig. 2.12(b). To violate the propagation condition, either pair 0 and 6 must be nonequivalent or pair 3 and 3 must be nonequivalent. Since each state is equivalent to itself, the pair 3 and 3 is automatically equivalent.

To investigate the possibility that 0 and 6 are nonequivalent, we add a new row to the state-equivalence table and label the row with that pair. The result is shown in Fig. 2.12(c). The process is now repeated on this new row. First we test 0 and 6 for the compatibility condition. Here we find that 0 and 6 are nonequivalent as 6 is accepting and 0 is rejecting. The test is over and we know that the original pair 0 and 7 are not equivalent. The state-equivalence table can be used to compute a distinguishing sequence. The row 0, 6 was entered because of input y applied to 0, 7 and so the distinguishing sequence is y.

Now we test the states 0 and 1 to see if they are equivalent. We initialize our state-equivalence table with pair 0, 1. This pair is compatible so we compute the effects of each input and enter these states in the table. The result is Fig. 2.13(a). Our hopes for the nonequivalence of states 0 and 1 depend on showing the nonequivalence of pair 0, 2, or of pair 3, 5. So we add a table row for each of these pairs. The result is Fig. 2.13(b).

Fixing our attention on row 0, 2, we note that this pair is compatible and so we compute the next state pairs in order to investigate propagation. The result is shown in Fig. 2.13(c). Of the two new table entries, only one gives a new row, namely pair 3, 7. The other entry, pair 0, 2, is already in the table and need not be repeated. The fact that pair 0, 2 has been generated twice by the method means that there are two input sequences that lead from the initial pair 0, 1 to the pair 0, 2. A distinguishing sequence for pair 0, 2 preceded by either of these sequences will be a distinguishing sequence for pair 0, 1. However, since we only need one distinguishing sequence for pair 0, 1 to prove their nonequivalence, we only need one entry for pair 0, 2 in the table. As a consequence, the only new row for our table is row 3, 7.

Continuing down the list of rows, we next consider row 3, 5. We find that these states are compatible. The next pairs are computed, namely 6, 6 and 5, 7. Since state 6 is equivalent to itself, the only new row is 5, 7. At this point, our table looks like Fig. 2.13(d). Continuing this procedure, we find no

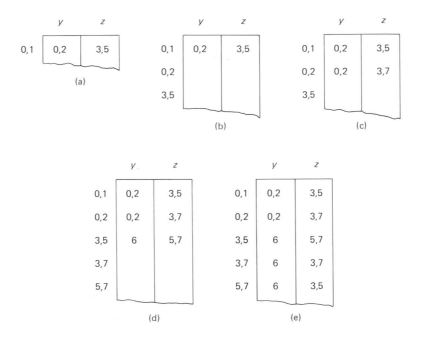

Figure 2.13

incompatible pairs, and no new pairs to be tested for compatibility. The table has been completed, as shown in Fig. 2.13(e), and the search for a distinguishing sequence has failed. State 0 and 1 must therefore be equivalent.

The general procedure may be described as follows:

1. Begin a state-equivalence table with one column for each input symbol. Label the first row with the pair of states to be tested.

2. Take a row of the state-equivalence table whose table entries have not been filled in and test the pair of states which label the row to see if they are compatible. If they are not compatible, the original pair of states is not equivalent and the procedure ends. If they are compatible, compute the effect of applying each input symbol to this state pair and write the resulting state pairs into the corresponding table entry of the row under consideration.

3. For each table entry completed in step 2, there are three possibilities. If the table entry is a state pair in which the two states are the same, no action is required for that pair. If the table entry is a state pair which has already been used to label a row, no action is required for that pair either. If the table entry is a pair of distinct states which has not been used to label a row, then a new row must be added for this new state pair. The order of the states in a

state pair is unimportant in this case and the pair s, t is to be considered the same as pair t, s. After the appropriate action has been taken for each state pair in the given row, go on to step 4.

4. If all entries in the state-equivalence table have been filled in, the original pair of states and all state pairs generated during the test are equivalent and the test is over. If the table is incomplete, at least one row of the state-equivalence table must still be processed and step 2 is applied.

Because every pair generated in a completed state-equivalence table is a pair of equivalent states, the test often yields more information than originally intended. Returning to our last example, we see from Fig. 2.13(e) that in addition to the equivalence of pair 0, 1 which was the pair being tested, we have proved the equivalence of pairs 0, 2 and 3, 5 and 3, 7 and 5, 7. From the transitive property of state equivalence, the equivalence of 0, 2 and 0, 1 implies the equivalence of 1, 2. Thus states 0, 1 and 2 are all equivalent to each other. Similarly, states 3, 5, and 7 are equivalent to each other.

This equivalence information can now be used to simplify the machine. We unite states 0, 1 and 2 into a single state which we call A and unite states 3, 5 and 7 into a single state which we call B. Substituting these new names into Fig. 2.11, and discarding redundant rows, we obtain the simpler equivalent machine of Fig. 2.14.

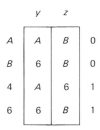

	y	z	
A	A	B	0
B	6	B	0
4	A	6	1
6	6	B	1

Figure 2.14

2.9 EXTRANEOUS STATES

There may be some states in a machine that can never be reached by any possible input sequence when the machine is initially in its starting state. In Fig. 2.15(a), s_4 is such a state since there are no transitions to it in the table.

States such as s_4 are called *extraneous* states. The rows corresponding to these states can be simply removed from the transition table to yield the transition table of a machine which is equivalent to the given one but has fewer states. This has been done in Fig. 2.15(b).

	0	1	
s_0	s_1	s_5	0
s_1	s_2	s_7	1
s_2	s_2	s_5	1
s_3	s_5	s_7	0
s_4	s_5	s_6	0
s_5	s_3	s_1	0
s_6	s_8	s_0	1
s_7	s_0	s_1	1
s_8	s_3	s_6	0

(a)

	0	1	
s_0	s_1	s_5	0
s_1	s_2	s_7	1
s_2	s_2	s_5	1
s_3	s_5	s_7	0
s_5	s_3	s_1	0
s_6	s_8	s_0	1
s_7	s_0	s_1	1
s_8	s_3	s_6	0

(b)

	0	1	
s_0	s_1	s_5	0
s_1	s_2	s_7	1
s_2	s_2	s_5	1
s_3	s_5	s_7	0
s_5	s_3	s_1	0
s_7	s_0	s_1	1

(c)

Figure 2.15

For a given machine it is quite simple to prepare a list of all nonextraneous states.

1. Initialize the list with the starting state.
2. Add to the list all states that can be reached from the starting state under single inputs.
3. For every new state on the list, also add any unlisted states that can be reached from the new state.

When no new states can be added by this procedure, one has obtained all the nonextraneous states and the remaining states can be deleted from the machine. Since each step in the procedure adds at least one state to the list of nonextraneous states, the number of steps in the procedure is bounded by the number of states in the given machine.

As an example, consider the machine of Fig. 2.15(a). Starting with s_0, we see that s_1 and s_5 are attainable after one input. State s_1 leads to s_2 and s_7; state s_5 leads to s_3 and s_1. Thus we know that s_0, s_1, s_5, s_2, s_7, and s_3 are attainable and we will have to see if s_2, s_7, and s_3 lead to any new states. A check of these states reveals that no new states are attainable and hence the remaining states s_4, s_6, and s_8 are extraneous. These three states can therefore be eliminated to obtain the equivalent machine of Fig. 2.15(c).

2.10   REDUCED MACHINES

We say that a machine is *reduced* if it has no extraneous states and if no two of its states are equivalent to each other. If a machine is not reduced, then an equivalent machine with fewer states can be obtained by either discarding some extraneous states or by combining two equivalent states as discussed in the preceeding two sections. This reduction process can be repeated until a reduced machine is obtained. Thus every finite-state machine has an equivalent reduced machine. The reduced machine obtained by this method has fewer states than the original (unless the original was already reduced) and can be implemented more compactly than the original on a computer.

By performing these reductions in various ways or by starting with different equivalent machines, one might conceivably obtain reduced machines that appear to be different. However, these machines will in fact be identical in every respect except for the names that are used for the states.

To illustrate this equivalence, we show two reduced machines in Fig. 2.16(a) and 2.16(b). Applying the test of Section 2.8 to the pair of starting states $(A, 1)$, we construct the state-equivalence table of Fig. 2.17 and find

	0	1	
A	B	C	1
B	D	A	0
C	B	B	1
D	C	D	0

(a)

	0	1	
1	3	4	1
2	4	2	0
3	2	1	0
4	3	3	1

(b)

	0	1	
(A)	1	3	4	1
(B)	3	2	1	0
(C)	4	3	3	1
(D)	2	4	2	0

(c)

Figure 2.16

	0	1
$A,1$	$B,3$	$C,4$
$B,3$	$D,2$	$A,1$
$C,4$	$B,3$	$B,3$
$D,2$	$C,4$	$D,2$

Figure 2.17

that the following pairs are equivalent.

$$(A, 1), (B, 3), (C, 4), (D, 2).$$

This means that the machines are equivalent and the pairs tell us which state names are equivalent. Substituting these new names into Fig. 2.16(a), we obtain Fig. 2.16(c) which is the same as Fig. 2.16(b) except for the order of the rows.

These two machines are thus identical except for the names of the states. To see that this will be true for any two equivalent reduced machines, M and N, consider what happens when one applies the equivalence test of Section 2.8 to M and N. First the state-equivalence table is initialized with the state pair consisting of the starting state of M and the starting state of N. Subsequent pairs generated in the test will of necessity consist of one state from M and one state from N. Each state of M can only be paired with at most one state of N and vice versa, for if state m of M were equivalent to two states n_1 and n_2 of N, the states n_1 and n_2 would be equivalent to each other contrary to our assumption that machine N is reduced. Furthermore, each state m of M will be paired with at least one state of N and vice versa because the input sequence which causes machine M to enter state m will also cause the pair of starting states in the equivalence table to go to a pair that contains state m. We conclude therefore that each state of M is equivalent to exactly one state of N and vice versa. This means that M and N are the same except for names.

We have shown that if one disregards state names, there is only one reduced machine for a given recognition problem. This means that no matter what recognizer one initially finds for a recognition problem and no matter how the state reductions are accomplished, there is only one possible reduced machine that can be found. This reduced machine is the minimal machine whose existence was asserted in the beginning of Section 2.7.

2.11   OBTAINING THE MINIMAL MACHINE

A finite-state machine can be converted into a minimal equivalent machine by deleting the extraneous states and combining the equivalent states. Section 2.9 gives an efficient method for finding the extraneous states. However, the method given in Section 2.8 for testing state equivalence is inconvenient to use for reducing machines since it deals with only two states at a time. Here we give a more efficient method for finding and combining equivalent states. This method is of considerable practical importance since minimal finite-state machines are used for most applications so as to minimize storage requirements.

The new method is referred to as the "separation method" since the objective is to separate or partition the states into disjoint subsets or *blocks,*

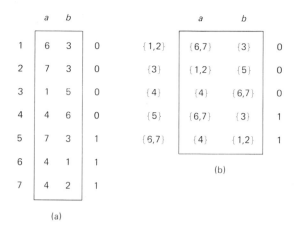

	a	b	
1	6	3	0
2	7	3	0
3	1	5	0
4	4	6	0
5	7	3	1
6	4	1	1
7	4	2	1

(a)

	a	b	
{1,2}	{6,7}	{3}	0
{3}	{1,2}	{5}	0
{4}	{4}	{6,7}	0
{5}	{6,7}	{3}	1
{6,7}	{4}	{1,2}	1

(b)

Figure 2.18

such that nonequivalent states fall into separate blocks. The method is illustrated by its application to the machine of Fig. 2.18(a).

The states are first separated into two blocks; one containing the accepting states and the other containing the rejecting states. For our example, this initial partition P_0 is given by

$$P_0 = (\{1, 2, 3, 4\}, \{5, 6, 7\})$$

because 1, 2, 3, and 4 are rejecting states and 5, 6, and 7 are accepting states. None of the states in the first block are equivalent to any of the states in the second block because such pairs of states violate the compatibility condition (see Section 2.8).

Now observe what happens to the states in block $\{1, 2, 3, 4\}$ under input a. States 3 and 4 go into states contained in the first block (i.e., states 1 and 4, respectively) whereas states 1 and 2 go into states of the second block (i.e., states 6 and 7, respectively). This means that for any state in set $\{1, 2\}$ and any state in $\{3, 4\}$, the corresponding next states under input a will be nonequivalent. This is a violation of the propagation condition and so we can conclude that no state in set $\{1, 2\}$ is equivalent to any state in set $\{3, 4\}$. This enables us to construct a new partition.

$$P_1 = (\{1, 2\}, \{3, 4\}, \{5, 6, 7\})$$

with the property that states from different blocks are always nonequivalent. We say that partition P_1 has been obtained from partition P_0 by *separating* block $\{1, 2, 3, 4\}$ *with respect* to input a.

We now try to find a block of P_1 and an input such that the block may be separated with respect to the input and a new partition thereby obtained.

This new partition will also have the property that states from different blocks are guaranteed to be nonequivalent. We repeat this process until no further separations are possible. Since we are not specifying an order for testing blocks and inputs to see if a separation is possible, the sequence of partitions obtained might develop in any number of different ways. The final partition will, however, be the same in any case. For our example, the continuations after P_1 might be as follows:

Separating $\{3, 4\}$ of P_1 with respect to a:

$$P_2 = (\{1, 2\}, \{3\}, \{4\}, \{5, 6, 7\}).$$

Separating $\{5, 6, 7\}$ of P_2 with respect to either a or b:

$$P_3 = (\{1, 2\}, \{3\}, \{4\}, \{5\}, \{6, 7\}).$$

Partition P_3 cannot be separated further. To see this observe that all the states in block $\{1, 2\}$ go into states in block $\{6, 7\}$ under input a and into states of block $\{3\}$ under input b. Similarly, block $\{6, 7\}$ goes into blocks $\{4\}$ and $\{1, 2\}$ under a and b, respectively. The other blocks have one element each and so are automatically excluded from further separation.

When the procedure is finished, the states within any given block are equivalent. In the example, states 1 and 2 are equivalent and states 6 and 7 are equivalent. To see why such states must be equivalent, one can reason as follows: Because no additional separations are possible, single inputs applied to states in the same block result in states that are again in the same block. Since this is true for all blocks and all single inputs, it must be also true when these inputs are combined to form input sequences. Because the initial partition separated the accepting and rejecting states, any block of a subsequent partition contains either all accepting or all rejecting states. Thus if a distinguishing sequence exists for a pair of states, it must carry them into different blocks. We conclude therefore that states in the same block of the final partition cannot have distinguishing sequences and that they must be equivalent.

The blocks of the final partition can be used to construct a new machine which is equivalent to the original and which has no two equivalent states. For our example, this machine is shown in Fig. 2.18(b). The state set of the new machine is the set of blocks of the final partitions. The transitions for the new machine are obtained from the old by observing which blocks follow which under each input. Thus in Fig. 2.18(b), the entry for state $\{1, 2\}$ under input a is state $\{6, 7\}$ because the states in block $\{1, 2\}$ of final partition P_3 go into states in block $\{6, 7\}$ under input a. The starting state of the new machine is simply the block which contains the starting state of the original machine and the accepting states are those blocks which contain accepting states of the original machine.

In the case of Fig. 2.18(b), the machine has no extraneous states and is therefore the minimal machine for Fig. 2.18(a). In general, the separation procedure must be accompanied by the removal of extraneous states in order to get the minimal machine. It does not matter which of these two procedures is done first.

We now attempt to reduce the machine of Fig. 2.7 which we designed to recognize the strings that can follow the word INTEGER in a FORTRAN statement. First we note that the machine has no extraneous states. Then we apply the separation procedure. First we construct our initial partition P_0 by separating the accepting and rejecting states;

$$P_0 = (\{1, 3, 4, 5, 6, 8, E\}, \{2, 7\}).$$

Separating $\{1, 3, 4, 5, 6, 8, E\}$ with respect to input v:

$$P_1 = (\{1, 8\}, \{3, 4, 5, 6, E\}, \{2, 7\}).$$

Separating $\{3, 4, 5, 6, E\}$ with respect to input) :

$$P_2 = (\{1, 8\}, \{3, 5, E\}, \{4, 6\}, \{2, 7\}).$$

Separating $\{3, 5, E\}$ with respect to input v:

$$P_3 = (\{1, 8\}, \{3, 5\}, \{E\}, \{4, 6\}, \{2, 7\}).$$

Separating $\{2, 7\}$ with respect to input (:

$$P_4 = (\{1, 8\}, \{3, 5\}, \{E\}, \{4, 6\}, \{2\}, \{7\})$$

No further separations are possible and so P_4 is the final partition showing equivalent states. Letting the symbols A, B, and C represent the blocks $\{1, 8\}$, $\{3, 5\}$, and $\{4, 6\}$, respectively, and letting 2, 7 and E represent the corresponding one-element blocks, we obtain the transition table of Fig. 2.19 which is the minimal machine for the machine of Fig. 2.7. Thus we have

		v	c	,	(	)	
{1,8}	A	2	E	E	E	E	0
	2	E	E	A	B	E	1
{3,5}	B	C	C	E	E	E	0
{4,6}	C	E	E	B	E	7	0
	7	E	E	A	E	E	1
	E	E	E	E	E	E	0

Figure 2.19

obtained a six-state machine to do the work of the nine-state machine of our original design.

Recalling the interpretations of the states given in Section 2.5, we can interpret the equivalence classes as follows:

$\{1, 8\}$ — nonempty list of items must begin

$\{3, 5\}$ — a dimension must be given

$\{4, 6\}$ — a dimension has just been specified.

With experience, one learns to spot usages that result in the same situation and thus obtain a smaller initial machine. However, no matter how many unnecessary states are initially included, the machine can be reduced by these algorithms to the minimal finite-state machine.

2.12   NONDETERMINISTIC MACHINES

We now introduce the automata theory concept of a *nondeterministic* machine. It is easy to get confused by the terminology itself since the English-language concept of a machine virtually excludes its use with the adjective "nondeterministic." So the first thing to keep in mind is that a nondeterministic machine is not a machine in the sense that it can be conveniently interpreted as modeling the behavior of a physical device. A second source of confusion is that the term "nondeterministic" suggests randomness, but there is nothing random about a nondeterministic machine. So the second thing to keep in mind is that no probabilities are involved.

A nondeterministic machine is simply a formalism for defining sets of sequences. The word "machine" is used in the name because the formalism is a generalization of the formalism for defining ordinary deterministic machines. The nondeterministic finite-state recognizers are important because:

1. it is sometimes easier to find a nondeterministic description of a given set;

2. there is a procedure for converting a nondeterministic finite-state recognizer into an ordinary finite-state recognizer.

A nondeterministic finite-state recognizer is similar to the ordinary recognizer except that the transition function specifies a set of states instead of a single state and a set of starting states is given instead of a single starting state. Thus the machine is defined by the following statement:

A *nondeterministic finite state recognizer* is described by:

1. a finite set of input symbols,

2. a finite set of states,

3. a transition function δ which assigns a set of new states to every combination of state and input,

4. a subset of the states designated as starting states,

5. a subset of the states designated as accepting states.

If state s_{new} is in the set of new states assigned by the transition function to state s_{old} for input symbol x, then we write

$$s_{old} \xrightarrow{\;x\;} s_{new}$$

We can certainly use this symbolism even if we choose not to interpret it as the transition of a real machine. An input sequence is said to be *accepted* by the machine if it can be used to connect a starting state with an accepting state. For example, if the relations

$$s_0 \xrightarrow{\;x_1\;} s_1 \xrightarrow{\;x_2\;} s_2 \xrightarrow{\;x_3\;} s_3$$

hold for some machine where s_0 is a starting state and s_3 an accepting state, then we would say that input sequence $x_1 x_2 x_3$ is accepted by the machine.

Restating the last paragraph a little more formally, we have the following definition:

An input sequence of length n is *accepted* by a nondeterministic finite-state recognizer if and only if one can find a sequence of states $s_0 \ldots s_n$ such that s_0 is a starting state, s_n is an accepting state, and for all i, such that $0 < i \leqslant n$, the state s_i is in the set of new states assigned by the transition function to the state s_{i-1} for the ith element of the input sequence.

The transition table method of representing finite-state recognizers is easily generalized to a method of representing nondeterministic finite-state recognizers. Only two changes are required. First, each table entry must contain a set of states. We indicate this set simply by listing the elements without the use of set brackets. The second change is that we indicate the starting states with arrows beside the corresponding row labels. If these arrows are omitted, we understand that there is only one starting state, namely the state corresponding to the first row.

Figure 2.20 shows a transition table representing a nondeterministic finite-state recognizer. The state set is $\{A, B, C\}$, the input set $\{0, 1\}$, the accepting states are $\{B, C\}$ and the starting states are $\{A, B\}$. The transitions are:

$$\delta(A, 0) = \{A, B\}, \qquad \delta(A, 1) = \{C\},$$
$$\delta(B, 0) = \{B\}, \qquad \delta(B, 1) = \{C\},$$
$$\delta(C, 0) = \{\,\} \qquad\qquad \delta(C, 1) = \{A, C\}.$$

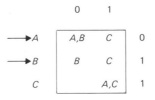

Figure 2.20

One sequence accepted by this machine is 11 because

$$B \xrightarrow{1} C \xrightarrow{1} C$$

and B is a starting state and C is an accepting state. The existence of this one transition sequence for input sequence 11 suffices to show that the input sequence is accepted, and the existence of other transition sequences such as

$$B \xrightarrow{1} C \xrightarrow{1} A$$

from a starting state to a nonaccepting state are of no consequence.

One of the nondeterministic transitions, namely $\delta(C, 0)$, is to the empty set. This simply means that no continuations are allowed for state C under input 0. Such an entry may prevent there being any transition sequence for some input sequence. In this example, 10 is such a sequence since the 1 carries either starting state into state C where the continuation set is empty. Such input sequences are simply rejected along with all the other sequences which cannot be used to transform a starting state into an accepting state.

The "operation" of a nondeterministic machine can be interpreted in two ways. We illustrate with the machine of Fig. 2.20. Assume the machine is in state A and an input sequence is applied beginning with input 0. Then one can imagine that either:

1. The machine makes a choice, going either to A or to B, which are the new states corresponding to old state A and input 0. The machine continues to operate in this fashion, and there may be many choices. If there is any sequence of choices under which the input sequence causes the machine to end up in an accepting state, then the machine is said to accept the input. We emphasize that only one sequence of choices reaching an accepting state is required and the machine accepts even if there are many other sequences of choices that do not lead to an accepting state.

2. The machine splits into two machines, one in state A and one in state B. As the inputs continue, each machine splits further, according to the possibilities in the transition table. When the inputs are completed, the sequence is accepted if one of the resulting machines is in an accepting state.

These two interpretations are equivalent and both are useful for under-standing the nondeterministic machine. But the purpose of the machine is not to model these situations. The purpose is to specify the set of input sequences that are accepted.

Example

We design a nondeterministic machine with input alphabet
$$\{A, E, G, N, R, Y\}$$

which accepts only the two sequences GREEN and GRAY. Using the tech-nique of labeling symbols, we find the following obvious usages.

$$
\begin{aligned}
s_0 &\;-\text{starting state}\\
G_1 &\;-\text{G in GREEN}\\
R_1 &\;-\text{R in GREEN}\\
E_1 &\;-\text{first E in GREEN}\\
E_2 &\;-\text{second E in GREEN}\\
N &\;-\text{N in GREEN}\\
G_2 &\;-\text{G in GRAY}\\
R_2 &\;-\text{R in GRAY}\\
A &\;-\text{A in GRAY}\\
Y &\;-\text{Y in GRAY}
\end{aligned}
$$

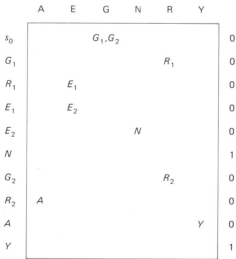

	A	E	G	N	R	Y	
s_0			G_1,G_2				0
G_1					R_1		0
R_1		E_1					0
E_1		E_2					0
E_2				N			0
N							1
G_2					R_2		0
R_2	A						0
A						Y	0
Y							1

Figure 2.21

The usages are then made into the transition table of Fig. 2.21. The nondeterminism appears in two ways. First, since either the G in GREEN or the G in GRAY could be used after the starting state, we simply put both G_1 and G_2 in that transition table entry. Secondly, there are many places where a given letter cannot be the valid continuation of a word and these places are simply left blank or empty indicating that no continuation is allowed. This saves us the trouble of introducing an error state as we did in Section 2.5, where we were trying to get a deterministic table directly from the usages.

2.13 EQUIVALENCE OF NONDETERMINISTIC AND DETERMINISTIC FINITE-STATE RECOGNIZERS

The concept of nondeterministic finite-state recognizers becomes a matter of practical importance because of the following fact:

> For every nondeterministic finite-state recognizer, there is an equivalent deterministic finite-state recognizer which accepts exactly the same input sequences as does the nondeterministic machine.

In this section we show how this equivalent deterministic machine can be found.

The basic idea of the construction is that after any particular input sequence, the state of the deterministic machine will represent the set of all states of the nondeterministic machine that can be reached from the starting states after applying that sequence. The transitions for the deterministic machine are obtained from the nondeterministic transitions by computing the set of states that can follow the given set under the various single inputs. The acceptability of a sequence is determined by whether the final deterministic state it reaches represents a set of nondeterministic states that includes at least one accepting state. The resulting deterministic machine is finite state because there are only a finite number of subsets of nondeterministic states.

If the nondeterministic machine has n states, then the equivalent deterministic machine we have just described could in principle have 2^n states, one for each subset of the original state set. In practice, many of these subsets represent extraneous states. In the procedure given below, we build transitions only for those subsets that are actually needed.

The procedure is given by the five steps below. Let M_n be the nondeterministic machine and M_d the deterministic equivalent machine to be constructed.

1. Label the first row of the transition table for M_d with the set of starting states of M_n. Apply step 2 to this set.

2. Given a set of states S labeling a transition table row of M_d for which the transitions have not been computed, compute those states of M_n that can be reached from S under each input symbol x and enter these next state sets in the corresponding table entry for M_d. Expressed symbolically, if δ is the nondeterministic transition function, the deterministic transitions δ' are given by the formula:

$$\delta'(S, x) = \{s \mid s \text{ is in } \delta(t, x) \text{ for some } t \text{ in } S\}$$

3. For each new set generated by the transitions of step 2, determine if it has already been used to label a row of M_d. If a set has not been used, then create a new row with that set as label. If a row has already been used as a label, no action is required.

4. If there is some row of M_d for which transitions have not been computed, go back and apply step 2 to that row. If all transitions have been computed, go on to step 5.

5. Mark a row as an accepting state of M_d if and only if the row name contains an accepting state of the nondeterministic machine. Otherwise, mark the row as a rejecting state.

We illustrate this procedure with the nondeterministic machine of Fig. 2.20. Applying step 1, the result is Fig. 2.22(a). Applying step 2 to $\{A,B\}$, we find that $\delta'(\{A, B\}, 0) = \{A, B\}$ and $\delta'(\{A, B\}, 1) = \{C\}$. See Fig. 2.22(b).

Applying step 3, we see that there is already a row for $\{A, B\}$ but not for $\{C\}$. We therefore create a new row for $\{C\}$ thereby obtaining the configuration in Fig. 2.22(c).

Going to step 4, we find that we must now apply step 2 to $\{C\}$. After doing this, step 3 tells us that 2 more rows are required (Fig. 2.22d). Applying step 2 to $\{A, C\}$ and to the empty set $\{\ \}$ gives us transitions to sets which are already state names. This result is shown in Fig. 2.22(e).

Now step 4 tells us to go on to step 5. State $\{A, B\}$ is marked as accepting because it contains accepting state B; states $\{C\}$ and $\{A, C\}$ are marked accepting because they contain accepting state C. The empty set of course does not contain an accepting state and so is marked as rejecting.

The result is shown in Fig. 2.22(f) which displays the complete deterministic machine equivalent to the original nondeterministic one. As a reminder that the sets in Fig. 2.22(f) are simply the state names of the new machine, we substitute in a new set of names to get the state table of Fig. 2.22(g), which is just the same machine in a simpler notation.

As a second example, we apply the procedure to the machine of Fig. 2.21. The result is shown in Fig. 2.23. Since most of the transitions are to the empty set$\{\ \}$, we use a blank in the table to represent this state instead of cluttering the table with the symbol $\{\ \}$. This state, corresponding to the

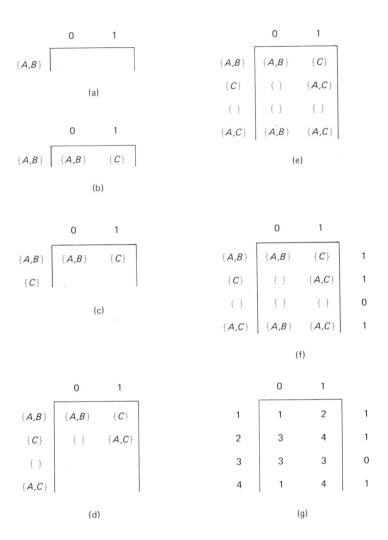

Figure 2.22

empty set, is actually the error state introduced in Section 2.5; it is a rejecting state that goes into itself for all inputs and is entered only if there are no acceptable continuations of a given input sequence.

In theory, the ten-state nondeterministic machine of Fig. 2.21 might require a deterministic version with 1024 states, one for each subset of the ten states, but in actuality, only nine states were required; this is less than the original. Thus we see that generating only the required subsets is an extremely useful technique.

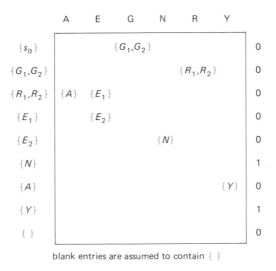

	A	E	G	N	R	Y	
$\{s_0\}$			$\{G_1,G_2\}$				0
$\{G_1,G_2\}$					$\{R_1,R_2\}$		0
$\{R_1,R_2\}$	$\{A\}$	$\{E_1\}$					0
$\{E_1\}$		$\{E_2\}$					0
$\{E_2\}$				$\{N\}$			0
$\{N\}$							1
$\{A\}$						$\{Y\}$	0
$\{Y\}$							1
$\{\ \}$							0

blank entries are assumed to contain { }

Figure 2.23

Looking at the transition table of Fig. 2.23, we see that no distinction need be made between usages G_1 and G_2 or R_1 and R_2. The algorithm has saved us the trouble of including these considerations when creating our original recognizer.

Although the procedure ensures that no extraneous states occur in the deterministic machine, the deterministic machine may not turn out to be minimal. In this last example, states (N) and (Y) are clearly equivalent and could be combined.

2.14 EXAMPLE: MINI-BASIC CONSTANTS

We have seen how to use finite-state machines to specify sets of sequences and how to make these machines into processors which can output "YES" if the input sequence is accepted or "NO" if the sequence is rejected. In practice, finite-state processors must do more than give a simple yes or no answer. Automata theory cannot tell us how to extend finite-state recognizers into special-purpose processors since the requirements of such processors vary too much from application to application. Thus we reach the point where the compiler designer must use his creativity to complete the job. This last step from recognizer to practical processor is usually a matter of augmenting the transitions with short routines.

To see how a recognizer can be extended into a practical processor, we design a processor that recognizes MINI BASIC constants and converts them into bit patterns which are their internal representation as floating-point numbers. In Chapter 4 this construction is incorporated into the lexical box of the MINI-BASIC compiler.

The first step in computing the bit pattern is to represent the number as two integers which we will call the "integer part" and the "exponent part."

The exponent part tells us the power of ten by which the integer part should be multiplied to obtain the actual number. Thus the number 12.35E14 will be represented by integer part 1235 and exponent part 12. Next we convert this pair of integers into an appropriate bit pattern. Since the details of this step are highly dependent on the particular machine, we will merely assume that we have such a routine and say no more about it. We also assume that the implementor can modify our routines to account for any overflow that might occur in constructing the integers.

Since the MINI-BASIC lexical analyzer will treat a unary + or − as a separate symbol, the optional sign which may precede a constant is not part of this example. We are designing a machine to process unsigned MINI-BASIC constants.

For this example, the input set of the recognizer is not the set of MINI-BASIC characters, but consists of only four symbols; namely,

DIGIT . E SIGN

We assume a preprocessor is supplied to translate the MINI-BASIC characters into these four input symbols. Specifically, we assume this translation of MINI-BASIC characters is as follows:

1. Each of the digits 0, 1, 2, 3, 4, 5, 6, 7, 8, and 9 is translated into a pair consisting of the symbol DIGIT and the value of the digit.

2. Each of the signs + and − is translated into a pair consisting of the symbol SIGN and an indication as to which sign it is.

3. The letter E is translated into the symbol E and . into ., each with no value part.

The MINI-BASIC lexical box design of Chapter 4 includes a similar preprocessing of the character set.

Writing down several sequences, we are able to spot seven usages:

3 8 . 7 E − 3   . 9 E 2 1

1 1 2 3 4 5 6   7 3 4 6 6

These usages may be described as:

1. digit before optional decimal point,

2. optional decimal point,

3. digit after decimal point,
4. letter E,
5. sign of exponent,
6. digit of exponent,
7. decimal point requiring decimal digits.

The one aspect of this list of usages that may not be obvious is the need to distinguish between usages 2 and 7. The difference is that usage 2 does not have to be followed by a digit and could be followed by nothing or by an E as in the sequences 38. and 38.E-21. Usage 7 must be followed by a digit since sequences such as .E-21 or a decimal point standing alone are not considered to be well-formed constants.

Next we introduce a starting state 0 and use this state together with the usages to make a transition table. As usual, the transitions are filled in according to which usages can follow which and, in the case of transitions from the starting state, which usages can begin a sequence. The usages that can end a sequence are marked as accepting states. The result is shown in Fig. 2.24(a). The machine is, in fact, deterministic if we interpret the blanks as a transition to an unlisted error state.

We see that the machine is not reduced since states 2 and 3 are equivalent and we elect to combine these into a single state which we call $\overline{23}$. The result is Fig. 2.24(b). A check of this transition table reveals that it is reduced.

The next step in designing a processor is to add the endmarker as input and give each transition a separate name. The result is shown in Fig. 2.25.

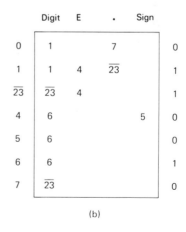

(a)

(b)

Figure 2.24

	Digit	E	ə	sign	⊣
0	1a		7		
1	1b	4a	$\overline{23}$c		YES1
$\overline{23}$	$\overline{23}$a	4b			YES2
4	6a			5	
5	6b				
6	6c				YES3
7	$\overline{23}$b				

Figure 2.25

Since the original transition table had two transitions to state 1, we have called these transitions 1a and 1b to distinguish them in the processing routines to be described later. Transitions to $\overline{23}$, 4, and 6 are similarly distinguished. The accepting entries under the endmarker are also given distinct names.

The mechanical part of the design has been completed and the ad hoc part begins. The transitions of the machine are interpreted as calls on routines or pieces of code that must be executed when the transitions occur. It is up to the designer to describe these routines so as to accomplish the desired result which in this case is the translation of the input sequence into an "integer part" and an "exponent part."

To carry out the transformation, we use four variables which we call NUMBER REGISTER, EXPONENT REGISTER, COUNT REGISTER, and SIGN REGISTER. The purposes of these variables are:

NUMBER REGISTER – to accumulate "integer part,"

EXPONENT REGISTER – to accumulate "exponent part,"

COUNT REGISTER – to count places after decimal point,

SIGN REGISTER – to remember sign of exponent.

We now supply the routines for each transition. Our descriptions are in English. The implementer can convert the routines into a program for his particular machine. In order to have any understanding of these routines, one must keep in mind the interpretation of the states and the location of the transitions in the table. For example, 1a is seen as the action taken when an initial digit is encountered and 1b is the action taken when a subsequent digit is encountered. The transition routines are as follows:

  1*a*: Put value of digit into NUMBER REGISTER.
        Get input and do state 1 transition.

  1*b*: Multiply contents of NUMBER REGISTER by 10.
        Add value of digit and save in NUMBER REGISTER.
        Get input and do state 1 transition.

$\overline{23}$*a*: Increment COUNT REGISTER by 1.
        Multiply contents of NUMBER REGISTER by 10.
        Add value of digit and save in NUMBER REGISTER.
        Get input and do state $\overline{23}$ transition.

$\overline{23}$*b*: Initialize COUNT REGISTER with 1.
        Put value of digit in NUMBER REGISTER.
        Get input and do state $\overline{23}$ transition.

$\overline{23}$ *c*: Initialize COUNT REGISTER with 0.
        Get input and do state $\overline{23}$ transition.

  4*a*: Initialize COUNT REGISTER with 0.
        Get input and do state 4 transition.

  4*b*: Get input and do state 4 transition.

   5: If operator is +, set SIGN REGISTER to +1.
        If operator is −, set SIGN REGISTER to −1.
        Get input and do state 5 transition.

  6*a*: Set SIGN REGISTER to +1.
        Put value of digit into EXPONENT REGISTER.
        Get input and do state 6 transition.

  6*b*: Put value of digit into EXPONENT REGISTER.
        Get input and do state 6 transition.

  6*c*: Multiply contents of EXPONENT REGISTER by 10.
        Add value of digit and save in EXPONENT REGISTER.
        Get input and do state 6 transition.

   7: Get input and do state 7 transition.

YES1: Set EXPONENT REGISTER to 0.
        Exit from machine.

YES2: Set EXPONENT REGISTER to minus the value in COUNT REG-
        ISTER.
        Exit from machine.

YES3: If SIGN REGISTER is −1, negate EXPONENT REGISTER.
        Subtract COUNT REGISTER from EXPONENT REGISTER.
        Exit from machine.

It should be noted that when we specify "Get input and do state s transition," we do not mean to imply that this should be implemented in a particular way. We merely mean that state s and the next input are to be used to select the next transition.

Also note that we wrote our routines without taking advantage of commonality such as can be found in the routines for $6a$ and $6b$. This was done for expository purposes whereas in practice we would write something like:

$6a$: Set SIGN REGISTER to $+1$.

$6b$: Put value of digit into EXPONENT REGISTER.
    Get input and do state 6 transition.

To make a complete processor, one needs to fill in the blank transition table entries with calls on error routines. We will not discuss here what these routines should be.

To see how the machine works and to achieve some confidence that it does, in fact, work, we now construct some test programs. At the very minimum, these test programs should cause each transition to be used at least once. One set that exercises all transitions consists of the following four programs:

47.2E-13   4E6   .8   3

The effect of these programs on the processor is shown in Fig. 2.26. Each row of the figure is a snapshot showing the input symbol read, the transition it caused, and the new values of the variables which resulted from the transition routines.

Note that if this processor is implemented as a computer program, these three test programs can be used for debugging purposes. In fact the debugging programs and their results can be specified by the designer with a high degree of confidence that if these programs run correctly, the processor is behaving correctly.

In order to check out the error routines, which presumably print out error messages to the MINI-BASIC programmer, it is necessary to supply an input sequence for each of the transitions to the error state. For instance the transition from state 4 with input E can be checked with the input sequence

DIGIT E E

The main point of this example is that the theory has enabled us to break a large problem (i.e., how to process sequences) into a bunch of little problems (i.e., how to augment transitions). Each of the solutions to these small problems can be expressed in a few lines.

Input	Transition	Number	New value of registers		
			Exponent	Count	Sign
4	1a	4	—	—	—
7	1b	47	—	—	—
.	$\overline{23}c$	47	—	0	—
2	$\overline{23}a$	472	—	1	—
E	4b	472	—	1	—
—	5	472	—	1	−1
1	6b	472	1	1	−1
3	6c	472	13	1	−1
⊣	YES3	472	−14	1	−1
4	1a	4	—	—	—
E	4a	4	—	0	—
6	6a	4	6	0	+1
⊣	YES3	4	6	0	+1
.	7	—	—	—	—
8	$\overline{23}b$	8	—	1	—
⊣	YES2	8	−1	1	—
3	1a	3	—	—	—
⊣	YES1	3	0	—	—

Figure 2.26

2.15 REFERENCES

The model of a finite-state machine was introduced by Huffman [1954], Moore [1956], and Mealy [1955], all of whom dealt with machine reduction. A highly abstract view of machines is given in Rabin and Scott [1959]; they also present the results on nondeterministic machines discussed here. Many of the original papers on finite-state machines have been reprinted in Moore [1964]. Books by Ginsburg [1962] and Hartmanis and Stearns [1966] give a detailed mathematical presentation of some aspects of finite-state machines. Other books containing a large amount of material on finite-state machines are Hennie [1968], Minsky [1967], Booth [1967], Harrison [1965], and Gill [1962].

PROBLEMS

1. Design a finite-state machine that will recognize the words

GO TO

where there can be an arbitrary number of blanks (including zero) between GO and TO.

2. a) Find the shortest sequence recognized by this machine.

b) Exhibit four other sequences recognized by this machine.

c) Exhibit four sequences that are rejected by this machine.

	0	1	
A	D	A	0
B	A	C	0
C	A	F	0
D	B	C	0
E	B	C	1
F	E	A	1

3. First design finite-state recognizers for the sets of sequences of 1's and 0's described below. Then convert each recognizer to a processor with an end-marker. Finally make the processors detect acceptable and unacceptable sequences as soon as possible.

a) The number of 1's is even and the number of 0's is odd.

b) There are an even number of 0's between occurrences of a 1.

c) There are an odd number of occurrences of the pattern 00, overlaps being allowed.

d) Every occurrence of the pattern 11 is followed by a 0.

e) Every third symbol is a 1.

f) There is at least one 1.

4. Design a finite-state machine whose input alphabet is {0, 1} and that accepts exactly the following set of sequences:

a) All input sequences

b) No input sequences

c) The input sequence 101

d) The two input sequences 01 and 0100

e) All sequences ending in a 1 and beginning with a 0

f) All sequences that contain no 1's

g) All sequences containing exactly three 1's

h) All sequences in which every 1 is immediately preceded by and followed by a 0.

i) The null sequence and 011

j) All sequences except the null sequence.

5. a) Design a finite-state machine that will recognize the following three ALGOL 60 reserved words:

STEP, STRING, SWITCH

b) Estimate how many states would be required to recognize all the ALGOL 60 reserved words.

6. Describe in words the set of sequences recognized by each of these machines.

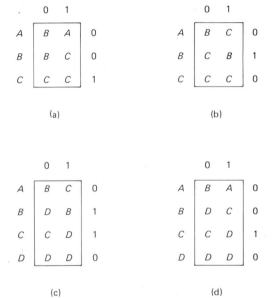

	0	1	
A	B	A	0
B	B	C	0
C	C	C	1

(a)

	0	1	
A	B	C	0
B	C	B	1
C	C	C	0

(b)

	0	1	
A	B	C	0
B	D	B	1
C	C	D	1
D	D	D	0

(c)

	0	1	
A	B	A	0
B	D	C	0
C	C	D	1
D	D	D	0

(d)

	1	*	c	
A	B	F	F	0
B	F	C	F	0
C	C	D	C	0
D	E	C	C	0
E	F	F	F	1
F	F	F	F	0

(e)

7. For each of these machines, find the input sequence, or sequences, of shortest total length that will cause:

a) each state to be visited at least once,

b) each transition to occur at least once.

	0	1	
A	C	B	0
B	D	B	1
C	A	E	0
D	A	A	0
E	F	E	1
F	E	A	1

	0	1	
A	A	E	0
B	B	D	0
C	C	F	1
D	D	B	1
E	B	F	1
F	F	C	0

8. Find a distinguishing sequence (if one exists) for this pair of machines.

	0	1	
A	A	B	1
B	C	D	0
C	B	A	1
D	A	B	0

	0	1	
A	A	D	1
B	A	D	0
C	B	A	1
D	C	B	0

9. Find the extraneous states in this machine.

	0	1	2	
A	C	E	G	0
B	J	E	G	1
C	J	A	H	0
D	F	A	G	1
E	E	J	H	0
F	D	I	A	1
G	H	A	J	0
H	G	J	B	1
I	D	F	G	0
J	B	H	G	1

10. Find the minimal equivalent transition table for each of the given machines.

	0	1	
s_1	s_1	s_3	0
s_2	s_7	s_4	1
s_3	s_6	s_5	0
s_4	s_1	s_4	1
s_5	s_1	s_4	0
s_6	s_7	s_6	1
s_7	s_7	s_3	0

(a)

	x	y	
1	4	1	1
2	5	1	1
3	4	5	0
4	2	6	0
5	1	7	0
6	1	4	1
7	2	5	1

(b)

	A	C	E	L	
INIT	Error	C	Error	Error	0
C	CA	Error	CE	Error	0
CA	Error	Error	Error	CAL	0
CAL	Error	Error	Error	CALL	0
CALL	Error	Error	Error	Error	1
CE	Error	Error	Error	CEL	0
CEL	Error	Error	Error	CELL	0
CELL	Error	Error	Error	Error	1
Error	Error	Error	Error	Error	0

(c)

11. Convert the machine of Fig. 2.19 to a processor with endmarker that detects errors as soon as possible.

12. Write an error message for each error transition of the machine of Fig. 2.19.

13. Many ALGOL 60 compilers have the restriction that in own array declarations the array bounds must be integer constants. Typical declarations of this form are:

OWN REAL ARRAY A1 [4 : 6]
OWN INTEGER ARRAY A2 [−1: 3, 12 :+4, 171 : 173]

a) Design a finite-state machine that will recognize that portion of the declaration after the identifier. Assume the input alphabet is:

$$[\quad] \quad : \quad , \quad - \quad + \quad d$$

where d is the token for a digit.

b) Convert this machine to a processor with endmarker that detects errors as soon as possible.

c) Find a set of sequences that will cause all the transitions of this machine to occur at least once.

14. Describe in words the set of sequences recognized by each of these nondeterministic machines.

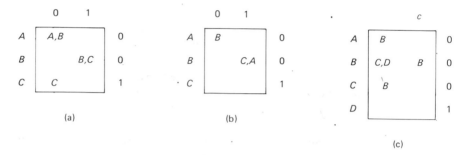

(a)   (b)   (c)

15. Find a deterministic machine that is equivalent to this nondeterministic machine.

	a	b	
1	2,3	2	0
2		1	0
3	1	3	1

16. Design a finite-state machine that will accept just those sequences that can be built up from the subsequences

GO , GOTO , TOO , ON

Repetitions are allowed, but overlaps are not. Thus one acceptable sequence is

GOONGOTOONGOTOOON

You may wish to first design a nondeterministic machine and later make it deterministic.

17. Consider a language that consists of arithmetic expressions using the operators + and − (both unary and binary), and ∗ and /, but no parentheses. Assume the operands are either integer constants (e.g., 314) or identifiers which consist of a sequence of letters and digits beginning with a letter (e.g., D12).

a) Utilizing the usage method, design the minimal finite-state recognizer for these expressions. Assume the input alphabet is

$$+ - * / l \, d$$

where l is the symbol for a letter and d is the symbol for a digit.

b) Assume the arithmetic operations are carried out strictly from left to right so that, for example, the value of

$$3 + 5 * 2$$

is 16. Design the ad hoc procedures that must be added to this recognizer to produce the machine instructions for these expressions. Assume the run-time addresses of the identifiers are known.

18. a) Design a finite-state machine which will recognize the set of Roman numerals representing numbers less than 2,000.

b) Convert this machine into a processor that recognizes the Roman numerals and converts them into the corresponding bit pattern.

c) Supply a set of sequences that exercises all the transitions of this processor, and describe the operation of the machine for these sequences.

d) Add error messages to the processor, preferably in Latin.

19. a) Find a set of input sequences, different than that given in the text, that exercises all the transitions of the machine of Fig. 2.25.

b) For the above sequences, draw a chart similar to those of Fig. 2.26.

20. a) Write an error message for each error transition of the machine of Fig. 2.25.

b) Find a set of input sequences that exercises all the error transitions of the machine of Fig. 2.25.

21. Write a program in your favorite language that will implement the machine of Fig. 2.25 and all the routines required for its transitions.

22. Design the transition table of a finite-state machine with input alphabet consisting of the twenty-eight symbols ONE, TWO, THREE, ... NINE, TEN, ELEVEN, ..., NINETEEN, TWENTY, THIRTY, ..., NINETY, HUNDRED and output alphabet consisting of the ten symbols 0, 1, 2, ..., 9 which will accept as input the English language representation of any number from 1 to 999 (for example, EIGHT HUNDRED THIRTY FIVE) and translate the input into the equivalent representation with numerals (835).

23. These two machines accept sets S_1 and S_2 respectively.

a) Design nondeterministic machines for the sets

   i) S_1 UNION S_2,

   ii) S_1 INTERSECTION S_2.

b) Find the minimal deterministic machines equivalent to the above nondeterministic machines.

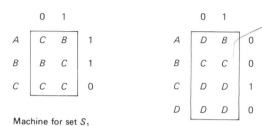

	0	1	
A	C	B	1
B	B	C	1
C	C	C	0

Machine for set S_1

	0	1	
A	D	B	0
B	C	C	0
C	D	D	1
D	D	D	0

Machine for set S_2

24. Consider the set of all two state recognizers with input alphabet $\{0, 1\}$.

   a) How many machines are in this set?

   b) How many nonequivalent machines are in this set?

   c) Describe in words the set of sequences recognized by each of these nonequivalent machines.

25. In some applications, a finite-state machine does not have a designated starting state. It can be started in any of its states by some external means. Two such machines are equivalent if for each state in one machine there is an equivalent state in the other, and vice versa. Describe a procedure that takes such a machine and finds the minimal equivalent machine.

26. a) Assume that k is the length of the shortest distinguishing sequence for some pair of states in a finite-state machine. Show that if $k \geq 1$, then there are two other states in the machine whose shortest distinguishing sequence is of length $k - 1$.

   b) Show that if two states in an n-state machine are not equivalent, then they have a distinguishing sequence of length $n - 2$ or less.

   c) Draw the transition table of a 6-state machine such that the length of the shortest distinguishing sequence for two of the states is 4.

27. Consider two finite-state machines M_1 and M_2 with a number of states N_1 and N_2, respectively. Show that a nondeterministic finite-state machine that recognizes the union of the sets recognized by M_1 and M_2 need never have more than $N_1 + N_2$ states.

28. A finite-state machine is said to be strongly connected if, and only if, given any two states s_1 and s_2, there is some input sequence that will take the machine from s_1 to s_2.
Show that for an N state machine this sequence never need be longer than $N - 1$ symbols.

29. A debugging sequence for a finite-state machine is an input sequence that causes all state transitions to occur at least once. Show that for an N-state strongly

connected [See Problem 28] machine with I inputs, a debugging sequence never need be longer than $N^2 I$ symbols.

30. Show that a finite-state machine cannot recognize all sequences of the form

$$1^n 0^n$$

(i.e., some number of 1's followed by the same number of zeros). These sequences are analogous to left and right parentheses in expressions. Hint: Assume the machine has only r states. Observe that if $n > r$, then in processing the string of 1's the machine must be in some state at least twice.

31. a) Give an example of two equivalent machines, M and N, where some state in M has more than one equivalent state in N.

   b) Give an example of two equivalent machines, M and N, where there is a state in M with no equivalent state in N.

32. How would you test for the equivalence of two states of a nondeterministic machine?

33. a) Design a finite-state machine that recognizes chemical formulas composed of the eight elements H, C, N, O, SI, S, CL, and SN. The formulas are written with commas separating consecutive elements. The elements can appear in any order and in any combination. The formulas need not represent compounds that actually exist. Some sample sequences are:

   H2, O

   O, H7

   SN, S, O4

   CL

   N, H4, C7, H5, O2

   O2

   There are nine input symbols:

   C H I L N O S , d

   where d is the token for a digit.

   b) Design a finite-state processor that calculates the molecular weight of the compound represented by the input sequence.

3
Implementing Finite-State Machines

3.1 INTRODUCTION

In the previous chapter we discussed finite-state machines from a fairly theoretical viewpoint giving only limited attention to their intended use as one of the basic building blocks of a compiler. In this chapter, we consider some of the problems of implementing a finite-state machine or processor as a computer program or subroutine. This material is also relevant to the implementation of the general machine models discussed in later chapters since these models use finite-state machines as their central control.

Throughout this chapter, there are three interrelated considerations:

1. how to represent the inputs, states, and transitions of a finite-state processor given the often-conflicting goals of having an implementation which executes quickly and which requires only a small amount of computer memory;

2. how to handle certain specific recurrent compilation problems;

3. how to break up a design problem to obtain machines that are easy to implement.

Some finite-state machine problems involve recognizing only a finite set of words. The essence of these problems is that the compiler must detect the occurrence of some word from this set and then take some action dependent on which word was detected. In MINI-BASIC for example, statements may begin with any of nine words (LET, IF, GOTO, etc.) and it is important for the compiler to determine which word if any begins each line and take the action appropriate for the given statement type. We call a problem of this nature an "identification" problem since the action of the compiler depends

61

on the identity of the specific word embedded in the machine's input sequence. Because identification problems may involve an enormous number of states, special implementation techniques must often be employed to handle such situations. For this reason it is frequently advisable to design the compiler so that the identification problem is handled by a separate dedicated subprocessor.

There are some word identification problems that, strictly speaking, cannot be handled by a finite-state machine. Consider the commonly occurring problem of recognizing variables or identifiers in some language and associating them with their corresponding symbol-table entries. To use the ordinary finite-state machine methods for this problem would require allocating some states and a symbol-table entry for every allowable identifier. However, for most languages the set of allowable identifiers is infinite or so large that it might as well be considered infinite. For example in ALGOL where identifiers can consist of an arbitrary number of symbols the number of allowable identifiers is infinite while in FORTRAN where identifiers can be as long as six symbols the number of allowable identifiers is finite but so astronomically large that it is infinite for all practical purposes. (By contrast, in MINI-BASIC identifiers are limited to only two symbols and the number of allowable identifiers is both finite and manageable.)

For those languages where the number of allowable identifiers is infinite or essentially so, it is clearly not possible to allocate storage space or a symbol-table entry for each possible identifier. This situation can be handled with the concept of an *expanding finite-state machine.* As such a machine scans its input sequence it allocates the required storage space and symbol-table entry for an identifier if and when that identifier is first encountered in the program. If that identifier is encountered again in the program, the machine uses the finite-state word-identification techniques to identify it. Then when a new identifier appears the machine expands itself again and so on. While such a machine is not strictly speaking a finite-state machine, many of the finite-state analysis and design concepts still apply.

Most identification techniques have potential utility both in the identification of prestored sets and for the identification of expanding sets. Thus, when discussing these specialized identification techniques, we must consider ease of expansion in addition to the usual considerations of time and space requirements.

3.2   REPRESENTING THE INPUT SET

In order to simulate a finite-state machine, we must encode its input set in a suitable manner. The most flexible arrangement is to represent the input symbols by a set of consecutive integers starting with 0 or 1. This encoding works well with all the techniques we will discuss for implementing transitions. However, some of these techniques will also work for arbitrary input encodings.

If the input to the finite-state machine is the output of some other box of the compiler, then it is generally a simple matter to design the box supplying inputs to do so in the form most suitable for the finite-state machine. The only place in the compiler design where the input encoding is likely to cause a problem is in the routine that reads the characters in the source program itself. We concentrate the remainder of this section on this case.

If the character set of a source program were used directly as input to some finite-state processor with many states, the machine would have a large transition table since the alphanumeric characters alone make up a set of 36 characters and many character sets are several times this size. A convenient way to reduce the size of the transition table is to process the source characters with a serial connection of two machines: the first machine is a transliterator whose only task is to reduce the input set to a manageable size; the second machine does the remainder of the processing. This kind of an interconnection is shown in Fig. 3.1(a).

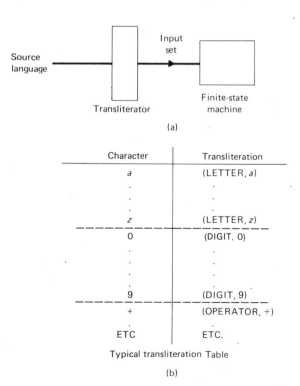

(a)

Character	Transliteration
a	(LETTER, a)
.	.
.	.
z	(LETTER, z)
0	(DIGIT, 0)
.	.
.	.
9	(DIGIT, 9)
+	(OPERATOR, +)
.	.
ETC	ETC.

Typical transliteration Table

(b)

Figure 3.1

The input-output relation of a transliterator can be expressed as a table similar to Fig. 3.1(b) which gives the translation of each character in the source language. We call the output of this translation a *character token*. Such a token usually consists of a class part and value part. Thus the letter *a* might have class LETTER and value *a* while the operator + might have class OPERATOR and value +. The class part of the character token is to be used as input by the second machine and the value part is to be available to the transition routines of the second machine. The need for such preprocessing of characters was suggested in Chapter 2. (Recall, for example, the constant processor.)

A transliterator is simply a one-state processor although there is hardly any need to analyze it as one. It is of course implemented as a routine which finds the translation of each input character in a table. On many computers, this can be done with only one or two instructions. The set of character token classes is generally represented by a set of consecutive integers since they represent the possible inputs to the second machine.

3.3   REPRESENTING THE STATE

There are two basic ways in which a program simulating a finite-state machine can remember the state of the simulated machine. The first is to keep a number, corresponding to the current state, stored in some register or memory location of the computer. We call this the *explicit* method as the state is explicitly given by some variable. The second basic method is to have separate portions of the program for each state. Thus the fact that the simulated machine is in a given state is "remembered" by the fact that the simulating program is executing a segment of code that "belongs" to that state. We call this the *implicit* method.

The choice between the explicit and implicit methods is simply one of programming convenience. The important point is that the word "state" is not intended to imply a specific implementation technique.

3.4   SELECTING THE TRANSITIONS

The heart of a simulation program for a finite-state processor is the technique used for selecting the transitions. That is, for a given state and next input, the program must carry out the transition specified by the transition table. Thus, the information in the transition table must be stored or otherwise incorporated into the simulation program.

We will assume for the moment that the state is being implicitly remembered. In this case, the correct row of the transition table is implicitly known and the problem reduces to that of finding the transition on the basis of the input alone. This problem must of course be solved separately for each state.

We consider two approaches to the problem of selecting a transition when given an input. We call these the "transition-vector" and "transition-list" methods.

In the *transition-vector method,* the address or label information of which transition routine to transfer to is kept as a vector in consecutive memory locations, one for each input symbol. The next input is used as an index to select the element of the vector which·gives the transition. For this method to work, the input set must be represented in a suitable form, such as a set of consecutive integers. An example of such a vector can be seen in Fig. 3.2(b) which is the transfer vector for state *A* of Fig. 3.2(a). This method has the

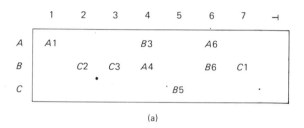

	1	2	3	4	5	6	7	⊣
A	*A*1			*B*3		*A*6		
B		*C*2	*C*3	*A*4		*B*6	*C*1	
C					*B*5			

(a)

Address of *A*1	Address of error routine	Address of error routine	Address of *B*3	Address of error routine	Address of *A*6	Address of error routine	Address of error routine

(b)

Input	Transition
1	*A*1
6	*A*6
4	*B*3

Default = Error Routine

(c)

Fig. 3.2 (a) Processor design; (b) Transition vector; (c) Transition list

advantage that the appropriate transition routine can be selected very quickly. The space requirement is one storage location for each element of the row. This method can be implemented in most high-level languages using a switch or computed go to.

In the *transition-list method,* the input symbols are divided into two classes: one class for which individual transitions are to be assigned to each input and one class for which all inputs have a common transition (usually an error routine). For the first class, the correspondence between input symbol and transition-routine address is kept as a list of ordered pairs. The common transition for inputs of the second class is remembered separately and is called the *default transition.*

When each new input symbol is applied, the list is searched to find that symbol and the corresponding transition. If the search fails, a transition is made to the default routine. This method can be used even if the input is not an index.

Figure 3.2(c) shows a transition list for state *A* of the processor in Fig. 3.2(a). The default case applies to the inputs 2, 3, 5, 7, and end marker thereby combining five table entries into a single piece of information.

The average time required to select a transition by the transition-list method depends on the length of the list and the relative frequency with which the input symbols appear in source programs. Naturally, it pays to have the pairs for the most frequent inputs near the beginning of the list. Nevertheless, the required time is always worse than the transition-vector method and gets poorer as the list becomes long. The list method requires very little space when the list is short; however, when the list is long, the list method may require more storage than the vector method since storage space is required for both the label of the transition routine and the input symbol that causes it. Thus this method is most effectively used when space is at a premium and the transition table contains many standard error conditions.

The machine simulation may of course employ a mixture of these two methods. In the example of Fig. 3.2(a), the transfer-vector method would be the preferred method of selecting the transition for state *B* whereas the transition-list method would be a space saver for state *C*.

When the state of the simulated machine is being kept explicitly, the principles of vectors and lists still apply, but more variations are possible. One possibility is to use the state as an index for transferring to one of the routines already described. Another is to store the transition table as a single two-dimensional array indexed by a combination of state and input. There is also the possibility of using the list method to choose elements from the columns of the transition table instead of from the rows. We do not advocate one method over another; the designer is advised to select the method he thinks is most suitable for his particular problem and computer.

3.5 WORD IDENTIFICATION—MACHINE APPROACH

This is the first of six sections dealing with identification problems. We begin with the *word-identification problem* in which we assume that some finite set of words over some input alphabet has been specified and that we are given some input word and asked to identify which member (if any) of the given set is the same as the input word. In this section, we solve this problem by designing a finite-state processor which, when presented with the input word and an endmarker, will tell us the identity of the input word. In subsequent sections, we consider alternatives to this approach.

The most common application of a word-identification machine in compilers is in the lexical box. One way such a machine could be used is illustrated in Fig. 3.3 which shows its use in a hypothetical lexical box. The master machine knows that a particular sequence of letters occurring at a certain place in the program should be a word and ships those letters, one at a time, to the word-identification machine for analysis. When the master machine detects that the word is completed, it sends an endmarker to the word-identification machine to see what the word is. We assume that the letters have been transliterated into character tokens of type LETTER with a value identifying the letter. Each input-symbol LETTER applied to the master machine causes it to apply the value of the letter as input to the word-identification machine, and to make some specified transition.

If a word-identification machine is to be used in this manner, the language must be such that the master machine knows which input symbols should go together to form a word. Some identification problems are not this

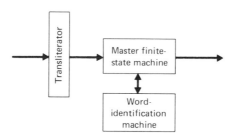

Fig. 3.3 Possible lexical-box organization

straightforward. In Section 3.10, we discuss the application of word-identification techniques to some situations that are less clear cut.

A machine to identify a set of words can be designed by introducing a state for each subsequence which is the prefix of some word in the set. This set of prefixes includes the null sequence which is a prefix of every word in the set and the words themselves since each word is a prefix of itself. Because the procedure is easier done than said, we demonstrate it in the following example.

Consider the problem of designing a finite-state processor which has input set {A, B, C, D, E} plus an endmarker and is to identify the set {ACE, BAD, BADE, BED}. A processor for this set is shown in Fig. 3.4. The states of the machine are named after the sequence of inputs that have been seen up to that point. Thus the starting state is ϵ which is the sequence seen before any inputs are applied, and the sequence BE will cause the machine to enter state *BE*. Table entries such as "ACE" mean that the machine has identified the corresponding word. Blank entries indicate an error exit which prints something like INPUT WORD NOT IN SET. Alternatively, one can have a transition to an error state which postpones the message until the erroneous word is completed. No processing is associated with the transitions other than the actions required to change state.

Since this particular word identification problem involves only five letters and ten states, the processor could easily be implemented using either

	A	B	C	D	E	⊣
ϵ	A	B				
A			AC			
B	BA				BE	
AC					ACE	
BA				BAD		
BE				BED		
ACE						"ACE"
BAD					BADE	"BAD"
BED						"BED"
BADE						"BADE"

Figure 3.4

the transition-vector method or the transition-list method. The word-recognition problems that arise in practice, however, are frequently of a much larger scale. For example, the input set generally involves all 26 letters or all 36 alphanumerics. The number of words to be identified can also be larger. The transition table could thus have thousands of entries and the transition-vector implementation would be ruled out on space considerations.

Thinking in terms of the transition-list method, we observe that the vast majority of transition table entries contain the error condition. This is characteristic of most word identification problems encounterd in practice and is due to the fact that each state represents a word prefix and can therefore be reached in only one way. For example, the state *BAD* can only be reached from state *BA* and can only be reached with input D. The number of transitions leaving a given state is equal to or less than the number of words in the set that have that prefix. For example the state *BAD* has two transitions, one to *BADE* and one to "BAD", while the state *BA* has only one transition, to *BAD,* even though there are two words with prefix BA. Therefore the transition-list method can be used effectively for fairly large word-identification problems, regardless of the size of the input alphabet.

Because of the simple nature of the transition routines, the machine can be implemented even more easily than suggested by our previous discussion of the transition-list method. In cases like this, where the transitions are merely transitions and not transition routines, it is convenient to represent the state as a pointer to its transition list. Since there are no transition routines, it is not necessary to associate the label of a transition routine with each transition. Instead, the transition lists are used to associate each non-error input with a pointer to the transition list for the next state. The transition is carried out simply by replacing the current-state transition-list pointer by the next-state transition-list pointer obtained from the table. The information associated with the endmarker entries in the transition list must be an index or symbol-table pointer which indicates which word has been found.

Applying these techniques to our example, we obtain the list structure shown in Fig. 3.5. The starting state is represented by a pointer to list 1. The processor takes the next input symbol and searches the current state's list until it finds either the input symbol or the ERROR symbol. For example, if the first input is C, the processor first compares the C with the A and B on list 1. It then sees the ERROR indicator and executes an error routine. If however the first input is B, the processor matches it with the B on list 1 and sets the state pointer to list 3 (the list for state *B*). Then if the next input is E, the processor sets the state pointer to list 6 (the list for state *BE*). Assuming the next input is D, the state pointer is set to list 9 (the list for state *BED*). Finally, if the next input is an endmarker, the processor matches it with the

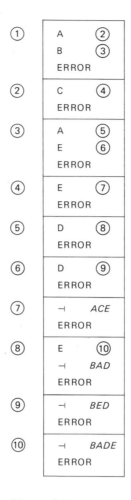

Figure 3.5

endmarker on list 9 and then finds a symbol-table pointer or other indicator of the word "BED" in the table. Observe that the list structure has one entry for each nonerror transition and one ERROR entry for each state with at least one error transition.

Suppose now that we wish to expand the table of Fig. 3.5 so that the corresponding machine would also recognize the word ADD. Two more transition lists would have to be added, one for state AD and one for state ADD. In addition, *list 2 would have to be lengthened* in order to record the transition from state A to state AD. Such an expansion is easy at design time but would be very difficult at compile time. Thus this implementation can be used to handle the recognition of a fixed set of words but cannot be used effectively to recognize an expanding set. There is, however, a variation of this list implementation which is ideally suited for such compile-time expansions.

To obtain an expandable list implementation, we observe that there are really two lists associated with each symbol in the lists. One is the transition list to be used if a match with the input symbol is found and one is a list of additional symbols to be checked if the input fails to match the symbol in the table. The location of the first list is given by the associated pointer and the second list is understood to begin in the next memory location. To achieve expandability, one merely reverses these conventions. The next state transition list will be understood as beginning in the next consecutive location and the beginning of the list of additional symbols to be checked will be remembered by a pointer. The list layout for our example, is shown in Fig. 3.6(a).

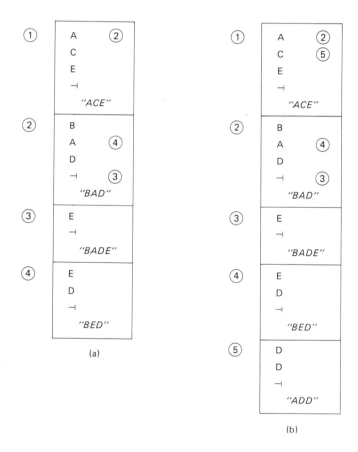

(a)

(b)

Figure 3.6

In this new implementation, the symbols may be paired with a next test pointer or a blank. The blank indicates that there are no further symbols to be matched and that an error must have occurred. For example, if the first input is C, the processor compares the C with the A in list 1. Because C is not A and because the A is associated with a pointer to list 2, the processor then compares C with the B in list 2. Again the symbols do not match, but this time there is a blank associated with the symbol in the table. The processor concludes that there is no word beginning with C and executes its error routine. In contrast with Fig. 3.5, the endmarker may also be associated with a list pointer (e.g., list 2) or a blank (e.g., list 1). When a match is found with an endmarker, the word identification is found in the next word. Observe that this list structure has one entry for each nonerror transition and one entry for each word in the set being recognized.

Now consider what happens when we wish to expand the machine to include the word ADD. This means that after input A, a D will be allowed in addition to the input C. A new list is appended to remember what is supposed to happen after the D and a pointer to this list is entered in the blank field associated with the C. The result is Fig. 3.6(b). Notice that the only new space required to expand the list can be added at the end of the used storage and thus the original storage does not have to be restructured to accommodate the change. Thus this last implementation is easily expanded at compile time.

3.6   WORD IDENTIFICATION—INDEX APPROACH

In the previous section, we discussed the solution of the word-identification problem by means of a finite-state machine. Now we consider a number of methods for solving this problem without machine simulation. All of these methods are based on storing the set of words to be recognized as some type of list or table, and then, when a word is applied as input, determining whether or not that word is in the list. In this section we consider the possibility of computing an index from the inputs which enables one to access the table directly.

As an example, consider the problem of identifying MINI-BASIC variables. A MINI-BASIC variable is either a single letter or a letter followed by a digit. Altogether, there are exactly 286 allowable MINI-BASIC variables. As this is a small number, one can afford to have a table entry for each allowable variable. The variable identification problem is then reduced to the problem of converting the variable to an index which denotes its position in the table. One way to do this is to set the index from 1 to 26 according to the letter input. Then if the next input symbol is an optional digit d, the number $26 * (d + 1)$ is added to the index. This means for example that variable Z would be number 26, A0 would be 27, and Z9 would be number 286.

In the general case, suppose that a recognizer can only be presented with a finite number of possible input words. Assume also that we are willing to allocate some storage space for each of the possible words. Finally suppose that for each of the possible words we can quickly calculate a unique integer, say between 1 and M. This integer is called the index of the word. Then a table can be stored in contiguous memory locations so that the jth entry in the table is reserved for the word whose index is j. Such a table is sometimes called an indexed table, and is similar to a one-dimensional array where the index serves as the subscript. An input word is processed by calculating its index and then looking in the table entry that has been reserved for that index.

Three conditions must be present before this index method can be applied. First, the number of words cannot be too large. This would rule out, for example, the set of FORTRAN variables because this set has over a billion elements. Second, the index must be easy to compute. This could rule out even small sets of reserved words for which there is no good way to construct an index. Third, the size of the set must be fixed at design time, since the method of computing the index cannot be conveniently altered in midcompilation. Considering these three conditions, it is apparent that this method cannot often be used. However, when it can be applied, the identification is achieved with a minimal expenditure of time.

When the purpose of the identification is to associate a word with its symbol-table entry, the correspondence between index and symbol-table entries can be achieved in at least two ways:

1. The index can be used to index the symbol table directly. In this case, the word with index i is assigned to the ith symbol-table entry.
2. The index can be used to index a pointer table which contains pointers to the symbol table. To find the symbol-table entry for the word with index i, take the pointer from the ith entry of the pointer table.

The second method permits one to assign symbol-table entries only to those words actually found in a given program. To achieve this, the pointer table is initialized with zeros which are interpreted to mean that no symbol-table entry has been assigned. When a word is encountered for the first time, this fact is detected by the zero in the pointer-table entry. A symbol-table entry is then created for that word and a pointer to it placed in the pointer table.

The second method requires less storage space under the frequently plausible assumptions that symbol-table entries require more space than pointer-table entries and that none of the individual programs being compiled use a high percentage of the allowable words. The second method also allows one to assign variable-size symbol-table entries. On the other hand, the second method may involve some extra computer time to access the symbol table.

3.7   WORD IDENTIFICATION—LINEAR-LIST APPROACH

Probably the most straightforward method of word identification is to build up a copy of the word from the inputs and then compare it with each item on the stored list until a match (if any) is found. The method is easily adapted to expanding set situations since all one has to do in that case is append the new word to the list. The space requirement is simply that there be enough space to store the list of words. The one drawback of this method is that searching a long list can be very time consuming. Assuming that one word is as likely as another, one would expect on the average to search halfway through the list to find a given word on the list. To be exact, if there are M words, the expected number of comparisons required to find one of these words selected at random is $(M + 1)/2$.

There are two common ways of storing lists of words, one using *consecutive storage* and one using *linked storage*. In the first method, the next item on the list is found by going to the next consecutive storage location. To be expandable, vacant space must be reserved at the end of the list. In the *linked-list method* each word has a pointer to the next word. To be expandable, there must be vacant space available, but the space need not be physically at the end of the given list. A single block of vacant space can therefore be used to service several linked lists at once.

3.8   WORD IDENTIFICATION—ORDERED-LIST APPROACH

The time required to search a long list can be shortened considerably if the items on the list are stored in some order such as alphabetical. Suppose, for example, that we have a list of M words arranged alphabetically and stored in consecutive storage locations and suppose we want to find the list location (if any) of some input word. The method of the previous section would require an average of $(M + 1)/2$ comparisons to find the word and would require M comparisons if the word were not on the list. By taking advantage of the list's ordering we can reduce the number of comparisons to about log M comparisons. This is done as follows:

1. Begin the search by comparing the input word with the middle word on the list. If the list has an even number of words, then either of the two middle words will do. If the input word matches the middle word, the search is over. If the input does not match, then, since the list is ordered, the comparison determines whether the input word comes *before* or *after* the middle.

2. If the order dictates that the input should come before the middle, there are two possibilities. If the middle word is also the first word as might happen with lists of length 1 or 2, then we know the input word is not on the list. If the middle word is not also the first word, then there is a new list to be searched, namely the list of words from the first word to the word just before the middle. This new list is no more than half as long as the original so the problem has been cut in half by a single comparison. We now reapply step 1 to search this new list.

3. If the order dictates that the input comes after the middle, then an analysis similar to step 2 applies to the list of words appearing after the middle. Again step 1 is applied to this sublist.

As an example, Fig. 3.7 shows how a list of 18 identifiers is searched for the word STEP, which is found in five tries. Since the list has 18 members, we can use either the ninth or the tenth as the middle member. We arbitrarily select the ninth, INTEGER, and compare it with the input word. Since the input word is alphabetically greater than the middle word, we have a new list consisting of words 10 through 18. We now compare the input word with STRING, the middle word on the new list. Since the input word is smaller,

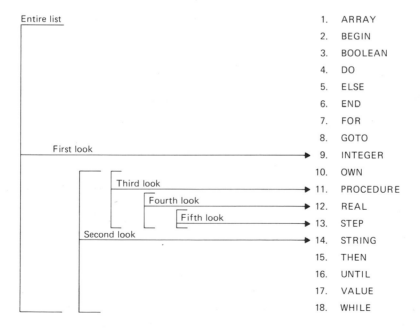

Figure 3.7

we get a new list consisting of words 10 through 13. Similarly, each of the subsequent comparisons in the search cuts the size of the list by a factor of two until STEP is found after five comparisons.

If instead the input word is STOP, the procedure continues in the same way except that when we get to the final list of length 1 (consisting of the word STEP) the input word is greater than the middle word on the list. Since the middle word is also the last word, there is no new list. We therefore know that the input word is not on the original list.

Of course, some words can be found on the list in fewer than five tries. For instance the input word INTEGER would be found on the first try.

In general the effect of step 1 is to either find a match or to reduce the list of words to be searched by one half. Assuming the original list has M words, this reduction by one half can only be done about $\log_2 M$ times and then the list will have been reduced to a single element. Clearly, by that time the word will have been found or it will be known that it is not in the list.

The exact bound on the number of comparisons is

$$1 + \text{the largest integer less than or equal to } \log_2 M.$$

This procedure is therefore called the *logarithmic-search method*. It is also frequently called the *binary-search method*.

When implementing this procedure, some work is involved in computing the middle. This makes each step in the procedure a little longer to execute than the steps of the straightforward list approach. However, the fact that only $\log_2 M$ steps are required instead of M or $M/2$ steps implies that for even moderately large M, the logarithmic method is faster.

The principle disadvantage of the logarithmic procedure is that the list is not easy to expand. The reason for this is that new words cannot be arbitrarily added to the end but must be inserted in the place dictated by the order.

The logarithmic procedure can also be adopted to linked storage if one is willing to assign two pointers to each word. One of the pointers is used to point to the middle of the words that come before the given word and one pointer is used to point to the middle of the words that come after the given word. Such a linking for the list in Fig. 3.7 is shown in Fig. 3.8. Notice that the layout is in the form of a tree. To find the word FOR, comparisons would first be made with the words INTEGER, DO, END, and FOR in that order.

Using the tree-like linked storage, it is possible to add words without disrupting the storage layout. For example, the word ASK could be attached to ARRAY and the word FOX attached to GOTO. Unfortunately, the resulting search times need no longer conform to the logarithmic time bound. The word FOX, for example, would require 6 comparisons. If one wishes to expand the word set and preserve the logarithmic search time, one has to be

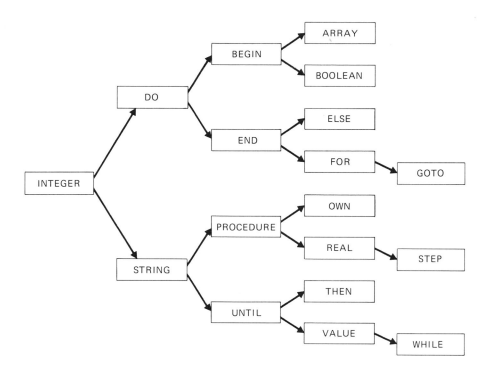

Figure 3.8

prepared to reorganize the whole tree structure as different words become the middle word. Thus this linked approach is expandable only in a limited sense.

3.9 WORD IDENTIFICATION—HASH-CODING APPROACH

When faced with a large and expanding set of words to identify, an ideal approach would be one that is easily expanded, has modest space requirements, and requires (on the average) only a few comparisons to locate a word. Each of the methods of the last three sections is deficient in at least one of these counts. Now we consider a hybrid method which does well against all these criteria. This method represents our recommendation among a set of techniques known as hash-coding or scatter-storage techniques.

The identification is carried out in two steps as follows:

1. The input word is used to compute an index as in the index-approach of Section 3.6. In this case, however, many words may have the same index.

This index is then used to retrieve a list pointer from a *list-pointer table*. If this pointer is zero indicating a null list, then the input word is not in the set. Otherwise, step 2 is applied.

2. The pointer obtained from the list pointer table points to a linked list of words, namely those words which yield the computed index value. This list is searched until either a match is found or the end of the list is reached. In the latter event, the input word is not in the set and may be added simply by linking it to the last item on the list.

In the literature, the hash-coding method is sometimes described using the imagery of "buckets." Each index is said to point to a bucket or hash bucket and all the words having that index are said to be in the same bucket.

As an example, we have taken the words from the list of Fig. 3.7 and shown a possible hash implementation in Fig. 3.9. In this example, the index is computed by adding the numeric equivalents of the first two letters and taking the remainder modulo 7. For example, the index for ARRAY is determined by adding 1 ($=A$) and 18 ($=R$) and then dividing the result (19) by 7 to obtain the remainder 5. This means that the list (if any) containing the word ARRAY will be the list found in cell 5 of the list pointer table.

In general, the implementation of this hash procedure involves two important considerations, namely:

1. the method of computing the index,
2. the size of the list-pointer table.

As these factors can have a noticeable impact on the speed and memory requirements of the procedure (and, in fact of the entire compiler), we discuss these points at some length.

The only reason for computing the index is to cut down the lengths of the lists that have to be searched. Ideally, we would like the lists to be of equal length. Unfortunately, the designer must select the method of computing the index *before* he knows what words will be added to the list during a given compilation. Considering this fact, the best that can be hoped for is that the new words will fall into the given lists with equal probability and that the list selections are independent of any programming conventions used in the source program. The design objective is to find an index selection method with these pseudo-random properties.

As an example of a not-so-random index-selection procedure, consider what happens if we are processing identifiers and decide to assign each word to one of 26 lists according to the first letter. Since the English language has many more words that begin with the letter R than begin with the letter O, one might expect the R list to contain many more entries than the O list. Such an imbalance would be further aggravated by a FORTRAN program-

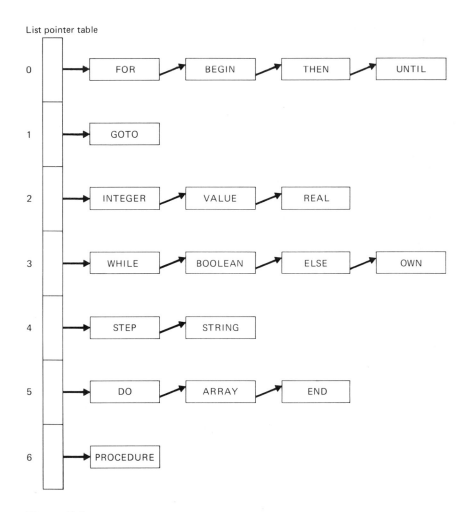

List pointer table

Figure 3.9

mer who decided to name all his integer variables with names that begin with *I*. Although far from ideal from the viewpoint of dividing lists, this index selection method might be used for some applications because the index is easy to compute.

The two-letter indexing method used above in the example of Fig. 3.9 is better than the single-letter method in that it tends to fill the lists more evenly. However, a programmer might use many names with the same beginning (e.g., ALPHA1, ALPHA2, ALPHA3, etc.) thereby degrading the compiler performance. A faster search might be obtained if the index were based on the sum of all the letters. However, the extra work required to compute the index might wash out the savings in search time. Thus cost of indexing must be balanced against cost of searching.

The most random-like indexing procedures are obtained in practice by treating the bit pattern of the input word as a single number or (for long words) as a series of numbers which are combined (e.g. added) to get a single number. The number is then reduced in some way to get an index of the desired size. One way to do this is to divide the number by some constant and use the remainder. Since division by small numbers may yield somewhat predictable remainders (e.g., they might all be even) it is important that the randomizing divisor not be a multiple of some small number. For this reason, a prime number is usually chosen as the randomizing divisor. An alternative indexing method is to square the number and extract the middle bits. The middle bits are used to ensure that the calculation involves all bits of the original number. Methods such as these for calculating an index with pseudo-random properties are sometimes referred to as *hash functions*.

Now we come to the question as to how large to make the list-pointer table. Assuming that the words are indeed placed on the lists in a random manner, the question of table size can be studied in a very quantitative manner. Suppose that the list pointer table has room for C pointers and suppose that M words have been entered randomly. If the input word is chosen randomly from among the M words, the expected number of comparisons to find the input word is

$$1 + (M - 1)/2C$$

(New input words require M/C comparisons to determine that they are not in the set.) If we know the number of words with which we will be dealing, the formula tells us the exact effect of the table size. Figure 3.10 shows the result of the formula evaluated for some values of M and C.

		Number of words (M)			
		20	100	500	1000	5000
	10	1.95	5.95	25.95	50.95	250.95
	50	1.19	1.99	5.99	10.99	50.99
Table size (C)	100	1.10	1.50	3.50	5.60	26.00
	200	1.05	1.25	2.25	3.50	13.50
	500	1.02	1.10	1.50	2.00	6.00
	1000	1.01	1.05	1.25	1.50	3.50

Fig. 3.10 Values of $1 + (M - 1)/2C$

Suppose we are interested in the efficiency of processing 500 different words, and want to compare the merits of 500 lists with the merits of having only 100 lists. The advantage of having only 100 lists is that one saves the space required to store the extra 400 pointers. The disadvantage is that more comparisons will (on the average) be required to identify a word. The exact saving is seen from Fig. 3.10 to be 2 comparisons (i.e., 3.50 vs. 1.50). The decision comes down to choosing between 400 extra pointers or 2 extra comparisons per word to be identified.

These extra comparisons must of course be evaluated in terms of the time required to accomplish them on the computer on which the compiler will run. The saving in time will occur each time a search is made during a compilation which could easily be several times per line of program. The time saved could well be a noticeable fraction of the entire compile time. These savings will of course be less if the number of words is smaller than 500 and will be larger if the word set is larger. It is wise, therefore, to make this analysis for several different numbers of words to get a feeling for the variety of speed savings that might result. Generally speaking, the conclusion is inescapable that one should be generous with the table size.

3.10   PREFIX DETECTION

As we pointed out in Section 3.5, word-identification procedures are well suited for use with a master machine which knows which symbols belong to a potential word to be identified and when such a word is over. In other words, they may be applied when the boundaries of a proposed word can be detected by a master machine. The presence of distinct word boundaries occurs in English for example where the words in each sentence must be separated by spaces or other punctuation. Distinct word boundaries also occur in many programming languages where blanks are required between consecutive alphanumeric entities. In those cases of distinct word boundaries, the word-identification subprocessor serves the main process in the same way that a dictionary helps someone reading a natural language.

An example of a word problem with nondistinct boundaries is the problem of identifying MINI-BASIC reserved words. This is an outgrowth of the convention that spaces have no significance in the MINI-BASIC language. To see this, consider the MINI-BASIC statement:

$$10 \text{ FORK} = \text{STOP}$$

Here the word boundaries can only be detected from a knowledge of the reserved word set, for example that there is a reserved word FOR and not a reserved work FORK. In fact, this same character string is also a valid FORTRAN statement but with different word boundaries. If spaces were required as punctuation, the statement would have to be written as

$$10 \text{ FOR } K = S \text{ TO } P$$

In order to solve identification problems of this nature, we now study a specific identification problem which we refer to as the *prefix-detection problem*. We assume that some finite set of words over some input alphabet has been specified and that we will be given an input sequence which presumably begins with some word in the set. We are asked to detect the element of the sequence (if any) at which the word ends and to exit to a routine appropriate to the word found. The given word set can be thought of as the set of allowable prefixes that may begin a valid input sequence. We want to detect the ending of a prefix and determine which prefix it is. In order to have a well-defined problem, we assume that no word in the given set is the prefix of any other word in the set.

First, consider the possibility of doing the detection with a finite-state processor. As with the word-identification problem, such a processor can be designed based on the idea of introducing a state for each subsequence which is the prefix of some word in the set. In this case, however, it is not necessary to have states corresponding to the words themselves. The technique is best explained with an example.

Consider the prefix-detection problem of detecting prefixes from the set {FIT, FIN, TIN} in sequences over the alphabet {F, I, T, N}. The associated finite-state prefix-detection processor is shown in Fig. 3.11a. It has three kinds of transition entries: transitions to new states, exits to routines for words in the given set (e.g., exit "FIT") and exits to an error routine indicated in the table by blanks. When the detector is used under the control of some other processor, the machine is not required to process the endmarker and that column of the table may be dropped. To contrast prefix detection with word identification, the corresponding word-identification processor is shown in Fig. 3.11b.

To implement the prefix-detection machine, the observations made in Section 3.5 about the word-identification machine apply almost without change.

The differences in the two problems become more apparent when one considers the problem of doing prefix detection with the list approach. The basic idea of the list approach is to construct the potential word as the inputs are read and then search a list to see if the word is on the list of words to be identified. This is no longer possible in the prefix case because the end of the prefix cannot be detected without knowing the specific prefix that occurs. Some modification is therefore required and the obvious change is to carry out a search after each input symbol. In this way, each input is treated as a possible prefix ending and the prefix is detected as soon as it occurs. To avoid

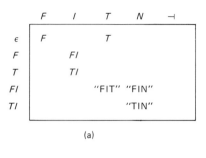

(a)

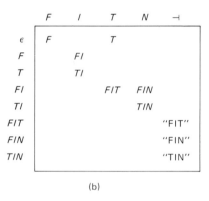

(b)

Fig. 3.11 (a) Prefix-detection processor; (b) Word-identification processor

searching a long list over and over, one can have a separate list of prefixes for each of the possible prefix lengths. Thus, when the first input symbol is received, the compiler searches only the prefixes of length one. When the second symbol is received, the compiler searches only the prefixes of length two, etc. In this way, at most one comparison will have to be made for each of the possible prefixes. As before, hashing and ordering could also be employed to speed up the searching.

If one attempts to apply the index method to the prefix-detection problem, the same difficulties arise. One cannot decide when to compute and use the index. It is conceivable that the index could be computed after each input but it is hard to imagine a set of sequences that might arise in practice where such a procedure would be a logical choice.

We have seen that the *prefix-detection problem* is essentially a variation of the *word-identification problem* in which the beginning of the word is known but the ending can only be determined by considering the specific words in the prefix set. This problem and its solution are adequate to describe the lexical box for the MINI-BASIC compiler. However, there are identification problems that occur in other languages where the word boundaries are even less distinct.

3.11   REFERENCES

Many of the methods presented in this chapter are part of the folklore of programming and were used before their appearance in the published literature. A good discussion of hash-coding techniques prior to 1968 is given in Morris [1968]. A discussion of the chaining method of handling collisions in hash coding is given in Johnson [1961]. A survey of solutions to the word-identification problem, primarily for nonexpandable sets, is given in Price [1971]. Solutions to the identification problem similar to the transition-list approach are described in de la Briandais [1959], Fredkin [1960], Scidmore and Weinberg [1963], and Sussenguth [1963]. The binary-search method with an expandable word set is discussed in Hibbard [1962], Foster [1965], and Martin and Ness [1972]. Searching is discussed in great depth in Knuth [1973]. See also Severance [1974] and Nievergelt [1974].

PROBLEMS

1. Describe how you would implement transliteration using the following languages:
   a) FORTRAN,
   b) APL,
   c) the assembly language of your favorite computer.

2. Construct the transition lists for the machine of Fig. 2.19.

3. Describe how you would implement the transition-vector method using the following languages:
   a) FORTRAN,
   b) ALGOL 60,
   c) PL/I,
   d) APL,
   e) the assembly language of your favorite computer.

4. It is possible to have transition vectors and lists for the inputs instead of for the states. Find a machine for which it makes a difference in terms of storage space whether there is a transition list for each state or for each input.

   (Hint: The default transition for a particular list need not be the error transition.)

5. a) Revise Fig. 3.5 and Fig. 3.6(a) to add the words DEAD, BA, and ACED.
   b) Add the word ϵ to the above.

6. Why will the implementation technique of Fig. 3.6 work for word-identification problems but not for arbitrary finite-state machines?

7. Estimate the amount of storage required to recognize the reserved words in ALGOL 60 using:
   a) the transition-list method,
   b) the linear-list method,
   c) the transition-vector method.

8. The set of words to be recognized is:

   ARRAY, ARCTAN, B1, B2, B3, DOG, CAT, DOGFIGHT.

   Draw a diagram of the structure of each of the following recognizers for this set:
   a) transition-list method,
   b) expandable transition-list method,
   c) ordered-list method.

9. Extended BASIC allows the following kinds of variables:
   1. simple variables—a single letter or a single letter followed by a single digit;
   2. subscripted variables—a single letter followed by a left parenthesis, an expression, and a right parenthesis;
   3. string variables—a single letter followed by a dollar sign.

   Note that the same letter can be used in the name of all three kinds of variable in the same program (for example, A, A1, A$ and A(1)). Design an indexing scheme based on the characters in the name of a variable that will give a unique index to every possible variable.

10. Modify Fig. 3.9 so that a logarithmic search can be performed on each list.

11. For each of the following procedures, describe what must be done to delete a word from the set to be recognized:
    a) transition-list method,
    b) expandable transition-list method,
    c) index method,
    d) linear list,
    e) ordered list,
    f) hash coding.

12. Consider a hash-coding scheme where the identifiers (inputted in the order given below) are:

    ABCD, ABDC, DCBA, FAD, ZEB, BARK,
    BUG, RATS, MICE, CATS, DOGS, ZEUS

    We wish to apply the hash function

    $$R \bmod 13$$

    where R is the binary number made up of the ASCII representation of the word. Draw the hash table after inputting all twelve words.

13. Design an efficient word-identification scheme for the reserved words in COBOL.

14. A hypothetical stock-market system has a symbol-table entry for each company on the New York Exchange. Design a searching procedure that takes a two- or three-letter code, such as IBM or GE, and finds the symbol-table entry for the corresponding company. Estimate the average searching time for your procedure.

15. Assume that a given language allows n possible identifiers, but that in some specific program only k identifiers are used. Assume that the symbol-table entry for each of the k identifiers occupies b storage locations. Assume also that a pointer occupies one storage location. Calculate the space required for the indexed table method of Section 3.6 using:

   a) the direct method, where the indexed table contains space for a symbol-table entry for each index;

   b) the indirect method where the indexed table contains a pointer to the symbol-table entry.

   Show that method a) requires less storage than method b) when

   $$k/n \geq 1 - 1/b$$

16. Suppose that we use a hashing scheme where, whenever the hash table is 80% full, we double the size of the hash table, get a new hash function for the new table, and rehash all the old entries into the new table. Show that for a program with m identifiers (each occurring once in the program), the average number of comparisons (including the time required for rehashing) using this scheme is proportional to m.

17. In hash coding, if the size of the list pointer table is C and k different words have been entered on the linked lists, then the average number of words on a linked list is k/C. Using this result, derive the formula

   $$1 + (M - 1)/2C$$

   given in Section 3.9.

18. Consider a variation of the logarithmic-search technique where, at each stage, the remaining portion of the list is divided into thirds; the input word is compared with the words 1/3 and 2/3 down the list; and the third of the list in which the input word lies is then selected for the next stage. Find the maximum number of comparisons per search using this technique and compare it with the binary logarithmic method of Section 3.8.

4
MINI-BASIC
Lexical Box

4.1 THE TOKEN SET

In this chapter, we carry out a fairly detailed design for a MINI-BASIC lexical box based on a finite-state machine. As a first step, we specify an interface to go between the lexical box and the syntax box. A token set for this interface is shown in Fig. 4.1. The table shows both the class of the token and its associated value. To the right of each table entry are some sample character sequences which lead to the given token. The token classes have been given suggestive names but they would be represented inside the compiler by numbers.

We assume that some routine named CREATE TOKEN is supplied which interfaces with the syntax box. As far as the lexical box design is concerned, CREATE TOKEN could be a routine for writing the token in an intermediate file or it could be a routine which tells the syntax box that its next output is ready. As we plan to compile MINI-BASIC in a single pass, the latter interpretation is the one that applies although the design is valid for either a one pass or a multipass situation.

When the routine CREATE TOKEN is called, we assume that the variable called CLASS REGISTER has been assigned some number representing the class of the token being created and the value part will be available in some variable depending on the specific token class involved. In order to specify these variables and to elaborate upon the choice of tokens, we discuss each of the tokens individually.

The token LINE is used to indicate the line number at the beginning of a statement. Its value is a pointer to a symbol-table entry for the line number. This pointer will be placed in a variable called POINTER REGISTER.

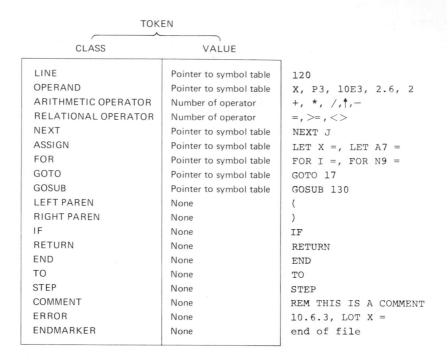

TOKEN		
CLASS	VALUE	
LINE	Pointer to symbol table	120
OPERAND	Pointer to symbol table	X, P3, 10E3, 2.6, 2
ARITHMETIC OPERATOR	Number of operator	+, *, /,↑,−
RELATIONAL OPERATOR	Number of operator	=, >=, <>
NEXT	Pointer to symbol table	NEXT J
ASSIGN	Pointer to symbol table	LET X =, LET A7 =
FOR	Pointer to symbol table	FOR I =, FOR N9 =
GOTO	Pointer to symbol table	GOTO 17
GOSUB	Pointer to symbol table	GOSUB 130
LEFT PAREN	None	(
RIGHT PAREN	None	)
IF	None	IF
RETURN	None	RETURN
END	None	END
TO	None	TO
STEP	None	STEP
COMMENT	None	REM THIS IS A COMMENT
ERROR	None	10.6.3, LOT X =
ENDMARKER	None	end of file

Figure 4.1

The token OPERAND is used to indicate the occurrence of a constant or of a variable within an expression. It is not used for those occurrences of variables immediately after the words NEXT, FOR, and LET. These exceptions are treated separately in the NEXT, FOR and ASSIGN tokens. The value of the OPERAND token is a pointer to a table entry for the variable or constant. This pointer will be located in POINTER REGISTER.

The token ARITHMETIC OPERATOR indicates occurrences of the symbols $+$, $-$, $*$, $/$, and $↑$. These operators will be numbered 1 through 5, respectively. The number of a given operator will be its value and will be found in a variable called the VALUE REGISTER. The number will actually be placed there directly by a transliteration routine.

The token RELATIONAL OPERATOR indicates occurrences of the operators $=$, $<$, $>$, $<=$, $>=$, and $<>$ which are assigned the numbers 1 through 6 respectively. The number for a given relational operator will be placed in a variable called RELATIONAL REGISTER.

The token "NEXT" represents the word NEXT and the variable that follows it. Its value is a pointer to the symbol-table entry corresponding to the variable, and is placed in POINTER REGISTER in the same way as for the token OPERAND. The interface could have been specified so that the characters NEXT K3 would be represented by two tokens, one for NEXT and the other for K3. However we have chosen to use only a single token to represent the same information. This choice was made to reduce the number of times the CREATE TOKEN routine has to be invoked and to impress upon the reader the fact that the tokens used inside the compiler need not be the same tokens used in the programming manual to explain the language to humans. In effect, we are doing a small syntactic action in the lexical box in order to be more efficient. In making decisions of this nature, we rely on an understanding of the capabilities of finite-state machines and not on a heuristic interpretation of the words "lexical" and "syntactic."

The token ASSIGN represents the word LET followed by a variable followed by an equal sign. Its value is a pointer to the symbol-table entry for the variable and is placed in POINTER REGISTER. Again we are using the lexical box to compress the information in the source statement. One token is being used to describe what the programming reference manual would explain in terms of three words.

The token "FOR" represents the word FOR followed by a variable followed by an equal sign. Its value is a pointer to the symbol-table entry for the variable and is placed in POINTER REGISTER. This token is a variation of the ASSIGN token.

The token "GOTO" represents the word GOTO and the line number which follows it. Again we combine two concepts into a single token. The value of the token is a pointer to the symbol-table entry of the line number and is placed in POINTER REGISTER.

The token "GOSUB" represents the word GOSUB followed by a line number. As with the LINE and GOTO tokens, the value is a pointer to the symbol-table entry of the line number and is placed in POINTER REGISTER.

The tokens LEFT PAREN and RIGHT PAREN represent the left and right parenthesis respectively. They have no value.

The tokens IF, RETURN, END, TO, and STEP represent the corresponding reserved words. These tokens have no value part.

The token COMMENT represents the word REM and the remaining characters on that line. It has no value part. This token is used by the syntax box to detect misplaced comments such as, for example, in the statement:

13 IF A1 REM THIS IS ABSURD

The lexical box generates the token COMMENT to allow the syntax box to verify the correct placement.

The token ERROR is used by the lexical box to tell the syntax box that an error has been detected. This enables the syntax box to avoid issuing a second error message. This token will be generated whenever the lexical box is unable to decompose a source statement into a meaningful sequence of tokens. The ERROR token might be issued if reserved words were misspelled (e.g., RETARN) or if constants were malformed (e.g., 3.6E.3) or if variables and constants were jumbled together (e.g., A3.E2). The token ERROR has no value.

The token ENDMARKER is issued when the end of file is encountered. It has no value part. The information required by the CREATE TOKEN routine is summarized in Fig. 4.2 which gives the variables mentioned in the discussion of the token set and describes their use.

CLASS REGISTER — Class of token

POINTER REGISTER — For pointer to symbol-table entry

VALUE REGISTER — For the number of an arithmetic operator

RELATIONAL REGISTER — For the number of a relational operator

Fig. 4.2 Information for CREATE TOKEN routine

4.2   THE IDENTIFICATION PROBLEMS

Having laid out the interface between the lexical and syntax boxes, we now concentrate on the design problems internal to the lexical box. To begin the design, we formulate a plan for solving the four identification problems involved, namely:

1. the detection of reserved words,
2. the identification of variables,
3. the identification of line numbers,
4. the identification of relational operators.

We discuss each of these in turn.

The detection of reserved words fits the description of a prefix detection problem discussed in Section 3.10. We have a finite set of words, namely {END, FOR, GOSUB, GOTO, IF, LET, NEXT, REM, RETURN, STEP, TO}. We can detect where these words begin but cannot detect where they end without considering the specific set of words involved. The solution we have selected is based on simulating the corresponding prefix-detection machine. The specifics of our plan are shown in Fig. 4.3. We use a transition vector for the transition due to the first letter and then use transition lists (in

				Character value	Transition	Alternative
A			①	N	B 1d	
B			②	D	A 2q	
C			③	O	B 1d	
D			④	R	F 1b	
E	①		⑤	O	B 1d	
F	③		⑥	T	B 1d	⑧
G	⑤		⑦	O	E 1a	
H			⑧	S	B 1d	
I	⑪		⑨	U	B 1d	
J			⑩	B	E 1b	
K			⑪	F	A 2r	
L	⑫		⑫	E	B 1d	
M			⑬	T	F 1a	
N	⑭		⑭	E	B 1d	
O			⑮	X	B 1d	
P			⑯	T	C 1a	
Q			⑰	E	B 1d	
R	⑰		⑱	T	B1d	㉒
S	㉓		⑲	U	B1d	
T	㉖		⑳	R	B 1d	
U			㉑	N	A2s	
V			㉒	M	G 1a	
W			㉓	T	B 1d	
X			㉔	E	B 1d	
Y			㉕	P	A 2t	
Z			㉖	O	A 2u	

Starting vector   Detection table

Fig. 4.3 Reserved-word detector

a manner similar to that of Fig. 3.6) for subsequent transitions. When a reserved word begins, the first letter is used to index into the Starting Vector.

This action corresponds to the first transition of the prefix-detection machine. Each table entry is a pointer for indexing the Detection Table. The Detection Table contains transition lists for processing further letters. For example, an initial G results in the selection of pointer ⑤ from the Starting

Vector and this pointer points to the information in the Detection Table which is used to detect occurrences of the words GOTO and GOSUB. The Starting Vector contains zero for those letters such as A, that do not begin reserved words. An appropriate error routine is called if the first letter selects an entry containing zero.

The Detection Table has three parts. One part contains a representation of a letter, one part contains the label of a transition routine, and one part contains either a pointer or a zero indicating no pointer. When a letter is found, it is compared with the letter in the current table entry. If there is a match, a transfer is made to the transition routine specified by the label entry. If a match is not found, the pointer field is used to find a new table entry on which the entire matching process is repeated. The table entries linked together in this fashion correspond to a transition list for the corresponding prefix-detection machine. The transition routines whose labels appear in the table are described with the main lexical analyzer routines listed later. The routine $B1d$ has the effect of incrementing the pointer to the current entry in the Detection Table, so that it points to the next entry. Thus, if the letter G is followed by the letter O, the O will cause the current table pointer to change from ⑤ to ⑥. Entry ⑥ is the first item on the transition list for the state corresponding to the prefix GO. The other transition routines listed in the table correspond to exits from the prefix detection routine. Each of these exits is filled in with the label of a transition routine appropriate for the particular reserved word which has been detected. The system used to name these labels is the same as that used for the main lexical analyzer and is described later.

The identification of variables will be done by indexing into the symbol table. We assume the first 286 locations of the table have been preallocated for the 286 possible variables. The remaining part of the symbol table is available for entries concerning constants, labels, etc. When the letter part of a variable is seen, the corresponding number 1 through 26 is added to the base address of the symbol table and the result is placed in POINTER REGISTER.

If the letter is followed by a digit d, the quantity $26 * (d + 1)$ is added to POINTER REGISTER. This method of indexing MINI-BASIC variables was discussed in Section 3.6.

The identification of line numbers will be achieved by constructing the numerical value of the line number as the characters of the line number are processed by the machine. Recall that the value part of the LINE token is a pointer to the symbol-table entry for that line number. Thus we must associate each mention of a given line number with the same symbol-table entry. This will be done by a list-searching technique on the list of line-number symbol-table entries. The list-searching technique we use is that of hashing.

The hash function will be the remainder after dividing the numerical value of the line number by a prime number, say P. The number P is a parameter of the design, and can be easily changed depending on such factors as the allowable storage space in the compiler and the expected size of the source program to be compiled. Initially we select P to be 101.

The identification of relational operators is an identification problem on the set $\{=, <, >, <=, >=, <>\}$. We will base the identification on an index method which relies on the fact that each word consists of either one or two symbols. When the first symbol is encountered, a corresponding number from 1 thorugh 3 is entered in RELATIONAL REGISTER. If and when a second symbol is encountered its corresponding number is placed in VALUE REGISTER. Then the number of the corresponding two-symbol operator is looked up in a table called the Relational Table. The details of this method are laid out in Fig. 4.4. Figure 4.4(a) shows the selected correspondence between relational operators and numbers; Fig. 4.4(b) shows the Relational Table itself. The zero entries correspond to situations such as $=\ =$ where the combination of symbols is an error. Notice that one need only change some table entries to give the illegal combinations, $=>$, $=<$, and $><$ their natural meaning. Often a particular design will make certain language extensions trivial to implement.

Value	Meaning
1	$=$
2	$<$
3	$>$
4	$<=$
5	$>=$
6	$<>$

(a)

VALUE REGISTER

	1 (=)	2 (<)	3 (>)
1 (=)	0	0	0
2 (<)	4 (<=)	0	6 (<>)
3 (>)	5 (>=)	0	0

RELATIONAL REGISTER

(b)

Fig. 4.4 (a) Values of RELATIONAL OPERATOR token; (b) Relational table

	Character tokens				Character tokens	
	Class	Value			Class	Value
A	LETTER	1		0	DIGIT	0
B	LETTER	2		1	DIGIT	1
C	LETTER	3		2	DIGIT	2
D	LETTER	4		3	DIGIT	3
E	LETTER	5		4	DIGIT	4
F	LETTER	6		5	DIGIT	5
G	LETTER	7		6	DIGIT	6
H	LETTER	8		7	DIGIT	7
I	LETTER	9		8	DIGIT	8
J	LETTER	10		9	DIGIT	9
K	LETTER	11		+	ARITH-OP	1
L	LETTER	12		−	ARITH-OP	2
M	LETTER	13		*	ARITH-OP	3
N	LETTER	14		/	ARITH-OP	4
O	LETTER	15		↑	ARITH-OP	5
P	LETTER	16		=	REL-OP	1
Q	LETTER	17		<	REL-OP	2
R	LETTER	18		>	REL-OP	3
S	LETTER	19		(	LEFT-PAR	−
T	LETTER	20		)	RIGHT-PAR	−
U	LETTER	21		.	DOT	−
V	LETTER	22			BLANK	−
W	LETTER	23		(RO)	BLANK	
X	LETTER	24		(LF)	BLANK	
Y	LETTER	25		(CR)	LINE-END	
Z	LETTER	26		⊠	FILE-END	

Fig. 4.5 Transliteration

4.3   THE TRANSLITERATOR

In specifying a transliterator, we try to keep in mind the economy of having a small set of character tokens. The transliteration is specified in Fig. 4.5. The interface of the transliterator with the computer operating system and with the rest of the lexical box is not laid out in detail here but is implied when we make the statement "get input and do state *A* transition." We assume that the transliterator will place the value part of the character tokens in the variable VALUE REGISTER. To elaborate upon the choice of character tokens, we now discuss them individually.

The character token LETTER is used to represent all letters and the value part is used to indicate which letter. The letters are lumped together because, with one exception, they can be used more or less interchangeably. The one exception is the letter E when used as the exponent part of a constant. Thus if we see the characters 10E we expect the E to be followed by a number specifying an exponent whereas if we see the characters 10S we expect the S to be the first letter of a reserved word (presumably the word STEP). One perfectly reasonable solution is to have a special character token class for the letter E keeping its value 5. However, we have decided on the alternative plan of checking for the letter E in the specific machine transitions where this is important. The resulting saving of a column in the lexical-box transition table is not really significant in this rather small machine but we wish to show the reader this technique. The value part of the token becomes the internal representation of the letters and it is these values that are actually used in the Detection Table of Fig. 4.3.

The character token DIGIT is used to represent all digits. They are assigned their natural values since we plan to do arithmetic operations on those values when processing constants and line numbers.

The character token ARITH-OP represents the arithmetic operators. The value of each arithmetic operator is the same as for the corresponding ARITHMETIC OPERATOR lexical token.

The character tokens LEFT-PAR, RIGHT-PAR, and DOT represent respectively left parenthesis, right parenthesis, and period. They have no value part.

The character token BLANK represents a blank, a rubout, and a line feed. This encoding of rubout and line feed requires some explanation. We are assuming that the source programs are to be prepared in some teletype environment where the end of a line is represented by some combination of rubouts with a carriage return and line feed. Our plan for dealing with this system is to treat the rubouts and line feed as blanks and treat the carriage return as the end of line symbol. The reader unfamiliar with these symbols can safely forget that they exist as they are not involved elsewhere in the design.

The character token LINE-END represents the symbol carriage return and denotes the fact that a line is over.

The character token FILE-END is the signal to the lexical box that there are no more characters in the input. The method of obtaining this token depends on the specific details of the computer operating-system conventions and does not affect the design. We assume that some means can be found for producing this token at the proper time and do not consider the problem further.

	LETTER	DIGIT	ARITH-OP	REL-OP	LEFT-PAR	RIGHT-PAR	DOT	BLANK	LINE-END	FILE-END	
A1	C2a	E2a	A2a	H1a	A2h	A3b	D6	A1	A1	EXIT1	Start of line
A2	B1a	D1a	A2a	H1a	A2h	A3b	D6	A2	A1	EXIT1	Look for var, const, OP, CR,), (
A3	B1a	D1a			A2h	A3b	D6	A3	A1	EXIT1	Look for Res, OP, CR,), (
B1	M1							B1			Detect reserved word
C1	C2d							C1			Look for variable
C2	B1b	A3a	A2g	H1b	A2k	A3c		C2	A1a	EXIT2	Finish variable
D1	M2	D1b	A2c	H1c	A2ℓ	A3d	D2c	D1	A1b	EXIT3	Finish integer part
D2	M3	D2a	A2d	H1d	A2m	A3e		D2	A1c	EXIT4	Finish decimal part
D3		D5a	D4a					D3			After letter E
D4		D5b						D4			After E and sign
D5	B1c	D5c	A2e	H1e	A2n	A3f		D5	A1d	EXIT5	Finish exponent part
D6		D2b						D6			After leading decimal point
E1		E2b						E1			Look for line number
E2	B1e	E2c	A2f	H1f	A2j	A3g		E2	A1e	EXIT6	Rest of line number
F1	F2a			A2o				F1			Look for variable =
F2		F3a		A2o				F2			Rest of variable
F3								F3			Look for =
G1	G1	G1	G1	G1	G1	G1	G1	G1	A1	EXIT1	Find CR
H1	C2b	D1c	A2g	A2p	A2k	A3c	D6a	H1	A1a	EXIT2	Finish relational operator

Figure 4.6

We are ignoring the possibility that there may be other characters allowed by the operating system but not used in the MINI-BASIC character set. For example, the input sequence might include a comma. Such characters could be transliterated into a new token which causes an error everywhere except in a comment. However, we assume for simplicity sake that we are only dealing with the characters mentioned in Fig. 4.5.

4.4   THE LEXICAL BOX

The finite-state machine which comprises the main unit of the lexical box is shown in Fig. 4.6. States which serve a similar purpose have been named with the same first letter and have been grouped together within the transition table. We now discuss these groups of states so that the reader can understand how the machine works.

The states $A1$, $A2$, and $A3$ might be described as control states. They are used to represent those situations in which one lexical token has just been completed and another is about to begin. The state $A1$ is the starting state and is used at the beginning of a line where the first token must be a line number. To see the need for two other control states, consider the MINI-BASIC statement:

$$30 \text{ IF } G < \text{ G } 1 * (G + 1) \text{ GOTO } 10$$

The letter G appears four times in this statement. The first three times (i.e., after the reserved word IF, after the relational operator, and after the left parenthesis), the letter G is a beginning of a MINI-BASIC variable. The last occurrence of G (i.e., after the right parenthesis) is not the beginning of a variable but is the first letter of a reserved word. The state $A2$ is used for those situations in which a letter should be the first letter of a variable and state $A3$ is used where a letter should be the beginning of a reserved word. The state used is determined by the previous lexical token. Without such a discrimination, one might find the lexical box trying to translate GOTO as OPERAND G followed by OPERAND O followed by OPERAND T followed by OPERAND O.

Our descriptions of the transition routines given at the end of this section are organized so that routines that correspond to transitions to the same state are adjacent. In the case of the control states, many of the transitions leading to these states call for actions required to complete the previous token. To appreciate the purposes of these particular routines, the reader is advised to look at the state from which the transition is made.

The state $B1$ is used for detecting reserved words. It uses a variable DETECTION REGISTER to store its pointer to the Detection Table of Fig. 4.3 (described earlier). When the input is a letter, the next state is determined by the transition $M1$ which selects the next state from the Detection Table. The specification of $M1$ is given after the other transition routines.

The states $C1$ and $C2$ are for finding an occurrence of a variable. They are used to compute the value part of the tokens OPERAND and NEXT. State $C1$ is for finding the letter part and $C2$ is for detecting the optional digit that might follow the letter. In many cases one cannot tell that a variable is beginning until after the first letter is seen. In these cases, state $C2$ is entered directly and the transition routine must include the work normally done when state $C1$ is entered. This includes loading CLASS REGISTER with the name of the token being processed as this information would otherwise be quickly lost. State $C1$ is only used after the word NEXT.

The states $D1$ through $D6$ are used to compute the value part of MINI-BASIC constants. These states correspond to the states 1, $\overline{23}$, 4, 5, 6, and 7 in the processor of Section 2.14. As in Section 2.14, we use the four variables NUMBER REGISTER, EXPONENT REGISTER, COUNT REGISTER, and SIGN REGISTER for intermediate calculations. We assume there is a routine COMPUTE CONSTANT which obtains a new symbol-table entry, uses NUMBER REGISTER and EXPONENT REGISTER to construct the internal representation of the constant, stores this representation in the new table entry, and places a pointer to that table entry in POINTER REGIS-TER. The transition routines are essentially those of Section 2.14. The three exit routines YES1, YES2, and YES3 of Section 2.14 are used as routines here except that they are no longer exit routines. They have been renamed YES1D, YES2D, and YES3D to show their association with the constant processing states $D1$ through $D6$. They are called at places in the code that process situations in which it is apparent that the constant is over and that the next token is beginning. For example in the MINI-BASIC statement

$$512 \text{ IF } 3 > (X + 10.3) / 2E3 \text{ GOTO } 10$$

there are three constants and the lexical box cannot tell that the last symbol of the constants has been seen until it encounters the symbol that follows, namely the symbols $>$,) , and G. In other words, the 3 might have been 37, the 10.3 might have been 10.31, and the 2E3 might have been 2E30. In each of the three cases, the transition routines must both finish processing the constant and begin processing the next lexical token. Thus the corresponding transition routines (i.e., $H1c$, $A3e$, and $B1c$) first call the appropriate YES routine to finish the constant and then the transition routines begin the work for the next token.

The states $E1$ and $E2$ are for processing line numbers. They are used to compute the value part of the tokens LINE, GOTO, and GOSUB. The state $E1$ is for detecting the first digit of the line number and $E2$ is for processing the remainder of the line number. As the digits are encountered, the corresponding integer is accumulated in a variable named LINE REGISTER.

When the line number is completed, a routine YES1E is called to find the corresponding symbol-table entry and place a pointer to the symbol-table entry in POINTER REGISTER. This routine must be called after the symbol following the line number is encountered as was the case with the other YES routines.

The states $F1$, $F2$, and $F3$ are used to detect a variable followed by an equal sign and are used to compute the value part of the tokens ASSIGN and FOR. State $F1$ finds the letter part of the variables, $F2$ looks for the optional digit, and $F3$ looks for the equal sign after the optional digit. They use POINTER REGISTER in the same way as do $C1$ and $C2$.

State $G1$ is used to find the LINE-END after the word REM is detected. It has the effect of deleting the comment. State $G1$ can also be entered after a lexical error is detected in order to resume normal lexical processing at the next line.

State $H1$ is used after the character token REL-OP is encountered and it is used to see if a second REL-OP follows. The identification of relational operators has already been discussed.

There are some additional entries in the transition table of the lexical analyzer where error routines could have been used. An example of this is the RIGHT-PAR entry in the table for state $A2$. Since state $A2$ is only entered after an arithmetic or relational operator or left parenthesis or the words END, IF, RETURN, STEP, and TO, we know that a right parenthesis cannot follow in any well-formed statement. We have decided, however, that the lexical box should create a RIGHT-PAREN token and continue as if nothing unusual had happened. The syntax box will of course detect the error and put out a message. As a general rule, we create tokens whenever the lexical symbol boundaries are clear cut and let the syntax box detect the errors. We do this because we assume the syntax box has more information about what the user is doing and can give a more meaningful error message.

There are three transition routines for which the next state is determined using information other than the information that the machine is in a given state. These are the routines $M1$, $M2$, and $M3$. The next state for transition $M1$ is determined by consulting the Detection Table so that different actions can be taken when a reserved word is completed. The transitions $M2$ and $M3$ determine the next state on the basis of whether or not the next letter is the letter E. Both these actions have been discussed above.

The transition routines have been specified in a way that is oriented toward coding the transitions with the states represented implicity. For example, the specification of the $A1b$ transition is given by three statements ending with "Get input and do state $A1$ transition." The second statement is labeled with $A1a$, since the last two statements happen to be a specification of the transition $A1a$ and the two routines could share common code at this point. Routines oriented toward explicit state representations might begin with a statement such as "Set state to $A1$" and then transfer to statements shared by transitions to other states. The final statement might be "Get input and do transition."

The specification of the transition table entries are given below. Blank entries represent places for error routines. These routines are not specified in detail. We assume only that they cause the token ERROR to be created and that they put the machine in state $G1$ to continue the lexical analysis. If the input is FILE-END, we assume that the error routine is an exit.

$A1b$: Do YES1D routine

$A1a$: CREATE TOKEN

$A1$: Get input and do state $A1$ transition

$A1c$: Do YES2D routine

   Goto $A1a$

$A1d$: Do YES3D routine

   Goto $A1a$

$A1e$: Do YES1E routine

   Goto $A1a$

$A2c$: Do YES1D routine

$A2g$: CREATE TOKEN

$A2a$: Load CLASS REGISTER with ARITHMETIC OPERATOR

$A2b$: CREATE TOKEN

$A2$: Get input and do state $A2$ transition

$A2d$: Do YES2D routine

   Goto $A2g$

$A2e$: Do YES3D routine

   Goto $A2g$

$A2f$: Do YES1E routine

   Goto $A2g$

$A2j$: Do YES1E routine

$A2k$: CREATE TOKEN

$A2h$: Load CLASS REGISTER with LEFT PAREN

   CREATE TOKEN

   Get input and do state $A2$ transition

$A2l$: Do YES1D routine

   Goto $A2k$

A2m: Do YES2D routine

Goto *A2k*

A2n: Do YES3D routine

Goto *A2k*

A2o: If VALUE REGISTER does not contain 1 (i.e., if operator is not
=) then goto an error routine

If VALUE REGISTER does contain 1, goto *A2b*

A2p: Use RELATIONAL REGISTER and VALUE REGISTER to obtain a number from the Relational Table (Fig. 4.4(b))

If number is zero, goto error routine

Put number into RELATIONAL REGISTER

Goto *A2b*

A2q: Load CLASS REGISTER with END

Goto *A2b*

A2r: Load CLASS REGISTER with IF

Goto *A2b*

A2s: Load CLASS REGISTER with RETURN

Goto *A2b*

A2t: Load CLASS REGISTER with STEP

Goto *A2b*

A2u: Load CLASS REGISTER with TO

Goto *A2b*

A3a: Add 1 to contents of VALUE REGISTER and multiply by 26

Add result to contents of POINTER REGISTER

CREATE TOKEN

A3: Get input and do state *A3* transition

A3d: Do YES1D routine

A3c: CREATE TOKEN

A3b: Load CLASS REGISTER with RIGHT PAREN

CREATE TOKEN

Get input and do state *A3* transition

A3e: Do YES2D routine

Goto *A3c*

A3f: Do YES3D routine

Goto *A3c*

A3g: Do YES1E routine
Goto *A3c*

B1c: Do YES3D routine
B1b: CREATE TOKEN
B1a: Load DETECTION REGISTER with pointer from Starting Vector using VALUE REGISTER as index
If DETECTION REGISTER contains zero, goto error routine
B1: Get input and do state *B1* transition
B1d: Increment DETECTION REGISTER
Get input and do state *B1* transition
B1e: Do YES1E routine
Goto *B1b*

C1a: Load CLASS REGISTER with NEXT
C1: Get input and do state *C1* transition
C2b: CREATE TOKEN
C2a: Load CLASS REGISTER with OPERAND
C2d: Load POINTER REGISTER with base address of symbol table plus contents of VALUE REGISTER
C2: Get input and do state *C2* transition

D1c: CREATE TOKEN
D1a: Load CLASS REGISTER with OPERAND
Put number in VALUE REGISTER into NUMBER REGISTER
Get input and do state *D1* transition
D1b: Multiply contents of NUMBER REGISTER by 10
Add number in VALUE REGISTER to NUMBER REGISTER
D1: Get input and do state *D1* transition
D2a: Increment COUNT REGISTER by 1
Multiply contents of NUMBER REGISTER by 10
Add number in VALUE REGISTER to NUMBER REGISTER
D2: Get input and do state *D2* transition

D2b: Initialize COUNT REGISTER with 1

Put number in VALUE REGISTER into NUMBER REGISTER

Get input and do state *D2* transition

D2c: Initialize COUNT REGISTER with 0

Get input and do state *D2* transition

D3a: Initialize COUNT REGISTER with 0

D3: Get input and do state *D3* transition

D4a: If VALUE REGISTER contains 1 (i.e., if operator is +), set SIGN REGISTER to +1

If VALUE REGISTER contains 2 (i.e., if operator is −), set SIGN REGISTER to −1

If VALUE REGISTER contains number larger than 2, goto some error routine

D4: Get input and do state *D4* transition

D5a: Set SIGN REGISTER to +1

D5b: Put number in VALUE REGISTER into EXPONENT REGISTER

D5: Get input and do state *D5* transition

D5c: Multiply contents of EXPONENT REGISTER by 10

Add number in VALUE REGISTER to EXPONENT REGISTER

Get input and do state *D5* transition

D6a: CREATE TOKEN

D6: Load CLASS REGISTER with OPERAND

Get input and do state *D6* transition

E1a: Load CLASS REGISTER with GOTO

E1: Get input and do state *E1* transition

E1b: Load CLASS REGISTER with GOSUB

Get input and do state *E1* transition

E2a: Load CLASS REGISTER with LINE

E2b: Load LINE REGISTER with contents of VALUE REGISTER

E2: Get input and do state *E2* transition

E2c: Multiply contents of LINE REGISTER by 10

Add contents of VALUE REGISTER to LINE REGISTER

Get input and so state $E2$ transition

$F1a$: Load CLASS REGISTER with ASSIGN

 $F1$: Get input and do state $F1$ transition

$F1b$: Load CLASS REGISTER with FOR

Get input and do state $F1$ transition

$F2a$: Load POINTER REGISTER with base address of symbol table plus contents of VALUE REGISTER

 $F2$: Get input and do state $F2$ transition

$F3a$: Add 1 to contents of VALUE REGISTER and multiply by 26

Add result to contents of POINTER REGISTER

 $F3$: Get input and do state $F2$ transition

$G1a$: Load CLASS REGISTER with COMMENT

CREATE TOKEN

 $G1$: Get input and do state $G1$ transition

$H1c$: Do YES1D routine

$H1b$: CREATE TOKEN

$H1a$: Put contents of VALUE REGISTER into RELATIONAL REGISTER

Load CLASS REGISTER with RELATIONAL OPERATOR

 $H1$: Get input and do state $H1$ transition

$H1d$: Do YES2D routine

Goto $H1b$

$H1e$: Do YES3D routine

Goto $H1b$

$H1f$: Do YES1E routine

Goto $H1b$

 $M1$: Compare character value pointed at by DETECTION REGISTER with VALUE REGISTER

If values are equal, goto transition routine pointed at by DETECTION REGISTER

Load DETECTION REGISTER with alternate value pointed at by DETECTION REGISTER

If DETECTION REGISTER contains zero, goto error routine

Goto *M*1

*M*2: If VALUE REGISTER does not contain the number 5 (i.e., if the letter is not E) then do YES1D routine and goto *B*1*b*

If number is 5, goto *D*3*a*

*M*3: If VALUE REGISTER does not contain the number 5 (i.e., if the letter is not E) then do YES2D routine and goto *B*1*b*

If number is 5, goto *D*3

EXIT3: Do YES1D routine

EXIT2: CREATE TOKEN

EXIT1: Load CLASS REGISTER with ENDMARKER

CREATE TOKEN

Exit from lexical box

EXIT4: Do YES2D routine

Goto EXIT2

EXIT5: Do YES3D routine

Goto EXIT2

EXIT6: Do YES1E routine

Goto EXIT2

Routines associated with constant processing

YES1D: Set EXPONENT REGISTER to 0

COMPUTE CONSTANT

Return

YES2D: Set EXPONENT REGISTER to minus value in COUNT REGISTER

COMPUTE CONSTANT

Return

YES3D: If SIGN REGISTER is -1, negate EXPONENT REGISTER

Subtract COUNT REGISTER from EXPONENT REGISTER

COMPUTE CONSTANT

Return

Routine for searching line numbers

YES1E: (Hash coding is used. The hash index is calculated by dividing the line number by a constant P. For the initial stages of the design we let P equal 101. The index is used to select from a List Pointer Table (see Section 3.9) a pointer to the linked list of symbol-table entries for the line numbers with the same index. We are concerned with only two parts of these symbol-table entries: the LINE NUMBER part that contains the line number and the NEXT ENTRY part that contains a pointer to the next entry on the list. If the list does not contain an entry for the line number for which we are searching (possibly because the list is empty), then we create a new symbol-table entry, fill it in, and place it at the beginning of the list for its index.)

Compute remainder obtained when LINE REGISTER is divided by P.

Load POINTER REGISTER with contents of List Pointer Table entry indexed by remainder just computed

YES1ELOOP: If POINTER REGISTER contains zero then

        Begin

        (no more entries on list)

        Get new symbol-table entry

        Load POINTER REGISTER with pointer to new entry

        Load LINE NUMBER part of new entry with contents of LINE REGISTER

        Load NEXT ENTRY part of new entry with contents of the selected List Pointer Table entry

        Load selected List Pointer Table entry with pointer to new symbol-table entry

        Return

        End

If LINE NUMBER part of symbol-table entry pointed to by POINTER REGISTER equals contents of LINE REGISTER then (Line Number found) return

> Otherwise (Line Number not found—look at next entry in list) load POINTER REGISTER with contents of NEXT ENTRY part of symbol-table entry pointed to by POINTER REGISTER, and goto YES1ELOOP

The design of any significant piece of software should include the means for testing and debugging it. Accordingly we include the following program which causes every nonerror transition and visits all the code in the lexical box. Note that this is not a legal MINI-BASIC program, but the errors in it are not detected by the lexical box.

The correct token-string output for this program can be obtained by a hand simulation of the lexical box (see problem 4.9). If this token string is in fact produced by some implementation of the design the designer can have a high degree of confidence that the programming was done correctly. If this token string is not produced, an error has been discovered and the designer may wish to provide a table of the correct values of the contents of the various internal variables of the lexical box for debugging purposes. This was done for the constant processor in Section 2.14 but is omitted here.

```
 1   REM DEBUGGING PROGRAM FOR LEXICAL BOX
 2   REM A1 + = ( ).
13   LET F 1 = 7 / — (63 < > 9)) = * < (
14   LET G = — 3 TO .65 + .01 = .1) + .8( .6
20   F OR I = .3 E 6 8 STEP . 3E + 6 = 1.3E — 1) (1.3E9
23   IF 10 E6 + 3E1 (1E1 GOTO 1 2 = H I >
40   NEXT E3
42   + A ↑ B ( C ) 2 ( D
45   GOSUB 1) GOTO 6
50   ( 9
52   ) . 6 RETURN ) END > = < = < )
 60 7
54 =J0+K1+L2+M3+N4+O5+P6+Q7+R8+S9+T+U+V+W+X+Y+Z
```

PROBLEMS

1. Specify the contents of each of the variables of the lexical box as each of the characters in the statement is processed.

010   IF X >= Y1 + 2E3 GOTO 20

2. Design error messages for each of the blank entries in the lexical box.

3. Indicate the changes that would be required in the design of the lexical box if the following changes were made in the transliteration table of Fig. 4.5.

E	E	5
+	+	1
−	−	2
=	=	1

4. Indicate the changes that would be required in the design of the lexical box if the output token set was changed to distinguish between the unary and binary use of the + and − signs. In Fig. 4.1 the lexical token ARITHMETIC OPERATOR would be retained for the +, −, *, /, ↑ operators used in a binary fashion (e.g., 1 + 1) but a new token UNARY OPERATOR would be used for the +, − operators used in a unary fashion (e.g., −1). The same values for + and − would be used.

5. Find a MINI-BASIC program that exercises all the transitions in Fig. 4.6 which can be exercised by a legal MINI-BASIC program.

6. The lexical box accepts all legal MINI-BASIC programs and many illegal ones. Find all the transitions in Fig. 4.6 which can be changed to transitions to the error state so that the new box will still accept all legal MINI-BASIC programs.

7. The lexical box accepts such illegal statements as:

    IF X1 = X2 GOSUB 10

However, this statement is "meaningful" and would be a potential extension of MINI-BASIC. Find three other illegal but meaningful statements.

8. Indicate how the routines in Section 4.4 would be changed if the explicit method for remembering states were used.

9. What is the token set produced by the lexical box for the debugging sequence given at the end of Section 4.4?

10. Design a lexical box for the MINI-BASIC language under the restriction that spaces count—i.e., reserved words, variables, and constants must be separated by spaces.

11. Program the lexical box in your favorite language.

12. Design a lexical box for the machine of Problem 2.22. The inputs to the lexical box are the characters a, b, ..., z. The outputs are the tokens ONE, TWO, ..., TEN, ..., TWENTY, ..., NINETY, HUNDRED.

13. Design a lexical box for the SNOBOL language.

14. Design a lexical box for your favorite assembly language.

15. Design a lexical box for MORSE CODE. The inputs are "dot", "dash", and "space". The outputs are tokens for all the alphanumerics and punctuation marks for which there are codes.

5

Pushdown
Machines

5.1 DEFINITION OF A PUSHDOWN MACHINE

A finite-state machine can only carry out computational tasks that require a fixed and finite amount of memory. However, there are many tasks in a compiler that cannot be performed under this restriction and, hence, a more-complex automaton model is needed. Consider, for example, the task of processing the parentheses in arithmetic expressions. An arithmetic expression may begin with any number of left parentheses and the compiler must check that the expression has exactly that number of balancing right parentheses. Each of the leading left parentheses in an expression must represent a distinct usage since each such usage requires a different number of balancing right parentheses to complete the expression. Stated differently, the compiler must effectively count the left parentheses in order to balance them. Obviously, one cannot use a finite set of states to remember the number of right parentheses required since the set of these numbers is infinite. In order to systematically solve this expression problem and a host of other compiler problems, there is a need to incorporate more powerful machine models within a compiler.

To obtain more powerful machines, the memory capability of the finite-state machine is augmented by an additional information-storage mechanism. One method of storing information, which has been found very useful for compilers and which is easy to implement, is that of "stacking." Operationally, the essential feature of stacking is that symbols can be added or deleted from the storage one at a time and that the symbol removed from storage is always the most recently entered symbol in the storage. The symbols can be pictured as being stored like a stack of plates in a cafeteria. Clean plates are added to the top of the stack by the cafeteria staff and are removed from the top of the stack by the customers. Thus, the customer always takes the most recently cleaned plate from the stack. The terminology of information stacking follows this cafeteria image. When information is added to the stack, we say that information is being "pushed onto" the stack. When information is removed, we say it is "popped off." The most recent information is said to be on the "top" of the stack. Although this imagery is useful, it is not meant to suggest in detail how a stack should be implemented within a compiler.

We depict a stack in Fig. 5.1(a). The bottom symbol is $\triangledown$ and the top symbol is C. The order of the symbols tells us the order they were entered in the stack. First the $\triangledown$ was entered, then the lower A, then the B, then the upper A, and finally the C. If one pushes the symbol D on this stack, the result is Fig. 5.1(b) with D as the top stack symbol. If, instead, one pops the top symbol C, the result is Fig. 5.1(c) with A exposed as the top stack symbol. With either of these operations, only the top of the stack is affected while the lower symbols remain unchanged. The symbol $\triangledown$ is a special symbol used to mark the bottom of the stack, and is called the *bottommarker*. It is used exclusively at the bottom of the stack and is never popped off. Thus, if the top stack symbol is $\triangledown$, as in Fig. 5.1(d), it is known that the stack has no other symbols. In this case, we say that the stack is empty. The stack in Fig. 5.1(a) can also be displayed as a string in either of the two following ways:

1. $C\ A\ B\ A\ \triangledown$

2. $\triangledown\ A\ B\ A\ C$

In the first line, the stack is represented using a "top symbol on the left" convention and the second line uses a "top symbol on the right" convention. The bottommarker makes it apparent which convention is being used.

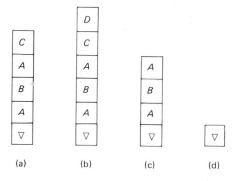

(a)   (b)   (c)   (d)

Figure 5.1

One automaton model employing the stacking principle is the *pushdown machine.* It combines the memory capabilities of a finite-state machine and a pushdown stack in a very elementary way. The pushdown machine can be in one of a finite number of states and it has a stack on which it can store and retrieve information.

As with a finite-state machine, the processing of an input sequence is carried out in a series of small steps. Each step may alter the memory configuration by changing its state and pushing or popping its stack. However, unlike the finite-state machine, a pushdown machine may take several steps to process a single input symbol. As a part of the control that determines each step, the machine decides whether it is finished processing the current input symbol, in which case it obtains the next input symbol, or whether the next step should use the current input symbol. Figure 5.2 shows one of the memory configurations that could occur while some hypothetical pushdown machine is processing the sequence 100110. For expository purposes, the input sequence is pictured as being written in the cells of a file or the squares of a tape with a pointer to the input symbol currently being processed.

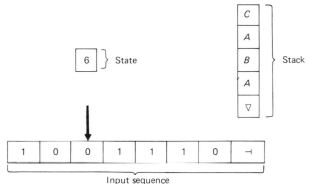

Figure 5.2

Each step in the processing is determined by a set of rules using three pieces of information:

1. the state,
2. the top stack symbol,
3. the current input symbol.

The set of these rules is referred to as the control. In Fig. 5.2, the information available to the control is that the state is state 6, the top stack symbol is *C,* and the current input is 0.

On the basis of the information available to it, the control selects either an exit (which ends the processing) or a transition. A transition consists of three parts: a stack operation, a state operation, and an input operation. The allowable operations are as follows:

Stack operations

1. Push a specified stack symbol.
2. Pop the top stack symbol.
3. Leave the stack unchanged.

State operation

1. Change to some specified state.

Input operations

1. Obtain the next input symbol and make it the current input symbol.
2. Retain the present input symbol as the current input symbol.

To process an input sequence, the pushdown machine is started in some specified state with a specified stack and with the first input symbol as the current input. The machine then carries out the operations called for by its control. If an exit is called for, the processing stops. If a transition is called for, then a new current input, top stack symbol, and state are obtained and the control is called upon to carry out another operation.

In order for the control rules to make sense, the machine must not ask for a next symbol if the current input is the endmarker and must not pop the stack if the top stack symbol is the bottommarker. Since the bottommarker is to be used exclusively at the bottom of the stack, the machine must also not ask that a bottommarker be pushed.

We now recapitulate how to specify a pushdown machine. A pushdown machine is specified by the following five items:

1. a finite set of *input symbols* which includes an endmarker;
2. a finite set of *stack symbols* which includes a bottommarker;
3. a finite set of *states* which includes a starting state;
4. a *control* which assigns an exit or transition to each combination of input symbol, stack symbol, and state. The nonexit transitions consist of a stack operation, a state operation, and an input operation as specified above. Operations which ask for inputs beyond the endmarker or which push or pop the bottommarker are excluded;

5. a *starting stack* which may be specified in "top symbol on right" notation as the bottommarker followed by a (possibly null) sequence of other stack symbols.

A pushdown machine will be called a *pushdown recognizer* if it has two exits, ACCEPT and REJECT. A sequence of symbols from the input alphabet (excluding the endmarker) will be said to be *accepted* by the recognizer if that sequence followed by the endmarker causes the machine started in its starting state and starting stack to execute a series of transitions resulting in the exit ACCEPT. Other sequences will be said to be *rejected.*

When we describe the transitions of a pushdown machine, we denote the operations using the words POP, PUSH, STATE, ADVANCE, and RETAIN in the following manner:

POP means pop the top stack symbol.

PUSH(A) where A is a stack symbol means push the symbol A on the stack.

STATE(s) where s is a state means that state s is to be used as the next state.

ADVANCE means that the next input is to be used as the current input. In some implementations, this might mean "advancing" the input pointer.

RETAIN means that the current input is to be retained.

When we want to specify a transition which leaves the stack unchanged, we note this fact by the absence of the words POP or PUSH. Although the RETAIN operation is basically the absence of an ADVANCE operation, we always write the input operation explicitly to make the reader aware of what is happening. We omit the word STATE from our specifications if the machine has exactly one state.

We now describe how to use a pushdown recognizer for the parentheses problem. Each time a left parenthesis is found, an A will be pushed on the stack. When a matching right parenthesis is found, an A will be popped from the stack. The sequence will be rejected if a right parenthesis is found when the stack is empty (i.e., if there are extra right parentheses) or if the sequence ends with an A on the stack (i.e., if there are extra left parentheses). The sequence is accepted if, when the sequence ends, the stack is empty. The full specifications follow:

1. input set is $\{(\ ,\ ),\ \dashv\}$
2. stack symbol set is $\{A,\ \nabla\}$

3. state set is $\{s\}$ where s is the starting state
4. transitions are:

$$\text{(, }A, s = \text{PUSH}(A), \text{STATE}(s), \text{ADVANCE}$$
$$\text{(, }\nabla, s = \text{PUSH}(A), \text{STATE}(s), \text{ADVANCE}$$
$$\text{), }A, s = \text{POP}, \text{STATE}(s), \text{ADVANCE}$$
$$\text{), }\nabla, s = \text{REJECT}$$
$$\dashv, A, s = \text{REJECT}$$
$$\dashv, \nabla, s = \text{ACCEPT}$$

where the combinations of input symbol, stack symbol, and state are displayed to the left of the equal signs and the transitions are shown on the right.

5. starting stack is ∇

To see this machine in action, we show, in Fig. 5.3, how it processes the input sequence:

$$(( ) ( ))$$

The figure shows each step of the processing beginning with the starting configuration in Fig. 5.3(a) and ending with acceptance in Fig. 5.3(h). This kind of stack movie consumes a great deal of space so we prefer to represent the sequence of operations more compactly as follows:

a: ∇	$[s]$	$(( ) ( )) \dashv$
b: ∇A	$[s]$	$( ) ( )) \dashv$
c: ∇AA	$[s]$	$) ( )) \dashv$
d: ∇A	$[s]$	$( )) \dashv$
e: ∇AA	$[s]$	$)) \dashv$
f: ∇A	$[s]$	$) \dashv$
g: ∇	$[s]$	$\dashv$
h: ACCEPT		

In this linear representation of the stack movie, we put the stack on the left, the state in the middle, and the unprocessed portion of the input string on the right. This partial input string includes the current input symbol and the symbols which follow. To see the entire input sequence, one must refer back to the initial configuration. The information available to the control is immediately apparent since the top stack symbol is immediately to the left of the state and the current input is immediately to the right. Many of the pushdown machines that arise in practice have only one state (as does this example) and in these cases, we usually elect to omit the state information.

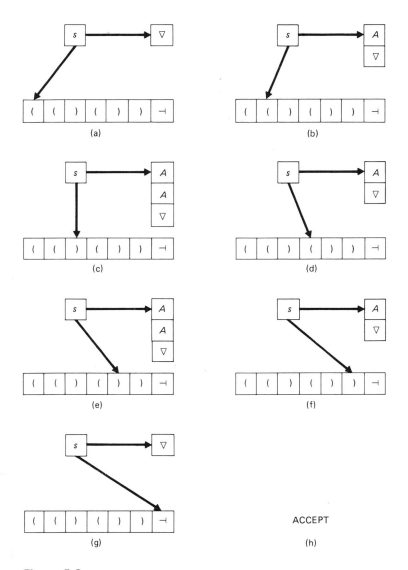

Figure 5.3

The control of this one-state machine can be represented in a control table such as Fig. 5.4, which shows the action of the machine for each combination of input symbol and top stack symbol. The column headings of the table are the input symbols, the row headings are the stack symbols, and the appropriate actions appear in the row-column intersections. Since this particular machine has only one state, the state information is omitted.

	(	)	⊣
A	PUSH(*A*) ADVANCE	POP ADVANCE	REJECT
▽	PUSH(*A*) ADVANCE	REJECT	ACCEPT

Figure 5.4

We use control tables in this format (i.e., with columns for input symbols and rows for stack symbols) as our standard representation of a one-state pushdown machine.

5.2 SOME NOTATION FOR SETS OF SEQUENCES

In order to give some examples of processing sets of sequences by pushdown machines, we introduce some descriptive notation. We begin by defining three operations on sets of sequences. These operations combine sets of sequences to obtain other sets of sequences. The three operations are union, concatenation, and Kleene star.

Union.   If P and Q are sets of sequences, the union of P and Q is the set of sequences that are in either P or Q or in both. Although the usual set notation for union is $P \cup Q$, in automata applications the union is usually expressed as $P + Q$. Some examples of union are:

$$\{FOR,IF,THEN\} + \{DO,IF\} = \{FOR,IF,THEN,DO\}$$
$$\{AB, X3\} + \{Y, \epsilon\} = \{AB, X3, Y, \epsilon\}$$

{all sequences of 0's and 1's beginning with a 0 and ending with a 1}
  + {all sequences of 0's and 1's beginning with a 0 and ending with a 0}
  = {all sequences of 0's and 1's beginning with a 0}
{simple variables in ALGOL} + {subscripted variables in ALGOL}
  = {variables in ALGOL}

Concatenation.   The concatenation of two sequences is defined as the sequence obtained by the juxtaposition (or placing together) of their symbols. For instance, the concatenation of ENVIRON and MENT results in the sequence ENVIRONMENT. The length of the resulting sequence is the sum of the lengths of the two sequences being concatenated. Since the null sequence has zero length, the effect of concatenating it with any sequence is to leave the sequence unchanged. For instance, the concatenation of MENT and ϵ is still the sequence of length four, MENT.

Concatenation can be extended from an operation on sequences to an operation on sets of sequences. If P and Q are sets of sequences, then the concatenation of P and Q is the set consisting of all possible concatenations of sequences from P with sequences from Q. The notation for concatenations is $P \cdot Q$. However, we can usually leave out the dot and write PQ. Some examples of concatenation are:

$\{10\}\{1, 00\} = \{101, 1000\}$

$\{AB, X, ABY\}\{\epsilon, Y\} = \{AB, X, ABY, XY, ABYY\}$

$\{$all letters$\}\{$all sequences of letters and digits$\}$

     $= \{$all sequences consisting of a letter followed by a sequence of letters and digits$\}$

The concatenation of a set R with itself, namely RR or $R \cdot R$, is also written as R^2. For example, $\{0, 11\}^2 = \{00, 011, 110, 1111\}$. Similarly, R^i for positive integer i represents the set R concatenated with itself i times. It is convenient to say that R concatenated with itself zero times is the set $\{\epsilon\}$. Thus:

$$R^0 = \{\epsilon\}$$

This definition is consistent with the law of exponents, namely

$$R^i \cdot R^j = R^{i+j}$$

and one can see that concatenation is treated notationally in much the same way as multiplication.

Kleene Star. It is useful to have a notation for the set of all sequences made up of symbols from a given alphabet. If A represents the set of alphabet symbols, then we say that A^* represents the set of all sequences made up of symbols from A. In particular A^* is always assumed to contain the null sequence ϵ.

As an example $\{0, 1\}^*$ represents the set of all sequences over the alphabet set $\{0, 1\}$.

The asterisk used in this way is called the *Kleene star* operator or sometimes just the *star* operator.

The Kleene star can be generalized from an operation on alphabets to an operation on other sets of sequences. For instance, $\{IF, THEN\}^*$ represents an infinite set of sequences including ϵ, IF, THEN, IFIF, THENIFTHEN, and IFTHENIFIF. Expressed symbolically, if R is a set of sequences, we define the set R^* by the infinite series

$$R^* = R^0 + R^1 + R^2 + \dots .$$

The $+$ in this expression is, of course, the union operator discussed above.

There is a widely used variant of the Kleene star known as the *Kleene plus*. Given a set of sequences A, we define the set A^+ by the equation

$$A^+ = AA^*$$

Thus, A^+ can be expressed as

$$A^+ = A^1 + A^2 + A^3 + \ldots .$$

The set A^+ is exactly the same as the set A^* except that A^+ only contains the sequence ϵ if the set A contains ϵ.

These three operations have the property that if they are applied to regular sets, the result is a regular set. (A regular set is a set that can be recognized by a finite-state machine.) In fact any regular set over a given alphabet can be expressed as the result of these three operations applied to the alphabet symbols. In the remainder of this section we introduce some extensions to these operations which can be used to obtain nonregular sets.

The first extension allows the use of variables in the exponent notation for sets. A simple example of this is

$$\{1^n \, 0^n\} \qquad n > 0$$

By this notation, we mean the set consisting of some number of 1's followed by the same number of 0's. Some members of this set are

$$10$$
$$111000$$
$$111111110000000$$

Stated in general terms, the notational technique is to use letters as exponents and then express the relationships among these exponents with numerical side conditions.

Another example is the formula

$$\{1^n \, 0^m\} \qquad n \geq m > 0$$

It defines the set consisting of sequences of some number of 1's followed by an equal or lesser number of 0's, including, for example, the sequences

$$111000$$
$$1110$$

Similarly, the set

$$\{a^n \, b^m \, c^m \, d^n\} \qquad n > 0, m > 0$$

consists of sequences of some number of a's followed by some number of b's, followed by some number of c's, followed by some number of d's, where the number of a's equals the number of d's and the number of b's equals the number of c's. Members of this set include

$$abbccd$$
$$aaabbbbcccccddd$$

A second notational technique is to use the superscript r to denote the reverse of a sequence. Thus, for example

$$(a\ b\ c)^r = c\ b\ a$$

Using this reversal operator, we can write formulas such as

$$\{ww^r\} \qquad w \text{ in } (0 + 1)^*$$

which represents the set of sequences consisting of an arbitrary sequence of 0's and 1's followed by that sequence in reverse. This is precisely the set of sequences of even length that read the same from left to right as they read from right to left. Sample sequences are:

$$1110110111$$
$$0000$$

Although these new notational methods are capable of expressing nonregular sets and enable us to describe the actions of some specific pushdown machines, they are not general enough to describe real programming languages. For this reason, the examples and problems of this chapter lack the immediate practical motivation of programming languages. Nevertheless, they should be sufficient to develop some intuitive appreciation of pushdown machine processing.

5.3 AN EXAMPLE OF PUSHDOWN RECOGNITION

In order to provide a second example of pushdown recognition, one which involves more than one state, we consider the problem of recognizing the set

$$\{0^n\ 1^n\} \qquad n > 0.$$

As a first step in designing a pushdown recognizer, we formulate a recognition plan in English:

> The initial sequence of 0's is pushed onto the stack. Then as each 1 appears, one of the 0's is popped off the stack. Acceptance occurs if and only if the stack is empty when the sequence is complete. If an occurrence of the symbol 0 occurs after the first occurrence of a 1, the sequence is rejected at once.

To carry out this plan, we need a stack symbol to represent the input symbol 0. Although we can use 0 itself as the stack symbol, we elect to use the symbol Z in order to avoid confusion. The processing is divided into two phases. The first is a "pushing" phase where the initial 0's are stored on the stack. These 0's are represented by the stack symbol Z. The second phase is a "popping" phase where an occurrence of the symbol 1 causes Z to be removed from the stack and where the occurrence of an input 0 is cause for immediate rejection of the sequence. In order for the machine to "remember" which phase it is in, we use two states, s_1 and s_2 to represent the two respective phases.

Before specifying the pushdown control in detail, we show a stack movie of the machine accepting the sequence 0 0 0 1 1 1 to see how the machine should operate. This movie is shown in Fig. 5.5(a). We also show a movie in Fig. 5.5(b) of the machine rejecting the sequence 0 0 1 0 1 1. After configuration 3, in Fig. 5.5(b), the machine switches to state s_2 to remember that it has entered the popping phase. The occurrence of the input 0 then triggers rejection.

One convenient way to exhibit the control is to give a set of control tables, one for each state, with each control table in the format of the standard one-state table. A pair of control tables for the present example is shown in Fig. 5.6. To find the action for a given combination of state, input, and stack symbols, first find the control table for the given state and then use

1:	$\triangledown$	$[s_1]$	0 0 0 1 1 1 $\dashv$
2:	$\triangledown$ Z	$[s_1]$	0 0 1 1 1 $\dashv$
3:	$\triangledown$ Z Z	$[s_1]$	0 1 1 1 $\dashv$
4:	$\triangledown$ Z Z Z	$[s_1]$	1 1 1 $\dashv$
5:	$\triangledown$ Z Z	$[s_2]$	1 1 $\dashv$
6:	$\triangledown$ Z	$[s_2]$	1 $\dashv$
7:	$\triangledown$	$[s_2]$	$\dashv$
8:	ACCEPT		

(a)

1:	$\triangledown$	$[s_1]$	0 0 1 0 1 1 $\dashv$
2:	$\triangledown$ Z	$[s_1]$	0 1 0 1 1 $\dashv$
3:	$\triangledown$ Z Z	$[s_1]$	1 0 1 1 $\dashv$
4:	$\triangledown$ Z	$[s_2]$	0 1 1 $\dashv$
5:	REJECT		

(b)

Figure 5.5

State s_1

	0	1	⊣
Z	STATE(s_1) PUSH(Z) ADVANCE	STATE(s_2) POP ADVANCE	REJECT
▽	STATE(s_1) PUSH(Z) ADVANCE	REJECT	REJECT

State s_2

	0	1	⊣
Z	REJECT	STATE(s_2) POP ADVANCE	REJECT
▽	REJECT	REJECT	ACCEPT

Starting stack: ▽

Figure 5.6

the input and stack symbols to look up the action in the selected control table. In Fig. 5.6, combination s_2, 1, Z calls for the operations STATE(s_2), POP, ADVANCE.

To summarize, the full specifications of a pushdown machine to recognize the set $\{0^n 1^n\}$ for $n > 0$ are as follows:

1. input set $\{0, 1, \dashv\}$
2. stack symbol set $\{Z, \nabla\}$
3. state set $\{s_1, s_2\}$ where s_1 is the starting state
4. transitions as shown in Fig. 5.6
5. starting stack ∇

5.4   EXTENDED STACK OPERATIONS

There are actually many different ways of defining a class of machine models whose transitions are selected by the input, state, and top stack symbols, and whose operations affect only the top of the stack. It is customary to refer to any of these models as a "pushdown machine." Thus, the machine model of Section 5.1 is just an example of a pushdown machine model. When confusion might result, we refer to the kind of pushdown machine defined in Section 5.1 as a *primitive pushdown machine*.

There are several reasons for beginning the study of pushdown machines with the primitive model. One reason is that this model exhibits the principles of pushdown processing in their simplest form. A second reason is that it is a mathematically defined concept that can be used to prove theorems or to solve the problems at the end of this chapter. It serves as our standard model in the sense that the word "pushdown machine" is reserved for machines which employ a stack in a similar way, and which have the same processing capabilities (e.g., can recognize the same sets) as the primitive machines.

The reason we call the primitive machine "primitive" is that the transitions involve, at most, one push or pop operation. These operations might be the ones used to actually build a pushdown machine as a piece of hardware. However, these operations are unnaturally restrictive if one wishes to use a pushdown machine as the basis of a software design. In this section, we consider stack operations from a software point of view.

Once a transition has been selected on the basis of state, stack, and input, the sensible thing to do from a programming viewpoint is to get as much work done as possible before reaccessing the control information and selecting a new transition. In other words, the designer may wish to associate more general routines with the transitions and not confine the stack manipulation to a single pop or push. Suppose, for example, that the designer wishes to push two symbols on the stack. He could, if so inclined, push the first symbol and enter a state whose single purpose is to cause the machine to push the second symbol during the next machine transition. However, this two-transition approach is inefficient and unnatural when compared with the obvious approach of having one transition routine do both of the push operations. Since a transition with two push operations can be simulated by two transitions of a primitive machine, we are happy to call pushing two symbols an "extended stack operation" and will continue to use the term pushdown machine for a device that pushes two symbols at once.

The methods of this book involve many types of transition routines. The effect of any of these routines can, in principle, be achieved by a combination of primitive transitions and so we still refer to the machines using them as "pushdown machines."

In this section, we introduce an extended stack operation called the REPLACE operation and illustrate how it can be used. Other extended operations will be introduced in later chapters as they are needed.

The effect of the REPLACE operation is to pop the top stack symbol and then do a sequence of push operations. To specify the sequence of symbols to be pushed onto the stack, the REPLACE operation must be expressed with a sequence as its argument. Thus, we write

$$\text{REPLACE}(A \ B \ C)$$

if the sequence to be pushed is $A\ B\ C$. This is equivalent to the series of operations

$$POP$$
$$PUSH(A)$$
$$PUSH(B)$$
$$PUSH(C)$$

Thus, the left symbol of the sequence is the first pushed on the stack and is placed below the other symbols in the sequence. If REPLACE($A\ B\ C$) is applied to the stack

$$\nabla\ X\ Y\ Z$$

the new stack is

$$\nabla\ X\ Y\ A\ B\ C$$

The REPLACE operator is used extensively and systematically in later chapters. At this point, we regard it simply as a shorthand for a sequence of primitive stack operations that a programmer might wish to include as part of a single transition routine.

To illustrate the use of the REPLACE operator, we return to the problem of recognizing the set $\{0^n\ 1^n\}$ for $n > 0$. In Section 5.3, we observed that a recognizer could be designed employing a "push phase" and a "pop phase." We designed such a machine using the control state to remember the phase. Now we design another pushdown machine for the same problem.

The new pushdown machine uses the same counting techniques as the previous machine. A Z is pushed on the stack for each occurrence of input 0 and is popped for each occurrence of input 1. However, a new strategy is employed to distinguish between the push and pop phases. During the push phase, a new stack symbol X is kept on top of the stack. The only purpose of this symbol is to remind the control that it is in the push phase. When the first 1 is encountered, the X is popped and the machine starts matching the Z's with the 1's. The availability of the REPLACE routine enables us to carry out this plan with only a single state, as shown in Fig. 5.7. A stack movie for the recognition of $0\ 0\ 0\ 1\ 1\ 1$ is provided in Fig. 5.8. This movie can be compared with Fig. 5.5(a) which shows the same sequence processed by the previously designed machine.

The REPLACE operator is used when the top stack symbol is an X and the input is 0. In one operation, it removes the unwanted X from the top of the stack, places a Z on the stack to record the occurrence of the 0, and then places another X on top to denote the fact that the machine is to remain in the "push phase."

	0	1	⊣
X	REPLACE(ZX) ADVANCE	POP RETAIN	REJECT
Z	REJECT	POP ADVANCE	REJECT
▽	REJECT	REJECT	ACCEPT

Starting stack: ▽ X

Figure 5.7

This is our first example where the input operation RETAIN is used. It appears in the transition in which the X is popped off the stack and the "pop phase" begins. The input symbol 1 is retained so that it can be checked against the underlying stack symbol.

Comparing Fig. 5.7 with the previous machine of Fig. 5.6, we see that the new machine requires only two pieces of information (input and stack symbol) whereas the old machine requires the usual three pieces of information. On the other hand, the new machine has more complex stack operations.

Unlike the situation for finite-state machines, there is no concept of a unique "reduced pushdown machine" and the choice among competing pushdown machines is correspondingly more difficult. At the time this book is being written, it is not even known whether or not there exists a general algorithm for deciding if two pushdown recognizers accept the same set. In any event, this example makes clear that there may be several attractive pushdown designs for the same problem and that there is even some choice between what information is remembered by the state and what information is stored on the stack.

1:	▽ X	0 0 0 1 1 1 ⊣
2:	▽ Z X	0 0 1 1 1 ⊣
3:	▽ Z Z X	0 1 1 1 ⊣
4:	▽ Z Z Z X	1 1 1 ⊣
5:	▽ Z Z Z	1 1 1 ⊣
6:	▽ Z Z	1 1 ⊣
7:	▽ Z	1 ⊣
8:	▽	⊣
9:	ACCEPT	

Figure 5.8

5.5 TRANSLATIONS WITH PUSHDOWN MACHINES

A pushdown recognizer is called a *pushdown translator* if it produces an output sequence while doing its recognition. In order for the machine to produce an output sequence, the control is permitted an *output operation* along with the usual state, input, and stack operations. In the absence of an output operation, it is assumed that no output is intended. If we wish to output the sequence AB, we write

$$\text{OUT}(AB)$$

in the specification of the corresponding pushdown transition.

In order to see how the OUT operation can be used, consider the problem of translating an arbitrary sequence of 1's and 0's into a sequence of the form $1^n 0^m$ where n and m are the number of 1's and 0's respectively in the sequence. For example, the sequence 0 1 1 0 1 1 should be translated into 1 1 1 1 0 0 because the sequence has four 1's and two 0's.

One plan for doing this translation is to output the 1's immediately as they are inputted and to push a 0 on the stack whenever 0 is encountered. When the endmarker is encountered, the machine is to pop off the 0's and use them for output. The control table for a one-state machine that implements this plan is shown in Fig. 5.9.

A stack movie of this machine processing the sequence 0 1 0 1 1 is shown in Fig. 5.10. If a transition calls for an output, we write this operation on the line between the configuration causing the transition and the configuration assumed after the transition.

In this example, the set recognized by the machine is simply $(0 + 1)^*$, the set of all sequences. The stack in this case is not used to achieve recognition and serves only to achieve the translation. The 0's are being pushed for the sole purpose of outputting them later. In the next example, we use the stack for both recognition and translation.

	0	1	⊣
0	PUSH(0) ADVANCE	OUT(1) ADVANCE	OUT(0) POP RETAIN
▽	PUSH(0) ADVANCE	OUT(1) ADVANCE	ACCEPT

Starting stack: ▽

Figure 5.9

1:	∇	0 1 0 1 1 $\dashv$
2:	∇ 0	1 0 1 1 $\dashv$
	OUT(1)	
3:	∇ 0	0 1 1 $\dashv$
4:	∇ 0 0	1 1 $\dashv$
	OUT(1)	
5:	∇ 0 0	1 $\dashv$
	OUT(1)	
6:	∇ 0 0	$\dashv$
	OUT(0)	
7:	∇ 0	$\dashv$
	OUT(0)	
8:	∇	$\dashv$
9:	ACCEPT	

Figure 5.10

Consider the problem of recognizing the set

$$\{w\ 2\ w^r\} \qquad w \text{ in } (0 + 1)*$$

and translating each sequence $w\ 2\ w^r$ into the sequence $1^n\ 0^m$ where n and m are the number of the 1's and 0's respectively in w. Thus,

$$0\ 1\ 0\ 1\ 1\ 2\ 1\ 1\ 0\ 1\ 0$$

is to be translated into

$$1\ 1\ 1\ 0\ 0$$

To do this translation, we design a pushdown machine which operates in two phases. The first phase is a pushing phase which occurs prior to encountering a 2. During this phase the input symbols 0 and 1 are stored on the stack as they appear in the input sequence. In addition, a symbol 1 is outputted whenever input 1 is encountered. The second phase is a popping phase used after input symbol 2. During this phase, input symbols are compared with the stack symbols to verify that they correspond. This ensures that the sequence after the 2 is indeed the reverse of the sequence before the 2. As these symbols are being matched, an output of 0 is produced for each 0 encountered. The phase of the pushdown machine is remembered by the state. A pair of control tables implementing this plan is shown in Fig. 5.11 using states named PHASE1 and PHASE2.

Figure 5.12 shows the machine in action as it rejects input sequence 0 0 1 2 1 0 1. Because the sequence is rejected, we say that it has no translation, even though the pushdown machine produced some output prior to the discovery of the input symbol 1 which did not match the corresponding symbol of the sequence before the 2.

	0	1	2	⊣
0	STATE(PHASE1) PUSH(0) ADVANCE	STATE(PHASE1) PUSH(1) OUT(1) ADVANCE	STATE(PHASE2) ADVANCE	REJECT
1	STATE(PHASE1) PUSH(0) ADVANCE	STATE(PHASE1) PUSH(1) OUT(1) ADVANCE	STATE(PHASE2) ADVANCE	REJECT
▽	STATE(PHASE1) PUSH(0) ADVANCE	STATE(PHASE1) PUSH(1) OUT(1) ADVANCE	STATE(PHASE2) ADVANCE	REJECT

(a)

	0	1	2	⊣
0	STATE(PHASE2) POP OUT(0) ADVANCE	REJECT	REJECT	REJECT
1	REJECT	STATE(PHASE2) POP ADVANCE	REJECT	REJECT
▽	REJECT	REJECT	REJECT	ACCEPT

(b)

Starting stack: ▽

Fig. 5.11 (a) Table for starting state PHASE1; (b) Table for state PHASE2

```
1:  ▽              PHASE1      0 0 1 2 1 0 1 ⊣
2:  ▽ 0            PHASE1        0 1 2 1 0 1 ⊣
3:  ▽ 0 0          PHASE1          1 2 1 0 1 ⊣
        OUT(1)
4:  ▽ 0 0 1        PHASE1            2 1 0 1 ⊣
5:  ▽ 0 0 1        PHASE2              1 0 1 ⊣
6:  ▽ 0 0          PHASE2                0 1 ⊣
        OUT(0)
7:  ▽ 0            PHASE2                  1 ⊣
8:  REJECT
```

Figure 5.12

	0	1	⊣
A	PUSH(*B*) RETAIN	POP ADVANCE	POP RETAIN
B	POP RETAIN	PUSH(*B*) RETAIN	REJECT
▽	PUSH(*A*) ADVANCE	PUSH(*B*) ADVANCE	ACCEPT

Starting stack: ▽

Figure 5.13

5.6 CYCLING

One danger in the use of a pushdown machine is that it may operate indefinitely without ever exiting. For instance, consider the one-state machine of Fig. 5.13. A stack movie for this machine confronted with input sequence 0 0 1 is shown in Fig. 5.14. With top stack symbol *A* and input symbol 0, the machine pushes a *B* while retaining the input symbol. However, the *B* is immediately popped off while still retaining the same input symbol. The machine thus cycles indefinitely without ever exiting or advancing to the next input symbol.

A similar situation arises for input sequence 1 1 0, as shown in Fig. 5.15. With *B* as the top stack symbol and 1 as the input symbol, the machine pushes another *B* while still retaining the 1 as the input symbol. Thus, the machine is in a cycle where it just keeps on pushing *B*'s without exiting or advancing the input pointer.

In designing a pushdown machine for use with a compiler, one must be certain that the machine can never cycle, even with input sequences that are not acceptable. Should the machine cycle, the compiler itself would loop and fail to complete its task.

Nevertheless, the problem of cycling is not a major compiler design problem. All the usual design procedures, including those given in this book, do in fact produce machines that never cycle. Furthermore, even when a pushdown machine is designed in an ad hoc manner, the heuristics of the design are usually sufficient to convince oneself that the machine cannot cycle.

Although not usually needed, there are methods of testing each combination of state, input, and stack symbol to see if it begins a cycle. A full

```
1:  ▽           0 0 1⊣
2:  ▽A            0 1⊣
3:  ▽AB           0 1⊣
4:  ▽A            0 1⊣
5:  ▽AB           0 1⊣
6:  ▽A            0 1⊣
7:  ▽AB           0 1⊣
                   .
                   .
                   .
```

Figure 5.14

```
1:  ▽           1 1 0 ⊣
2:  ▽B            1 0 ⊣
3:  ▽BB           1 0 ⊣
4:  ▽BBB          1 0 ⊣
5:  ▽BBBB         1 0 ⊣
                   .
                   .
                   .
```

Figure 5.15

treatment of this subject appears in Hopcroft and Ullman [1969], pages 168–170.

5.7 REFERENCES

Pushdown stacks have been used in programming from early times and are part of the folklore of the area. The use of a pushdown machine in compiling is described in Ershov [1959] and Bauer and Samelson [1959, 1960]. A formalization of a nondeterministic pushdown machine appears in Oettinger [1961]. The deterministic pushdown machines of this chapter are considered in Schutzenberger [1963], Fischer [1963], and Ginsburg and Greibach [1966]. They are also discussed in the text Hopcroft and Ullman [1969].

PROBLEMS

1. a) Exhibit three sequences in the set recognized by this one-state pushdown machine.

b) For each of these sequences, show the stack movie for its acceptance.

	a	b	c	⊣
A	PUSH(A) ADVANCE	REJECT	POP ADVANCE	REJECT
B	PUSH(C) ADVANCE	POP RETAIN	PUSH(A) ADVANCE	REJECT
C	PUSH(B) RETAIN	PUSH(C) ADVANCE	POP ADVANCE	REJECT
▽	PUSH(A) ADVANCE	PUSH(B) ADVANCE	REJECT	ACCEPT

Starting stack: ▽

2. Describe in words the set of sequences recognized by this one-state pushdown machine. (Compare with Fig. 5.4.)

	(	)	⊣
A	PUSH(A) ADVANCE	POP ADVANCE	POP RETAIN
▽	PUSH(A) ADVANCE	REJECT	ACCEPT

Starting stack: ▽

3. Design a (primitive) pushdown recognizer for each of the following sets of sequences:

a) $\{1^n \, 0^m\}$ $n > m > 0$;

b) $\{1^n \, 0^m\}$ $n \geq m > 0$;

c) $\{1^n \, 0^m\}$ $m > n > 0$;

d) $\{1^n \, 0^n\} + \{0^m \, 1^{2m}\}$ $n, m > 0$ where $+$ denotes union;

e) $\{1^n \, 0^n \, 1^m \, 0^m\}$ $n, m \geq 0$;

f) $\{1^n \, 0^m \, 1^m \, 0^n\}$ $n, m \geq 1$

g) an arbitrary sequence of 1's and 0's such that the number of 1's equals the number of 0's

h) $b_i \, 2 \, (b_{i+1})^r$

where b_i is a sequence of 1's and 0's that is the binary representation of the number i (for instance, the member of this language for $i = 48$ is 110000210011).

4. a) For cach of the sets in Problem 3, exhibit a sequence of length greater than 3.

   b) Show the stack movie as each sequence is recognized by the machine found in Problem 3.

5. Design a (primitive) pushdown machine that will recognize the complement of the set recognized by the machine of Fig. 5.6.

6. Write computer programs that will implement the pushdown machine of Fig. 5.7 using each of the following languages:

   a) FORTRAN — write subroutines to perform the POP and REPLACE operations.

   b) LISP

   c) The assembly language of some computer using a register as the pointer to the top of the stack. Write macros to perform the POP and REPLACE operations.

7. Repeat Problems 3 and 4 using the REPLACE operation. Try to find machines with only one state.

8. Exhibit three sequences that are accepted by the following one-state pushdown machine and show the corresponding stack movies.

	0	1	⊣
A	REPLACE(AA) ADVANCE	POP ΛDVΛNCE	REJECT
▽	REJECT	REJECT	ACCEPT

Starting stack: ▽ A

9. Consider the following new extended stack operation:

   POP(n) where n is any positive integer. This operation pops the top n symbols off the stack. If there are fewer than n symbols on the stack, excluding the bottommarker, the machine rejects the input sequence.

   a) Show that POP(n) can be simulated by a primitive pushdown machine.

   b) Using this new operation, design pushdown machines that will recognize each of the following sets:

   i. $\{1^{2m} 0^m\}$ $m > 0$

   ii. $\{1^{2m} 0^m\} \cup \{1^n 2^n\}$ $m > 0, n > 0$

10. Show a stack movie for each of the pushdown machines of Figs. 5.6, 5.7, 5.9, and 5.11, processing the null sequence.

11. Find a set of input sequences that exercise all the transitions of the machines of Figs. 5.6 and 5.7.

12. Using the REPLACE operation, design a one-state translator that performs the same translation as Fig. 5.11.

13. Design (general) pushdown machines that will perform each of the following translations:

   a) $1^n 0^m$ into $1^n 0^{2n}$ where $n > 0, m > 0$

   b) $1^n 0^m 1^m 0^n$ into $1^m 0^{n+m}$ where $m > 0, n > 0$

   c) b_1 into $(b_{1+1})^r$

   where b_i is a sequence of 1's and 0's that is the binary representation of the number i.

   d) $1^m 0^n$ into:

   $$1^{m-n}   \text{if } m > n$$
   $$0^{n-m}   \text{if } m < n$$
   $$\epsilon   \text{if } m = n$$

   (Part d) is analogous to producing error messages for incorrect parentheses count.)

14. Show that any finite-state recognizer can be simulated by a one-state pushdown recognizer.

15. Show that each of the following pushdown machines never cycles for any input sequence.

	0	1	2	3	⊣
A	POP ADVANCE	PUSH(A) ADVANCE	REJECT	POP ADVANCE	ACCEPT
B	PUSH(B) ADVANCE	ACCEPT	POP ADVANCE	ACCEPT	REJECT
▽	PUSH(A) ADVANCE	PUSH(B) ADVANCE	REJECT	PUSH(A) ADVANCE	ACCEPT

Starting stack: ▽

	a	b	c	⊣
C	PUSH(C) ADVANCE	ACCEPT	PUSH(D) ADVANCE	ACCEPT
D	POP ADVANCE	PUSH(C) RETAIN	POP RETAIN	POP RETAIN
▽	PUSH(C) RETAIN	REJECT	PUSH(D) ADVANCE	ACCEPT

Starting stack: ▽

16. For each of the following cases show that a pushdown machine with the given properties never cycles for any input.

    a) Every nonexit transition contains an ADVANCE operation.

    b) RETAIN operations only occur in POP transitions.

17. Find two input sequences, one starting with 0 and the other starting with 1, for which the following machine cycles:

	0	1	2	3	⊣
A	ACCEPT	PUSH(A) RETAIN	PUSH(B) ADVANCE	PUSH(A) ADVANCE	REJECT
B	POP ADVANCE	ACCEPT	REJECT	PUSH(C) RETAIN	POP ADVANCE
C	PUSH(E) RETAIN	PUSH(A) ADVANCE	PUSH(D) RETAIN	POP RETAIN	REJECT
D	ACCEPT	PUSH(D) ADVANCE	PUSH(E) ADVANCE	ACCEPT	ACCEPT
E	PUSH(C) RETAIN	REJECT	ACCEPT	PUSH(E) ADVANCE	PUSH(D) ADVANCE
▽	PUSH(A) ADVANCE	PUSH(D) ADVANCE	PUSH(A) ADVANCE	PUSH(B) ADVANCE	ACCEPT

Starting stack: ▽

18. Redesign the machine of Fig. 5.13 so as to obtain another machine that accepts the same language, but which never cycles.

19. Indicate why a pushdown machine cannot recognize each of the following sets:

    a) $\{1^n \, 0^n \, 1^n\}$ $\qquad n > 0$

    b) $\{w \, w^r\}$ where w is a sequence of 1's and 0's

    c) $\{1^n \, 0^n\} + \{1^n \, 0^{2n}\}$ $\qquad n > 0$

20. Design a pushdown machine that will accept the set of LISP S-expressions. The input vocabulary of the machine is:

$$\{\text{ATOM}, (,), \cdot, \dashv\}$$

21. Suppose that a pushdown machine has the property that there is a constant such that for all input sequences the number of symbols on the stack never exceeds the constant. Show that such a pushdown machine can be simulated by a finite-state machine.

22. Give an example of a set of sequences that can be recognized by a pushdown machine that uses both ADVANCE and RETAIN in its transitions but cannot be recognized by any pushdown machine that only uses ADVANCE.

23. Show that a pushdown machine that pushes the bottommarker can be simulated by a pushdown machine that does not push the bottommarker.

24. Show that any pushdown machine can be simulated by a pushdown machine whose stack alphabet consists of a bottommarker and two other symbols.

25. Show that for every $k > 1$, there exists a set of sequences that can be recognized by a primitive pushdown machine with k states, but cannot be recognized by any primitive pushdown machine with $k - 1$ states.

26. One way to augment a finite-state machine is by the use of the RETAIN operation in its transitions. Show that finite-state recognizers using the RETAIN operation can recognize only regular sets.

27. Show that if a set of sequences is accepted by a pushdown machine, then its complement is also accepted by some pushdown machine.

28. Show that given a pushdown machine and a finite-state recognizer, a pushdown machine can be obtained that recognizes the intersection of the sets accepted by the two given machines.

29. Give an example of a set of sequences that can be recognized by a pushdown machine whose stack alphabet contains a bottommarker and two other symbols but cannot be recognized by any pushdown machine whose stack alphabet consists of a bottommarker and a single additional symbol.

30. How would you test a pushdown machine to determine whether or not all input sequences lead to an exit?

31. Design a pushdown machine that will accept the set of FORTRAN logical expressions using the operators .AND. , .OR. , and .NOT. with constant operands .TRUE. and .FALSE. and such that the expressions have the value .TRUE. . For example, one such expression is

.TRUE. .AND. .NOT. (.FALSE. .OR. (.FALSE. .AND. .TRUE.))

The input vocabulary of the machine is

{ .TRUE. ,   .FALSE. ,   .NOT. ,   .AND. ,   .OR. ,   ),   (, ⊣}

6
Context-Free Grammars

6.1 INTRODUCTION

In this chapter, we present a method of defining sets of sequences based on the concept of a *context-free grammar*. Unlike the previous methods given for describing such sets, the context-free methods are powerful enough to describe almost all of the so-called syntactic features of programming languages. Indeed context-free grammars are often used in language manuals to describe a programming language.

Using a particular set-description method to describe a programming language can be a valuable step in the design of a compiler for the language if there are systematic methods of converting the set description into a program that processes the set. In the case of context-free grammars, we will develop in later chapters methods of converting certain context-free grammars into pushdown machines that recognize and even translate the sets defined by the grammars. Before these methods can be explained, we must understand how sets are defined by context-free grammars (Chapter 6) and how translations can be defined in terms of these grammars (Chapter 7).

6.2 FORMAL LANGUAGES AND FORMAL GRAMMARS

Many of the concepts in this chapter are analogous to concepts used in discussing natural languages such as English. Some of the definitions introduced in this chapter were in fact originally developed with natural languages in mind.

The most basic concept is that of a *language*. For theoretical purposes the word "language" is synonymous with the term "set of sequences". Thus we might think of the FORTRAN IV language as being the set of sequences specified by some official set of specifications. Most interesting languages, like FORTRAN IV, consist of an infinite set of sequences.

To distinguish between the use of the word "language" as meaning a precisely specified set of sequences and the use of the word "language" as used in every day nontechnical conversation, one sometimes refers to a set of sequences as a *formal language*.

In order to attack problems of languages and language processing in a mathematical way, we must confine ourselves to sets of sequences that can be specified in some precise way. There are many ways of precisely specifying such sets. One way, for example, is to define a language as the set accepted by some kind of a sequence recognizer such as a finite-state or pushdown machine. Another approach is the use of methods that can be thought of as grammatical.

The term "formal grammar" is applied to any formal-language specification based on "grammatical rules" whereby sequences can be generated or analyzed in a way analogous to the use of grammars in the study of natural languages. In this chapter, we are concerned with a specific kind of formal grammar, called a context-free grammar.

6.3 FORMAL GRAMMARS—AN EXAMPLE

In this section, we give a specific formal grammar that looks something like an English grammar and which defines a formal language consisting of four English sentences.

The formal grammar uses certain entities that are like parts of speech.

⟨sentence⟩

⟨subject⟩

⟨verb⟩

⟨object⟩

⟨noun⟩

⟨article⟩

We enclose these in pointed brackets to distinguish them from the actual dictionary words that make up the sequences in the language. In our example, the dictionary contains the following five words or symbols.

THE

BOY

GIRL

SEES

.   (period)

The grammar has certain rules that tell how sequences in the language can be made up from these symbols. One such rule is:

1. ⟨sentence⟩ → ⟨subject⟩ ⟨verb⟩ ⟨object⟩.

The interpretation of this rule is: "An example of a sentence is a subject followed by a verb followed by an object followed by a period." The grammar could well have other rules giving other examples of sentences. This particular grammar does not have such rules.

The remaining rules are:

2. ⟨subject⟩ → ⟨article⟩ ⟨noun⟩
3. ⟨object⟩ → ⟨article⟩ ⟨noun⟩
4. ⟨verb⟩   → SEES
5. ⟨article⟩ → THE
6. ⟨noun⟩   → BOY
7. ⟨noun⟩   → GIRL

We now use this grammar to generate or derive a sentence in the language. By rule 1, an example of a sentence in the language is

⟨subject⟩ ⟨verb⟩ ⟨object⟩ .

Since, by rule 2, an example of a subject is

⟨article⟩ ⟨noun⟩

these can be substituted for ⟨subject⟩ to obtain the following example of a sentence

⟨article⟩ ⟨noun⟩ ⟨verb⟩ ⟨object⟩ .

Similarly we can use rule 3 to substitute for ⟨object⟩ to obtain

⟨article⟩ ⟨noun⟩ ⟨verb⟩ ⟨article⟩ ⟨noun⟩ .

Now we can use rule 5 to substitute for ⟨article⟩ in both places to obtain

THE ⟨noun⟩ ⟨verb⟩ THE ⟨noun⟩.

Finally we can use rule 4 to substitute for ⟨verb⟩ and rules 6 and 7 to substitute for the two occurrences of ⟨noun⟩ to obtain a complete sentence:

THE BOY SEES THE GIRL.

The derivation can be shown pictorially as a tree (see Fig. 6.1). The tree shows which rules were applied to the various intermediate entities but conceals the order in which the rules were applied. Thus the tree demonstrates that the resulting sequence is independent of the order in which substitutions are made for intermediate entities. The tree is sometimes said to display the "syntactic structure" of the sentence.

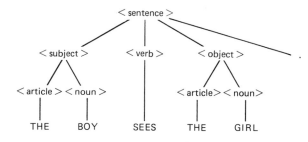

Figure 6.1

The idea of a derivation suggests other interpretations of a rule such as

⟨subject⟩ → ⟨article⟩ ⟨noun⟩

Instead of saying "an example of a ⟨subject⟩ is an ⟨article⟩ followed by a ⟨noun⟩" we might say ⟨subject⟩ "generates" (or "derives" or "can be replaced by") ⟨article⟩ ⟨noun⟩.

This grammar can also be used to derive three other sentences, namely:

THE GIRL SEES THE BOY.

THE GIRL SEES THE GIRL.

THE BOY SEES THE BOY.

These three sentences together with the one sentence derived previously are the only sentences that can be derived from the grammar. We say that the set consisting of these four sequences is the language specified by (or generated by, or derived from) the grammar.

6.4 CONTEXT-FREE GRAMMARS

The grammar given in the last section is a simple example of the class of grammars that is our main concern: the context-free grammars. In this section we define this type of grammar and introduce the conventional notation for its description.

The entities such as ⟨sentence⟩, ⟨verb⟩, etc., that are analogous to parts of speech are called *nonterminal symbols* or *nonterminals.* A context-free grammar can be specified to have any finite number of nonterminals. For programming languages, the nonterminals may be such entities as ⟨statement⟩, ⟨arithmetic expression⟩, etc.

The entities such as THE, BOY, etc., which are analogous to dictionary words are called *terminal symbols* or *terminals.* A context-free grammar can be specified to have any finite number of terminals. For programming languages, the terminals are the actual words and symbols in the language, such as DO, $+$, etc.

The rules of the grammar are sometimes called *productions* and are of the general form:

Any single nonterminal $\rightarrow$ any finite sequence of terminals and nonterminals

The sequence on the right of the arrow can be the null sequence. An example of such a production is

$$\langle A \rangle \rightarrow \epsilon$$

We sometimes refer to a production with a null righthand side as an epsilon production. A context-free grammar can have any finite set of productions. An example of a production in a programming language is

$$\langle \text{statement} \rangle \rightarrow \text{IF } \langle \text{Boolean expression} \rangle \text{ THEN } \langle \text{statement} \rangle$$

One of the nonterminals is specified to be the *starting nonterminal* or *starting symbol* from which derivations of sequences in the language must start. For a natural language this nonterminal might be ⟨sentence⟩; for a programming language it might be ⟨program⟩. We frequently use ⟨S⟩ for the starting symbol.

Summarizing the above, a context-free grammar is specified by

a) a finite set of nonterminals;

b) a finite set of terminals which is disjoint from the set of nonterminals;

c) a finite set of productions of the form

$$\langle A \rangle \rightarrow \alpha$$

where ⟨A⟩ is a nonterminal and α is a sequence (possibly the null sequence) of terminals and nonterminals — nonterminal ⟨A⟩ is called the lefthand side of the production and α is called the right-hand side;

d) a starting symbol which is one of the nonterminals.

If the set of productions of a grammar is given without specifying a set of nonterminals or terminals, it is assumed that the grammar has precisely those nonterminals and terminals that appear in the productions. For example, assume we are given the following four productions:

1. $S \rightarrow a \, A \, b \, S$
2. $S \rightarrow b$
3. $A \rightarrow S \, A \, c$
4. $A \rightarrow \epsilon$

In the absence of other specifications, it is assumed that the nonterminal set is $\{S, A\}$ as these are the symbols that appear on the lefthand side of the productions. It is also assumed that the terminal set is $\{a, b, c\}$ as these are the other symbols used in the productions. The symbol ϵ in production 4, of course, represents the null sequence and is not a symbol of the grammar. Production 4 could be written without ϵ as

4. $A \rightarrow$

Using the conventions of the previous paragraph, it is often possible to specify a grammar by giving the productions and the starting nonterminal. The nonterminal and terminal set need only be given explicitly if they differ from the sets implied by the conventions. For example, if we wished the terminal set of the last example to be $\{a, b, c, d\}$, we would have to say so explicitly. In this event, a recognizer for the language would have to include d as an input even though none of the acceptable sequences include that symbol.

In order that nonterminal and terminal symbols be readily distinguished, we adopt the convention of defining nonterminals with pointed brackets. Following this convention, the productions just given would be written as in Fig. 6.2. Under this convention one can look at any string of symbols such as $a \langle A \rangle b \langle S \rangle$ and see which are nonterminals and which are terminals.

Although the notation we have used for describing grammars is quite common in the literature, there is another frequently used notation called *Backus-Naur Form* or *BNF*. In this notation, the $\rightarrow$ is replaced by $::=$ and this symbol can be followed by any number of righthand sides separated by a $|$. Also the nonterminals must be defined with pointed brackets. Using

BNF, we would rewrite the grammar of Fig. 6.2 as

$$\langle S \rangle ::= a \langle A \rangle b \langle S \rangle \mid b$$
$$\langle A \rangle ::= \langle S \rangle \langle A \rangle c \mid \epsilon$$

The idea of combining righthand sides can, of course, be used with the →
notation but we prefer to use separate lines for clarity and so that we can
number each line as in Fig. 6.2 for reference purposes.

1. $\langle S \rangle \rightarrow a \langle A \rangle b \langle S \rangle$
2. $\langle S \rangle \rightarrow b$
3. $\langle A \rangle \rightarrow \langle S \rangle \langle A \rangle c$
4. $\langle A \rangle \rightarrow \epsilon$

Figure 6.2

6.5   DERIVATIONS

In this section, we discuss in greater depth how grammars are used to generate the sequences in a language.

The rules of a grammar are used to define a special kind of string
substitution. This substitution is accomplished by replacing a specific nonterminal in some given string of terminals and nonterminals with the righthand side of a production which has the specified nonterminal as its lefthand
side. We sometimes say that the production is *applied* to the nonterminal in
the string.

For example, consider the following grammar with starting nonterminal
$\langle S \rangle$

1. $\langle S \rangle \rightarrow a \langle A \rangle \langle B \rangle c$
2. $\langle S \rangle \rightarrow \epsilon$
3. $\langle A \rangle \rightarrow c \langle S \rangle \langle B \rangle$
4. $\langle A \rangle \rightarrow \langle A \rangle b$
5. $\langle B \rangle \rightarrow b \langle B \rangle$
6. $\langle B \rangle \rightarrow a$

If we are given the string

$$a \langle A \rangle \langle B \rangle c$$
$$\uparrow$$

and we wish to apply production 5 to the nonterminal $\langle B \rangle$ pointed to by the arrow the result of the corresponding substitution is

$$a \langle A \rangle \, b \, \langle B \rangle \, c$$

We express this substitution by writing

$$a \langle A \rangle \, \langle B \rangle \, c \Rightarrow a \, \langle A \rangle \, b \, \langle B \rangle \, c$$
$$\underset{5}{\uparrow}$$

In this notation, the vertical arrow points to the nonterminal to be replaced, the number under the arrow indicates the production to be applied, and the symbol $\Rightarrow$ is used to separate the *before* string from the *after* string.

Sometimes this notation is used without the vertical arrow to indicate just the before and after strings. For instance, one might write

$$a \langle A \rangle \, \langle B \rangle \, c \Rightarrow a \, \langle A \rangle \, b \, \langle B \rangle \, c$$

as a shorthand for "string $a \langle A \rangle \, b \, \langle B \rangle \, c$ can be obtained from string $a \langle A \rangle \, \langle B \rangle \, c$ as the result of one substitution."

However this abbreviated notation is not always sufficient to describe the substitution involved. For instance the same after string can also be obtained by the substitution

$$a \langle A \rangle \, \langle B \rangle \, c \Rightarrow a \, \langle A \rangle \, b \, \langle B \rangle \, c$$
$$\underset{4}{\uparrow}$$

A series of substitutions is called a *derivation*. For instance the string *acabac* can be obtained from the starting nonterminal by the following derivation.

$$\langle S \rangle \Rightarrow a \langle A \rangle \, \langle B \rangle \, c \Rightarrow a \, \langle A \rangle \, b \, \langle B \rangle \, c \Rightarrow a \, c \, \langle S \rangle \, \langle B \rangle \, b \, \langle B \rangle \, c$$
$$\underset{1}{\uparrow} \qquad \underset{4}{\uparrow} \qquad \underset{3}{\uparrow} \qquad \underset{6}{\uparrow}$$

$$\Rightarrow a \, c \, \langle S \rangle \, a \, b \, \langle B \rangle \, c \Rightarrow a \, c \, a \, b \, \langle B \rangle \, c \Rightarrow a \, c \, a \, b \, a \, c$$
$$\underset{2}{\uparrow} \qquad\qquad\qquad \underset{6}{\uparrow}$$

Each of the strings of terminals and nonterminals that appears in a derivation is called an *intermediate string* of the derivation. Thus, in the above derivation, there are seven intermediate strings, counting the initial and final strings. (In the literature an intermediate string derived from the starting symbol is sometimes called a "sentential form.")

We frequently use the word "derivation" without specifying the initial string of the derivation. In such cases, the initial string is assumed to be the starting nonterminal. If a different initial string is meant, it is explicitly indicated.

To assert the existence of a derivation from one string to another string we use the symbol

$$\overset{*}{\Rightarrow}$$

For instance we write

$$\langle S \rangle \overset{*}{\Rightarrow} a\,c\,a\,b\,a\,c$$

to mean that "string *acabac* can be obtained from string $\langle S \rangle$ by a derivation," or equivalently, that "from string $\langle S \rangle$, the string *acabac* can be derived."

For purposes of uniformity, we allow the number of substitutions in a derivation to be zero. For instance

$$b\,\langle A \rangle\,c$$

can be regarded as a derivation of length zero where $b \langle A \rangle c$ is both the initial and final string. Therefore, for any string α, we can write

$$\alpha \overset{*}{\Rightarrow} \alpha$$

since α can be obtained from itself by a length zero sequence of substitutions.

The "$*$" is analogous to the Kleene star in that it suggests zero or more uses of the relation $\Rightarrow$. If one wishes to exclude the rather trivial zero length derivation, one replaces the $*$ by a $+$ and writes

$$\langle S \rangle \overset{+}{\Rightarrow} a\,c\,a\,b\,a\,c$$

to mean that "string *acabac* can be obtained from string $\langle S \rangle$ by a derivation of length greater than zero."

We define the language specified by a grammar to be the set of terminal strings that can be derived from the starting symbol of the grammar. Sometimes, one says that the language is "defined by," "generated from," or "derived from" the grammar. Any language that can be specified by a context-free grammar is called a *context-free language*.

For the grammar given above, *acabac* can be derived from the starting symbol of the grammar, and therefore *acabac* is in the language specified by the grammar. On the other hand, inspection of the grammar reveals that the string *bb* cannot possibly be derived from $\langle S \rangle$; therefore, *bb* is not in the language specified by the grammar.

6.6   TREES

We have defined the context-free language specified by a grammar to be the set of terminal strings that can be derived from the starting symbol. Given a derivation of a string in a context-free language, it is possible to construct an associated *derivation tree*. This construction is carried out by interpreting the substitutions in the derivation as tree-building operations. This tree construction is easier to demonstrate than to describe, so we illustrate with an example.

The previous section contains a grammar and a derivation of the terminal string *acabac* according to the grammar. This derivation can be used to construct an associated derivation tree as shown in Fig. 6.3 where each step in the derivation is shown together with an associated tree. In Fig. 6.3(a), the starting symbol $\langle S \rangle$ is associated with a one node tree $\langle S \rangle$. When production 1 is applied to symbol $\langle S \rangle$, that symbol is replaced by the righthand side of production 1, namely $a \langle A \rangle \langle B \rangle c$. The corresponding tree-building action is to add the symbols a, $\langle A \rangle$, $\langle B \rangle$, and c as tree nodes attached below the symbol being replaced. The result is Fig. 6.3(b). The derivation and associated tree construction continue until Fig. 6.3(g) is achieved. The final tree is then said to be a derivation tree associated with the terminal string *acabac*.

The derivation tree shows which productions were applied during the derivation and to which occurrence of a nonterminal they were applied. However, the tree does not provide information about the order in which the productions were applied except for the obvious implication that the productions for each node must have been used before the productions for the nonterminal nodes below it. Thus in the tree of Fig. 6.3(g), one can see that production 4 was used before production 3 but one cannot tell the order in which production 2 and the two applications of production 6 were used.

Because the associated tree may conceal the order of substitution, there may be many derivations associated with the same derivation tree. For example, the tree in Fig. 6.3 (g) is also associated with the derivation

$$\langle S \rangle \Rightarrow a \langle A \rangle \langle B \rangle c \Rightarrow a \langle A \rangle b \langle B \rangle c \Rightarrow a c \langle S \rangle \langle B \rangle b \langle B \rangle c$$
$$\quad\uparrow \qquad\quad \uparrow \qquad\qquad \uparrow \qquad\qquad\quad \uparrow$$
$$\quad 1 \qquad\quad 4 \qquad\qquad 3 \qquad\qquad\quad 2$$

$$\Rightarrow a c \langle B \rangle b \langle B \rangle c \Rightarrow a c a b \langle B \rangle c \Rightarrow a c a b a c$$
$$\qquad\uparrow \qquad\qquad\qquad\qquad \uparrow$$
$$\qquad 6 \qquad\qquad\qquad\qquad 6$$

This particular derivation is called a *leftmost derivation* because at each step the substitution was performed on the leftmost nonterminal symbol. For each tree, there is a unique leftmost derivation since the convention of selecting the leftmost nonterminal determines a unique place to perform a substitution and the tree determines a unique production to use for the substitution.

For each tree there is also a unique *rightmost derivation* obtained by the convention that a substitution is always made at the rightmost nonterminal.

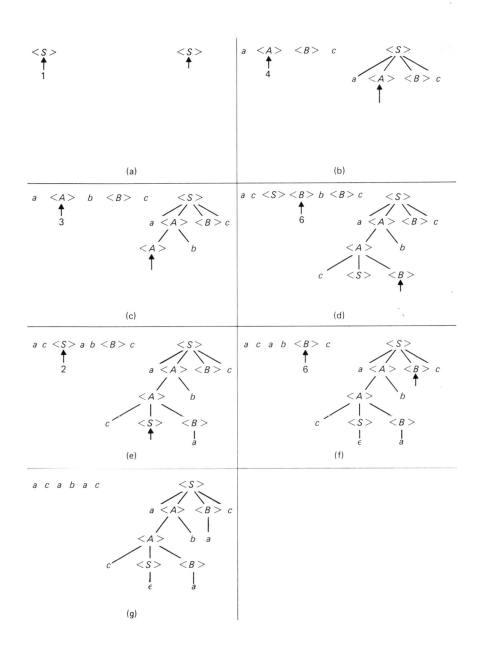

Figure 6.3

The rightmost derivation for the tree of Fig. 6.3(g) is

$$\langle S \rangle \Rightarrow a \langle A \rangle \langle B \rangle c \Rightarrow a \langle A \rangle a c \Rightarrow a \langle A \rangle b a c$$

$$\begin{array}{cccc} \uparrow & \uparrow & \uparrow & \uparrow \\ 1 & 6 & 4 & 3 \end{array}$$

$$\Rightarrow a c \langle S \rangle \langle B \rangle b a c \Rightarrow a c \langle S \rangle a b a c \Rightarrow a c a b a c$$

$$\begin{array}{cc} \uparrow & \uparrow \\ 6 & 2 \end{array}$$

Many language-processing methods deal exclusively with leftmost or rightmost derivations since these derivations are very suitable for systematic treatment. In discussing these cases, we write

$$\alpha \Rightarrow_L \beta$$

to mean that "string β can be obtained from string α as the result of one leftmost substitution," and we write

$$\alpha \Rightarrow_R \beta$$

to mean that "string β can be obtained from string α as the result of one rightmost substitution." In these cases, the substitution can be deduced from the two intermediate strings. It is clear for example that

$$a \langle A \rangle \langle B \rangle c \Rightarrow_L a \langle A \rangle b \langle B \rangle c$$

can only result from substitution

$$a \langle A \rangle \langle B \rangle c \Rightarrow a \langle A \rangle b \langle B \rangle c$$

$$\begin{array}{c} \uparrow \\ 4 \end{array}$$

and that

$$a \langle A \rangle \langle B \rangle c \Rightarrow_R a \langle A \rangle b \langle B \rangle c$$

can only result from substitution

$$a \langle A \rangle \langle B \rangle c \Rightarrow a \langle A \rangle b \langle B \rangle c$$

$$\begin{array}{c} \uparrow \\ 5 \end{array}$$

We also write

$$\alpha \overset{*}{\Rightarrow}_L \beta$$

if there is a leftmost derivation of β from α and write

$$\alpha \overset{*}{\Rightarrow}_R \beta$$

if there is a rightmost derivation.

A string in a language may have more than one tree because the string may have different derivations which yield distinct trees. This is in fact the case for our example *acabac*. In addition to the tree of Fig. 6.3(g) which has been redrawn in Fig. 6.4(a), it also has the tree of Fig. 6.4(b) obtained from the following derivation:

$$\langle S \rangle \Rightarrow a \langle A \rangle \langle B \rangle\, c \Rightarrow a \langle A \rangle\, b \langle B \rangle\, c \Rightarrow a\, c\, \langle S \rangle \langle B \rangle\, b \langle B \rangle\, c$$

    ↑   ↑   ↑   ↑

    1   5   3   6

$$\Rightarrow a\, c\, \langle S \rangle\, a\, b \langle B \rangle\, c \Rightarrow a\, c\, a\, b \langle B \rangle\, c \Rightarrow a\, c\, a\, b\, a\, c$$

            ↑   ↑

            2   6

In this derivation, even the intermediate strings are the same as in our original derivation. However, this derivation uses production 5 when the original used production 6 and the associated trees are clearly different.

In cases like this where one string can have several trees, the grammar is said to be *ambiguous*.

The discussion up to this point can be summarized as follows:

1. Corresponding to each string derived from a given context-free grammar, there are one or more derivation trees.

2. Corresponding to each derivation tree, there are one or more derivations.

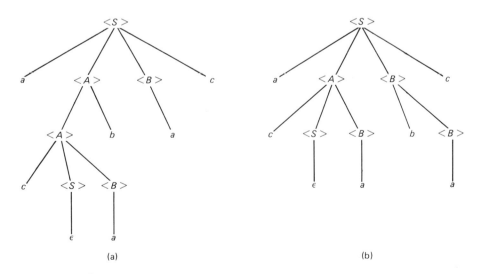

(a)   (b)

Figure 6.4

3. Corresponding to each derivation tree, there is a unique rightmost derivation and a unique leftmost derivation.

4. If each string derived from a given context-free grammar has only one derivation tree, the grammar is said to be unambiguous; otherwise it is said to be ambiguous.

6.7   A GRAMMAR FOR MINI-BASIC CONSTANTS

It is frequently necessary to find a context-free grammar for some language that is only specified in some informal way. We demonstrate how this might be done by finding a grammar for MINI-BASIC constants.

We give the nonterminals names corresponding to the strings that can be derived from them. The starting nonterminal is ⟨constant⟩.

The MINI-BASIC manual describes two forms of constants: those with and without the E, representing power of 10. Those without the E will be derived from the production

1. ⟨constant⟩ → ⟨decimal number⟩

where ⟨decimal number⟩ generates a sequence of digits with an optional decimal point. Constants with the E will be derived from the production

2. ⟨constant⟩ → ⟨decimal number⟩ E ⟨integer⟩

where ⟨decimal number⟩ is the same as before and ⟨integer⟩ generates a sequence of digits preceded by an optional sign.

To complete the grammar we need productions for ⟨decimal number⟩ and ⟨integer⟩. We begin with ⟨integer⟩.

3. ⟨integer⟩ → + ⟨unsigned integer⟩
4. ⟨integer⟩ → − ⟨unsigned integer⟩
5. ⟨integer⟩ → ⟨unsigned integer⟩

where ⟨unsigned integer⟩ generates a sequence of digits.

The productions for ⟨unsigned integer⟩ are

6. ⟨unsigned integer⟩ → d ⟨unsigned integer⟩
7. ⟨unsigned integer⟩ → d

where d represents an arbitrary digit. It is easy to see that these two productions generate the required sequence of digits.

The productions for ⟨decimal number⟩ can be expressed in terms of the nonterminal ⟨unsigned integer⟩.

8. ⟨decimal number⟩ → ⟨unsigned integer⟩
9. ⟨decimal number⟩ → ⟨unsigned integer⟩ .

10. ⟨decimal number⟩ → . ⟨unsigned integer⟩
11. ⟨decimal number⟩ → ⟨unsigned integer⟩ . ⟨unsigned integer⟩

   Production 8 is for numbers without a decimal point; production 9 is for numbers with the decimal point after the last digit; production 10 is for numbers with the decimal point at the beginning; and production 11 is for numbers with digits on each side of the decimal point. The righthand sides of these productions only use the nonterminal ⟨unsigned integer⟩ whose productions have already been given. All nonterminals are thus accounted for and the grammar is complete.

   As an example, the constant

$$3.1 \text{ E} - 21$$

can be generated from the following leftmost derivation

   ⟨constant⟩ ⟹ ⟨decimal number⟩ E ⟨integer⟩ ⟹
   ⟨unsigned integer⟩ . ⟨unsigned integer⟩ E ⟨integer⟩ ⟹
   3. ⟨unsigned integer⟩ E ⟨integer⟩ ⟹
   3.1 E ⟨integer⟩ ⟹
   3.1 E − ⟨unsigned integer⟩ ⟹
   3.1 E − 2 ⟨unsigned integer⟩ ⟹
   3.1 E − 21

The corresponding derivation tree is shown in Fig. 6.5.

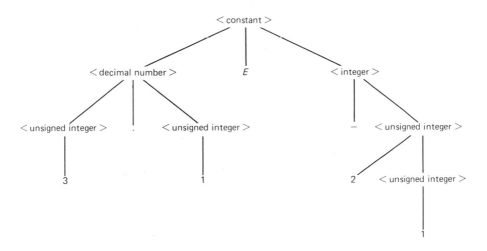

Figure 6.5

6.8   A GRAMMAR FOR S-EXPRESSIONS IN LISP

As another example we find a grammar for S-expressions in LISP. In the LISP manual, S-expressions are defined recursively in terms of other S-expressions and atoms which are analogous to identifiers:

> "An S-expression is either an atom or a left parenthesis followed by an S-expression followed by a dot followed by an S-expression followed by a right parenthesis."

Using ATOM as a terminal symbol, a grammar for S-expressions is:

$$\langle S \rangle \rightarrow \text{ATOM}$$
$$\langle S \rangle \rightarrow (\, \langle S \rangle \cdot \langle S \rangle \,)$$

This grammar demonstrates two of the nice features of context-free languages–that they can handle nested parentheses, and that they can define sets of strings in a recursive fashion.

A sample derivation in this grammar is

$$\langle S \rangle \Rightarrow (\langle S \rangle \cdot \langle S \rangle) \Rightarrow ((\langle S \rangle \cdot \langle S \rangle) \cdot \langle S \rangle) \Rightarrow ((\text{ATOM} \cdot \langle S \rangle) \cdot \langle S \rangle) \Rightarrow$$
$$((\text{ATOM} \cdot (\langle S \rangle \cdot \langle S \rangle)) \cdot \langle S \rangle) \Rightarrow$$
$$((\text{ATOM} \cdot (\text{ATOM} \cdot \langle S \rangle)) \cdot \langle S \rangle) \Rightarrow$$
$$((\text{ATOM} \cdot (\text{ATOM} \cdot \text{ATOM})) \cdot \langle S \rangle) \Rightarrow$$
$$((\text{ATOM} \cdot (\text{ATOM} \cdot \text{ATOM})) \cdot \text{ATOM})$$

A corresponding derivation tree is shown in Fig. 6.6

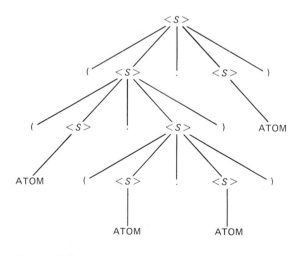

Figure 6.6

6.9   A GRAMMAR FOR ARITHMETIC EXPRESSIONS

In addition to specifying which sequences are in a language, a grammar can sometimes be used to display a certain "structure" of the language. For example, consider the grammar

1. $\langle E \rangle \rightarrow \langle E \rangle + \langle T \rangle$
2. $\langle E \rangle \rightarrow \langle T \rangle$
3. $\langle T \rangle \rightarrow \langle T \rangle * \langle F \rangle$
4. $\langle T \rangle \rightarrow \langle F \rangle$
5. $\langle F \rangle \rightarrow \langle F \rangle \uparrow \langle P \rangle$
6. $\langle F \rangle \rightarrow \langle P \rangle$
7. $\langle P \rangle \rightarrow (\langle E \rangle)$
8. $\langle P \rangle \rightarrow I$

where $\langle E \rangle$ is the starting symbol and I represents any integer. This grammar, which is based on the grammar for arithmetic expressions given in the ALGOL 60 report, generates all ALGOL 60 arithmetic expressions using integers and the binary operators $+$, $*$, and $\uparrow$. Figure 6.7 shows a derivation tree based on this grammar for the expression

$$1 + 2 * 3 + (5 + 6) * 7$$

where the integers are considered instances of the terminal symbol I.

A specification of a programming language must indicate not only which sequences are in the language, but also how they are to be executed. Therefore, the specification of arithmetic expressions includes rules for determining the operands of each operator in the expression. For instance, the operands of the first $+$ in the above expression are the integer 1 and the result of evaluating the subexpression $2 * 3$. Observe that in Fig. 6.7, the subexpression $1 + 2 * 3$ is generated from a single node labeled with an $\langle E \rangle$ and that this node has three descendants: an $\langle E \rangle$ that generates the operand 1, the $+$, and a $\langle T \rangle$ that generates the subexpression $2 * 3$. Similarly each of the other operators in the tree descends from a node whose other two nodes generate the operands of the operator. Thus the tree reflects which parts of the input sequence form subexpressions that are to be evaluated and what the operands of each operator are. In this sense, the tree displays the "structure" of the expression.

6.10   DIFFERENT GRAMMARS FOR THE SAME LANGUAGE

For any context-free language, there are an infinite number of grammars that generate that language. Although most of these grammars are need-

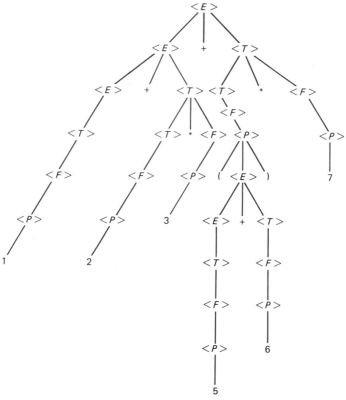

Figure 6.7

lessly complex, it frequently happens that there are several different grammars which might be considered useful for describing some particular language.

For example, the following grammar, with starting symbol $\langle E \rangle$, generates the same arithmetic expression language as the grammar of Section 6.9.

1. $\langle E \rangle \rightarrow \langle T \rangle \langle E\text{-list} \rangle$
2. $\langle E\text{-list} \rangle \rightarrow + \langle T \rangle \langle E\text{-list} \rangle$
3. $\langle E\text{-list} \rangle \rightarrow \epsilon$
4. $\langle T \rangle \rightarrow \langle F \rangle \langle T\text{-list} \rangle$
5. $\langle T\text{-list} \rangle \rightarrow * \langle F \rangle \langle T\text{-list} \rangle$
6. $\langle T\text{-list} \rangle \rightarrow \epsilon$
7. $\langle F \rangle \rightarrow \langle P \rangle \langle F\text{-list} \rangle$

8. $\langle F\text{-list}\rangle \rightarrow \uparrow \langle P\rangle \langle F\text{-list}\rangle$

9. $\langle F\text{-list}\rangle \rightarrow \epsilon$

10. $\langle P\rangle \rightarrow (\,\langle E\rangle\,)$

11. $\langle P\rangle \rightarrow I$

In fact, nonterminals $\langle E\rangle$, $\langle T\rangle$, $\langle F\rangle$, and $\langle P\rangle$ generate the same sequences in both grammars.

First observe that both grammars have the same productions for nonterminal $\langle P\rangle$. Now consider nonterminal $\langle F\rangle$. Both grammars embody the concept that an $\langle F\rangle$ is a $\langle P\rangle$ with zero or more $\uparrow\langle P\rangle$'s appended to it. In the grammar of Section 6.9, n applications of production 5 followed by an application of production 6 generate a list of $(n + 1)$ $\langle P\rangle$'s separated by $\uparrow$'s. For example

$$\langle F\rangle \Rightarrow \langle F\rangle \uparrow \langle P\rangle \Rightarrow \langle F\rangle \uparrow \langle P\rangle \uparrow \langle P\rangle \Rightarrow$$
$$\langle P\rangle \uparrow \langle P\rangle \uparrow \langle P\rangle$$

In the new grammar the same string is generated by an application of production 7 followed by n applications of production 8 followed by an application of production 9. For example

$$\langle F\rangle \Rightarrow \langle P\rangle \langle F\text{-list}\rangle \Rightarrow \langle P\rangle \uparrow \langle P\rangle \langle F\text{-list}\rangle \Rightarrow$$
$$\langle P\rangle \uparrow \langle P\rangle \uparrow \langle P\rangle \langle F\text{-list}\rangle \Rightarrow \langle P\rangle \uparrow \langle P\rangle \uparrow \langle P\rangle$$

The nonterminal $\langle F\text{-list}\rangle$ is introduced to generate the list of zero or more $\uparrow\langle P\rangle$'s. Production 8 generates one $\uparrow \langle P\rangle$ followed by $\langle F\text{-list}\rangle$ to generate more. Production 9 generates a list of zero items.

The "structure" of an expression is reflected in the grammar. The right operand of each $\uparrow$ is generated from the $\langle P\rangle$ immediately following the $\uparrow$ in production 8. The left operand of each $\uparrow$ is generated from the string of $\langle P\rangle$'s and $\uparrow$'s preceding the occurrence of $\langle F\text{-list}\rangle$ to which production 8 is applied.

Next consider the nonterminal $\langle T\rangle$. Both sets of productions embody the concept that a $\langle T\rangle$ is an $\langle F\rangle$ followed by a list of zero or more $*$ $\langle F\rangle$'s. The nonterminal $\langle T\text{-list}\rangle$ is introduced to generate the list of zero or more items. Productions 4, 5, and 6 provide for the first item, the list continuation, and the list termination.

Nonterminal $\langle E\rangle$ has a similar interpretation arising from productions 1, 2, and 3.

6.11 REGULAR SETS AS CONTEXT-FREE LANGUAGES

Two classes of languages have been introduced in this book: regular sets and context-free languages. In this section we show that context-free languages are the more powerful concept. In particular we demonstrate the following fact:

Any regular set can be described by a context-free grammar.

This is, of course, another way of saying that regular sets are also context-free languages.

Suppose that one is given a finite-state recognizer for some regular set. A context-free grammar for that set can be obtained from the machine description as follows:

1. The input set of the machine is used as the terminal set of the grammar.
2. The state set of the machine is used as the nonterminal set and the starting state is used as the starting nonterminal.
3. If the machine has a transition from state A to state B under input x, then the grammar is given the rule

$$A \rightarrow x\,B$$

4. If A is an accepting state of the machine, then the grammar is given the rule

$$A \rightarrow \epsilon$$

To see that this construction results in a grammar for the set of sequences generated by the machine, interpret the nonterminal corresponding to state Z as

⟨string accepted by the machine started in state Z⟩.

The production $A \rightarrow x\,B$ constructed in Step 3 is then interpreted as saying

an example of a string accepted by the machine starting in state A is an x followed by an example of a string accepted by the machine started in state B.

The production $A \rightarrow \epsilon$ constructed in step 4 is interpreted as saying

an example of a string accepted by the machine started in (accepting) state A is the null string.

Thus the productions express simple truths about how the finite-state machine works.

Under the interpretations just given, derivations correspond in a one-to-one fashion with the actions of the finite-state machine. As an example, we show a machine in Fig. 6.8(a) and the grammar constructed from the machine in Fig. 6.8(b). The sequence *aba* is accepted by the machine because it causes the following transition sequence

$$S \xrightarrow{a} A \xrightarrow{b} A \xrightarrow{a} B$$

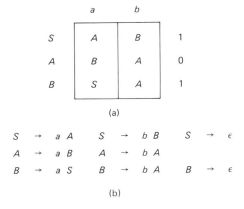

(a)

S	$\rightarrow$	$a\ A$		S	$\rightarrow$	$b\ B$		S	$\rightarrow$	ϵ
A	$\rightarrow$	$a\ B$		A	$\rightarrow$	$b\ A$				
B	$\rightarrow$	$a\ S$		B	$\rightarrow$	$b\ A$		B	$\rightarrow$	ϵ

(b)

Figure 6.8

where S is the starting state and B is an accepting state. A corresponding derivation is obtained by applying the corresponding production for each transition and then removing the final nonterminal by applying an epsilon production. Thus the corresponding derivative of *aba* is

$$S \Rightarrow aA \Rightarrow abA \Rightarrow abaB \Rightarrow aba$$

Conversely, if one wants to find the state transitions corresponding to a given derivation, the nonterminal and rightmost terminal at each step give the new state and the input used to reach that state. Thus derivation

$$S \Rightarrow bB \Rightarrow baS \Rightarrow ba$$

implies the state transitions

$$S \xrightarrow{b} B \xrightarrow{a} S$$

and the application of the final epsilon production implies that final state S is an accepting state.

6.12   RIGHT-LINEAR GRAMMARS

Consider a special-form grammar in which the productions have one of the two forms

$$\langle A \rangle \rightarrow x\ \langle B \rangle \qquad \text{or} \qquad \langle A \rangle \rightarrow \epsilon$$

where x is a single terminal symbol. The procedure of the previous section can be reversed to obtain a finite-state recognizer to recognize the language generated by any grammar of the special form. Specifically, the inverse procedure is as follows:

1. the terminal set of the grammar is used as the input set of the machine;

2. the nonterminal set of the grammar is used as the state set of the machine and the starting nonterminal is used as the starting state;

3. if the grammar has a rule

$$\langle A \rangle \rightarrow x \langle B \rangle$$

then the machine is given a transition from state $\langle A \rangle$ to state $\langle B \rangle$ under input x;

4. if the grammar has a rule

$$\langle A \rangle \rightarrow \epsilon$$

then $\langle A \rangle$ is made an accepting state.

The result of this construction is a nondeterministic machine with one starting state. The construction of the previous section is valid for this kind of nondeterministic machine although it was presented as a procedure for deterministic machines. Applying the procedure to the grammar of Fig. 6.8(b), one gets Fig. 6.8(a). Derivation steps and machine transitions correspond as before.

Knowing that grammars of the above special form generate regular sets can be useful for spotting problems that can be done on a finite-state machine and the procedure can be used to obtain the machine. For example, the identifiers in ALGOL 60 can be described by the following grammar with starting nonterminal $\langle$identifier$\rangle$:

$$\langle \text{identifier} \rangle \rightarrow l \, \langle \text{letters and digits} \rangle$$
$$\langle \text{letters and digits} \rangle \rightarrow l \, \langle \text{letters and digits} \rangle$$
$$\langle \text{letters and digits} \rangle \rightarrow d \, \langle \text{letters and digits} \rangle$$
$$\langle \text{letters and digits} \rangle \rightarrow \epsilon$$

where l and d represent letter and digit respectively. As the grammar has the special form, it is immediately apparent that it can be recognized by a finite-state machine. The procedure gives the nondeterministic machine of Fig. 6.9.

Grammars of the above special form are by no means the only grammars that generate regular sets. Another easily recognized class of grammars

Figure 6.9

known to generate regular sets is the class known as "right-linear" grammars. A grammar is called *right linear* if the righthand side of each production has at most one instance of a nonterminal and this nonterminal is the rightmost symbol of the righthand side. Symbolically, the productions of a right linear grammar have one of the two forms

$$\langle A \rangle \rightarrow w \langle B \rangle \qquad \text{or} \qquad \langle A \rangle \rightarrow w$$

where $\langle A \rangle$ and $\langle B \rangle$ are nonterminals and w is a string of terminal symbols.

An example of a right-linear grammar is the following grammar with starting symbol $\langle S \rangle$:

1. $\langle S \rangle \rightarrow a \langle A \rangle$
2. $\langle S \rangle \rightarrow b\,c$
3. $\langle S \rangle \rightarrow \langle A \rangle$
4. $\langle A \rangle \rightarrow a\,b\,b \langle S \rangle$
5. $\langle A \rangle \rightarrow c \langle A \rangle$
6. $\langle A \rangle \rightarrow \epsilon$

Productions 1, 3, 4, and 5 have the form $\langle A \rangle \rightarrow w \langle B \rangle$ and productions 2 and 6 have the form $\langle A \rangle \rightarrow w$. In productions 3 and 6, w is the null string.

Right-linear grammars are easily transformed into grammars of the special form previously discussed. We show how this is done on the current example. Production 4 is of the wrong form because the nonterminal is preceded by three terminals instead of one. To cure this, replace the production by the three productions:

$$\langle A \rangle \quad \rightarrow a \langle bbS \rangle$$
$$\langle bbS \rangle \rightarrow b \langle bS \rangle$$
$$\langle bS \rangle \quad \rightarrow b \langle S \rangle$$

each of the correct form. The result is that we now have

$$\langle A \rangle \Rightarrow a \langle bbS \rangle \Rightarrow a\,b \langle bS \rangle \Rightarrow a\,b\,b \langle S \rangle$$

instead of the single production:

$$\langle A \rangle \rightarrow a\,b\,b \langle S \rangle$$

One reason that production 2 has the wrong form is that its terminal symbols are not followed by a nonterminal. To cure this, we replace it by the two productions

$$\langle S \rangle \rightarrow b\,c \langle \text{epsilon} \rangle$$
$$\langle \text{epsilon} \rangle \rightarrow \epsilon$$

The new production for $\langle S \rangle$ must now be transformed by the technique used previously for production 4.

Finally, we have production 3 which is the wrong form because the righthand side is a single nonterminal. To cure this, we replace production 3 by the productions of the form

$$\langle S \rangle \rightarrow \text{righthand side of a production for } \langle A \rangle$$

for all productions for $\langle A \rangle$.

The resulting new grammar is as follows:

1. $\langle S \rangle \rightarrow a \langle A \rangle$
2a. $\langle S \rangle \rightarrow b \langle c \text{ epsilon} \rangle$
2b. $\langle c \text{ epsilon} \rangle \rightarrow c \langle \text{epsilon} \rangle$
2c. $\langle \text{epsilon} \rangle \rightarrow \epsilon$
3a. $\langle S \rangle \rightarrow a \langle bbS \rangle$
3b. $\langle S \rangle \rightarrow c \langle A \rangle$
3c. $\langle S \rangle \rightarrow \epsilon$
4a. $\langle A \rangle \rightarrow a \langle bbS \rangle$
4b. $\langle bbS \rangle \rightarrow b \langle bS \rangle$
4c. $\langle bS \rangle \rightarrow b \langle S \rangle$
5. $\langle A \rangle \rightarrow c \langle A \rangle$
6. $\langle A \rangle \rightarrow \epsilon$

The transformed grammar can now be used to build a finite-state recognizer as shown in Fig. 6.10.

Although the transformed right-linear grammar is ideally suited for building a finite-state recognizer, the original untransformed grammar is probably preferable for describing the set to humans because it has fewer productions and nonterminals.

	a	b	c	
→ $<S>$	$<A>, <bbS>$	$<c\ epsilon>$	$<A>$	1
$<c\ epsilon>$			$<epsilon>$	0
$<epsilon>$				1
$<A>$	$<bbS>$		$<A>$	1
$<bbS>$		$<bS>$		0
$<bS>$		$<S>$		0

Figure 6.10

Sometimes, particularly after the application of a grammatical transformation technique, a grammar contains a production of the form:

$$\langle A \rangle \rightarrow \langle A \rangle$$

Such productions say that a nonterminal is an example of itself. These productions serve no useful purpose and can be deleted from the grammar without affecting the language generated.

The transformation techniques of this section can be combined into a single procedure to convert a right-linear grammar into the special form described at the beginning of the section.

1. If there are productions of the form

$$\langle A \rangle \rightarrow w$$

where w is a nonnull string of terminals, invent a new nonterminal, say $\langle \text{epsilon} \rangle$, and add the production:

$$\langle \text{epsilon} \rangle \rightarrow \epsilon$$

Then replace each of the $\langle A \rangle \rightarrow w$ productions with production:

$$\langle A \rangle \rightarrow w \langle \text{epsilon} \rangle$$

2. Replace each production of the form

$$\langle A \rangle \rightarrow a_1 \ldots a_n \langle B \rangle$$

for $n > 1$, with productions

$$\langle A \rangle \rightarrow a_1 \langle a_2 \ldots a_n B \rangle$$
$$\langle a_i \ldots a_n B \rangle \rightarrow a_i \langle a_{i+1} \ldots a_n B \rangle \text{ for } 1 < i < n$$
$$\langle a_n B \rangle \rightarrow a_n \langle B \rangle$$

where $\langle a_i \ldots a_n B \rangle$ for $1 < i \leq n$ are new nonterminals.

3. If there is a nonterminal $\langle B \rangle$ such that there are productions of the form

$$\langle A \rangle \rightarrow \langle B \rangle$$

first delete the production

$$\langle B \rangle \rightarrow \langle B \rangle$$

if it is present and then if there are any remaining productions having $\langle B \rangle$ as the righthand side, replace them with productions of the form

$$\langle A \rangle \rightarrow y$$

for all combinations of $\langle A \rangle$ and righthand side y such that there are productions

$$\langle A \rangle \rightarrow \langle B \rangle \text{ and } \langle B \rangle \rightarrow y$$

Repeat step 3 if there are any remaining productions whose righthand side consists of a single nonterminal.

The effect of step 3 is to completely eliminate nonterminal $\langle B \rangle$ as an isolated righthand side. Once step 3 has eliminated a particular nonterminal as a righthand side then subsequent applications of step 3 to other nonterminals cannot reintroduce that nonterminal as a righthand side. Consequently, step 3 need only be applied once for each nonterminal appearing as a righthand side.

It sometimes happens that steps in the procedure produce duplicate productions. For example, consider the following grammar with starting symbol $\langle S \rangle$

1. $\langle S \rangle \rightarrow a \, b \, \langle A \rangle$
2. $\langle A \rangle \rightarrow b \, b \, \langle A \rangle$
3. $\langle A \rangle \rightarrow b \, \langle S \rangle$
4. $\langle S \rangle \rightarrow \epsilon$

Step 1 of the procedure need not be applied since there are no productions of the appropriate form. Step 2 applies to both productions 1 and 2 and the result is

1a. $\langle S \rangle \rightarrow a \, \langle bA \rangle$
1b. $\langle bA \rangle \rightarrow b \, \langle A \rangle$
2a. $\langle A \rangle \rightarrow b \, \langle bA \rangle$
2b. $\langle bA \rangle \rightarrow b \, \langle A \rangle$
3. $\langle A \rangle \rightarrow b \, \langle S \rangle$
4. $\langle S \rangle \rightarrow \epsilon$

However, productions 1b and 2b are identical and one copy should be discarded. Step 3 does not apply to this grammar as it already has the desired form.

As a further illustration, we now apply the procedure to the following grammar with starting symbol $\langle S \rangle$:

1. $\langle S \rangle \rightarrow a \, \langle A \rangle$
2. $\langle S \rangle \rightarrow \langle A \rangle$
3. $\langle A \rangle \rightarrow \langle S \rangle$
4. $\langle A \rangle \rightarrow \epsilon$

Steps 1 and 2 of the procedure do not apply. Applying step 3 to nonterminal $\langle A \rangle$ gives the productions

1. $\langle S \rangle \rightarrow a \, \langle A \rangle$

2a. $\langle S \rangle \rightarrow \langle S \rangle$

2b. $\langle S \rangle \rightarrow \epsilon$

3. $\langle A \rangle \rightarrow \langle S \rangle$

4. $\langle A \rangle \rightarrow \epsilon$

Applying step 3 to nonterminal $\langle S \rangle$, we first discard production 2a and then replace production 3 by two new productions. The new grammar is

1. $\langle S \rangle \rightarrow a \langle A \rangle$

2b. $\langle S \rangle \rightarrow \epsilon$

3a. $\langle A \rangle \rightarrow a \langle A \rangle$

3b. $\langle A \rangle \rightarrow \epsilon$

4. $\langle A \rangle \rightarrow \epsilon$

Productions 3b and 4 are duplicates so one of them should be dropped resulting in a four-production grammar of the desired form.

Because of the procedure for converting right-linear grammars to the special form, we can assert the following fact:

The language generated by a right-linear grammar is regular.

To see how right-linear grammars might arise in practice, consider ALGOL 60 variable declarations, which are of the form

$$\text{TYPE IDENT, IDENT, \ldots, IDENT}$$

where TYPE and IDENT are lexical tokens. These declarations are described rather compactly by the right-linear grammar:

$\langle \text{declaration} \rangle \rightarrow$ TYPE IDENT $\langle \text{declared variable list} \rangle$

$\langle \text{declared variable list} \rangle \rightarrow$, IDENT $\langle \text{declared variable list} \rangle$

$\langle \text{declared variable list} \rangle \rightarrow \epsilon$

6.13   ANOTHER GRAMMAR FOR MINI-BASIC CONSTANTS

A grammar for MINI-BASIC constants was given in Section 6.7. Now we derive a second grammar by applying the procedure of Section 6.11 to a finite-state recognizer for MINI-BASIC constants.

A recognizer for unsigned MINI-BASIC constants was developed in Section 2.14 and was shown in Fig. 2.24(b). For this example, we explicitly add an error state, ER, to obtain the recognizer of Fig. 6.11. The names of the input symbols have been changed to conform to Section 6.7.

Applying the procedure of Section 6.11 to this transition table gives a grammar with 40 productions of the form $\langle A \rangle \rightarrow x \langle B \rangle$ and three of the

	d	E	.	+	−	
0	1	ER	7	ER	ER	0
1	1	4	$\overline{23}$	ER	ER	1
$\overline{23}$	$\overline{23}$	4	ER	ER	ER	1
4	6	ER	ER	5	5	0
5	6	ER	ER	ER	ER	0
6	6	ER	ER	ER	ER	1
7	$\overline{23}$	ER	ER	ER	ER	0
ER	ER	ER	ER	ER	ER	0

Figure 6.11

form $\langle A \rangle \rightarrow \epsilon$. However, closer inspection reveals that this size is somewhat misleading. Consider the productions that apply to the nonterminal $\langle ER \rangle$. These may be found by inspecting the row for state $\langle ER \rangle$ in the transition table and are specifically:

$$\langle ER \rangle \rightarrow d \langle ER \rangle$$
$$\langle ER \rangle \rightarrow E \langle ER \rangle$$
$$\langle ER \rangle \rightarrow . \langle ER \rangle$$
$$\langle ER \rangle \rightarrow + \langle ER \rangle$$
$$\langle ER \rangle \rightarrow - \langle ER \rangle$$

It is evident from these productions that the nonterminal $\langle ER \rangle$ cannot be used in the derivation of any string of terminals since any substitution for nonterminal $\langle ER \rangle$ simply results in a new string containing nonterminal $\langle ER \rangle$. In fact, the interpretation of nonterminal $\langle ER \rangle$ as

$$\langle \text{string accepted by the machine started in state ER} \rangle$$

indicates that it does not generate any terminal strings at all since ER is an error state with the property that once the machine enters state ER, it will never subsequently accept any sequence. Thus, if nonterminal $\langle ER \rangle$ is ever introduced in a derivation all subsequent intermediate strings must contain $\langle ER \rangle$ and cannot be terminal strings.

Because nonterminal $\langle ER \rangle$ does not generate any terminal strings we can eliminate from the grammar all productions containing $\langle ER \rangle$ on either the left or right side. Since $\langle ER \rangle$ cannot be involved in the generation of any string in the language, elimination of $\langle ER \rangle$ and all its productions from the grammar cannot possibly have any effect on the language generated by the grammar.

After eliminating all the productions containing $\langle ER \rangle$ the 43 original productions reduce to the following 16.

$$\langle 0 \rangle \rightarrow d \langle 1 \rangle$$
$$\langle 0 \rangle \rightarrow . \langle 7 \rangle$$
$$\langle 1 \rangle \rightarrow d \langle 1 \rangle$$
$$\langle 1 \rangle \rightarrow E \langle 4 \rangle$$
$$\langle 1 \rangle \rightarrow . \langle \overline{23} \rangle$$
$$\langle 1 \rangle \rightarrow \epsilon$$
$$\langle \overline{23} \rangle \rightarrow d \langle \overline{23} \rangle$$
$$\langle \overline{23} \rangle \rightarrow E \langle 4 \rangle$$
$$\langle \overline{23} \rangle \rightarrow \epsilon$$
$$\langle 4 \rangle \rightarrow d \langle 6 \rangle$$
$$\langle 4 \rangle \rightarrow + \langle 5 \rangle$$
$$\langle 4 \rangle \rightarrow - \langle 5 \rangle$$
$$\langle 5 \rangle \rightarrow d \langle 6 \rangle$$
$$\langle 6 \rangle \rightarrow d \langle 6 \rangle$$
$$\langle 6 \rangle \rightarrow \epsilon$$
$$\langle 7 \rangle \rightarrow d \langle \overline{23} \rangle$$

In order to use this grammar as a means of communicating the form of MINI-BASIC constants, the nonterminals should be given more suggestive names. One possibility is as follows:

$\langle 0 \rangle = \langle \text{constant} \rangle$

$\langle 1 \rangle = \langle \text{digits with optional decimal and exponent} \rangle$

$\langle \overline{23} \rangle = \langle \text{decimal digits and optional exponent} \rangle$

$\langle 4 \rangle = \langle \text{integer} \rangle$

$\langle 5 \rangle = \langle \text{unsigned integer} \rangle$

$\langle 6 \rangle = \langle \text{digits} \rangle$

$\langle 7 \rangle = \langle \text{decimal integer and optional exponent} \rangle$

6.14   EXTRANEOUS NONTERMINALS

In the last section, we came upon an example of a nonterminal which could not be used in the derivation of a terminal string and which could therefore be discarded from the grammar along with all productions involving that nonterminal. Nonterminals which do not generate any terminal strings are called *dead nonterminals*.

In the previous section, the nonterminal $\langle ER \rangle$ was dead because each production with $\langle ER \rangle$ on the lefthand side also had $\langle ER \rangle$ on the righthand side. Nonterminals can also be dead for more subtle reasons. Consider for example the following grammar with starting symbol $\langle S \rangle$:

1. $\langle S \rangle \rightarrow a \langle S \rangle a$
2. $\langle S \rangle \rightarrow b \langle A \rangle d$
3. $\langle S \rangle \rightarrow c$
4. $\langle A \rangle \rightarrow c \langle B \rangle d$
5. $\langle A \rangle \rightarrow a \langle A \rangle d$
6. $\langle B \rangle \rightarrow d \langle A \rangle f$

Here, both $\langle A \rangle$ and $\langle B \rangle$ are dead nonterminals. A string with symbol $\langle A \rangle$ can be changed to a string with symbol $\langle B \rangle$ by applying production 4 and a $\langle B \rangle$ can be changed back to $\langle A \rangle$ using production 6. But no matter how one substitutes, a string with an $\langle A \rangle$ or $\langle B \rangle$ is always transformed into a string with an $\langle A \rangle$ or $\langle B \rangle$. The productions involving $\langle A \rangle$ and $\langle B \rangle$ can therefore be eliminated from the grammar leaving only productions 1 and 3. Productions 1 and 3 generate the same terminal strings as productions 1 through 6.

A similar situation occurs when there are nonterminals that cannot be reached from the starting nonterminal. Consider for example the following grammar with starting nonterminal $\langle S \rangle$:

1. $\langle S \rangle \rightarrow a \langle S \rangle b$
2. $\langle S \rangle \rightarrow c$
3. $\langle A \rangle \rightarrow b \langle S \rangle$
4. $\langle A \rangle \rightarrow a$

Neither of the two productions with starting symbol $\langle S \rangle$ as a lefthand side (i.e., productions 1 and 2) has the symbol $\langle A \rangle$ on the righthand side. No string derived from symbol $\langle S \rangle$ can contain an $\langle A \rangle$. Therefore $\langle A \rangle$ cannot be used to derive a string from an $\langle S \rangle$, even though $\langle A \rangle$ itself is not dead. Nonterminal $\langle A \rangle$ and its productions can be eliminated from the grammar leaving only productions 1 and 2. Nonterminals which do not appear in any string derived from the starting symbol are called *unreachable nonterminals*.

Nonterminals which are either dead or unreachable are called *extraneous*. When a grammar is obtained by mechanical means such as by using the procedure of Section 6.11, there is often a possibility that extraneous nonterminals have been created. Such grammars should generally be checked to see if they can be simplified by eliminating extraneous nonterminals. Even with grammars that are made by hand, extraneous nonterminals frequently arise when the designer makes an error. Because of this, a search for extraneous nonterminals can often be useful in debugging a handmade grammar. For these reasons, we now describe a procedure for detecting extraneous nonterminals.

The procedure consists of two parts, one to detect dead nonterminals and one to detect unreachable nonterminals. The procedure for dead nonterminals should be done first since the elimination of dead nonterminals from the grammar may cause other nonterminals to become unreachable.

We call a symbol alive if it is either a terminal symbol or a nonterminal symbol from which a terminal string can be derived (i.e., if it is not a dead nonterminal). The procedure for detecting dead nonterminals is based on the following property of alive symbols

> **Property A:**   If all symbols on the righthand side of a production
> are alive, then so is the symbol on the lefthand side.

To see that this property must hold, observe that given such a production, a terminal string for the symbol on the lefthand side can be obtained by first applying the given production and then replacing each nonterminal in the righthand side with one of the strings that makes it alive.

The basic idea of the procedure is to start a list of nonterminals "known to be alive" and then use Property A to detect other alive nonterminals and expand the list. The steps of the procedure are as follows:

1. Make a list of nonterminals that have at least one production with no nonterminals on the righthand side.

2. If a production is found such that all the nonterminals on the righthand side are on the list, then the nonterminal on the lefthand side of the production is added to the list.

3. When no further nonterminals can be added to the list using rule 2, then the list is the list of all alive nonterminals and all nonterminals not on the list are dead.

The fact that the list obtained from step 3 contains only alive nonterminals is due to the fact that nonterminals are only added when they are known to be alive by Property A. To see that all alive nonterminals must appear on the list, observe that given a sequence of productions used to derive a terminal string from a given nonterminal, the production sequence can be used in reverse to show that all nonterminals involved are alive by Property A.

To see the procedure in action, consider the grammar of Fig. 6.12(a) with starting symbol $\langle S \rangle$. By step 1, $\langle C \rangle$ can be placed on the list because of production 9. Then $\langle A \rangle$ can be added by step 2 because of production 5. Finally, $\langle S \rangle$ can be added because of production 2. Further attempts to

1. $\langle S \rangle \rightarrow a \langle A \rangle \langle B \rangle \langle S \rangle$
2. $\langle S \rangle \rightarrow b \langle C \rangle \langle A \rangle \langle C \rangle d$ 2. $\langle S \rangle \rightarrow b \langle C \rangle \langle A \rangle \langle C \rangle d$
3. $\langle A \rangle \rightarrow b \langle A \rangle \langle B \rangle$
4. $\langle A \rangle \rightarrow c \langle S \rangle \langle A \rangle$ 4. $\langle A \rangle \rightarrow c \langle S \rangle \langle A \rangle$
5. $\langle A \rangle \rightarrow c \langle C \rangle \langle C \rangle$ 5. $\langle A \rangle \rightarrow c \langle C \rangle \langle C \rangle$
6. $\langle B \rangle \rightarrow b \langle A \rangle \langle B \rangle$
7. $\langle B \rangle \rightarrow c \langle S \rangle \langle B \rangle$
8. $\langle C \rangle \rightarrow c \langle S \rangle$ 8. $\langle C \rangle \rightarrow c \langle S \rangle$
9. $\langle C \rangle \rightarrow c$ 9. $\langle C \rangle \rightarrow c$

           (a)   (b)

Figure 6.12

apply step 2 fail and so we know that the alive nonterminals are $\langle C \rangle$, $\langle A \rangle$, and $\langle S \rangle$ and the remaining nonterminal $\langle B \rangle$ is dead. Eliminating all productions involving the dead nonterminal $\langle B \rangle$ gives the grammar of Fig. 6.12(b).

    A symbol is called *reachable* in a grammar if it appears in a string derived from the starting nonterminal (i.e., if it is not unreachable). The procedure for detecting unreachable nonterminals is based on the following property of reachable symbols:

> **Property B.** If the nonterminal on the lefthand side of a production is reachable, then so are all the symbols on the righthand side.

This property holds because the righthand-side symbols can be reached by first deriving a string containing the lefthand side and then applying the given production. The basic idea of the procedure is to start a list of nonterminals "known to be reachable" and then use Property B to detect other reachable nonterminals and expand the list. The steps of the procedure are as follows.

    1. Make a one-element list of nonterminals consisting of the starting nonterminal.

    2. If a production is found such that the lefthand side is on the list, then the nonterminals appearing on the righthand side are added to the list.

    3. When no further nonterminals can be added to the list using rule 2, then the list is the list of all reachable nonterminals and all nonterminals not on the list are unreachable.

    The list obtained from step 3 contains only reachable nonterminals since nonterminals are only added when known to be reachable by Property B. All reachable nonterminals must be on the final list as the sequence of produc-

1. $\langle S \rangle \rightarrow a \langle A \rangle \langle B \rangle$	1. $\langle S \rangle \rightarrow a \langle A \rangle \langle B \rangle$
2. $\langle S \rangle \rightarrow \langle E \rangle$	2. $\langle S \rangle \rightarrow \langle E \rangle$
3. $\langle A \rangle \rightarrow d \langle D \rangle \langle A \rangle$	3. $\langle A \rangle \rightarrow d \langle D \rangle \langle A \rangle$
4. $\langle A \rangle \rightarrow e$	4. $\langle A \rangle \rightarrow e$
5. $\langle B \rangle \rightarrow b \langle E \rangle$	5. $\langle B \rangle \rightarrow b \langle E \rangle$
6. $\langle B \rangle \rightarrow f$	6. $\langle B \rangle \rightarrow f$
7. $\langle C \rangle \rightarrow c \langle A \rangle \langle B \rangle$	
8. $\langle C \rangle \rightarrow d \langle S \rangle \langle D \rangle$	
9. $\langle C \rangle \rightarrow a$	
10. $\langle D \rangle \rightarrow e \langle A \rangle$	10. $\langle D \rangle \rightarrow e \langle A \rangle$
11. $\langle E \rangle \rightarrow f \langle A \rangle$	11. $\langle E \rangle \rightarrow f \langle A \rangle$
12. $\langle E \rangle \rightarrow g$	12. $\langle E \rangle \rightarrow g$
(a)	(b)

Figure 6.13

tions used to reach a given nonterminal can be used with Property B to show that all nonterminals in the sequence of productions are placed on the list.

As an example of the procedure, consider the grammar of Fig. 6.13(a) with starting symbol $\langle S \rangle$. By rule 1, we begin with starting symbol $\langle S \rangle$ on the list. Applying rule 2 to the productions with $\langle S \rangle$ on the lefthand side, namely productions 1 and 2, we find that nonterminals $\langle A \rangle$, $\langle B \rangle$, and $\langle E \rangle$ must be added to the list. Applying rule 2 to production 3, we find that $\langle D \rangle$ must also be added. Checking the other productions does not give any additional nonterminals and we conclude that $\langle S \rangle$, $\langle A \rangle$, $\langle B \rangle$, $\langle D \rangle$, and $\langle E \rangle$ are reachable and the remaining nonterminal $\langle C \rangle$ is unreachable. Dropping the productions involving $\langle C \rangle$, we get the simplified grammar in Fig. 6.13(b).

Finally, we illustrate the two procedures together using the grammar of Fig. 14(a), with starting symbol $\langle S \rangle$. Applying the procedure for dead nonterminals, we discover that $\langle A \rangle$ and $\langle B \rangle$ are dead. Eliminating the productions involving these dead nonterminals gives the grammar of Fig. 6.14(b).

1. $\langle S \rangle \rightarrow a\,c$	1. $\langle S \rangle \rightarrow a\,c$
2. $\langle S \rangle \rightarrow b \langle A \rangle$	5. $\langle C \rangle \rightarrow b \langle C \rangle$
3. $\langle A \rangle \rightarrow c \langle B \rangle \langle C \rangle$	6. $\langle C \rangle \rightarrow d$
4. $\langle B \rangle \rightarrow a \langle S \rangle \langle A \rangle$	(b)
5. $\langle C \rangle \rightarrow b \langle C \rangle$	
6. $\langle C \rangle \rightarrow d$	
	1. $\langle S \rangle \rightarrow a\,c$
(a)	(c)

Figure 6.14

Now testing for unreachable nonterminals, we find that $\langle C \rangle$ is unreachable. Eliminating the productions involving $\langle C \rangle$ gives us the grammar of Fig. 6.14(c). It is now evident that the language generated from the grammar of Fig. 6.14(a) consists of the one string ac. Observe that nonterminal $\langle C \rangle$ becomes unreachable only after production 3 is eliminated. Thus if the test for unreachable nonterminals were performed before the test for dead nonterminals, the full simplification would not be achieved.

6.15   A MINI-BASIC GRAMMAR FOR THE MINI-BASIC LANGUAGE MANUAL

The MINI-BASIC Language Manual of Appendix A is designed to explain the MINI-BASIC language to people with no formal language skills. The approach used is to explain the language structures by means of example. It is hoped that by looking at a few examples, the reader can write arbitrary constructions of a given form. The weakness of such a scheme is that the reader may nevertheless be confused as to exactly what is allowed. To assist the more sophisticated user, it is good practice to supplement the elementary description with a context-free grammar for the language so that the reader familiar with formal languages can determine more exactly what language constructs are permitted. In this section, we give a MINI-BASIC grammar which might be suitable as an appendix to the MINI-BASIC manual.

The terminals of the grammar are the characters that normally go into a MINI-BASIC program. The blank character is not part of the terminal set as the rule "spaces are ignored" is best understood without being built into the grammar.

Starting Nonterminal

The starting nonterminal is called $\langle$statement list$\rangle$ and has two productions:

  1. $\langle$statement list$\rangle \rightarrow \langle$number$\rangle \ \langle$statement$\rangle$ Ⓒ︎Ⓡ︎ $\langle$statement list$\rangle$
  2. $\langle$statement list$\rangle \rightarrow \langle$number$\rangle$ END Ⓒ︎Ⓡ︎

The symbol Ⓒ︎Ⓡ︎ stands for the character "carriage return." These productions ensure that the program is a list of statements preceded by line numbers and that the last statement is the END statement.

Now we consider each of the statements.

Null Statement

A line can contain no statement at all.

  3. $\langle$statement$\rangle \rightarrow \epsilon$

Assignment Statement

  4. $\langle$statement$\rangle \rightarrow$ LET $\langle$variable$\rangle = \langle$expression$\rangle$

GOTO Statement

  5. ⟨statement⟩ → GOTO ⟨number⟩

IF Statement

  6. ⟨statement⟩ → IF ⟨expression⟩ ⟨relational operator⟩ ⟨expression⟩
                   GOTO ⟨number⟩

GOSUB Statement

  7. ⟨statement⟩ → GOSUB ⟨number⟩

RETURN Statement

  8. ⟨statement⟩ → RETURN

FOR Statement

  9. ⟨statement⟩ → FOR ⟨variable⟩ = ⟨expression⟩ TO ⟨expression⟩
 10. ⟨statement⟩ → FOR ⟨variable⟩ = ⟨expression⟩ TO ⟨expression⟩ STEP
                ⟨expression⟩

NEXT Statement

 11. ⟨statement⟩ → NEXT ⟨variable⟩

REM Statement

 12. ⟨statement⟩ → REM ⟨characters⟩

Because there are so many characters we do not bother to give productions for the nonterminal ⟨characters⟩, but merely observe that it generates an arbitrary sequence composed of any characters except ⒸⓇ .

Expressions

The grammar for expressions is a larger version of that given in Section 6.9. Productions 13 and 14 generate the unary + and − operators.

 13. ⟨expression⟩ → + ⟨term⟩
 14. ⟨expression⟩ → − ⟨term⟩
 15. ⟨expression⟩ → ⟨expression⟩ + ⟨term⟩
 16. ⟨expression⟩ → ⟨expression⟩ − ⟨term⟩
 17. ⟨expression⟩ → ⟨term⟩
 18. ⟨term⟩ → ⟨term⟩ * ⟨factor⟩
 19. ⟨term⟩ → ⟨term⟩ / ⟨factor⟩
 20. ⟨term⟩ → ⟨factor⟩
 21. ⟨factor⟩ → ⟨factor⟩ ↑ ⟨primary⟩

22. ⟨factor⟩ → ⟨primary⟩
23. ⟨primary⟩ → (⟨expression⟩)
24. ⟨primary⟩ → ⟨variable⟩
25. ⟨primary⟩ → ⟨unsigned constant⟩

Numbers and Constants

26. ⟨number⟩ → ⟨digit⟩ ⟨digits⟩
27. ⟨digits⟩ → ⟨digit⟩ ⟨digits⟩
28. ⟨digits⟩ → ε

Productions for ⟨digit⟩ will be given later.

29. ⟨unsigned constant⟩ → ⟨number⟩ ⟨exponent⟩
30. ⟨unsigned constant⟩ → ⟨number⟩ . ⟨digits⟩ ⟨exponent⟩
31. ⟨unsigned constant⟩ → . ⟨number⟩ ⟨exponent⟩
32. ⟨exponent⟩ → E + ⟨number⟩
33. ⟨exponent⟩ → E − ⟨number⟩
34. ⟨exponent⟩ → E ⟨number⟩
35. ⟨exponent⟩ → ε

Variables

36. ⟨variable⟩ → ⟨letter⟩
37. ⟨variable⟩ → ⟨letter⟩ ⟨digit⟩

Other Productions

To conserve space, we write several productions on one line

38 − 43. ⟨relational operator⟩   → = | <> | < | <= | > | >=
44 − 53. ⟨digit⟩   → 0 | 1 | 2 | 3 | 4 | 5 | 6 | 7 | 8 | 9
54 − 79. ⟨letter⟩ → A | B | C | D | E | F | G | H | I | J | K | L |M |
                N | O | P | Q | R | S | T | U | V | W | X | Y | Z

   Some aspects of the MINI-BASIC language are not specified by this grammar; for example,

   a) no two lines of a MINI-BASIC program can begin with the same line number;

   b) the line number used in a GOTO, IF, or GOSUB statement must actually occur at the beginning of some line in the program;

c) each FOR statement must have a corresponding NEXT statement with the same variable, and these statements must be properly nested.

Published context-free grammars for other common programming languages such as ALGOL and PL/I also give an incomplete specification. Usually, a programming language is specified by a context-free grammar plus additional informal descriptive material. The programming language is then defined to consist of those sequences that can be generated by the grammar *and* satisfy the additional restrictions specified in the descriptive material. Hence the grammar alone generates all the programs in the language plus some additional programs not in the language; for example, the MINI-BASIC grammar generates some programs where two lines have the same line number.

Customarily those features of the language that are described by the grammar in its manual are called *syntactic* or *grammatical* features and those features not described by its grammar are called *semantic* features. In the language manual the semantic features are usually described informally in a natural language such as English.

The words "syntactic" and "semantic" should be not taken too seriously. When different grammars are used to describe the same programming language, some features of the language that are not described by one grammar (and hence might be called semantic) may be described by another grammar (and hence would be syntactic for that grammar). As an example of this situation, the grammar actually used in the syntax box of our MINI-BASIC compiler (as given in Sections 10.1 and 12.8) does describe grammatically the requirement that each FOR statement have a matching NEXT statement.

However there are some aspects of programming languages that cannot possibly be described by a context-free grammar. For instance if line numbers are allowed to be arbitrarily long, it can be proved that no context-free grammar generates exactly those MINI-BASIC programs satisfying the restriction that no two lines begin with the same line number. As another example, a context-free grammar cannot generate exactly those ALGOL programs satisfying the restriction that identifiers are not declared more than once in the same block.

There are other aspects of programming languages that *can* be described by a context-free grammar, but only by a grammar that is excessively large. For instance it *is* possible to find a grammar that generates the MINI-BASIC programs satisfying the restriction that each FOR statement and its matching NEXT statement actually use the same variable. However, this grammar would be quite large; hence we choose to describe this restriction by non-grammatical means.

In practice, context-free grammars are only used to specify as much of a programming language as can be done compactly. For the remaining aspects, informal descriptive methods are used.

6.16 REFERENCES

Context-free grammars were first formalized by Chomsky [1956, 1957, 1959]. Many of the properties of context-free languages first appeared in Bar-Hillel, Perles, and Shamir [1961]. The relationship between regular sets and right-linear grammars is developed in Chomsky and Miller [1958]. A survey of context-free grammars is given in Chomsky [1963]. The first use of Backus-Naur Form to describe a programming language is in Naur, et al. [1960, 1962]. Ginsburg [1966] is a mathematical text that is completely devoted to context-free languages. Methods for obtaining a recognizer for any context-free grammar are discussed in Aho and Ullman [1972a].

PROBLEMS

1. Find a context-free grammar that will generate each of the following languages:
   a) $\{1^n 0^m\}$ for $n > m > 0$;
   b) $\{1^n 0^n 1^m 0^m\}$ for $n, m \geq 0$;
   c) $\{1^n 0^m 1^m 0^n\}$ for $n, m \geq 0$;
   d) $\{1^n 0^n\} \cup \{0^m 1^m\}$ for $n, m \geq 0$;
   e) $\{1^{3n+2} 0^n\}$ for $n \geq 0$;
   f) $\{w \, a \, w^r\}$ where w is an arbitrary sequence of 1's and 0's;
   −g) All sequences of 1's and 0's containing an equal number of each;
   h) All sequences of 1's and 0's containing an equal number of each and such that each subsequence beginning at the left end contains at least as many 1's as 0's;
   −i) $\{1^n 0^m 1^p\}$ for $n + p > m \geq 0$.

2. A context-free grammar generates the following derivation tree.

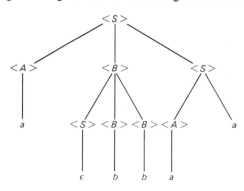

a) Give the leftmost derivation corresponding to this derivation tree.

b) How many different derivations correspond to this derivation tree?

c) Draw a derivation tree for the terminal string *ab*.

3. Describe the language generated by each of the following grammars with starting nonterminal $\langle S \rangle$.

a) $\langle S \rangle \rightarrow 1\,0\,\langle S \rangle\,0$

$\langle S \rangle \rightarrow a\,\langle A \rangle$

$\langle A \rangle \rightarrow b\,\langle A \rangle$

$\langle A \rangle \rightarrow a$

b) $\langle S \rangle \rightarrow \langle S \rangle\,\langle S \rangle$

$\langle S \rangle \rightarrow 1\,\langle A \rangle\,0$

$\langle A \rangle \rightarrow 1\,\langle A \rangle\,0$

$\langle A \rangle \rightarrow \epsilon$

c) $\langle S \rangle \rightarrow 1\,\langle A \rangle$

$\langle S \rangle \rightarrow \langle B \rangle\,0$

$\langle A \rangle \rightarrow 1\,\langle A \rangle$

$\langle A \rangle \rightarrow \langle C \rangle$

$\langle B \rangle \rightarrow \langle B \rangle\,0$

$\langle B \rangle \rightarrow \langle C \rangle$

$\langle C \rangle \rightarrow 1\,\langle C \rangle\,0$

$\langle C \rangle \rightarrow \epsilon$

d) $\langle S \rangle \rightarrow B\,\langle A \rangle\,\langle D \rangle\,C$

$\langle D \rangle \rightarrow \langle G \rangle\,I$

$\langle A \rangle \rightarrow A\,\langle G \rangle\,S$

$\langle G \rangle \rightarrow \epsilon$

e) $\langle S \rangle \rightarrow a\,\langle S \rangle\,\langle S \rangle$

$\langle S \rangle \rightarrow a$

4. Which of the following sequences can be derived from the given grammar with starting nonterminal $\langle S \rangle$? In each case give a leftmost derivation, a rightmost derivation, and a derivation tree.

$$\langle S \rangle \rightarrow a\,\langle A \rangle\,c\,\langle B \rangle$$

$$\langle S \rangle \rightarrow \langle B \rangle\,d\,\langle S \rangle$$

$$\langle B \rangle \rightarrow a\,\langle S \rangle\,c\,\langle A \rangle$$

$$\langle B \rangle \rightarrow c\,\langle A \rangle\,\langle B \rangle$$

$$\langle A \rangle \rightarrow \langle B \rangle\,a\,\langle B \rangle$$

$$\langle A \rangle \rightarrow a\,\langle B \rangle\,c$$

$$\langle A \rangle \rightarrow a$$

$$\langle B \rangle \rightarrow b$$

a) *aacb*

b) *aababcbadcd*

c) *aacbccb*

d) *aacabcbcccaacdca*

e) *aacabcbcccaacbca*

5. Find a context-free grammar for expressions in the Lambda Calculus as described in the following paragraph:

An expression in Lambda Calculus is a variable or the symbol λ followed by a variable followed by an expression or a left parenthesis followed by an expression followed by an expression followed by a right parenthesis.

6. Is it possible for a sequence to have two leftmost derivations, but only one rightmost derivation?

7. Show that if a language is context free, then the language obtained by regarding the endmarker as a terminal symbol and inserting it at the end of every sequence in the original language is also context free.

8. Find a context-free grammar for the two IF statements in FORTRAN.

9. Find a context-free grammar for the IF statement in COBOL.

10. Draw the derivation tree for the following ALGOL program using the standard grammar in the ALGOL report (Naur [1963]):

$$\textbf{begin integer } A1;$$
$$A1 := 12; \textbf{ end}$$

11. Find a context-free grammar for a statement in SNOBOL.

12. Find a context-free grammar for regular expressions (Hennie [1968]) using the $+$ and $*$ operators and indicating concatenation with juxtaposition.

13. Describe the language generated by the following grammar and draw the derivation tree for three of the sequences in its language.

$$\langle E \rangle \rightarrow \langle P \rangle \langle R \rangle$$
$$\langle P \rangle \rightarrow (\langle E \rangle)$$
$$\langle P \rangle \rightarrow I$$
$$\langle R \rangle \rightarrow + \langle P \rangle \langle R \rangle$$
$$\langle R \rangle \rightarrow * \langle P \rangle \langle R \rangle$$
$$\langle R \rangle \rightarrow \uparrow \langle P \rangle \langle R \rangle$$
$$\langle R \rangle \rightarrow \epsilon$$

14. Find a grammar which generates the same set of arithmetic expressions as the grammar of Section 6.9, but which has only one nonterminal.

15. a) Find a context-free grammar for Boolean expressions made up of Boolean variables, constants, parentheses, and the NOT, OR, and AND operators. Assume the usual precedence of NOT before AND and AND before OR.

b) Add to your grammar Boolean primaries consisting of an arithmetic expression followed by a relational operator ($>$, $\geq$, $=$, $\neq$, $<$, $\leq$) followed by another arithmetic expression.

16. Find a right-linear grammar for the language recognized by the lexical box of the MINI-BASIC compiler.

17. The language recognized by this machine is denoted by L

	0	1	
A	B	A	0
B	C	B	1
C	B	A	0

Find right-linear grammars for the languages
a) $L + \epsilon$
b) $L \cdot L$
c) $L *$
d) $L ^+$

18. Consider the grammar
$$S \to S\, a$$
$$S \to S\, b$$
$$S \to a$$
a) Find a right-linear grammar that generates the same language.
b) Draw the derivation tree for the sequence $ababb$ according to both grammars.

19. Find right-linear grammars for the languages and/or machines described in the following problems from Chapter 2.

a) 1	e) 13	i) 17
b) 3	f) 14	j) 18
c) 4	g) 15	k) 22
d) 6	h) 16	l) 23

20. Show that the following two right-linear grammars generate the same language.
a) (starting nonterminal $\langle X \rangle$)
$$\langle X \rangle \to 0$$
$$\langle X \rangle \to 0 \langle Y \rangle$$
$$\langle X \rangle \to 1 \langle Z \rangle$$
$$\langle Y \rangle \to 0 \langle X \rangle$$
$$\langle Y \rangle \to 1 \langle Y \rangle$$
$$\langle Y \rangle \to 1$$
$$\langle Z \rangle \to 0 \langle Z \rangle$$
$$\langle Z \rangle \to 1 \langle X \rangle$$

b) (starting nonterminal $\langle A \rangle$)

$\langle A \rangle \rightarrow 0 \langle B \rangle$ $\langle D \rangle \rightarrow 0 \langle A \rangle$

$\langle A \rangle \rightarrow 1 \langle E \rangle$ $\langle D \rangle \rightarrow 1 \langle D \rangle$

$\langle B \rangle \rightarrow 0 \langle A \rangle$ $\langle D \rangle \rightarrow \epsilon$

$\langle B \rangle \rightarrow 1 \langle F \rangle$ $\langle E \rangle \rightarrow 0 \langle C \rangle$

$\langle B \rangle \rightarrow \epsilon$ $\langle E \rangle \rightarrow 1 \langle A \rangle$

$\langle C \rangle \rightarrow 0 \langle C \rangle$ $\langle F \rangle \rightarrow 0 \langle A \rangle$

$\langle C \rangle \rightarrow 1 \langle A \rangle$ $\langle F \rangle \rightarrow 1 \langle B \rangle$

                                          $\langle F \rangle \rightarrow \epsilon$

21. Find the extraneous nonterminals in the following grammar with starting non-terminal $\langle S \rangle$

$\langle S \rangle \rightarrow a \langle A \rangle \langle B \rangle \langle C \rangle$

$\langle S \rangle \rightarrow b \langle C \rangle \langle E \rangle \langle S \rangle$

$\langle S \rangle \rightarrow a \langle E \rangle$

$\langle A \rangle \rightarrow b \langle E \rangle$

$\langle A \rangle \rightarrow \langle S \rangle \langle C \rangle \langle D \rangle$

$\langle A \rangle \rightarrow d$

$\langle B \rangle \rightarrow d \langle F \rangle \langle S \rangle$

$\langle B \rangle \rightarrow a \langle B \rangle \langle C \rangle$

$\langle C \rangle \rightarrow a \langle E \rangle \langle S \rangle$

$\langle C \rangle \rightarrow b \langle E \rangle$

$\langle D \rangle \rightarrow a \langle A \rangle \langle C \rangle$

$\langle D \rangle \rightarrow d$

$\langle E \rangle \rightarrow a \langle C \rangle \langle E \rangle$

$\langle E \rangle \rightarrow \epsilon$

$\langle F \rangle \rightarrow \langle A \rangle \langle B \rangle$

$\langle F \rangle \rightarrow a \langle F \rangle$

22. Find a right-linear grammar with no extraneous nonterminals corresponding to each of the machines in Fig. 6.15.

23. What is the value of each of the following expressions in MINI-BASIC? What is their value in FORTRAN (making the lexical change of replacing ↑ with **)?

a) $- 2 \uparrow 2$

b) $2 + 2 / 2 + 2$

c) $- 2 * 2$

	0	1	
A	A,B		
B		C	1
C	C	B,C	
D		C,D	1

(a)

	0	1	
A	B	G	0
B	I	F	1
C	A	B	0
D	F	D	0
E	C	H	0
F	H	F	0
G	A	B	1
H	D	F	0
I	D	A	0

(b)

Figure 6.15

d) $2 \uparrow 2 / 2 \uparrow 2$

e) $2 \uparrow 2 \uparrow 2 \uparrow 2$

24. Describe in words the language generated by this grammar with $\langle E \rangle$ as the starting symbol:

$\langle E \rangle \rightarrow \langle E \rangle \langle T \rangle +$

$\langle E \rangle \rightarrow \langle T \rangle$

$\langle T \rangle \rightarrow \langle T \rangle \langle F \rangle *$

$\langle T \rangle \rightarrow \langle F \rangle$

$\langle F \rangle \rightarrow \langle F \rangle \langle P \rangle \uparrow$

$\langle F \rangle \rightarrow \langle P \rangle$

$\langle P \rangle \rightarrow \langle E \rangle$

$\langle P \rangle \rightarrow I$

25. Find a grammar for arithmetic expressions similar to that of Section 6.9 except that unary plus and minus operators are allowed before every number or variable (for example $3 * - 4$ is allowed) with each of the following interpretations:

a) the same precedence as binary addition and subtraction (for example $- 2 \uparrow 2 = -(2 \uparrow 2) = -4$);

b) the unary operators are always carried out first (for example $-2 \uparrow 2 = (-2) \uparrow 2 = 4$).

26. Draw the derivation tree corresponding to the grammar of Section 6.15 for the following MINI-BASIC programs.

    a) 05 LET X1 = −4 + 3 * (+1 − 7)

       10 END
    b) 12 FOR X1 = 1 TO 12

       22 FOR X2 = 1 TO 10

       24 LET X1 = X2 + 1

       25 NEXT X2

       26 NEXT X1

       27 END

27. Using the terminal alphabet of the grammar of Section 6.9, write a grammar that generates all strings composed from these terminals that are not arithmetic expressions (according to the grammar of Section 6.9).

28. In ordinary algebra, variables are single letters and hence the multiplication operator can often be omitted (for example $2z$ denotes two times z). Find a context-free grammar for polynomials made up of numbers, single-letter variables, and $+$, $-$, and $\uparrow$ operators with multiplication implied between adjacent variables or between an adjacent integer and variable.

29. Given two context-free grammars, G_1 and G_2 that generate languages L_1 and L_2, describe general procedures that will give a context-free grammar for:

    a) $L_1 \cup L_2$

    b) $L_1 \cdot L_2$

    c) $L_1{}^*$

    Use the grammars directly in your procedure.

30. Find a context-free grammar that will generate the FORMAT statement in FORTRAN (excluding the Hollerith field).

31. Find a context-free grammar for the BASIC language as described in some convenient manual. Which features of the language are not described by your grammar?

32. Find a context-free grammar that will generate S-expressions in LISP using

    a) dot notation,

    b) list notation,

    c) LISP metalanguage.

33. Suppose that a MINI-BASIC program could only use the three line numbers 1, 2, and 3. Write a context-free grammar that generates all MINI-BASIC programs satisfying the requirements that each line begins with a distinct line number and that the line number used in a GOTO, IF, or GOSUB statement actually occurs at the beginning of some line in the program.

34. How would you determine whether the language generated by a grammar contains an infinite number of sequences?

35. How would you determine if a grammar generates any terminal sequences at all?

36. Show that if a context-free language does not contain the null string, there exists a context-free grammar for that language with no epsilon productions.

37. Give an example of a grammar with no terminal symbols, but whose language contains at least one sequence.

38. Give an example of a grammar for which each sequence in the language has an infinite number of derivation trees.

39. What property must a grammar have if every derivation tree has only one corresponding derivation?

40. a) Suppose that we write $x \Longleftrightarrow y$ if either $x \Rightarrow y$ or $y \Rightarrow x$. Also suppose that $\overset{*}{\Longleftrightarrow}$ represents zero or more uses of the relation $\Longleftrightarrow$. Give an example of a context-free grammar with starting symbol $\langle S \rangle$ for which the set of terminal strings w such that $\langle S \rangle \overset{*}{\Rightarrow} w$ is different from the set of terminal strings w such that $\langle S \rangle \overset{*}{\Longleftrightarrow} w$.

    b) What would the "derivation tree" for a "derivation" using the relation $\Longleftrightarrow$ look like?

41. Show that the language $a^* + b^*$ cannot be generated by any context-free grammar with a single nonterminal.

42. Show that for each grammar there exists a constant such that every sequence in the language has a derivation with a number of steps less than the constant times the length of the sequence.

43. Find a context-free grammar that will generate all the well-formed formulas in the propositional calculus.

44. Give a procedure that will test two right-linear grammars to determine whether or not they generate the same language.

45. Draw the derivation trees for each of the following expressions according to the grammars of Section 6.9 and 6.10.

    a) $I * I + I$

    b) $I * (I + I)$

    c) $I + (I * I) \uparrow I + I$

7
Syntax-Directed Processing

7.1   INTRODUCTION

In our study of finite-state machines, we developed the theory around problems of recognition. When finite-state machines were applied to practical problems, such aspects of the processing as generating outputs and computing values were handled informally by the use of transition routines specified in an *ad hoc* manner. Since the required *ad hoc* routines almost always turned out to be short and fairly straightforward to design, we judged the theory of finite-state recognition to be adequate theoretical knowledge for the design of finite-state processors.

In subsequent chapters, we deal with the recognition of context-free languages by pushdown machines. Unlike the finite-state case, *ad hoc* extensions of a pushdown recognizer are sufficiently difficult to design that the theory of context-free recognition by itself does not provide adequate theoretical knowledge for the design of compilers. The purpose of this chapter is to establish a theoretical basis of context-free-language processing beyond the theory of recognition, and provide a framework that easily accommodates *ad hoc* extensions.

The design methods of subsequent chapters are all based on techniques in which the processing of a context-free language is specified in terms of the processing of each individual production. The adjective "syntax-directed" is commonly used to describe processing specified by this technique. The syntax-directed methods of this book are based on the mathematical concept of a "translation grammar" which is introduced in Section 7.3 and the concept of an "attributed translation grammar" in Section 7.7.

181

7.2 POLISH NOTATION

Throughout this chapter the problem of translating arithmetic expressions is used as an illustrative example. In this section we present a specific example of what one might translate expressions into.

The usual method of writing arithmetic expressions as described by the grammar of Section 6.9 is known as *infix notation*. There are, however, other notations for describing how arithmetic quantities should be combined. One such method is a notation known as *postfix Polish* notation, developed by the Polish mathematician, J. Lukasiewicz.

In postfix Polish notation, each operator is written immediately after its operands. The set of Polish expressions with operators + and * can be generated by the grammar

$$\langle\text{operand}\rangle \rightarrow \langle\text{operand}\rangle \, \langle\text{operand}\rangle \, +$$
$$\langle\text{operand}\rangle \rightarrow \langle\text{operand}\rangle \, \langle\text{operand}\rangle \, *$$
$$\langle\text{operand}\rangle \rightarrow I$$

where I denotes any variable. For purposes of discussion, these variables are represented by small Italic letters.

Every expression written in infix notation has an equivalent expression written in postfix Polish notation. For example, the postfix Polish for

$$a * b \quad \text{is} \quad a \, b \, *$$

and for

$$a * b + c \quad \text{is} \quad a \, b * c +$$

The derivation tree for this last string is shown in Fig. 7.1. The expression consists of the operand $ab*$ (i.e., the product of a and b) the operand c and the operator $+$.

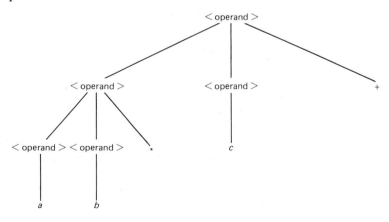

Figure 7.1

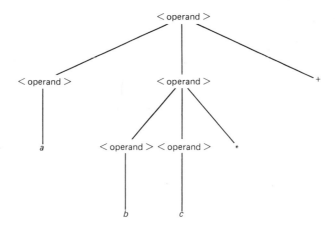

Figure 7.2

As another example the infix expression

$$a + b * c \qquad \text{has} \qquad a\, b\, c * +$$

as its corresponding postfix Polish expression. The derivation tree for this string is shown in Fig. 7.2. The expression consists of the operand a, the operand $bc*$, and the operator $+$.

Postfix Polish notation has no parentheses, even when corresponding infix expressions must be parenthesized. For example the infix expression

$$(a + b) * c \qquad \text{is written as} \qquad a\, b + c *$$

As a final example, the postfix Polish for

$$a + b * (c + d) * (e + f) \qquad \text{is} \qquad a\, b\, c\, d + *\, e f + * +$$

Postfix Polish notation provides an alternate language for expressing mathematical formulas. Some compilers have a syntax box which literally translates infix expressions into Polish expressions. Many other compilers make a translation similar to Polish. Such a translation is discussed later in this chapter.

7.3 TRANSLATION GRAMMARS

Suppose we want to devise a processor that takes infix expressions as input and prints the equivalent postfix Polish expressions. We wish the design to be based on a recognizer which calls a printing routine each time a symbol is to be put out. Although we do not yet have a detailed recognition plan, we can envision how the processing might take place. Suppose, for example, that the input sequence were

$$a + b * c$$

A possible scenario of processor input and output activities is:

READ(*a*) PRINT(*a*) *READ(+)* READ(*b*) PRINT(*b*) READ(*) READ(*c*)
PRINT(*c*) PRINT(*) PRINT(+)

This is a plausible scenario because the symbols *a*, *b*, and *c* are printed as soon as they are known and operators are printed as soon as both operands have been printed.

The word READ should not be interpreted too literally as many machines do not have a READ operation. The primitive pushdown machine, for example, advances to an input, retains it for an indefinite number of transitions, and then advances beyond the input.

The sequence of input and output actions can be described without the words READ and PRINT as follows:

$$a \; \{a\} \; + \; b \; \{b\} \; * \; c \; \{c\} \; \{*\} \; \{+\}$$

The read operations are represented by the input symbols themselves and the outputs represented by symbols enclosed in braces. This sequence is an example of what we call an *activity sequence*. The output resulting from the specified PRINT operations is the sequence of symbols in the braces, namely *abc*$*$+. For the purpose of making a mathematical translation model, a pair of braces and the output they enclose are treated as a single symbol called an *action symbol*. Thus the activity sequence shown above has five action symbols, namely {*a*}, {*b*}, {*c*}, {*}, and {+}. In this example, we think of these action symbols as the names of routines which print the enclosed output symbols. In other applications, action symbols are used to represent more general *ad hoc* routines.

The above activity sequence merely suggests how one particular infix expression might be processed. To show how *all* infix expressions might be processed, a *set* or *language* of activity sequences can be described. Our goal is to describe such languages using context-free grammars. We now develop such a description for the current example. Specifically, we derive a context-free grammar which describes a set of activity sequences suitable for translating infix into postfix Polish.

The usual starting point for developing a context-free description of an activity sequence language is the grammar for the input language since it already describes the input portion of the activity. A grammar for infix expressions, with starting nonterminal $\langle E \rangle$, is:

1. $\langle E \rangle \rightarrow \langle E \rangle + \langle T \rangle$
2. $\langle E \rangle \rightarrow \langle T \rangle$

3. $\langle T \rangle \rightarrow \langle T \rangle * \langle P \rangle$
4. $\langle T \rangle \rightarrow \langle P \rangle$
5. $\langle P \rangle \rightarrow (\langle E \rangle)$
6. $\langle P \rangle \rightarrow a$
7. $\langle P \rangle \rightarrow b$
8. $\langle P \rangle \rightarrow c$

For expository purposes, the grammar has been supplied with three specific variable names, a, b, and c. To construct a grammar for activity sequences, we simply describe the activities appropriate for each righthand side.

For example, to print an a after an a is read, production 6 is changed to:

$$\langle P \rangle \rightarrow a \; \{a\}$$

To print the add operator after printing both its operands, production 1 is changed to:

$$\langle E \rangle \rightarrow \langle E \rangle + \langle T \rangle \; \{+\}$$

This new production can be interpreted as saying "an example of processing an $\langle E \rangle$ is processing an $\langle E \rangle$, reading a $+$, processing a $\langle T \rangle$, and printing a $+$." When similar changes are made in the other productions, the new grammar becomes

1. $\langle E \rangle \rightarrow \langle E \rangle + \langle T \rangle \; \{+\}$
2. $\langle E \rangle \rightarrow \langle T \rangle$
3. $\langle T \rangle \rightarrow \langle T \rangle * \langle P \rangle \; \{*\}$
4. $\langle T \rangle \rightarrow \langle P \rangle$
5. $\langle P \rangle \rightarrow (\langle E \rangle)$
6. $\langle P \rangle \rightarrow a \; \{a\}$
7. $\langle P \rangle \rightarrow b \; \{b\}$
8. $\langle P \rangle \rightarrow c \; \{c\}$

This new grammar is an example of what we call a *translation grammar*.

Because of the correspondence between the productions of the infix grammar and productions of the translation grammar, the derivation of an input sequence using the infix grammar can be used to obtain an activity sequence for that input using the translation grammar. This is done simply by applying the corresponding productions in corresponding places. As an example, consider the infix expression $(a + b) * c$. A leftmost derivation of this string is obtained by applying the sequence of productions 2, 3, 4, 5, 1, 2, 4, 6, 4, 7, 8. This same sequence of productions from the translation grammar applied to the corresponding nonterminals (in this case the leftmost nonterminals) gives a derivation of an activity sequence for that input sequence. The corresponding derivations are

$$\langle E \rangle \Rightarrow \langle T \rangle \Rightarrow \langle T \rangle * \langle P \rangle \Rightarrow \langle P \rangle * \langle P \rangle$$
$$\Rightarrow (\langle E \rangle) * \langle P \rangle \Rightarrow (\langle E \rangle + \langle T \rangle) * \langle P \rangle$$
$$\overset{*}{\Rightarrow} (a + b) * c$$

$$\langle E \rangle \Rightarrow \langle T \rangle \Rightarrow \langle T \rangle * \langle P \rangle \{*\} \Rightarrow \langle P \rangle * \langle P \rangle \{*\}$$
$$\Rightarrow (\langle E \rangle) * \langle P \rangle \{*\} \Rightarrow (\langle E \rangle + \langle T \rangle \{+\}) * \langle P \rangle \{*\}$$
$$\overset{*}{\Rightarrow} (a \{a\} + b \{b\} \{+\}) * c \{c\} \{*\}$$

Several of the more trivial steps in the derivation are not shown. They occur when the symbol $\overset{*}{\Rightarrow}$ appears.

We formalize the ideas introduced above as a mathematical model using the following definitions:

A *translation grammar* is a context-free grammar in which the set of terminal symbols is partitioned into a set of *input symbols* and a set of *action symbols*. The strings in the language specified by a translation grammar are called *activity sequences*.

An example of a translation grammar is the following:

input symbols = $\{a, b, c\}$

action symbols = $\{x, y, z\}$

nonterminal symbols = $\{\langle A \rangle, \langle B \rangle\}$

starting nonterminal = $\langle A \rangle$

productions = $\langle A \rangle \rightarrow a \langle A \rangle x \langle B \rangle$

$\langle A \rangle \rightarrow z$

$\langle B \rangle \rightarrow \langle B \rangle c$

$\langle B \rangle \rightarrow b y$

In order that action symbols be readily distinguished from nonterminal and input symbols, we adopt the convention of defining action symbols with braces. Under this convention, one can look at any string of symbols and see which symbols are nonterminals, which are inputs, and which are actions. For example, if the grammar just given had been constructed with action symbols $\{x\}$, $\{y\}$, and $\{z\}$ instead of x, y, and z, the set of productions would be

$\langle A \rangle \rightarrow a \langle A \rangle \{x\} \langle B \rangle$

$\langle A \rangle \rightarrow \{z\}$

$\langle B \rangle \rightarrow \langle B \rangle c$

$\langle B \rangle \rightarrow b \{y\}$

and the occurrences of terminals, nonterminals, and action symbols would easily be distinguished.

There are many applications, for example, infix to Polish translation, in which we intend each action symbol to represent a routine which outputs the symbol within the braces. When this interpretation is intended, we refer to the grammar as a *string translation grammar*. Thus, the term "string translation grammar" indicates that a given translation grammar is intended to describe the translation of input strings into output strings. This is in contrast with the general interpretation of action symbols as representing arbitrary routines.

7.4 SYNTAX-DIRECTED TRANSLATIONS

Mathematically, we regard a *translation* as a set of pairs, where the first element of each pair comes from a set of things being translated from and the second element comes from a set of things being translated into. In the translations discussed in this book, the first element of a pair is a sequence from some input language and the second element is a sequence representing a translation of the input. When the pairs are obtained in a grammatical fashion, the translation is sometimes called a syntax-directed translation.

In this section, we use the activity sequence concept as the basis of a class of syntax-directed translations. First we state how an activity sequence can be used to specify a pair:

> Given an activity sequence of input and action symbols, we use the term *input part* to refer to that sequence of input symbols obtained from the activity sequence by deleting all action symbols, and we use the term *action part* to refer to that sequence of action symbols obtained from the activity sequence by deleting all input symbols. We say that the input part is *paired with* the action part.

Under this definition, the activity sequence

$$a \ \{a\} + b \ \{b\} * c \ \{c\} \ \{*\} \ \{+\}$$

discussed in the previous section pairs input sequence $a + b * c$ with action sequence $\{a\} \ \{b\} \ \{c\} \ \{*\} \ \{+\}$.

Given a translation grammar, a set of pairs can be obtained by pairing the input part of each activity sequence with the action part. This set of pairs is called the translation defined by the given translation grammar.

Under this definition, the translation defined by the infix to Polish translation grammar of the previous section is the set of pairs for which the first element is an infix expression and the second element is a sequence of action symbols which says how an equivalent Polish expression can be printed.

Certain translation grammars have the property that the same input sequence can appear in more than one activity sequence or be paired with more than one action sequence. This situation is discussed more fully in Section 7.11. Here we merely note that our interest is almost exclusively in cases where each input sequence is part of only one activity sequence and hence has only one translation.

In discussing translations, we frequently use the concept of an *input grammar:*

> Given a translation grammar, the grammar obtained by deleting all action symbols from the productions in the given grammar is called the *input grammar* for that translation grammar. The language specified by the input grammar is called the *input language.*

For the infix-to-Polish example, the input grammar is simply the grammar for infix expressions. For the grammar used to illustrate the definition of a translation grammar, the input grammar is:

$$\langle A \rangle \rightarrow a \langle A \rangle \langle B \rangle$$
$$\langle A \rangle \rightarrow \epsilon$$
$$\langle B \rangle \rightarrow \langle B \rangle \; c$$
$$\langle B \rangle \rightarrow b$$

For any translation grammar, the input language is nothing more than the set of input sequences. The input grammar therefore describes the set of sequences for which the translation grammar defines translations.

Although we have defined an input grammar as being obtained from a translation grammar, the normal course of events in designing a compiler is somewhat different. First the language to be processed is described with an input grammar, and then the action symbols are inserted into the productions to describe the desired processing.

Given a translation grammar, an *action grammar* can be obtained by deleting all input symbols. Thus, a translation grammar can be viewed as translating from one context-free language, the input language, to another context-free language, the action language. However, the action-grammar concept has no further significance in this book.

In the case of a string translation grammar, we think of an action-symbol sequence as being synonymous with the corresponding output sequence. In the infix-to-Polish example, we think of action sequence

$$\{a\} \; \{b\} \; \{c\} \; \{*\} \; \{+\}$$

as being synonymous with output sequence

$$a \; b \; c \; * \; +$$

and might refer to either string as a translation of input string

$$a + b * c$$

Thus a string translation grammar can be interpreted as specifying a translation of an input language into an output language.

A given translation can be specified by many different translation grammars. For example the translation of infix-to-Polish expressions discussed in Section 7.3 can also be described using the following translation grammar based on the input grammar of Section 6.10.

1. $\langle E \rangle \rightarrow \langle T \rangle \, \langle E\text{-list} \rangle$
2. $\langle E\text{-list} \rangle \rightarrow \, + \langle T \rangle \, \{+\} \, \langle E\text{-list} \rangle$
3. $\langle E\text{-list} \rangle \rightarrow \epsilon$
4. $\langle T \rangle \rightarrow \langle P \rangle \, \langle T\text{-list} \rangle$
5. $\langle T\text{-list} \rangle \rightarrow * \langle P \rangle \, \{*\} \, \langle T\text{-list} \rangle$
6. $\langle T\text{-list} \rangle \rightarrow \epsilon$
7. $\langle P \rangle \rightarrow (\langle E \rangle)$
8. $\langle P \rangle \rightarrow a \, \{a\}$
9. $\langle P \rangle \rightarrow b \, \{b\}$
10. $\langle P \rangle \rightarrow c \, \{c\}$

As described in Section 6.10, the $\langle T \rangle$ in production 2 generates the right operand of the $+$ operator. Hence the proper place to emit the $+$ is directly after this $\langle T \rangle$. Similar reasoning applies to the emitting of the $*$ in production 5. The leftmost derivation of the activity sequence for input sequence $(a + b) * c$ according to this grammar is:

$\langle E \rangle \Rightarrow \langle T \rangle \, \langle E\text{-list} \rangle$
$\quad \Rightarrow \langle P \rangle \, \langle T\text{-list} \rangle \, \langle E\text{-list} \rangle$
$\quad \Rightarrow (\langle E \rangle) \, \langle T\text{-list} \rangle \, \langle E\text{-list} \rangle$
$\quad \Rightarrow (\langle T \rangle \, \langle E\text{-list} \rangle) \, \langle T\text{-list} \rangle \, \langle E\text{-list} \rangle$
$\quad \Rightarrow (\langle P \rangle \, \langle T\text{-list} \rangle \, \langle E\text{-list} \rangle) \, \langle T\text{-list} \rangle \, \langle E\text{-list} \rangle$
$\quad \Rightarrow (a \, \{a\} \, \langle T\text{-list} \rangle \, \langle E\text{-list} \rangle) \, \langle T\text{-list} \rangle \, \langle E\text{-list} \rangle$
$\quad \Rightarrow (a \, \{a\} \, \langle E\text{-list} \rangle) \, \langle T\text{-list} \rangle \, \langle E\text{-list} \rangle$
$\quad \Rightarrow (a \, \{a\} + \langle T \rangle \, \{+\} \, \langle E\text{-list} \rangle) \, \langle T\text{-list} \rangle \, \langle E\text{-list} \rangle$
$\quad \Rightarrow (a \, \{a\} + \langle P \rangle \, \langle T\text{-list} \rangle \, \{+\} \, \langle E\text{-list} \rangle) \, \langle T\text{-list} \rangle \, \langle E\text{-list} \rangle$
$\quad \Rightarrow (a \, \{a\} + b \, \{b\} \, \langle T\text{-list} \rangle \, \{+\} \, \langle E\text{-list} \rangle) \, \langle T\text{-list} \rangle \, \langle E\text{-list} \rangle$
$\quad \Rightarrow (a \, \{a\} + b \, \{b\} \, \{+\} \, \langle E\text{-list} \rangle) \, \langle T\text{-list} \rangle \, \langle E\text{-list} \rangle$
$\quad \Rightarrow (a \, \{a\} + b \, \{b\} \, \{+\} \,) \, \langle T\text{-list} \rangle \, \langle E\text{-list} \rangle$

$$\Rightarrow (a \{a\} + b \{b\} \{+\}) * \langle P \rangle \{*\} \langle T\text{-list} \rangle \langle E\text{-list} \rangle$$
$$\Rightarrow (a \{a\} + b \{b\} \{+\}) * c \{c\} \{*\} \langle T\text{-list} \rangle \langle E\text{-list} \rangle$$
$$\Rightarrow (a \{a\} + b \{b\} \{+\}) * c \{c\} \{*\} \langle E\text{-list} \rangle$$
$$\Rightarrow (a \{a\} + b \{b\} \{+\}) * c \{c\} \{*\}$$

7.5 EXAMPLE—SYNTHESIZED ATTRIBUTES

In the previous sections, we have discussed translations of symbol strings into symbol strings. The symbols involved were all taken from finite sets and did not embody the concept that symbols should have both a class part and a value part. In effect, string translation grammars only have the power to describe the translation of class parts. Now we begin to extend the translation-grammar concept to include value parts as well. The extended concept is called an "attributed grammar" and is described in full in Section 7.7. Here we present a specific attributed grammar to illustrate the concept of a "synthesized attribute."

The basic idea behind the attributed-grammar concept is that value parts are associated with all nodes of a derivation tree, both terminal and nonterminal. The relationships between the input and output values are then expressed on a production-by-production basis in terms of the values appearing on the tree. To illustrate how such relationships might be expressed, we consider a simple example.

Suppose there is a lexical box that supplies input set

$$\{(,), +, *, c\}$$

where c is a token representing a constant and has a value part which is the value of that constant as constructed by the lexical box. Now we consider the problem of designing a syntax box that accepts arithmetic expressions made up of symbols in this input set and outputs the numerical value of the expression. The correspondence between the class parts of the inputs and outputs can be expressed by the following string translation grammar with starting symbol $\langle S \rangle$:

1. $\langle S \rangle \rightarrow \langle E \rangle$ {ANSWER}
2. $\langle E \rangle \rightarrow \langle E \rangle + \langle T \rangle$
3. $\langle E \rangle \rightarrow \langle T \rangle$
4. $\langle T \rangle \rightarrow \langle T \rangle * \langle P \rangle$
5. $\langle T \rangle \rightarrow \langle P \rangle$
6. $\langle P \rangle \rightarrow (\langle E \rangle)$
7. $\langle P \rangle \rightarrow c$

Output symbol ANSWER is to have a value part which is a number. The desired relation between the values of the input tokens and the output token, ANSWER, can be expressed in English: "The value part of ANSWER is the numerical value of the input expression." The objective of this example is to find a mathematical way of expressing the relationship described by that English sentence.

Consider now the specific input sequence

$$(c_3 + c_9) * (c_2 + c_{41})$$

where the value parts of the input symbols as supplied by the lexical box are indicated by subscripts. The prescribed output sequence for this input is, of course,

$$ANSWER_{516}$$

Figure 7.3(a) shows the derivation tree corresponding to the input sequence. We are seeking a method whereby an input sequence and derivation tree can be used to specify value parts of output symbols.

The most natural way to discuss the value of the given input expression is to discuss the value of each of its parts. Since each occurrence of nonterminals $\langle E \rangle$, $\langle T \rangle$, and $\langle P \rangle$ in the derivation tree represents a subexpression of the input expression, the natural value to assign a given occurrence is the numerical value of the subexpression it generates. In Fig. 7.3(b), we show the derivation tree of Fig. 7.3(a) with each nonterminal $\langle E \rangle$, $\langle T \rangle$, and $\langle P \rangle$ labeled with the value of its subexpression and the output symbol labeled with the desired output value.

To specify how values should be placed on derivation trees obtained from this grammar, we first specify how to obtain the value of each nonterminal node given the values of its immediate descendants. The specification is done by associating with each production for $\langle E \rangle$, $\langle T \rangle$, or $\langle P \rangle$ a rule for computing the value of a node corresponding to the lefthand nonterminal, given the values of the immediate descendant nodes corresponding to the symbols on the righthand side.

For instance, the rule for the production

$$\langle E \rangle \rightarrow \langle E \rangle + \langle T \rangle$$

is that the value of the $\langle E \rangle$ on the lefthand side is equal to the sum of the value of the $\langle E \rangle$ on the righthand side and the value of the $\langle T \rangle$. Applying this rule to the leftmost parenthesized $\langle E \rangle$ in the tree of the example, we see that the value of the $\langle E \rangle$ on the righthand side is 3 and the value of the $\langle T \rangle$ is 9. We, therefore, conclude that the value of the $\langle E \rangle$ on the lefthand side is 12, and we attach the value 12 to the corresponding node of the tree.

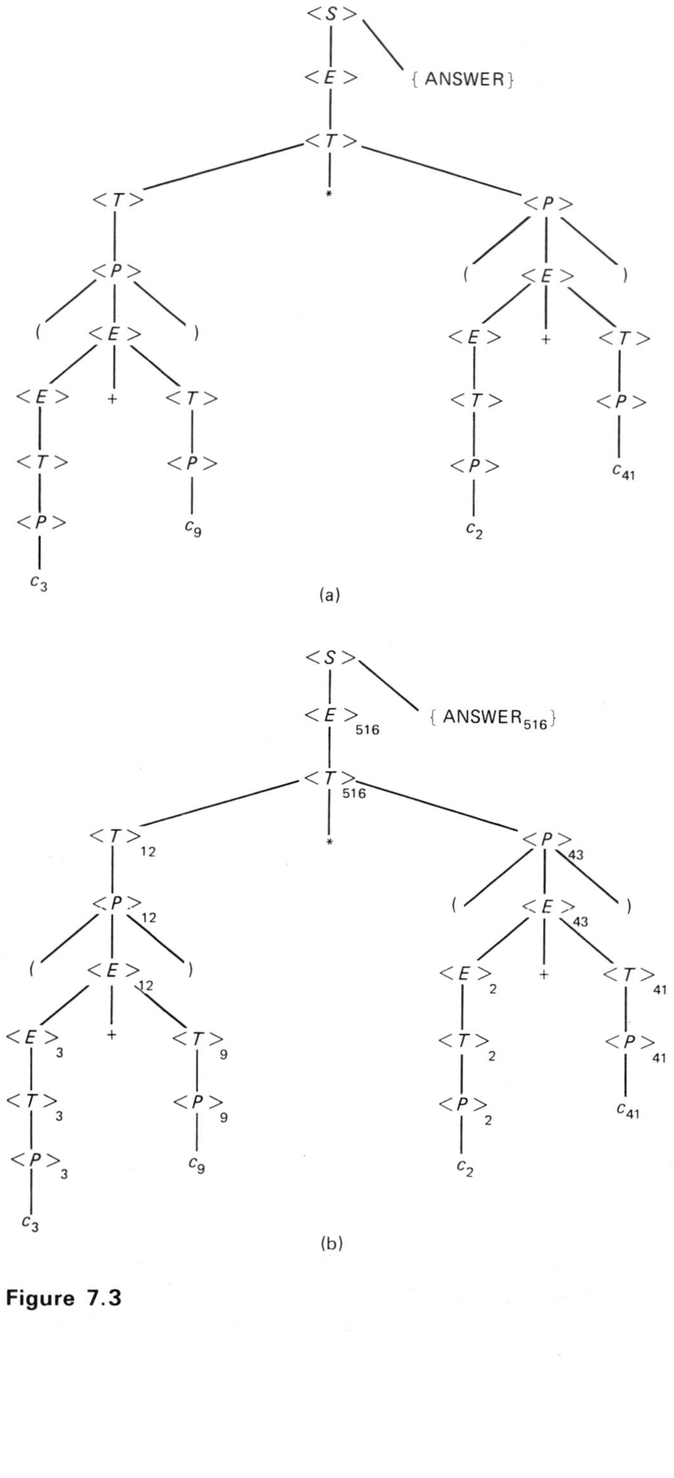
<S>
<E>
{ANSWER}
<T>
<T>
*
<P>
<P>
(
<E>
)
<E>
+
<T>
<T>
<P>
<P>
c3
c9
c2
c41
(a)
<S>
<E>516
{ANSWER516}
<T>516
<T>12
<P>43
<P>12
<E>43
<E>12
<E>2
<T>41
<E>3
<T>9
<T>2
<P>41
<T>3
<P>9
<P>2
<P>3
c3
c9
c2
c41
(b)

Figure 7.3

The rule for the production

$$\langle E \rangle \rightarrow \langle T \rangle$$

is that the value of the $\langle E \rangle$ is equal to the value of the $\langle T \rangle$. The rule for

$$\langle T \rangle \rightarrow \langle T \rangle * \langle P \rangle$$

is that the value of the $\langle T \rangle$ on the lefthand side is equal to the product of the value of the $\langle T \rangle$ on the righthand side and the value of the $\langle P \rangle$. The rule for

$$\langle T \rangle \rightarrow \langle P \rangle$$

is that the value of $\langle T \rangle$ equals the value of $\langle P \rangle$. The rule for

$$\langle P \rangle \rightarrow (\langle E \rangle)$$

is that the value of $\langle P \rangle$ equals the value of $\langle E \rangle$. The rule for

$$\langle P \rangle \rightarrow c$$

is that the value of $\langle P \rangle$ equals the value of c.

Finally, for the production

$$\langle S \rangle \rightarrow \langle E \rangle \ \{\text{ANSWER}\}$$

we supply the rule that the value of ANSWER is equal to the value of $\langle E \rangle$.

In this example, the rules associated with the productions specify how to compute the numerical value of an expression. In this sense, they reflect the "meaning" of the productions. However, the technique of associating rules with each production can be used to specify values that do not necessarily reflect the apparent "meaning" of the input sequence. For instance, the rules for the productions might be used to associate a table entry with each node of the tree.

Continuing with the example, to express the above rules in a more mathematical notation, we can write each production giving a distinct name to each value occurring in the production and then state the rules for the production in terms of these names. For instance, production 2 and the rule for calculating the value of $\langle E \rangle$ can be written

2. $\langle E \rangle_p \rightarrow \langle E \rangle_q + \langle T \rangle_r$
    $p \leftarrow q + r$

where the assignment symbol $\leftarrow$ indicates that attribute p is computed by evaluating the expression on the right (i.e., $q + r$).

The remaining productions in the grammar and their associated rules can be written as

3. $\langle E \rangle_p \rightarrow \langle T \rangle_q$

    $p \leftarrow q$

4. $\langle T \rangle_p \rightarrow \langle T \rangle_q * \langle P \rangle_r$

    $p \leftarrow q * r$

5. $\langle T \rangle_p \rightarrow \langle P \rangle_q$

    $p \leftarrow q$

6. $\langle P \rangle_p \rightarrow (\langle E \rangle_q)$

    $p \leftarrow q$

7. $\langle P \rangle_p \rightarrow c_q$

    $p \leftarrow q$

1. $\langle S \rangle \rightarrow \langle E \rangle_q \{\text{ANSWER}_r\}$

    $r \leftarrow q$

The use of variable names is local to each production, and the use of the same letter such as p in two different productions has no significance. We could just as well have written production 4 as

$$\langle T \rangle_{\text{Zeus}} \rightarrow \langle T \rangle_{\text{Merlin}} * \langle P \rangle_{\text{Hedgehog}}$$
$$\text{Zeus} \leftarrow \text{Merlin} * \text{Hedgehog}$$

The above productions together with their evaluation rules are examples of "attributed productions" and, taken together with starting nonterminal $\langle S \rangle$, constitute an "attributed" grammar. In attribute terminology, the value parts of the above symbols are called "attributes." In later examples, we see that a value part can in fact be a vector of attributes.

In this example, the value of each nonterminal attribute is determined by the symbols below it in a derivation tree. This upward evaluation is reflected by the fact that all the nonterminal attribute evaluation rules associated with the productions tell how to compute the attribute of the lefthand side given the attribute values of the symbols on the right. Attributes whose values are given in this bottom up fashion are traditionally called "synthesized" attributes. In the next section we give an example of nonterminal attributes being passed down a derivation tree.

One final comment on notation. We ordinarily write our action symbols with attributes outside the braces and our standard notation would be

$$\{\text{ANSWER}\}_5 \text{ instead of } \{\text{ANSWER}_5\}$$

However, in cases such as this example where the action symbol has been constructed by putting braces around an output symbol, we take the liberty of placing the attribute inside the braces to suggest that it be emitted as part of the enclosed output symbol.

7.6   EXAMPLE—INHERITED ATTRIBUTES

We now illustrate how attribute information can be specified to flow down a derivation tree. Consider the following grammar with starting symbol ⟨declaration⟩:

1. ⟨declaration⟩ → TYPE *V* ⟨variable list⟩
2. ⟨variable list⟩ → , *V* ⟨variable list⟩
3. ⟨variable list⟩ → ε

This grammar generates declaration statements similar to those found in many programming languages.

Assume there is a lexical box that supplies the three tokens

$$V \qquad \text{TYPE} \qquad ,$$

where *V* is the token for variable and has a value part which is a pointer to the symbol-table entry for that variable; and TYPE is a token with a value part that denotes which one of the types REAL, INTEGER, or BOOLEAN is to be associated with the variables on the list.

In processing the declaration of each variable, the job of the syntax box is to call a procedure SET-TYPE which enters the type, REAL, INTEGER, or BOOLEAN, into the proper field of the symbol-table entry for that variable. An appropriate time to call SET-TYPE is directly after the variable is inputted to the syntax box. This timing is described by the following string translation grammar which uses action symbol {SET-TYPE} to denote the calling of SET-TYPE.

1. ⟨declaration⟩ → TYPE *V* {SET-TYPE} ⟨variable list⟩
2. ⟨variable list⟩ → , *V* {SET-TYPE} ⟨variable list⟩
3. ⟨variable list⟩ → ε

We assume procedure SET-TYPE has two arguments: a pointer to the symbol-table entry for the variable, and the type of the variable. A call on SET-TYPE might thus be expressed as

$$\text{SET-TYPE(pointer, type)}$$

We want to add attributes and attribute evaluation rules to the above grammar so that activity sequences will show input symbols with their value parts as attributes, and so that occurrences of action symbol {SET-TYPE} will have two attributes showing the arguments of the corresponding call on procedure SET-TYPE. Thus occurrences of {SET-TYPE} will have the form

$$\{SET\text{-}TYPE\}_{\text{pointer, type}}$$

The attributed action symbol {SET-TYPE} is a good illustration of the differences between an attribute and a value part. The symbol has two attributes, namely the pointer and the type, but it has only one value part, namely the pair (pointer, type). The attribute concept is thus a refinement of the value-part concept. As we get into the specifics of the attributed grammar model, we deal exclusively with attributes.

Returning to the problem of generating the desired attributed activity sequence, consider how occurrences of {SET-TYPE} can obtain their attributes. In production 1, the job is easy since the attributes of {SET-TYPE} can be obtained from inputs TYPE and V of that production. In production 2, the type is not available, and must be passed somehow using nonterminal attributes. To this end, we let ⟨variable list⟩ have an attribute representing the type, and the desired activity sequences are generated from the following attributed productions:

1. ⟨declaration⟩ $\rightarrow$ TYPE$_t$ V_p {SET-TYPE}$_{p1,\ t1}$ ⟨variable list⟩$_{t2}$
   $$(t2,\ t1) \leftarrow t \qquad p1 \leftarrow p$$
2. ⟨variable list⟩$_t \rightarrow$, V_p {SET-TYPE}$_{p1,\ t1}$ ⟨variable list⟩$_{t2}$
   $$(t2,\ t1) \leftarrow t \qquad p1 \leftarrow p$$
3. ⟨variable list⟩$_t \rightarrow \epsilon$

The notation $(t2,\ t1) \leftarrow t$ means that t is assigned to both $t2$ and $t1$. Figure 7.4 shows the attributed derivation tree for the sequence

$$\text{TYPE}_{\text{REAL}}\ V_1,\ V_2,\ V_3$$

as specified by the grammar.

Note that in Fig. 7.4, the attribute values of the occurrences of nonterminal ⟨variable list⟩ are obtained from symbols above it or from symbols in the same righthand side. The value REAL is obtained from input symbol TYPE, is passed to the uppermost occurrence of ⟨variable list⟩, and is then passed down to other occurrences. This downward evaluation is reflected in the fact that all the nonterminal evaluation rules associated with the productions tell how to compute the attributes of righthand side occurrences of a nonterminal. Attributes whose values are given in this top-down fashion are traditionally called "inherited" attributes.

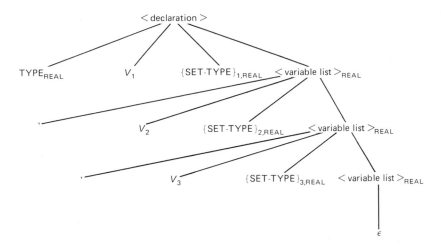

Figure 7.4

  Contrasting the examples of this and the last section, we see that synthesized attribute information is passed up the derivation tree whereas inherited attribute information is passed down. Synthesized attributes have rules associated with lefthand occurrences of a nonterminal whereas inherited attributes have rules associated with righthand occurrences.

  We make one final comment on notation. In contrast to the symbol {ANSWER} of Section 7.5, the action symbol {SET-TYPE} was not constructed by putting an output symbol in braces. Consequently, we stayed with the standard notation of placing action symbol attributes outside the braces.

7.7 ATTRIBUTED TRANSLATION GRAMMARS

Having presented two attributed translation grammars in Section 7.5 and 7.6, we now state precisely what we mean by the term "attributed translation grammar." The definition of attributed grammars incorporates both inherited and synthesized nonterminal attributes as illustrated in the previous examples. Both types are allowed within the same grammar. The definition also distinguishes between synthesized and inherited action-symbol attributes. The action-symbol attributes in the previous examples were all of the inherited type having their values given from above by rules associated with the righthand side occurrences of the action symbol. Synthesized action-symbol attributes are not strictly necessary for specifying translations, but they take on an important role in Chapter 9.

An *attributed translation grammar* is a translation grammar for which the following additional specifications are made:

1. Each input, nonterminal, and action symbol has an associated finite set of attributes, and each attribute has a (possibly infinite) set of permissible values.

2. Each nonterminal and action symbol attribute is classified as being either *inherited* or *synthesized.*

3. Rules for inherited attributes are specified as follows:

   a) For each occurrence of an inherited attribute on the righthand side of a given production, there is an associated rule which describes how to compute a value for that attribute as a function of certain other attributes of symbols occurring in the left- or righthand sides of the given production.

   b) An initial value is specified for each inherited attribute of the starting symbol.

4. Rules for synthesized attributes are specified as follows:

   a) For each occurrence of a synthesized nonterminal attribute on the lefthand side of a given production, there is an associated rule which describes how to compute a value for that attribute as a function of certain other attributes of symbols occurring in the left- or righthand sides of the given production.

   b) For each synthesized action-symbol attribute, there is an associated rule which describes how to compute a value for that attribute as a function of certain other attributes of the action symbol.

Part 1 of the definition says that the input, nonterminal, and action symbols are to be attributed symbols. In making our grammatical specifications, we usually write attributes as subscripts. Each occurrence of a symbol in our specifications is shown with one subscript per attribute.

Part 2 of the definition requires that each nonterminal and action symbol attribute be specified as either synthesized or inherited. This specification is required to indicate whether the attribute value is to be computed by rules meeting the specifications of part 3 or by rules meeting the specifications of part 4. Notationally, we display the symbols with their attributes and say how each attribute is classified. For example, we might write

$$\langle X \rangle_{a,\ b,\ c} \quad \text{SYNTHESIZED } a, c \quad \text{INHERITED } b$$

or

$$\{\text{DOUBLE}\}_{p,\ r} \quad \text{SYNTHESIZED } p \quad \text{INHERITED } r$$

For synthesized attributes of action symbols, the statement that an attribute is synthesized should be accompanied by a rule in accord with Section (b) of rule 4. For example, the attribute specification for action symbol {DOU-BLE} above might include the rule

$$p \leftarrow 2 * r$$

for computing the value of synthesized attribute p.

Section (a) of part 3 and Section (a) of part 4 describe the attribute-evaluation rules that are to be associated with the productions. Section (a) of part 3 refers to inherited attributes of both nonterminals and action symbols since either can occur in a righthand side. To specify the rules associated with a given production, we display the production with a name given to each attribute of each symbol in the production. The attribute names are then used as variables with which to describe the rules.

For example, if $\langle X \rangle$ has three attributes, $\langle Y \rangle$ and $\{Z\}$ two attributes each, and b one attribute, the production

$$\langle X \rangle \rightarrow b \langle Y \rangle \{Z\}$$

might be written as

$$\langle X \rangle_{p,q,r} \rightarrow b_s \langle Y \rangle_{y,u} \{Z\}_{v,w}$$

If q and r were the only synthesized attributes on the left, thereby requiring an evaluation rule under Section (a) of part 4, and if y and v were the only inherited attributes on the right, thereby requiring an evaluation rule under Section (a) of part 3, the above production might be accompanied by rules

$$q \leftarrow \text{SIN}(u + w)$$
$$(r, v) \leftarrow s * u$$
$$y \leftarrow p$$

By custom, we write our rules as assignment statements. The lefthand side of each assignment is always a single attribute or a list of attributes enclosed in parentheses. The righthand side is always some expression. The interpretation is that the value of the righthand expression is to be assigned to each attribute that is part of the lefthand side. The second of the above rules thus assigns the product $s * u$ to both r and v.

Attributed translation grammars are to be used to define attributed derivation trees and then attributed activity sequences and attributed translations. The trees are defined by the following tree construction procedures:

1. Use the underlying unattributed translation grammar to construct a derivation tree for an activity sequence of unattributed input and action symbols.

2. Assign attribute values to the occurrences of input symbols in the derivation tree.

3. Initialize the starting symbol in the derivation tree with the initial inherited attributes.

4. Compute the values of the attributes of the symbols in the derivation tree by repeatedly applying the following until it can no longer be applied: Find an attribute not yet on the tree for which the arguments of its rule are already on the tree; compute the value of the attribute and add this value to the derivation tree.

5. If step 4 results in a tree in which each symbol has an attribute value assigned to each of its attributes, we say that the resulting tree is *complete*. Otherwise we call the tree *incomplete*.

To illustrate the steps, we return to Fig. 7.3 and the grammar of Section 7.5. Figure 7.3(a) shows a derivation tree constructed in step 1 with attribute values assigned to the four occurrences of input *c* as required by step 2. Step 3 applies vacuously because the starting symbol has no attributes; hence Fig. 7.3(a) is also the result of the first three steps. Applying step 4 then changes the tree from Fig. 7.3(a) to the tree of Fig. 7.3(b). This resulting tree is complete since all occurrences of symbols that have an attribute have a value assigned to that attribute.

We note that parts 3 and 4 of the attributed grammar definition guarantee that each attribute of each nonterminal and each action symbol in a derivation tree has an associated evaluation rule. Because each symbol in a derivation tree either is associated with the righthand side of a production (i.e., the production which attaches the symbol to its parent in the tree) or is designated as the root of the tree (in which case the symbol is an occurrence of the starting symbol), each inherited attribute of a given symbol must have a rule under one of the sections of part 3. Because each nonterminal symbol in a derivation tree is associated with a lefthand side, Section (a) of part 4 guarantees that each synthesized nonterminal attribute has a rule. Finally, Section (b) of part 4 guarantees a rule for each synthesized action symbol attribute.

It is important to realize that although each attribute in a tree has an evaluation rule, there is no guarantee that the evaluation can take place and that a complete tree can be obtained. A rule can only be used after values have been obtained for its arguments, and a circular dependence of one attribute on another can sometimes occur. If an attributed grammar is such that the steps 1 through 5 of the tree-building procedure always result in a complete tree, then the grammar is called *well defined*. For purposes of compiler design, we only deal with well-defined attributed grammars.

Knuth [1968] provides a test for deciding if a given attributed grammar is well defined. We do not use this test in this book because our design methods, given later, involve other constraints which themselves imply that the grammar is well defined. We have no applications for grammars which are not well defined.

Given an attributed translation grammar and a derivation tree obtained from that grammar, the sequence of attributed input and action symbols obtained from the derivation tree is an *attributed activity sequence*. The attributed action part of this activity sequence is called a translation of the attributed input part. The set of attributed input part and action part pairs obtainable from the given attributed grammar is called the *attributed translation* specified by that grammar. If an attributed translation grammar has an unambiguous input grammar, then each attributed input sequence has at most one derivation tree and at most one attributed translation.

In many applications, action symbols are constructed by putting output symbols in braces. It is intended that each action symbol represent a routine which outputs the symbol within the braces using the attributes of the action symbol as the attributes of the output. When this interpretation is intended, we refer to the grammar as an *attributed string translation grammar*. This is in contrast with the more general interpretation of attributed action symbols as representing arbitrary routines which use the attributes as arguments.

In the case of an attributed string translation grammar, we think of a sequence of attributed action symbols as being synonymous with the corresponding sequence of attributed output symbols. Thus an attributed string translation grammar can be interpreted as specifying a translation of an attributed input language into an attributed output language. When using attributed string translation grammars, we prefer to write attributed action symbols with attributes displayed inside the braces as subscripts of the enclosed output symbol. Thus if output symbol ADD had three attributes p, q, and r, we would write $\{ADD_{p,q,r}\}$ instead of $\{ADD\}_{p,q,r}$. This choice of notation is made for aesthetic reasons and has no technical significance.

7.8 A TRANSLATION OF ARITHMETIC EXPRESSIONS

In this section we construct an attributed translation grammar to describe the processing of arithmetic expressions by the syntax box of a compiler organized according to the naive model of Section 1.2. According to the naive model, the output of the syntax box is a string of atoms and some tables. It was suggested in Section 1.2 that the atoms for binary operations might have a value part consisting of three pointers to table entries. The entries referenced by these pointers would contain information about the two operands and the result of the operation. We follow that suggestion here and so the desired translation of

$$a + b$$

is

$$\text{ADD}(p_a, p_b, p_r)$$

where p_a and p_b are pointers to table entries representing a and b respectively and p_r is a pointer to a table entry representing the result of the add operation.

Figure 7.5 shows the complete translation of the expression

$$(a + b) * (a + c)$$

including both the atom string and the table entries. The input to the syntax box is not literally this expression but is a string of lexical tokens produced by the lexical box when presented with this expression. We assume each variable is represented by a lexical token of class I (for identifier) and that the value part of this token is a pointer to a corresponding table entry. In the figure, the value parts are indicated by subscripts.

The table entries in Fig. 7.5 are shown as belonging to a single table, but some implementations might have the identifiers and partial results in separate tables, particularly if the identifier entries are created by the lexical box and the partial-result entries by the syntax box. Furthermore, the actual values of the pointers to the table entries might be different than shown in Fig. 7.5, depending on the order in which the table entries are reserved. For instance, it is quite possible for b to have position 1 and a to have position 2.

In general, we want the atom strings produced by the syntax box to have the following properties.

Expression:	$(a + b) * (a + c)$
Input:	$(I_1 + I_2) * (I_1 + I_4)$
Output:	ADD(1, 2, 3) ADD(1, 4, 5) MULT(3, 5, 6)

Table entries:		
①	IDENTIFIER	a
②	IDENTIFIER	b
③	PARTIAL RESULT	
④	IDENTIFIER	c
⑤	PARTIAL RESULT	
⑥	PARTIAL RESULT	

Figure 7.5

1. Each binary operation in the input sequence is represented by an atom.
2. The atoms in the atom string are in the same order as the operations are to be performed at execution time.
3. Each atom has three pointers to table entries:
   a) the left operand,
   b) the right operand,
   c) the result of the operation.

To see that this proposed syntax box output does in fact provide enough information for the code generator to do its job, let us consider briefly how the code generator can use this output to generate a suitable sequence of machine-language instructions.

The atoms serve as instructions to the code generator as to what operations are to be performed at execution time. The table entries can be used by the code generator to store and retrieve information about the run-time location of variables and partial results. For example, when the code generator processes the ADD(1, 2, 3) atom in the atom string of Fig. 7.5, it can use the table entry at location 3 to store the run-time location of the partial result. This information can be retrieved when the code generator encounters the MULT(3, 5, 6) atom so that the code generated to do the multiplication will fetch its left operand from the correct run-time location.

Returning to the problem of the syntax-box design, we wish to specify a translation into the proposed set of atoms. As a first step we design a translation grammar which specifies when the atoms should be put out. We introduce the action symbols {ADD} and {MULT} corresponding to the ADD and MULT atoms.

We decide that we want the syntax box to put out each atom as soon as possible. The correct time to produce the ADD atom is after the two operands of a + have been processed since processing these operands might require the putting out of atoms that should precede the ADD in the atom string. Similarly, the MULT atom should be put out after the two operands of a * have been processed. This timing is achieved by placing {ADD} and {MULT} at the extreme right of the corresponding productions, thus obtaining the following translation grammar with starting nonterminal $\langle E \rangle$:

$$\langle E \rangle \rightarrow \langle E \rangle + \langle T \rangle \{\text{ADD}\}$$
$$\langle E \rangle \rightarrow \langle T \rangle$$
$$\langle T \rangle \rightarrow \langle T \rangle * \langle P \rangle \{\text{MULT}\}$$
$$\langle T \rangle \rightarrow \langle P \rangle$$
$$\langle P \rangle \rightarrow (\langle E \rangle)$$
$$\langle P \rangle \rightarrow I$$

This placement of {ADD} and {MULT} is the same as the placement of {+} and {*} in the Polish translation of Section 7.3.

Using this grammar for the input sequence

$$(a + b) * (a + c)$$

translated in Fig. 7.5, the specified activity sequence is

$$(a + b \,\{\text{ADD}\}) * (a + c \,\{\text{ADD}\}) \,\{\text{MULT}\}$$

and the corresponding output part is

$$\text{ADD} \qquad \text{ADD} \qquad \text{MULT}$$

which is the order in which the atoms should be put out.

We now invent attributes and rules to make this grammar into an attributed string translation grammar from which suitable values for the output symbols can be computed.

The basic plan is to let each nonterminal have a single synthesized attribute which is a pointer to a table entry representing the expression it generates. Input symbol I has a single attribute which is a pointer to its table entry as supplied by the lexical box. Each output symbol, ADD or MULT, has three (inherited) attributes, a pointer each for its left operand, right operand, and result. To illustrate the attributes associated with a specific

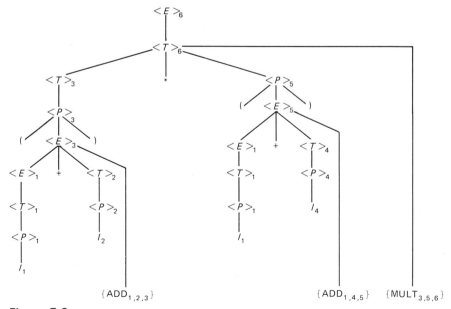

Figure 7.6

derivation tree, Fig. 7.6 shows the derivation tree and attributes for input sequence

$$(a + b) * (a + c)$$

used in Fig. 7.5 to illustrate the translation.

A translation grammar to carry out this plan is the following:

$$\langle E \rangle_x \qquad \text{SYNTHESIZED } x$$
$$\langle T \rangle_x \qquad \text{SYNTHESIZED } x$$
$$\langle P \rangle_x \qquad \text{SYNTHESIZED } x$$
$$\{\text{ADD}_{y,z,p}\} \qquad \text{INHERITED } y, z, p$$
$$\{\text{MULT}_{y,z,p}\} \qquad \text{INHERITED } y, z, p$$

Starting symbol: $\langle E \rangle$

1. $\langle E \rangle_x \rightarrow \langle E \rangle_q + \langle T \rangle_r \ \{\text{ADD}_{y,z,p}\}$
   $\quad (x, p) \leftarrow \text{NEWT} \quad y \leftarrow q \quad z \leftarrow r$

2. $\langle E \rangle_x \rightarrow \langle T \rangle_p$
   $\quad x \leftarrow p$

3. $\langle T \rangle_x \rightarrow \langle T \rangle_q * \langle P \rangle_r \ \{\text{MULT}_{y,z,p}\}$
   $\quad (x, p) \leftarrow \text{NEWT} \quad y \leftarrow q \quad z \leftarrow r$

4. $\langle T \rangle_x \rightarrow \langle P \rangle_p$
   $\quad x \leftarrow p$

5. $\langle P \rangle_x \rightarrow (\ \langle E \rangle_p \ )$
   $\quad x \leftarrow p$

6. $\langle P \rangle_x \rightarrow I_p$
   $\quad x \leftarrow p$

The expression

$$(x, p) \leftarrow \text{NEWT}$$

in production 1 is intended to indicate that p and x are to be computed by calling a system procedure NEWT which supplies a pointer to some unused table entry. This pointer is used as both the third attribute of output symbol ADD and the attribute of lefthand side $\langle E \rangle$.

7.9   TRANSLATION OF SOME MINI-BASIC STATEMENTS

In the last section we used an attributed grammar to specify a translation of arithmetic expressions into atoms. To illustrate how these productions might be used as part of a larger translation, we now give attributed productions for two MINI-BASIC statements which involve expressions.

First consider the assignment statement which we assume is specified by the production

$$\langle statement \rangle \rightarrow \text{LET VARIABLE} = \langle expression \rangle$$

As in the last section, we assume terminal VARIABLE has one attribute which is a pointer to a table entry for the variable, and we assume nonterminal $\langle expression \rangle$ has one synthesized attribute which is a pointer to a table entry for the expression. We introduce a new atom for assignment

$$\text{ASSIGN}(x, y)$$

where x is a pointer to the table entry for the variable and y is a pointer to the table entry for the expression. As an example, the translation of

$$\text{LET } A = B + C$$

is illustrated in Fig. 7.7.

Treating the two pointers of ASSIGN as inherited attributes, the translation of the assignment statement can be specified by the attributed production

$$\langle statement \rangle \rightarrow \text{LET VARIABLE}_{\text{VAR1}} = \langle expression \rangle_{\text{EXP1}}$$

$$\{\text{ASSIGN}_{\text{VAR2,EXP2}}\}$$

$$\text{VAR2} \leftarrow \text{VAR1} \qquad \text{EXP2} \leftarrow \text{EXP1}$$

Now consider the IF statement, which we assume is specified by the production

$$\langle statement \rangle \rightarrow \text{IF } \langle expression \rangle \text{ RELATIONAL OPERATOR } \langle expression \rangle$$

$$\text{GOTO NUMBER}$$

The terminal RELATIONAL OPERATOR has a single attribute that denotes the relational operator it represents. The terminal NUMBER has an

Statement:	LET A = B + C
Input:	LET VARIABLE$_1$ = VARIABLE$_2$ + VARIABLE$_3$
Output:	ADD$_{2,3,4}$ ASSIGN$_{1,4}$

Table entries:			
	①	IDENTIFIER	A
	②	IDENTIFIER	B
	③	IDENTIFIER	C
	④	PARTIAL RESULT	

Figure 7.7

```
Statement:      IF A7 * B < 32 GOTO 360
Input:          IF VARIABLE₁ * VARIABLE₂ RELATIONAL OPERATOR<
                CONSTANT₄ GOTO NUMBER₅
Output:         MULT₁,₂,₃ CONDJUMP₃,₄,<,₅
Table entries:  (1)    IDENTIFIER      A7
                (2)    IDENTIFIER      B
                (3)    PARTIAL RESULT
                (4)    CONSTANT        32
                (5)    LINE NUMBER     360
```

Figure 7.8

attribute which is a pointer to a table entry for the line number involved. Nonterminal ⟨expression⟩ is to have the same synthesized attribute as before. We introduce a new atom

$$\text{CONDJUMP}(a, b, c, d)$$

(conditional jump) where a is a pointer to the table entry for the first expression, b is a pointer to the table entry for the second expression, c denotes the relational operator involved, and d is a pointer to the table entry for the line number. As an example, the translation of

$$\text{IF A7 * B} < 32 \text{ GOTO 360}$$

is illustrated in Fig. 7.8. The atom CONDJUMP tells the code generator to produce code to perform the relational operation indicated by c on the expressions denoted by a and b and if the relation is satisfied to transfer control to the line denoted by d.

The translation can be specified by the attributed production

$$\langle\text{statement}\rangle \rightarrow \text{IF } \langle\text{expression}\rangle_{E1} \text{ RELATIONAL OPERATOR}_{R1}$$
$$\langle\text{expression}\rangle_{E2} \text{ GOTO NUMBER}_{LN1} \{\text{CONDJUMP}_{E3, E4, R2, LN2}\}$$
$$E3 \leftarrow E1 \qquad E4 \leftarrow E2 \qquad R2 \leftarrow R1 \qquad LN2 \leftarrow LN1$$

where the attributes of CONDJUMP are inherited.

7.10   ANOTHER ATTRIBUTED TRANSLATION GRAMMAR FOR EXPRESSIONS

Any given attributed translation can be described by many attributed translation grammars. In this section we use the alternate grammar for arithmetic expressions given in Section 6.10 as the input grammar of an attributed translation grammar that describes the same translation into ADD and MULT atoms described in Section 7.8. This example demonstrates a number of new ways to use attributes.

We begin with a somewhat simpler example based on the following input grammar with starting symbol $\langle E \rangle$.

1. $\langle E \rangle \rightarrow I \langle R \rangle$
2. $\langle R \rangle \rightarrow + I \langle R \rangle$
3. $\langle R \rangle \rightarrow - I \langle R \rangle$
4. $\langle R \rangle \rightarrow \epsilon$

We assume that I represents an identifier and has a value part consisting of a pointer to a table entry for the identifier.

This grammar generates a list of I's separated by $+$'s and $-$'s. The generated language is in fact the set of unparenthesized expressions over identifiers using only the binary operators $+$ and $-$.

Suppose we wish to translate an input sequence into an atom sequence similar to that described in Sections 1.2 and 7.8. Specifically, we wish to use the atoms ADD and SUBTRACT. Each atom is to have a value consisting of three pointers for the left operand, right operand, and result. We wish to output each atom immediately after its two operands have been processed. In production 2, the right operand of the $+$ is the I, so we wish to output the ADD atom for the $+$ immediately after the I. Similarly, in production 3, we wish to output the SUBTRACT atom for the $-$ immediately after the I. The timing of the output symbols is specified by the following string translation grammar.

1. $\langle E \rangle \rightarrow I \langle R \rangle$
2. $\langle R \rangle \rightarrow + I \{\text{ADD}\} \langle R \rangle$
3. $\langle R \rangle \rightarrow - I \{\text{SUBTRACT}\} \langle R \rangle$
4. $\langle R \rangle \rightarrow \epsilon$

Now we add attributes to the grammar to specify the three pointers of each atom. Nonterminal $\langle R \rangle$ is given an inherited attribute that is a pointer to the table entry for the partial result preceding the $\langle R \rangle$. Specifically, the attributed translation grammar is the following:

$$\langle R \rangle_p \qquad \text{INHERITED}_p$$

Attributes of action symbols are INHERITED.

1. $\langle E \rangle \rightarrow I_{p1} \langle R \rangle_{p2}$
   $$p2 \leftarrow p1$$

2. $\langle R \rangle_{p1} \rightarrow + I_{q1} \{ADD_{p2,q2,r1}\} \langle R \rangle_{r2}$
   $(r2, r1) \leftarrow NEWT \qquad p2 \leftarrow p1 \qquad q2 \leftarrow q1$
3. $\langle R \rangle_{p1} \rightarrow - I_{q1} \{SUBTRACT_{p2,q2,r1}\} \langle R \rangle_{r2}$
   $(r2, r1) \leftarrow NEWT \qquad p2 \leftarrow p1 \qquad q2 \leftarrow q1$
4. $\langle R \rangle_r \rightarrow \epsilon$

As an example, an attributed derivation tree for the input sequence

$$I_1 - I_2 + I_3$$

is shown in Fig. 7.9(a). In this figure we assume that the system procedure NEWT supplies the values 4 and 5 for the partial-result table entries.

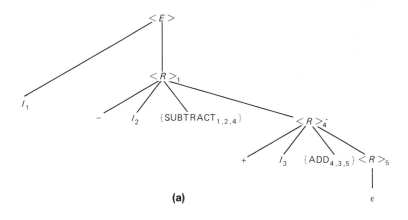

(a)

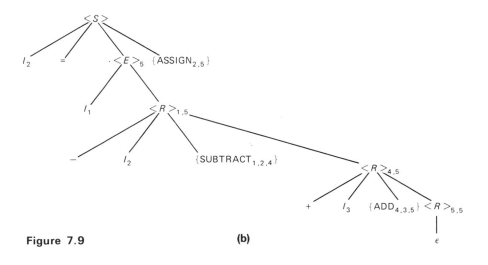

Figure 7.9   (b)

Observe that the attribute of $\langle R \rangle$ is a pointer to the table entry for the partial result of the subexpression preceding the $\langle R \rangle$. This partial result is also the left operand of the first operator generated by the $\langle R \rangle$ if such an operator exists.

Suppose now that an assignment statement is generated by the following production

$$\langle S \rangle \to I = \langle E \rangle$$

with the previous productions for $\langle E \rangle$ and suppose we wish to translate an assignment statement into an atom string ending with the ASSIGN atom, as described in Section 7.9. We decide we want $\langle E \rangle$ to have a synthesized attribute that equals a pointer to the table entry for the expression generated by $\langle E \rangle$. We change the grammar to the following grammar, with starting symbol $\langle S \rangle$.

$$\langle E \rangle_t \qquad \text{SYNTHESIZED } t$$
$$\langle R \rangle_{p,t} \qquad \text{INHERITED } p \qquad \text{SYNTHESIZED } t$$

Attributes of action symbols are INHERITED.

5. $\langle S \rangle \to I_{p1} = \langle E \rangle_{q1} \, \{\text{ASSIGN}_{p2,q2}\}$
   $p2 \leftarrow p1 \qquad q2 \leftarrow q1$

1. $\langle E \rangle_{t2} \to I_{p1} \, \langle R \rangle_{p2,t1}$
   $p2 \leftarrow p1 \qquad t2 \leftarrow t1$

2. $\langle R \rangle_{p1,t2} \to + \, I_{q1} \, \{\text{ADD}_{p2,q2,r1}\} \, \langle R \rangle_{r2,t1}$
   $(r2, r1) \leftarrow \text{NEWT} \qquad p2 \leftarrow p1 \qquad q2 \leftarrow q1 \qquad t2 \leftarrow t1$

3. $\langle R \rangle_{p1,t2} \to - \, I_{q1} \, \{\text{SUBTRACT}_{p2,q2,r1}\} \, \langle R \rangle_{r2,t1}$
   $(r2, r1) \leftarrow \text{NEWT} \qquad p2 \leftarrow p1 \qquad q2 \leftarrow q1 \qquad t2 \leftarrow t1$

4. $\langle R \rangle_{p1,p2} \to \epsilon$
   $p2 \leftarrow p1$

As an example, the attributed derivation tree for the input sequence

$$I_2 = I_1 - I_2 + I_3$$

is shown in Fig. 7.9(b). Observe that in the application of production 4, the synthesized attribute of $\langle R \rangle$ is computed as being equal to the inherited attribute of $\langle R \rangle$. This value is then passed up the tree as the synthesized attribute of the lefthand nonterminal of productions 2, 3, and 1 and is used as an attribute of the ASSIGN atom.

Now we turn our attention to the grammar of Section 6.10 using only binary $+$ and $*$.

1. $\langle E \rangle \to \langle T \rangle \, \langle E\text{-list} \rangle$

2. $\langle E\text{-list}\rangle \rightarrow + \langle T\rangle \langle E\text{-list}\rangle$
3. $\langle E\text{-list}\rangle \rightarrow \epsilon$
4. $\langle T\rangle \rightarrow \langle P\rangle \langle T\text{-list}\rangle$
5. $\langle T\text{-list}\rangle \rightarrow * \langle P\rangle \langle T\text{-list}\rangle$
6. $\langle T\text{-list}\rangle \rightarrow \epsilon$
7. $\langle P\rangle \rightarrow (\langle E\rangle)$
8. $\langle P\rangle \rightarrow I$

Suppose we wish to translate expressions in this grammar into ADD and MULT atoms as in Section 7.8. As before we wish to output the atom for

$$\langle E\rangle_p \qquad \text{SYNTHESIZED } p$$
$$\langle T\rangle_p \qquad \text{SYNTHESIZED } p$$
$$\langle P\rangle_p \qquad \text{SYNTHESIZED } p$$
$$\langle E\text{-list}\rangle_{p,q} \qquad \text{INHERITED } p \quad \text{SYNTHESIZED } q$$
$$\langle T\text{-list}\rangle_{p,q} \qquad \text{INHERITED } p \quad \text{SYNTHESIZED } q$$

Attributes of action symbols are INHERITED.

1. $\langle E\rangle_{t2} \rightarrow \langle T\rangle_{p1} \langle E\text{-list}\rangle_{p2,t1}$
   $p2 \leftarrow p1 \qquad t2 \leftarrow t1$
2. $\langle E\text{-list}\rangle_{p1,t2} \rightarrow + \langle T\rangle_{q1} \{\text{ADD}_{p2,q2,r1}\} \langle E\text{-list}\rangle_{r2,t1}$
   $(r2, r1) \leftarrow \text{NEWT} \qquad p2 \leftarrow p1 \qquad q2 \leftarrow q1 \qquad t2 \leftarrow t1$
3. $\langle E\text{-list}\rangle_{p1,p2} \rightarrow \epsilon$
   $p2 \leftarrow p1$
4. $\langle T\rangle_{t2} \rightarrow \langle P\rangle_{p1} \langle T\text{-list}\rangle_{p2,t1}$
   $p2 \leftarrow p1 \qquad t2 \leftarrow t1$
5. $\langle T\text{-list}\rangle_{p1,t2} \rightarrow * \langle P\rangle_{q1} \{\text{MULT}_{p2,q2,r1}\} \langle T\text{-list}\rangle_{r2,t1}$
   $(r2, r1) \leftarrow \text{NEWT} \qquad p2 \leftarrow p1 \qquad q2 \leftarrow q1 \qquad t2 \leftarrow t1$
6. $\langle T\text{-list}\rangle_{p1,p2} \rightarrow \epsilon$
   $p2 \leftarrow p1$
7. $\langle P\rangle_{p2} \rightarrow (\langle E\rangle_{p1})$
   $p2 \leftarrow p1$
8. $\langle P\rangle_{p2} \rightarrow I_{p1}$
   $p2 \leftarrow p1$

Figure 7.10

each operator immediately after its right operand has been processed. This time, however, the right operand, instead of being just an I, can be an entire subexpression. Thus in production 2, the right operand of the $+$ operator is generated from the $\langle T \rangle$ following the $+$. Hence the timing for emitting the atoms is given by the string translation grammar:

1. $\langle E \rangle \rightarrow \langle T \rangle \langle E\text{-list} \rangle$
2. $\langle E\text{-list} \rangle \rightarrow + \langle T \rangle \{\text{ADD}\} \langle E\text{-list} \rangle$
3. $\langle E\text{-list} \rangle \rightarrow \epsilon$
4. $\langle T \rangle \rightarrow \langle P \rangle \langle T\text{-list} \rangle$
5. $\langle T\text{-list} \rangle \rightarrow * \langle P \rangle \{\text{MULT}\} \langle T\text{-list} \rangle$
6. $\langle T\text{-list} \rangle \rightarrow \epsilon$
7. $\langle P \rangle \rightarrow (\langle E \rangle)$
8. $\langle P \rangle \rightarrow I$

Attributes can be added to this grammar using the same reasoning as in the similar examples; we let $\langle E \rangle$, $\langle T \rangle$, and $\langle P \rangle$ each have a synthesized attribute corresponding to the table entry for their result. The resulting grammar is shown in Fig. 7.10.

The attributed-derivation tree for the expression

$$I_1 + I_2 * I_3$$

is shown in Fig. 7.11.

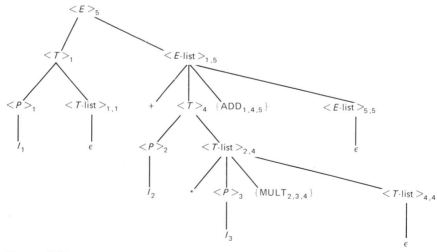

Figure 7.11

7.11 AMBIGUOUS GRAMMARS AND MULTIPLE TRANSLATIONS

As explained in Section 6.6, a grammar is called *ambiguous* if there exists a string in the language for which there is more than one derivation tree. For example, using the grammar

$$\langle E \rangle \rightarrow \langle E \rangle \, t \, \langle E \rangle$$
$$\langle E \rangle \rightarrow x$$

The string *xtxtx* has two derivation trees corresponding to the leftmost derivations

$$\langle E \rangle \Rightarrow \langle E \rangle \, t \, \langle E \rangle \Rightarrow \langle E \rangle \, t \, \langle E \rangle \, t \, \langle E \rangle \Rightarrow x \, t \, \langle E \rangle \, t \, \langle E \rangle$$
$$\Rightarrow x \, t \, x \, t \, \langle E \rangle \Rightarrow x \, t \, x \, t \, x$$
$$\langle E \rangle \Rightarrow \langle E \rangle \, t \, \langle E \rangle \Rightarrow x \, t \, \langle E \rangle \Rightarrow x \, t \, \langle E \rangle \, t \, \langle E \rangle$$
$$\Rightarrow x \, t \, x \, t \, \langle E \rangle \Rightarrow x \, t \, x \, t \, x$$

The two derivation trees are shown in Fig. 7.12. When ambiguous grammars are made into translation grammars by adding action symbols, certain input strings may have more than one translation. In the present example, this occurs when output symbols *T* and *X* are added to obtain string translation grammar:

$$\langle E \rangle \rightarrow \langle E \rangle \, t \, \langle E \rangle \, \{T\}$$
$$\langle E \rangle \rightarrow x \, \{X\}$$

The two derivations shown above yield different activity sequences for input sequence *xtxtx*, namely:

$$x \, \{X\} \, t \, x \, \{X\} \, \{T\} \, t \, x \, \{X\} \, \{T\} \qquad \text{and} \qquad x \, \{X\} \, t \, x \, \{X\} \, t \, x \, \{X\} \, \{T\} \, \{T\}$$

The output parts of these activity sequences are *XXTXT* and *XXXTT*, respectively. Interpreting *t* as a binary operator and *x* as an operand, the two

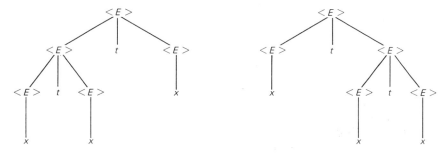

Figure 7.12 Two derivation trees for *xtxtx*

output sequences represent two Polish expressions which are evaluated differently. The first translation calls for the left operation to be done first as in $(xtx)tx$ and the second calls for the right operation to be done first as in $xt(xtx)$.

From the standpoint of compiler design, ambiguous translations are of dubious value since a compiler can produce only a single translation for a given input sequence. One possible interpretation is that the person specifying the ambiguous translation is willing to have the compiler produce either translation. This might occur in the present example if the binary operation t was really addition since, mathematically:

$$(x_1 + x_2) + x_3 = x_1 + (x_2 + x_3)$$

It would certainly not occur if the operation were subtraction since:

$$(x_1 - x_2) - x_3 \neq x_1 - (x_2 - x_3)$$

In any event, the most useful syntax-processing techniques are based on grammars which are known to be unambiguous, so we treat ambiguity as an evil to be avoided.

Given an ambiguous grammar for some context-free language, it is sometimes but not always possible to find an unambiguous grammar for the same language. In the current example, there are many unambiguous alternative grammars including the following two:

$$\langle E \rangle \rightarrow \langle E \rangle \ t \ \langle T \rangle$$
$$\langle E \rangle \rightarrow \langle T \rangle$$
$$\langle T \rangle \rightarrow x$$

and

$$\langle E \rangle \rightarrow \langle T \rangle \ t \ \langle E \rangle$$
$$\langle E \rangle \rightarrow \langle T \rangle$$
$$\langle T \rangle \rightarrow x$$

The first of these grammars is suitable for defining translations in which the leftmost operation is done first; the second is suitable for doing the rightmost operation first.

Mathematically, a translation grammar may specify many translations for a given input sequence and one should refer to any *one* output sequence as being *a* translation of the corresponding input sequence. In the unambiguous case, it is quite proper to refer to *the* translation. As most of the grammars we deal with are unambiguous, we sometimes refer to *the* translation without going through the ritual of pointing out that the particular grammar under consideration is in fact unambiguous.

To see how ambiguity might sneak up on an unsuspecting language designer, suppose one designed a grammar which included the two product-ions

$$\langle S \rangle \rightarrow \text{if } \langle B \rangle \text{ then } \langle S \rangle \text{ else } \langle S \rangle$$
$$\langle S \rangle \rightarrow \text{if } \langle B \rangle \text{ then } \langle S \rangle$$

where $\langle S \rangle$ is short for $\langle$statement$\rangle$ and $\langle B \rangle$ is short for $\langle$Boolean expres-sion$\rangle$. The preliminary version of ALGOL 60 actually allowed these con-structs but now the ALGOL grammar restricts the kind of statement that can follow the word **then.** The intended interpretation of each production is clear, but the meaning of the language is ambiguous since there are two derivation trees corresponding to

$$\langle S \rangle \overset{*}{\Rightarrow} \text{if } \langle B \rangle \text{ then if } \langle B \rangle \text{ then } \langle S \rangle \text{ else } \langle S \rangle$$

as shown in Fig. 7.13. Using the interpretation suggested by Fig. 7.13(a), the statement

if true then if false then PRINT("X") **else** PRINT("Y")

would cause a "Y" to be printed as output whereas the execution of the statement as suggested by Fig. 7.13(b) would not result in any output. This suggests that the grammar should be redesigned to exclude one of these interpretations.

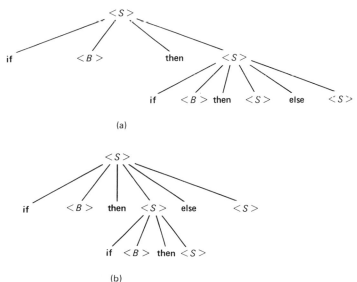

Figure 7.13

7.12 REFERENCES

Syntax-directed translations were first used in Irons [1961, 1963a], and further expounded in Cheatham and Sattley [1964]. The use of action routines is also implied in Brooker and Morris [1960, 1962]. Mathematical models of syntax-directed translations have been developed and studied in Petrone [1965], Culik [1966], Paull [1967], Younger [1967], Lewis and Stearns [1968], Aho and Ullman [1969a, 1969b], and Vere [1970]. Attributed grammars with synthesized and inherited attributes were introduced and studied in Knuth [1968a]. The specific model of attributed translation grammars presented in this chapter was introduced in Lewis, Rosenkrantz, and Stearns [1974].

PROBLEMS

1. What is the value of the following postfix Polish expressions:

a) $3\ 7\ 11\ +\ *\ 4\ -$

b) $16\ 9\ 5\ 2\ *\ +\ *$

c) $1\ 2\ 3\ -\ 4\ 5\ *\ 6\ 7\ +\ *\ +\ -$

2. Find the translation into postfix Polish of the expression

$$a + b * c * (b + a) * (c + a)$$

according to the translation grammar of Section 7.3.

3. Suppose that in postfix Polish notation the symbol $-$ was used for both unary and binary subtraction. Show that in this case the expression

$$7\ 5\ -\ -$$

would have two different interpretations yielding different values.

4. Find a string translation grammar that will translate MINI-BASIC arithmetic expressions as defined in the grammar of Section 6.15 into postfix Polish. The Polish expressions should use different symbols for the unary and binary operators.

5. Find a string translation grammar that will translate postfix Polish arithmetic expressions using addition (unary and binary), multiplication, and exponentiation into infix notation.

6. In prefix Polish notation, the operators occur before their operands, so that for instance the infix expression

$$a + b * c$$

has as its corresponding prefix Polish expression

$$+ a * bc$$

For expressions involving $+$ and $*$ and variables find a string translation grammar that specifies the translation of:

a) infix expressions into prefix Polish,

b) prefix Polish expressions into postfix Polish,

c) postfix Polish expressions into prefix Polish,

d) prefix Polish expressions into infix.

7. Find the translation of the sequence

POLISH

according to the following string translation grammar with starting symbol $\langle S \rangle$.

$\langle S \rangle \rightarrow P \{LU\} \langle S \rangle \langle H \rangle$

$\langle S \rangle \rightarrow \{K\} O \langle D \rangle L$

$\langle S \rangle \rightarrow \{W\} IS \langle E \rangle$

$\langle S \rangle \rightarrow \epsilon$

$\langle D \rangle \rightarrow \langle T \rangle \{AS\} \langle K \rangle$

$\langle K \rangle \rightarrow \langle T \rangle \{IE\}$

$\langle E \rangle \rightarrow \langle T \rangle \{IC\}$

$\langle H \rangle \rightarrow \langle S \rangle \langle U \rangle \{Z\} \langle Y \rangle$

$\langle Y \rangle \rightarrow H$

$\langle T \rangle \rightarrow \epsilon$

$\langle U \rangle \rightarrow \epsilon$

8. Find a string translation grammar that will accept as input an arbitrary sequence of 0's and 1's and produce as output

a) the reverse of the input sequence,

b) the null sequence ϵ,

c) the input sequence itself,

d) the sequence $0^n 1^m$, where n is the number of 0's in the input sequence and m is the number of 1's in the input sequence.

9. Find a string translation grammar corresponding to each of the translations described in Problem 13 of Chapter 5.

10. Find a string translation grammar that will translate infix arithmetic expressions into functional notation, so that, for example

$$a + b \text{ becomes } f_+(a, b)$$

and

$$a + b * c \text{ becomes } f_+(a, f_*(b, c))$$

where f_+ and f_* are single symbols.

11. What does the following string translation grammar do?

$$\langle S \rangle \rightarrow \{C\} EN \{HI\} G L \{N\} I \{E\} S \{SE\} H$$

12. Two of the activity sequences generated by a particular translation grammar are

$$\{x\} \{y\} b \{z\}$$

and:

$$\{q\} a \{x\} \{y\} b \{z\} \{x\} \{x\} \{y\} b \{z\} \{y\}$$

The input grammar obtained by deleting the action symbols from the translation grammar is

$\langle S \rangle \rightarrow a \langle S \rangle \langle S \rangle$

$\langle S \rangle \rightarrow b$

What is the translation grammar?

13. List all the pairs belonging to the syntax directed translation defined by the following translation grammar with starting symbol $\langle S \rangle$.

$\langle S \rangle \rightarrow \langle A \rangle \{x\} \ c \ \langle B \rangle \{y\}$

$\langle S \rangle \rightarrow \{y\} \ d \ \{x\} \ c \ \{z\} \ b$

$\langle A \rangle \rightarrow \langle B \rangle \ a \ \{y\}$

$\langle A \rangle \rightarrow d$

$\langle B \rangle \rightarrow b \ \{x\}$

14. Find a string translation grammar that will accept as input any sequence accepted by the following finite-state machine and produce as output the state sequence of the machine while processing that input. For instance, the input sequence 1010 should be translated into $ABBCD$.

	0	1	
A	A	B	0
B	B	C	1
C	D	A	0
D	A	D	1

15. Find a string translation grammar that will translate the FORTRAN logical IF statement into ALGOL.

16. Find a string translation grammar that will translate FORTRAN Boolean expressions into ALGOL Boolean expressions which have the same value.

17. Find a string translation grammar that will translate IF statements in ALGOL into IF statements in PL/I.

18. Find string translation grammars that will translate ADD, SUBTRACT, MULTIPLY and DIVIDE statements in COBOL into MINI-BASIC.

19. Find the atom string and table that will result when the expression

$$a + b * c * (b + a) * (c + a)$$

is translated according to the attributed grammar in Section 7.8.

20. Consider the following attributed grammar with starting symbol $\langle S \rangle$ whose starting inherited attribute is 1.

$\langle S \rangle_{p,q}$ SYNTHESIZED p INHERITED q

$\langle A \rangle_{p,q}$ SYNTHESIZED p INHERITED q

Attributes of action symbols are INHERITED.

1. $\langle S \rangle_{p4,q1} \to a_{p1} \langle S \rangle_{t1,p2} \, b_{s1} \, \{c_{q2,p3}\} \, \langle A \rangle_{r1,q3} \, \{d_{r2,s2,t2}\}$
   $\qquad (p2,\ p3,\ p4) \leftarrow p1 \qquad (q2,\ q3) \leftarrow q1 \qquad s2 \leftarrow s1 \qquad t2 \leftarrow t1 \qquad r2 \leftarrow r1$

2. $\langle S \rangle_{p2,p1} \to \epsilon$
   $\qquad p2 \leftarrow p1$

3. $\langle A \rangle_{p3,t1} \to \langle S \rangle_{p1,t2} \, b_{q1} \, \langle A \rangle_{r1,q2} \, \langle A \rangle_{s1,q3} \, \{f_{r2,s2,p2}\}$
   $\qquad (p2,\ p3) \leftarrow p1 \qquad (q2,\ q3) \leftarrow q1 \qquad r2 \leftarrow r1 \qquad s2 \leftarrow s1 \qquad t2 \leftarrow t1$

4. $\langle A \rangle_{p2,q1} \to \{e_{q2}\} \, c_{p1}$
   $\qquad p2 \leftarrow p1 \qquad q2 \leftarrow q1$

and input sequence:

$$a_1 \, b_2 \, a_3 \, b_4 \, c_5 \, b_2 \, c_6 \, c_7$$

a) Draw the derivation tree for the input sequence with the attributes on all the symbols.

b) What is the prescribed action sequence?

21. For the following attributed string translation grammar with starting non-terminal $\langle S \rangle$

$\langle T \rangle_{u,v,w,x} \qquad$ INHERITED u, $v \qquad$ SYNTHESIZED w, x

Attributes of action symbols are INHERITED.

$\langle S \rangle \to d \, \langle T \rangle_{p,q,r,s}$

$\qquad p \leftarrow r$

$\qquad q \leftarrow s$

$\langle T \rangle_{u,v,w,x} \to a_y \, \{g_z\} \, \langle T \rangle_{p,q,r,s} \, \{h_t\}$

$\qquad z \leftarrow r$

$\qquad p \leftarrow u + y$

$\qquad q \leftarrow v + 3 * y$

$\qquad t \leftarrow v$

$\qquad w \leftarrow r + 1$

$\qquad x \leftarrow s + 5$

$\langle T \rangle_{u,v,w,x} \to b_y \, \{f_z\}$

$\qquad z \leftarrow v$

$\qquad w \leftarrow y$

$\qquad x \leftarrow u$

Find the attributed derivation tree and activity sequence for the input sequence:

$$d \, a_2 \, a_1 \, a_4 \, b_5$$

22. Consider the following attributed string translation grammar,

$\langle S \rangle_{i,s} \qquad$ INHERITED $i \qquad$ SYNTHESIZED s

with starting value of $i = 3$:

Attributes of action symbols are INHERITED.

$$\langle S \rangle_{i,s} \rightarrow a_x \{f_y\} \{g_z\}$$

$y \leftarrow x + i$

$z \leftarrow y + x$

$s \leftarrow z$

$$\langle S \rangle_{i,s} \rightarrow b_x \{f_y\} \{g_z\}$$

$y \leftarrow z$

$z \leftarrow s$

$s \leftarrow y$

$$\langle S \rangle_{i,s} \rightarrow c_x \{f_y\} \{g_z\}$$

$y \leftarrow z + 1$

$z \leftarrow s + 1$

$s \leftarrow y + 1$

$$\langle S \rangle_{i,s} \rightarrow d_x \{h_y\} \langle S \rangle_{j,t}$$

$y \leftarrow i + t$

$j \leftarrow i$

$s \leftarrow t$

$$\langle S \rangle_{i,s} \rightarrow e_x \langle S \rangle_{j,t} \{f_y\}$$

$y \leftarrow x$

$j \leftarrow t$

$s \leftarrow t$

Find the attributed derivation tree and activity sequence, if they exist, for each of the following input sequences.

a) a_6 b) $a_1 a_2$ c) $d_3 a_2$

d) b_4 e) c_9 f) $d_1 d_2 d_3 d_4 a_5$

g) $e_2 d_1 d_2 d_3 d_4 a_5$

23. Find an attributed string translation grammar that will accept as input, a list written in *list notation* in **LISP** and translate it into the *S*-expression in LISP that represents the same list. For example, the list

$$(A \ B \ (C \ D))$$

translates into:

$$(A \cdot (B \cdot ((C \cdot (D \cdot NIL)) \cdot NIL)))$$

24. Consider the following grammar for conditional statements taken from the ALGOL-60 report.

1. $\langle \text{conditional statement} \rangle \rightarrow \langle \text{if statement} \rangle$

2. $\langle \text{conditional statement} \rangle \rightarrow \langle \text{if statement} \rangle$ **else** $\langle \text{statement} \rangle$

3. $\langle$if statement$\rangle \rightarrow \langle$if clause$\rangle \, \langle$unconditional statement$\rangle$

4. $\langle$if clause$\rangle \rightarrow$ **if** $\langle$Boolean expression$\rangle$ **then**

Assume $\langle$Boolean expression$\rangle$ has a synthesized attribute which is a pointer to the table entry for its result. Assume the existence of the following three atoms:

LABEL(p) where p is a pointer to a table entry corresponding to the label. This atom is put out at places in the program to which control is to be passed by transfer atoms.

JUMP(p) where p is a pointer to a table entry for a label. This atom causes code to be generated that transfers control to the label.

JUMPFALSE(q, p) where q is a pointer to a table entry for the result of a Boolean expression and p is a pointer to a table entry for a label. This atom causes a conditional transfer of control. JUMPFALSE causes code to be generated that tests the value of the Boolean expression and, if it is false, transfers control to the label.

Using these atoms, add attributes to the above grammar to obtain an attributed grammar that specifies an appropriate translation into atoms.

25. Suppose a language has a WHILE statement of the form

$$\langle\text{statement}\rangle \rightarrow \text{WHILE} \, \langle\text{Boolean expression}\rangle \, \text{DO} \, \langle\text{statement}\rangle$$

with the following interpretation:

The Boolean expression is evaluated. If it is true, the statement is executed; otherwise control is passed around the statement. After the statement is executed (assuming it does not transfer out of the WHILE statement) the Boolean expression is reevaluated and the process repeats.

a) Using the atoms defined in Problem 24, find an attributed grammar that specifies an appropriate translation into atoms.

b) Still using this attributed grammar, what is the translation of

$$\text{WHILE } x > y \text{ DO WHILE } z > x \text{ DO } x = x + 4$$

Define appropriate atoms for the Boolean expressions and the assignment statement.

26. A drunken computer scientist wrote the following attributed grammar. Find the errors and inconsistencies in the grammar

$\langle B \rangle_x$ INHERITED x

$\langle C \rangle_x$ SYNTHESIZED x

$\langle D \rangle_{a,b}$ INHERITED a, b

Attributes of action symbols are INHERITED.

1. $\langle A \rangle \rightarrow a_x \, b_y$

        $y \leftarrow x$

2. $\langle A \rangle \rightarrow c_{y1} \, \langle D \rangle_{y2,y3}$

         $(y2, y3) \leftarrow y1$

3. $\langle A \rangle \to a_x \langle D \rangle_{y1,y2}$

$\qquad y2 \leftarrow y1$

4. $\langle B \rangle \to b_{x1} \{FLOP_{x2}\}$

$\qquad x2 \leftarrow x1$

5. $\langle C \rangle_x \to \epsilon$

6. $\langle C \rangle_{p2} \to d_{q1} \langle A \rangle_{q2} \{NIP_{p1,q3}\}$

$\qquad (q2, q3) \leftarrow q1 \qquad p2 \leftarrow p1$

7. $\langle D \rangle_{p1,q3} \to \langle B \rangle_q \langle C \rangle \langle D \rangle_{q2,p2}$

$\qquad (q2, q3) \leftarrow q1 \qquad p2 \leftarrow p1$

8. $\langle D \rangle_{r,s3} \to a_{s1} \langle C \rangle_{s2} \langle B \rangle_t$

$\qquad (s2, s3) \leftarrow s1$

9. $\langle D \rangle \to a_{x,y} \langle C \rangle_{z1} \langle C \rangle_{z2}$

$\qquad z2 \leftarrow z1$

27. a) Add attributes to the following grammar

$\quad\langle integer \rangle \to digit \langle more\ digits \rangle$

$\quad\langle more\ digits \rangle \to digit \langle more\ digits \rangle$

$\quad\langle more\ digits \rangle \to \epsilon$

so that nonterminal $\langle integer \rangle$ has a synthesized attribute that is equal to the value of the integer it generates. Assume that input symbol "digit" has an attribute that is a number between 0 and 9.

b) Find an attributed grammar for MINI-BASIC constants (the language generated by the grammar of Section 6.7) so that the starting nonterminal has a synthesized attribute equal to the value of the constant.

28. Consider the following translation grammar, where c is a token representing a constant and has a value part which is the value of the constant. The starting symbol is $\langle S \rangle$.

$\langle S \rangle \to \langle E \rangle \{ANSWER\}$

$\langle E \rangle \to \langle P \rangle \langle R \rangle$

$\langle R \rangle \to + \langle P \rangle \langle R \rangle$

$\langle R \rangle \to - \langle P \rangle \langle R \rangle$

$\langle R \rangle \to \epsilon$

$\langle P \rangle \to c$

$\langle P \rangle \to (\langle E \rangle)$

Add attributes to this grammar so that $\{ANSWER\}$ has an attribute that is equal to the numerical value of the expression.

29. Find an attributed grammar for expressions over constants using the binary operators $+$, $-$, $*$, and $/$, and parentheses. The operators are to be carried out strictly from left to right except for the usual rules for parenthesized expressions. For instance the expression

$$3 + 4 * 5$$

is equivalent to

$$(3 + 4) * 5$$

and has the value 35. The grammar is to have one action symbol {ANSWER} which appears in the production for the starting symbol, and which has an attribute that is equal to the numerical value of the expression.

30. Suppose that in the assignment statements described in Section 7.9, $+$ and $-$ associate from right to left instead of from left to right. Thus for input sequence

$$\text{LET } I_2 = I_1 - I_2 + I_3$$

the atom string might be

$$\text{ADD}_{2,3,4} \quad \text{SUBTRACT}_{1,4,5} \quad \text{ASSIGN}_{2,5}$$

Add output symbols and attributes to each of the following grammars so as to specify this attributed translation.

a) $\langle S \rangle \rightarrow \text{LET } I = \langle E \rangle$

$\langle E \rangle \rightarrow I + \langle E \rangle$

$\langle E \rangle \rightarrow I - \langle E \rangle$

$\langle E \rangle \rightarrow I$

b) $\langle S \rangle \rightarrow \text{LET } I = \langle E \rangle$

$\langle E \rangle \rightarrow I \langle R \rangle$

$\langle R \rangle \rightarrow + I \langle R \rangle$

$\langle R \rangle \rightarrow - I \langle R \rangle$

$\langle R \rangle \rightarrow \epsilon$

31. Add attributes to the following grammar, so that $\langle \text{declaration} \rangle$ has a synthesized attribute that is equal to the number of identifiers following the word "REAL."

$\langle \text{declaration} \rangle \rightarrow \text{REAL } I \langle \text{identifier list} \rangle$

$\langle \text{identifier list} \rangle \rightarrow , I \langle \text{identifier list} \rangle$

$\langle \text{identifier list} \rangle \rightarrow \epsilon$

32. It is possible for an attribute to be a string and for the rule specifying an attribute to involve the concatenation of strings.

a) Show that given any context-free grammar, it is possible to add attributes to the grammar so that the starting symbol has a synthesized attribute equal to the generated string.

b) For some computers, it is desirable to translate expressions into an atom string using the atoms ADD, SUBTRACT, MULT, and DIVIDE such that the translation of the right operand of $-$ and $/$ appears before the translation of the left operand. Add attributes to the following grammar

$\langle S \rangle \rightarrow \langle E \rangle \; \{\text{OUTSTRING}\}$

$\langle E \rangle \rightarrow \langle E \rangle + \langle T \rangle$

$\langle E \rangle \rightarrow \langle E \rangle - \langle T \rangle$

$\langle E \rangle \rightarrow T$

$\langle T \rangle \rightarrow \langle T \rangle * \langle P \rangle$

$\langle T \rangle \rightarrow \langle T \rangle \, / \, \langle P \rangle$

$\langle T \rangle \rightarrow \langle P \rangle$

$\langle P \rangle \rightarrow (\, \langle E \rangle \,)$

$\langle P \rangle \rightarrow I$

so that output symbol OUTSTRING has an attribute that is equal to the desired atom string. For instance, if the input is

$$I * I - I / I$$

the output should be

$$\text{OUTSTRING}_{\text{DIVIDE,MULT,SUBTRACT}}$$

c) Add attributes to the grammar given in part *b* so that the attribute of OUTSTRING is an appropriate attributed string. For instance, if the input is

$$I_1 * I_2 - I_3 / I_4$$

the output should be

$$\text{OUTSTRING}_{\text{DIVIDE(3,4,5)MULT(1,2,6)SUBTRACT(6,5,7)}}$$

Assume appropriate table pointers are obtained by calling function NEWT.

33. Draw the derivation tree according to the grammar of Fig. 7.10 for the input sequence

$$(I_1 + I_2) * (I_3 + I_4)$$

34. In ALGOL-60, the arithmetic expression

$$\text{if } x > y \text{ then } 1 \text{ else } 2 + 3$$

could conceivably have two meanings denoted by the parenthesized forms:

$$\text{if } x > y \text{ then } 1 \text{ else } (2 + 3)$$

$$(\text{if } x > y \text{ then } 1 \text{ else } 2) + 3$$

Show that the grammar in the ALGOL-60 report is not ambiguous and find the intended meaning.

35. For the string translation grammar

$$\langle E \rangle \rightarrow \langle E \rangle - \langle E \rangle \; \{-\}$$

$$\langle E \rangle \rightarrow I \; \{I\}$$

where I represents any variable, what are the possible output sequences for the input sequence

$$a - b - c - d$$

36. Give an example of a string translation grammar where an input string can have an infinite number of possible output strings.

37. Given any grammar, show how to find a string translation grammar whose activity sequences have an input part consisting of a sequence generated by the given grammar and an output part consisting of the sequence of production names used in a leftmost derivation of the input part by the given grammar.

38. a) Find an attributed translation grammar that will translate expressions over identifiers using $+$ and $*$ but not parentheses into the assembly language of some computer. Assume the existence of a storage location $T1$ for temporary results. For instance, the expression

$$I_A * I_B + I_C * I_D$$

might be translated into

$$\text{LOAD}_A$$
$$\text{MULT}_B$$
$$\text{STORE}_{T1}$$
$$\text{LOAD}_C$$
$$\text{MULT}_D$$
$$\text{ADD}_{T1}$$

The attribute of an I is the name of the identifier.

b) Repeat Part (a) for expressions with parentheses allowed. Assume the existence of an unbounded number of storage locations $T1$, $T2$, $T3$, ... for temporary results.

39. a) Show that if a translation grammar has an unambiguous input grammar, then the length of the action part of any activity sequence is bounded by a constant times the length of the input part.

b) Show, by example, that this is not necessarily true if the input grammar is ambiguous.

40. The string translation grammar given below with starting symbol $\langle S \rangle$ has only one activity sequence whose input part is the same as its output part. Find this activity sequence.

$$\langle S \rangle \rightarrow \langle S \rangle \langle Y \rangle$$
$$\langle S \rangle \rightarrow \langle X \rangle \langle S \rangle \langle X \rangle \{e\}$$
$$\langle S \rangle \rightarrow \{a\} \langle Z \rangle \langle Z \rangle \{a\}$$
$$\langle Y \rangle \rightarrow a$$
$$\langle Y \rangle \rightarrow e$$
$$\langle X \rangle \rightarrow g \langle Y \rangle \{g\}$$
$$\langle Z \rangle \rightarrow b \{rb\}$$
$$\langle Z \rangle \rightarrow r$$

41. A certain grammar has the nonterminal $\langle \text{declaration} \rangle$ which generates the word REAL followed by a list of identifiers separated by commas. The value part of each identifier is a pointer to a table entry for the identifier. Nonterminal $\langle \text{declaration} \rangle$ has an inherited attribute that equals the next available run-time location to be used for variables declared in the list.

For each variable on the list, the syntax box is to call an action routine, named FILLINENTRY. This routine has two parameters, a pointer to a table entry for an identifier and the runtime location for the identifier. The address of the location for each variable is to be one greater than the address for the previously declared variable.

Find an attributed grammar specifying the action-routine calls with the proper parameters.

8
Top-Down Processing

8.1 INTRODUCTION

In previous chapters, we viewed context-free grammars and translation grammars as a way to specify languages and their translations. Now we begin a study of when and how the specified recognition and translation can be carried out by a pushdown machine. This problem of actually performing a translation is, of course, the primary concern of compiler design.

Virtually all design methods based on context-free grammars result in processors which somehow "use" the grammar in the sense that the processor's actions can be interpreted as the recognition of individual productions in a derivation tree. Any processor whose operation involves the recognition of productions is called a *parser*. The word "parsing" is borrowed from natural-language grammarians who use it to refer to the analysis or diagramming of natural-language sentences.

Parsing methods can be divided into two categories: top down and bottom up. Each category is characterized by the order in which the productions on the derivation tree are recognized. Broadly speaking, top-down processors recognize productions higher up in the tree before those lower down, while bottom-up processors recognize lower productions before higher ones. This distinction will be clarified as the methods are considered in more detail.

Pushdown machines can be designed using either a top-down or a bottom-up approach. However, with either approach not all context-free languages can be recognized nor can all syntax-directed translations be performed by a pushdown machine. Each method imposes restrictions on the form of the input grammar and translation grammar that can be processed and the kind of communication allowed between action routines.

We begin our study of pushdown machine processing with the top-down approach. Top-down parsing with a pushdown machine is sometimes called *deterministic top-down parsing* as contrasted to some other techniques which are referred to as "nondeterministic top-down parsing" or "top-down parsing with backtrack."

We assume throughout this chapter that the grammars under consideration have no extraneous nonterminals. Thus we assume that each production and nonterminal can be used in the derivation of some sentence in the language. This assumption is an insignificant restriction since the deletion from a grammar of extraneous nonterminals and productions involving them does not change the language to be recognized or the translation to be performed.

8.2   AN EXAMPLE

In this section we illustrate some principles of top-down pushdown processing by exhibiting a one-state pushdown recognizer for the following grammar with starting nonterminal $\langle S \rangle$:

1. $\langle S \rangle \rightarrow d \langle S \rangle \langle A \rangle$
2. $\langle S \rangle \rightarrow b \langle A \rangle c$
3. $\langle A \rangle \rightarrow d \langle A \rangle$
4. $\langle A \rangle \rightarrow c$

The stack symbols of the pushdown machine are the nonterminals, certain terminals from the grammar and the bottommarker. Specifically, the set of stack symbols is

$$\{ \langle S \rangle, \langle A \rangle, c, \nabla \}$$

At every step in the processing the stack represents an assertion about the sequence of inputs remaining. Specifically, it represents the assertion that the entire input sequence is acceptable if and only if the sequence of remaining terminals (including the current input if it is not the endmarker) can be derived from the string of symbols on the stack. For example if the stack

$$\langle S \rangle \langle A \rangle c \langle A \rangle \nabla$$

occurs during the course of processing an input sequence, this stack is an assertion that the total input sequence is acceptable if and only if the sequence of inputs remaining to be processed is an example of an $\langle S \rangle$ followed by an example of an $\langle A \rangle$ followed by a c followed by another $\langle A \rangle$ followed by an endmarker.

Before exhibiting the control table, we now show how the pushdown machine uses its stack in recognizing the sequence:

$$d\ b\ c\ c\ d\ c$$

The fact that sequence *dbccdc* is in the language defined by the grammar can be seen from the leftmost derivation

$$\langle S \rangle \Rightarrow d \langle S \rangle \langle A \rangle \Rightarrow d\ b \langle A \rangle\ c \langle A \rangle \Rightarrow$$
$$d\ b\ c\ c \langle A \rangle \Rightarrow d\ b\ c\ c\ d \langle A \rangle \Rightarrow d\ b\ c\ c\ d\ c$$

or from the derivation tree shown in Fig. 8.1.

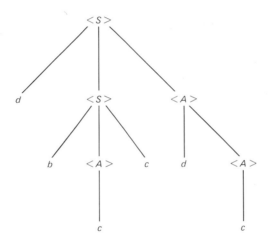

Figure 8.1

To begin the processing, the stack is initialized with:

$$\langle S \rangle\ \nabla$$

This initialization is simply an assertion that the input sequence itself must (if acceptable) be an example of starting nonterminal $\langle S \rangle$ followed by an endmarker. This starting stack combined with the sample input sequence is the starting configuration shown in line 1 of the stack movie in Fig. 8.2. The movie has an extra column on the right which is to be ignored in the present discussion. No states are indicated since the machine only has one state.

$$
\begin{array}{llll}
1\text{:} & \triangledown \langle S \rangle & d\,b\,c\,c\,d\,c \dashv & 1 \\
2\text{:} & \triangledown \langle A \rangle \langle S \rangle & b\,c\,c\,d\,c \dashv & 2 \\
3\text{:} & \triangledown \langle A \rangle \, c \, \langle A \rangle & c\,c\,d\,c \dashv & 4 \\
4\text{:} & \triangledown \langle A \rangle \, c & c\,d\,c \dashv & c \Rightarrow c \\
5\text{:} & \triangledown \langle A \rangle & d\,c \dashv & 3 \\
6\text{:} & \triangledown \langle A \rangle & c \dashv & 4 \\
7\text{:} & \triangledown & \dashv & \\
8\text{:} & \text{ACCEPT} & &
\end{array}
$$

Figure 8.2

From the starting configuration, the machine must make a transition based on the fact that the top stack symbol is $\langle S \rangle$ and the current input is d. The top stack symbol says that the remaining inputs must (if acceptable) begin with an example of an $\langle S \rangle$ and the current input says that the remaining inputs begin with d. We conclude that the initial $\langle S \rangle$ must begin with input d. There are two productions that might be applied to an $\langle S \rangle$ to derive the required example of an $\langle S \rangle$, namely productions 1 and 2. However, a sequence beginning with d cannot be obtained by first applying production 2 because the righthand side of production 2 begins with b and all sequences derived from the righthand side of production 2 must therefore begin with b. The inescapable conclusion is that the required $\langle S \rangle$ is a sequence obtained by first applying production 1 to $\langle S \rangle$. Because the righthand side of this production is $d\langle S \rangle\langle A \rangle$, we know that the required $\langle S \rangle$ must consist of a d (the current input) followed by an $\langle S \rangle$ followed by an $\langle A \rangle$. To record this fact, the pushdown machine advances the input and replaces the $\langle S \rangle$ on top of the stack with an $\langle S \rangle$ and an $\langle A \rangle$, the $\langle S \rangle$ above the $\langle A \rangle$. By making this transition, the machine is in effect asserting that the sequence of symbols after the d is an example of an $\langle S \rangle$ followed by an example of an $\langle A \rangle$ followed by examples of whatever grammatical symbols happen to be on the stack below the replaced $\langle S \rangle$. In this case, there are no grammatical symbols below the replaced $\langle S \rangle$ and the stack becomes simply

$$\langle S \rangle \, \langle A \rangle \, \triangledown$$

which asserts that the remaining inputs must (if acceptable) be an example of $\langle S \rangle$ followed by an example of $\langle A \rangle$. The new machine configuration is shown in line 2 of Fig. 8.2.

The machine now sees top stack symbol $\langle S \rangle$ and current input b. This time the only possibility is that the required $\langle S \rangle$ be derived by first applying production 2 since that is the only production that can be applied to an $\langle S \rangle$ to derive a sequence beginning with b. Thus the remaining terminals must be a *b* followed by an example of $\langle A \rangle$ followed by a *c* followed by a sequence derived from the grammatical symbols below the $\langle S \rangle$ on top of the stack. The pushdown machine records this fact by advancing the input to account for the *b* and then replacing the $\langle S \rangle$ on top of the stack with $\langle A \rangle c$ to obtain stack

$$\langle A \rangle \; c \; \langle A \rangle \; \triangledown$$

The new configuration is line 3 of Fig. 8.2.

Now the machine sees from top stack symbol $\langle A \rangle$ that the remaining inputs begin with an example of an $\langle A \rangle$ and it sees from current input *c* that this example of an $\langle A \rangle$ begins with a *c*. Since the righthand side of production 3 begins with *d*, the example of $\langle A \rangle$ is derived from an initial application of production 4. Because the righthand side of production 4 is simply *c*, the current input must itself be the required example of an $\langle A \rangle$. The terminals after *c* must be a sequence described by the stack symbols below the top $\langle A \rangle$. This fact is recorded by popping the $\langle A \rangle$ and advancing to the next input. The result is line 4 of Fig. 8.2.

The top stack symbol is *c* indicating that the sequence of remaining inputs must begin with *c*. The current input symbol is in fact the required *c*. The machine notes this fact by popping stack symbol *c* and advancing the input. The result is line 5 of Fig. 8.2.

The top stack symbol is now $\langle A \rangle$ and the current input *d*. Only production 3 can be used to begin a derivation from $\langle A \rangle$ of a sequence beginning with *d*. Thus we conclude that the remaining sequence must be *d* followed by $\langle A \rangle$ followed by whatever is below the top stack symbol $\langle A \rangle$. The machine records this fact by advancing the input and replacing the $\langle A \rangle$ on top of the stack with $\langle A \rangle$. The result is line 6 of Fig. 8.2.

Now the top stack symbol is $\langle A \rangle$ and the current input is *c*. This situation was discussed above and, as before, the machine advances the input and pops the $\langle A \rangle$. The result is line 7 of Fig. 8.2.

The top stack symbol is now $\triangledown$ which says that the original sequence is acceptable if and only if the remaining terminal sequence is null. The current input is the endmarker and so there are indeed no more terminal symbols. The machine therefore uses exit ACCEPT, and the processing is complete.

Each time a nonterminal appeared on top of the stack, a transition was made to record the inference that only one particular production could be applied to the top stack symbol for purposes of generating a string of terminals beginning with the current input symbol. The rightmost column of the stack movie in Fig. 8.2 shows the number of that one applicable production. The notation $c \Rightarrow c$ is used in row 4 where terminal *c* was the top stack symbol and the transition was based on the fact that "an example of a *c* is a *c*."

Past inputs	Stack	Intermediate string in the leftmost derivation
1:	$\langle S \rangle \triangledown$	$\langle S \rangle$
2: d	$\langle S \rangle \langle A \rangle \triangledown$	$d \langle S \rangle \langle A \rangle$
3: $d\,b$	$\langle A \rangle\, c \langle A \rangle \triangledown$	$d\,b \langle A \rangle\, c \langle A \rangle$
4: $d\,b\,c$	$c \langle A \rangle \triangledown$	$d\,b\,c\,c \langle A \rangle$
5: $d\,b\,c\,c$	$\langle A \rangle \triangledown$	
6: $d\,b\,c\,c\,d$	$\langle A \rangle \triangledown$	$d\,b\,c\,c\,d \langle A \rangle$
7: $d\,b\,c\,c\,d\,c$	$\triangledown$	$d\,b\,c\,c\,d\,c$

Figure 8.3

The order in which the productions are used in the processing, namely 1, 2, 4, 3, 4, is the same order as the productions used in the leftmost derivation of the terminal string. The relationship between the configurations of the pushdown machine and the leftmost derivation is shown graphically in Fig. 8.3. For each of the recognition steps shown in Fig. 8.2, Fig. 8.3 shows the sequence of inputs already processed, the stack displayed using the "top on the left" convention and the intermediate string corresponding to a step in the leftmost derivation.

The relationship between the recognition step and the intermediate string is that the intermediate string is just the past input sequence and the stack concatenated into a single string.

Steps 4 and 5 correspond to the same derivation step because the machine transition between these steps involves the comparison of two terminals rather than the use of a production.

Because of the relationship between derivation steps and machine configurations, the top stack symbol of each configuration can be thought of as corresponding to a symbol in the derivation tree. This correspondence is shown in Fig. 8.4. Figure 8.4(a) shows the stack movie of Fig. 8.2 repeated with a subscript added to each stack symbol. The subscript indicates the line of the stack movie at which the stack symbol becomes the top stack symbol. Using the correspondence, shown in Fig. 8.3, between the stack movie and the leftmost derivation, these same subscripts can be added to the nonterminals in the leftmost derivation, yielding:

$$\langle S \rangle_1 \Rightarrow d \langle S \rangle_2 \langle A \rangle_5 \Rightarrow d\,b \langle A \rangle_3\, c_4 \langle A \rangle_5 \Rightarrow$$
$$d\,b\,c\,c_4 \langle A \rangle_5 \Rightarrow d\,b\,c\,c_4\,d \langle A \rangle_6 \Rightarrow d\,b\,c\,c_4\,d\,c$$

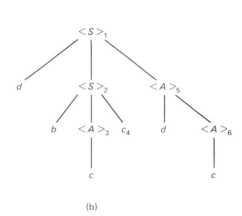

1:    ▽ $<S>_1$ $d\ b\ c\ c\ d\ c\ \dashv$

2:    ▽ $<A>_5\ <S>_2$ $b\ c\ c\ d\ c\ \dashv$

3:    ▽ $<A>_5\ c_4\ <A>_3$ $c\ c\ d\ c\ \dashv$

4:    ▽ $<A>_5\ c_4$ $c\ d\ c\ \dashv$

5:    ▽ $<A>_5$ $d\ c\ \dashv$

6:    ▽ $<A>_6$ $c\ \dashv$

7:    ▽ $\dashv$

(a)

(b)

Figure 8.4

Marking the tree of Fig. 8.1 with the subscripts of this derivation yields the tree of Fig. 8.4(b). The correspondence between subscripts of Fig. 8.4 is more than just a correspondence between symbols. It is also a correspondence between productions used by the machine and productions applied in building the tree. For example, production 1 was used by the machine when $\langle S \rangle_1$ was the top stack symbol and production 1 was also applied to $\langle S \rangle_1$ in building the tree. This correspondence also carries over to the righthand sides. Thus $\langle S \rangle_2$ and $\langle A \rangle_5$ are the symbols the machine used to replace $\langle S \rangle_1$ on the stack and they also are the symbols immediately below $\langle S \rangle_1$ on the tree. Thus the pushdown machine can be thought of as "visiting" the non-terminals on the tree or as "parsing" the input, even though no representation of the tree is actually constructed during the processing.

The numbers used as subscripts in Fig. 8.4(b) display the order in which the corresponding tree symbols were processed by the pushdown machine. In all cases, each symbol in the tree was processed before those below it. Hence the name top-down parsing. In cases where neither of two given symbols is above the other (e.g., $\langle A \rangle_3$ and $\langle A \rangle_5$), the leftmost is always processed first.

Because the pushdown stack contains a description of the remaining sequence of inputs (if the input sequence is acceptable) the stack is sometimes referred to as a "prediction" about the future inputs. Similarly, the analysis is sometimes called "predictive parsing" instead of top-down parsing. During the parsing, the top stack symbol is sometimes called the "goal" and the job of the machine thought of as finding a subsequence of inputs that is an example of this predicted goal.

At each step in the analysis of the sample input, we inspected the grammar and deduced what stack and input operations should be carried out in order to maintain the interpretation that the stack represents an assertion about what the future terminals ought to be. Now we exhibit a one-state pushdown machine to carry out the indicated stack and input operations. The machine makes use of the extended stack operation REPLACE in addition to the primitive pushdown-machine operations. Recall that the REPLACE operation is written using the top-symbol-on-right convention.

The control table of the pushdown machine is shown in Fig. 8.5. The inputs are made up of the terminals of the grammar and the endmarker. The stack symbols consist of the bottommarker and the nonterminal and terminal symbols needed to make assertions about the remaining inputs. The nonexit entries are the stack and input operations we deduced as correct during the analysis of the sample input sequence. For example, if $\langle S \rangle$ is the top stack symbol and d is the input symbol, we deduced in the example that the required example of an $\langle S \rangle$ could only be derived from production 1 and therefore the top $\langle S \rangle$ should be replaced by an $\langle A \rangle$ and an $\langle S \rangle$ and the

	d	b	c	$\dashv$
$\langle S \rangle$	REPLACE ($\langle A \rangle \langle S \rangle$) ADVANCE	REPLACE ($c \langle A \rangle$) ADVANCE	REJECT	REJECT
$\langle A \rangle$	REPLACE ($\langle A \rangle$) ADVANCE	REJECT	POP ADVANCE	REJECT
c	REJECT	REJECT	POP ADVANCE	REJECT
∇	REJECT	REJECT	REJECT	ACCEPT

Starting stack: $\nabla \langle S \rangle$

Figure 8.5

input advanced. Thus we have entered REPLACE ($\langle A \rangle \langle S \rangle$), ADVANCE as the table entry for $\langle S \rangle$ and *d*.

The REJECT entries mark situations in which the top stack symbol and current input are contradictory. Thus the entry for stack symbol $\langle S \rangle$ and input *c* is marked REJECT because there is no way in which an example of an $\langle S \rangle$ can start with terminal *c* and therefore the input sequence cannot be acceptable.

8.3 *S*-GRAMMARS

The chief concern of this chapter is the problem of obtaining top-down recognizers from grammars. In particular we are interested in pushdown machines which operate on the principle that the stack always contains a string of terminals and nonterminals from which the set of acceptable input continuations can be derived. Machines of this type are of great practical significance since they are easy to implement, operate rapidly, and do not require excessively large amounts of memory. Also, as we will show later, machines of this type are easily extended to accommodate a large variety of syntax-directed translations.

Unfortunately, not all context-free grammars are suitable for top-down analysis by a pushdown machine since for many grammars, the set of all acceptable input continuations cannot always be represented by a single string of nonterminal and terminal symbols. In this chapter, we are concerned with classes of grammars for which top-down pushdown recognizers can be found. In this section we introduce one such class, the so called *s*-grammars.

A context-free grammar is called an *s-grammar* if and only if the following two conditions hold:

1. the righthand side of each production begins with a terminal symbol;

2. if two productions have the same lefthand side, then their righthand sides begin with different terminal symbols.

It is very easy to inspect a grammar to see if it is an *s*-grammar. For example, the grammar

1. $\langle S \rangle \rightarrow a \langle T \rangle$
2. $\langle S \rangle \rightarrow \langle T \rangle b \langle S \rangle$
3. $\langle T \rangle \rightarrow b \langle T \rangle$
4. $\langle T \rangle \rightarrow b a$

is obviously not an s-grammar because the righthand side of production 2 does not begin with a terminal as required by condition 1 and also because productions 3 and 4 violate condition 2. On the other hand, the grammar

1. $\langle S \rangle \rightarrow a\, b\, \langle R \rangle$
2. $\langle S \rangle \rightarrow b\, \langle R \rangle\, b\, \langle S \rangle$
3. $\langle R \rangle \rightarrow a$
4. $\langle R \rangle \rightarrow b\, \langle R \rangle$

obviously is an s-grammar since each production is of the form required by condition 1, the righthand sides of the two productions with lefthand side $\langle S \rangle$ begin with different terminal symbols as required by condition 2, and the two productions with lefthand side $\langle R \rangle$ also satisfy condition 2.

A context-free language may have many grammars, some of which are s-grammars and some of which are not. For example, the two sets of productions just given with starting nonterminal $\langle S \rangle$ both specify the same language, yet one is an s-grammar and the other is not. On the other hand, there are many context-free languages which do not have any s-grammars.

The grammar in the previous section was an s-grammar and a corresponding pushdown control table was designed by introducing a REPLACE or POP operation for each production in the grammar and filling the other table entries with ACCEPT, REJECT, or POP as appropriate. These control-table-design techniques may be applied to all s-grammars by using the following rules:

Given an s-grammar, a one-state pushdown recognizer is specified as follows:

1. The input set is the terminal set of the grammar augmented with an endmarker.

2. The stack symbol set consists of the bottommarker, the nonterminal symbols of the grammar, and those terminal symbols that appear in the righthand side of productions in positions other than at the extreme left.

3. The starting stack consists of the bottommarker and the starting nonterminal.

4. The control is described by a one-state control table having rows labeled with stack symbols, columns with input symbols, and entries as described below.

5. A table entry is made for each production in the grammar. The productions have the form

$$\langle A \rangle \rightarrow b\, \alpha$$

where $\langle A \rangle$ is a nonterminal, b is a terminal, and α is a string of nonterminals and terminals. Corresponding to this production the entry for row $\langle A \rangle$ and column b is

$$\text{REPLACE}(\alpha^r), \text{ADVANCE}$$

where α^r is the sequence α reversed to conform to the top-symbol-on-right convention. If the production is just $\langle A \rangle \rightarrow b$, POP can be used instead of REPLACE(ϵ).

6. If terminal b is a stack symbol, then the table entry for row b and column b is:

$$\text{POP, ADVANCE}$$

7. The table entry for the bottommarker row and the endmarker column is:

$$\text{ACCEPT}$$

8. All table entries not described by 5, 6, and 7 above are:

$$\text{REJECT}$$

The two conditions in the definition of *s*-grammars ensure that these rules will always work. Condition 1 says that the productions have the asserted form and condition 2 implies that when carrying out Rule 5, no two productions give specifications for the same entry. Therefore, we conclude that:

> If a language has an *s*-grammar, then it can be recognized by a one-state pushdown machine using the extended stack operation REPLACE.

Application of the rules to the *s*-grammar of this section produces the control table shown in Fig. 8.6(a).

A pushdown machine designed according to the above rules can be thought of as "using" the *s*-grammar from which it was designed. When a transition specified by rule 5 is carried out, we can say that the machine is "using" the corresponding production or that the machine is "applying" the production to the symbol on top of the stack. The intuitive meaning of the words "use" and "apply" depends on one's image of how the machine operates.

If we imagine that the machine is carrying out a leftmost derivation (as in Fig. 8.3), then we think of the machine applying the production to the leftmost nonterminal symbol of an intermediate string. This leftmost nonterminal matches the top stack symbol and the resulting intermediate string is the string obtained by replacing that symbol with the righthand side of the production being "used."

	a	b	⊣
<S>	REPLACE (<R>b) ADVANCE	REPLACE (<S>b<R>) ADVANCE	REJECT
<R>	POP ADVANCE	REPLACE (<R>) ADVANCE	REJECT
b	REJECT	POP ADVANCE	REJECT
▽	REJECT	REJECT	ACCEPT

Starting stack: ▽ <S>

(a)

	a	b	⊣
<S>	# 1	# 2	REJECT
<R>	# 3	# 4	REJECT
b	REJECT	POP ADVANCE	REJECT
▽	REJECT	REJECT	ACCEPT

Starting stack: ▽ <S>

# 1	REPLACE (<R>b), ADVANCE
# 2	REPLACE (<S>b<R>), ADVANCE
# 3	POP, ADVANCE
# 4	REPLACE (<R>), ADVANCE

(b)

Figure 8.6

If we imagine that the machine is building a derivation tree, then we think of the machine as applying the production to the leftmost nonterminal for which branches must still be drawn in the partially constructed tree. This nonterminal matches the top stack symbol, and the righthand side of the production is added to the tree.

If we imagine that the machine is making predictions about subsequent inputs, then we think of the machine as using the production to make a prediction about the inputs to follow.

If we imagine that the machine is making assertions about the required form of the remaining inputs, then we think of the machine as using the production to revise its assertion. The special conditions imposed on the grammar ensure that the revised assertion is correct.

The imagery of applying productions is reinforced if the control table is displayed as in Figure 8.6(b). In this figure, only the number of the production is shown in the table and a description of the transition for that production is shown below the table. For example, the table entry for stack symbol $\langle S \rangle$ and input a is " #1" indicating that production 1 should be applied. The transition for this production is

$$\text{REPLACE}(\langle R \rangle \ b), \text{ADVANCE}$$

as shown in the figure by the explanations below the control table.

As an alternative to the intuition of applying productions, the nonexit transitions of the pushdown machine can be thought of as "matching" the current input with an occurrence of that input in the righthand side of a production.

Transitions described by rule 5 represent the matching of the current input with the leftmost symbol in the righthand side of the corresponding production. Transitions described by rule 6 represent the matching of the current input with the terminal symbol on top of the stack; this stack symbol represents a symbol in the righthand side of the production used by the transition which pushed that symbol.

The transitions of Fig. 8.6(b) can be optimized somewhat for implementation purposes. For example, transition #2 calls for replacing $\langle S \rangle$ with $\langle S \rangle$ $b \langle R \rangle$. It would be more efficient to simply push $b \langle R \rangle$ on top of the existing $\langle S \rangle$. Thus one might write:

$$\#2 \quad \text{PUSH}(b \ \langle R \rangle), \text{ADVANCE}$$

Similarly, transition #4 calls for replacing $\langle R \rangle$ by $\langle R \rangle$ and could be replaced by:

$$\#4 \quad \text{ADVANCE}$$

These simple optimization techniques apply to a number of the examples, but we do not point them out for each example.

8.4   TOP-DOWN PROCESSING OF TRANSLATION GRAMMARS

We now consider the problem of performing a syntax-directed string translation specified by a string translation grammar. In particular, we consider the case of string translation grammars for which the input grammar is an *s*-grammar. We show that such string translations can always be done by a pushdown machine which is a straightforward extension of the standard pushdown recognizer for the s-grammar as constructed by the rules of the previous section. The techniques for modifying the pushdown recognizer to obtain a translator are powerful enough to apply to the other classes of top-down parsable grammars described later in this chapter.

The method of modifying the standard pushdown machine is to take each transition where a given input grammar production is used (i.e., where rule 5 of the construction applies) and modify the transition to account for the corresponding translation grammar production. We first illustrate how this is done for a particular example.

Suppose that a string translation grammar has been specified and suppose that one of its productions is

$$\langle A \rangle \rightarrow \{v\}\, a\, \{w\}\, \langle B \rangle\, \{x\}\, c\, \{y\}\, \langle D \rangle\, \{z\}$$

corresponding to input production

$$\langle A \rangle \rightarrow a\, \langle B \rangle\, c\, \langle D \rangle$$

Suppose further that the input grammar is an s-grammar. The standard pushdown recognizer for the s-grammar uses the given production in its transition for top stack symbol $\langle A \rangle$ and current input a. The specified transition rule is

$$\text{REPLACE}(\langle D \rangle\, c\, \langle B \rangle),\ \text{ADVANCE}$$

Our goal is to modify this transition in a way that will ensure output symbols v, w, x, y, and z are put out at appropriate times. The modification involves two different strategies, one for outputs v and w and one for outputs x, y, and z.

The v and w are taken care of by adding the output operation $\text{OUT}(vw)$ to the given transition specification. This transition is an appropriate time to put out these symbols since the action symbols $\{v\}$ and $\{w\}$ are adjacent to the terminal a in the righthand side of the translation grammar production and this is the transition which matches the terminal a of the production with the current input a.

The symbols x, y, and z cannot, in general, be put out as part of the given transition since the translation grammar tells us that outputs w and x are separated in the output string by a translation of a string derived from nonterminal $\langle B \rangle$.

To ensure that these outputs do get accomplished at an appropriate time, the REPLACE operation is changed to push additional symbols on the stack along with the symbols $\langle D \rangle$, c, and $\langle B \rangle$ required for recognition. A picture of the stack before and after the REPLACE operation is shown in Fig. 8.7. The new stack symbols are action symbols corresponding to output

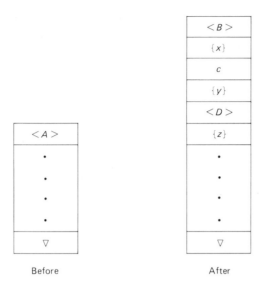

Before   After

Figure 8.7

symbols x, y, and z for which the output operation must be deferred. When an action symbol becomes the top stack symbol, we specify that the machine should put out the corresponding output symbol, pop the action symbol off the stack, and retain the current input.

The "after" stack in Fig. 8.7 can be interpreted as the following prediction: first an example of a $\langle B \rangle$ will be encountered and translated; then an x will be put out; then the current input will be verified to be a c, and the input will be advanced; then y will be put out; then $\langle D \rangle$ translated; and finally a z put out. Assuming the input sequence is acceptable so that these predictions do happen, the x and y will be put out in their proper place between the translation of the $\langle B \rangle$ and the translation of the $\langle D \rangle$. The correct translation of the production will then have been produced.

The transition for the modified pushdown machine can be described as

$$\text{OUT}(vw), \text{REPLACE}(\{z\} \langle D \rangle \{y\} c \{x\} \langle B \rangle), \text{ADVANCE}$$

The sequence of symbols pushed on the stack is simply a picture of the righthand side of the production with certain beginning symbols removed because they can be accounted for in the transition itself.

To get a better idea of how the translation works suppose the complete translation grammar has starting symbol $\langle A \rangle$ and productions

1. $\langle A \rangle \rightarrow \{v\}\, a\, \{w\}\, \langle B \rangle\, \{x\}\, c\, \{y\}\, \langle D \rangle\, \{z\}$
2. $\langle A \rangle \rightarrow b$

3. $\langle B \rangle \rightarrow c \; \{r\}$
4. $\langle B \rangle \rightarrow a \; \{m\} \; \langle A \rangle$
5. $\langle D \rangle \rightarrow c \; \langle D \rangle \; \{n\}$
6. $\langle D \rangle \rightarrow \{s\} \; b$

The problems involved in deriving the correct transition routines are all special cases of the problems already discussed in connection with the sample production which is production 1 of this grammar. The resulting pushdown control is shown in Fig. 8.8.

Notice that rows have been included in Fig. 8.8 to explain what happens when one of the action symbols $\{x\}$, $\{y\}$, $\{z\}$ and $\{n\}$ is the top stack symbol. For each row the action taken is independent of the input; so all entries in that row are the same. This independence is emphasized in the figure by treating these action rows as a single entry.

Figure 8.9 shows a stack movie of the pushdown machine translating

$$a \; c \; c \; b \text{ into } v \; w \; r \; x \; y \; s \; z.$$

Between each pair of adjacent stack configurations is a list of output operations (if any) which occurred during that transition.

	a	b	c	$\dashv$
$<A>$	# 1	# 2	REJECT	REJECT
$<B>$	# 4	REJECT	# 3	REJECT
$<D>$	REJECT	# 6	# 5	REJECT
c	REJECT	REJECT	POP ADVANCE	REJECT
∇	REJECT	REJECT	REJECT	ACCEPT
$\{x\}$	OUT(x), POP, RETAIN			
$\{y\}$	OUT(y), POP, RETAIN			
$\{z\}$	OUT(z), POP, RETAIN			
$\{n\}$	OUT(n), POP, RETAIN			

Starting stack: ∇ $<A>$

\# 1   OUT(vw), REPLACE($\{z\}<D>\{y\}$ c $\{x\}$ $<B>$), ADVANCE
\# 2   POP, ADVANCE
\# 3   OUT(r), POP, ADVANCE
\# 4   OUT(m), REPLACE($<A>$), ADVANCE
\# 5   REPLACE($\{n\}<D>$), ADVANCE
\# 6   OUT(s), POP, ADVANCE

Figure 8.8

1: $\nabla \langle A \rangle$		$a\,c\,c\,b \dashv$
	OUT(vw)	
2: $\nabla \{z\}\langle D\rangle \{y\}c\{x\}\langle B\rangle$		$c\,c\,b \dashv$
	OUT(r)	
3: $\nabla \{z\}\langle D\rangle \{y\}c\{x\}$		$c\,b \dashv$
	OUT(x)	
4: $\nabla \{z\}\langle D\rangle \{y\}c$		$c\,b \dashv$
5: $\nabla \{z\}\langle D\rangle \{y\}$		$b \dashv$
	OUT(y)	
6: $\nabla \{z\}\langle D\rangle$		$b \dashv$
	OUT(s)	
7: $\nabla \{z\}$		$\dashv$
	OUT(z)	
8: ∇		$\dashv$
9:	ACCEPT	

Figure 8.9

Now we state the general rules for specifying a top-down pushdown translator for a translation specified by a translation grammar with an input grammar that is an s-grammar.

1. The input set is the input set of the grammar augmented with an end-marker.

2. The stack symbol set consists of the bottommarker, the nonterminal symbols of the grammar, those input symbols appearing in the righthand side of productions of the input grammar in positions other than the extreme left, and certain action symbols as required by rule 5.

3. The starting stack consists of the bottommarker and the starting nonterminal.

4. The control is described by a one-state control table having rows labeled with stack symbols, columns with input symbols, and entries as described below.

5. A table entry is made for each production in the grammar. The productions have the form

$$\langle A \rangle \rightarrow \xi\,b\,\psi\,\alpha$$

where $\langle A \rangle$ is a nonterminal, b a terminal, ξ and ψ are (possibly null) sequences of action symbols, and α is a sequence of action, nonterminal, and terminal symbols that does not begin with an action symbol. Corresponding to this production, the entry for row $\langle A \rangle$ and column b is:

$$\text{OUT}(\overline{\xi\psi}),\ \text{REPLACE}(\alpha^r),\ \text{ADVANCE}$$

The notation $\overline{\xi\psi}$ is used to represent the string of output symbols corresponding to the string of action symbols $\xi\psi$ (i.e., $\overline{\xi\psi}$ is $\xi\psi$ with the braces deleted). If $\xi\psi$ is null, the OUT is omitted and if α is null, the REPLACE is simply POP.

6. If terminal b is a stack symbol, then the table entry for row b and column b is:

$$\text{POP, ADVANCE}$$

7. The table entry for the bottommarker row and endmarker column is ACCEPT.

8. If action symbol $\{x\}$ is a stack symbol, then all table entries for row $\{x\}$ are:

$$\text{OUT}(x),\ \ \text{POP},\ \ \text{RETAIN}$$

9. All table entries not described by 5, 6, 7, and 8 above are REJECT.

The rules above are simply the indicated extension of the rules given in the last section for obtaining a top-down recognizer.

The condition that the input grammar be an s-grammar ensures that Rule 5 does not give two specifications for the same transition. The construction implies that the following is true:

> Given a string translation grammar whose input grammar is an s-grammar, the specified string translation can be performed by a one-state pushdown machine using the extended stack operation REPLACE.

The pushdown machine constructed above for string translations can serve as the basic machine for treating certain other kinds of syntax-directed processing. The operations which output a symbol can easily be replaced by operations which call a routine. Thus if a translation grammar is given in which action symbols represent the names of action routines to be called, and for which the input grammar is an s-grammar, a pushdown machine to call these routines in the order specified by the grammar can easily be obtained from the standard machine for printing out the names of the routines. Thus the timing problem for the routine calls is solved algorithmically for s-grammars and the programmer's efforts can be focused on writing the routines themselves. In Chapter 9 we will discuss the problem of writing these routines and the problem of communicating information among these routines.

8.5 *q*-GRAMMARS

Consider the following grammar with starting nonterminal $\langle S \rangle$:

1. $\langle S \rangle \rightarrow a \langle A \rangle \langle S \rangle$
2. $\langle S \rangle \rightarrow b$
3. $\langle A \rangle \rightarrow c \langle A \rangle \langle S \rangle$
4. $\langle A \rangle \rightarrow \epsilon$

This grammar is not an *s*-grammar because the righthand side of production 4 does not begin with a terminal. Nevertheless, it is still possible for a pushdown machine to "use" this grammar to maintain a stack which asserts the form of the remaining inputs (if acceptable). To illustrate this process we now show how a machine can process the sequence

$$a\,a\,c\,b\,b$$

which is in the language specified by the grammar (see the derivation tree of Fig. 8.10).

    The pushdown machine begins with initial stack $\nabla \langle S \rangle$ since the entire input sequence must be an example of an $\langle S \rangle$. Looking at top stack symbol $\langle S \rangle$ and current input a, the machine applies production 1 because production 1 begins with a; the alternative production for nonterminal $\langle S \rangle$,

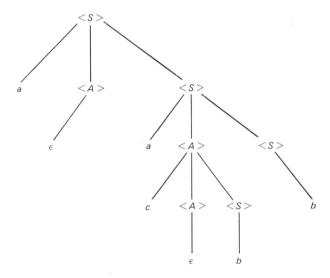

Figure 8.10

$$
\begin{array}{lll}
1: & \triangledown \langle S \rangle & a\,a\,c\,b\,b \dashv \\
2: & \triangledown \langle S \rangle \langle A \rangle & a\,c\,b\,b \dashv \\
3: & \triangledown \langle S \rangle & a\,c\,b\,b \dashv \\
4: & \triangledown \langle S \rangle \langle A \rangle & c\,b\,b \dashv \\
5: & \triangledown \langle S \rangle \langle S \rangle \langle A \rangle & b\,b \dashv \\
6: & \triangledown \langle S \rangle \langle S \rangle & b\,b \dashv \\
7: & \triangledown \langle S \rangle & b \dashv \\
8: & \triangledown & \dashv \\
9: & \text{ACCEPT} &
\end{array}
$$

Figure 8.11

production 2, begins with b. The result is line 2 of the stack movie of Fig. 8.11.

Up to this point, the behavior of the machine and the reasoning behind this behavior has been the same as with an s-grammar. This similarity is due to the fact that the productions with lefthand side $\langle S \rangle$ satisfy the s-grammar conditions. The configuration in line 2 is the first place where the ϵ-production must be taken into account. The top stack symbol $\langle A \rangle$ says that the remaining inputs must begin with an example of an $\langle A \rangle$ and the current input a says that the remaining inputs begin with an a. The required example of an $\langle A \rangle$ cannot be derived by applying production 3 since production 3 begins with c and the current input is not c. The only explanation is that the required $\langle A \rangle$ is obtained by applying production 4 (i.e., the required $\langle A \rangle$ is ϵ) and that the current input a is the beginning terminal of a string obtained from a symbol further down the stack.

An application of production 4 consists of popping the top symbol $\langle A \rangle$ off the stack, because the example of the $\langle A \rangle$ (i.e., ϵ) has been seen. The current input is retained since it is still the first of the inputs to be generated from symbols remaining on the stack. The result is line 3 of Fig. 8.11.

The transition from line 3 to line 4 is the same as that between lines 1 and 2 and need not be discussed further.

In line 4, the top stack symbol is $\langle A \rangle$ and the current input is c. On the surface, it appears that the current input can be explained in two different ways. One explanation is that the required example of an $\langle A \rangle$ is obtained by first applying production 3 and that the current input c matches the c on the righthand side of production 3. The second explanation is that the $\langle A \rangle$ is in fact ϵ obtained from production 4 and that the current input c is generated by some symbol below the top stack symbol $\langle A \rangle$. However, a more penetrating analysis of the situation reveals that there are no intermediate strings in the language in which an example of an $\langle A \rangle$ is immediately followed by an instance of *c* and the second explanation therefore cannot be correct. Hence only production 3 can be used in deriving an acceptable string of remaining inputs.

To see why an example of an $\langle A \rangle$ cannot be followed by a *c*, observe that each occurrence of $\langle A \rangle$ in the righthand side of a production is followed by an instance of nonterminal $\langle S \rangle$. Therefore, the terminals which can follow an occurrence of $\langle A \rangle$ are precisely those terminals that can begin an example of $\langle S \rangle$, namely *a* (using production 1), or *b* (using production 2), but not *c*.

To see the futility of applying production 4 in the specific situation of the example, consider what would happen if production 4 were applied to line 4 of the stack movie. In this event, line 5 of the movie would be

$$5: \quad \nabla \ \langle S \rangle \qquad c \ c \ b \ \dashv$$

and the processing would have to terminate due to the fact that an $\langle S \rangle$ cannot begin with a *c*. Again we see that production 3, not production 4, must be applied to line 4.

The transition from line 4 to line 5 in Fig. 8.11 shows the result of applying production 3. In line 5, production 4 is applied because the only explanation of current input *b* is that the required $\langle A \rangle$ is ϵ and the *b* is part of the sequence generated by some lower stack symbols. The remaining steps of the stack movie follow from *s*-grammar logic.

A control table to carry out this procedure is shown in Fig. 8.12. The entry for stack symbol $\langle A \rangle$ and input $\dashv$ represents a new situation. The same reasoning that led to an application of production 4 at line 2 of the stack movie suggests that this entry be filled in with an application of pro-

	a	*b*	*c*	$\dashv$
$\langle S \rangle$	# 1	# 2	REJECT	REJECT
$\langle A \rangle$	# 4	# 4	# 3	# 4
∇	REJECT	REJECT	REJECT	ACCEPT

Starting stack: ∇ $\langle S \rangle$

1 REPLACE($\langle S \rangle \langle A \rangle$), ADVANCE
2 POP, ADVANCE
3 REPLACE($\langle S \rangle \langle A \rangle$), ADVANCE
4 POP, RETAIN

Figure 8.12

duction 4. However, no intermediate string can be derived from

$$\langle S \rangle \dashv$$

in which an instance of $\langle A \rangle$ is immediately followed by $\dashv$. Therefore applying production 4 cannot lead to acceptance of the input sequence. To be more specific, because each occurrence of $\langle A \rangle$ in the righthand side of a production is followed by an instance of nonterminal $\langle S \rangle$, the symbol below $\langle A \rangle$ on the stack is always $\langle S \rangle$. If the transition for $\langle A \rangle$ and $\dashv$ applies production 4, then the next move of the machine will be the transition for $\langle S \rangle$ and $\dashv$, which is REJECT. Therefore, the entry for $\langle A \rangle$ and $\dashv$ could just as well be REJECT. In fact, applying production 4 is a futile but harmless gesture, and the entry for $\langle A \rangle$ and $\dashv$ can be either REJECT, or POP, RETAIN. Since there is no theoretical basis for choosing one alternative over the other, the choice, in practice, is made on the basis of which choice is easiest to implement or which choice leads to a better error message.

To simplify future discussions, we now introduce the concept of the "follow set" of a nonterminal:

Given a context-free grammar with starting symbol $\langle S \rangle$ and a nonterminal $\langle X \rangle$, we define

$$\text{FOLLOW}(\langle X \rangle)$$

to be the set of input symbols that can immediately follow an $\langle X \rangle$ in an intermediate string derived from $\langle S \rangle \dashv$. This set is called the *follow set* of $\langle X \rangle$.

FOLLOW($\langle X \rangle$) is simply the set of input symbols that can follow an example of $\langle X \rangle$ in an acceptable input sequence.

In our previous analysis, we observed that nonterminal $\langle A \rangle$ could only be followed by a or b. Now we can express this fact by the equation

$$\text{FOLLOW}(\langle A \rangle) = \{a, b\}$$

From this fact we can conclude that it is useless to apply the ϵ-production to stack symbol $\langle A \rangle$ for current inputs not in the follow set (i.e., for inputs c and $\dashv$). On the other hand there do exist input sequences containing examples of an $\langle A \rangle$ followed by a and b. Consequently it is necessary for the pushdown machine to apply the ϵ-production to $\langle A \rangle$ for current inputs a and b, but this is not necessary for c and $\dashv$.

We have now isolated two circumstances in which a given production must be applied for a given stack symbol $\langle A \rangle$ and given input symbol b. One case is that the given production has the form

$$\langle A \rangle \rightarrow b\,\alpha$$

and the other case is that the production is

$$\langle A \rangle \rightarrow \epsilon$$

and b is in the follow set of $\langle A \rangle$. To discuss these situations simultaneously, we introduce the concept of the selection set of a production:

If a production of a grammar has the form

$$\langle A \rangle \rightarrow b \, \alpha$$

where b is a terminal symbol and α is a string of terminal and nonterminal symbols, we define:

$$\mathrm{SELECT}(\langle A \rangle \rightarrow b \, \alpha) = \{b\}$$

If a production has the form

$$\langle A \rangle \rightarrow \epsilon$$

we define:

$$\mathrm{SELECT}(\langle A \rangle \rightarrow \epsilon) = \mathrm{FOLLOW}(\langle A \rangle)$$

If p is the number of a production

$$\langle A \rangle \rightarrow \alpha$$

we sometimes write

$$\mathrm{SELECT}(p)$$

instead of:

$$\mathrm{SELECT}(\langle A \rangle \rightarrow \alpha)$$

The set $\mathrm{SELECT}(p)$ is called the *selection set* for production p.

The selection set simply gives the inputs for which a pushdown control must apply a production. For the example:

$$\mathrm{SELECT}(1) = \mathrm{SELECT}(\langle S \rangle \rightarrow a \, \langle A \rangle \, \langle S \rangle) = \{a\}$$
$$\mathrm{SELECT}(2) = \mathrm{SELECT}(\langle S \rangle \rightarrow b) = \{b\}$$
$$\mathrm{SELECT}(3) = \mathrm{SELECT}(\langle A \rangle \rightarrow c \, \langle A \rangle \, \langle S \rangle) = \{c\}$$
$$\mathrm{SELECT}(4) = \mathrm{SELECT}(\langle A \rangle \rightarrow \epsilon) = \mathrm{FOLLOW}(\langle A \rangle) = \{a, b\}$$

The reason we were able to design a top-down pushdown recognizer is that for every combination of nonterminal and input, the input was in the selection set of at most one production for the nonterminal.

We now wish to define a particular class of grammars, more general than the *s*-grammars, that includes the grammar of the example and whose grammars can be recognized by top-down pushdown recognizers. We call a member of this class a "*q*-grammar."

A context free grammar is called a *q-grammar* if and only if the following two conditions hold:

1. The righthand side of each production is either ϵ or begins with a terminal symbol.

2. Productions with the same lefthand side have disjoint selection sets.

Condition 1 is simply a statement that the productions are restricted to the two forms for which we have defined selection sets. Condition 2 says that there are no conflicting requirements in designing a top-down control table. The example satisfies the two conditions because it has the correct form and because

$$\text{SELECT}(1) \cap \text{SELECT}(2) = \{a\} \cap \{b\} = \{\ \}$$

and

$$\text{SELECT}(3) \cap \text{SELECT}(4) = \{c\} \cap \{a, b\} = \{\ \}$$

The rules given in Section 8.3 for constructing a pushdown recognizer from an *s*-grammar are easily extended to a set of rules for *q*-grammars. Rule 5 should be replaced by the following two rules:

5′. A production is "applied" whenever the stack symbol is its lefthand side and the input is in its selection set. To apply a production of the form

$$\langle A \rangle \rightarrow b\ \alpha$$

where *b* is a terminal and α is a string of terminals and nonterminals, use the transition:

$$\text{REPLACE}(\alpha^r),\ \text{ADVANCE}$$

If the production is just

$$\langle A \rangle \rightarrow b$$

POP can be used instead of REPLACE(ϵ). To apply a production of the form

$$\langle A \rangle \rightarrow \epsilon$$

use the transition:

$$\text{POP, RETAIN}$$

5″. If there is an ϵ-production for nonterminal $\langle A \rangle$ and no entry for stack symbol $\langle A \rangle$ and input b is implied by rule 5', then the entry can either "apply" the ϵ-production or REJECT.

As a second example, consider the following grammar with starting symbol $\langle S \rangle$:

1. $\langle S \rangle \rightarrow a \langle A \rangle$
2. $\langle S \rangle \rightarrow b$
3. $\langle A \rangle \rightarrow c \langle S \rangle a$
4. $\langle A \rangle \rightarrow \epsilon$

For this grammar, $\langle A \rangle$ can be followed by either a or $\dashv$ as demonstrated by the intermediate strings

$$a\,c\,a\,\langle A \rangle\,a \dashv \quad \text{and} \quad a\,\langle A \rangle \dashv$$

The selection sets are as follows:

$$\text{SELECT}(1) = \{a\} \qquad \text{SELECT}(2) = \{b\}$$
$$\text{SELECT}(3) = \{c\} \qquad \text{SELECT}(4) = \{a, \dashv\}$$

Because SELECT(1) and SELECT(2) are disjoint and SELECT(3) and SE-LECT(4) are disjoint, the grammar is a q-grammar. The control table obtained from the rules is shown in Fig. 8.13. According to rule 5″, the entry for stack symbol $\langle A \rangle$ and input b can be filled in with either POP, RETAIN (i.e., #4) or REJECT. Both alternatives are mentioned in Fig. 8.13.

The entry for stack symbol $\langle A \rangle$ and input $\dashv$ must under rule 5' be POP, RETAIN. This entry is used by the machine in recognizing sequence a.

	a	b	c	$\dashv$
$<S>$	# 1	# 2	REJECT	REJECT
$<A>$	# 4	# 4 or REJECT	# 3	# 4
a	POP ADVANCE	REJECT	REJECT	REJECT
∇	REJECT	REJECT	REJECT	ACCEPT

Starting stack: $\nabla\ <S>$

1 REPLACE($<A>$), ADVANCE
2 POP, ADVANCE
3 REPLACE($a <S>$), ADVANCE
4 POP, RETAIN

Figure 8.13

The set of rules for constructing the recognizer for a q-grammar establishes the following fact:

> If a language has a q-grammar, then it can be recognized by a one-state pushdown machine using the extended stack operation REPLACE.

The principles of Section 8.4 are easily extended to obtain a top-down pushdown translator for a string translation grammar whose input grammar is a q-grammar. The extension concerns productions of the form

$$\langle A \rangle \rightarrow \xi$$

where ξ is a string of action symbols. The corresponding input production is:

$$\langle A \rangle \rightarrow \epsilon$$

To cover this case, the pushdown translator transitions that apply this production should be

$$\text{OUT}(\bar{\xi}), \text{POP}, \text{RETAIN}$$

where $\bar{\xi}$ is the output string implied by action string ξ. With this addition, the construction establishes the following fact:

> Given a string translation grammar whose input grammar is a q-grammar, the specified string translation can be performed by a one-state pushdown machine using the extended stack operation REPLACE.

As an example, consider the following translation grammar with starting symbol $\langle S \rangle$:

1. $\langle S \rangle \rightarrow a \; \{x\} \; \langle A \rangle \; \{y\}$
2. $\langle S \rangle \rightarrow b \; \{z\}$
3. $\langle A \rangle \rightarrow c \; \langle S \rangle \; \{v\} \; a$
4. $\langle A \rangle \rightarrow \{w\}$

The input grammar for this translation grammar is the q-grammar whose recognizer is shown in Fig. 8.13. The control table of the pushdown machine that performs the specified translation is shown in Fig. 8.14.

8.6   LL(1) GRAMMARS

In the previous section, we introduced the concept of a selection set for grammars in which the righthand sides of the productions either begin with a terminal or are null. The selection set for a production specifies which input

	a	b	c	⊣
<S>	# 1	# 2	REJECT	REJECT
<A>	# 4	# 4 or REJECT	# 3	# 4
a	POP ADVANCE	REJECT	REJECT	REJECT
▽	REJECT	REJECT	REJECT	ACCEPT
{y}	OUT(y), POP, RETAIN			
{v}	OUT(v), POP, RETAIN			

Starting stack: ▽ <S>

1 OUT(x), REPLACE({y}<A >), ADVANCE
2 OUT(z), POP, ADVANCE
3 REPLACE(a {v}<S >), ADVANCE
4 OUT(w), POP, RETAIN

Figure 8.14

symbols require the application of the production when the lefthand side is the top stack symbol. In the event that there are no combinations of stack and input symbols where the application of two different productions are required, we call the grammar a q-grammar and use the selection sets to design a pushdown control. In this section, we generalize the concept of selection set to apply to context-free productions of arbitrary form.

In the previous section we found two conditions under which an input symbol b is in the selection set of a production with lefthand side $\langle A \rangle$:

1. the righthand side of the production begins with b;
2. the righthand side of the production is ϵ and b is in FOLLOW($\langle A \rangle$).

In this section, we generalize these two conditions by generalizing the concept of "the righthand side beginning with b" and "the righthand side being ϵ." These generalizations permit us to define selection sets for productions in which the righthand side begins with a nonterminal. A grammar for which these generalized selection sets imply at most one production for each combination of stack and input symbol is called an "LL(1) grammar."

Suppose we are trying to construct a top-down pushdown recognizer for some grammar that contains the production:

$$\langle A \rangle \rightarrow b \, \langle A \rangle \, \langle S \rangle$$

We reason that any sequence derived from an $\langle A \rangle$ starting with this production must begin with b. We conclude that this production should only be applied if the top stack symbol is $\langle A \rangle$ and the current input is b. The relevant fact about this production is not that its righthand side begins with b, but that any sequence derived from the righthand side must begin with b. If we discuss productions in terms of what sequences their righthand sides generate, we find that we can discuss righthand sides that do not begin with a terminal.

Suppose for example that we are trying to construct a top-down pushdown recognizer for a grammar that contains the production:

$$\langle S \rangle \rightarrow \langle A \rangle \, b \, \langle B \rangle$$

Suppose further that an analysis of the grammar reveals that each terminal string that can be derived from righthand side $\langle A \rangle \, b \, \langle B \rangle$ begins with one of the four terminals in the set:

$$\{a, b, c, e\}$$

We can conclude that this production should only be applied if the top stack symbol is $\langle S \rangle$ and the current input is one of the four symbols a, b, c, or e. The word "apply" in this case means replacing the $\langle S \rangle$ on top of the stack with the righthand side and retaining the input. Specifically, the transition is

$$\text{REPLACE}(\langle B \rangle \, b \, \langle A \rangle), \text{RETAIN}$$

The REPLACE operation represents an assertion that the required $\langle S \rangle$ must be an $\langle A \rangle$ followed by a b followed by a $\langle B \rangle$. The current input must be retained because it is still part of the sequence represented by symbols on the stack.

In order to facilitate the discussion, we introduce the concept of FIRST:

Given a context-free grammar and an intermediate string α of symbols from the grammar, we define

$$\text{FIRST}(\alpha)$$

to be the set of terminal symbols that occur at the beginning of intermediate strings derived from α.

A procedure for computing FIRST is given in the next section, but the FIRST of a given intermediate string can frequently be computed by inspection.

To illustrate FIRST with a specific context-free grammar, Fig. 8.15 shows a grammar with the value of FIRST computed for each of the righthand sides. The computation of FIRST for productions 2, 5, 7, and 8 is trivial because their righthand sides begin with a terminal. Their FIRST sets are one element sets containing the beginning terminal.

1. $<S> \rightarrow <A> b <B>$ FIRST($<A> b <B>$) = $\{a, b, c, e\}$

2. $<S> \rightarrow d$ FIRST(d) = $\{d\}$

3. $<A> \rightarrow <C> <A> b$ FIRST($<C> <A> b$) = $\{a, e\}$

4. $<A> \rightarrow <B>$ FIRST($<B>$) = $\{c\}$

5. $<B> \rightarrow c <S> d$ FIRST($c <S> d$) = $\{c\}$

6. $<B> \rightarrow \epsilon$ FIRST(ϵ) = $\{ \}$

7. $<C> \rightarrow a$ FIRST(a) = $\{a\}$

8. $<C> \rightarrow e d$ FIRST($e d$) = $\{e\}$

Starting nonterminal: $<S>$

Figure 8.15

The computation for production 6 is also trivial. Because no strings can be derived from ϵ except ϵ itself, there are no symbols in FIRST(ϵ).

For production 3, FIRST($\langle C \rangle \langle A \rangle b$) consists of those terminals that begin productions for $\langle C \rangle$, namely a (from production 7) and e (from production 8).

For production 4, FIRST($\langle B \rangle$) is only c (by applying production 5) since an application of production 6 results in ϵ.

The computation of FIRST($\langle A \rangle b \langle B \rangle$) for production 1 is more complicated. The initial $\langle A \rangle$ can begin with a $\langle C \rangle$ or a $\langle B \rangle$ (productions 3 and 4) and these nonterminals can begin with c, a, and e (productions 5, 7, and 8). Therefore, the initial $\langle A \rangle$ can generate strings beginning with c, a, and e and these terminals must be in FIRST($\langle A \rangle b \langle B \rangle$). Because the initial $\langle A \rangle$ can go into ϵ, the b following the $\langle A \rangle$ can be the first symbol in a derived string and therefore b must also be in FIRST($\langle A \rangle b \langle B \rangle$). Specifically, b is in FIRST because $\langle A \rangle b \langle B \rangle$ generates $b \langle B \rangle$ as follows:

$$\langle A \rangle b \langle B \rangle \Rightarrow \langle B \rangle b \langle B \rangle \Rightarrow b \langle B \rangle$$

Given a production p with lefthand side $\langle A \rangle$ and righthand side α, we know that if b is in FIRST(α), a sequence beginning with b can be generated from $\langle A \rangle$ by first applying production p. Hence b must be included in the selection set for p. Conversely, if b is not in FIRST(α), there is no way a sequence beginning with b can be generated from $\langle A \rangle$ starting with production p. Thus the concept of "b is in FIRST(righthand side)" plays the same role in constructing selection sets as the concept "the righthand side begins with b" did in the previous section. It characterizes the situations under which a production should be applied for purposes of generating a sequence beginning with the current input.

Now we consider the problem of characterizing the situations in which a production should be applied in order to generate ϵ from the top stack symbol. We have already discussed this problem in connection with ε-productions. For the current example of Fig. 8.15, we know that the ε-production 6 should be applied to $\langle B \rangle$ for all inputs in:

$$\text{FOLLOW}(\langle B \rangle) = \{b, d, \dashv\}$$

The inclusion of b, d, and $\dashv$ in this set is demonstrated by the following derivations:

$$\langle S \rangle \dashv \Rightarrow \langle A \rangle \, b \, \langle B \rangle \dashv \Rightarrow \langle B \rangle \, b \, \langle B \rangle \dashv$$
$$\langle S \rangle \dashv \Rightarrow \langle A \rangle \, b \, \langle B \rangle \dashv \Rightarrow \langle A \rangle \, b \, c \, \langle S \rangle \, d \dashv \Rightarrow \langle A \rangle \, b \, c \, \langle A \rangle \, b \, \langle B \rangle \, d \dashv$$

The first derivation shows $\langle B \rangle$ followed by b and $\dashv$ and the second derivation shows $\langle B \rangle$ followed by d.

There is a second production in the grammar which can be applied for purposes of generating ε, namely production 4. Although production 4 is not itself an ε-production, it can be used to generate ε from $\langle A \rangle$ as follows:

$$\langle A \rangle \Rightarrow \langle B \rangle \Rightarrow \epsilon$$

Thus the application of production 4 must be considered whenever the top stack symbol is $\langle A \rangle$ and the current input is in FOLLOW($\langle A \rangle$). It can be computed that:

$$\text{FOLLOW}(\langle A \rangle) = \{b\}$$

In order to simplify the discussion about righthand sides going into ε, we introduce the concept of nullable strings and productions.

A string α of symbols from a grammar is called *nullable* if and only if:

$$\alpha \overset{*}{\Rightarrow} \epsilon$$

A production from the grammar is called *nullable* if and only if its righthand side is nullable.

In the current example, there are two nullable productions, namely productions 4 and 6. The concept of "a righthand side being nullable" is the promised generalization of "a righthand side being ε." The nullable productions play the role that ε-productions played in the study of q-grammars.

Combining the case in which a production is applied to generate a sequence beginning with the current input with the case in which one is applied to generate ε, we now define selection sets for productions of arbitrary form as follows:

Given a production

$$\langle A \rangle \rightarrow \alpha$$

where α is a string of terminals and nonterminals, we define:

$$\text{SELECT}(\langle A \rangle \rightarrow \alpha) = \text{FIRST}(\alpha)$$

if α is not nullable and

$$\text{SELECT}(\langle A \rangle \rightarrow \alpha) = \text{FIRST}(\alpha) \cup \text{FOLLOW}(\langle A \rangle)$$

if α is nullable. If p is the number of the production, we sometimes write

$$\text{SELECT}(p)$$

instead of:

$$\text{SELECT}(\langle A \rangle \rightarrow \alpha)$$

This definition is consistent with the previous definition of SELECT. If the righthand side of a production begins with a terminal,

$$\langle A \rangle \rightarrow b \, \alpha$$

the production is not nullable and

$$\text{SELECT}(\langle A \rangle \rightarrow b \, \alpha) = \text{FIRST}(b \, \alpha) = \{b\}$$

which is the same selection set as described in the definition of the previous section. If we have ϵ-production

$$\langle A \rangle \rightarrow \epsilon$$

then this production is nullable and

$$\text{SELECT}(\langle A \rangle \rightarrow \epsilon) = \text{FIRST}(\epsilon) \cup \text{FOLLOW}(\langle A \rangle) = \text{FOLLOW}(\langle A \rangle)$$

because $\text{FIRST}(\epsilon)$ is the empty set and so again this new definition is consistent with the earlier definition.

Returning to the example, the computations of the selection sets for the two nullable productions are as follows:

$$\text{SELECT}(4) = \text{FIRST}(\langle B \rangle) \cup \text{FOLLOW}(\langle A \rangle) = \{c\} \cup \{b\} = \{c, b\}$$
$$\text{SELECT}(6) = \text{FIRST}(\epsilon) \cup \text{FOLLOW}(\langle B \rangle) = \{\,\} \cup \{b, d, \dashv\}$$
$$= \{b, d, \dashv\}$$

For the other productions, the selection sets are just the FIRST sets shown in Fig. 8.15, that is:

$$\text{SELECT}(1) = \text{FIRST}(\langle A \rangle \, b \, \langle B \rangle) = \{a, b, c, e\}$$

Having computed the selection set for each production of the example, we can specify a control table for a pushdown machine recognizer. We specify that each production be "applied" in those entries of the control table

	a	b	c	d	e	⊣
$<S>$	# 1	# 1	# 1	# 2	# 1	REJECT
$<A>$	# 3	# 4	# 4	REJECT	# 3	REJECT
$<B>$	REJECT	# 6	# 5	# 6	REJECT	# 6
$<C>$	# 7	REJECT	REJECT	REJECT	# 8	REJECT
b	REJECT	POP ADVANCE	REJECT	REJECT	REJECT	REJECT
d	REJECT	REJECT	REJECT	POP ADVANCE	REJECT	REJECT
▽	REJECT	REJECT	REJECT	REJECT	REJECT	ACCEPT

Starting stack: ▽ $<S>$

#1   REPLACE($<B>b<A>$), RETAIN
#2   POP, ADVANCE
#3   REPLACE($b<A><C>$), RETAIN
#4   REPLACE($<B>$), RETAIN
#5   REPLACE($d<S>$), ADVANCE
#6   POP, RETAIN
#7   POP, ADVANCE
#8   REPLACE(d), ADVANCE

Figure 8.16

whose stack symbol is the lefthand side of the production and whose input symbol is in the selection set of the production. In the example there are no table entries where two different productions should be applied and the control table of Fig. 8.16 results. From our previous reasoning, it is clear that this machine indeed recognizes the given language.

Now we wish to define an LL(1) grammar as one in which this approach to control table specification always succeeds:

A context-free grammar is called an *LL(1) grammar* if and only if productions with the same lefthand side have disjoint selection sets.

The rules given in Section 8.3 for constructing a pushdown recognizer can now be extended to LL(1) grammars. Rule 5 should be replaced by the following two rules:

5′. A production is applied whenever the stack symbol is its lefthand side and the input is in its selection set. To apply a production of the form

$$\langle A \rangle \rightarrow b\, \alpha$$

where b is a terminal and α a string of terminals and nonterminals, use the transition:

$$\text{REPLACE}(\alpha^r), \text{ADVANCE}$$

To apply a production of the form

$$\langle A \rangle \rightarrow \alpha$$

where α is a string of terminals and nonterminals not beginning with a terminal, use the transition:

$$\text{REPLACE}(\alpha^r), \text{RETAIN}$$

When α is ϵ, POP may be used instead of REPLACE(ϵ).

5″. If there is a nullable production for nonterminal $\langle A \rangle$ and no entry for stack symbol $\langle A \rangle$ and input b is implied by rule 5′, then either the nullable production can be applied or the sequence can be rejected.

The set of rules for constructing a recognizer establishes the following fact:

If a language has an LL(1) grammar, it can be recognized by a one-state pushdown machine using the extended stack operation REPLACE.

As a second example we design a recognizer for arithmetic expressions over + and *, based on the grammar of Section 6.10

1. $\langle E \rangle \rightarrow \langle T \rangle \langle E\text{-list} \rangle$
2. $\langle E\text{-list} \rangle \rightarrow + \langle T \rangle \langle E\text{-list} \rangle$
3. $\langle E\text{-list} \rangle \rightarrow \epsilon$
4. $\langle T \rangle \rightarrow \langle P \rangle \langle T\text{-list} \rangle$
5. $\langle T\text{-list} \rangle \rightarrow * \langle P \rangle \langle T\text{-list} \rangle$
6. $\langle T\text{-list} \rangle \rightarrow \epsilon$
7. $\langle P \rangle \rightarrow (\langle E \rangle)$
8. $\langle P \rangle \rightarrow I$

This grammar is LL(1) with selection sets:

$$\text{SELECT}(1) = \text{FIRST}(\langle T \rangle \langle E\text{-list} \rangle) = \{I, (\}$$
$$\text{SELECT}(2) = \text{FIRST}(+ \langle T \rangle \langle E\text{-list} \rangle) = \{+\}$$
$$\text{SELECT}(3) = \text{FOLLOW}(\langle E\text{-list} \rangle) = \{), \dashv\}$$
$$\text{SELECT}(4) = \text{FIRST}(\langle P \rangle \langle T\text{-list} \rangle) = \{I, (\}$$
$$\text{SELECT}(5) = \text{FIRST}(*\langle P \rangle \langle T\text{-list} \rangle) = \{*\}$$
$$\text{SELECT}(6) = \text{FOLLOW}(\langle T\text{-list} \rangle) = \{+,), \dashv\}$$
$$\text{SELECT}(7) = \text{FIRST}((\langle E \rangle)) = \{(\}$$
$$\text{SELECT}(8) = \text{FIRST}(I) = \{I\}$$

	I	+	*	(	)	⊣
<E>	# 1	REJECT	REJECT	# 1	REJECT	REJECT
<T>	# 4	REJECT	REJECT	# 4	REJECT	REJECT
<P>	# 8	REJECT	REJECT	# 7	REJECT	REJECT
<E-list>	REJECT	# 2	REJECT	REJECT	# 3	# 3
<T-list>	REJECT	# 6	# 5	REJECT	# 6	# 6
)	REJECT	REJECT	REJECT	REJECT	POP ADVANCE	REJECT
▽	REJECT	REJECT	REJECT	REJECT	REJECT	ACCEPT

Starting stack: ▽ <E>

```
# 1  REPLACE(<E-list><T>), RETAIN
# 2  REPLACE(<E-list><T>), ADVANCE
# 3  POP, RETAIN
# 4  REPLACE(<T-list><P>), RETAIN
# 5  REPLACE(<T-list><P>), ADVANCE
# 6  POP, RETAIN
# 7  REPLACE( )<E>), ADVANCE
# 8  POP, ADVANCE
```

Figure 8.17

▽ $\langle E \rangle$	$I + I * I \dashv$
▽ $\langle E\text{-list} \rangle \langle T \rangle$	$I + I * I \dashv$
▽ $\langle E\text{-list} \rangle \langle T\text{-list} \rangle \langle P \rangle$	$I + I * I \dashv$
▽ $\langle E\text{-list} \rangle \langle T\text{-list} \rangle$	$+ I * I \dashv$
▽ $\langle E\text{-list} \rangle$	$+ I * I \dashv$
▽ $\langle E\text{-list} \rangle \langle T \rangle$	$I * I \dashv$
▽ $\langle E\text{-list} \rangle \langle T\text{-list} \rangle \langle P \rangle$	$I * I \dashv$
▽ $\langle E\text{-list} \rangle \langle T\text{-list} \rangle$	$* I \dashv$
▽ $\langle E\text{-list} \rangle \langle T\text{-list} \rangle \langle P \rangle$	$I \dashv$
▽ $\langle E\text{-list} \rangle \langle T\text{-list} \rangle$	$\dashv$
▽ $\langle E\text{-list} \rangle$	$\dashv$
▽	$\dashv$

ACCEPT

Figure 8.18

The processor is shown in Fig. 8.17. Figure 8.18 shows a stack movie of this processor accepting the expression:

$$I + I * I$$

The principles of Section 8.4 are easily extended to perform string translations specified by string translation grammars which have LL(1) input grammars. The extension concerns productions of the form

$$\langle A \rangle \rightarrow \xi\, \alpha$$

where ξ is a string of action symbols and α is either ϵ or a string beginning with a nonterminal. In this second case the transitions which apply this production should be

$$\text{OUT}(\bar{\xi}), \text{REPLACE}(\alpha^r), \text{RETAIN}$$

where $\bar{\xi}$ is the output string implied by action string ξ. With this addition, the construction establishes the following fact:

> Given a string translation grammar whose input grammar is an LL(1) grammar, the specified string translation can be performed by a one-state pushdown machine using the extended stack operation REPLACE.

To illustrate this construction, consider the following grammar with starting symbol $\langle S \rangle$

1. $\langle S \rangle \rightarrow \{x\}\, \langle A \rangle\, \{y\}$
2. $\langle S \rangle \rightarrow a\, \{y\}$
3. $\langle A \rangle \rightarrow \{z\}$
4. $\langle A \rangle \rightarrow b\, \langle S \rangle\, \{z\}\, c\, \langle A \rangle$

The selection sets for the input grammar are:

$$\text{SELECT}(1) = \text{FIRST}(\langle A \rangle) \cup \text{FOLLOW}(\langle S \rangle) = \{b\} \cup \{c, \dashv\}$$
$$= \{b, c, \dashv\}$$
$$\text{SELECT}(2) = \text{FIRST}(a) = \{a\}$$
$$\text{SELECT}(3) = \text{FIRST}(\epsilon) \cup \text{FOLLOW}(\langle A \rangle) = \{\ \} \cup \{c, \dashv\}$$
$$= \{c, \dashv\}$$
$$\text{SELECT}(4) = \text{FIRST}(b\, \langle S \rangle\, c\, \langle A \rangle) = \{b\}$$

The resulting pushdown machine is shown in Fig. 8.19.

The relationship between LL(1) grammars and q-grammars can be expressed by the following fact:

> Given an LL(1) grammar, a q-grammar can be obtained for the same language.

	a	b	c	$\dashv$
$<S>$	# 2	# 1	# 1	# 1
$<A>$	# 3 or REJECT	# 4	# 3	# 3
c	REJECT	REJECT	POP ADVANCE	REJECT
∇	REJECT	REJECT	REJECT	ACCEPT
$\{y\}$	OUT(y), POP, RETAIN			
$\{z\}$	OUT(z), POP, RETAIN			

Starting stack: ∇ $<S>$

1   OUT(x), REPLACE($\{y\}<A>$), RETAIN
2   OUT(y), POP, ADVANCE
3   OUT(z), POP, RETAIN
4   REPLACE($<A>c\{z\}$ $<S>$), ADVANCE

Figure 8.19

The corresponding q-grammar can be found by the method of "corner substitution" described in Appendix C.

The name "LL(1)" comes from the fact that the machine begins scanning on the <u>L</u>eft, it detects an occurrence of a production when it gets to the <u>L</u>eftmost symbol derived from that production, and the decision is made looking at <u>one</u> input. Top down parsing can also be discussed using "selection sets" made up of input sequences of length k in which case one refers to LL(k) grammars. The practical applications of LL(k) grammars for k greater than 1 are so rare that this case is not discussed further.

8.7   FINDING SELECTION SETS

In this section we give a procedure for finding the selection sets for the productions of a given grammar. This procedure enables one to test a grammar to see if it is LL(1) and, if it is, to construct a top-down pushdown recognizer. This section assumes an understanding of the appendix on relations (Appendix B). The appendix may be read independently of any other material in this book.

Recall that we are assuming the grammars under consideration have no extraneous nonterminals. In effect, we assume that as a preliminary step a given grammar is tested by the procedure of Section 6.14 and that extraneous nonterminals are discarded or the grammar otherwise rewritten.

The procedure for finding selection sets is summarized in Fig. 8.20. The figure can be regarded as a table of contents for this section. Later parts of the section define the relations shown in the figure and explain each step of the procedure.

Using the given grammar:

1. Find the nullable nonterminals and productions.
2. Construct the relation BEGINS-DIRECTLY-WITH.
3. Compute the relation BEGINS-WITH.
4. Compute the FIRST set for each nonterminal.
5. Compute the FIRST set for each production.
6. Construct the relation IS-FOLLOWED-DIRECTLY-BY.
7. Construct the relation IS-DIRECT-END-OF.
8. Compute the relation IS-END-OF.
9. Compute the relation IS-FOLLOWED-BY.
10. Extend IS-FOLLOWED-BY to include endmarker.
11. Compute the FOLLOW set for each nullable nonterminal.
12. Compute the selection sets.

Fig. 8.20 Procedure for finding selection sets

Step 1 in the procedure for finding selection sets is to identify the nullable nonterminals and productions. This is easily accomplished by the following:

1. From the given grammar, delete all productions which have a terminal symbol as part of their righthand sides. (Since ϵ is not a terminal symbol, this step does not delete any ϵ-productions.)

2. From the grammar obtained in step 1, determine which of the nonterminals are alive and which are dead according to the procedure given in Section 6.14.

3. The nullable nonterminals are those found to be alive in step 2 and the nullable productions are those for which the symbols on the righthand side are nullable.

The procedure works because it identifies those nonterminals from which terminal sequences can be derived using productions without terminal symbols. The only terminal sequence that can be generated by such a derivation is the null sequence.

To illustrate the procedure, consider the following grammar with starting nonterminal $\langle S \rangle$:

1. $\langle S \rangle \rightarrow \langle A \rangle \langle B \rangle$
2. $\langle S \rangle \rightarrow b \langle C \rangle$
3. $\langle A \rangle \rightarrow \epsilon$
4. $\langle A \rangle \rightarrow b$
5. $\langle B \rangle \rightarrow \epsilon$
6. $\langle B \rangle \rightarrow a \langle D \rangle$
7. $\langle C \rangle \rightarrow \langle A \rangle \langle D \rangle$
8. $\langle C \rangle \rightarrow b$
9. $\langle D \rangle \rightarrow a \langle S \rangle$
10. $\langle D \rangle \rightarrow c$

Deleting the productions containing a terminal symbol gives the following grammar:

1. $\langle S \rangle \rightarrow \langle A \rangle \langle B \rangle$
3. $\langle A \rangle \rightarrow \epsilon$
5. $\langle B \rangle \rightarrow \epsilon$
7. $\langle C \rangle \rightarrow \langle A \rangle \langle D \rangle$

Applying step 2 reveals that $\langle S \rangle$, $\langle A \rangle$, $\langle B \rangle$ are alive and hence nullable and that $\langle C \rangle$ and $\langle D \rangle$ are not. The nullable productions are thus productions 1, 3, and 5.

Step 2 of the selection-set procedure is the construction of a relation called BEGINS-DIRECTLY-WITH. This relation is defined on the symbols of the grammar for which we wish to compute the selection sets. Intuitively, we say that

A BEGINS-DIRECTLY-WITH *B*

if a sequence beginning with *B* can be obtained from *A* by applying exactly one production and then optionally replacing nullable nonterminals with ϵ. This relation can be expressed as follows:

If A and B are symbols in a given grammar, we write

$$A \text{ BEGINS-DIRECTLY-WITH } B$$

if and only if there is a production of the form

$$A \rightarrow \alpha\, B\, \beta$$

where α is a nullable string and β an arbitrary string.

It is important to realize that a production can have the form

$$A \rightarrow \alpha\, B\, \beta$$

with nullable α in more than one way.

Suppose for example that the production is:

$$\langle A \rangle \rightarrow \langle V \rangle\, \langle X \rangle\, \langle Y \rangle\, \langle Z \rangle$$

It is seen to have the form $A \rightarrow \alpha\, B\, \beta$ by taking

$$A = \langle A \rangle,\ \alpha = \epsilon,\ B = \langle V \rangle,\ \beta = \langle X \rangle\, \langle Y \rangle\, \langle Z \rangle$$

and so

$$\langle A \rangle \text{ BEGINS-DIRECTLY-WITH } \langle V \rangle$$

However, if $\langle V \rangle$ is nullable, then the form is also satisfied with

$$A - \langle A \rangle,\ \alpha = \langle V \rangle,\ B = \langle X \rangle,\ \beta = \langle Y \rangle\, \langle Z \rangle$$

and it is also true that

$$\langle A \rangle \text{ BEGINS-DIRECTLY-WITH } \langle X \rangle$$

If, in addition, $\langle X \rangle$ is nullable, the form is also satisfied with

$$A = \langle A \rangle,\ \alpha = \langle V \rangle\, \langle X \rangle,\ B = \langle Y \rangle,\ \beta = \langle Z \rangle$$

and then

$$\langle A \rangle \text{ BEGINS-DIRECTLY-WITH } \langle Y \rangle$$

Finally, if it were also true that $\langle Y \rangle$ were nullable, then

$$\langle A \rangle \text{ BEGINS-DIRECTLY-WITH } \langle Z \rangle$$

would be true even though $\langle Z \rangle$ happens to be the rightmost symbol of the righthand side.

This approach can be summarized by a very simple procedure for constructing a matrix or graph for the relation BEGINS-DIRECTLY-WITH:

For each production

$$A \rightarrow \alpha$$

and each symbol B in righthand side α, determine if the symbols (if any) to the left of B in α are all nullable. If they are, mark the matrix or graph to indicate

$$A \text{ BEGINS-DIRECTLY-WITH } B$$

We now illustrate the above procedure by constructing the matrix representation of BEGINS-DIRECTLY-WITH for the following grammar with starting nonterminal $\langle A \rangle$. This grammar is used as an example for the remainder of this section.

1. $\langle A \rangle \rightarrow \langle B \rangle \langle C \rangle c$
2. $\langle A \rangle \rightarrow e \langle D \rangle \langle B \rangle$
3. $\langle B \rangle \rightarrow \epsilon$
4. $\langle B \rangle \rightarrow b \langle C \rangle \langle D \rangle \langle E \rangle$
5. $\langle C \rangle \rightarrow \langle D \rangle a \langle B \rangle$
6. $\langle C \rangle \rightarrow c a$
7. $\langle D \rangle \rightarrow \epsilon$
8. $\langle D \rangle \rightarrow d \langle D \rangle$
9. $\langle E \rangle \rightarrow e \langle A \rangle f$
10. $\langle E \rangle \rightarrow c$

A trivial calculation reveals that the nullable nonterminals are $\langle B \rangle$ and $\langle D \rangle$ and the nullable productions are 3 and 7.

From an inspection of production 1, we conclude that:

$$\langle A \rangle \text{ BEGINS-DIRECTLY-WITH } \langle B \rangle$$

and, because $\langle B \rangle$ is nullable, that:

$$\langle A \rangle \text{ BEGINS-DIRECTLY-WITH } \langle C \rangle$$

Because $\langle C \rangle$ is not nullable, no further conclusions can be made from production 1. Continuing with the other productions, we infer the following relationships:

$\langle A \rangle$ BEGINS-DIRECTLY-WITH e by production 2.
$\langle B \rangle$ BEGINS-DIRECTLY-WITH b by production 4.
$\langle C \rangle$ BEGINS-DIRECTLY-WITH $\langle D \rangle$ and a by production 5.
$\langle C \rangle$ BEGINS-DIRECTLY-WITH c by production 6.
$\langle D \rangle$ BEGINS-DIRECTLY-WITH d by production 8.

⟨*E*⟩ BEGINS-DIRECTLY-WITH *e*   by production 9.

⟨*E*⟩ BEGINS-DIRECTLY-WITH *c*   by production 10.

To record these relationships in a matrix, we prepare a blank table with rows and columns labeled with the symbols in the grammar. Then a 1 is entered in the table for each of the relationships. Thus because of production 1, the ⟨*B*⟩ and ⟨*C*⟩ entries of row ⟨*A*⟩ are marked with a 1. The location of all the 1 entries is shown in Fig. 8.21(a).

Step 3 of the procedure is the computation of the relation BEGINS-WITH defined as follows:

If *A* and *B* are symbols in a given grammar, we write

$$A \text{ BEGINS-WITH } B$$

if and only if there is a string beginning with *B* that can be derived from *A*.

Because any derivation sequence going from *A* to a string beginning with *B* can be expressed as a (possibly zero length) series of BEGINS-DIRECTLY-WITH steps, the relation BEGINS-WITH is the reflexive transitive closure of the relation BEGINS-DIRECTLY-WITH. Hence step 3 of the procedure is the computation of the reflexive transitive closure by a method such as that described in Appendix B. For the example, the resulting matrix representation of BEGINS-WITH is shown in Fig. 8.21(b), where the symbol ∗ in the matrix indicates the pairs added to the BEGINS-DIRECTLY-WITH relation by the closure procedure.

Step 4 is the computation of FIRST(⟨*A*⟩) for each nonterminal ⟨*A*⟩. The set FIRST(⟨*A*⟩) is simply the set of terminals *b* such that

$$⟨A⟩ \text{ BEGINS-WITH } b$$

For each row of the matrix for BEGINS-WITH, the marked terminal columns indicate which terminals are in the FIRST set of the row symbol. Thus in the example

$$\text{FIRST}(⟨A⟩) = \{a, b, c, d, e\}$$
$$\text{FIRST}(⟨B⟩) = \{b\}$$
$$\text{FIRST}(⟨C⟩) = \{a, c, d\}$$
$$\text{FIRST}(⟨D⟩) = \{d\}$$
$$\text{FIRST}(⟨E⟩) = \{c, e\}$$

Step 5 is the computation of FIRST for the righthand side of each production. This computation is easily done with the information obtained in step 4.

Starting with production 1 of the example, because ⟨*B*⟩ is nullable and ⟨*C*⟩ is not,

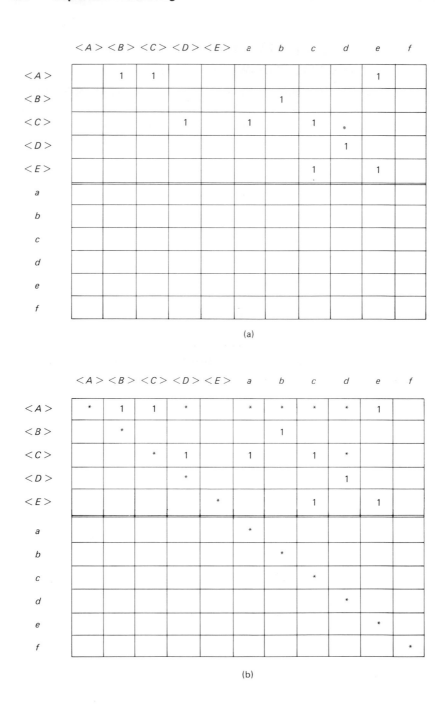

(a)

(b)

Fig. 8.21 (a) BEGINS-DIRECTLY-WITH; (b) BEGINS-WITH

1. FIRST($\langle B \rangle \langle C \rangle c$) = FIRST($\langle B \rangle$) $\cup$ FIRST($\langle C \rangle$) = $\{a, b, c, d\}$

Similarly, we compute as follows for each righthand side:

2. FIRST($e \langle D \rangle \langle B \rangle$) = FIRST($e$) = $\{e\}$
3. FIRST(ϵ) = $\{ \}$
4. FIRST($b \langle C \rangle \langle D \rangle \langle E \rangle$) = FIRST($b$) = $\{b\}$
5. FIRST($\langle D \rangle a \langle B \rangle$) = FIRST($\langle D \rangle$) $\cup$ FIRST(a) = $\{a, d\}$
6. FIRST($c\ a$) = FIRST(c) = $\{c\}$
7. FIRST(ϵ) = $\{ \}$
8. FIRST($d \langle D \rangle$) = FIRST(d) = $\{d\}$
9. FIRST($e \langle A \rangle f$) = FIRST(e) = $\{e\}$
10. FIRST(c) = $\{c\}$

The only symbol that can begin a string derived from terminal t is the terminal t itself. Thus it is not necessary to have rows in the BEGINS-WITH matrix for the terminal symbols, since we can remember the relation

$$t \text{ BEGINS-WITH } t$$

without displaying this fact in the matrix. The double lines in Fig. 8.21 thus separate the information actually needed from the information displayed for expository purposes.

Step 6 is the construction of a relation called IS-FOLLOWED-DIRECTLY-BY. This relation is defined as follows

We write
$$A \text{ IS-FOLLOWED-DIRECTLY-BY } B$$

if and only if there is a production of the form

$$D \rightarrow \alpha\ A\ \beta\ B\ \gamma$$

where A and B are symbols, β is a nullable string, and α and γ are arbitrary strings.

A given righthand side may yield suitable combinations of A and B in many different ways. In the example, production 4 yields 4 pairs, namely

$$b \text{ IS-FOLLOWED-DIRECTLY-BY } \langle C \rangle$$
$$\langle C \rangle \text{ IS-FOLLOWED-DIRECTLY-BY } \langle D \rangle$$
$$\langle D \rangle \text{ IS-FOLLOWED-DIRECTLY-BY } \langle E \rangle$$
$$\langle C \rangle \text{ IS-FOLLOWED-DIRECTLY-BY } \langle E \rangle$$

The last relation holds because the definition is satisfied with

$$\alpha = b,\ A = \langle C \rangle,\ \beta = \langle D \rangle,\ B = \langle E \rangle, \text{ and } \gamma = \epsilon.$$

The construction of a matrix or a graph for the relation IS-FOLLOWED-DIRECTLY-BY can be achieved by the systematic application of the following procedure:

For each production

$$D \rightarrow \alpha$$

and each pair of symbols A and B in righthand side α, determine if the string separating A and B is nullable. If it is and A is to the left of B, mark the matrix or graph to indicate

A IS-FOLLOWED-DIRECTLY-BY B

Returning to the example, we have already determined the implications of production 4. The calculation of the IS-FOLLOWED-DIRECTLY-BY relationships is equally straightforward for the other productions and marking the corresponding entries in a matrix results in Fig. 8.22.

Step 7 is the construction of a relation IS-DIRECT-END-OF defined as follows:

If A and B are symbols in a given grammar, we write

A IS-DIRECT-END-OF B

	<A>	<B>	<C>	<D>	<E>	a	b	c	d	e	f
<A>											1
<B>			1								
<C>				1	1		1				
<D>		1			1	1					
<E>											
a		1									
b			1								
c					1						
d			1								
e	1	1		1							
f											

Fig. 8.22 IS-FOLLOWED-DIRECTLY-BY

if and only if there is a production of the form

$$B \rightarrow \alpha \ A \ \beta$$

where β is a nullable string and α an arbitrary string.

The relation IS-DIRECT-END-OF is simply a right-to-left version of the relation BEGINS-DIRECTLY-WITH and can be constructed by systematic application of the following simple procedure:

For each production

$$B \rightarrow \alpha$$

and each symbol A in righthand side α determine if the symbols to the right of A in α are all nullable. If they are, mark the matrix or graph to indicate:

$$A \text{ IS-DIRECT-END-OF } B$$

Now we compute IS-DIRECT-END-OF for the example. Considering production 2, we see that:

$$\langle B \rangle \text{ IS-DIRECT-END-OF } \langle A \rangle$$

and because $\langle B \rangle$ is nullable:

$$\langle D \rangle \text{ IS-DIRECT-END-OF } \langle A \rangle$$

and because $\langle D \rangle$ is also nullable:

$$e \text{ IS-DIRECT-END-OF } \langle A \rangle$$

Production 4 yields only the relationship:

$$\langle E \rangle \text{ IS-DIRECT-END-OF } \langle B \rangle$$

because rightmost symbol $\langle E \rangle$ is not nullable. After considering all the productions, the resulting pairs are those indicated by 1's in the matrix of Fig. 8.23(a).

Step 8 is the computation of a relation, IS-END-OF, defined as follows:

If A and B are symbols in a given grammar, we write

$$A \text{ IS-END-OF } B$$

if and only if there is a string ending with A that can be derived from B.

The relation IS-END-OF is the reflexive transitive closure of IS-DIRECT-END-OF for the same reasons BEGINS-WITH is the reflexive transitive closure of BEGINS-DIRECTLY-WITH. Applying the reflexive

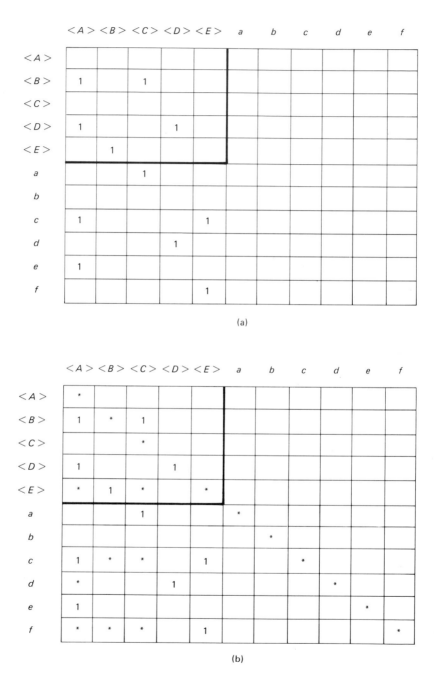

(a)

(b)

Fig. 8.23 (a) IS-DIRECT-END-OF; (b) IS-END-OF

transitive-closure procedure to the matrix for IS-DIRECT-END-OF results in the addition of pairs marked with ∗ in Fig. 8.23(b).

Step 9 is the computation of a relation called IS-FOLLOWED-BY. This relation is defined as follows:

Given a grammar with starting symbol $\langle S \rangle$, we write

$$A \text{ IS-FOLLOWED-BY } B$$

if and only if there is a string that can be derived from $\langle S \rangle$ in which there is an occurrence of symbol A immediately followed by an occurrence of symbol B.
If A and B are symbols such that

$$A \text{ IS-FOLLOWED-BY } B$$

then there must be symbols X and Y such that

$$A \text{ IS-END-OF } X \text{ IS-FOLLOWED-DIRECTLY-BY } Y \text{ BEGINS-WITH } B$$

Given a derivation tree for a sequence with A followed by B, the X and Y can be found by tracing up the tree from A and B until a common righthand side is found. As an illustration, Fig. 8.24 shows a derivation tree for the sequence

$$b \langle C \rangle \ e \ e \langle D \rangle f \langle C \rangle \ c$$

using the grammar of the example. To find the X and Y which explain

$$\langle D \rangle \text{ IS-FOLLOWED-BY } f$$

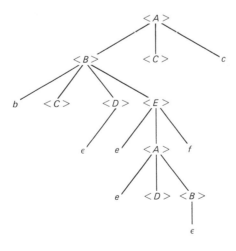

Figure 8.24

trace $\langle D \rangle$ and f back to their common righthand side, namely $e \langle A \rangle f$. Because the $\langle D \rangle$ came from $\langle A \rangle$ and f from f, we take $X = \langle A \rangle$ and $Y = f$ and write

$\langle D \rangle$ IS-END-OF $\langle A \rangle$ IS-FOLLOWED-DIRECTLY-BY f BEGINS-WITH f

A similar analysis for

$\langle C \rangle$ IS-FOLLOWED-BY e

reveals

$\langle C \rangle$ IS-END-OF $\langle C \rangle$ IS-FOLLOWED-DIRECTLY-BY $\langle E \rangle$ BEGINS-WITH e

It should now be apparent that IS-FOLLOWED-BY is the product relation

IS-END-OF · IS-FOLLOWED-DIRECTLY-BY · BEGINS-WITH

This product can be computed using the procedure of Appendix B. Computing this product for the present example gives the matrix of Fig. 8.25 (excluding the column marked $\dashv$).

In order to determine which selection sets contain the endmarker, we must note which symbols can be followed by $\dashv$ in a string derived from $\langle S \rangle \dashv$ where $\langle S \rangle$ is the starting symbol. Obviously, these are precisely the symbols that can end an $\langle S \rangle$ so we extend IS-FOLLOWED-BY to include

	<A>	<B>	<C>	<D>	<E>	a	b	c	d	e	f	⊣
<A>											1	1
<B>			1	1	1	1		1	1	1	1	1
<C>			1	1				1	1	1		
<D>		1			1	1	1	1		1	1	1
<E>			1	1	1	1		1	1	1	1	1
a		1	1	1			1	1	1	1		
b			1	1		1		1	1			
c			1	1	1	1		1	1	1	1	1
d		1	1	1	1	1		1	1	1	1	1
e	1	1	1	1		1	1	1	1	1	1	1
f			1	1	1	1		1	1	1	1	1

Fig. 8.25 IS-FOLLOWED-BY

the endmarker by defining

$$A \text{ IS-FOLLOWED-BY } \dashv$$

if and only if

$$A \text{ IS-END-OF } \langle S \rangle$$

where $\langle S \rangle$ is the starting symbol.

This information is already contained in the starting symbol column of the matrix for the relation IS-END-OF as computed in step 8. Step 10 can thus be accomplished by appending this column to the IS-FOLLOWED-BY matrix computed in step 9 and labeling the column as the endmarker column. For the current example, Fig. 8.25 shows the result of appending the starting symbol $(\langle A \rangle)$ column to the matrix computed in step 9. The appended column appears as the rightmost column separated from the original matrix by the double line.

Step 11 is the computation of the FOLLOW set for each nullable nonterminal, and is easily done once the IS-FOLLOWED-BY relation has been computed. In the example, the nullable nonterminals are $\langle B \rangle$ and $\langle D \rangle$. From the rows for $\langle B \rangle$ and $\langle D \rangle$ in Fig. 8.25, we see that

$$\text{FOLLOW}(\langle B \rangle) = \{a, c, d, e, f, \dashv\}$$
$$\text{FOLLOW}(\langle D \rangle) = \{a, b, c, e, f, \dashv\}$$

The relation IS-FOLLOWED-BY need only be constructed for these two rows, and Fig. 8.25 actually contains much unneeded information. In fact, because we only calculate FOLLOW sets for nonterminals, we only need those parts of Figs. 8.23 and 8.22 indicated by the heavy lines.

Step 12 is the computation of the selection sets which can now be obtained from the computed values of FIRST and FOLLOW. For the example, the selection sets are

$$\begin{aligned}
\text{SELECT}(1) &= \text{FIRST}(\langle B \rangle \langle C \rangle c) = \{a,b,c,d\} \\
\text{SELECT}(2) &= \text{FIRST}(e \langle D \rangle \langle B \rangle) = \{e\} \\
\text{SELECT}(3) &= \text{FIRST}(\epsilon) \cup \text{FOLLOW}(\langle B \rangle) = \{a,c,d,e,f,\dashv\} \\
\text{SELECT}(4) &= \text{FIRST}(b \langle C \rangle \langle D \rangle \langle E \rangle) = \{b\} \\
\text{SELECT}(5) &= \text{FIRST}(\langle D \rangle a \langle B \rangle) = \{a,d\} \\
\text{SELECT}(6) &= \text{FIRST}(c \, a) = \{c\} \\
\text{SELECT}(7) &= \text{FIRST}(\epsilon) \cup \text{FOLLOW}(\langle D \rangle) = \{a,b,c,e,f,\dashv\} \\
\text{SELECT}(8) &= \text{FIRST}(d \langle D \rangle) = \{d\} \\
\text{SELECT}(9) &= \text{FIRST}(e \langle A \rangle f) = \{e\} \\
\text{SELECT}(10) &= \text{FIRST}(c) = \{c\}
\end{aligned}$$

For each nonterminal, the selection sets of productions with that nonterminal as lefthand side are disjoint. Therefore, the language is LL(1) and a topdown pushdown recognizer can be obtained.

8.8   ERROR PROCESSING IN TOP-DOWN PARSING

Compilers often encounter input sequences that are not in the language being recognized. We call these sequences *nonsentences.*

When confronted with a nonsentence, a compiler must detect that an error has occurred (i.e., that the input is a nonsentence). Moreover, the compiler is expected to produce a list of error messages indicating what errors the programmer might have made.

The number and wording of the error messages for a given nonsentence are usually a matter of judgment and are often debatable. In fact, different compilers for the same programming language often produce different error messages for the same nonsentence.

A pushdown recognizer detects that its input sequence is a nonsentence the first time it encounters a REJECT entry in its control table. At this point the compiler is expected to produce an error message describing what mistake the programmer might have made. Furthermore, the compiler is expected to somehow modify the configuration of the pushdown machine so that the processing of the input sequence can be continued and, if appropriate, additional messages can be produced. This modification process is termed *error recovery.* Commonly the REJECT entries in the control table, instead of being just exits, contain calls on routines which produce the error messages and perform the error recovery. The top-down recognizers we have been studying can usually produce helpful error messages because they have a special property we call the "prefix property." Given a pushdown recognizer and a nonsentence, we refer to a symbol of that nonsentence as the *offending symbol* if it is the current input when the recognizer rejects. A pushdown recognizer is said to have the *prefix property* if, for all nonsentences, the sequence of symbols to the left of the offending symbol is the prefix of some acceptable input string. In other words, a recognizer has the prefix property if the offending symbol is the first input inconsistent with the hypothesis that the input sequence is going to be acceptable. Thus a pushdown recognizer with the prefix property detects an error at the earliest possible input.

The machines defined in this chapter all have the prefix property, since the sequence of symbols to the left of the offending symbol can be made into an acceptable string by adding any terminal string derivable from that intermediate string which is on the stack at the time of rejection.

When a recognizer has the prefix property, good error messages are often obtained by assuming the error occurred at or near the offending symbol. To produce an appropriate error message, the compiler can analyze the input string and stack contents at the time of rejection. Frequently an extensive analysis is not made and the error message is based only on the top stack symbol and the current input. The top stack symbol says what the compiler was looking for, and the input says what it found. Thus a conceivable format for the message is

"I WAS LOOKING FOR (THE BEGINNING OF) A _____ , BUT INSTEAD I FOUND A _____ ."

where the first dash contains the name of the top stack symbol (suitably paraphrased to be intelligible to the user) and the second dash contains the name of the input symbol. The error message might not use these exact words, but the form summarizes the information on which the error message is based.

Typically the error message also contains the line or card number and the character position of the offending symbol.

As an example of error-message design consider the s-grammar

1. $\langle S \rangle \rightarrow a$
2. $\langle S \rangle \rightarrow (\langle S \rangle \langle R \rangle$
3. $\langle R \rangle \rightarrow , \langle S \rangle \langle R \rangle$
4. $\langle R \rangle \rightarrow)$

with starting symbol $\langle S \rangle$. This grammar generates LISP-like expressions, such as

$$a$$
$$(a, (a, a))$$
$$((a, (a, a), (a, a)), a)$$

Assume that these expressions have been called "S-expressions" in the language manual and that the programmer is familiar with the term S-expression when it appears in an error message.

Figure 8.26 shows a control table obtained by applying the procedure of Section 8.3 to the grammar. For convenience, the REJECT entries in Fig. 8.26 have been labeled with letters a through j. We begin the error processing design by choosing error messages for each of the REJECT entries.

Experience indicates that frequently several entries in a given row of the table can share the same error message. Hence we consider each row separately. Row $\langle S \rangle$ has three REJECT entries namely a, b, and c. Because

	a	,	(	)	⊣
$\langle S \rangle$	# 1	REJECT a	# 2	REJECT b	REJECT c
$\langle R \rangle$	REJECT d	# 3	REJECT e	# 4	REJECT f
▽	REJECT g	REJECT h	REJECT i	REJECT j	ACCEPT

Starting stack: ▽ $\langle S \rangle$

\# 1 POP, ADVANCE
\# 2 REPLACE($\langle R \rangle \langle S \rangle$), ADVANCE
\# 3 REPLACE($\langle R \rangle \langle S \rangle$), ADVANCE
\# 4 POP, ADVANCE

Figure 8.26

examples of nonterminal $\langle S \rangle$ are known to the user as *S*-expressions, the message for entries *a* and *b* can be

_____ OCCURS WHEN S-EXPRESSION EXPECTED

where the dash is filled with the input symbol. This message would be somewhat inappropriate for entry *c* since replacing the dash with END-MARKER or EXPRESSION END would not mean much to the average user. Looking at some typical input sequences where the message for entry *c* would be produced

$$\dashv$$
$$(\dashv$$
$$(a , \dashv$$

we decide on the message:

S-EXPRESSION INCOMPLETE

Now consider the row for nonterminal $\langle R \rangle$. Because the average user will probably not know anything about nonterminal $\langle R \rangle$, there is no point in mentioning it in the error message. An alternative to mentioning a nonterminal is to mention the inputs which could begin an acceptable continuation. In this case, the acceptable continuations begin with comma or right parenthesis so an appropriate message might be:

_____ OCCURRED WHEN COMMA OR RIGHT PARENTHESIS EX-
PECTED

However, if we are less conservative, we can give a more explicit message indicating the probable cause of the error. This entails a risk that the mes-

a, b: ____ OCCURS WHEN S-EXPRESSION EXPECTED

c: S-EXPRESSION INCOMPLETE

d, e: MISSING COMMA

f: MISSING RIGHT PARENTHESIS

g,h,i,j: ____ OCCURS AFTER END OF S-EXPRESSION

Figure 8.27

sage will be inappropriate. All the sequences which cause the machine to use entries *d* and *e* have an example of $\langle S \rangle$ followed by "*a*" or "(". Some typical sequences that would involve entries *d* and *e*, with the offending symbol underlined, are:

$$(a \underline{a}) \dashv$$
$$((a) \underline{a}) \dashv$$
$$(a \underline{(} a)) \dashv$$
$$((a) \underline{(} a)) \dashv$$

For each sequence, inserting a comma before the offending symbol would allow the machine to continue processing, while inserting a right parenthesis (the other input for stack symbol $\langle R \rangle$) would not. Hence we select the error message

MISSING COMMA

for entries *d* and *e*. This message should indicate to the user how his program is incorrect even if it does not accurately describe his mistake. For instance if he mistakenly typed a left parenthesis instead of a right parenthesis, he might produce the sequence:

$$((a \underline{(} , a)$$

Even for this sequence the programmer would probably not be misled by a message containing the line number and character position of the left parenthesis, plus the words MISSING COMMA.

For entry *f* we select the message

MISSING RIGHT PARENTHESIS

since a right parenthesis is clearly missing, as illustrated by the sample sequence

$$(a , a \dashv$$

The error entries *g, h, i,* and *j* in the bottommarker row of the table correspond to situations in which the recognizer thinks the *S*-expression is over, but there are additional input symbols. An appropriate message is

____ OCCURS AFTER END OF S-EXPRESSION.

The selected error messages are summarized in Fig. 8.27.

Now we consider the problem of error recovery. Our approach is to design error-recovery routines which adjust the input and stack and then continue processing as if no error had occurred. If the pushdown machine subsequently encounters another REJECT entry, it then adds that entry's error message to the list of error messages produced thus far and uses that entry's recovery procedure. We hope that the restored configuration after the first error is "right" in the sense that it corresponds to a configuration that would have resulted if the programmer had not made the first error and that therefore, if any error messages are produced after the recovery they represent additional mistakes that the programmer would like called to his attention. The risk is that the restored configuration is "wrong" and that the compiler might later generate bogus error messages which annoy the programmer because they do not seem to correspond to additional mistakes in the program. Any attempt at error recovery therefore represents a compromise between the desire to detect as many errors as possible and the desire to avoid bogus messages.

First, we consider an approach to error recovery that might be characterized as being "local" in nature. The idea is to fill in each of the REJECT

	a	,	(	)	$\dashv$
$<S>$	# 1	a	# 2	b	c
$<R>$	d	# 3	e	# 4	f
∇	g	h	i	j	ACCEPT

Starting stack: $\nabla <S>$

```
# 1: POP, ADVANCE
# 2: REPLACE(<R><S>), ADVANCE
# 3: REPLACE(<R><S>), ADVANCE
# 4: POP, ADVANCE
a, b: PRINT ( _____ OCCURS WHEN S-EXPRESSION EXPECTED)
      POP, RETAIN
   c: PRINT (S-EXPRESSION INCOMPLETE)
      EXIT
d, e: PRINT (MISSING COMMA)
      REPLACE(<R><S>), RETAIN
   f: PRINT (MISSING RIGHT PARENTHESIS)
      EXIT
g, i: PRINT ( _____ OCCURS AFTER END OF S-EXPRESSION)
      PUSH(<R><S>), RETAIN
   h: PRINT ( _____ OCCURS AFTER END OF S-EXPRESSION)
      PUSH(<R>), RETAIN
   j: PRINT ( _____ OCCURS AFTER END OF S-EXPRESSION)
      ADVANCE
```

Figure 8.28

$$\nabla \langle S \rangle \qquad\qquad (\, a \, , \, , \, a \dashv$$
$$\nabla \langle R \rangle \, \langle S \rangle \qquad\qquad a \, , \, , \, a \dashv$$
$$\nabla \langle R \rangle \qquad\qquad , \, , \, a \dashv$$
$$\nabla \langle R \rangle \, \langle S \rangle \qquad\qquad , \, a \dashv$$

PRINT(4, "COMMA OCCURS WHEN S-EXPRESSION EXPECTED")

$$\nabla \langle R \rangle \qquad\qquad , \, a \dashv$$
$$\nabla \langle R \rangle \, \langle S \rangle \qquad\qquad a \dashv$$
$$\nabla \langle R \rangle \qquad\qquad \dashv$$

PRINT(6, "MISSING RIGHT PARENTHESIS")

EXIT

(a)

$(a \, , \, , \, a$

↑

COMMA OCCURS WHEN S-EXPRESSION EXPECTED

$(a \, , \, , \, a$

↑

MISSING RIGHT PARENTHESIS

(b)

Figure 8.29

entries in the control table with ordinary stack and input operations. If a particular error is detected, first the error message is produced, then the indicated stack and input operations are performed, and finally the usual processing is resumed. The designer selects the operations for each error entry individually based on intuition as to what the error might be and how the stack and input might best be adjusted to resume the processing.

Figure 8.28 shows the complete control table with a reasonable recovery routine specified for each error entry. Note that we have used the notation PUSH( ) for pushing a sequence of symbols in one operation.

It sometimes happens that a single offending symbol can cause two error messages. In the present example the first symbol in the input sequence

$$, \, a \,) \dashv$$

would first cause entry a to be used and, after the recovery procedure for entry a, would cause entry h to be used. However we clearly do not want to print the message for entry h. Therefore we adopt the convention that, if a single input symbol produces several messages, only the first one will be printed.

As an example of error recovery in action, Fig. 8.29(a) shows a stack movie of the machine of Fig. 8.28 processing the input sequence:

$$(a , , a$$

The movie assumes that the messages are prepared by a routine named PRINT that has two parameters: the position of the offending symbol and the words of the message. The messages might actually be displayed to the programmer in a format such as that of Fig. 8.29(b), where the input sequence is printed with an arrow pointing to the offending symbol.

Many compilers classify each error as being either "fatal" or "nonfatal." For fatal errors, the error routine takes some action which prevents the compiler from generating object code and executing the program. For nonfatal errors, the error routine does not take such an action and, if no subsequent fatal errors are detected, the compilation and execution will proceed to completion. In general, nonfatal errors are those for which the compiler designer feels the recovery routine is highly likely to correct the error. The wording of the messages for nonfatal errors usually indicates that only a warning is being given.

In the present example, this type of error correction might be attempted for entries d and e. The error message might be changed to the warning message

"ASSUMED MISSING COMMA"

We now discuss an approach to error recovery that might be characterized as "global." This second approach might be used when the designer has insufficient confidence in the accuracy of any local recovery routines or when the memory requirements do not allow individual recovery routines for each error entry.

The basic idea is to scan ahead in the input sequence until one of a set of "trustworthy" input symbols is found. The error recovery then depends on that symbol and on the top stack symbol. Two types of trustworthy symbols can be considered.

Synchronizing Symbols

A synchronizing symbol is one for which the designer has reasonable confidence that he or she knows how to restart the processing. A set of synchronizing symbols for a given language might include certain punctuation symbols such as comma and semicolon and certain reserved words such as END or THEN.

During error recovery, when the scanning routine finds one of the synchronizing symbols, the stack is popped until a stack symbol is found to which that synchronizing symbol can correctly be applied. The processing is continued from that point.

One simple example of recovery based on synchronizing symbols occurs in those compilers which skip to the next line or the next statement whenever an error is detected. The synchronizing symbols are the statement separators and the "new line" symbols. The recovery procedures for MINI-BASIC (Section 10.4) and for many FORTRAN compilers are of this type.

Beginning Symbols

A beginning symbol is one whose occurrence enables the designer to predict the next several nonterminals or terminals even though he may not be able to restart the processor.

For example, suppose the S-expression grammar were part of a larger grammar which did not use parentheses in any other context. Then, when a left parenthesis occurs in the input, the designer is confident that an S-Expression is starting even though it may not be possible to completely resynchronize the stack and input.

During error recovery, if the scanning routine finds a left parenthesis, we can predict that the left parenthesis begins an $\langle S \rangle$. The recovery procedure does

$$\text{PUSH}(\{\text{ERROR}\} \ \langle S \rangle)$$

and then normal pushdown processing continues with the left parenthesis being applied to the $\langle S \rangle$. The symbol $\{\text{ERROR}\}$ is a new action symbol which functions somewhat like a fake bottommarker. When $\{\text{ERROR}\}$ becomes the top stack symbol, we know that the prediction has been verified. The action taken is to pop $\{\text{ERROR}\}$ off the stack and resume scanning for another synchronizing or beginning symbol.

In general, when a beginning symbol is found, the recovery procedure pushes $\{\text{ERROR}\}$ and the symbols that it can predict. Other examples of beginning symbols occur in languages in which certain reserved words always begin statements.

It should be emphasized that in global recovery procedures, the sets of synchronizing and beginning symbols must be considered together. For example, frequently a certain symbol can be used as a synchronizing symbol only if another specific symbol is used as a beginning symbol.

In the S-Expression grammar, for example, an error-recovery scheme based only on using comma and right parentheses as synchronizing symbols would not work, since if the scanning routine scanned over a left parenthesis looking for a comma, the parenthesis count would be incorrect. However, if left parentheses is considered to be a beginning symbol, then this combination of beginning and synchronizing symbols would be satisfactory.

The recovery techniques outlined above are by no means the only ones that might be used and other routines, particularly of the global type, may be invented to match the peculiar characteristics of a given language. Error recovery is more of an art than a science and the techniques of this section must be regarded as examples rather than as universal procedures.

8.9   METHOD OF RECURSIVE DESCENT

We have discussed how certain kinds of grammars can be recognized and translated in a top-down manner by a pushdown machine. In this section, we present an alternative, but related, method of recognizing and translating these grammars. This alternative method is known as *recursive descent* and is oriented toward situations in which the programming of the compiler is to be done in one of the high-level languages (such as ALGOL and PL/I) that allow recursive procedures. (A procedure is recursive if it can call on itself, either directly or indirectly through a chain of other procedure calls.)

The basic idea of recursive descent is that each nonterminal of the grammar has a corresponding procedure which recognizes an example of that nonterminal. These procedures call on each other when appropriate. The stacking mechanism of the pushdown machine is thus supplanted by the procedure-calling mechanism of the high-level language.

As an example, consider the following q-grammar with starting nonterminal $\langle S \rangle$:

1. $\langle S \rangle \rightarrow a \langle A \rangle \langle S \rangle$
2. $\langle S \rangle \rightarrow b$
3. $\langle A \rangle \rightarrow c \langle A \rangle \langle S \rangle b$
4. $\langle A \rangle \rightarrow \epsilon$

Procedures for recognizing the language generated by this grammar are shown in Fig. 8.30. The procedures for $\langle S \rangle$ and $\langle A \rangle$ are called PROCS and PROCA respectively. They assume the availability of a procedure called ADVANCE which advances the input and assigns the new input symbol to a variable named INP.

The procedure PROCS for $\langle S \rangle$ starts out by making the same decision as would be made by a pushdown recognizer when confronted with top stack symbol $\langle S \rangle$. The procedure inspects the current input and selects a production to be applied. Figure 8.30 shows this selection as being accomplished by a kind of computed goto statement. The table next to the goto shows a label to be transferred to for each value of INP. We assume there is an error routine labeled REJECT.

Label $P1$ marks the code for production 1. The first thing this code does is call ADVANCE. It does this for the same reason that the pushdown recognizer would do an ADVANCE when applying production 1. The current input has been matched with the leftmost symbol of the righthand side

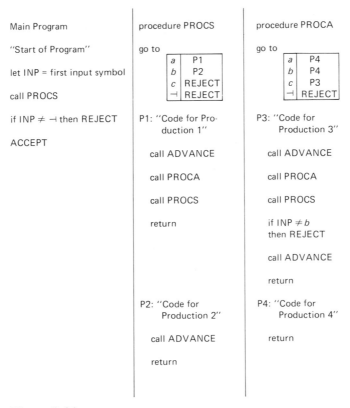

Main Program	procedure PROCS	procedure PROCA

Main Program

"Start of Program"

let INP = first input symbol

call PROCS

if INP ≠ ⊣ then REJECT

ACCEPT

procedure PROCS

go to

a	P1
b	P2
c	REJECT
⊣	REJECT

P1: "Code for Pro-
       duction 1"

call ADVANCE

call PROCA

call PROCS

return

P2: "Code for
       Production 2"

call ADVANCE

return

procedure PROCA

go to

a	P4
b	P4
c	P3
⊣	REJECT

P3: "Code for
       Production 3"

call ADVANCE

call PROCA

call PROCS

if INP ≠ b
then REJECT

call ADVANCE

return

P4: "Code for
       Production 4"

return

Figure 8.30

and the input must be advanced so that the remaining inputs can be pro-
cessed. The pushdown machine would also push an $\langle S \rangle$ and an $\langle A \rangle$ on the
stack because these are the next symbols that must be found in the input
sequence. The procedure PROCS finds these sequences simply by calling
PROCA to find an example of an $\langle A \rangle$ and then PROCS to find an example
of an $\langle S \rangle$. Since the righthand side of production 1 has been accounted for
after these calls are completed, the procedure then does a return.

The code at $P2$ for production 2 is very simple. The current input is
known to be the sought after example of $\langle S \rangle$, so the input is advanced and
the procedure returns.

The procedure PROCA for $\langle A \rangle$ starts out by selecting a production to be
applied. This decision is based on the following equations:

$$\text{SELECT}(3) = \{c\}$$
$$\text{SELECT}(4) = \text{FOLLOW}(\langle A \rangle) = \{a, b\}$$

The code for production 3 is located at *P3*. It first calls ADVANCE, then calls PROCA, and then calls PROCS. After the call on PROCS, the code reaches a point where the current input should be a *b* matching the *b* in the righthand side of the production. To test this, INP is checked to see if the current input is in fact *b*. If it is not, control is passed to the rejection routine. If the current input is *b*, the program continues by advancing the input because the *b* is part of the example of an ⟨*A*⟩ that PROCA has found. Since the complete righthand side is now accounted for, the procedure returns. The code for production 4 of P4 is trivial. There is no input operation since the current input must still be accounted for and no procedure calls since the righthand side is null. Thus the only action is return.

Main Program	procedure PROCS	procedure PROCA
"Start of Program"	go to	go to
let INP = first input symbol		
call PROCS		
if INP ≠ ⊣ then REJECT	P1: "Code for Production 1"	P3: "Code for Production 3"
ACCEPT		
	call ADVANCE	call ADVANCE
	call PROCA	call OUT(*y*)
	call OUT(*x*)	call PROCA
	call PROCS	call PROCS
	return	call OUT(*v*)
		if INP ≠ *b* then REJECT
		call ADVANCE
		return
	P2: "Code for Production 2"	P4: "Code for Production 4"
	call ADVANCE	call OUT(*w*)
	call OUT(*z*)	return
	return	

PROCS go to table:

a	P1
b	P2
c	REJECT
⊣	REJECT

PROCA go to table:

a	P4
b	P4
c	P3
⊣	REJECT

Figure 8.31

A main program to initiate the calling of the procedures is also shown in Fig. 8.30. The duty of this program is to ensure that the input sequence consists of an example of an $\langle S \rangle$ followed by an endmarker. It begins by assigning the first input symbol to INP. Next it calls PROCS and then it verifies that the resulting current input is the endmarker.

The procedures can be easily expanded to do transitions described by a string translation grammar for which the given grammar is an input grammar. For instance, suppose actions are added to the grammar, yielding the following set of productions:

1. $\langle S \rangle \rightarrow a \langle A \rangle \{x\} \langle S \rangle$
2. $\langle S \rangle \rightarrow b \{z\}$
3. $\langle A \rangle \rightarrow c \{y\} \langle A \rangle \langle S \rangle \{v\} b$
4. $\langle A \rangle \rightarrow \{w\}$

The procedures of Fig. 8.30 are modified by adding outputs in places corresponding to the actions added to the grammar. The result is the set of procedures shown in Fig. 8.31.

Recursive descent can be used for any LL(1) grammar. Each nonterminal in the grammar has a corresponding procedure which begins with a computed goto and contains code for each of the productions for the nonterminal. For those input symbols that are in the selection set of a production, the computed goto transfers control to the code for the production. For the remaining input symbols, control is passed to REJECT, or optionally to the code for a nullable production if the nonterminal has one.

The code for a production contains an operation for each symbol on the righthand side of that production. These operations appear in the same order as the symbols appear in the production. After the last operation, the code contains a return from the procedure.

The operation for the various kinds of symbols that can appear in the righthand side of a production of a string translation grammar are:

1. for an action symbol, the operation is an OUT of that symbol;

2. for a terminal that is the first nonaction symbol of the production, the operation is ADVANCE;

3. for other terminals, the operation is a test and ADVANCE;

4. for nonterminals, the operation is a call on the corresponding procedure.

Observe that the recursive procedure for a nonterminal is very similar to the row for that nonterminal in a top-down pushdown recognizer.

The implementation of recursive descent in a high-level language provides the advantage of ease in programming and debugging. In particular, there is no need for the programmer to create and maintain a stack.

Nevertheless, stacking is an essential ingredient of recursive descent since the implementation of the high-level language itself must include a run-time stack or its equivalent. In particular, a stack of return addresses must be maintained during the execution of the program so that each call on a given recursive procedure is able to return control to the place from which it was called. In fact, most high-level languages have more complex stacking mechanisms than those required to implement pushdown machines. Consequently, a straightforward implementation of a pushdown machine is likely to be more efficient than recursive descent in both time and space.

8.10   REFERENCES

The initial work on top-down processing dealt with "nondeterministic top-down" processing. Therefore the word top-down appearing with no qualifiers in the literature frequently refer to the nondeterministic case.

S-grammars were formalized and studied by Korenjak and Hopcroft [1966]. LL grammars were formalized by Lewis and Stearns [1968] and also studied by Kurki-Suonio [1969], Wood [1969a, 1969b], and Rosenkrantz and Stearns [1970]. Grau [1961] describes the use of recursive procedures in a compiler. Some sophisticated error-recovery techniques are described in Irons [1963b] and Freeman [1964].

PROBLEMS

1. An s-grammar generates the following derivation tree:

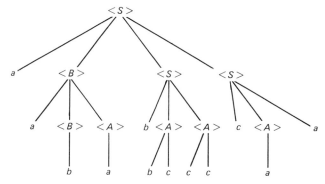

Draw the stack movie of the top-down pushdown recognizer for the grammar processing the following input sequences:

a) *a a b a b b c c c c a a*

b) *c b*

c) *c c c a*

d) *b a a c*

2. For each of the following languages, find an s-grammar and the corresponding top-down pushdown recognizer:

a) $\{1^n\ m\ 0^n\}$ $\hspace{4cm}$ $n \geq 0$

b) $\{w\ m\ w^r\}$ $\hspace{4cm}$ w in $(0 + 1)*$

c) $\{1^n\ m\ 0^n\} \cup \{m\ 1^n\ m\ 0^{2n}\}$ $\hspace{2cm}$ $n > 0$

d) $\{1^n\ m\ 0^n\ 1^p\ m\ 0^p\}$ $\hspace{2.5cm}$ $n > 0, p \geq 0$

e) $\{1^n\ 0^n\}$ $\hspace{4cm}$ $n > 0$

Draw the stack movie as the machine of part d) recognizes the string:

$$1\ 1\ m\ 0\ 0\ 1\ m\ 0$$

3. A top-down processor for the following grammar

1. $\langle S \rangle \rightarrow a\ \langle S \rangle\ \langle S \rangle$
2. $\langle S \rangle \rightarrow b\ \langle S \rangle$
3. $\langle S \rangle \rightarrow c\ \langle S \rangle\ \langle S \rangle\ \langle S \rangle$
4. $\langle S \rangle \rightarrow d$

recognizes the productions in a given sequence in the order:

$$1, 4, 3, 2, 4, 2, 1, 4, 2, 4, 4$$

What is that sequence?

4. The following stack movie corresponds to the top-down pushdown recognizer for an s-grammar. Draw the derivation tree for the input sequence of the movie.

$\triangledown\ \langle S \rangle$	$a\ d\ b\ a\ b\ a\ b \dashv$
$\triangledown\ b\ \langle D \rangle$	$d\ b\ a\ b\ a\ b \dashv$
$\triangledown\ b\ \langle D \rangle\ a\ \langle S \rangle$	$b\ a\ b\ a\ b \dashv$
$\triangledown\ b\ \langle D \rangle\ a$	$a\ b\ a\ b \dashv$
$\triangledown\ b\ \langle D \rangle$	$b\ a\ b \dashv$
$\triangledown\ b\ a$	$a\ b \dashv$
$\triangledown\ b$	$b \dashv$
$\triangledown$	$\dashv$

ACCEPT

5. Show that no sequence in the language generated by an s-grammar can be a prefix of any other sequence in the language.

6. For each of the following languages, find a q-grammar and the corresponding top-down pushdown recognizer

a) $\{1^n\}$ $\hspace{1.5cm}$ $n > 0$

b) $\{1^n\ 0^n\}$ $\hspace{1.2cm}$ $n \geq 0$

c) $\{1^n\ 0^m\}$ $\hspace{1.2cm}$ $0 < n \leq m$

Indicate, without proof, why these languages do not have s-grammars.

7. The following machine was designed using the methods of this chapter.

a) Find the grammar that was used to design the machine.

b) Which entries in the table could be changed to REJECT without affecting the language being recognized.

	a	b	c	d	⊣
\<S\>	# 1	# 2	# 2	# 2	# 2
\<A\>	# 2	# 3	# 2	# 2	# 2
\<B\>	# 4	# 4	# 5	# 6	# 4
▽	# 4	# 4	# 4	# 4	# 7

Starting stack: ▽\<S\>

#1   REPLACE(\<B\> \<A\>), ADVANCE
#2   POP, RETAIN
#3   REPLACE(\<B\> \<A\> \<S\>), ADVANCE
#4   REJECT
#5   REPLACE(\<B\>), ADVANCE
#6   POP, ADVANCE
#7   ACCEPT

8. For each of the translations described in Problem 5.13(a) and (b):

a) design a string translation grammar for which the input grammar is a q-grammar;

b) using this grammar design the control table of a one-state pushdown machine that will perform the translation.

9. Design the control table for the pushdown machine that recognizes top-down the languages generated by each of the following grammars, with starting symbol $\langle S \rangle$:

a) $\langle S \rangle \rightarrow a \langle A \rangle \langle B \rangle$
   $\langle S \rangle \rightarrow b \langle B \rangle \langle S \rangle$
   $\langle S \rangle \rightarrow \epsilon$
   $\langle A \rangle \rightarrow c \langle B \rangle \langle S \rangle$
   $\langle A \rangle \rightarrow \epsilon$
   $\langle B \rangle \rightarrow d \langle B \rangle$
   $\langle B \rangle \rightarrow e$

b) $\langle S \rangle \rightarrow a \langle A \rangle b \langle B \rangle b \langle S \rangle$
   $\langle S \rangle \rightarrow \epsilon$
   $\langle A \rangle \rightarrow a \langle B \rangle \langle C \rangle$
   $\langle A \rangle \rightarrow b \langle A \rangle$
   $\langle B \rangle \rightarrow a \langle B \rangle$
   $\langle B \rangle \rightarrow \epsilon$
   $\langle C \rangle \rightarrow c \langle C \rangle$
   $\langle C \rangle \rightarrow \epsilon$

c) Draw the stack movie of the machine of part b) as it recognizes the sequences:

   $a\ a\ a\ b\ a\ b$

   $a\ a\ b\ b\ a\ a\ b\ b$

10. A certain q-grammar generates the two strings

    $BABY$

    $BBBB$

    When the string $BABY$ is applied to the one-state pushdown machine that recognizes this grammar top down, the sequence of stack configurations is as shown below. (Notice that the indication of which input symbol is applied to which stack configuration has been carefully omitted.)

    $\nabla \langle S \rangle$

    $\nabla \langle S \rangle \langle C \rangle$

    $\nabla \langle S \rangle Y \langle S \rangle \langle C \rangle$

    $\nabla \langle S \rangle Y \langle S \rangle$

    $\nabla \langle S \rangle Y$

    $\nabla \langle S \rangle$

    ∇

    Draw the stack configurations that would result if the string $BBBB$ is presented to this machine.

11. Write a program in your favorite language to implement the pushdown machines of:

    a) Fig. 8.6

    b) Fig. 8.8

    c) Fig. 8.12

    d) Fig. 8.16

    Use one of the methods given in Chapter 3 to implement the control table, and use an array with some type of pointer to implement the stack.

12. Given an arbitrary grammar, show how to find a string translation grammar describing the translation from leftmost derivations (represented as a sequence of production names) into sequences generated by the derivations.

13. For any context-free grammar show how to find a pushdown machine which will accept as input the sequence of productions used in the leftmost derivation of some sentence in the language and which will produce as output:

    a) the reverse of the sequence of productions used in the rightmost derivation;

    b) the string generated by the derivation;

    c) the translation defined on that grammar by an arbitrary translation grammar.

14. For the following grammar with starting symbol $\langle S \rangle$:

    $\langle S \rangle \rightarrow a \langle A \rangle \langle B \rangle$

    $\langle S \rangle \rightarrow b \langle A \rangle$

    $\langle S \rangle \rightarrow \epsilon$

    $\langle A \rangle \rightarrow a \langle A \rangle b$

$$\langle A \rangle \to \epsilon$$

$$\langle B \rangle \to b \langle B \rangle$$

$$\langle B \rangle \to c$$

a) find FOLLOW of each of the nonterminals;

b) find SELECT of each of the productions;

c) determine if this is a q-grammar.

15. Design a pushdown machine for each of the following string translation grammars with starting symbol $\langle S \rangle$

$$\langle S \rangle \to a \ \{x\} \ \langle B \rangle \ \{h\} \ \{a\} \ c$$

$$\langle S \rangle \to \{a\} \ b \ \{a\}$$

$$\langle B \rangle \to c \ \{x\} \ \{y\} \ \langle B \rangle \ \langle B \rangle \ \{e\}$$

$$\langle B \rangle \to a \ \{b\} \ \{c\} \ d \ \{e\} \ f \ \{y\}$$

(a)

$$\langle S \rangle \to 3 \ \{\text{THREE}\} \ \langle \text{erp} \rangle \ \langle S \rangle \ \{\text{VOID}\}$$

$$\langle S \rangle \to \{y\} \ \{z\} \ 4$$

$$\langle \text{erp} \rangle \to \epsilon$$

$$\langle \text{erp} \rangle \to 2 \ \{\text{TWO}\} \ \langle S \rangle \ \langle \text{erp} \rangle$$

(b)

$$\langle S \rangle \to \{A\} \ \langle \text{noon} \rangle \ \{Y\} \ Y$$

$$\langle S \rangle \to X \ \{\text{ORB}\}$$

$$\langle \text{noon} \rangle \to \{\text{NIB}\} \ Q \ \langle \text{noon} \rangle$$

$$\langle \text{noon} \rangle \to \{\text{BLAZB}\}$$

(c)

16. Given any LL(1) grammar, show how to find a string translation grammar which will translate any sentence in the language into the sequence of production names used in its derivation in the order that these productions would be recognized by a top-down recognizer.

17. An LL(1) grammar generates the following derivation tree:

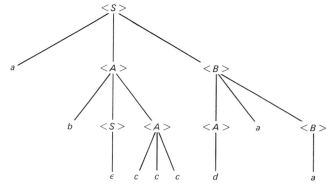

Draw the stack movie of the top-down pushdown recognizer for the grammar processing the following input sequences:

a) $a\,b\,c\,c\,c\,d\,a\,a$

b) ϵ

c) $a\,c\,c\,c$

d) $a\,d\,a\,b$

18. Suppose a grammar contains the production

$$\langle A \rangle \to \alpha$$

(where α is a sequence of terminals and nonterminals) and that this production is nullable. Show that if $\text{FIRST}(\alpha)$ and $\text{FOLLOW}(\langle A \rangle)$ are not disjoint, then the grammar cannot be LL(1).

19. Show that given an LL(1) grammar with starting symbol $\langle S \rangle$ (and no extraneous nonterminals), the grammar remains LL(1) if a different nonterminal is designated to be the starting symbol.

20. State whether or not each of the following stack movies can correspond to a top-down pushdown recognizer.

$\nabla\,\langle S \rangle$	$a\,b\,a\,c \dashv$	$\nabla\,\langle S \rangle$	$a\,b\,a\,c \dashv$
$\nabla\,c\,\langle S \rangle\,\langle B \rangle$	$b\,a\,c \dashv$	$\nabla\,\langle B \rangle\,\langle S \rangle\,\langle B \rangle$	$b\,a\,c \dashv$
$\nabla\,c\,\langle S \rangle$	$a\,c \dashv$	$\nabla\,\langle B \rangle\,\langle S \rangle$	$b\,a\,c \dashv$
$\nabla\,c$	$c \dashv$	$\nabla\,\langle B \rangle$	$a\,c \dashv$
∇	$\dashv$	$\nabla\,c$	$c \dashv$
ACCEPT		∇	$\dashv$
		ACCEPT	
(a)		(b)	

$\nabla\,\langle S \rangle$	$a\,a\,a\,b \dashv$	$\nabla\,\langle S \rangle$	$\dashv$
$\nabla\,\langle B \rangle\,\langle S \rangle$	$a\,a\,b \dashv$	∇	$\dashv$
$\nabla\,\langle B \rangle\,\langle B \rangle\,\langle S \rangle$	$a\,b \dashv$	REJECT	
$\nabla\,\langle B \rangle\,\langle B \rangle\,\langle B \rangle\,\langle S \rangle$	$b \dashv$		
$\nabla\,\langle B \rangle\,\langle B \rangle\,\langle B \rangle$	$b \dashv$		
$\nabla\,\langle B \rangle\,\langle B \rangle$	$\dashv$		
$\nabla\,\langle B \rangle$	$\dashv$		
∇	$\dashv$		
ACCEPT			
(c)		(d)	

∇ ⟨S⟩	$a\,b\,c\,d \dashv$	∇ ⟨S⟩	$a\,b \dashv$
∇ ⟨S⟩	$b\,c\,d \dashv$	∇	$b \dashv$
∇ ⟨S⟩	$c\,d \dashv$	∇	$\dashv$
∇ ⟨S⟩	$d \dashv$	ACCEPT	
∇ ⟨S⟩	$\dashv$		
∇	$\dashv$		
ACCEPT			

(e)	(f)

21. Find all the nullable nonterminals in the following grammar:

$$\langle S \rangle \rightarrow a \langle B \rangle \langle D \rangle$$
$$\langle S \rangle \rightarrow \langle A \rangle \langle B \rangle$$
$$\langle S \rangle \rightarrow \langle D \rangle \langle A \rangle \langle C \rangle$$
$$\langle S \rangle \rightarrow b$$
$$\langle A \rangle \rightarrow \langle S \rangle \langle C \rangle \langle B \rangle$$
$$\langle A \rangle \rightarrow \langle S \rangle \langle A \rangle \langle B \rangle \langle C \rangle$$
$$\langle A \rangle \rightarrow \langle C \rangle b \langle D \rangle$$
$$\langle A \rangle \rightarrow c$$
$$\langle A \rangle \rightarrow \epsilon$$
$$\langle B \rangle \rightarrow c \langle D \rangle$$
$$\langle B \rangle \rightarrow d$$
$$\langle B \rangle \rightarrow \epsilon$$
$$\langle C \rangle \rightarrow \langle A \rangle \langle D \rangle \langle C \rangle$$
$$\langle C \rangle \rightarrow c$$
$$\langle D \rangle \rightarrow \langle S \rangle a \langle C \rangle$$
$$\langle D \rangle \rightarrow \langle S \rangle \langle C \rangle$$
$$\langle D \rangle \rightarrow f\,g$$

22. Can two nullable productions in an LL(1) grammar have the same lefthand side?

23. Describe how the procedure for finding selection sets given in Section 8.7 can be simplified in the case of q-grammars.

24. For the following grammar with starting symbol ⟨S⟩:

$$\langle S \rangle \rightarrow a \langle A \rangle \langle B \rangle b \langle C \rangle \langle D \rangle$$
$$\langle S \rangle \rightarrow \epsilon$$
$$\langle A \rangle \rightarrow \langle A \rangle \langle S \rangle d$$
$$\langle A \rangle \rightarrow \epsilon$$
$$\langle B \rangle \rightarrow \langle S \rangle \langle A \rangle c$$

$\langle B \rangle \rightarrow e \langle C \rangle$

$\langle B \rangle \rightarrow \epsilon$

$\langle C \rangle \rightarrow \langle S \rangle f$

$\langle C \rangle \rightarrow \langle C \rangle g$

$\langle C \rangle \rightarrow \epsilon$

$\langle D \rangle \rightarrow a \langle B \rangle \langle D \rangle$

$\langle D \rangle \rightarrow \epsilon$

a) find FOLLOW of each of the nonterminals;

b) find SELECT of each of the productions;

c) determine if this is an LL(1)-grammar.

25. Write a program in ALGOL or PL/I that implements the recursive-descent procedure for the pushdown machines of

a) Fig. 8.6

b) Fig. 8.8

c) Fig. 8.12

d) Fig. 8.16

26. Show how to implement a procedure similar to recursive descent using a language, such as FORTRAN, that does not allow recursive procedure calls. Use a stack to keep track of return points. Demonstrate your procedure on the pushdown machine of Fig. 8.12.

27. Show how to extend the ideas of Section 8.9 to design a recursive-processing method for implementing a general primitive pushdown machine (i.e., a multistate machine with stack operations PUSH and POP).

28. For each REJECT entry of Fig. 8.26:

a) find the shortest input sequence that reaches that entry.

b) For each sequence found in Part a) delete the offending symbol and find the shortest sequence that can be concatenated with the prefix sequence to form a correct sentence.

29. a) Find a set of sequences that will visit all the entries, including the REJECT entries, in the control table of Fig. 8.28.

b) List all the error messages that would be produced for each of your sequences.

30. Draw the stack movie and list all the error messages that would be put out by the machine of Fig. 8.28 given the input sequence

$$, a , a\, a\, (\, a , , (\,) \, a , , ,$$

31. Do you think it would be advisable to change the error-recovery routine for entry a of Fig. 8.28 to:

a) REPLACE($\langle R \rangle$ $\langle S \rangle$), ADVANCE

b) POP, ADVANCE

c) ADVANCE

32. Find three sequences for which the local error-recovery procedure of Fig. 8.28 does a poor job. Describe what went wrong.

33. Find a context-free grammar for the set of sequences that reaches the accept entry in the machine of Fig. 8.28.

34. In the following grammar with starting symbol $\langle E \rangle$ the operator ↑ means exponentiation. In the expressions generated from this grammar, the exponentiation is to be done from left to right except that operations within parentheses are to be done first.

1. $\langle E \rangle \rightarrow a \langle R \rangle$
2. $\langle E \rangle \rightarrow (\langle E \rangle) \langle R \rangle$
3. $\langle R \rangle \rightarrow \uparrow a \langle R \rangle$
4. $\langle R \rangle \rightarrow \epsilon$

a) Show that this grammar is q.

b) Design the q-grammar recognizer.

c) Design the complete error-processing portion of the processor including error messages and local error-recovery routines.

35. For the following ALGOL-like grammar with starting symbol $\langle \text{statement} \rangle$

1. $\langle \text{statement} \rangle \rightarrow$ **begin** $\langle \text{declarations} \rangle \langle \text{statement list} \rangle$ **end**
2. $\langle \text{declarations} \rangle \rightarrow d ; \langle \text{declarations} \rangle$
3. $\langle \text{declarations} \rangle \rightarrow \epsilon$
4. $\langle \text{statement list} \rangle \rightarrow s \langle \text{more statements} \rangle$
5. $\langle \text{statement list} \rangle \rightarrow \epsilon$
6. $\langle \text{more statements} \rangle \rightarrow ; \langle \text{statement list} \rangle$
7. $\langle \text{more statements} \rangle \rightarrow \epsilon$

a) Show that the grammar is q.

b) Design the q-grammar recognizer.

c) Design an appropriate set of error messages.

d) Design local error-recovery routines.

e) Design global error-recovery routines.

36. a) Design a q-grammar for S-expressions in LISP.

b) Design the control table of the top-down pushdown recognizer corresponding to your grammar.

c) Design error messages for all the error entries in the table.

d) Design local error-recovery routines.

37. a) Show that every regular set has a q-grammar.

   b) Find a regular set that has no s-grammar.

   c) Show that for any regular set R, the language $R \dashv$, where $\dashv$ is regarded as a terminal symbol, has an s-grammar.

38. A finite-state translator is a finite-state recognizer which is augmented so that a specified output can occur at each transition. Show that the input-output relation of such a device can always be characterized by a string translation grammar for which the input grammar is a q-grammar.

39. Find a q-grammar for each of the following constructions in ALGOL. Do not carry the derivation below the level of ⟨Boolean expression⟩ or ⟨arithmetic expression⟩ or, in the case of the **for** statement, ⟨statement⟩.

   a) Array declarations

   b) Switch declarations

   c) **for** statements

40. a) Indicate why the following language does not have an LL-grammar.

$$\{1^n \, 0^n\} \cup \{1^n \, 2^n\} \qquad n > 0$$

   b) Design a one-state pushdown recognizer (using the REPLACE operation) for this language.

41. Show that pushdown machines designed according to the procedures of Sections 8.4, 8.5, and 8.6 will never cycle.

42. Show that all s-grammars, q-grammars, and LL(1) grammars are unambiguous.

43. a) Convert the LL(1) grammar from Fig. 8.15 into a q-grammar for the same language.

   b) Describe a procedure that will convert any LL(1) grammar into a q-grammar for the same language.

44. The following two grammars with starting symbol ⟨S⟩ generate the same language:

Grammar 1:

1. ⟨S⟩ → ⟨B⟩ ⟨A⟩
2. ⟨A⟩ → ⟨B⟩ ⟨S⟩
3. ⟨A⟩ → d
4. ⟨B⟩ → a ⟨A⟩
5. ⟨B⟩ → b ⟨S⟩
6. ⟨B⟩ → c

Grammar 2:

1. $\langle S \rangle \to a \langle A \rangle \langle A \rangle$
2. $\langle S \rangle \to b \langle S \rangle \langle A \rangle$
3. $\langle S \rangle \to c \langle A \rangle$
4. $\langle A \rangle \to a \langle A \rangle \langle S \rangle$
5. $\langle A \rangle \to b \langle S \rangle \langle S \rangle$
6. $\langle A \rangle \to c \langle S \rangle$
7. $\langle A \rangle \to d$

Grammar 2 was obtained from Grammar 1 by substituting for $\langle B \rangle$, in productions 1 and 2, all the righthand sides of productions for $\langle B \rangle$. $\langle B \rangle$ then became unreachable and was deleted.

1. Show that Grammar 1 is LL(1) and Grammar 2 is q.
2. Design pushdown machines corresponding to each grammar.
3. Compare the stack movies of each machine recognizing:

$$a\ b\ c\ d\ b\ c\ d\ c\ c\ d\ d$$

4. Compare the time and memory requirements of each machine.

45. Assume $\langle A \rangle$ is a nullable nonterminal that can be used to generate at least two terminal strings. Show that in an LL(1) grammar, no production can have two adjacent occurrences of $\langle A \rangle$ in its righthand side. In other words, no production can be of the form

$$\langle B \rangle \to \alpha \langle A \rangle \langle A \rangle \beta$$

where α and β are arbitrary strings of terminals and nonterminals.

46. Show that the top-down pushdown machine recognizer of an LL(1) grammar performs its recognition using a number of operations bounded by a constant times the number of input symbols.

47. a) Show that the following grammar is not LL(1):

$$\langle S \rangle \to \langle S \rangle\ a$$
$$\langle S \rangle \to b$$

b) A nonterminal $\langle X \rangle$ is said to be *left recursive* if:

$$\langle X \rangle \overset{+}{\Rightarrow} \langle X \rangle\ w$$

Show that if a grammar has any left recursive nonterminals, that grammar is not LL(1).

48. Draw the stack movie as the processor of Fig. 8.17 processes each of the following sequences

a) $I * (I + I + I) * I + I$

b) $I + (I * I)\ I$

49. a) Show that the REJECT entry in the ⟨E-list⟩ row and $*$ column of the control table of Fig. 8.17 is never accessed even for incorrect input sequences.

b) Design error messages for each REJECT entry in Fig. 8.17 that can be accessed.

50. a) Find an LL(1) grammar for arithmetic expressions using binary operators $+$, $-$, $*$, $/$, $\uparrow$.

b) Add productions to your grammar to include unary $+$ and $-$.

c) Design processors for the grammars of Parts a) and b).

51. Corresponding to the following grammar with starting symbol ⟨Boolean expression⟩:

⟨Boolean expression⟩ → ⟨Boolean expression⟩ ∨ ⟨Boolean factor⟩

⟨Boolean expression⟩ → ⟨Boolean factor⟩

⟨Boolean factor⟩ → ⟨Boolean factor⟩ ∧ ⟨Boolean secondary⟩

⟨Boolean factor⟩ → ⟨Boolean secondary⟩

⟨Boolean secondary⟩ → ¬ ⟨Boolean primary⟩

⟨Boolean secondary⟩ → ⟨Boolean primary⟩

⟨Boolean primary⟩ → (⟨Boolean expression⟩)

⟨Boolean primary⟩ → I

a) find an LL(1) grammar that generates the same language;

b) insert an appropriate action symbol for each operator;

c) design a pushdown processor;

d) draw the stack movie as this machine processes:

$$\neg I \vee I \wedge I$$

52. Design a recursive-descent parser corresponding to the arithmetic-expression recognizer of Fig. 8.17.

53. Design a processor to perform the translation of infix to Polish arithmetic expressions given in Section 7.3.

54. Consider the following two translation grammars, each with starting symbol ⟨F⟩:

⟨F⟩ → ⟨F⟩ ↑ ⟨P⟩ {EXP}   ⟨F⟩ → ⟨P⟩ ↑ ⟨F⟩ {EXP}

⟨F⟩ → ⟨P⟩   ⟨F⟩ → ⟨P⟩

⟨P⟩ → (⟨F⟩)   ⟨P⟩ → (⟨F⟩)

⟨P⟩ → I ⟨P⟩ → I

a) Write the activity sequence and derivation tree according to both grammars for input sequence:

$$I \uparrow I \uparrow I$$

(In the first grammar ↑ is said to be a "left associative" operator; in the second grammar it is a "right associative operator.")

b) Find LL(1) grammars generating the same activity sequences as the above grammars.

55. Write an LL(1) grammar that generates the same language as each of the following grammars

a) 1. ⟨program⟩ → **begin** ⟨statement list⟩ **end**
   2. ⟨statement list⟩ → ⟨statement list⟩; ⟨statement⟩
   3. ⟨statement list⟩ → ⟨statement⟩
   4. ⟨statement⟩ → s

   Starting symbol: ⟨program⟩

b) 1. ⟨identifier⟩ → ⟨letter⟩
   2. ⟨identifier⟩ → ⟨identifier⟩ ⟨letter⟩
   3. ⟨identifier⟩ → ⟨identifier⟩ ⟨digit⟩
   4. ⟨letter⟩ → A
   5. ⟨letter⟩ → B
   6. ⟨digit⟩ → 3
   7. ⟨digit⟩ → 4

   Starting symbol: ⟨identifier⟩

56. Find an LL(1) grammar for MINI-BASIC expressions assuming each of the following changes in the language.

a) Whenever unary operators are allowed, as many unary operators as desired can be used. Thus

$$2 + (-\ -4 + 5)$$

is allowed and equals 11.

b) All operations are carried out from left to right, except that operations within parentheses are carried out before those outside the parentheses. Thus $3 + 2 * 7$ equals 35.

c) All operations are carried out from right to left except that operations within parentheses are carried out before those outside.

d) Unary $+$ and $-$ are allowed in front of any operand and are carried out before any other operations. Thus

$$3 * -4 \uparrow 2$$

is allowed and equals 48.

57. Consider the following grammar with starting symbol ⟨A⟩.

⟨A⟩ → ⟨A⟩ c ⟨B⟩
⟨A⟩ → c ⟨C⟩
⟨A⟩ → ⟨C⟩
⟨B⟩ → b ⟨B⟩

$\langle B \rangle \rightarrow I$

$\langle C \rangle \rightarrow \langle C \rangle \, a \, \langle B \rangle$

$\langle C \rangle \rightarrow \langle B \rangle \, b \, \langle B \rangle$

$\langle C \rangle \rightarrow \langle B \rangle$

a) Show that the grammar is unambiguous.

b) Find an LL(1) grammar for this language.

58. Design a top-down parsing procedure for each of the following LL(2) grammars with starting symbol $\langle S \rangle$.

    a) $\langle S \rangle \rightarrow a \, b \, \langle S \rangle \, a$

       $\langle S \rangle \rightarrow a \, a \, \langle A \rangle \, b$

       $\langle S \rangle \rightarrow b$

       $\langle A \rangle \rightarrow b \, a \, \langle A \rangle \, b$

       $\langle A \rangle \rightarrow b$

    b) $\langle S \rangle \rightarrow a \, \langle S \rangle \langle A \rangle$

       $\langle S \rangle \rightarrow \epsilon$

       $\langle A \rangle \rightarrow b \, \langle B \rangle$

       $\langle A \rangle \rightarrow c \, c$

       $\langle B \rangle \rightarrow b \, d$

       $\langle B \rangle \rightarrow \epsilon$

59. Describe an error-recovery procedure for the recursive descent method of Section 8.9.

60. Show that if a language and its complement are each generated by q-grammars, they are both finite-state languages.

9
Top-Down Processing of Attributed Grammars

9.1 INTRODUCTION

In this chapter, we show how to design a pushdown device for performing translations described by a certain class of attributed grammars. The grammars to which these methods apply can be described informally as having a top-down parsable input grammar and top-down parsable rules. By "top-down parsable grammar," we mean a grammar that can be recognized by a machine of the type discussed in the previous chapter, specifically an LL(1) grammar. By "top-down parsable rules" we mean that the rules can be computed during a top-down parse, specifically that the rules are "L-attributed" as discussed in Section 9.2.

The design procedure is presented as an algorithm to be applied to attributed string translation grammars. The resulting pushdown devices are machines which process strings of attributed input symbols and which, for each input string, either produce an output string which is a translation of the input or reject the input as not being in the input language. However, the techniques are easily extended to general situations because the action of producing an attributed output can be replaced by the action of calling a routine which uses the attributes as arguments.

9.2 L-ATTRIBUTED GRAMMARS

In this section, we present a class of grammars called L-attributed grammars. The purpose of the L-attributed property is to ensure that attributes can be evaluated in an orderly way suitable for top-down processing. In Section 9.5, we show how to obtain an augmented pushdown machine to perform the

translation specified by an L-attributed grammar that has a top-down parsable (LL(1)) input grammar.

An attributed translation grammar is called *L-attributed* if and only if
the following three conditions hold:

1. For each attribute-evaluation rule associated with an inherited attribute
of some given symbol in the righthand side of some given production, each
argument of that rule is either an inherited attribute of the lefthand side or
an arbitrary attribute of some righthand side symbol appearing to the left of
the given symbol.

2. For each attribute-evaluation rule associated with a synthesized attribute of the lefthand side of some given production, each argument of that
rule is either an inherited attribute of the given lefthand side or an arbitrary
attribute of some righthand side symbol.

3. For each attribute-evaluation rule associated with a synthesized attribute of an action symbol, each argument of that rule is an inherited attribute
of the given action symbol.

Recall the definition of attributed translation grammars given in Section
7.7. That definition contained four parts, and parts 3 and 4 each had two
sections, a) and b). Rules 1, 2, and 3 above are restrictions on Sections 3a, 4a,
and 4b respectively. The only evaluation rules not constrained by the above
three conditions are the initialization rules of Section 3b.

An attributed grammar can be tested for the L-attributed property by
independently inspecting each of the productions (to check conditions 1 and
2) and each of the action symbol specifications (to check condition 3). These
inspections themselves consist of independent inspections of the various
attribute-evaluation rules.

To illustrate the testing, suppose a grammar contains the production

$$\langle A \rangle_{I1,S2,S3} \rightarrow \langle B \rangle_{I4} \langle C \rangle_{S5} \langle D \rangle_{S6,I7,I8} \langle E \rangle_{I9}$$

where $I1, I4, I7, I8,$ and $I9$ are inherited attributes, $S2, S3, S5,$ and $S6$ are
synthesized attributes, and attribute evaluation rules are given for $S2, S3, I4,$
$I7, I8,$ and $I9$. The test for this production consists of checking to see that the
rules for $I4, I7, I8,$ and $I9$ satisfy condition 1 and that the rules for $S2$ and $S3$
satisfy condition 2.

Under condition 1, the evaluation rule for $I4$ may use only $I1$ as an
argument. Thus the rule could be

$$I4 \leftarrow f(I1) \quad \text{or} \quad I4 \leftarrow 328 \quad \text{or} \quad (I4, I7) \leftarrow I1$$

but could not be

$$I4 \leftarrow S2 \quad \text{or} \quad I4 \leftarrow g(S6, I4)$$

Similarly, the arguments of the rules for $I7$ and $I8$ must be from the set $\{I1,$ $I4, S5\}$ and the arguments of the rule for $I9$ must be from the set $\{I1, I4, S5,$ $S6, I7, I8\}$. Under condition 2, the attribute-evaluation rules for $S2$ and $S3$ can use any attributes except $S2$ and $S3$ themselves.

Condition 3 is used to test the attribute-evaluation rules associated with action-symbol specifications and is carried out by inspecting the argument list to make sure that no synthesized attribute is used as an argument of an evaluation rule.

We sometimes use the term L-attributed to apply to rules, productions, or action symbols. We call a rule L-attributed if it satisfies whichever one of the three conditions is appropriate. We call a production or an action symbol L-attributed if all its associated attribute-evaluation rules are L-attributed. An attributed grammar is thus L-attributed if all its productions and action symbols are L-attributed.

The importance of condition 1 is that it causes inherited attributes of a given symbol to depend only on information to the symbol's *left*. (The "L" in "L-attributed" stands for *left*.) This is helpful for top-down attribute processing because each symbol is processed before the inputs to its right are read. Conditions 2 and 3 are added to ensure that circular dependencies are avoided. Together, the three conditions ensure that given a production such as $\langle A \rangle \rightarrow \langle B \rangle \langle C \rangle$, the attributes of $\langle A \rangle$, $\langle B \rangle$, and $\langle C \rangle$ can be evaluated in the following order:

1. inherited attributes of $\langle A \rangle$;
2. inherited attributes of $\langle B \rangle$;
3. synthesized attributes of $\langle B \rangle$;
4. inherited attributes of $\langle C \rangle$;
5. synthesized attributes of $\langle C \rangle$;
6. synthesized attributes of $\langle A \rangle$.

9.3   SIMPLE ASSIGNMENT FORM

We generally write attribute rules as assignment statements in which a function is evaluated using certain attribute values as arguments and the result is assigned to one or more other attributes. For example, assignment statement

$$x \leftarrow f(y, z)$$

requires that f be evaluated using the values of the attributes y and z as arguments and that the value of f be assigned to attribute x. However, in certain simple cases (namely identity and constant functions), the righthand sides of the assignments show no function evaluation. Instead, they simply show the value of one attribute or constant assigned to other attributes. Two examples are

$$x \leftarrow y \quad \text{and} \quad (x, y, z) \leftarrow 17$$

An attribute-evaluation rule is a *copy rule* if and only if it is of the form

$$x \leftarrow y \quad \text{or} \quad (x_1, \ldots, x_n) \leftarrow y$$

where the lefthand side is a single attribute or list of attributes and the righthand side y is either an attribute or a constant. The righthand side is called the *source* of the copy rule, and each attribute on the lefthand side is called a *sink* of the copy rule.

It is sometimes possible to consolidate two copy rules into a single rule. For example

$$(x, y) \leftarrow z \quad \text{and} \quad (a, b) \leftarrow y$$

can be written as the single rule

$$(a, b, x, y) \leftarrow z$$

because the source y of the second rule is assigned the value of z by the first rule. Similarly,

$$x \leftarrow z \quad \text{and} \quad (a, b) \leftarrow z$$

can be written as

$$(x, a, b) \leftarrow z$$

because their sources are identical. Note that in both cases, the sinks are consolidated into a single lefthand side.

A set of copy rules is *independent* if and only if the source of each rule of the set does not appear anywhere in any of the other rules of the set.

Two independent copy rules cannot be consolidated.

The concept of independent copy rules gives us the basic concept of this section:

An attributed grammar is in *simple assignment form* if and only if:

a) the only rules which are not copy rules are rules for computing synthesized attributes of action symbols;

b) the set of copy rules associated with each production is independent.

In Section 9.5 we show how to take an L-attributed grammar in simple assignment form and design a pushdown machine to perform the attributed translation. In this section, we are concerned with the following problem: "Given an L-attributed grammar, find an 'equivalent' L-attributed grammar in simple assignment form." The meaning of equivalent here is discussed later.

Given a production for which one of the associated rules is not a copy rule, a simple technique allows the construction of a production which achieves the same effect but which has only copy rules. To illustrate this technique, consider the attributed production

$$\langle A \rangle \rightarrow a_R \langle B \rangle_S \langle C \rangle_I$$
$$I \leftarrow f(R, S)$$

where I is inherited and S synthesized. The associated attribute rule is, of course, not a copy rule as it requires the evaluation of function f.

The first step is to invent a new action symbol to represent the evaluation of function f. We use an obvious name for this action symbol, namely $\{f\}$. We give $\{f\}$ two inherited attributes, one for each argument of f, and one synthesized attribute.

The value of the synthesized attribute is to be obtained by applying f to the inherited attributes. A complete specification of $\{f\}$ is therefore

$$\{f\}_{I1,I2,S1} \quad \text{INHERITED } I1, I2 \quad \text{SYNTHESIZED } S1$$
$$S1 \leftarrow f(I1, I2)$$

The second step is to alter the production itself by

1. inserting the new action symbol $\{f\}$ into the righthand side;
2. introducing new copy rules which match the arguments of f (i.e., R and S) with the inherited attributes of $\{f\}$;
3. introducing a new copy rule matching the synthesized attribute of $\{f\}$ with the attribute to which the value computed by f is assigned (i.e., I);
4. discarding the rule involving f.

This step does not specify a unique resulting production because the choice of variable names and the location of the inserted symbol are discretionary. However, one possible result of this step is replacement production:

$$\langle A \rangle \rightarrow a_R \langle B \rangle_S \{f\}_{I1,I2,S1} \langle C \rangle_I$$
$$I1 \leftarrow R \qquad I2 \leftarrow S \qquad I \leftarrow S1$$

Note how the original rule using f has been replaced by three copy rules, two which copy arguments and one which copies the result. The number of noncopy rules has been reduced and simple assignment form has been reached. This new production has the same effect as the old production in the sense that both productions generate the same attributed input sequences, and both specify the same value for the attribute I. In this sense, both productions result in the same compilation.

The new production does not generate the same translation in a formal sense since the new production adds action symbol $\{f\}$ to the action sequence. The new action sequences can be thought of as enhanced to show the "actions" of evaluating the function f.

Having illustrated a technique for obtaining simple assignment forms, we now consider how to make the technique work in a manner which preserves the L-attributed property. In our illustration, we made a seemingly arbitrary decision to insert the $\{f\}$ between the $\langle B \rangle$ and $\langle C \rangle$. However, this is in fact the only insert position which preserves the L-attributed property of the original production.

Suppose, for example, that $\{f\}$ had been inserted before the $\langle B \rangle$, as in production:

$$\langle A \rangle \rightarrow a_R \; \{f\}_{I1,I2,S1} \; \langle B \rangle_S \; \langle C \rangle_I$$
$$I1 \leftarrow R \qquad I2 \leftarrow S \qquad I \leftarrow S1$$

This is a simple assignment form, but the inherited attribute $I2$ is a function of an attribute appearing to its right, a violation of L-attributedness. A necessary requirement is that the inserted symbol be to the right of all righthand side symbols supplying values for its inherited attributes.

Now suppose that $\{f\}$ had been inserted to the right of $\langle C \rangle$, as in:

$$\langle A \rangle \rightarrow a_R \; \langle B \rangle_S \; \langle C \rangle_I \; \{f\}_{I1,I2,S1}$$
$$I1 \leftarrow R \qquad I2 \leftarrow S \qquad I \leftarrow S1$$

Then inherited attribute I is a function of an attribute to its right and again the L-attributed property is violated. A necessary requirement is that the new symbol be placed to the left of any righthand side symbol whose attribute is assigned the function value.

For this example, the two necessary requirements dictate a unique position for inserting into the righthand side. If the requirements allow a choice of positions, the leftmost of the permitted positions is often more efficient since certain leftmost action symbols need not be made into stack symbols in the pushdown machine that performs the processing. If the requirements disallow all choices, the grammar is not L-attributed in the first place.

To illustrate the technique on a complete grammar, consider the L-attributed grammar of Fig. 9.1. Input symbol C of this grammar represents a constant having a value part which is the arithmetic value of the constant.

$\langle E \rangle_p$ SYNTHESIZED p
$\{\text{ANSWER}_r\}$ INHERITED r

1. $\langle S \rangle \rightarrow \langle E \rangle_p \{\text{ANSWER}_r\}$
   $\quad r \leftarrow p$
2. $\langle E \rangle_p \rightarrow + \langle E \rangle_q \langle E \rangle_r$
   $\quad p \leftarrow q + r$
3. $\langle E \rangle_p \rightarrow * \langle E \rangle_q \langle E \rangle_r$
   $\quad p \leftarrow q * r$
4. $\langle E \rangle_p \rightarrow C_q$
   $\quad p \leftarrow q$
Starting symbol: $\langle S \rangle$

Figure 9.1

$\langle E \rangle_p$ SYNTHESIZED p
$\{\text{ANSWER}_r\}$ INHERITED r
$\{\text{ADD}\}_{A1,A2,R}$ INHERITED $A1, A2$ SYNTHESIZED R
                          $R \leftarrow A1 + A2$
$\{\text{MULT}\}_{A1,A2,R}$ INHERITED $A1, A2$ SYNTHESIZED R
                          $R \leftarrow A1 * A2$

1. $\langle S \rangle \rightarrow \langle E \rangle_p \{\text{ANSWER}_r\}$
   $\quad r \leftarrow p$
2. $\langle E \rangle_p \rightarrow + \langle E \rangle_q \langle E \rangle_r \{\text{ADD}\}_{A1,A2,R}$
   $\quad A1 \leftarrow q \qquad A2 \leftarrow r \qquad p \leftarrow R$
3. $\langle E \rangle_p \rightarrow * \langle E \rangle_q \langle E \rangle_r \{\text{MULT}\}_{A1,A2,R}$
   $\quad A1 \leftarrow q \qquad A2 \leftarrow r \qquad p \leftarrow R$
4. $\langle E \rangle_p \rightarrow C_q$
   $\quad p \leftarrow q$
Starting symbol: $\langle S \rangle$

Figure 9.2

The grammar generates prefix Polish expressions over constants. The translation is similar to the translation of infix expressions over constants given in Section 7.5.

In order to put this grammar into simple assignment form, we must eliminate the two noncopy rules $p \leftarrow q + r$ and $p \leftarrow q * r$. The "functions" here are addition and multiplication and we invent action symbols {ADD} and {MULT} to represent them. To maintain L-attributedness, action symbol {ADD} must be placed at the extreme right of the righthand side because one argument of the addition is the attribute r of the rightmost $\langle E \rangle$.

The attribute getting the result of the addition is not a consideration in the placement of {ADD} since it is not associated with a righthand side symbol. The L-attributed simple assignment grammar which results is shown in Fig. 9.2.

Once a set of copy rules has been obtained for a production, it is a simple matter to consolidate the rules into an independent set of rules. If the source of a copy rule is found elsewhere in another rule, the rules are simply combined as illustrated at the beginning of this section.

We now present the ideas discussed above as a single procedure for converting an L-attributed grammar to an L-attributed simple-assignment-form grammar suitable for the machine-design methods of Section 9.5.

1. For each function $f(x_1, \ldots, x_n)$ in an attribute-evaluation rule associated with some production of the grammar, create a corresponding action symbol $\{f\}$ specified as follows:

$$\{f\}_{x_1, \ldots, x_n, p} \qquad \text{INHERITED } x_1, \ldots, x_n \qquad \text{SYNTHESIZED } p$$
$$p \leftarrow f(x_1, \ldots, x_n)$$

2. For each noncopy rule

$$(z_1, \ldots, z_m) \leftarrow f(y_1, \ldots, y_n)$$

associated with a grammatical production, find symbols $a_1, \ldots, a_n, r$ which do not appear elsewhere in the production and insert the symbol

$$\{f\}_{a_1, \ldots, a_n, r}$$

into the righthand side of the production subject to conditions stated below. Replace the noncopy rule by the following $(n + 1)$-copy rules:

$$a_i \leftarrow y_i \qquad \text{for each argument } y_i$$
$$(z_1, \ldots, z_m) \leftarrow r$$

The restrictions on placing the inserted action symbol are as follows:

a) The action symbol must be placed to the right of all righthand side symbols having one of the arguments $y_1, \ldots, y_n$ as attributes.

b) The action symbol must be placed to the left of any righthand side symbol having an attribute from list $(z_1, \ldots, z_m)$ as one of its attributes.

c) Within constraints a) and b), there may be a choice of insert points and the choice can be made at the discretion of the designer. The leftmost position should be given prime consideration as it may avoid the use of a corresponding stack symbol in the pushdown machine that implements the translation.

3. Two copy rules for the same production should be consolidated if the source of one rule appears in the other rule. This consolidation is accomplished by discarding the rule with the redundant source and merging its sinks with the sinks of the retained rule.

One final note about simple assignment form: in later examples, we treat parameterless function procedures as though they are constants and allow them to appear as the source of simple-assignment-form attribute rules. For instance we allow the production

$$\langle A \rangle \rightarrow \langle B \rangle_x \, \langle C \rangle_y$$
$$(x, y) \leftarrow \text{NEWT}$$

One should, however, be cautious about this liberty since if two calls of the parameterless function procedure can return different values, then separate occurrences of the function name are treated as separate constants, and their attribute rules cannot be combined. For instance in production:

$$\langle A \rangle \rightarrow \langle B \rangle_x \, \langle C \rangle_y \, \{d_z\}$$
$$x \leftarrow \text{NEWT} \qquad (y, z) \leftarrow \text{NEWT}$$

we cannot combine the two assignments into one assignment:

$$(x, y, z) \leftarrow \text{NEWT}$$

9.4   AN EXAMPLE OF AN AUGMENTED MACHINE

In this section, we present an example of an augmented machine. In all our augmented machines, we use stack symbols which consist of a *name part* and an associated set of *fields*. The fields of any symbol on the stack are storage locations which are available for storing and retrieving information during the lifetime of that symbol (i.e., from push to pop). For expository purposes, we imagine a stack symbol with n fields as being represented on the pushdown stack by $(n + 1)$ cells where the top cell contains the symbol name and the lower cells represent the fields. Figure 9.3 shows such a picture of stack

$$\nabla\ C\ A\ B\ A$$

where A has two fields, B one field, and C no fields.

Now consider the grammar of Fig. 9.2. If the attributes are deleted and the grammar treated as if it were an ordinary string translation grammar, the top-down design method for LL(1) grammars gives the pushdown machine of Fig. 9.4. We now augment this machine to get an augmented pushdown machine that processes the attributes in the manner specified.

In the augmented processor, the stack symbols have one field for each attribute of the corresponding grammatical symbol. Thus {ADD} and {MULT} have three fields, $\langle E \rangle$ and {ANSWER} have one field, and $\langle S \rangle$ and ∇ have no fields. Their layout is explained in Fig. 9.5. It is important to realize that the field of a symbol on the stack need not contain the value of the corresponding attribute. In fact, the synthesized attribute fields never contain the associated attribute value. They are used to store pointers. Inherited attribute fields are initially blank, but they do receive the corresponding attribute value sometime before the stack symbol becomes the top stack symbol. The machine works in such a way that each top stack symbol field corresponding to an inherited attribute will contain the value of that attribute, and each top stack symbol field corresponding to a synthesized

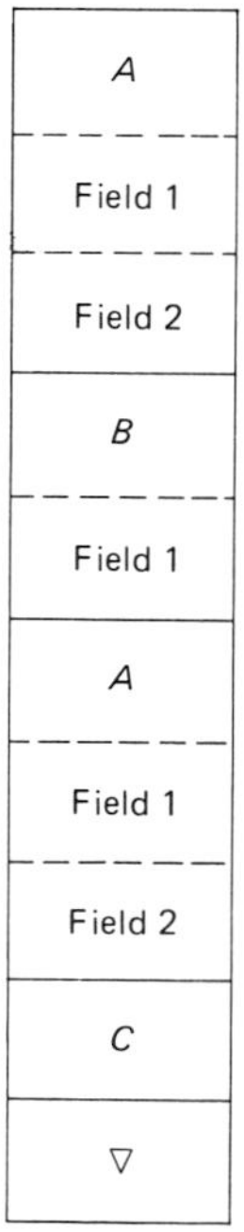

Figure 9.3

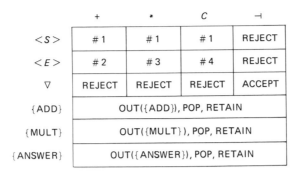

	+	*	C	⊣
\<S\>	# 1	# 1	# 1	REJECT
\<E\>	# 2	# 3	# 4	REJECT
▽	REJECT	REJECT	REJECT	ACCEPT
{ADD}	OUT({ADD}), POP, RETAIN			
{MULT}	OUT({MULT}), POP, RETAIN			
{ANSWER}	OUT({ANSWER}), POP, RETAIN			

Starting stack: ▽ \<S\>

# 1	REPLACE({ANSWER}\<E\>), RETAIN
# 2	REPLACE({ADD}\<E\>\<E\>), ADVANCE
# 3	REPLACE({MULT}\<E\>\<E\>), ADVANCE
# 4	POP, ADVANCE

Figure 9.4

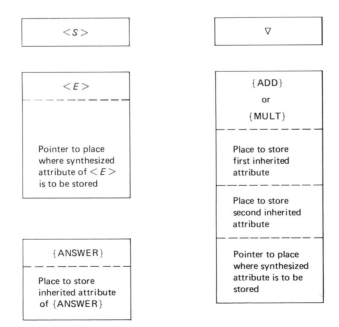

Figure 9.5

attribute will contain a pointer to the place where the value of that attribute should be stored.

The control table for the augmented machine is shown in Fig. 9.6. Figure 9.7 displays before and after pictures of two of the augmented replacements.

To understand the machine, first consider the stack movie of Fig. 9.8, which corresponds to the processing of input sequence

$$C_4 \dashv$$

Configuration Fig. 9.8(a) shows the initial stack and input string. The transition from Fig. 9.8(a) to Fig. 9.8(b) represents an application of production 1 (Fig. 9.2) achieved by transition routine #1. The copy rule associated with production 1 specifies that the inherited attribute of {ANSWER} is equal to the synthesized attribute of the symbol $\langle E \rangle$. In general, when

	+	*	c	$\dashv$
$\langle S \rangle$	# 1	# 1	# 1	REJECT
$\langle E \rangle$	# 2	# 3	# 4	REJECT
∇	REJECT	REJECT	REJECT	ACCEPT
{ADD}	Add contents of first two fields and store sum in location pointed to by third field POP, RETAIN			
{MULT}	Multiply contents of first two fields and store product in location pointed to by third field POP, RETAIN			
{ANSWER}	OUT(ANSWER with contents of field) POP, RETAIN			

Starting stack: $\nabla \ \langle S \rangle$

1 REPLACE $\langle S \rangle$ as shown in Figure 9.7(a)
RETAIN

2 REPLACE $\langle E \rangle$ as shown in Figure 9.7(b)
ADVANCE

3 REPLACE $\langle E \rangle$ as shown in Figure 9.7(b) using {MULT}
instead of {ADD}
ADVANCE

4 Place current input value in location pointed to by
field of $\langle E \rangle$
POP, ADVANCE

Figure 9.6

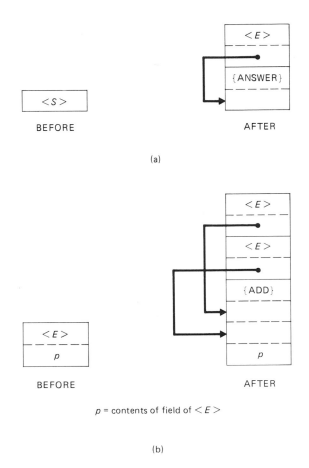

(a)

(b)

p = contents of field of $\langle E \rangle$

Figure 9.7

production 1 is applied, the value of the synthesized attribute of $\langle E \rangle$ cannot be determined, since the value can depend on input symbols not yet read. The machine leaves the field of stack symbol {ANSWER} blank, but provides for its subsequently being filled in by placing a pointer to it in the field of stack symbol $\langle E \rangle$. The task of computing the synthesized attribute of $\langle E \rangle$ and storing it in the field of {ANSWER} is left to the processing of symbol $\langle E \rangle$. Because the $\langle E \rangle$ is processed before {ANSWER} becomes the top stack symbol, the blank field will be filled in before {ANSWER} becomes the top stack symbol.

The transition from Fig. 9.8(b) to Fig. 9.8(c) is achieved by transition routine #4. The copy rule associated with production 4 specifies that the synthesized attribute of the $\langle E \rangle$ equals the attribute of the current input

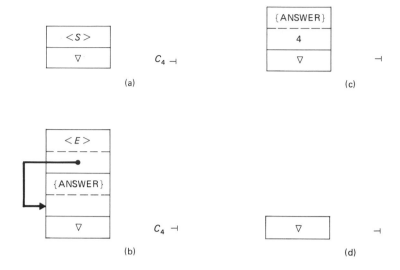

Figure 9.8

symbol. The value of the current input C_4 is copied into the location pointed to by the field of $\langle E \rangle$, thereby filling in the field of {ANSWER}. The transition from Fig. 9.8(c) to Fig. 9.8(d) causes $ANSWER_4$ to be emitted, and configuration Fig. 9.8(d) causes ACCEPT.

We further explain the machine with a commentary on how it processes the input sequence

$$+ * C_2\ C_3\ C_5 \dashv$$

Expressed in infix, this input calls for the evaluation of $(2 * 3) + 5$ which has value 11. A stack movie of this processing is shown in Fig. 9.9. The transition from Fig. 9.9(a) to Fig. 9.9(b) is identical to the transition from Fig. 9.8(a) to Fig. 9.8(b).

The transition from Fig. 9.9(b) to Fig. 9.9(c) is achieved by transition routine #2. The transition implements the copy rule,

$$p \leftarrow R$$

of production 2 (and ensures that the synthesized attribute of the $\langle E \rangle$ in Fig. 9.9(b) will be stored in the location pointed to by the field of the $\langle E \rangle$ in Fig. 9.9(b)) by copying the pointer from the field of the old $\langle E \rangle$ into the third field of {ADD}. When the addition is finally performed (in the transition from Fig. 9.9(h) to Fig. 9.9(i)) the resulting sum will be copied into the field of {ANSWER}. The stack in Fig. 9.9(c) also has two $\langle E \rangle$'s as called for by the production, one for each operand of the addition. The fields of the $\langle E \rangle$'s are initialized with pointers so that the values of the operands can be copied into fields of {ADD} and the addition can eventually be performed. As each of these $\langle E \rangle$'s is processed, its attribute will be placed in the corresponding field of {ADD}, hence {ADD} will have all three fields properly filled in when it reaches the top of the stack.

The transition from Fig. 9.9(c) to Fig. 9.9(d) is achieved by transition routine #3 which applies production 3. The {MULT} is set up in the same

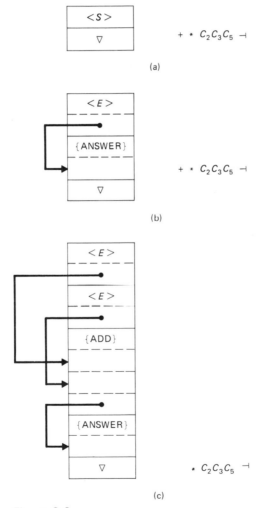

(a)

(b)

(c)

Figure 9.9

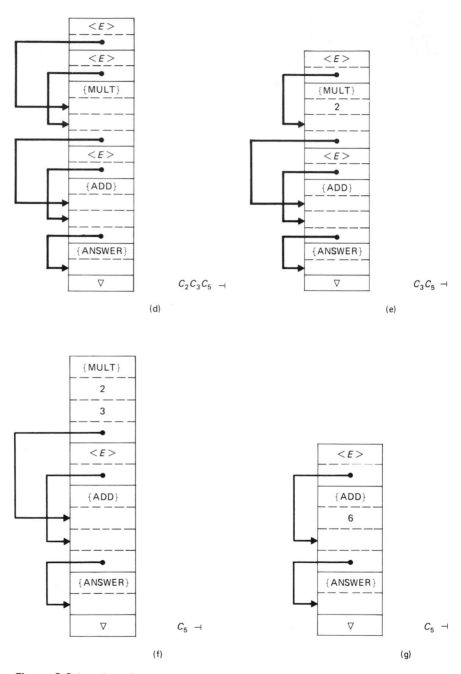

Figure 9.9 (continued)

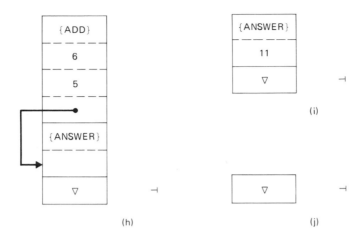

Figure 9.9 (continued)

way as {ADD} was previously. The pointer in {MULT} is obtained from the top symbol $\langle E \rangle$ of configuration Fig. 9.9(c) and will enable the result of the multiplication to be passed to the {ADD}.

The transition from Fig. 9.9(d) to Fig. 9.9(e) is achieved by transition routine #4 which applies production 4. The value of the current input C_2 is copied into the field pointed to by the top symbol $\langle E \rangle$. The first operand of the {MULT} has thus been discovered.

The transition from Fig. 9.9(e) to Fig. 9.9(f) results in the discovery of the second operand of {MULT} and, for the first time, the top stack symbol is an action symbol.

The transition from Fig. 9.9(f) to Fig. 9.9(g) is achieved by the action symbol routine. The routine causes the values in the inherited attribute fields (i.e., the operands) to be multiplied and the result to be placed in the field pointed to by the synthesized attribute field. We note that no output is emitted even though output was specified in the unaugmented machine (Fig. 9.4). The reason for this omission is that {MULT} was artificially introduced in Section 9.3 in order to obtain simple assignment form. Since we do not really want such an output, we do not emit it. Our augmented machine is actually performing the string translation specified by the grammar of Fig. 9.1 from which Fig. 9.2 was obtained.

The transition from Fig. 9.9(g) to Fig. 9.9(h) is simply the discovery of the second operand of {ADD} and the transition from Fig. 9.9(h) to Fig. 9.9(i) is the performance of that addition. At last {ANSWER} has its attribute value. The transition from Fig. 9.9(i) to Fig. 9.9(j) causes ANSWER$_{11}$ to be emitted and configuration Fig. 9.9(j) causes ACCEPT.

9.5   THE AUGMENTED PUSHDOWN MACHINE

We now address the following problem:

> Given a simple-assignment-form, L-attributed grammar with an LL(1) input grammar, design a pushdown device which performs the described translation.

First we use the methods of Chapter 8 to design a pushdown processor for the unattributed string translation grammar which is obtained from the given attributed string translation grammar by deleting the attributes. This machine is referred to as the "unaugmented machine" and is to be modified into a processor for the attributed grammar by augmenting its stack symbols with fields and augmenting the transitions to compute attributes and fill in fields.

According to the construction in Chapter 8, the stack symbols of the unaugmented machine correspond to symbols in the given grammar. In the augmented machine, each stack symbol is augmented with a field for each attribute of the corresponding grammatical symbol.

The plan for using the augmented stack symbols follows closely the ideas illustrated in Section 9.4. By the time a stack symbol becomes the top symbol, its fields will be filled in as follows:

1. If the corresponding attribute is inherited, the field will contain the value of the attribute.

2. If the corresponding attribute is synthesized, the field will contain a pointer to a linked list of inherited attribute fields where the attribute is to be stored.

3. Input symbol attributes are treated like synthesized attributes.

The fields for synthesized and input attributes are initialized with a pointer at the time they are first pushed, and remain unchanged throughout the lifetime of the corresponding stack symbol.

The fields for inherited attributes are initialized with either the value of that attribute or a list pointer (or end-of-list marker). In the latter case, the field is a member of a list pointed to by a synthesized or input attribute field and will be filled in with the attribute value before reaching the top of the stack.

By custom, our figures use a blank field, which we call a null pointer, and which serves as an end-of-list marker. Thus the "after" picture in Fig. 9.7(a) shows the synthesized attribute field of $\langle E \rangle$ pointing to a one-element list. The list is one element long because the attribute of $\langle E \rangle$ is only copied to one inherited attribute. If we had a given grammar with a symbol $\langle A \rangle$ having one synthesized attribute and if a situation arose during processing in which the synthesized value of top stack symbol $\langle A \rangle$ was supposed to be assigned to three other fields, the stack might look like Fig. 9.10. This figure shows the field of $\langle A \rangle$ pointing to a list of three elements: the second field of $\langle C \rangle$, the field of $\langle D \rangle$, and the field of $\langle F \rangle$. In cases, such as in Section 9.4, when a pointer always points to a list with one member, some increase in efficiency can be achieved if the machine is designed so that it does not search the list for the end-of-list marker.

Starting Configuration. The processing begins with the starting symbol and the bottommarker on the stack. The fields of the starting stack symbol are initialized as part of the stack initialization. The fields corresponding to inherited attributes are initialized with the initial values specified as part of the attributed grammar. The fields corresponding to synthesized attributes are initialized with the null pointer. Because of this initialization, the inherited attribute fields of the initial top stack symbol are filled with attribute values and the synthesized attribute fields filled with a linked-list pointer; hence there is conformity with the planned use of attribute fields.

When designing a machine for purposes other than simple string translation, the designer may wish to have the ACCEPT routine make use of the synthesized attributes of the starting nonterminal. In such cases, each field of the starting stack symbol corresponding to a synthesized attribute can be initialized with a pointer to a linked list of locations (usually one location) where the attribute is to be stored for use by the ACCEPT routine.

Input Symbol on Top. When the top stack symbol is an input symbol and the stack symbol matches the current input (the nonerror case) the attributes of the current input are matched up with corresponding attribute fields of the top stack symbol. Each of these attribute fields contain a pointer to a list of stack fields where the attribute value is needed. The normal action of the pushdown machine (namely POP, ADVANCE) is augmented so that each attribute of the current input is copied into all fields in the list of fields pointed to by the corresponding field of the top stack symbol.

Action Symbol on Top. When the top stack symbol is an action symbol, the pushdown machine transition is augmented for attribute processing as follows:

1. the values of the inherited attributes are retrieved from the corresponding fields of the top stack symbol;

2. the values of the synthesized attributes are computed from the inherited attributes using the attribute rules associated with the action symbol;

3. the value of each synthesized attribute is placed in each field of the list of fields pointed to by the corresponding field of the top stack symbol.

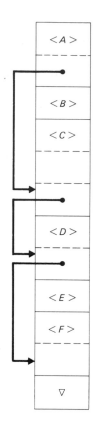

Figure 9.10

In the case where a string translation is being performed, the attributes are also used to emit a corresponding attributed output symbol. Generally, the attributes may be used for whatever purpose the designer desires.

One case deserving special mention is the situation where a strict string translation was originally intended, but additional action symbols had to be introduced to get the grammar into simple assignment form. In this case the translation originally intended can be performed simply be emitting only the original output symbols and not performing any output activity when the additional symbols are encountered.

In addition to the attribute processing and the outputting described above, the transition routine for an action symbol also does the usual POP, RETAIN of the unaugmented machine.

Nonterminal on Top.   When the top stack symbol is a nonterminal, the unaugmented machine performs a transition based on the production it recognizes. This transition replaces the stack symbol by a string of symbols and perhaps performs some output (or other activities) associated with the action symbols which are part of the applied production but which are not pushed on the stack (e.g., the ξ and ψ of rule 5 in the procedure of Section 8.4, and the ξ referred to in the Section 8.6 discussion of translations).

The augmented machine pushes the same string of symbols on the stack and produces the same output symbols. However the augmented transition may require some attribute evaluation associated with the unpushed action symbols, some activity to fill in the fields of the pushed symbols, and some activity to enter attribute values into certain fields of symbols buried in the stack.

The sources in attribute rules associated with a production of a simple-assignment-form grammar can only be constants, inherited attributes of the lefthand side, input symbol attributes, or synthesized attributes of righthand side symbols. The sources can be divided into six categories as indicated in Table 9.1. The table indicates, depending on the category of a source, whether the value of the source will be available during the transition routine for the production and, if so, how the value of the source can be obtained by the transition routine. The sources described by the second category in the table are available because the transition routine which applies the production will evaluate all attributes of unpushed action symbols (by means described in rule 1 below).

The sinks can only be synthesized attributes of the lefthand side of the production, and inherited attributes of righthand side symbols. The sinks can be divided into three categories, as indicated in the Table 9.2. The table indicates, depending on the category of a sink, which stack field attributes must be filled in because of the occurrence of that sink in a particular copy rule.

The augmented actions associated with a given production of the grammar are described by the following:

Rule 1. For each action symbol in the production which is not pushed on the stack, its synthesized attributes are computed from its associated attribute-evaluation rules and the associated attributed output symbols are emitted (or other associated actions taken).

The augmented machine processes the unpushed action symbols in left-to-right order. Thus actions associated with a given unpushed action symbol are performed after actions associated with action symbols to its left and prior to actions associated with unpushed action symbols to its right.

Rule 2. If the source of a copy rule is "available" (i.e., falls in one of the first four categories listed in Table 9.1), then the augmented machine places its value into certain fields of symbols on the stack. These fields to be filled in are indicated for each sink by Table 9.2. Table 9.1 describes in detail where the augmented machine obtains the available value for storage in sink fields.

Rule 3.   If the source of a copy rule is "not available" (i.e., falls in one of the last two categories in Table 9.1), then the source is an attribute of a symbol to be pushed on the stack, and the augmented machine fills in the corresponding field of the pushed symbol with a pointer to a list of fields. The augmented machine creates this list by linking together all fields "indicated" for each sink by Table 9.2.

To illustrate Rule 1, suppose that the top stack symbol is $\langle A \rangle$, that the current input is a, and that the augmented machine must apply the following production:

$$\langle A \rangle_{I1} \rightarrow \{NEW\}_{S1} \quad a_X \quad \{f\}_{I2,I3,I4,S2} \quad \{OUT_{I5,I6}\} \quad \langle others \rangle$$
$$(I5, I4) \leftarrow I1 \qquad I2 \leftarrow S1 \qquad I3 \leftarrow X \qquad I6 \leftarrow S2$$

where $S1$ and $S2$ are synthesized and $I1$, $I2$, $I3$, $I4$, $I5$ and $I6$ are inherited. We assume $\{NEW\}$ and $\{f\}$ were added by the methods of Section 9.3 to convert the grammar into simple assignment form. Thus $\{NEW\}$ computes its synthesized attribute by applying parameterless procedure NEW, and $\{f\}$ computes its synthesized attribute by applying f to its inherited attributes. We assume name $\{OUT\}$ is output symbol OUT in braces and that the purpose of action symbol $\{OUT\}$ is to emit OUT with appropriate output values. (This interpretation of $\{OUT\}$ is emphasized by displaying the attributes inside the braces.)

TABLE 9.1   SOURCE AVAILABILITY

Source	Availability
Inherited attribute of lefthand side	Value is in corresponding field of top stack symbol
Synthesized attribute of unpushed action symbol	Value is computed by augmented transition in accordance with rule 1
Attribute of unpushed input symbol	Value is part of current input
Constant	Always available
Synthesized attribute of symbol to be pushed	Not available
Attribute of input symbol to be pushed	Not available

TABLE 9.2   SINK FIELDS

Sink	Fields
Inherited attribute of a symbol to be pushed	Corresponding field of symbol to be pushed
Synthesized attribute of the production's lefthand side	All fields on list of fields pointed to by corresponding field of stack symbol
Inherited attribute of an unpushed action symbol	No fields

The unaugmented machine action for the sample production pushes only $\langle$others$\rangle$ on the stack which leaves {NEW}, {f}, and {OUT} as unpushed action symbols to be accommodated by Rule 1. Taking the symbols in left-to-right order, the augmented machine must take the following steps:

1. compute $S1$ by calling parameterless function NEW;
2. compute $S2$ by calling $f(I2, I3, I4)$, where $I2$ equals the value $S1$ computed in step 1, $I3$ equals the value of the current input, and $I4$ equals the value stored in the field of top stack symbol $\langle A \rangle$;
3. emit attributed symbol $\text{OUT}_{I5,I6}$, where $I5$ equals the value stored in the field of top stack symbol $\langle A \rangle$ and $I6$ equals the value of $S2$ computed in step 2.

Notice that any order of evaluation other than left to right would be impossible here. The evaluation of f requires that NEW be called first to obtain $S1$. The emitting of OUT requires that f be evaluated first in order to compute OUT's second attribute. The L-attributed property ensures that, for any L-attributed production, the unpushed actions can successfully be carried out in left-to-right order.

To illustrate Rule 2, suppose the production to be applied is

$$\langle A \rangle_{I1,S1,S2} \rightarrow a_X \quad \{g\}_{I2,S3} \quad \langle B \rangle_{I3} \quad \{\text{OUT}_{I4,I5}\} \quad \langle C \rangle_{I6,I7}$$
$$(I4, I2) \leftarrow I1 \qquad (S1, I6, I3) \leftarrow S3$$
$$(S2, I7) \leftarrow X \qquad I5 \leftarrow 36$$

where $I1$, $I2$, $I3$, $I4$, $I5$, $I6$, and $I7$ are inherited and $S1$, $S2$, and $S3$ are synthesized. According to the unaugmented construction, symbols $\langle B \rangle$, {OUT}, and $\langle C \rangle$ are pushed on the stack and a and {g} are not pushed. The source of each copy rule is "available." The actions required by Rule 2 are as follows:

1. For assignment $(I4, I2) \leftarrow I1$, take the value of $I1$ from the inherited attribute field of top stack symbol $\langle A \rangle$ and put the value in the first field (the $I4$ field) of the symbol $\{OUT\}$ to be pushed on the stack. No field assignment is required for $I2$ of unpushed $\{g\}$. That attribute was accounted for by Rule 1.

2. For assignment $(S2, I7) \leftarrow X$, take the value of the current input and store it in the second field of the $\langle C \rangle$ to be pushed on the stack and in all fields on the list of fields pointed to by the third field of top stack symbol $\langle A \rangle$.

3. For assignment $(S1, I6, I3) \leftarrow S3$, take the value of $S3$ previously computed by the augmented machine (an action taken for unpushed action symbol $\{g\}$ in accordance with Rule 1) and put that value in the field of the $\langle B \rangle$ to be pushed, the first field of the $\langle C \rangle$ to be pushed, and all the fields on the list of fields pointed to by the second field of top stack symbol $\langle A \rangle$.

4. For assignment $I5 \leftarrow 36$, put value 36 in the second field of the $\{OUT\}$ to be pushed on the stack.

To illustrate Rule 3, suppose that the production recognized is

$$\langle A \rangle_{S1,S2} \rightarrow a \quad \langle B \rangle_{S3} \quad z_X \quad \{g\}_{I1,S4} \quad \langle C \rangle_{I2,I3}$$
$$S2 \leftarrow S3 \quad (I2, I1) \leftarrow X \quad (S1, I3) \leftarrow S4$$

where $S1$, $S2$, $S3$, and $S4$ are synthesized and $I1$, $I2$, and $I3$ are inherited.

We note that $\langle B \rangle$, z, $\{g\}$, and $\langle C \rangle$ are to be pushed whereas a is not. The source in each assignment is "not available." The actions required by Rule 3 are:

1. For assignment $S2 \leftarrow S3$, the pointer from the second field of top stack symbol $\langle A \rangle$ is placed in the field of the $\langle B \rangle$ to be pushed. This makes the field of $\langle B \rangle$ associated with $S3$ point to the list of fields "indicated" by $S2$.

2. For assignment $(I2, I1) \leftarrow X$, the first fields of the $\{g\}$ and $\langle C \rangle$ to be pushed are linked together in a list (these are the two fields indicated by $I1$ and $I2$) and a pointer to the list is placed in the field of the z to be pushed (i.e., the field associated with attribute X).

3. For the assignment $(S1, I3) \leftarrow S4$, the list of indicated items consists of the second field of the $\langle C \rangle$ to be pushed and all the fields of the list pointed to by the first field of top stack symbol $\langle A \rangle$. From an implementation standpoint, the list is conveniently obtained by attaching the field of $\langle C \rangle$ to the beginning of the list taken from $\langle A \rangle$ (i.e., by moving the pointer from $\langle A \rangle$ to the field of $\langle C \rangle$). No matter how the list is obtained, a pointer to the new list must be placed in the second field of the $\{g\}$ to be pushed, the field corresponding to source $S4$.

We note that each field on each list of fields occurs below the symbol having the pointer to the list. It is important that each list pointer occur above its items, because otherwise a symbol could reach the top of the stack without the value of an inherited attribute having been stored into an inherited-attribute field. The L-attributed condition ensures that, for any L-attributed production, the list pointers created by Rule 3 are always placed above the items on the list. It is not necessary that the list items themselves occur in the same order as in the stack, although we customarily show them that way.

It is possible that Rule 3 might call for the merging of two lists as in the example

$$\langle A \rangle_{S1,S2} \to a \, \langle B \rangle_{S3}$$
$$(S1, \, S2) \leftarrow S3$$

where $S1$, $S2$, and $S3$ are synthesized. We expect this case to be rare in practice.

It is also possible that a pushed input symbol attribute or synthesized attribute of a pushed symbol is not the source of any attribute rule at all. An example is

$$\langle A \rangle \to a \, \langle B \rangle_S \, b_Z$$

where S is a synthesized attribute. For this production, the transition routine would place null pointers in the fields of pushed stack symbols $\langle B \rangle$ and b.

Summary. The above construction can be applied to any L-attributed grammar in simple assignment form which has an LL(1) input grammar. If we take an L-attributed grammar with an LL(1) input grammar and convert it into simple assignment form by adding extra action symbols (the method of Section 9.3), the augmented machine for the new grammar can be made to perform the originally specified translation by the simple technique of not emitting output for the extra action symbols. This gives the following conclusion:

> Given an L-attributed string translation grammar which has an LL(1) input grammar, a top-down pushdown processor can be designed to perform the translation specified by the grammar.

9.6   EXAMPLE OF A CONDITIONAL STATEMENT

Suppose we want to design a syntax box for a language whose grammar includes the three productions

1. $\langle S \rangle \rightarrow$ IF V V $\langle S \rangle$ $\langle$ifrem$\rangle$
2. $\langle$ifrem$\rangle \rightarrow$ ENDIF
3. $\langle$ifrem$\rangle \rightarrow$ ELSE $\langle S \rangle$ ENDIF

where V represents a variable and has a value part which is a symbol table pointer. IF, ENDIF, and ELSE are lexical tokens with no value part. We assume the grammar has more productions than have been shown but we only wish to discuss the problems associated with translating these three productions. Nonterminal $\langle S \rangle$ is intended to generate statements in the language and production 1 generates the IF statements.

Because there are two productions for $\langle$ifrem$\rangle$, there are essentially two kinds of IF statements, namely

IF V V $\langle S \rangle$ ENDIF

IF V V $\langle S \rangle$ ELSE $\langle S \rangle$ ENDIF

In the first type of IF statement, if the two variables are equal, the statement $\langle S \rangle$ is to be executed and then control is to pass to whatever statement comes after the ENDIF. If the variables are not equal, control is to be passed directly to the statement after the ENDIF without executing the statement $\langle S \rangle$. In the second type of IF statement, exactly one of the two statements $\langle S \rangle$ is to be executed and then control passed to the statement beyond the ENDIF. If the two variables are equal, the first $\langle S \rangle$ is to be executed and if the variables are not equal, the second $\langle S \rangle$ is to be executed.

We assume three atoms are available for describing to the code generator the desired transfer of control. These atoms are LABEL, JUMP, and JUMPN. The use of these atoms in translating the two types of IF statements is shown in Fig. 9.11 (a) and (b).

The atom LABEL is put out at places in the program where control is to be passed by certain transfer atoms. Such an atom might also be put out where the programmer uses a label in his program; but, in the context of the three productions under discussion, the label atom is put out to mark control points implied by the nature of the IF statements. The atom LABEL has as its value a pointer to a table entry used by the code generator to pass information among the atoms that reference a given label.

The JUMP atom marks the places where code to cause an unconditional transfer is to be generated. The value of the JUMP atom is a pointer to the table entry for the label to which control is to be transferred. Each JUMP atom will therefore have the same pointer as some corresponding LABEL atom.

The JUMPN (jump on not equal) atom marks the places where code is to be generated for comparing two variables and then transferring if and only if the variables are not equal. The value part of JUMPN consists of

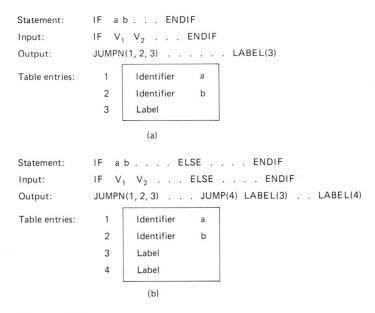

Statement: IF a b . . . ENDIF

Input: IF V_1 V_2 . . . ENDIF

Output: JUMPN(1, 2, 3) . . . . . . LABEL(3)

Table entries: 1 | Identifier | a
                  2 | Identifier | b
                  3 | Label

(a)

Statement: IF a b . . . . ELSE . . . . ENDIF

Input: IF V_1 V_2 . . . ELSE . . . . ENDIF

Output: JUMPN(1, 2, 3) . . . JUMP(4) LABEL(3) . . LABEL(4)

Table entries: 1 | Identifier | a
                  2 | Identifier | b
                  3 | Label
                  4 | Label

(b)

Figure 9.11

three pointers, the first two pointing to entries for the variables to be compared and the third pointing to the entry for the LABEL to which control should be transferred if the variables are not equal.

As a first step toward the syntax box design we expand productions 1, 2, and 3 into string translation productions which express the desired placement of the atoms. Since atom JUMPN uses the values of the two variables and must precede the translation of the first $\langle S \rangle$ the most obvious placement of {JUMPN} is between the V and $\langle S \rangle$ in production 1. Since the statement after the ELSE is to be preceded by JUMP and LABEL, {JUMP} and {LABEL} can be inserted between the ELSE and $\langle S \rangle$ of production 3.

The one atom whose placement is not immediately obvious is the LABEL for the end of the IF statement. There are two possible placements, each of which might be considered natural. One plan is to put {LABEL} at the end of production 1 because that position marks the end of the IF statement. The other plan is to put {LABEL} after each occurrence of terminal ENDIF in productions 2 and 3 since ENDIF also marks the end of the IF statement. Both plans are workable, but we only explore the second plan as it happens to give productions that are more convenient for adding attributes.

Summarizing the two previous paragraphs, the translations for productions 1, 2, and 3 are to be based on the following string translation productions.

1. $\langle S \rangle \rightarrow$ IF $V\ V$ {JUMPN} $\langle S \rangle$ $\langle$ifrem$\rangle$
2. $\langle$ifrem$\rangle \rightarrow$ ENDIF {LABEL}
3. $\langle$ifrem$\rangle \rightarrow$ ELSE {JUMP} {LABEL} $\langle S \rangle$ ENDIF {LABEL}

The next step in the syntax-box design is to add attributes and attribute rules to these string translation productions so as to make the productions L-attributed and in simple assignment form. We assume we have a table-entry allocation function routine NEWTL, which returns a pointer to a new table entry representing a label.

Input symbol V has one synthesized attribute, a pointer to its table entry. We let the atom JUMPN have three inherited attributes, one for each of its pointers. Similarly, we let JUMP and LABEL each have one inherited attribute. The label pointer that is the third attribute of the JUMPN in production 1 is to be used as the attribute of the appropriate LABEL atom in either production 2 or production 3. We let $\langle$ifrem$\rangle$ have an inherited attribute whose value is to be this pointer.

Having selected attributes for each symbol, the following attributed productions are constructed:

1. $\langle S \rangle \rightarrow$ IF $V_x V_y$ {JUMPN$_{x1,y1,z1}$} $\langle S \rangle$ $\langle$ifrem$\rangle_{z2}$
   $(z1, z2) \leftarrow$ NEWTL $x1 \leftarrow x$ $y1 \leftarrow y$
2. $\langle$ifrem$\rangle_z \rightarrow$ ENDIF {LABEL$_{z1}$}
   $z1 \leftarrow z$
3. $\langle$ifrem$\rangle_z \rightarrow$ ELSE {JUMP$_w$} {LABEL$_{z1}$} $\langle S \rangle$ ENDIF {LABEL$_{w1}$}
   $(w1, w) \leftarrow$ NEWTL $z1 \leftarrow z$

The rules are simply a description of the desired relationships among the pointers. The grammar is easily verified as L-attributed. Strictly speaking, the grammar is not in simple assignment form, since the attribute rules involve calling the parameterless function procedure NEWTL. However we can treat NEWTL as though it were a constant, and use the processor-design method of Section 9.5.

As a final step, we design the augmented transition routines for each production. For production 1, the augmented transition routine is:

1. Call NEWTL.
2. REPLACE as in Fig. 9.12.
3. ADVANCE.

For production 2, the transition is:

1. Output LABEL using the contents of the field of top stack symbol $\langle$ifrem$\rangle$ as its attribute.

2. POP.

3. ADVANCE.

For production 3 the transition routine is:

1. Call NEWTL.

2. Output JUMP with the result of NEWTL as its attribute.

3. Output LABEL using the contents of the field of top stack symbol ⟨ifrem⟩ as its attribute.

4. REPLACE ({LABEL} ENDIF ⟨S⟩) with the result of NEWTL placed in the field of {LABEL}.

5. ADVANCE.

When input V is the top stack symbol, and the current input is V, the value of the current input is placed in each field on the linked list of fields

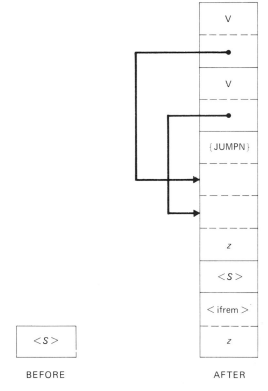

BEFORE   AFTER

z = Pointer to table entry returned by NEWTL

Figure 9.12

pointed to by the field of the stack symbol. Actually, this linked list has exactly one item so list tracing is not required.

9.7   EXAMPLE OF ARITHMETIC EXPRESSIONS

In this section we design a processor for the attributed arithmetic-expression grammar of Fig. 7.10. The input grammar for this attributed grammar was shown to be LL(1) in Section 8.6, and a pushdown recognizer for that input grammar was given in Fig. 8.17.

	/	+	*	(	)	⊣
$<E>$	# 1	REJECT	REJECT	# 1	REJECT	REJECT
$<T>$	# 4	REJECT	REJECT	# 4	REJECT	REJECT
$<P>$	# 8	REJECT	REJECT	# 7	REJECT	REJECT
$<E$-list$>$	REJECT	# 2	REJECT	REJECT	# 3	# 3
$<T$-list$>$	REJECT	# 6	# 5	REJECT	# 6	# 6
)	REJECT	REJECT	REJECT	REJECT	POP ADVANCE	REJECT
▽	REJECT	REJECT	REJECT	REJECT	REJECT	ACCEPT
{ADD}	OUT(ADD$_{p,q,r}$) using contents of three fields, POP, RETAIN					
{MULT}	OUT(MULT$_{p,q,r}$) using contents of three fields, POP, RETAIN					

Starting stack: Figure 9.14(a)

1   REPLACE as in Fig. 9.14(b), RETAIN

2   Call NEWT, REPLACE as in Fig. 9.14(c), ADVANCE

3   Put contents of first field of stack symbol into field pointed to by second field of stack symbol, POP, RETAIN

4   REPLACE as in Fig. 9.14(d), RETAIN

5   Call NEWT, REPLACE as in Fig. 9.14(e), ADVANCE

6   Put contents of first field of stack symbol into field pointed to by second field of stack symbol, POP, RETAIN

7   REPLACE as in Fig. 9.14(f), ADVANCE

8   Put value part of input into field pointed to by field of stack symbol, POP, ADVANCE

Figure 9.13

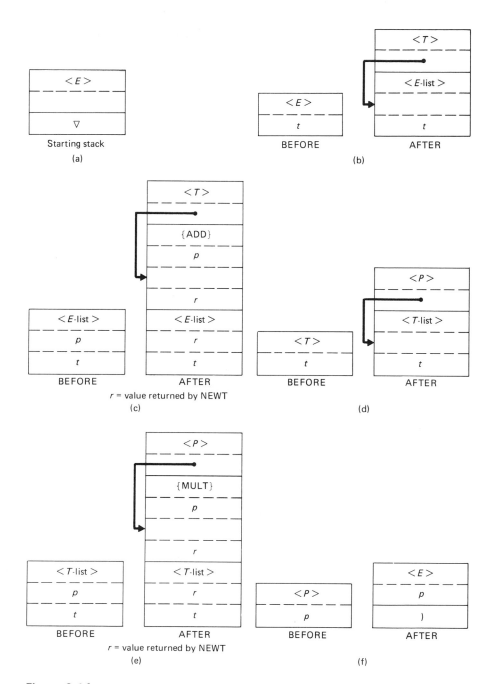

Figure 9.14

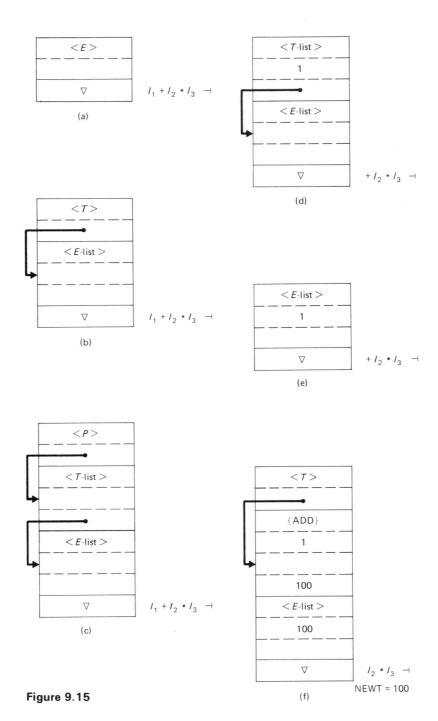

Figure 9.15

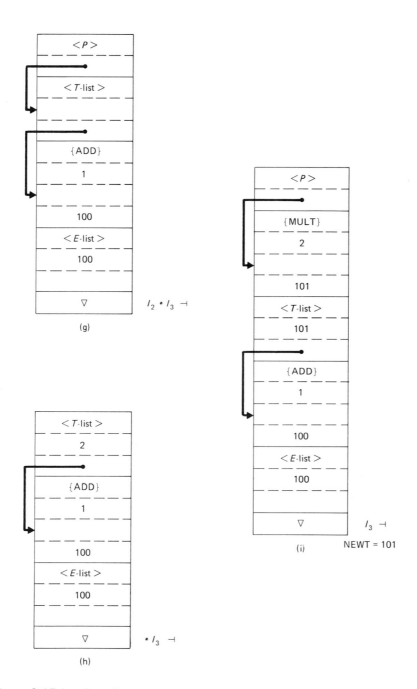

Figure 9.15 (continued)

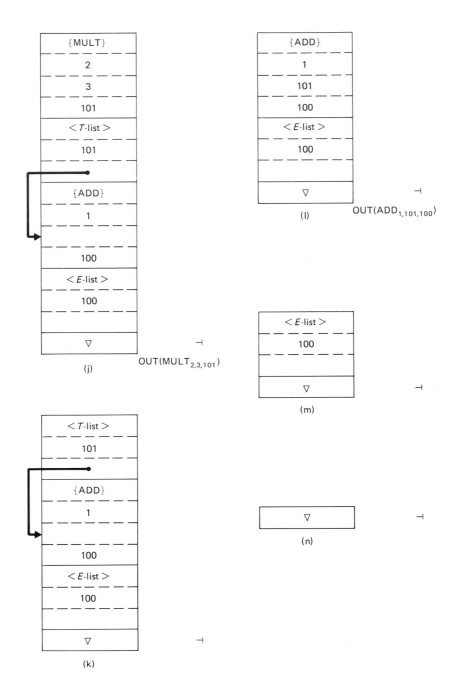

Figure 9.15 (continued)

The attributed grammar of Fig. 7.10 is already a simple-assignment-form L-attributed grammar so the methods of Section 9.5 can be applied directly. The resulting processor is shown in Figs. 9.13 and 9.14.

Figure 9.15 shows the processer processing the sequence

$$I_1 + I_2 * I_3 \dashv$$

9.8 RECURSIVE DESCENT FOR ATTRIBUTED GRAMMARS

In this section we show how the recursive-descent parsing method described in Section 8.9 can be extended to carry out L-attributed string translations. In the extended method, the procedure for a nonterminal has a parameter for each attribute of the nonterminal. For an inherited attribute, the corresponding actual parameter in the procedure call is the value of the attribute. For a synthesized attribute, the corresponding actual parameter is a variable to which we want the value of the synthesized attribute assigned. By the time the procedure returns, the parameter will be assigned the value of the synthesized attribute.

We assume the language in which the procedures are written contains a parameter-passing mechanism such that when a value is assigned to a formal parameter, this value is stored in the corresponding actual parameter. Parameter-passing mechanisms such as "call by name" in ALGOL 60 and "call by reference" in FORTRAN have this property.

The technique for extending the method of Section 8.9 uses the attribute names from the attributed productions as the names of variables and parameters. The naming of the attributes is thus linked to the implementation of the recursive-descent procedures, and certain attribute-naming conventions must be imposed in addition to the usual notational conventions employed for attributed translations.

One of the additional attribute-naming conventions is that all lefthand occurrences of a given nonterminal have the same list of attribute names. For example, it would be unsuitable for a grammar to have the two productions

$$\langle L \rangle_{a,b} \rightarrow e_i \langle R \rangle_{x,j} \langle L \rangle_{i,k}$$
$$\langle L \rangle_{x,y} \rightarrow \langle H \rangle_{z,w} \{ZAP_{k,q}\}$$

because one lefthand occurrence of $\langle L \rangle$ has attribute list a, b and the other has list x, y. In this situation, the designer should decide upon an attribute name list for nonterminal $\langle L \rangle$ and rename the attributes accordingly. For example, the designer may select list a, b as the "official" attribute name list for $\langle L \rangle$ and, by substituting a for x and b for y, express the second production as

$$\langle L \rangle_{a,b} \rightarrow \langle H \rangle_{z,w} \{ZAP_{k,q}\}$$

This change makes $\langle L \rangle_{a,b}$ the lefthand side of both $\langle L \rangle$ productions. We also employ the same name list when specifying which attributes are synthesized and which are inherited. For the example at hand, the selection of a, b as the official list for $\langle L \rangle$ would, if a were synthesized and b inherited, require that the specification be expressed as

$$\langle L \rangle_{a,b} \qquad \text{SYNTHESIZED } a \qquad \text{INHERITED } b$$

We note that the official attribute name list does not apply to righthand side occurrences of a nonterminal.

After lefthand-side and specification attributes have been renamed to conform to one another, a new notational convention may be employed to simplify or eliminate certain attribute-evaluation rules.

The new notational convention is as follows:

> If two attributes are to have the same value they may be given the same name, provided this is done without changing the attribute names of the lefthand side nonterminal.

We illustrate this convention with some examples. First consider the old notation production:

$$\langle S \rangle \rightarrow I_a \langle B \rangle_b \langle C \rangle_c$$
$$(b, c) \leftarrow a$$

Attributes a, b, and c are all given the same value by the copy rule and may be given any common name. Using name x, the production may be written in the new notation as:

$$\langle S \rangle \rightarrow I_x \langle B \rangle_x \langle C \rangle_x$$

This new attributed production has no associated evaluation rules at all. In the old notation, an explicit evaluation rule was required to show that the three attributes had the same value, but now this fact is shown by giving the attributes a common name.

Now consider production:

$$\langle L \rangle_I \rightarrow \langle A \rangle_S \{ f \}_T$$
$$(S, T) \leftarrow I$$

Here attributes I, S, and T can be given the same name, but the common name must be I in order not to change the lefthand side. Using this name, the production becomes

$$\langle L \rangle_I \rightarrow \langle A \rangle_I \{ f \}_I$$

and the need for a copy rule vanishes. Sometimes only a partial simplification is possible as for production:

$$\langle L \rangle_{I,S} \rightarrow a \, \langle B \rangle_X \, \langle C \rangle_Y$$
$$(S, X, Y) \leftarrow I$$

Here S, X, Y, and I have the same value, but they cannot be given the same name because both S and I are on the lefthand side. Nevertheless, several simplifications are possible including:

$$\langle L \rangle_{I,S} \rightarrow a \, \langle B \rangle_S \, \langle C \rangle_S$$
$$S \leftarrow I$$

A practical example of this case is the production

$$\langle E\text{-list} \rangle_{I,S} \rightarrow \epsilon$$
$$S \leftarrow I$$

which we have used in certain expression grammars.

Even noncopy rules can imply simplification. For example

$$\langle L \rangle_{I,S} \rightarrow a_X \, \langle R \rangle_Y$$
$$(S, Y) \leftarrow f(I, X)$$

can be simplified to:

$$\langle L \rangle_{I,S} \rightarrow a_X \, \langle R \rangle_S$$
$$S \leftarrow f(I, X)$$

because both S and Y are assigned a common value.

As a final example, consider:

$$\langle L \rangle_{I,S} \rightarrow a_V \, \langle A \rangle_{X1,Y1} \, \langle B \rangle_{R,X2,Y2}$$
$$(X1, X2) \leftarrow \text{NEWT} \quad (Y1, Y2) \leftarrow 74 \quad S \leftarrow g \, (X1, Y2, I) \quad R \leftarrow V$$

Giving $X1$ and $X2$ name X, giving $Y1$ and $Y2$ name Y, and giving R and V name V we obtain:

$$\langle L \rangle_{I,S} \rightarrow a_V \, \langle A \rangle_{X,Y} \, \langle B \rangle_{V,X,Y}$$
$$X \leftarrow \text{NEWT} \quad S \leftarrow g \, (X, Y, I) \quad Y \leftarrow 74$$

The new notation is introduced here because we plan to convert attribute lists directly into argument lists. The notation involves a certain penalty in that the flow of information becomes obscured. For example, if we see:

$$\langle L \rangle \rightarrow C \, \langle A \rangle_X \, \langle B \rangle_X$$

it is not immediately apparent whether the attribute of $\langle A \rangle$ is being assigned to the attribute of $\langle B \rangle$ or vice versa. If the attribute of $\langle A \rangle$ is assigned to $\langle B \rangle$, the production is L-attributed and the design method works. If, on the other hand, the attribute of $\langle B \rangle$ is assigned to $\langle A \rangle$, the production is not L-attributed and the design method fails. We can determine which attribute is assigned to which because we know that the synthesized attribute is being assigned to the inherited attribute, but we must refer back to the attribute specifications to make the distinction. Because the information flow is obscured by the new notation, we use the old notation for most descriptive purposes and switch over to the new notation only after we have an L-attributed grammar and want to apply this particular design technique.

We now describe the extensions to the method of Section 8.9 in detail. To illustrate the extensions, we apply them to the following L-attributed version of the string translation grammar from Section 8.9:

$\langle S \rangle_R$ INHERITED R

$\langle A \rangle_P$ SYNTHESIZED P

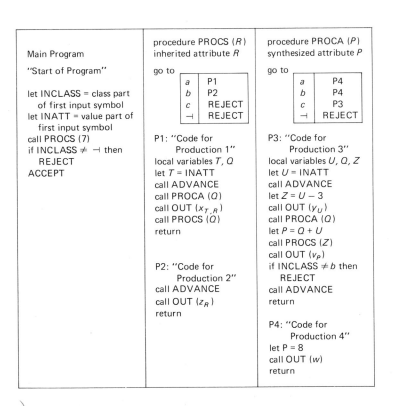

Figure 9.16

All action symbol attributes are INHERITED.

1. $\langle S \rangle_R \rightarrow a_T \langle A \rangle_Q \{x_{T,R}\} \langle S \rangle_Q$
2. $\langle S \rangle_R \rightarrow b \{z_R\}$
3. $\langle A \rangle_P \rightarrow c_U \{y_U\} \langle A \rangle_Q \langle S \rangle_Z \{v_P\}$ b

$$P \leftarrow Q + U$$
$$Z \leftarrow U - 3$$

4. $\langle A \rangle_P \rightarrow \{w\}$

$$P \leftarrow 8$$

The starting nonterminal is $\langle S \rangle$, and the starting value of its inherited attribute is 7.

The recursive-descent procedures for the unattributed grammar were presented in Fig. 8.31 and the extended version about to be derived is shown in Fig. 9.16. Figure 9.16 assumes there are two global variables INCLASS and INATT and a procedure ADVANCE. The procedure ADVANCE advances the input and assigns the class part of the input to INCLASS and the value part (if there is one) to INATT.

The extensions to the methods of Section 8.9 are described by eight rules which follow. The rules assume that the grammar is L-attributed, that the lefthand sides and specifications for each nonterminal use the same attribute names, and that common attribute names may have been used for attributes having the same value.

Rule 1. Formal Parameters.   The attribute name list associated with lefthand occurrences of a nonterminal becomes the formal parameter list of the corresponding procedure.

Rule 2. Parameter Specifications.   The INHERITED-SYNTHESIZED specifications become the formal parameter specifications, where INHERITED represents "call by value" and SYNTHESIZED "call by name" or "call by reference".

Rule 3. Local Variables.   In a production, attribute names other than those associated with lefthand occurrences become local variables of the corresponding procedure.

Rule 4. Code for Nonterminals.   For each procedure call corresponding to a righthand side occurence of a nonterminal, the attribute list of that occurrence is used as the actual parameter list.

Rule 5. Code for Input Symbols. For each occurrence of an input symbol in the grammar, code is inserted before the corresponding ADVANCE in the procedure so that each variable on the input-symbol attribute list is assigned a corresponding input attribute as found in some global variable used by the routine ADVANCE.

Rule 6. Code for Action Symbols. For each occurrence, code is inserted to compute the rules for any synthesized attributes of the action symbol and assign the results to the variables corresponding to the synthesized attributes. Then the attributed output symbol is put out.

Rule 7. Code for Attribute Rules. For each attribute-evaluation rule associated with a production, code is inserted to evaluate the righthand side of the rule and assign the result to each variable on the lefthand side of the rule. (The lefthand side will usually be a single variable if the "same-name" convention has been fully applied.) The code may be placed anywhere A) after the point where the attributes used by the rule have been computed and B) prior to the point where the computed value is first used.

Rule 8. Main Program. Each name of a synthesized attribute of the starting nonterminal becomes a local variable of the main program. The actual parameter list in the call of the starting nonterminal's procedure contains, for each inherited attribute, the initial value of that attribute, and for each synthesized attribute, the name of that attribute.

The effect of Rule 1 on Fig. 8.31 is that in Fig. 9.16 PROCS is specified with a parameter R which is the subscript of $\langle S \rangle$ in the production lefthand sides (productions 1 and 2) and PROCA is specified with a parameter P. The effect of Rule 2 is that R is specified inherited and P specified synthesized. The concepts "inherited" and "synthesized" must of course be translated into the corresponding concepts of the actual programming language being used, e.g., "value" and "name" if ALGOL is used.

The effect of Rule 3 is that PROCS has local variables T and Q and PROCA has U, Q, and Z. The method of declaring these local variables of course depends on the programming language being used.

The effect of Rule 4 is seen at each place in Fig. 9.16 when a nonterminal procedure is called. In the place corresponding to the occurrence of $\langle A \rangle$ in production 1, PROCA is called with parameter Q since Q is the attribute name associated with the occurrence of $\langle A \rangle$ in production 1.

The effect of Rule 5 is illustrated by the assignment $T = \text{INATT}$ in the code for production 1. This assignment occurs just prior to the call on AD-VANCE corresponding to the a_T in the righthand side of production 1. Input b has no associated assignment since b has no attributes.

The effect of Rule 6 for all action symbols is that attributes are put out with the corresponding output symbol.

According to Rule 7, the attribute rule $Z \leftarrow U - 3$ must be inserted after U is computed and before Z is used. The attribute rule $P \leftarrow Q + U$ must be inserted after Q and U are computed and before P is used. The L-attributed property of the given grammar ensures that such places can be found.

Rule 7 is analogous to Rule 2 of the procedure, given at the end of Section 9.3, for conversion into simple assignment form. Both rules describe the insertion of attribute evaluation rules into the righthand side of a production. The rules differ in that Rule 7 includes copy rules if any remain after employing the "same name" convention.

The effect of Rule 8 is that, in the main program, the actual parameter in the call of PROCS is the constant 7.

As mentioned in Section 8.9, the implementation of recursive descent in a high-level language is easy to program and debug. The procedure-calling mechanism of the language implements the required stacking of information. Using recursive descent for an attributed grammar has the additional feature that the parameter-passing mechanism of the high-level language implements the communication of attributes among symbols.

9.9 REFERENCES

The performing of attributed translations by pushdown machines is discussed in Lewis, Rosenkrantz, and Stearns (1974).

PROBLEMS

1. The following productions are part of an attributed grammar. In each production, attributes p, q, and r are inherited and s and t are synthesized. For each production, state which attributes the rules for p and r can depend on if the production is to be L-attributed.

   a) $\langle S \rangle_{s,q} \rightarrow a_u \langle S \rangle_{t,p} \langle A \rangle_r$

   b) $\langle S \rangle_{s,q} \rightarrow \{c_p\} b_u \langle S \rangle_{t,r}$

   c) $\langle S \rangle_{s,q} \rightarrow c_u \langle A \rangle_r \langle S \rangle_{t,p}$

2. Draw the stack movie as the sequence

$$+ * + C_1 \, C_2 + C_1 * C_3 \, C_2 \, C_4$$

   is processed by the machine of Fig. 9.6.

3. Rewrite each of the following productions in simple assignment form. The attributes whose names begin with I are inherited and those whose names begin with S are synthesized.

a) $\langle S \rangle_{S1,I1} \to \langle A \rangle_{S2} \quad \langle B \rangle_{S3,I2} \quad \langle C \rangle_{S4,I3} \quad \langle D \rangle_{S5,I4}$

$$I2 \leftarrow S2 * I1$$
$$I3 \leftarrow I1^2$$
$$I4 \leftarrow I2 * I3$$
$$S1 \leftarrow S2^2$$

b) $\langle S \rangle_{S1,I1} \to \epsilon$

$$S1 \leftarrow \text{SIN}(I1)$$

c) $\langle S \rangle_{S1,S2} \to \langle A \rangle_{S3} \quad \langle B \rangle_{I1} \quad \{\text{JOHN}\}_{I2,I3} \quad \langle C \rangle_{I4}$

$$I1 \leftarrow 3 * S3$$
$$I2 \leftarrow I1^2$$
$$(S2, I3) \leftarrow I2$$
$$I4 \leftarrow I3$$
$$S1 \leftarrow I4 + 2$$

4. Design a processor for the following grammar with starting symbol $\langle S \rangle$

$\langle E \rangle_p$ SYNTHESIZED p

All action symbol attributes are INHERITED.

1. $\langle S \rangle \to I_{p1} = \langle E \rangle_{r1} \{\text{ASSIGN}_{p2,r2}\}$
   $$p2 \leftarrow p1 \qquad r2 \leftarrow r1$$

2. $\langle E \rangle_{r2} \to +\langle E \rangle_{p1} \quad \langle E \rangle_{q1} \quad \{\text{ADD}_{p2,q2,r1}\}$
   $$(r2, r1) \leftarrow \text{NEWT} \qquad p2 \leftarrow p1 \qquad q2 \leftarrow q1$$

3. $\langle E \rangle_{r2} \to *\langle E \rangle_{p1} \quad \langle E \rangle_{q1} \quad \{\text{MULT}_{p2,q2,r1}\}$
   $$(r2, r1) \leftarrow \text{NEWT} \qquad p2 \leftarrow p1 \qquad q2 \leftarrow p1$$

4. $\langle E \rangle_{r2} \to I_{r1}$
   $$r2 \leftarrow r1$$

5. Design the processor for the following grammar and compare with the processor of the previous problem

$\langle E \rangle_p$ SYNTHESIZED p

$\{\text{ADD}_{p,q,r}\}$ SYNTHESIZED r INHERITED p, q
   $$r \leftarrow \text{NEWT}$$

$\{\text{MULT}_{p,q,r}\}$ SYNTHESIZED r INHERITED p, q
   $$r \leftarrow \text{NEWT}$$

$\{\text{ASSIGN}_{p,q}\}$ INHERITED p, q

1. $\langle S \rangle \to I_{p1} = \langle E \rangle_{r1} \{\text{ASSIGN}_{p2,r2}\}$
   $$p2 \leftarrow p1 \qquad r2 \leftarrow r1$$

2. $\langle E \rangle_{r2} \to + \langle E \rangle_{p1} \quad \langle E \rangle_{q1} \quad \{\text{ADD}_{p2,q2,r1}\}$
   $$p2 \leftarrow p1 \qquad q2 \leftarrow q1 \qquad r2 \leftarrow r1$$

3. $\langle E \rangle_{r2} \rightarrow {}^* \langle E \rangle_{p1}$ $\langle E \rangle_{q1}$ $\{MULT_{p2,q2,r1}\}$
   $p2 \leftarrow p1$ $\quad q2 \leftarrow q1$ $\quad r2 \leftarrow r1$

4. $\langle E \rangle_{r2} \rightarrow I_{r1}$
   $r2 \leftarrow r1$

6. Draw the "before" and "after" stack pictures corresponding to the two attributed productions for $\langle statement \rangle$ given in Section 7.9.

7. Consider the following L-attributed string translation grammar with starting symbol $\langle S \rangle$:

   $\langle S \rangle_{a,b}$ $\quad$ SYNTHESIZED a $\quad$ INHERITED b

   $\qquad\qquad\qquad\qquad\qquad$ starting value of $b = 1$

   $\langle A \rangle_{p,q}$ $\quad$ SYNTHESIZED p $\quad$ INHERITED q

   $\{g_t\}$ $\qquad$ SYNTHESIZED t $\qquad t \leftarrow$ NEWT

   attributes of $\{c\}$, $\{d\}$, and $\{f\}$ INHERITED

   1. $\langle S \rangle_{a,b} \rightarrow a_c \langle S \rangle_{d,e} b_f \{c_{g,h}\} \langle A \rangle_{i,j} \{d_{m,n,p}\}$
      $e \leftarrow c$ $\quad g \leftarrow b$ $\quad h \leftarrow f$ $\quad j \leftarrow b - c$
      $m \leftarrow i$ $\quad n \leftarrow j + 3$ $\quad p \leftarrow d$ $\quad a \leftarrow c + n$

   2. $\langle S \rangle_{p,q} \rightarrow \epsilon$
      $p \leftarrow q$

   3. $\langle S \rangle_{a,b} \rightarrow c_s \{c_{u,v}\} \langle S \rangle_{p,q} \{c_{d,e}\} b_t \{d_{f,g,h}\}$
      $u \leftarrow b$ $\quad v \leftarrow s$ $\quad q \leftarrow b - v$ $\quad e \leftarrow q$
      $(a, f, g) \leftarrow t$ $\quad (d, h) \leftarrow p$

   4. $\langle A \rangle_{p,q} \rightarrow d \langle S \rangle_{a,b} b_v \langle A \rangle_{r,s} \langle A \rangle_{c,d} \{g_t\} \{f_{m,n,u}\}$
      $b \leftarrow q$ $\quad m \leftarrow r$ $\quad (s, d, p) \leftarrow v$
      $n \leftarrow c$ $\quad u \leftarrow t$

   5. $\langle A \rangle_{p,q} \rightarrow \{c_{r,t}\} c_s$
      $r \leftarrow q$ $\quad p \leftarrow s$ $\quad t \leftarrow q + 3$

   a) Show that the input grammar is a q grammar.

   b) Put the grammar into simple assignment form.

   c) For each production, draw the "before" and "after" stack pictures for the pushdown processor.

   d) Complete the design of the processor.

8. Repeat the previous problem for the following L-attributed string translation grammar with starting symbol $\langle S \rangle$.

   $\langle A \rangle_p$ $\quad$ SYNTHESIZED p

   $\langle B \rangle_p$ $\quad$ INHERITED p

   $\{b_t\}$ $\quad$ INHERITED t

1. $\langle S \rangle \rightarrow a_p \langle A \rangle_q \langle B \rangle_r \langle A \rangle_s \{b_t\}$
$$r \leftarrow p + 2q$$
$$t \leftarrow r + s$$

2. $\langle A \rangle_p \rightarrow a_q \langle A \rangle_r \langle B \rangle_s \langle B \rangle_t \langle B \rangle_u \langle S \rangle$
$$s \leftarrow q + r$$
$$t \leftarrow q * s - 7$$
$$(u, p) \leftarrow r + t$$

3. $\langle A \rangle_p \rightarrow b$
$$p \leftarrow 13$$

4. $\langle B \rangle_p \rightarrow a_q \langle A \rangle_r \{b_t\}$
$$t \leftarrow p + q$$

9. Design the augmented pushdown machine for the following L-attributed string translation grammar, with starting symbol $\langle S \rangle$.

$\langle A \rangle_A$ SYNTHESIZED A

$\langle B \rangle_B$ INHERITED B

All output attributes are INHERITED.

$\langle S \rangle \rightarrow a_{M1} \langle A \rangle_{N1} \{d_{M2,N2}\} \langle B \rangle_{N3}$
$$M2 \leftarrow M1 \qquad (N3, N2) \leftarrow N1$$

$\langle S \rangle \rightarrow b_K \langle B \rangle_{R1} \{g_{R2}\}$
$$(R2, R1) \leftarrow 52$$

$\langle A \rangle_{Q4} \rightarrow a_p \langle A \rangle_{Q1} \{d_{Q2,Q3}\} \langle A \rangle_N$
$$(Q4, Q3, Q2) \leftarrow Q1$$

$\langle A \rangle_{R2} \rightarrow b_{T1} \{q_{T2}\} a_{R1}$
$$T2 \leftarrow T1 \qquad R2 \leftarrow R1$$

$\langle B \rangle_T \rightarrow a_Z \langle B \rangle_Y$
$$Y \leftarrow Z + T$$

$\langle B \rangle_{T1} \rightarrow \{d_{T2,L}\}$
$$T2 \leftarrow T1 \qquad L \leftarrow T1 - 5$$

10. a) State whether or not the grammar of Problem 7.21 is L-attributed.

   b) If it is L-attributed, draw the "before" and "after" picture for each production.

11. Add attributes and attribute rules to the following productions so as to get L-attributed productions for the translation described in Section 9.6.

   1. $\langle S \rangle \rightarrow$ IF V V {JUMPN} $\langle S \rangle$ $\langle$ifrem$\rangle$ {LABEL}
   2. $\langle$ifrem$\rangle \rightarrow$ ENDIF
   3. $\langle$ifrem$\rangle \rightarrow$ ELSE {JUMP} {LABEL} $\langle S \rangle$ ENDIF

12. a) Find an L-attributed translation grammar with an input q-grammar for the conditional statements of Problem 7.24.

   b) Design a processor for this grammar.

13. a) Find an L-attributed translation grammar with an input q-grammar for the WHILE statement of Problem 7.25.

   b) Design a processor for this grammar.

14. Design a processor that will perform the interpretation of expressions described in Problem 7.28.

15. Consider the following grammar for assignment statements:

   1. $\langle$assignment statement$\rangle \rightarrow$ IDENTIFIER $= \langle$rest of statement$\rangle$
   2. $\langle$rest of statement$\rangle \rightarrow$ IDENTIFIER $= \langle$rest of statement$\rangle$
   3. $\langle$rest of statement$\rangle \rightarrow \langle$expression$\rangle$
   4. $\langle$expression$\rangle \rightarrow + \langle$expression$\rangle \langle$expression$\rangle$
   5. $\langle$expression$\rangle \rightarrow * \langle$expression$\rangle \langle$expression$\rangle$
   6. $\langle$expression$\rangle \rightarrow$ IDENTIFIER

   A typical assignment statement is:

   $$I_1 = I_5 = + + * I_2 I_3 * I_5 I_4 I_1$$

   In executing these statements the expression is evaluated first and the assignment is then made from right to left (in the example, the assignment is made first to I_5 and then to I_1).

   a) Find an L-attributed translation grammar with an input q-grammar that will translate these statements into a suitable set of atoms with table pointers.

   b) Design a top-down processor based on this grammar.

   c) Show the stack movie as your machine processes the above statement.

16. Consider the grammar for assignment statements in the previous problem with the additional production:

   7. $\langle$expression$\rangle \rightarrow (\langle$assignment statement$\rangle)$

   A typical assignment statement in the new grammar is:

   $$I_5 = I_3 = + * I_8 I_2 * (I_5 = + I_2 * I_4 I_7) + I_2 I_6$$

   The statement is executed as before except that if a parenthesized assignment statement is encountered while evaluating an expression, that assignment statement is executed and then the value of its expression is used as the value of the parenthesized quantity. In the example the value of the parenthesized quantity is

   $$+ I_2 * I_4 I_7$$

   a) Design an L-attributed translation grammar with an input q-grammar that will translate these statements into a suitable set of atoms with table pointers.

   b) Design a top-down processor based on this grammar.

   c) Show the stack movie as your machine processes the above statement.

17. a) Find an L-attributed translation grammar with an input q-grammar that describes the input-output relation of the constant processor of Section 2.14.

b) Design the augmented pushdown machine for this grammar.

18. Draw the stack move as the processor of Fig. 9.13 processes the expression

$$I_1 * (I_2 + I_3)$$

19. Design an arithmetic expression processor similar to that of Fig. 9.13 except that:

a) unary minus is allowed;

b) exponentiation is allowed and is carried out from right to left.

20. Design a pushdown machine that will act as an interpreter for arithmetic expressions (over $+$ and $*$) using constants and written in infix form. The interpreter should be based on an L-attributed LL(1) grammar.

21. Design a recursive-descent interpreter for arithmetic expressions (over $+$ and $*$) written in infix form.

22. Design a recursive-descent processor for the following L-attributed string translation grammar with starting symbol $\langle S \rangle$.

$\langle S \rangle_q$ SYNTHESIZED q

$\langle A \rangle_{x,y,z}$ INHERITED x SYNTHESIZED y, z

All action symbol attributes are INHERITED.

$\langle S \rangle_q \rightarrow a_{x1} \langle A \rangle_{x,y,z} \langle S \rangle_{q1} \{b_w\}$
$\qquad w \leftarrow y * z + q1 \qquad x \leftarrow x1 \qquad q \leftarrow q1$

$\langle S \rangle_{r1} \rightarrow b \, a_y \{c_w\} \langle A \rangle_{u,r,x} \{b_v\}$
$\qquad w \leftarrow y + 3 \qquad r1 \leftarrow r$
$\qquad v \leftarrow r * x - w \qquad u \leftarrow w + 2$

$\langle A \rangle_{x,y,z1} \rightarrow a_q \{c_v\} \langle A \rangle_{x1,z,u} \langle A \rangle_{u,t,y1}$
$\qquad v \leftarrow x - q \qquad x1 \leftarrow x \qquad y \leftarrow y1 \qquad z1 \leftarrow z \qquad u \leftarrow 3$

$\langle A \rangle_{t,s,s1} \rightarrow b \, a_q \{b_{t1}\} a_{s2}$
$\qquad t1 \leftarrow t \qquad (s, s1) \leftarrow s2$

23. Design recursive-descent processors for the grammars of each of the following problems: 9.4, 9.5, 9.8, 9.11, 9.12, 9.13, 9.16

24. a) Find an L-attributed grammar for which the pushdown processor designed according to the methods of this chapter requires a number of operations proportional to the square of the number of symbols in the input sequence.

b) Modify the design method so that it requires a number of operations proportional to the number of symbols in the input sequence. Hint: Let each synthesized attribute have two fields, one pointing to each end of its linked list.

25. Consider the following attributed grammar

$\langle E \rangle_{p,s}$ SYNTHESIZED p, s

$\langle E \rangle_{p,s} \rightarrow + \langle E \rangle_{q,t} \langle E \rangle_{r,u}$

      $p \leftarrow \text{NEWT}$

      $s \leftarrow t \circ u \circ \text{ADD} \circ q \circ r \circ p$

$\langle E \rangle_{p,s} \rightarrow - \langle E \rangle_{q,t} \langle E \rangle_{r,u}$

      $p \leftarrow \text{NEWT}$

      $s \leftarrow u \circ t \circ \text{SUBTRACT} \circ q \circ r \circ p$

$\langle E \rangle_{p2,s} \rightarrow I_{p1}$

      $p2 \leftarrow p1$

      $s \leftarrow \epsilon$ (the null string)

where the first attribute of $\langle E \rangle$ is a pointer to a table entry, the second attribute is a string, $\circ$ denotes string concatenation, and the function routine NEWT returns a pointer to a new table entry.

a) Explain in English what this grammar does.

b) What is a translation of the input string:

$$- + I_a I_b - I_c + I_d I_e$$

c) Design a pushdown processor for this attributed grammar.

26. Show that given an L-attributed translation grammar and a derivation tree with the attributes of the input symbols filled in, all the attributes on the tree can be computed (by steps 3 and 4 of the activity-sequence construction of Section 7.7).

27. Consider the following grammar with starting symbol $\langle$GO TO statement$\rangle$.

1. $\langle$GO TO statement$\rangle \rightarrow$ GO TO $\langle$label expression$\rangle$

2. $\langle$label expression$\rangle \rightarrow$ IDENTIFIER

3. $\langle$label expression$\rangle \rightarrow$ IF VARIABLE THEN $\langle$label expression$\rangle$ ELSE

                $\langle$label expression$\rangle$

Assume IDENTIFIER is a token whose value part is a pointer to a table entry for a label and VARIABLE is a token whose value part is a pointer to a table entry for a variable.

At execution time the GO TO statement causes a transfer of control to a label. The label expression in production 1 is evaluated at execution time, and the value of that expression is the label to which control is transferred.

For label expressions described by production 2, the execution-time value of the expression is the label named by the identifier.

For label expressions described by production 3 the execution-time value of the expression is, if the VARIABLE equals 0, the value of the first label expression on the righthand side and, if not, the value of the second label expression.

Assume the following atoms are available:

a) LABEL(p) where p is a pointer to a table entry for a label. LABEL has two uses. It marks the place where the programmer has specified a label and it marks the place where the compiler has defined a label for its own purposes. The type of table entry pointed to by p is the same for both uses.

b) JUMP(p) where p is a pointer to a table entry for a label. JUMP generates code to cause an unconditional transfer of control to the label specified by p.

c) JUMPNZ(q, p) where p is a pointer to a table entry for a label and q is a pointer to a table entry for a variable. JUMPNZ generates code to transfer to the label specified by p if the variable specified by q is not zero.

   i) Find an L-attributed string translation grammar which specifies a translation of strings in this language into appropriate atom strings.

      As an example, the translation of

$$\text{GO TO IDENTIFIER}_7$$

     is

$$\text{JUMP(7)}$$

     and that of

$$\text{GO TO IF VARIABLE}_5 \text{ THEN IDENTIFIER}_{17} \text{ ELSE IDENTIFIER}_{11}$$

      might be

$$\text{JUMPNZ(5, 31) JUMP(17) LABEL(31) JUMP(11)}$$

     where 31 is a pointer to a table entry for a label defined by the compiler.

  ii) Design a processor based on this grammar.

 iii) Assume the following atom is available:

     JUMPZ(q, p) where q points to a table entry for a variable and p points to a table entry for a label. JUMPZ generates code to transfer to the label specified by p if the variable specified by q is equal to zero.

     Find an L-attributed grammar (perhaps involving a change in the input grammar) which specifies a translation into an atom string such that if the label expression after a THEN is an identifier, the JUMPZ atom is used with its second attribute being a pointer to the table entry for the identifier. For instance, the translation of

$$\text{GO TO IF VARIABLE}_5 \text{ THEN IDENTIFIER}_{17} \text{ ELSE IDENTIFIER}_{11}$$

     is

$$\text{JUMPZ(5, 17) JUMP(11)}$$

 iv) Assume that in addition to JUMPZ, the atom

$$\text{EQUATE-LABELS}(p, q)$$

     is available, where p is a pointer to a table entry for a label specified by the programmer and q is a pointer to a table entry for a label defined by the compiler. This atom indicates to the code generator that both labels mark the same place in the program.

Find an L-attributed grammar (perhaps involving a change in the input grammar) which specifies a translation into an atom string such that if the label expression after a THEN begins with IF, and the label expression after the ELSE is an identifier, then the JUMPNZ atom is used with a compiler-defined label that is subsequently equated to the programmer-specified label after the ELSE. For instance, the translation of:

GO TO IF VARIABLE$_7$ THEN IF VARIABLE$_5$ THEN IDENTIFIER$_{17}$ ELSE IDENTIFIER$_{11}$ ELSE IDENTIFIER$_{21}$

might be

JUMPNZ(7,31) JUMPZ(5,17) JUMP(11) EQUATE-LABELS(21,31)

where 31 is a pointer to a table entry for a label defined by the compiler.

28. a) In designing a processor for an L-attributed grammar, sometimes certain stack symbol fields can be replaced by global variables which are used to keep track of attribute values. Design an augmented pushdown processor for the grammar of Fig. 9.2 in which only stack symbols {ADD} and {MULT} have fields. These stack symbols are to have a single field which is used to store the value of the left operand. The processor is to also have a single global variable to keep the most recently obtained subexpression value.

b) Repeat Part a for the grammar of Fig. 7.10.

29. Consider the following attributed grammar:

$\langle E \rangle_r$ SYNTHESIZED r

All action symbol attributes are INHERITED.

1. $\langle S \rangle \rightarrow I_{p1} = \langle E \rangle_{r1} \{\text{ASSIGN}_{p2,r2}\}$
   $\quad p2 \leftarrow p1 \qquad r2 \leftarrow r1$

2. $\langle E \rangle_r \rightarrow + \langle E \rangle_{p1} \langle E \rangle_{q1} \{\text{ADD}_{p2,q2}\}$
   $\quad p2 \leftarrow p1 \qquad q2 \leftarrow q1$
   $\quad r \leftarrow \text{address of ADD atom}$

3. $\langle E \rangle_r \rightarrow * \langle E \rangle_{p1} \langle E \rangle_{q1} \{\text{MULT}_{p2,q2}\}$
   $\quad p2 \leftarrow p1 \qquad q2 \leftarrow q1$
   $\quad r \leftarrow \text{address of MULT atom}$

4. $\langle E \rangle_{r2} \rightarrow I_{r1}$
   $\quad r2 \leftarrow r1$

The atom string will begin in location 400, and the address of each atom in the string equals the address of the previous atom plus three.

a) Find the attributed translation of:

$$I_1 = + I_2 * + I_3 I_1 * I_4 I_5$$

b) Let $\langle E \rangle$ have two additional attributes, one inherited and one synthesized. The inherited attribute is to equal the address in the atom string of the first atom that might be produced by translating the $\langle E \rangle$. The synthesized attribute is to equal the address in the atom string of the next atom that is produced after the translation of the $\langle E \rangle$. Add rules to the grammar specifying the values of these attributes. Also change the rule for r in productions 2 and 3 so as to take advantage of these new attributes.

c) Design a processor for the above grammar.

30. Assume it is possible for a field of a stack symbol in an augmented pushdown machine to contain a pointer to a location in the part of the atom string that has already been produced.

a) Use this capability in the design of a processor for the following non-L-attributed grammar.

$$\langle S \rangle \rightarrow a \ \{c\}_y \ \langle S \rangle \ d_x$$
$$y \leftarrow x$$
$$\langle S \rangle \rightarrow b$$

b) Show that if an L-attributed grammar is modified by the insertion into the productions of output symbols having inherited attributes not satisfying part 1 of the definition of L-attributed grammars, the resulting translation can be performed by an augmented pushdown machine using the above capability.

31. Some compilers are designed so that the syntax box produces as its output some representation of the derivation tree of its input sequence. One representation is a data structure containing an atom for each node in the tree. As an example, the representation of the tree shown below is the data structure shown below. Each atom of the data structure consists of a class part and two attributes. The class part is the name of the terminal or nonterminal. The first attribute is a pointer to the leftmost immediate descendant, when one exists. When there are no descendants, as for a terminal or for a nonterminal to which an ϵ-production is applied, the first attribute is zero. The second attribute of each atom is a pointer to its next sibling on the right, when one exists. (All the direct descendants of a given node are said to be *siblings* of each other.) When there are no right siblings, as for the last symbol in a production or for the starting nonterminal, the second attribute is zero.

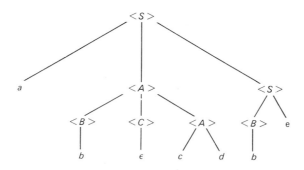

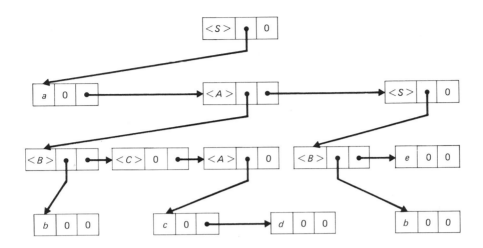

a) Find an L-attributed grammar that specifies the translation of each sequence generated by the following grammar, with starting symbol $\langle S \rangle$, into an atom string representing its tree.

$\langle S \rangle \rightarrow a \langle A \rangle \langle S \rangle$

$\langle S \rangle \rightarrow \langle B \rangle e$

$\langle A \rangle \rightarrow \langle B \rangle \langle C \rangle \langle A \rangle$

$\langle A \rangle \rightarrow c\ d$

$\langle B \rangle \quad \rightarrow b$

$\langle C \rangle \rightarrow \epsilon$

$\langle C \rangle \rightarrow a \langle B \rangle \langle B \rangle$

The atoms can be generated in any order you wish.

Hint: For the sample tree, the following output string might be generated:

1. $b\ (0, 0)$	8. $e\ (0, 0)$
2. $d\ (0, 0)$	9. $\langle B \rangle\ (7, 8)$
3. $c\ (0, 2)$	10. $\langle S \rangle\ (9, 0)$
4. $\langle A \rangle\ (3, 0)$	11. $\langle A \rangle\ (6, 10)$
5. $\langle C \rangle\ (0, 4)$	12. $a\ (0, 11)$
6. $\langle B \rangle\ (1, 5)$	13. $\langle S \rangle\ (12, 0)$
7. $b\ (0, 0)$	

The atoms have been numbered for convenience.

10
MINI-BASIC
Syntax Box

10.1   AN LL(1) GRAMMAR FOR MINI-BASIC

In this chapter we design a MINI-BASIC syntax box based on an L-attributed translation grammar whose input grammar is an LL(1) grammar. The job of the syntax box is to input a token string produced by the lexical box of Chapter 4 and to produce as output an atom string which will be used as input to the code generator described in Chapter 14.

We begin by discussing the LL(1) grammar underlying the translation. This grammar is shown in Fig. 10.1 and can be compared with the MINI-BASIC grammar given in Section 6.15.

The terminal set of the grammar in Fig. 10.1 is the set of tokens listed in Fig. 4.1, except that the five arithmetic operators are represented as distinct tokens rather than as one token. In studying the grammar, it is helpful to keep in mind the actual character strings corresponding to each of the tokens. For instance, the token ASSIGN corresponds to the word LET followed by a variable followed by $=$, and the token LINE corresponds to the line number at the beginning of a line.

Observe that production 9 generates both a FOR statement and its matching NEXT statement. Also observe that production 9 generates both forms of the FOR statement, since nonterminal ⟨step part⟩ generates either the null string or STEP followed by an expression.

It is readily verified that the grammar of Fig. 10.1 is in fact an LL(1) grammar.

Starting symbol: ⟨program⟩

Program Structure

1. ⟨program⟩ → LINE ⟨program body⟩ END
2. ⟨program body⟩ → ε

Null Statement

3. ⟨program body⟩ → LINE ⟨program body⟩

Assignment Statement

4. ⟨program body⟩ → ASSIGN ⟨expression⟩ ⟨more lines⟩

GOTO Statement

5. ⟨program body⟩ → GOTO ⟨more lines⟩

IF Statement

6. ⟨program body⟩ → IF ⟨expression⟩ RELATIONAL OPERATOR
   ⟨expression⟩ GOTO ⟨more lines⟩

GOSUB Statement

7. ⟨program body⟩ → GOSUB ⟨more lines⟩

RETURN Statement

8. ⟨program body⟩ → RETURN ⟨more lines⟩

FOR Statement

9. ⟨program body⟩ → FOR ⟨expression⟩ TO ⟨expression⟩
   ⟨step part⟩ ⟨more lines⟩ NEXT ⟨more lines⟩
10. ⟨step part⟩ → STEP ⟨expression⟩
11. ⟨step part⟩ → ε

REM Statement

12. ⟨program body⟩ → COMMENT ⟨more lines⟩

Line Number

13. ⟨more lines⟩ → LINE ⟨program body⟩

Expressions

14. ⟨expression⟩ → ⟨term⟩ ⟨E-list⟩
15. ⟨expression⟩ → + ⟨term⟩⟨E-list⟩
16. ⟨expression⟩ → − ⟨term⟩ ⟨E-list⟩
17. ⟨E-list⟩ → + ⟨term⟩ ⟨E-list⟩
18. ⟨E-list⟩ → − ⟨term⟩ ⟨E-list⟩
19. ⟨E-list⟩ → ε
20. ⟨term⟩ → ⟨factor⟩ ⟨T-list⟩
21. ⟨T-list⟩ → * ⟨factor⟩ ⟨T-list⟩
22. ⟨T-list⟩ → / ⟨factor⟩ ⟨T-list⟩
23. ⟨T-list⟩ → ε
24. ⟨factor⟩ → ⟨primary⟩ ⟨F-list⟩
25. ⟨F-list⟩ → ↑ ⟨primary⟩ ⟨F-list⟩
26. ⟨F-list⟩ → ε
27. ⟨primary⟩ → (⟨expression⟩)
28. ⟨primary⟩ → OPERAND

Fig. 10.1 LL(1) Grammar for MINI-BASIC syntax box

10.2 THE ATOM SET AND TRANSLATION GRAMMAR

Now we are ready to specify the atom set and the translation grammar. Figure 10.2 shows the complete atom set with descriptions of all the attributes.

ATOM SET				
NAME	ATTRIBUTES			
FINIS				
LINEN	Pointer to line number			
ASSIGN	Pointer to variable	Pointer to result of expression		
JUMP	Pointer to line number or label			
JUMPSAVE	Pointer to line number			
RETURNJUMP				
CONDJUMP	Pointer to result of expression	Pointer to result of expression	Name of relational operator	Pointer to line number
SAVE	Pointer to result of expression	Pointer to result of SAVE		
LABEL	Pointer to label			
TEST	Pointer to FOR variable	Pointer to result of SAVE for TO expression	Pointer to result of SAVE for STEP expression	Pointer to LABEL
INCR	Pointer to FOR variable	Pointer to result of SAVE for STEP expression		
ADD	Pointer to left operand	Pointer to right operand	Pointer to result	
SUBT	Pointer to left operand	Pointer to right operand	Pointer to result	

Fig. 10.2 Atom set

ATOM SET			
NAME	ATTRIBUTES		
MULT	Pointer to left operand	Pointer to right operand	Pointer to result
DIV	Pointer to left operand	Pointer to right operand	Pointer to result
EXP	Pointer to left operand	Pointer to right operand	Pointer to result
PLUS	Pointer to operand	Pointer to result	
NEG	Pointer to operand	Pointer to result	

Figure 10.2 (continued)

FINIS, the first atom in the figure, serves as the endmarker for the atom string. It is used as a message from the syntax box to the code generator indicating that the syntax processing is complete and that the syntax box current input is the endmarker. Upon receipt of the FINIS atom, the code generator generates code for ending the runtime program. The FINIS atom is produced by the exit routine of the syntax box and is not specified as a part of the translation grammar. Having FINIS put out by the exit routine ensures that FINIS is always the last atom put out, even if the syntax-box input is not syntactically correct and an error-recovery routine has been invoked.

The next atom

$$\text{LINEN}(p)$$

is to be put out whenever the lexical token LINE appears. The attribute p equals the value part of the token LINE, namely a pointer to the table entry for a line number. The appearance of this atom in the atom string enables the code generator to record the object-code address corresponding to the line number. The timing for producing LINEN can be expressed by

1. $\langle\text{program}\rangle \rightarrow$ LINE {LINEN} $\langle\text{program body}\rangle$ END
3. $\langle\text{program body}\rangle \rightarrow$ LINE {LINEN} $\langle\text{program body}\rangle$
13. $\langle\text{more lines}\rangle \rightarrow$ LINE {LINEN} $\langle\text{program body}\rangle$

When the syntax box encounters the token LINE, we also want it to record the value part of the token; so that, in case any errors are detected while processing that line, the line number can be printed as part of the error message. We assume a variable, named LINE NUMBER, is used by the syntax box to keep track of the current line number. We introduce a new action symbol {SET LINE NUMBER} whose corresponding action routine is to assign the value part of the token LINE to the variable LINE NUMBER. The timing for calling this action routine can be expressed by

1. ⟨program⟩ → LINE {LINEN} {SET LINE NUMBER}
   ⟨program body ⟩ END

3. ⟨program body⟩ → LINE {LINEN} {SET LINE NUMBER}
   ⟨program body⟩

13. ⟨more lines⟩ → LINE {LINEN} {SET LINE NUMBER}
   ⟨program body⟩

For expressions we use a translation similar to that in Section 7.4.

14. ⟨expression⟩ → ⟨term⟩ ⟨E-list⟩
15. ⟨expression⟩ → + ⟨term⟩ {PLUS} ⟨E-list⟩
16. ⟨expression⟩ → − ⟨term⟩ {NEG} ⟨E-list⟩
17. ⟨E-list⟩ → + ⟨term⟩ {ADD} ⟨E-list⟩
18. ⟨E-list⟩ → − ⟨term⟩ {SUBT} ⟨E-list⟩
19. ⟨E-list⟩ → ε
20. ⟨term⟩ → ⟨factor⟩ ⟨T-list⟩
21. ⟨T-list⟩ → * ⟨factor⟩ {MULT} ⟨T-list⟩
22. ⟨T-list⟩ → / ⟨factor⟩ {DIV} ⟨T-list⟩
23. ⟨T-list⟩ → ε
24. ⟨factor⟩ → ⟨primary⟩ ⟨F-list⟩
25. ⟨F-list⟩ → ↑ ⟨primary⟩ {EXP} ⟨F-list⟩
26. ⟨F-list⟩ → ε
27. ⟨primary⟩ → (⟨expression⟩)
28. ⟨primary⟩ → OPERAND

The purpose of the remaining atoms can be seen by considering each statement type individually. In Section 7.9 we designed the translation of the assignment statement and IF statement, using the atoms ASSIGN and CONDJUMP respectively. Here we use these same atoms with the same attributes. The relevant translation grammar productions are

4. ⟨program body⟩ → ASSIGN ⟨expression⟩ {ASSIGN}
   ⟨more lines⟩

6. ⟨program body⟩ → IF ⟨expression⟩ RELATIONAL OPERATOR
    ⟨expression⟩ GOTO {CONDJUMP}
    ⟨more lines⟩

The null statement and REM statement require no atoms as output. For the GOTO statement we use the atom

$$JUMP(p)$$

where p is a pointer to the table entry for the line number to which control is transferred (i.e., p equals the value part of the GOTO token). The timing for producing this atom is specified by

5. ⟨program body⟩ → GOTO {JUMP} ⟨more lines⟩

Next we consider the GOSUB and RETURN statements. Our plan for implementing subroutine calls at run time involves the use of a run-time stack on which return addresses are kept. Whenever a GOSUB is executed, control is transferred to the specified line number and the return address is pushed onto the run-time stack. Then, when a RETURN is executed, control is transferred to the address on the top of the run-time stack and this address is popped off the stack. The bottommarker of the stack is the address of a run-time error routine so that if more RETURN's are executed than GOSUB's, control will be passed to this error routine, which will print out an appropriate error message and stop the program.

To carry out this plan we use two atoms: JUMPSAVE(p), which is issued right after the lexical token GOSUB and RETURNJUMP which is issued right after the token RETURN. JUMPSAVE has one attribute, a pointer to the table entry for the line number to which control is to be transferred (i.e., the attribute equals the value part of the token GOSUB). JUMPSAVE causes code to be generated to effect the transfer and to push the return address on the run-time stack. RETURNJUMP has no attributes and causes code to be generated which pops the return address off the top of the run-time stack and transfers control to this address.

The timing for outputting these atoms is expressed by the productions

7. ⟨program body⟩ → GOSUB {JUMPSAVE} ⟨more lines⟩
8. ⟨program body⟩ → RETURN {RETURNJUMP} ⟨more lines⟩

Now we consider the FOR statement. To explain our translation of the FOR statements into atoms, we first describe our plan for implementing the FOR statement at run time. This plan is expressed in Fig. 10.3(a) in the form of a flow chart. The object code for the boxes is to be generated in the order in which the boxes appear in Fig. 10.3(a). At run time, we first compute the value of the initial expression and assign it to the FOR variable. Then we

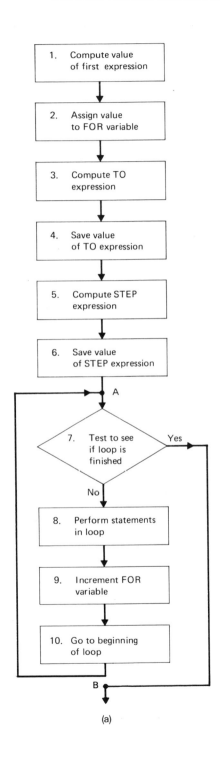

Figure 10.3   (a)

1. $<$ expression $>$
2.   {ASSIGN}
3. $<$ expression $>$
4.   {SAVE}
5. $<$ expression $>$ or 1
6.   {SAVE}
A.   {LABEL}
7.   {TEST}
8. $<$ more lines $>$
9.   {INCR}
10.   {JUMP}
B.   {LABEL}

(b)

Figure 10.3 (continued)

compute the value of the TO expression (i.e., the expression after the word TO) and save it for future use. Then we compute the value of the STEP expression and save its value. Now we carry out the test to see if statements in the loop should be performed. If these statements are performed, we increment the FOR variable after completing them and return to the beginning of the test. Note that computing and saving the TO and STEP expressions before the loop occurs in the flow chart ensures that the same values will be used for these expressions, even if some of the variables used in the computation are changed by one of the statements in the loop.

Our syntax-box plan for processing FOR/NEXT constructions is to put out one or more atoms for each box and each labeled node in the flow chart of Fig. 10.3(a). We now consider each box and labeled node and describe the desired translation into atoms. The discussion is summarized by Fig. 10.3(b).

Atoms for boxes 1 and 3 are produced from the two occurrences of $\langle$ expression $\rangle$ in production 9.

If production 10 is applied to $\langle$ step part $\rangle$ then atoms for box 5 are produced from the occurrence of $\langle$ expression $\rangle$ in production 10. If production 11 is applied to $\langle$ step part $\rangle$ then the expression for box 5 is the constant 1.

Code for box 2 is to be obtained from the atom ASSIGN already discussed. For boxes 4 and 6, we introduce an atom

$$SAVE(p, q)$$

where p is a pointer to a table entry for the expression being saved and q is a pointer to a table entry associated with the run-time location where the value is to be saved. We refer to the table entry pointed to by q as being for the result of the SAVE. The code generator handles the SAVE atom differently than the ASSIGN atom. When the first attribute of SAVE points to the table entry for a constant, the code generator does not generate any code but uses the constant itself in the code generated for other atoms involving the STEP expression. When the table entry is for a variable or an expression involving an operator, the SAVE generates code to store the value of the STEP expression in some location. This location is used in the code generated for other atoms involving the STEP expression.

Nodes A and B in the flow chart represent places to which control is to be passed. We refer to each of these control points as a label and give it a table entry. To enable the code generator to record the object-code address corresponding to each of these labels, nodes A and B are represented by atom

$$\text{LABEL}(p)$$

where p is a pointer to the table entry for the label. Note that a label is an entity created by the compiler and is not the same as a line number.

For box 7 we use the atom

$$\text{TEST}(p, q, r, s)$$

where p is a pointer to the table entry for the FOR variable, q is a pointer to the table entry for the SAVE corresponding to the TO expression, r is a pointer to the table entry for the SAVE corresponding to the STEP expression, and s is a pointer to the table entry for the label corresponding to node B in Fig. 10.3(a). The code generated from TEST implements the following algorithm where the names of the attributes are used to represent the corresponding run-time values.

$$\text{IF } (r \geq 0 \text{ and } p > q) \text{ or } (r < 0 \text{ and } p < q) \text{ THEN GO TO } s$$

Atoms for box 8 are to be obtained by processing the first occurrence of nonterminal ⟨more lines⟩ in the righthand side of production 9.

For box 9 we use the atom

$$\text{INCR}(p, q)$$

where p is a pointer to the table entry for the FOR variable and q is a pointer to the result of the SAVE of the STEP expression. The code generated from INCR adds the value of the STEP expression to the FOR variable.

For box 10 we use the atom

$$\text{JUMP}(p)$$

where p is a pointer to the table entry for the label corresponding to point A in the flow chart.

The flow chart for the FOR/NEXT construction describes what happens at run time and suggests which atoms to generate at compile time. However, in addition to generating these atoms, one additional action must be performed at compile time, namely checking that the FOR and NEXT variables are the same. To accomplish this checking we introduce an action routine

$$\{CHECK\}_{p,q,r}$$

where p and q equal the value part of the FOR and NEXT tokens respectively, and r is a pointer to the table entry for the line number of the FOR statement. The action of {CHECK} is to verify that p and q are equal. If they are not equal, a warning message is produced referring to the line number of the FOR statement. However, this is not considered a fatal error, and the compilation continues.

The correct timing for outputting the atoms and the calling of {CHECK} is expressed by the productions

9. ⟨program body⟩ → FOR ⟨expression⟩ {ASSIGN} TO
   ⟨expression⟩ {SAVE} ⟨step part⟩ {SAVE}
   {LABEL} {TEST} ⟨more lines⟩ NEXT
   {CHECK} {INCR} {JUMP} {LABEL}
   ⟨more lines⟩

10. ⟨step part⟩ → STEP ⟨expression⟩

11. ⟨step part⟩ → ε

10.3   AN L-ATTRIBUTED GRAMMAR

An L-attributed grammar is shown in Fig. 10.4. We assume the existence of three table-entry-allocating procedures NEWTR, NEWTSR, and NEWTL. NEWTR returns a pointer to a new table entry for a partial result, NEWTSR returns a pointer to a new table entry for the result of a SAVE atom, and NEWTL returns a pointer to a new table entry for a label. As we show in Chapter 14, each of these types of entries has certain fields needed by the code generator. Some of these fields are to be initialized by NEWTR, NEWTSR or NEWTL when the entries are allocated, but we defer discussion of this initialization until Chapter 14. Here we only need to know that NEWTR, NEWTSR, and NEWTL return appropriate pointers.

In production 11 we assume the ability to obtain a pointer to a previously prepared table entry for the constant 1.

All nonterminal attributes are SYNTHESIZED except

$\langle E\text{-list}\rangle_{p,t}$ INHERITED p SYNTHESIZED t

$\langle T\text{-list}\rangle_{p,t}$ INHERITED p SYNTHESIZED t

$\langle F\text{-list}\rangle_{p,t}$ INHERITED p SYNTHESIZED t

All action symbol attributes are INHERITED.

Description of Action Routine $\{\text{SET LINE NUMBER}\}_p$

$$\text{LINE NUMBER} \leftarrow p$$

Description of Action Routine $\{\text{CHECK}\}_{p,w,y}$

$$\text{IF } p \neq w \text{ THEN print warning message}$$

Starting symbol: $\langle$program$\rangle$

Program Structure

1. $\langle$program$\rangle \rightarrow \text{LINE}_{p1}$ $\{\text{LINEN}_{p2}\}$ $\{\text{SET LINE NUMBER}\}_{p3}$ $\langle$program body$\rangle$
   END

   $(p3, p2) \leftarrow p1$

2. $\langle$program body$\rangle \rightarrow \epsilon$

Null Statement

3. $\langle$program body$\rangle \rightarrow \text{LINE}_{p1}$ $\{\text{LINEN}_{p2}\}$ $\{\text{SET LINE NUMBER}\}_{p3}$
   $\langle$program body$\rangle$

   $(p3, p2) \leftarrow p1$

Assignment Statement

4. $\langle$program body$\rangle \rightarrow \text{ASSIGN}_{p1}$ $\langle$expression$\rangle_{q1}$ $\{\text{ASSIGN}_{p2,q2}\}$ $\langle$more lines$\rangle$

   $p2 \leftarrow p1 \quad q2 \leftarrow q1$

GOTO Statement

5. $\langle$program body$\rangle \rightarrow \text{GOTO}_{p1}$ $\{\text{JUMP}_{p2}\}$ $\langle$more lines$\rangle$

   $p2 \leftarrow p1$

IF Statement

6. $\langle$program body$\rangle \rightarrow \text{IF} \langle$expression$\rangle_{p1}$ RELATIONAL OPERATOR$_{r1}$
   $\langle$expression$\rangle_{q1}$ GOTO_{s1} $\{\text{CONDJUMP}_{p2,q2,r2,s2}\}$
   $\langle$more lines$\rangle$

   $p2 \leftarrow p1 \quad q2 \leftarrow q1 \quad r2 \leftarrow r1 \quad s2 \leftarrow s1$

GOSUB Statement

7. $\langle$program body$\rangle \rightarrow \text{GOSUB}_{p1}$ $\{\text{JUMPSAVE}_{p2}\}$ $\langle$more lines$\rangle$

   $p2 \leftarrow p1$

RETURN Statement

8. $\langle$program body$\rangle \rightarrow \text{RETURN}$ $\{\text{RETURN JUMP}\}$ $\langle$more lines$\rangle$

Fig. 10.4 L-attributed grammar for MINI-BASIC syntax box

FOR Statement

9. $\langle$program body$\rangle \rightarrow$ FOR$_{p1}$ $\langle$expression$\rangle_{q1}$ {ASSIGN$_{p2,q2}$} TO $\langle$expression$\rangle_{r1}$
$\qquad$ {SAVE$_{r2,s1}$} $\langle$step part$\rangle_{x1}$ {SAVE$_{x2,t1}$} {LABEL$_{u1}$}
$\qquad$ {TEST$_{p3,s2,t2,v1}$} $\langle$more lines$\rangle$ NEXT$_{w1}$ {CHECK}$_{p4,w2,y}$
$\qquad$ {INCR$_{p5,t3}$} {JUMP$_{u2}$} {LABEL$_{v2}$} $\langle$more lines$\rangle$

$\qquad$ (s2, s1) $\leftarrow$ NEWTSR $\qquad$ (t3, t2, t1) $\leftarrow$ NEWSTR
$\qquad$ (u2, u1) $\leftarrow$ NEWTL $\qquad$ (v2, v1) $\leftarrow$ NEWTL
$\qquad$ (p5, p4, p3, p2) $\leftarrow$ p1 $\qquad$ y $\leftarrow$ LINE NUMBER
$\qquad$ q2 $\leftarrow$ q1 $\qquad$ r2 $\leftarrow$ r1 $\qquad$ x2 $\leftarrow$ x1 $\qquad$ w2 $\leftarrow$ w1

10. $\langle$step part$\rangle_{p2} \rightarrow$ STEP $\langle$expression$\rangle_{p1}$
$\qquad$ p2 $\leftarrow$ p1

11. $\langle$step part$\rangle_{p} \rightarrow \epsilon$
$\qquad$ p equals a pointer to a table entry for the constant 1.

REM Statement

12. $\langle$program body$\rangle \rightarrow$ COMMENT $\langle$more lines$\rangle$

Line Number

13. $\langle$more lines$\rangle \rightarrow$ LINE$_{p1}$ {LINEN$_{p2}$} {SET LINE NUMBER}$_{p3}$
$\qquad\qquad$ $\langle$program body$\rangle$

$\qquad$ (p3, p2) $\leftarrow$ p1

Expressions

14. $\langle$expression$\rangle_{t2} \rightarrow \langle$term$\rangle_{p1}$ $\langle$E-list$\rangle_{p2,t1}$
$\qquad$ p2 $\leftarrow$ p1 $\qquad$ t2 $\leftarrow$ t1

15. $\langle$expression$\rangle_{t2} \rightarrow$ + $\langle$term$\rangle_{q1}$ {PLUS$_{q2,r1}$} $\langle$E-list$\rangle_{r2,t1}$
$\qquad$ q2 $\leftarrow$ q1 $\qquad$ t2 $\leftarrow$ t1
$\qquad$ (r2, r1) $\leftarrow$ NEWTR

16. $\langle$expression$\rangle_{t2} \rightarrow$ − $\langle$term$\rangle_{q1}$ {NEG$_{q2,r1}$} $\langle$E-list$\rangle_{r2,t1}$
$\qquad$ q2 $\leftarrow$ q1 $\qquad$ t2 $\leftarrow$ t1
$\qquad$ (r2, r1) $\leftarrow$ NEWTR

17. $\langle$E-list$\rangle_{p1,t2} \rightarrow$ + $\langle$term$\rangle_{q1}$ {ADD$_{p2,q2,r1}$} $\langle$E-list$\rangle_{r2,t1}$
$\qquad$ p2 $\leftarrow$ p1 $\qquad$ q2 $\leftarrow$ q1 $\qquad$ t2 $\leftarrow$ t1
$\qquad$ (r2, r1) $\leftarrow$ NEWTR

18. $\langle$E-list$\rangle_{p1,t2} \rightarrow$ − $\langle$term$\rangle_{q1}$ {SUBT$_{p2,q2,r1}$} $\langle$E-list$\rangle_{r2,t1}$
$\qquad$ p2 $\leftarrow$ p1 $\qquad$ q2 $\leftarrow$ q1 $\qquad$ t2 $\leftarrow$ t1
$\qquad$ (r2, r1) $\leftarrow$ NEWTR

19. $\langle$E-list$\rangle_{q1,q2} \rightarrow \epsilon$
$\qquad$ q2 $\leftarrow$ q1

Figure 10.4 (continued)

20. $\langle \text{term} \rangle_{t2} \rightarrow \langle \text{factor} \rangle_{p1} \langle T\text{-list} \rangle_{p2,t1}$
    $p2 \leftarrow p1 \qquad t2 \leftarrow t1$

21. $\langle T\text{-list} \rangle_{p1,t2} \rightarrow * \langle \text{factor} \rangle_{q1} \{ \text{MULT}_{p2,q2,r1} \} \langle T\text{-list} \rangle_{r2,t1}$
    $p2 \leftarrow p1 \qquad q2 \leftarrow q1 \qquad t2 \leftarrow t1$
    $(r2, r1) \leftarrow \text{NEWTR}$

22. $\langle T\text{-list} \rangle_{p1,t2} \rightarrow / \langle \text{factor} \rangle_{q1} \{ \text{DIV}_{p2,q2,r1} \} \langle T\text{-list} \rangle_{r2,t1}$
    $p2 \leftarrow p1 \qquad q2 \leftarrow q1 \qquad t2 \leftarrow t1$
    $(r2, r1) \leftarrow \text{NEWTR}$

23. $\langle T\text{-list} \rangle_{q1,q2} \rightarrow \epsilon$
    $q2 \leftarrow q1$

24. $\langle \text{factor} \rangle_{t2} \rightarrow \langle \text{primary} \rangle_{p1} \langle F\text{-list} \rangle_{p2,t1}$
    $p2 \leftarrow p1 \qquad t2 \leftarrow t1$

25. $\langle F\text{-list} \rangle_{p1,t2} \rightarrow \uparrow \langle \text{primary} \rangle_{q1} \{ \text{EXP}_{p2,q2,r1} \} \langle F\text{-list} \rangle_{r2,t1}$
    $p2 \leftarrow p1 \qquad q2 \leftarrow q1 \qquad t2 \leftarrow t1$
    $(r2, r1) \leftarrow \text{NEWTR}$

26. $\langle F\text{-list} \rangle_{q1,q2} \rightarrow \epsilon$
    $q2 \leftarrow q1$

27. $\langle \text{primary} \rangle_{p2} \rightarrow (\langle \text{expression} \rangle_{p1})$
    $p2 \leftarrow p1$

28. $\langle \text{primary} \rangle_{p2} \rightarrow \text{OPERAND}_{p1}$
    $p2 \leftarrow p1$

Figure 10.4 (continued)

10.4 THE SYNTAX BOX

The remainder of the design can be carried out using either the pushdown machine design technique or the method of recursive descent, both of which are discussed in Chapter 9. In this example we illustrate the pushdown machine techniques.

Figure 10.5 shows the transition table. The numbered entries correspond to transitions in which a production is applied. The Roman-lettered entries correspond to nonerror transitions for which the top stack symbol is the bottommarker or a terminal symbol of the translation grammar. The Greek-lettered entries correspond to errors. All entries that could optionally either apply a production or be error entries have been made error entries.

Figure 10.6 shows "before" and "after" stack pictures for all the productions whose transitions use the REPLACE operation. Figure 10.7 shows

	LINE	OPERAND	REL OPERATOR	NEXT	ASSIGN	FOR	GOTO	GOSUB	LEFT PAREN	RIGHT PAREN	IF	RETURN	END	TO	STEP	COMMENT	+	−	*	/	↓	ERROR	ENDMARKER
< program >	1	α	α	α	α	α	α	α	α	α	α	α	α	α	α	α	α	α	α	α	α	σ	τ1
< program body >	3	β	β	2	4	9	5	7	β	β	6	8	2	β	β	12	β	β	β	β	β	σ	τ2
< step part >	11	γ1	γ1	γ1	γ1	γ1	γ1	γ1	γ1	γ2	γ1	γ1	γ1	γ1	10	γ1	γ1	γ1	γ1	γ1	γ1	σ	τ2
< more lines >	13	14	δ	δ	δ	δ	δ	δ	14	δ	δ	δ	δ	δ	δ	δ	δ	δ	δ	δ	δ	σ	τ2
< expression >	ξ2	20	ξ1	ξ4	ξ4	ξ4	ξ1	ξ4	20	ξ3	ξ4	ξ4	ξ4	ξ1	ξ1	ξ4	15	16	ξ5	ξ5	ξ5	σ	τ3
< term >	ξ2	24	ξ1	ξ4	ξ4	ξ4	ξ1	ξ4	24	ξ3	ξ4	ξ4	ξ4	ξ1	ξ1	ξ4	ξ6	ξ6	ξ6	ξ6	ξ6	σ	τ3
< factor >	ξ2	28	ξ1	ξ4	ξ4	ξ4	ξ1	ξ4	27	ξ3	ξ4	ξ4	ξ4	ξ1	ξ1	ξ4	ξ6	ξ6	ξ6	ξ6	ξ6	σ	τ3
< primary >	ξ2	ξ7	ξ1	ξ4	ξ4	ξ4	ξ1	ξ4	ξ7	ξ3	ξ4	ξ4	ξ4	ξ1	ξ1	ξ4	ξ6	ξ6	ξ6	ξ6	ξ6	σ	τ3
< E-list >	19	ξ7	19	3	3	3	19	3	ξ7	19	3	3	3	19	19	3	17	18	3	3	3	3	3
< T-list >	23	ξ7	23	3	3	3	23	3	ξ7	23	3	3	3	23	23	3	23	23	21	22	3	3	3
< F-list >	26	ξ7	26	ξ4	ξ4	ξ4	26	ξ4	ξ7	26	ξ4	3	ξ4	26	26	ξ4	26	26	26	26	25	σ	τ2
REL OPERATOR	θ2	θ1	b	θ1	θ1	θ1	θ1	θ1	θ1	θ3	θ1	θ1	θ1	θ1	θ1	θ1	θ1	θ1	θ1	θ1	θ1	3	τ3
NEXT	3	3	3	b	3	3	b	3	3	3	3	3	λ	3	3	3	3	3	3	3	3	σ	3
GOTO	μ2	μ1	μ3	μ1	μ1	μ1	μ1	μ1	μ1	μ4	μ1	μ1	μ1	μ1	μ1	μ1	μ1	μ1	μ1	μ1	μ1	σ	τ3
RIGHT PAREN	ν2	ν1	ν1	ν1	ν1	ν1	ν1	ν1	ν1	a	ν1	ν1	ν1	ν1	ν1	ν1	ν1	ν1	ν1	ν1	ν1	3	τ3
END	3	3	3	3	3	3	3	3	3	3	3	3	a	3	3	3	3	3	3	3	3	σ	3
TO	π2	π1	π1	π1	π1	π1	π1	π1	π1	π3	π1	π1	π1	a	π4	π1	π1	π1	π1	π1	π1	σ	τ3
▷	ρ	ρ	ρ	ρ	ρ	ρ	ρ	ρ	ρ	ρ	ρ	ρ	ρ	ρ	ρ	ρ	ρ	ρ	ρ	ρ	ρ		c

Action symbols:

{ASSIGN}	d
{CONDJUMP}	e
{SAVE}	f
{LABEL}	g
{TEST}	h
{CHECK}	i
{INCR}	j
{JUMP}	k
{ADD}	ℓ
{SUBT}	m
{MULT}	n
{DIV}	o
{EXP}	p
{PLUS}	q
{NEG}	r

Figure 10.5

the transition routines referred to by the transition table. The machine uses the usual operations of REPLACE, POP, ADVANCE, and RETAIN.

The routine PRODUCEATOM interfaces with the code generator, producing its parameter as an atom. As far as the syntax box design is concerned, PRODUCEATOM could either write the atom in an intermediate file or could tell the code generator that the next atom is ready. Since we plan to compile MINI-BASIC in a single pass, the latter interpretation is the one that applies in this case.

The routine ERROR, described in Fig. 10.7, is called when an error is detected. The routine has a string as a parameter, and this string is printed out as an error message for the benefit of the MINI-BASIC programmer. As an example, transition routine α is:

ERROR("PROGRAM BEGINS INCORRECTLY")

The routine ERROR produces this message and adds a line number obtained from the variable LINE NUMBER. Thus if the error occurred in line 10, the message to the user might look like:

10: PROGRAM BEGINS INCORRECTLY

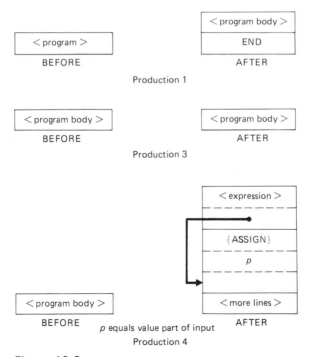

Figure 10.6

We assume the capability of inserting particular pieces of information into the error messages. For instance we frequently want to incorporate into a message a description of an offending input symbol, as illustrated by transition routine δ:

ERROR("UNEXPECTED $(input) AFTER STATEMENT COMPLETE")

When the message is printed, $(input) is replaced by a description of the input token. If the token is RELATIONAL OPERATOR, then $(input) is replaced by the particular operator involved, (e.g., =). If the token is OPERAND, then $(input) is replaced either by the word "CONSTANT" or by the name of the particular variable involved. For the other tokens, $(input) is replaced by the name of the token or some corresponding reserved word.

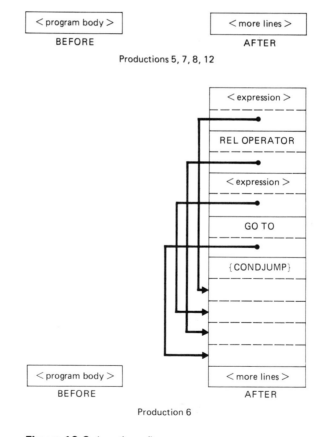

Productions 5, 7, 8, 12

Production 6

Figure 10.6 (continued)

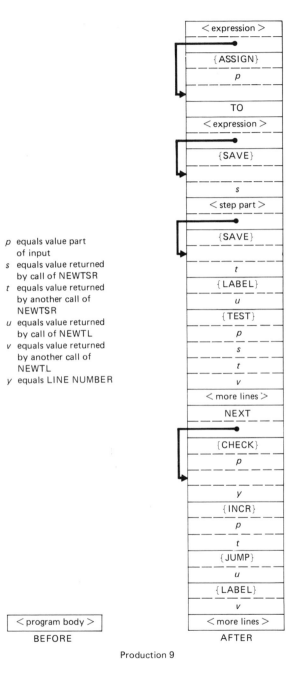

p equals value part
   of input
s equals value returned
   by call of NEWTSR
t equals value returned
   by another call of
   NEWTSR
u equals value returned
   by call of NEWTL
v equals value returned
   by another call of
   NEWTL
y equals LINE NUMBER

Production 9

Figure 10.6 (continued)

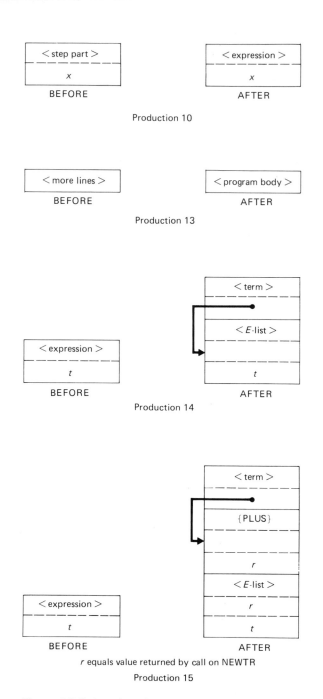

BEFORE

AFTER

Production 10

BEFORE

AFTER

Production 13

BEFORE

AFTER

Production 14

BEFORE

AFTER

r equals value returned by call on NEWTR

Production 15

Figure 10.6 (continued)

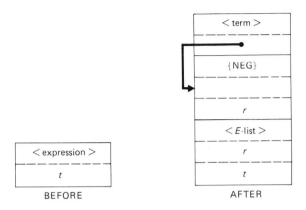

BEFORE   AFTER

r equals value returned by call on NEWTR

Production 16

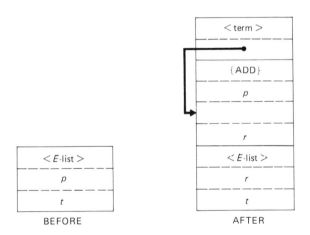

BEFORE   AFTER

r equals value returned by call on NEWTR

Production 17

Figure 10.6 (continued)

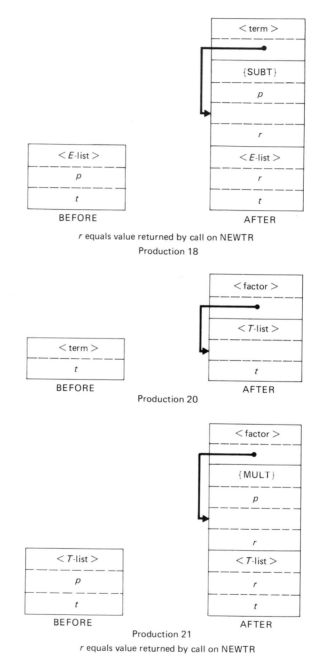

r equals value returned by call on NEWTR

Production 18

Production 20

Production 21

r equals value returned by call on NEWTR

Figure 10.6 (continued)

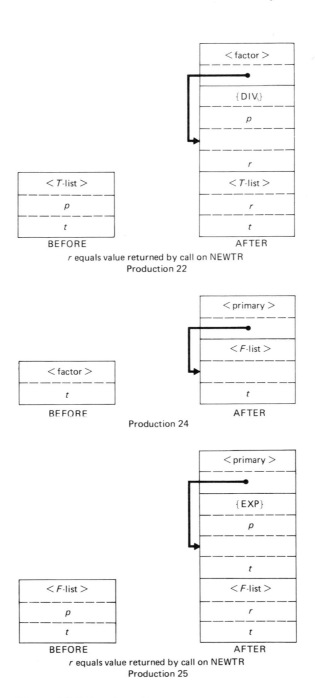

r equals value returned by call on NEWTR
Production 22

Production 24

r equals value returned by call on NEWTR
Production 25

Figure 10.6 (continued)

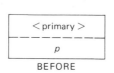 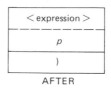

Production 27

Figure 10.6 (continued)

1: REPLACE as in Fig. 10.6 for Production 1.
PRODUCEATOM(LINEN$_p$) where p equals value part of input.
LINE NUMBER ← value part of input.
ADVANCE.

2: POP.
RETAIN.

3: REPLACE as in Fig. 10.6 for Production 3.
PRODUCEATOM(LINEN$_p$) where p equals value part of input.
LINE NUMBER ← value part of input.
ADVANCE.

4: REPLACE as in Fig. 10.6 for Production 4.
ADVANCE.

5: REPLACE as in Fig. 10.6 for Production 5.
PRODUCEATOM(JUMP$_p$) where p equals value part of input.
ADVANCE.

6: REPLACE as in Fig. 10.6 for Production 6.
ADVANCE.

7: REPLACE as in Fig. 10.6 for Production 7.
PRODUCEATOM(JUMPSAVE$_p$) where p equals value part of input.
ADVANCE.

8: REPLACE as in Fig. 10.6 for Production 8.
PRODUCEATOM(RETURNJUMP).
ADVANCE.

Figure 10.7

 9: REPLACE as in Fig. 10.6 for Production 9.
ADVANCE.

10: REPLACE as in Fig. 10.6 for Production 10.
ADVANCE.

11: Place a pointer to a table entry for the constant 1 into the field pointed to by the
field of top stack symbol ⟨step part⟩.
POP.
RETAIN.

12: REPLACE as in Fig. 10.6 for Production 12.
ADVANCE.

13: REPLACE as in Fig. 10.6 for Production 13.
PRODUCEATOM(LINEN$_p$) where p equals value part of input.
LINE NUMBER ← value part of input.
ADVANCE.

14: REPLACE as in Fig. 10.6 for Production 14.
RETAIN.

15: REPLACE as in Fig. 10.6 for Production 15.
ADVANCE.

16: REPLACE as in Fig. 10.6 for Production 16.
ADVANCE.

17: REPLACE as in Fig. 10.6 for Production 17.
ADVANCE.

18: REPLACE as in Fig. 10.6 for Production 18.
ADVANCE.

19: Put contents of first field of top stack symbol ⟨E-list⟩ into location pointed to by
second field.
POP.
RETAIN.

20: REPLACE as in Fig. 10.6 for Production 20.
RETAIN.

21: REPLACE as in Fig. 10.6 for Production 21.
ADVANCE.

Figure 10.7 (continued)

22: REPLACE as in Fig. 10.6 for Production 22.

ADVANCE.

23: Put contents of first field of top stack symbol $\langle T$-list$\rangle$ into location pointed to by second field.

POP.

RETAIN.

24: REPLACE as in Fig. 10.6 for Production 24.

RETAIN.

25: REPLACE as in Fig. 10.6 for Production 25.

ADVANCE.

26: Put contents of first field of top stack symbol $\langle F$-list$\rangle$ into location pointed to by second field.

POP.

RETAIN.

27: REPLACE as in Fig. 10.6 for Production 27.

ADVANCE.

28: Put value part of input symbol into location pointed to by field of top stack symbol $\langle$primary$\rangle$.

POP.

ADVANCE.

 a: POP.

ADVANCE.

 b: Place value part of input in location pointed to by field of top stack symbol.

POP.

ADVANCE.

 c: PRODUCEATOM(FINIS).

 d: PRODUCEATOM(ASSIGN$_{p,q}$) where p and q are contents of first two stack fields.

POP.

RETAIN.

 e: PRODUCEATOM(CONDJUMP$_{p,q,r,s}$) where p, q, r, and s are contents of first four stack fields.

POP.

RETAIN.

Figure 10.7 (continued)

f: PRODUCEATOM(SAVE$_{p,q}$) where p and q are contents of first two stack fields.

POP.

RETAIN.

g: PRODUCEATOM(LABEL$_p$) where p is contents of first stack field.

POP.

RETAIN.

h: PRODUCEATOM(TEST$_{p,q,r,s}$) where p, q, r, and s are contents of first four stack fields.

POP.

RETAIN.

i: IF contents of first field of stack symbol $\neq$ contents of second field
  THEN PRINT("NEXT VARIABLE DIFFERS FROM FOR VARIABLE ON LINE $(line number in table entry pointed to by third field) — ASSUMED FOR VARIABLE INTENDED").

POP.

RETAIN.

j: PRODUCEATOM(INCR$_{p,q}$) where p and q are contents of first two stack fields.

POP.

RETAIN.

k: PRODUCEATOM(JUMP$_p$) where p is contents of first stack field.

POP.

RETAIN.

ℓ: PRODUCEATOM(ADD$_{p,q,r}$), where p, q, and r are contents of first three stack fields.

POP.

RETAIN.

m: PRODUCEATOM(SUBT$_{p,q,r}$), where p, q, and r are contents of first three stack fields.

POP.

RETAIN.

n: PRODUCEATOM(MULT$_{p,q,r}$) where p, q, and r are contents of first three stack fields.

Figure 10.7 (continued)

POP.

RETAIN.

o: PRODUCEATOM($DIV_{p,q,r}$) where p, q, and r are contents of first three stack fields.

POP.

RETAIN.

p: PRODUCEATOM($EXP_{p,q,r}$) where p, q, and r are contents of first three stack fields.

POP.

RETAIN.

q: PRODUCEATOM($PLUS_{q,r}$) where q and r are contents of first two stack fields.

POP.

RETAIN.

r: PRODUCEATOM($NEG_{q,r}$) where q and r are contents of first two stack fields.

POP.

RETAIN.

α: ERROR("PROGRAM BEGINS INCORRECTLY")

β: ERROR("STATEMENT BEGINS INCORRECTLY")

$\gamma 1$: ERROR("UNEXPECTED $(input) NEAR END OF FOR STATEMENT")

$\gamma 2$: ERROR("EXTRA RIGHT PARENTHESIS IN EXPRESSION AFTER TO")

δ: ERROR("UNEXPECTED $(input) AFTER STATEMENT COMPLETE")

$\zeta 1$: ERROR("EXPRESSION INCOMPLETE – MISSING OPERAND")

$\zeta 2$: ERROR("STATEMENT INCOMPLETE")

$\zeta 3$: ERROR("MISSING OPERAND IN EXPRESSION")

$\zeta 4$: ERROR("UNEXPECTED $(input) FOLLOWS EXPRESSION")

$\zeta 5$: ERROR("EXPRESSION BEGINS WITH $(input)")

$\zeta 6$: ERROR("TWO OPERATORS IN A ROW IN EXPRESSION")

$\zeta 7$: ERROR("OPERATOR MISSING IN EXPRESSION")

$\theta 1$: ERROR("UNEXPECTED $(input) IN IF STATEMENT")

$\theta 2$: ERROR("IF STATEMENT INCOMPLETE")

$\theta 3$: ERROR("EXTRA RIGHT PARENTHESIS IN EXPRESSION AFTER IF")

λ: ERROR("FOR STATEMENTS INCORRECTLY NESTED – MISSING NEXT")

$\mu 1$: ERROR("UNEXPECTED $(input) IN IF STATEMENT")

Figure 10.7 (continued)

$\mu2$: ERROR("IF STATEMENT INCOMPLETE")

$\mu3$: ERROR("TWO RELATIONAL OPERATORS IN IF STATEMENT")

$\mu4$: ERROR("EXTRA RIGHT PARENTHESIS IN EXPRESSION AFTER RE-
LATIONAL OPERATOR")

$\nu1$: ERROR("MISSING RIGHT PARENTHESIS BEFORE \$(input)")

$\nu2$: ERROR("MISSING RIGHT PARENTHESIS AT END OF LINE")

ξ: ERROR("FOR STATEMENTS INCORRECTLY NESTED – EXTRA
NEXT")

$\pi1$: ERROR("UNEXPECTED \$(input) IN FOR STATEMENT")

$\pi2$: ERROR("FOR STATEMENT INCOMPLETE")

$\pi3$: ERROR("EXTRA RIGHT PARENTHESIS IN EXPRESSION AFTER $=$")

$\pi4$: ERROR("MISSING OR MISPLACED TO IN FOR STATEMENT")

ρ ERROR("PROGRAM CONTINUES AFTER END STATEMENT")

σ ERROR("")

$\tau1$: ERROR("NO PROGRAM")

$\tau2$: ERROR("MISSING END STATEMENT")

$\tau3$: ERROR("PROGRAM ENDS IN MIDDLE OF STATEMENT")

ω: ERROR("COMPILER ERROR")

Description of Routine ERROR

Print error message.

Set error flag to indicate an error has occurred.

Scan token string, including current token, until LINE or $\dashv$ is found.

If token is $\dashv$, end compilation.

Otherwise perform stack operation depending on top stack symbol

Stack Symbol	Operation
⟨program⟩	None
⟨program body⟩	None
⟨more lines⟩	None
END	PUSH(⟨program body⟩)
▽	PUSH(⟨program body⟩)
All others	POP until ⟨more lines⟩ is the top stack symbol. (Do not perform routines corresponding to action symbols).
RETAIN	

Figure 10.7 (continued)

Also in transition i for stack symbol {CHECK} we assume the ability to insert a line number in the warning message.

Note that in transition σ, ERROR is called with the null string as a parameter. In this case no error message is printed; an appropriate error message has already been produced by the lexical box.

After producing the error message, routine ERROR sets an error flag to indicate an error has occurred. All errors for which routine ERROR is called are fatal, and after the error flag is set, object code is no longer generated.

Routine ERROR also has the responsibility for error recovery. The method of error recovery used is based on the ideas of Section 8.8, using the tokens LINE and $\dashv$ as synchronizing symbols.

Entries labeled ω correspond to configurations that cannot occur, even for nonsentences. For instance, consider the entry for stack symbol $\langle T\text{-list}\rangle$ and input $\uparrow$. From productions 20, 21, and 22 we see that whenever $\langle T\text{-list}\rangle$ is pushed on the stack, $\langle \text{factor}\rangle$ is pushed above it. Production 24 is then applied to $\langle \text{factor}\rangle$, so that $\langle F\text{-list}\rangle$ becomes the stack symbol immediately above $\langle T\text{-list}\rangle$. As long as production 25 is applied to $\langle F\text{-list}\rangle$, the stack symbol immediately above $\langle T\text{-list}\rangle$ remains $\langle F\text{-list}\rangle$. The only way for $\langle T\text{-list}\rangle$ to be exposed as the top stack symbol is for an application of production 26 to pop $\langle F\text{-list}\rangle$ off the stack. Since production 26 is an ϵ-production, the current input symbol when production 26 is applied remains the current input symbol when $\langle T\text{-list}\rangle$ becomes the top stack symbol. Therefore whenever $\langle T\text{-list}\rangle$ is the top stack symbol, the current input symbol is one that causes production 26 to be applied to $\langle F\text{-list}\rangle$, i.e., the current input symbol is in the selection set of production 26. Since input symbol $\uparrow$ is not in this selection set, $\uparrow$ is never the current input when $\langle T\text{-list}\rangle$ is the top stack symbol. Furthermore, the error-recovery procedure never results in a situation in which $\langle T\text{-list}\rangle$ is the top stack symbol and $\uparrow$ the current input. Therefore, the table entry for $\langle T\text{-list}\rangle$ and $\uparrow$ should never be accessed, even for nonsentences. However, we fill this entry in with ω so that, in case this entry is somehow accessed, the message

COMPILER ERROR

will be printed, indicating an error in the design or coding of the compiler itself.

Figure 10.8 shows a MINI-BASIC program that causes every nonerror transition in the syntax box. The correct atom string for this program can be obtained by a hand simulation of the syntax-box design. If this atom string is in fact produced by some implementation of the design, the designer can have a high degree of confidence that the programming was done correctly.

```
10 REM DEBUGGING PROGRAM FOR SYNTAX BOX
20
30 LET X = 10 * 5
40 GOSUB 60
50 GOTO 70
60 RETURN
70 IF X = 0 GOTO 80
80 FOR X = 0 TO 10
90 FOR Y = X TO 20 STEP 2
100 NEXT Y
110 NEXT X
120 LET A = X ↑ 2 ↑ 3 * Y * 5 + Y * ( − Z ↑ 2 + 3)
130 LET B = A ↑ 2 / X / 7.1 − ((3 + X + A))
140 LET C = B − C − ( + Y / 2 ↑ 3 + 5 ) ↑ 2 − 4 * X ↑ 2 − 1
150 LET D = 3 * A + B ↑ (C ↑ B − 1) * X / Y + 1
160 LET E = A / B ↑ C / 2 − A ↑ 3 ↑ 4 / Y * B − 6
170 LET F = 37 ↑ (A ↑ B − C * A ↑ 4 ↑ 5 * D) + 3
180 END
```

Figure 10.8

10.5 A COMPACT MINI-BASIC EXPRESSION PROCESSOR

The top-down processors considered up to this point have the feature that each stack symbol represents a single grammatical symbol. For some grammars, it is profitable to design processors in which a single stack symbol represents several grammatical symbols, with fields of the stack symbol specifying precisely which grammatical symbol is represented by a particular occurrence of the stack symbol. In particular, symbol-compacting techniques are very useful in certain expression grammars. We now illustrate some of these techniques on a MINI-BASIC expression grammar.

As a preliminary step in our discussion, we show in Fig. 10.9 a MINI-BASIC expression grammar whose input grammar is identical with that used in the syntax box except for an added nonterminal $\langle P\text{-list}\rangle$ which generates only the null sequence. The technical reason for introducing the new grammar is that all productions with lefthand side $\langle E \rangle$, $\langle T \rangle$, $\langle F \rangle$, and $\langle P \rangle$ have righthand sides which end with a "list" nonterminal (i.e., $\langle E\text{-list}\rangle$, $\langle T\text{-list}\rangle$, $\langle F\text{-list}\rangle$, or $\langle P\text{-list}\rangle$). For reference purposes, the grammar is divided into four sections.

Section $\langle E \rangle$:

A1. $\langle E \rangle \rightarrow \langle T \rangle \langle E\text{-list} \rangle$

A2. $\langle E \rangle \rightarrow + \langle T \rangle \{\text{PLUS}\} \langle E\text{-list} \rangle$

A3. $\langle E \rangle \rightarrow - \langle T \rangle \{\text{NEG}\} \langle E\text{-list} \rangle$

A4. $\langle E\text{-list} \rangle \rightarrow + \langle T \rangle \{\text{ADD}\} \langle E\text{-list} \rangle$

A5. $\langle E\text{-list} \rangle \rightarrow - \langle T \rangle \{\text{SUBT}\} \langle E\text{-list} \rangle$

A6. $\langle E\text{-list} \rangle \rightarrow \epsilon$

Section $\langle T \rangle$:

A7. $\langle T \rangle \rightarrow \langle F \rangle \langle T\text{-list} \rangle$

A8. $\langle T\text{-list} \rangle \rightarrow * \langle F \rangle \{\text{MULT}\} \langle T\text{-list} \rangle$

A9. $\langle T\text{-list} \rangle \rightarrow / \langle F \rangle \{\text{DIV}\} \langle T\text{-list} \rangle$

A10. $\langle T\text{-list} \rangle \rightarrow \epsilon$

Section $\langle F \rangle$:

A11. $\langle F \rangle \rightarrow \langle P \rangle \langle F\text{-list} \rangle$

A12. $\langle F\text{-list} \rangle \rightarrow \uparrow \langle P \rangle \{\text{EXP}\} \langle F\text{-list} \rangle$

A13. $\langle F\text{-list} \rangle \rightarrow \epsilon$

Section $\langle P \rangle$:

A14. $\langle P \rangle \rightarrow (\langle E \rangle) \langle P\text{-list} \rangle$

A15. $\langle P \rangle \rightarrow I \langle P\text{-list} \rangle$

A16. $\langle P\text{-list} \rangle \rightarrow \epsilon$

Starting symbol: $\langle E \rangle$

Figure 10.9

Figure 10.10 shows a MINI-BASIC translation grammar whose input grammar is a q-grammar. This grammar generates the same activity sequences as the grammar of Fig. 10.9. In the new grammar, nonterminals $\langle E \rangle, \langle T \rangle, \langle F \rangle$, and $\langle P \rangle$ generate the same terminal strings as in the previous grammar. The grammar also contains ten nonterminals of the form $\langle X, Y \rangle$. Each of these nonterminals generates the same set of terminal strings as a certain string of list nonterminals from Fig. 10.9. The string of list nonterminals corresponding to each of the ten new nonterminals is shown in Fig. 10.11. Observe that for each new nonterminal of the form $\langle X, Y \rangle$, the last nonterminal in the corresponding string is $\langle X\text{-list} \rangle$ and the first is $\langle Y\text{-list} \rangle$. In addition to specifying the last list nonterminal in the string, the X in name $\langle X, Y \rangle$ identifies the section of the grammar where that symbol occurs. For instance, all occurrences of $\langle T, P \rangle$, on either the lefthand or righthand side of a production, are in Section $\langle T \rangle$ of the grammar.

Section $\langle E \rangle$:

B1. $\langle E \rangle \rightarrow (\langle E \rangle) \langle E, P \rangle$

B2. $\langle E \rangle \rightarrow I \langle E, P \rangle$

B3. $\langle E \rangle \rightarrow + \langle T \rangle \{PLUS\} \langle E, E \rangle$

B4. $\langle E \rangle \rightarrow - \langle T \rangle \{NEG\} \langle E, E \rangle$

B5. $\langle E, P \rangle \rightarrow + \langle T \rangle \{ADD\} \langle E, E \rangle$

B6. $\langle E, P \rangle \rightarrow - \langle T \rangle \{SUBT\} \langle E, E \rangle$

B7. $\langle E, P \rangle \rightarrow * \langle F \rangle \{MULT\} \langle E, T \rangle$

B8. $\langle E, P \rangle \rightarrow / \langle F \rangle \{DIV\} \langle E, T \rangle$

B9. $\langle E, P \rangle \rightarrow \uparrow \langle P \rangle \{EXP\} \langle E, F \rangle$

B10. $\langle E, P \rangle \rightarrow \epsilon$

B11. $\langle E, F \rangle \rightarrow + \langle T \rangle \{ADD\} \langle E, E \rangle$

B12. $\langle E, F \rangle \rightarrow - \langle T \rangle \{SUBT\} \langle E, E \rangle$

B13. $\langle E, F \rangle \rightarrow * \langle F \rangle \{MULT\} \langle E, T \rangle$

B14. $\langle E, F \rangle \rightarrow / \langle F \rangle \{DIV\} \langle E, T \rangle$

B15. $\langle E, F \rangle \rightarrow \uparrow \langle P \rangle \{EXP\} \langle E, F \rangle$

B16. $\langle E, F \rangle \rightarrow \epsilon$

B17. $\langle E, T \rangle \rightarrow + \langle T \rangle \{ADD\} \langle E, E \rangle$

B18. $\langle E, T \rangle \rightarrow - \langle T \rangle \{SUBT\} \langle E, E \rangle$

B19. $\langle E, T \rangle \rightarrow * \langle F \rangle \{MULT\} \langle E, T \rangle$

B20. $\langle E, T \rangle \rightarrow / \langle F \rangle \{DIV\} \langle E, T \rangle$

B21. $\langle E, T \rangle \rightarrow \epsilon$

B22. $\langle E, E \rangle \rightarrow + \langle T \rangle \{ADD\} \langle E, E \rangle$

B23. $\langle E, E \rangle \rightarrow - \langle T \rangle \{SUBT\} \langle E, E \rangle$

B24. $\langle E, E \rangle \rightarrow \epsilon$

Section $\langle T \rangle$:

B25. $\langle T \rangle \rightarrow (\langle E \rangle) \langle T, P \rangle$

B26. $\langle T \rangle \rightarrow I \langle T, P \rangle$

B27. $\langle T, P \rangle \rightarrow * \langle F \rangle \{MULT\} \langle T, T \rangle$

B28. $\langle T, P \rangle \rightarrow / \langle F \rangle \{DIV\} \langle T, T \rangle$

B29. $\langle T, P \rangle \rightarrow \uparrow \langle P \rangle \{EXP\} \langle T, F \rangle$

B30. $\langle T, P \rangle \rightarrow \epsilon$

B31. $\langle T, F \rangle \rightarrow * \langle F \rangle \{MULT\} \langle T, T \rangle$

B32. $\langle T, F \rangle \rightarrow / \langle F \rangle \{DIV\} \langle T, T \rangle$

B33. $\langle T, F \rangle \rightarrow \uparrow \langle P \rangle \{EXP\} \langle T, F \rangle$

B34. $\langle T, F \rangle \rightarrow \epsilon$

B35. $\langle T, T \rangle \rightarrow * \langle F \rangle \{MULT\} \langle T, T \rangle$

B36. $\langle T, T \rangle \rightarrow / \langle F \rangle \{DIV\} \langle T, T \rangle$

B37. $\langle T, T \rangle \rightarrow \epsilon$

Figure 10.10

Section $\langle F \rangle$:

B38. $\langle F \rangle \rightarrow (\langle E \rangle) \langle F, P \rangle$
B39. $\langle F \rangle \rightarrow I \langle F, P \rangle$
B40. $\langle F, P \rangle \rightarrow \uparrow \langle P \rangle \ \{EXP\} \ \langle F, F \rangle$
B41. $\langle F, P \rangle \rightarrow \epsilon$
B42. $\langle F, F \rangle \rightarrow \uparrow \langle P \rangle \ \{EXP\} \ \langle F, F \rangle$
B43. $\langle F, F \rangle \rightarrow \epsilon$

Section $\langle P \rangle$:

B44. $\langle P \rangle \rightarrow (\langle E \rangle) \langle P, P \rangle$
B45. $\langle P \rangle \rightarrow I \langle P, P \rangle$
B46. $\langle P, P \rangle \rightarrow \epsilon$

Starting symbol: $\langle E \rangle$

Figure 10.10 (continued)

Nonterminal	String
$\langle E, P \rangle$	$\langle P\text{-list} \rangle \ \langle F\text{-list} \rangle \ \langle T\text{-list} \rangle \ \langle E\text{-list} \rangle$
$\langle E, F \rangle$	$\langle F\text{-list} \rangle \ \langle T\text{-list} \rangle \ \langle E\text{-list} \rangle$
$\langle E, T \rangle$	$\langle T\text{-list} \rangle \ \langle E\text{-list} \rangle$
$\langle E, E \rangle$	$\langle E\text{-list} \rangle$
$\langle T, P \rangle$	$\langle P\text{-list} \rangle \ \langle F\text{-list} \rangle \ \langle T\text{-list} \rangle$
$\langle T, F \rangle$	$\langle F\text{-list} \rangle \ \langle T\text{-list} \rangle$
$\langle T, T \rangle$	$\langle T\text{-list} \rangle$
$\langle F, P \rangle$	$\langle P\text{-list} \rangle \ \langle F\text{-list} \rangle$
$\langle F, F \rangle$	$\langle F\text{-list} \rangle$
$\langle P, P \rangle$	$\langle P\text{-list} \rangle$

Figure 10.11

Section $\langle P \rangle$ of the new grammar is easy to understand. Under the naming conventions of Fig. 10.11, $\langle P, P \rangle$ is to be interpreted as $\langle P\text{-list} \rangle$, and the two section $\langle P \rangle$'s are seen to be identical.

Section $\langle F \rangle$ of the new grammar is understood by keeping in mind that

$\langle F, F \rangle$ represents $\langle F\text{-list} \rangle$

$\langle F, P \rangle$ represents $\langle P\text{-list} \rangle \ \langle F\text{-list} \rangle$

Each production is interpreted as representing several steps in a leftmost derivation using Fig. 10.9. For example, using productions A11 and A14 gives

$$\langle F \rangle \Rightarrow_L \langle P \rangle \ \langle F\text{-list} \rangle \Rightarrow_L (\langle E \rangle) \ \langle P\text{-list} \rangle \ \langle F\text{-list} \rangle$$

$\text{SELECT}(10) = \text{FOLLOW}(\langle E, P \rangle) = \{\}, \dashv\}$
$\text{SELECT}(16) = \text{FOLLOW}(\langle E, F \rangle) = \{\}, \dashv\}$
$\text{SELECT}(21) = \text{FOLLOW}(\langle E, T \rangle) = \{\}, \dashv\}$
$\text{SELECT}(24) = \text{FOLLOW}(\langle E, E \rangle) = \{\}, \dashv\}$
$\text{SELECT}(30) = \text{FOLLOW}(\langle T, P \rangle) = \{\}, \dashv, +, -\}$
$\text{SELECT}(34) = \text{FOLLOW}(\langle T, F \rangle) = \{\}, \dashv, +, -\}$
$\text{SELECT}(37) = \text{FOLLOW}(\langle T, T \rangle) = \{\}, \dashv, +, -\}$
$\text{SELECT}(41) = \text{FOLLOW}(\langle F, P \rangle) = \{\}, \dashv, +, -, *, /\}$
$\text{SELECT}(43) = \text{FOLLOW}(\langle F, F \rangle) = \{\}, \dashv, +, -, *, /\}$
$\text{SELECT}(46) = \text{FOLLOW}(\langle P, P \rangle) = \{\}, \dashv, +, -, *, /, \uparrow\}$

Figure 10.12

This two-step derivation is represented by production B38 using $\langle F, P \rangle$ to abbreviate $\langle P\text{-list} \rangle \langle F\text{-list} \rangle$. Production B39 is a similar representative of the derivation using productions A11 and A15. Production B40 is interpreted as representing the two-step derivation

$$\langle P\text{-list} \rangle \langle F\text{-list} \rangle \Rightarrow_L \langle F\text{-list} \rangle \Rightarrow_L \uparrow \langle P \rangle \{EXP\} \langle F\text{-list} \rangle$$

obtained by applying productions A16 and A12. Production B41 is interpreted as the two-step derivation

$$\langle P\text{-list} \rangle \langle F\text{-list} \rangle \Rightarrow_L \langle F\text{-list} \rangle \Rightarrow_L \epsilon$$

using productions A16 and A13. Production B42 represents the one-step derivation given by production A12. Production B43 is the one-step derivation given by production A13.

To understand section $\langle T \rangle$ keep in mind the interpretation of the new nonterminals. Production B25 is interpreted as

$$\langle T \rangle \overset{*}{\Rightarrow}_L (\langle E \rangle) \langle P\text{-list} \rangle \langle F\text{-list} \rangle \langle T\text{-list} \rangle$$

which is achieved in three steps using productions A7, A11, and A14. Production B31 is interpreted as

$$\langle F\text{-list} \rangle \langle T\text{-list} \rangle \overset{*}{\Rightarrow}_L * \langle F \rangle \{MULT\} \langle T\text{-list} \rangle$$

which is achieved using productions A13 and A8. Production B29 says

$$\langle P\text{-list} \rangle \langle F\text{-list} \rangle \langle T\text{-list} \rangle \overset{*}{\Rightarrow}_L \uparrow \langle P \rangle \{EXP\} \langle F\text{-list} \rangle \langle T\text{-list} \rangle$$

which is evident from productions A16 and A12. Production B34 says

$$\langle F\text{-list} \rangle \langle T\text{-list} \rangle \overset{*}{\Rightarrow}_L \epsilon$$

which is achieved from productions A13 and A10. Similar analysis shows valid interpretations for the other productions from section $\langle T \rangle$ and for section $\langle E \rangle$.

A routine computation of selection sets shows that the new grammar is a q-grammar. For reference, the selection sets for the ϵ-productions are presented in Fig. 10.12. The selection set of each unlisted production is, of course, the terminal symbol beginning the righthand side.

The grammar of Fig. 10.10 is more complex than the grammar of Fig. 10.9 in the sense that it has 14 nonterminals and 46 productions in contrast to

$$
a \begin{cases}
1. & \langle E_1 \rangle \to (\langle E_1 \rangle) \langle E_1, E_4 \rangle \\
25. & \langle E_2 \rangle \to (\langle E_1 \rangle) \langle E_2, E_4 \rangle \\
38. & \langle E_3 \rangle \to (\langle E_1 \rangle) \langle E_3, E_4 \rangle \\
44. & \langle E_4 \rangle \to (\langle E_1 \rangle) \langle E_4, E_4 \rangle
\end{cases}
$$

$$
b \begin{cases}
2. & \langle E_1 \rangle \to I \langle E_1, E_4 \rangle \\
26. & \langle E_2 \rangle \to I \langle E_2, E_4 \rangle \\
39. & \langle E_3 \rangle \to I \langle E_3, E_4 \rangle \\
45. & \langle E_4 \rangle \to I \langle E_4, E_4 \rangle
\end{cases}
$$

$$
c \{ \quad 3. \quad \langle E_1 \rangle \to + \langle E_2 \rangle \ \{\text{PLUS}\} \ \langle E_1, E_1 \rangle
$$

$$
d \{ \quad 4. \quad \langle E_1 \rangle \to - \langle E_2 \rangle \ \{\text{NEG}\} \ \langle E_1, E_1 \rangle
$$

$$
e \begin{cases}
22. & \langle E_1, E_1 \rangle \to + \langle E_2 \rangle \ \{\text{ADD}\} \ \langle E_1, E_1 \rangle \\
17. & \langle E_1, E_2 \rangle \to + \langle E_2 \rangle \ \{\text{ADD}\} \ \langle E_1, E_1 \rangle \\
11. & \langle E_1, E_3 \rangle \to + \langle E_2 \rangle \ \{\text{ADD}\} \ \langle E_1, E_1 \rangle \\
5. & \langle E_1, E_4 \rangle \to + \langle E_2 \rangle \ \{\text{ADD}\} \ \langle E_1, E_1 \rangle
\end{cases}
$$

$$
f \begin{cases}
23. & \langle E_1, E_1 \rangle \to - \langle E_2 \rangle \ \{\text{SUBT}\} \ \langle E_1, E_1 \rangle \\
18. & \langle E_1, E_2 \rangle \to - \langle E_2 \rangle \ \{\text{SUBT}\} \ \langle E_1, E_1 \rangle \\
12. & \langle E_1, E_3 \rangle \to - \langle E_2 \rangle \ \{\text{SUBT}\} \ \langle E_1, E_1 \rangle \\
6. & \langle E_1, E_4 \rangle \to - \langle E_2 \rangle \ \{\text{SUBT}\} \ \langle E_1, E_1 \rangle
\end{cases}
$$

$$
g \begin{cases}
19. & \langle E_1, E_2 \rangle \to * \langle E_3 \rangle \ \{\text{MULT}\} \ \langle E_1, E_2 \rangle \\
13. & \langle E_1, E_3 \rangle \to * \langle E_3 \rangle \ \{\text{MULT}\} \ \langle E_1, E_2 \rangle \\
7. & \langle E_1, E_4 \rangle \to * \langle E_3 \rangle \ \{\text{MULT}\} \ \langle E_1, E_2 \rangle \\
35. & \langle E_2, E_2 \rangle \to * \langle E_3 \rangle \ \{\text{MULT}\} \ \langle E_2, E_2 \rangle \\
31. & \langle E_2, E_3 \rangle \to * \langle E_3 \rangle \ \{\text{MULT}\} \ \langle E_2, E_2 \rangle \\
27. & \langle E_2, E_4 \rangle \to * \langle E_3 \rangle \ \{\text{MULT}\} \ \langle E_2, E_2 \rangle
\end{cases}
$$

Figure 10.13

8 nonterminals and 16 productions. However, the new grammar has the advantage that its derivation trees are much smaller.

As a further preliminary to explaining a compact processor, we now show in several steps how the grammar of Fig. 10.10 can be presented in a compact form. The first step is represented by the grammar of Fig. 10.13. It is simply Fig. 10.10 with the symbols renamed and the productions presented in a different order. Each production in Fig. 10.13 was obtained from the same numbered production of Fig. 10.10 by replacing letters E, T, F, and P by E_1, E_2, E_3, and E_4 respectively.

The productions in Fig. 10.13 are partitioned into ten groups labeled a through j. Within each group, the productions are identical except for subscripts. In Fig. 10.14, we show each group of productions represented by a single line. Each line consists of a production form and a numerical con-

$$h \begin{cases} 20.\ \langle E_1, E_2 \rangle \to / \langle E_3 \rangle \ \{\text{DIV}\} \ \langle E_1, E_2 \rangle \\ 14.\ \langle E_1, E_3 \rangle \to / \langle E_3 \rangle \ \{\text{DIV}\} \ \langle E_1, E_2 \rangle \\ 8.\ \langle E_1, E_4 \rangle \to / \langle E_3 \rangle \ \{\text{DIV}\} \ \langle E_1, E_2 \rangle \\ 36.\ \langle E_2, E_2 \rangle \to / \langle E_3 \rangle \ \{\text{DIV}\} \ \langle E_2, E_2 \rangle \\ 32.\ \langle E_2, E_3 \rangle \to / \langle E_3 \rangle \ \{\text{DIV}\} \ \langle E_2, E_2 \rangle \\ 28.\ \langle E_2, E_4 \rangle \to / \langle E_3 \rangle \ \{\text{DIV}\} \ \langle E_2, E_2 \rangle \end{cases}$$

$$i \begin{cases} 15.\ \langle E_1, E_3 \rangle \to \uparrow \langle E_4 \rangle \ \{\text{EXP}\} \ \langle E_1, E_3 \rangle \\ 9.\ \langle E_1, E_4 \rangle \to \uparrow \langle E_4 \rangle \ \{\text{EXP}\} \ \langle E_1, E_3 \rangle \\ 33.\ \langle E_2, E_3 \rangle \to \uparrow \langle E_4 \rangle \ \{\text{EXP}\} \ \langle E_2, E_3 \rangle \\ 29.\ \langle E_2, E_4 \rangle \to \uparrow \langle E_4 \rangle \ \{\text{EXP}\} \ \langle E_2, E_3 \rangle \\ 42.\ \langle E_3, E_3 \rangle \to \uparrow \langle E_4 \rangle \ \{\text{EXP}\} \ \langle E_3, E_3 \rangle \\ 40.\ \langle E_3, E_4 \rangle \to \uparrow \langle E_4 \rangle \ \{\text{EXP}\} \ \langle E_3, E_3 \rangle \end{cases}$$

$$j \begin{cases} 24.\ \langle E_1, E_1 \rangle \to \epsilon \\ 21.\ \langle E_1, E_2 \rangle \to \epsilon \\ 16.\ \langle E_1, E_3 \rangle \to \epsilon \\ 10.\ \langle E_1, E_4 \rangle \to \epsilon \\ 37.\ \langle E_2, E_2 \rangle \to \epsilon \\ 34.\ \langle E_2, E_3 \rangle \to \epsilon \\ 30.\ \langle E_2, E_4 \rangle \to \epsilon \\ 43.\ \langle E_3, E_3 \rangle \to \epsilon \\ 41.\ \langle E_3, E_4 \rangle \to \epsilon \\ 46.\ \langle E_4, E_4 \rangle \to \epsilon \end{cases}$$

Starting symbol: $\langle E_1 \rangle$

Figure 10.13 (continued)

straint on subscript i or on subscripts i and j. Each line means that a production of the grammar can be obtained by replacing i and j in the form by any values satisfying the numerical constraints. Thus, for example, line a represents four productions, one for each i satisfying $1 \leq i \leq 4$, and line g represents six productions.

The grammar can be compacted further than in Fig. 10.14 if we represent inputs and action symbols by subscripted symbols. To do this, replace operators $+$, $-$, $*$, $/$, and $\uparrow$ by OP_+, OP_-, OP_*, $OP_/$, and $OP_\uparrow$; replace action symbols {ADD}, {SUBT}, {MULT}, {DIV} and {EXP} by {$BINARY_+$}, {$BINARY_-$}, {$BINARY_*$}, {$BINARY_/$}, and {$BINARY_\uparrow$}; and replace {PLUS} and {NEG} by {$UNARY_+$} and {$UNARY_-$}. When this is done, each group of forms labeled I through V in Fig. 10.14 combines into a single form shown in Fig. 10.15.

The forms in Fig. 10.15 each have some of the variables i, j, and x as parameters. The most complex is form IV which has all three parameters. To see if there is a form IV production for particular values of i, j, and x, it is necessary to look up the value $m(x)$ from the table in the figure and check the relations $1 \leq i \leq m(x) \leq j \leq 4$. If the relations are satisfied, a production of the grammar is obtained by substituting i, j, x, and $m(x)$ into the form. If, for example, $i = 2$, $j = 3$, and $x = *$; the table indicates that $m(*) = 2$, the relations $1 \leq 2 \leq 2 \leq 3 \leq 4$ hold, and the result of substituting into the form gives

$$\langle E_2, E_3 \rangle \rightarrow OP_* \langle E_3 \rangle \{BINARY_*\} \langle E_2, E_2 \rangle$$

which is production 31 from either Fig. 10.13 or Fig. 10.10 under the new naming conventions.

Figures 10.16 and 10.17 show a processor based on the grammatical forms of Fig. 10.15. Stack symbols $\langle E \rangle$ and $\langle E, E \rangle$ each represent a set of nonterminals. $\langle E \rangle$ represents the $\langle E_i \rangle$ and $\langle E, E \rangle$ represents the $\langle E_i, E_j \rangle$ stack symbols. $\langle E \rangle$ and $\langle E, E \rangle$ have one and two fields respectively where values of i and of i and j are stored. The values of these fields indicate which $\langle E_i \rangle$ or $\langle E_i, E_j \rangle$ is actually represented by a particular occurrence of the stack symbol. Stack symbols {UNARY} and {BINARY} have one field to store the name of the operator.

The pushdown recognizer of Fig. 10.16 is designed to imitate a pushdown recognizer based on the grammar of Fig. 10.13. When the input symbol is in the selection set of a production for the nonterminal represented by the top stack symbol, that production is applied. The application of the production involves replacing the top stack symbol with stack symbols representing the appropriate symbols on the righthand side of the selected production.

$$\text{I} \begin{cases} \text{a. } \langle E_i \rangle \rightarrow (\langle E_1 \rangle) \langle E_i, E_4 \rangle & 1 \leq i \leq 4 \end{cases}$$

$$\text{II} \begin{cases} \text{b. } \langle E_i \rangle \rightarrow I \langle E_i, E_4 \rangle & 1 \leq i \leq 4 \end{cases}$$

$$\text{III} \begin{cases} \text{c. } \langle E_i \rangle \rightarrow + \langle E_2 \rangle \{\text{PLUS}\} \langle E_i, E_1 \rangle & i = 1 \\ \text{d. } \langle E_i \rangle \rightarrow - \langle E_2 \rangle \{\text{NEG}\} \langle E_i, E_1 \rangle & i = 1 \end{cases}$$

$$\text{IV} \begin{cases} \text{e. } \langle E_i, E_j \rangle \rightarrow + \langle E_2 \rangle \{\text{ADD}\} \langle E_i, E_1 \rangle & 1 \leq i \leq 1 \quad 1 \leq j \leq 4 \\ \text{f. } \langle E_i, E_j \rangle \rightarrow - \langle E_2 \rangle \{\text{SUBT}\} \langle E_i, E_1 \rangle & 1 \leq i \leq 1 \quad 1 \leq j \leq 4 \\ \text{g. } \langle E_i, E_j \rangle \rightarrow * \langle E_3 \rangle \{\text{MULT}\} \langle E_i, E_2 \rangle & 1 \leq i \leq 2 \quad 2 \leq j \leq 4 \\ \text{h. } \langle E_i, E_j \rangle \rightarrow / \langle E_3 \rangle \{\text{DIV}\} \langle E_i, E_2 \rangle & 1 \leq i \leq 2 \quad 2 \leq j \leq 4 \\ \text{i. } \langle E_i, E_j \rangle \rightarrow \uparrow \langle E_4 \rangle \{\text{EXP}\} \langle E_i, E_3 \rangle & 1 \leq i \leq 3 \quad 3 \leq j \leq 4 \end{cases}$$

$$\text{V} \begin{cases} \text{j. } \langle E_i, E_j \rangle \rightarrow \epsilon & 1 \leq i \leq j \leq 4 \end{cases}$$

Starting symbol: $\langle E_1 \rangle$

Figure 10.14

$$\text{I. } \langle E_i \rangle \rightarrow (\langle E_1 \rangle) \langle E_i, E_4 \rangle \qquad 1 \leq i \leq 4$$

$$\text{II. } \langle E_i \rangle \rightarrow I \langle E_i, E_4 \rangle \qquad 1 \leq i \leq 4$$

$$\text{III. } \langle E_i \rangle \rightarrow \text{OP}_x \langle E_2 \rangle \{\text{UNARY}_x\} \langle E_i, E_1 \rangle \qquad i = 1$$
$$x = + \text{ or } -$$

$$\text{IV. } \langle E_i, E_j \rangle \rightarrow \text{OP}_x \langle E_{m(x)+1} \rangle \{\text{BINARY}_x\} \langle E_i, E_{m(x)} \rangle$$
$$1 \leq i \leq m(x) \leq j \leq 4$$
$$x = +, -, *, /, \text{ or } \uparrow$$

x	$m(x)$
+	1
−	1
*	2
/	2
↑	3

$$\text{V. } \langle E_i, E_j \rangle \rightarrow \epsilon \qquad 1 \leq i \leq j \leq 4$$

Starting symbol: $\langle E_1 \rangle$

Figure 10.15

	OP_x		(	)	⊣
$<E>$ / i	#III	#II	#I	REJECT	REJECT
$<E,E>$ / i / j	#IV	REJECT	REJECT	#V	#V
)	REJECT	REJECT	REJECT	POP ADVANCE	REJECT
∇	REJECT	REJECT	REJECT	REJECT	ACCEPT
{UNARY} / y	OUT(UNARY$_y$) POP, RETAIN				
{BINARY} / y	OUT(BINARY$_y$) POP, RETAIN				

Starting stack:

$<E>$
1
∇

#I REPLACE as in Fig. 10.17(a), ADVANCE
#II REPLACE as in Fig. 10.17(b), ADVANCE
#III If $i = 1$ and ($x = +$ or $x = -$)
      then REPLACE as in Fig. 10.17(c), ADVANCE
      else REJECT
#IV Using value of m specified by following table

x	m
+	1
−	1
*	2
/	2
↑	3

    if $i \leq m$ and $m \leq j$
      then REPLACE as in Fig. 10.17(d), ADVANCE
      else do #V
#V POP, RETAIN

Figure 10.16

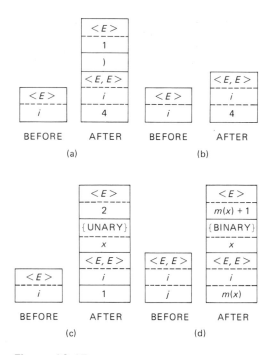

Figure 10.17

First consider transition #I for top stack symbol $\langle E \rangle$ and current input (. Each of the four nonterminals that might be represented by the top stack symbol has a form I production, and a pushdown recognizer based on Fig. 10.13 would apply the appropriate form I production to each of these four nonterminals. As shown in Fig. 10.17, the compacted processor fills in the fields of the new stack symbols so that they represent the symbols on the righthand side of the appropriate production.

Next consider transition #III for top stack symbol $\langle E \rangle$ and current input OP with value part x. For nonterminals of the form $\langle E_i \rangle$, the only productions whose selection sets include a terminal symbol of the form OP_x are the form III productions. However, the grammar only contains a form III production if $i = 1$ and $x = +$ or $-$. A machine based on Fig. 10.13 would apply a form III production only if the nonterminal represented by the top stack symbol has a form III production beginning with the terminal represented by the input symbol; otherwise it would reject. Therefore transition routine #III first checks to see if there is a form III production for the particular $\langle E \rangle$ and OP on hand. If there is, the field of $\langle E \rangle$ and value of OP are used to carry out a properly initialized replace operation. If there is no form III production, the transition rejects.

Now consider the case when the top of the stack is $\langle E, E \rangle$ and the current input is right parenthesis. None of the forms have a righthand side beginning with right parenthesis, so the only productions that might be applicable are the ϵ-productions given by form V. Right parenthesis is in the selection set of all the form V productions (Fig. 10.12), so if the represented nonterminal has a form V production, it should be applied. The constraint associated with form V, $1 \leq i \leq j \leq 4$ is satisfied by the i and j of all $\langle E_i, E_j \rangle$ in the grammar, so the represented nonterminal has a form V production and the machine need not check the constraint. Therefore, transition routine #V simply does POP, RETAIN.

In the case of top stack symbol $\langle E, E \rangle$ and current input I or left parenthesis, these inputs are not in the selection sets of any of the form V ϵ-productions, nor are they the first symbol of any other form. Therefore, the machine can optionally either reject or apply a form V production. The machine in Fig. 10.16 is designed to reject.

The most complex transition routine is #IV which occurs when $\langle E, E \rangle$ is on top of the stack and the current input is OP. In this case, there are two forms that might be applicable, form IV or form V. Form IV must be considered because its righthand side begins with OP, and form V must be considered because, for some values of i, j, and x, OP_x is in the follow set of $\langle E_i, E_j \rangle$ (e.g., $i = 3, j = 4, x = *$). The transition routine #IV begins by testing the fields of the top stack symbol and input symbol value to see if there is a form IV production for the particular $\langle E_i, E_j \rangle$ and OP_x under consideration. If there is, the top stack symbol is replaced by $\langle E, E \rangle$ {BINARY} $\langle E \rangle$ initialized with field values to match the righthand side of the particular form IV production for $\langle E_i, E_j \rangle$ that beings with OP_x. If there is no form IV production for the particular $\langle E_i, E_j \rangle$ and OP_x, the transition routine applies the form V ϵ-production. In some cases (e.g., $i = 3, j = 4$, $x = *$) OP_x is in the selection set of the form V production. In other cases (e.g., $i = 1, j = 2, x = \uparrow$), OP_x is not in the selection set of either the form IV or the form V production for $\langle E_i, E_j \rangle$ and the machine could optionally reject instead of applying the form V production.

The grammar of Fig. 10.14 or the forms of Fig. 10.15 can be made into an attributed grammar and the design of Figs. 10.16 and 10.17 converted into a compact translator for the attributed expression translation of Fig. 10.4.

PROBLEMS

1. Consider the MINI-BASIC program:

```
10 FOR X = 1 TO 100
20 LET Y = Y + X
30 NEXT X
40 END
```

a) Find the derivation tree for this program according to the grammar of Section 6.15.

b) Find the tree according to the grammar of Fig. 10.1.

c) Using the attributed grammar of Fig. 10.4, find the atom string and table output for this program.

d) Draw the stack movie as the pushdown processor of Fig. 10.5 processes this program.

2. Find the atom string output of the MINI-BASIC syntax box of Section 10.4 for the debugging program of Fig. 10.8.

3. a) Using the method of recursive descent, design a MINI-BASIC syntax box based on the attributed grammar of Fig. 10.4.

b) Write a program implementing this design in your favorite high-level language.

c) Debug your program using the MINI-BASIC program of Fig. 10.8; check to see that the output is correct for this program.

4. In the MINI-BASIC syntax box design of Section 10.4 explain why the error message for the entry labeled ξ in the transition table of Fig. 10.5 is appropriate.

5. Show why each of the entries marked ω in Fig. 10.5 cannot be reached even for nonsentences.

6. List the error messages that would be produced by the MINI-BASIC syntax box design of Section 10.4 for the following input sequence.

```
10 END
20 FOR A = 1 STEP 1 TO 2
30 FOR B = 2
40 LET Y = (B + (C * D)
50 NEXT A
60 IF A > B > C LET X = 6
70 GOSUB 65
80 GO TO 80
80 IF A = B GOSUB 80
```

7. Design a more sophisticated error-recovery procedure than that used in Section 10.4.

8. Find an incorrect MINI-BASIC program for which the error messages produced by the syntax-box design of Section 10.4 are misleading.

9. a) Assuming the MINI-BASIC lexical box of Chapter 4 is working correctly, which error entries in the transition table of Fig. 10.5 can never be reached?

b) Find a small set of MINI-BASIC programs that exercises all the reachable error transitions.

c) Based on the results of Part a), design an improved set of error messages.

10. a) Using your favorite language, implement the MINI-BASIC syntax box design of Section 10.4.

    b) Debug your program using the program of Fig. 10.8, and check to see that the output is correct for this program.

11. Show that the MINI-BASIC grammar given in Fig. 10.1 is an LL(1) grammar.

12. Consider the following productions for the FOR statement which replace productions 9, 10, and 11 in the MINI-BASIC grammar of Fig. 10.1.

    9′ ⟨program body⟩ → FOR ⟨expression⟩ TO ⟨expression⟩ ⟨step remainder⟩

    10′ ⟨step remainder⟩ → STEP ⟨expression⟩ ⟨more lines⟩ NEXT ⟨more lines⟩

    11′ ⟨step remainder⟩ → ⟨more lines⟩ NEXT ⟨more lines⟩

    a) Add atoms and attributes to these productions so that they define the same attributed translation as productions 9, 10, and 11 in Fig. 10.4.

    b) Discuss the advantages and disadvantages of using 9′, 10′, and 11′ instead of 9, 10, and 11.

13. a) Rewrite production 9 in Fig. 10.4 so that FOR/NEXT constructions generate atoms suitable for generating code to implement the run-time flow chart in Fig. 10.18 (instead of Fig. 10.3a).

    b) Draw the "before" and "after" stack pictures for the new productions.

    c) Discuss the relative merits of the two run-time flow charts.

14. Suppose that in adding attributes to production 9 in Fig. 10.4, the attributes of {SAVE} were defined as:

$$\{SAVE_{a,b}\} \quad\quad \text{INHERITED } a \quad\quad \text{SYNTHESIZED } b$$
$$b \leftarrow \text{NEWT}$$

Specify each of the following parts of the design:

    a) Production 9 of Fig. 10.4;

    b) the "before" and "after" stack pictures corresponding to Production 9;

    c) the transition routine for Production 9;

    d) routine f, which is called when {SAVE} is the top stack symbol.

15. a) Find an attributed translation grammar that specifies the processing performed by the MINI-BASIC lexical box designed in Chapter 4.

    b) Using this grammar, implement the lexical box with the method of recursive descent.

16. Sometimes when a nonterminal has one synthesized and one inherited attribute, the inherited attribute can be stored in the same location where the synthesized attribute is to be stored. The stack symbol for the nonterminal can have a single field, containing a pointer to this location.

    Show that the two attributes of ⟨E-list⟩, ⟨T-list⟩, and ⟨F-list⟩ in the MINI-BASIC design of Section 10.4 can be implemented in this way. Indicate all the required changes in the design, including the new "before" and "after" pictures and the new transition routines.

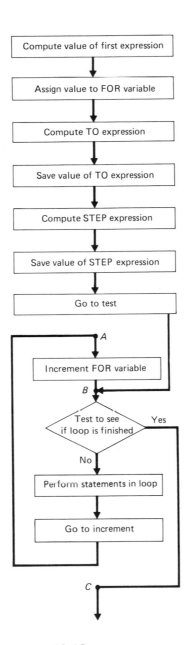

Figure 10.18

17. When a production is specified with several action symbols appearing consecutively, efficiencies can often be achieved by combining the action symbols into a single action symbol. In the MINI-BASIC syntax-box design of Section 10.4, this situation occurs in production 9 where the three action symbols {SAVE}, {LABEL}, and {TEST} occur consecutively and the action symbols {CHECK}, {INCR}, {JUMP}, and {LABEL} occur consecutively. These action symbols can be combined into two action symbols, say {SAVE-LABEL-TEST} and {CHECK-INCR-JUMP-LABEL}, and production 9 of the string translation grammar can be written:

9. $\langle$program body$\rangle \rightarrow$ FOR $\langle$expression$\rangle$ {ASSIGN} TO $\langle$expression$\rangle$ {SAVE} $\langle$step part$\rangle$ {SAVE-LABEL-TEST} $\langle$more lines$\rangle$ NEXT {CHECK-INCR-JUMP-LABEL} $\langle$more lines$\rangle$

Show how the design would change if this new production were used.

18. Consider the language generated by the following grammar with starting symbol $\langle B \rangle$.

$\langle B \rangle \rightarrow \langle B \rangle \vee \langle R \rangle$ {OR}
$\langle B \rangle \rightarrow \langle R \rangle$
$\langle R \rangle \rightarrow \langle E \rangle = \langle E \rangle$ {EQ}
$\langle R \rangle \rightarrow \neg \langle R \rangle$ {NOT}
$\langle R \rangle \rightarrow \langle E \rangle$
$\langle E \rangle \rightarrow \langle E \rangle + \langle T \rangle$ {ADD}
$\langle E \rangle \rightarrow \langle T \rangle$
$\langle T \rangle \rightarrow \langle T \rangle * \langle F \rangle$ {MULT}
$\langle T \rangle \rightarrow - \langle T \rangle$ {NEG}
$\langle T \rangle \rightarrow \langle F \rangle$
$\langle F \rangle \rightarrow \langle P \rangle \uparrow \langle F \rangle$ {EXP}
$\langle F \rangle \rightarrow \langle P \rangle$
$\langle P \rangle \rightarrow (\langle B \rangle)$
$\langle P \rangle \rightarrow I$

a) Find an LL(1) grammar for this language.

b) Find a q-grammar for this language.

c) Find a grammar for this language with a compact representation.

d) Design a compact processor for this language.

19. In some one-pass compilers, the partial result entries are kept in fields of the stack symbols. This approach is in contrast to the MINI-BASIC design of Section 10.4 in which the fields contain pointers to partial result entries. The only potential difficulty with using fields to contain result entries is that the lifetime from push to pop of the stack symbol containing the result entry must include the time during which the code generator needs access to the result entry.

Assume that in the MINI-BASIC compiler, the code generator only accesses result cells during the time between the processing of the atoms for which that cell is an attribute. Assume also that in processing the atoms for binary operators, the code generator can reuse one of the operand cells for the result cell.

Redesign the syntax box so that stack-symbol fields are used for the cells obtained by calls on NEWTL, NEWTR, and NEWTSR.

20. Show that whenever transition routine #IV of the machine of Fig. 10.16 is selected, the condition $m \leq j$ is satisfied. Consequently the condition need not be checked, and the j field of stack symbol $\langle E, E \rangle$ can be omitted from the processor.

21. a) Add attributes to the grammar of Fig. 10.15 to obtain the attributed translation of expressions specified in Fig. 10.4.

   b) Design a corresponding attributed version of the processor of Fig. 10.16.

   c) Design a corresponding recursive descent processor.

   d) Draw the stack movie as the processor of Part b) processes the input:

   $$I_4 \text{ OP}_\uparrow \text{ (OP}_- I_3 \text{ OP}_* I_6 \text{ OP}_+ I_4 \text{) OP}_/ I_2$$

11
Bottom-Up Processing

11.1 INTRODUCTION

In Chapters 6 and 7 we viewed context-free grammars and translation grammars as a way to specify languages and their translations. Now we are interested in studying when and how the specified recognition and translation can be carried by a pushdown machine. This processing can be done either "top down" or "bottom up." In Chapters 8 through 10 we presented the top-down approach, and in Chapters 11 through 13 we present the bottom-up approach. For the convenience of certain readers we have attempted to make the presentation of each of these approaches independent. Achieving this independence has necessitated a small amount of repetition of material. For example, much of the material in the remainder of this section is a repetition of material in Section 8.1.

Virtually all design methods based on context-free grammars result in processors which somehow "use" the grammar in the sense that the processor's actions can be interpreted as the recognition of individual productions in a derivation tree. Any processor whose operation involves the recognition of productions is called a *parser*. The word "parsing" is borrowed from natural language grammarians who use it to refer to the analysis or diagramming of natural language sentences.

Top down and bottom up are two categories of parsing methods. Each category is characterized by the order in which the productions in the derivation tree are recognized. Broadly speaking, top-down processors recognize productions higher up in the tree before those lower down, while bottom-up processors recognize lower productions before higher ones. This distinction will be clarified as the methods are considered in more detail.

Pushdown machines can be designed using either a top-down or a bottom-up approach. However, with either approach not all context-free languages can be recognized nor can all syntax-directed translations be performed by a pushdown machine. Each method imposes restrictions on the form of the input grammar and translation grammar that can be processed and on the kind of communication allowed between action routines.

We continue our study of pushdown machine processing with the bottom-up approach. Bottom-up parsing with a pushdown machine is sometimes called *deterministic bottom-up parsing* as contrasted to some other techniques which are referred to as "nondeterministic bottom-up parsing" or "bottom-up parsing with backtrack."

We assume throughout this chapter that the grammars under consideration have no extraneous nonterminals. Thus we assume that each production and nonterminal can be used in the derivation of some sentence in the language. This assumption is an insignificant restriction since the deletion from a grammar of extraneous nonterminals and productions involving them does not change the language to be recognized or the translation to be performed.

11.2 HANDLES

In this section, we present a concept that underlies bottom-up parsing. To begin, consider the grammar of Fig. 11.1. This grammar is unambiguous, so that each string in its language has a unique derivation tree and a unique rightmost derivation. Now consider the string

$$(((b) a (a)) (b))$$

This string has the derivation tree shown in Fig. 11.2 and the rightmost derivation shown in Fig. 11.3(a). At each step of the derivation in Fig. 11.3(a), the nonterminal pointed to by an arrow is replaced by the righthand side of the production whose number appears below the arrow.

In bottom-up parsing we are concerned with the reverse of a rightmost derivation. For the sample sequence, the reverse of the rightmost derivation is shown in Fig. 11.3(b). In each step of Fig. 11.3(b), an occurrence of the

1. $\langle S \rangle \rightarrow (\langle A \rangle \langle S \rangle)$
2. $\langle S \rangle \rightarrow (b)$
3. $\langle A \rangle \rightarrow (\langle S \rangle a \langle A \rangle)$
4. $\langle A \rangle \rightarrow (a)$
   Starting symbol: $\langle S \rangle$

Figure 11.1

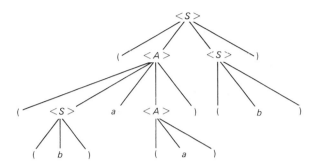

Figure 11.2

$\langle S \rangle \Rightarrow$
$\uparrow$
1

$(\langle A \rangle \langle S \rangle) \Rightarrow$ $(((b) a (a)) (b))$
$\uparrow$ 2
2

$(\langle A \rangle (b)) \Rightarrow$ $((\langle S \rangle a (a)) (b))$
$\uparrow$ 4
3

$((\langle S \rangle a \langle A \rangle) (b)) \Rightarrow$ $((\langle S \rangle a \langle A \rangle) (b))$
$\uparrow$ 3
4

$((\langle S \rangle a (a)) (b)) \Rightarrow$ $(\langle A \rangle (b))$
$\uparrow$ 2
2

$(((b) a (a)) (b))$ $(\langle A \rangle \langle S \rangle)$
                                        1

          (a) $\langle S \rangle$

                              (b)

Figure 11.3

righthand side of some production is replaced by the lefthand nonterminal of that production. Each occurrence of a righthand side that is replaced is underlined, and the number of the production involved is written below it. We call each underlined substring of Fig 11.3(b) a "handle" of the string in which it occurs, and the associated production a "handle production" of the string in which it occurs. For instance

$$(a)$$

is a handle and production 4 a handle production of the string:

$$(((\langle S \rangle a (a)) (b))$$

In general

> A *handle* of a string (of terminals and nonterminals) is the occurrence of the righthand side of the last production applied in a rightmost derivation of the string. A *handle production* of a string is the last production applied in a rightmost derivation of the string.

If a grammar is unambiguous, a string can have at most one rightmost derivation, and hence at most one handle and one handle production.

It is possible for a string to have no handle. For instance the string

$$(\, a \,) \,)$$

has no derivation at all with respect to the grammar of Fig. 11.1, and hence has no handle. The string

$$(\, (\, a \,) \, \langle S \rangle \,)$$

has the derivation

$$\langle S \rangle \; \Rightarrow \; (\, \langle A \rangle \, \langle S \rangle \,) \; \Rightarrow \; (\, (\, a \,) \, \langle S \rangle \,)$$
$$\underset{1}{\uparrow} \qquad\qquad \underset{4}{\uparrow}$$

but has no rightmost derivation and hence has no handle.

The rightmost derivation of Fig. 11.3(a) can be interpreted as building the derivation tree of Fig. 11.2. Replacing a nonterminal by the righthand side of one of its productions corresponds to adding the symbols on the righthand side as tree nodes attached below the node associated with the replaced nonterminal.

Similarly, Fig. 11.3(b) can be interpreted as *pruning* the derivation tree of Fig. 11.2. Figure 11.4 shows the derivation trees for the six strings occurring in Fig. 11.3(b). Figure 11.4(a) is the derivation tree for the first string, the initial terminal string. Figure 11.4(b) is the derivation tree for the second string

$$(\, (\, (\, \langle S \rangle \, a \, (\, a \,) \,) \, (\, b \,) \,)$$

Similarly for the rest of Fig. 11.4.

We use the word *leaf* to refer to a tree node that has no descendants. The string corresponding to each of the trees of Fig. 11.4 can be obtained by concatenating the leaves of the tree.

Each step in Fig. 11.3(b) consists of replacing an occurrence of the righthand side of a handle production by the lefthand side. The associated tree-pruning operation in Fig. 11.4 consists of deleting the tree leaves corresponding to the righthand side of the production. Because these leaves are the immediate descendants of the tree node corresponding to the lefthand

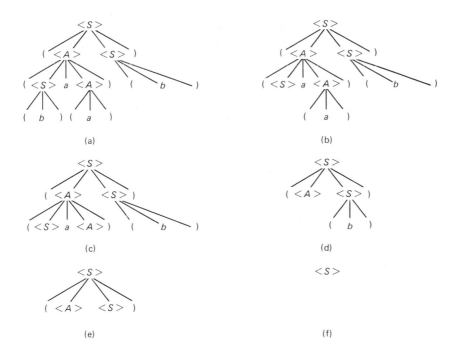

Figure 11.4

side nonterminal, this node becomes a leaf of the new tree and represents the occurrence of the lefthand nonterminal that replaces the righthand side in the string. For instance Fig. 11.4(b) is obtained from Fig. 11.4(a) by a pruning corresponding to production 2, in which leaves representing (*b*), the righthand side of production 2, are deleted. The deletion exposes as a leaf their common ancestor, a node labeled $\langle S \rangle$ (the lefthand side of production 2). Similarly each step in Fig. 11.3(b) corresponds to removing a righthand side from a tree thereby leaving a lefthand side pruned of its descendants.

A derivation tree may in general have several nodes that are "prunable" in the sense that all their descendants are leaves. However, in the reverse of a rightmost derivation, we always prune the leftmost prunable node. These leaves represent the handle of the intermediate string obtained by concatenating the leaves of the tree.

11.3 AN EXAMPLE

In this section, we illustrate some principles of bottom-up processing by exhibiting a pushdown machine that recognizes the language specified by the grammar of Fig. 11.1. The input alphabet of the machine is the terminal set of the grammar and the endmarker. The stack alphabet consists of a bottommarker, nonterminal symbols from the grammar, and terminals from the grammar.

The machine is designed so that if the input sequence is acceptable, then at every step in the processing, the string of terminals and nonterminals on the stack (using the top-symbol-on-right convention) concatenated with the string of remaining terminals (including the current input if it is not the endmarker) is an intermediate string in a rightmost derivation of the entire input string.

The pushdown machine uses five operations for manipulating the stack and input. These operations are named SHIFT, REDUCE(1), REDUCE(2), REDUCE(3), and REDUCE(4). The operation SHIFT pushes the current input on top of the stack and advances the input. The machine is designed so that SHIFT is never selected when the current input is endmarker. SHIFT does not alter the string obtained by concatenating the stack with the unprocessed inputs; it merely changes the current input from an unprocessed input to a stack symbol.

Considering now the REDUCE operations, the machine is designed so that operation REDUCE(p) for $p = 1, 2, 3,$ or 4 is only selected when the top of the stack matches the righthand side of production p. For example, operation REDUCE(1) is only selected when the top stack symbols are the righthand side of production 1, namely ($\langle A \rangle$ $\langle S \rangle$). Thus REDUCE (1) might be selected with any of the three following stacks:

$$\nabla\,(\,\langle A \rangle\,\langle S \rangle\,)$$
$$\nabla\,(\,(\,\langle S \rangle\,a\,(\,(\,\langle A \rangle\,\langle S \rangle\,)$$
$$\nabla\,(\,\langle S \rangle\,\langle S \rangle\,(\,\langle A \rangle\,\langle S \rangle\,)$$

The operation REDUCE(p) does one POP for each symbol on the righthand side of production p and then pushes the lefthand side. Operation REDUCE(1) thus does

$$\text{POP, POP, POP, POP, PUSH(}\ \langle S \rangle\ \text{)}$$

The result of applying REDUCE(1) to the three stacks given above is respectively

$$\nabla\,\langle S \rangle$$
$$\nabla\,(\,(\,\langle S \rangle\,a\,(\,\langle S \rangle$$
$$\nabla\,(\,\langle S \rangle\,\langle S \rangle\,\langle S \rangle$$

REDUCE(p) alters the string consisting of the stack concatenated with the unprocessed inputs by replacing an occurrence of the righthand side of production p by the lefthand side.

The reduce operations are not primitive pushdown machine operations; so the machine is not primitive. Another nonprimitive aspect of the machine is that occasionally several of the top stack symbols are used to select an operation. However, before discussing how the machine selects its operations, we show how the machine uses its stack to recognize the string

$$(((b)a(a))(b))$$

Recall that this is the string discussed in the previous section and that Fig. 11.3(b) shows the reverse of the rightmost derivation for this string.

Figure 11.5 shows the stack movie for this input sequence. The rightmost column in the figure gives the operation selected to produce the next configuration. Thus SHIFT is used at line 1 to obtain line 2 and REDUCE(2) is used at line 6 to obtain line 7.

The stack is initialized with $\triangledown$ as shown in line 1. The string of terminals and nonterminals represented by this stack concatenated with the unpro-

1. $\triangledown$	$(((b)a(a))(b))\dashv$	SHIFT
2. $\triangledown ($	$((b)a(a))(b))\dashv$	SHIFT
3. $\triangledown (($	$(b)a(a))(b))\dashv$	SHIFT
4. $\triangledown ((($	$b)a(a))(b))\dashv$	SHIFT
5. $\triangledown (((b$	$)a(a))(b))\dashv$	SHIFT
6. $\triangledown (((b)$	$a(a))(b))\dashv$	REDUCE(2)
7. $\triangledown ((\langle S\rangle$	$a(a))(b))\dashv$	SHIFT
8. $\triangledown ((\langle S\rangle a$	$(a))(b))\dashv$	SHIFT
9. $\triangledown ((\langle S\rangle a ($	$a))(b))\dashv$	SHIFT
10. $\triangledown ((\langle S\rangle a (a$	$))(b))\dashv$	SHIFT
11. $\triangledown ((\langle S\rangle a (a)$	$)(b))\dashv$	REDUCE(4)
12. $\triangledown ((\langle S\rangle a \langle A\rangle$	$)(b))\dashv$	SHIFT
13. $\triangledown ((\langle S\rangle a \langle A\rangle)$	$(b))\dashv$	REDUCE(3)
14. $\triangledown ((\langle A\rangle$	$(b))\dashv$	SHIFT
15. $\triangledown ((\langle A\rangle ($	$b))\dashv$	SHIFT
16. $\triangledown ((\langle A\rangle (b$	$))\dashv$	SHIFT
17. $\triangledown ((\langle A\rangle (b)$	$)\dashv$	REDUCE(2)
18. $\triangledown ((\langle A\rangle \langle S\rangle$	$)\dashv$	SHIFT
19. $\triangledown ((\langle A\rangle \langle S\rangle)$	$\dashv$	REDUCE(1)
20. $\triangledown \langle S\rangle$	$\dashv$	ACCEPT

Figure 11.5

cessed inputs is simply the input sequence itself:

$$(((b) a (a)) (b))$$

The handle of this string is the first occurrence of substring:

$$(b)$$

In order to change the represented string to a different string in a rightmost derivation, the machine seeks to replace the handle of the represented string by the corresponding lefthand nonterminal. The machine shifts the input symbols onto the stack until the handle is on top of the stack. This shifting operation is selected in lines 1 through 5 of Fig. 11.5. Finally in line 6, the handle is on top of the stack. The machine then selects the operation

$$REDUCE(2)$$

which replaces the handle by the lefthand nonterminal of production 2, namely $\langle S \rangle$. The resulting represented string is:

$$(((\langle S \rangle a (a)) (b))$$

This new string is the same as the second string in Fig. 11.3(b).

   The handle of this new string is the substring

$$(a)$$

In lines 7 through 10 of Fig. 11.5, the machine shifts input symbols until the handle is on top of the stack. Then in line 11, the machine selects RE-DUCE(4) which replaces the handle by the lefthand nonterminal of the handle production. The resulting string, as represented in line 12, is the same as the third string in Fig. 11.3(b).

   The machine continues in a similar manner until line 20 of Fig. 11.5 where the current input is endmarker and the stack contains only the starting symbol and the bottommarker. In this configuration, the machine accepts the input sequence, since the machine has verified that the input sequence can be derived from $\langle S \rangle$. At each step in the processing, the old represented string was either identical to the new represented string or could be derived from the new represented string by applying a single production. The history of intermediate strings represented by the stack and input describes a method of deriving the input string from $\langle S \rangle$ through a sequence of rightmost substitutions. In fact, the order of productions used by REDUCE is the reverse order of the productions used in the rightmost derivation.

   The pushdown machine is shown in Fig. 11.6. On the basis of the top stack symbol and current input, the control table selects one of the three transition routines IDENTIFY1, IDENTIFY2, or SHIFT. Observe that IDENTIFY1 is selected whenever the top stack symbol is a right parenthesis.

	(	a	b	)	⊣
$<S>$	SHIFT	SHIFT	SHIFT	SHIFT	IDENTIFY2
$<A>$	SHIFT	SHIFT	SHIFT	SHIFT	IDENTIFY2
(	SHIFT	SHIFT	SHIFT	SHIFT	IDENTIFY2
)	IDENTIFY1	IDENTIFY1	IDENTIFY1	IDENTIFY1	IDENTIFY1
b	SHIFT	SHIFT	SHIFT	SHIFT	IDENTIFY2
a	SHIFT	SHIFT	SHIFT	SHIFT	IDENTIFY2
▽	SHIFT	SHIFT	SHIFT	SHIFT	IDENTIFY2

Starting stack: ▽

IDENTIFY1: if top of stack is $(<A><S>)$ then REDUCE(1)
　　　　　else if top of stack is (b) then REDUCE(2)
　　　　　else if top of stack is $(<S>a<A>)$ then REDUCE(3)
　　　　　else if top of stack is (a) then REDUCE(4)
　　　　　else REJECT

IDENTIFY2: if top of stack is $▽<S>$ then ACCEPT
　　　　　else REJECT

SHIFT:　　　PUSH (current input), ADVANCE
REDUCE(1): POP, POP, POP, POP, PUSH $(<S>)$
REDUCE(2): POP, POP, POP, PUSH $(<S>)$
REDUCE(3): POP, POP, POP, POP, POP, PUSH $(<A>)$
REDUCE(4): POP, POP, POP, PUSH $(<A>)$

Figure 11.6

Transition routine IDENTIFY1 inspects several of the symbols on top of the stack and selects one of the REDUCE(p) operations or REJECT. REDUCE(p) is selected if the top several stack symbols match the righthand side of production p and REJECT is selected if the top of the stack fails to match a righthand side. Although Fig. 11.6 shows the selection performed by an *if-then-else* construction, the problem is really an identification problem similar to those discussed in Chapter 3, and the techniques of that chapter could be applied here.

The routine IDENTIFY2 checks to see if the stack is ▽ $\langle S \rangle$, accepts if it is, and rejects otherwise.

The basis of the machine's operation is that if the total input string is acceptable, the string represented by the stack and unprocessed inputs is an intermediate string in the rightmost derivation of the input string. The machine shifts inputs onto the stack until the top of the stack contains the handle of the represented string. The machine then does the REDUCE corresponding to the handle production. This REDUCE replaces the handle by the lefthand side of the handle production. In terms of pruning the associated derivation tree, the REDUCE corresponds to deleting the righthand-side tree leaves and thereby exposing the lefthand-side node as a leaf. Hence there is a correspondence between the tree node representing the lefthand side and the pushed stack symbol representing the lefthand side. The term *bottom up* is used to characterize this recognition procedure, because, for each nonterminal, the productions for its descendants are recognized before the production for the nonterminal itself.

The design of the machine for the given grammar is quite simple. Observe in Fig. 11.3(b) that each handle of an intermediate string contains the leftmost right parenthesis in the string. In general, since every production ends with a right parenthesis, a handle can only be on top of the stack when the top stack symbol is a right parenthesis. Since right parentheses only appear at the end of productions, a right parenthesis on top of the stack must be the end of a handle. Therefore, the machine performs IDENTIFY1 if and only if the top stack symbol is a right parenthesis. Furthermore, since every production begins with a left parenthesis, each handle must begin with a left parenthesis. Since left parentheses only appear at the beginning of productions, the topmost left parenthesis begins the handle that ends with a right parenthesis on top of the stack. Therefore, these two parentheses and enclosed stack symbols must constitute the righthand side of the handle production if there is any rightmost derivation at all (i.e., if the input sequence is acceptable). Finally, since no two productions have the same righthand side, the identification of the righthand side specifies a unique production.

As an example of how an unacceptable input sequence is rejected, Fig. 11.7 shows a stack movie of the machine of Fig. 11.6 processing the terminal sequence:

$$(\,(\,(\,b\,)\,a\,(\,a\,a\,)\,)\,(\,b\,)\,)$$

The stack, current input, and operation in the first nine configurations match the stack, current input, and operation in Fig. 11.5, because the two input sequences begin with the same eight inputs.

Consider line 6 of the two stack movies. In Fig. 11.5, the $(\,b\,)$ on top of the stack represents the handle of the stack concatenated with the remaining inputs. In Fig. 11.7, the $(\,b\,)$ on top of the stack is not a handle, because the stack concatenated with the remaining inputs cannot even be derived from $\langle S \rangle$ and therefore has no handle. The intuition that the machine operates by replacing handles applies only to the processing of acceptable sequences. In the processing of unacceptable sequences, the string represented by the stack and remaining inputs has no handle, and the operation of the machine can be described as replacing certain occurrences of the righthand side of productions by the lefthand side. In line 6 of the stack movie, with stack

$$\nabla\,(\,(\,(\,b\,)$$

and current input a, it is appropriate to perform REDUCE(2) because, if the represented string has a handle, that handle is $(\,b\,)$. The machine does not

1. $\triangledown$	$(((b)a(a\,a))(b))\dashv$	SHIFT
2. $\triangledown\,($	$((b)a(a\,a))(b))\dashv$	SHIFT
3. $\triangledown\,((\,$	$(b)a(a\,a))(b))\dashv$	SHIFT
4. $\triangledown\,(((\,$	$b)a(a\,a))(b))\dashv$	SHIFT
5. $\triangledown\,(((\,b$	$)a(a\,a))(b))\dashv$	SHIFT
6. $\triangledown\,(((\,b\,)$	$a(a\,a))(b))\dashv$	REDUCE(2)
7. $\triangledown\,((\,(\langle S\rangle$	$a(a\,a))(b))\dashv$	SHIFT
8. $\triangledown\,(((\langle S\rangle\,a$	$(a\,a))(b))\dashv$	SHIFT
9. $\triangledown\,(((\langle S\rangle\,a\,($	$a\,a))(b))\dashv$	SHIFT
10. $\triangledown\,(((\langle S\rangle\,a\,(\,a$	$a))(b))\dashv$	SHIFT
11. $\triangledown\,(((\langle S\rangle\,a\,(\,a\,a$	$))(b))\dashv$	SHIFT
12. $\triangledown\,(((\langle S\rangle\,a\,(\,a\,a\,)$	$)(b))\dashv$	REJECT

Figure 11.7

know if the unseen inputs are $(a))(b))$ as in Fig. 11.5 or $(a\,a))(b))$ as in Fig. 11.7 or any other sequence, and therefore it is inaccurate to say that the machine "knows" (b) is a handle.

Returning to Fig. 11.7, the machine continues until the configuration of line 12 is reached. At that point, IDENTIFY1 is performed. The $(a\,a)$ on top of the stack does not match the righthand side of any production, so IDENTIFY1 rejects.

In the processing of any input sequence, acceptable or not, the string represented by the stack and remaining inputs always generates the original input sequence since the stack and input are only manipulated by SHIFT and REDUCE(p). Since the machine only accepts when the represented string is $\langle S\rangle$, and there is no way for $\langle S\rangle$ to generate a sequence not in the language, the machine accepts sequences in the language only. The machine cannot cycle since the number of SHIFT and REDUCE operations performed in processing an input sequence is bounded by twice the length of the sequence. Therefore all sequences not in the language are rejected by the machine.

11.4   A SECOND EXAMPLE

In the previous section, we presented a pushdown machine for recognizing the language specified by the grammar of Fig. 11.1. In this section, we present a second pushdown machine for performing the same recognition. As was the case in the last section, the machine described here seeks to discover a rightmost derivation for a given input sequence. Both machines use their stack and unprocessed inputs to represent intermediate strings in a rightmost derivation. Both machines also manipulate their stack and current input with shift and reduce operations (although these operations require an added step in the new machine). However, the machines are considerably different in their mechanisms for deciding which shift or reduce operation to apply.

The machine of the last section inspects several of the top stack symbols in order to decide which REDUCE(p) operation to perform. The presence of a right parenthesis on top of the stack indicates that a handle should be on top of the stack but does not indicate which handle. The machine of this section uses an expanded stack alphabet which encodes extra information about the stack. Enough information is encoded so that the top stack symbol and current input are sufficient to determine if a handle is on top of the stack and, if so, determine the handle production without the machine having to inspect any symbols further down the stack. However the REDUCE corresponding to each production involves inspecting the stack symbol below the handle.

The stack alphabet of the new machine consists of the fourteen stack symbols shown in the second column of Fig. 11.8. For convenience, we write these stack symbols as grammatical symbols with subscripts, but in an implementation of the machine they are likely to be represented as fourteen consecutive integers.

Each stack symbol is thought of as both a *representation of a grammatical symbol* and an *encoding of a string,* as shown in Fig. 11.8. Each stack symbol represents the grammatical symbol obtained by deleting the subscript. Thus the three stack symbols $\langle S \rangle_1$, $\langle S \rangle_2$, and $\langle S \rangle_3$ all represent nonterminal $\langle S \rangle$ and stack symbol b_1 represents terminal b. Under this many-to-one representation of symbols, a pushdown stack can be interpreted as representing a string of terminals and nonterminals in essentially the same manner as in the last section. For example, the stack

$$\nabla \; (_1 \; \langle S \rangle_2 \; a_1$$

represents the string

$$(\; \langle S \rangle \; a$$

obtained by deleting the ∇ and subscripts.

In addition to representing a grammatical symbol, each stack symbol is regarded as an encoding of a string. For example, $\langle S \rangle_1$ is regarded as an encoding of the string

$$(\; \langle A \rangle \; \langle S \rangle$$

The rightmost symbol in each encoded string is always an instance of the grammatical symbol represented by the stack symbol.

Represented grammatical symbol	Stack symbol	Encoded string
a	a_1	$(<S>a$
	a_2	$(a$
b	b_1	$(b$
$($	$(_1$	$($
$)$	$)_1$	$(<A><S>)$
	$)_2$	(b)
	$)_3$	$(<S>a<A>)$
	$)_4$	(a)
$<S>$	$<S>_1$	$(<A><S>$
	$<S>_2$	$(<S>$
	$<S>_3$	$\nabla<S>$
$<A>$	$<A>_1$	$(<A>$
	$<A>_2$	$(<S>a<A>$
None	∇	∇

Figure 11.8

The bottommarker is a special case. It does not represent any grammatical symbol but is considered to be an encoding of the string consisting of the bottommarker itself.

The pushdown machine is designed so that a stack symbol is only pushed on the stack if its encoded string is consistent with the string represented by the new stack after the symbol is pushed.

We say that the encoded string of a given symbol on the stack is *consistent* with the string represented by the stack up to and including the given symbol if either:

a) the encoded string is a suffix of the string represented by the stack; or

b) the encoded string is identical to ∇ concatenated with the string represented by the stack.

For example, when the stack is

$$\nabla \; (_1 \; (_1 \; \langle S \rangle_2 \; a_1$$

the machine might push $\langle A \rangle_2$ producing stack

$$\nabla \; (_1 \; (_1 \; \langle S \rangle_2 \; a_1 \; \langle A \rangle_2$$

The newly pushed stack symbol is consistent with the new stack because the top four stack symbols represent the string encoded by symbol $\langle A \rangle_2$. Stack symbol $\langle A \rangle_1$ would be inconsistent because for the resulting stack

$$\nabla \; (_1 \; (_1 \; \langle S \rangle_2 \; a_1 \; \langle A \rangle_1$$

the string ($\langle A \rangle$ encoded by the top stack symbol is neither a suffix of the represented string

$$(\; (\; \langle S \rangle \; a \; \langle A \rangle$$

nor ∇ concatenated with the represented string.

The stack alphabet is designed so that the string encoded by each stack symbol except $\langle S \rangle_3$ and ∇ is a prefix of a righthand side of some production. Conversely, each nonnull prefix of a righthand side is encoded by a stack symbol. For example, the righthand side of production 1 is ($\langle A \rangle$ $\langle S \rangle$) which has four nonnull prefixes, namely

$$(\, , \qquad (\, \langle A \rangle \, , \qquad (\, \langle A \rangle \, \langle S \rangle \, , \qquad \text{and} \qquad (\, \langle A \rangle \, \langle S \rangle \,).$$

Note that the entire righthand side is considered a prefix. These four prefixes are encoded by the four stack symbols

$$(_1 \, , \qquad \langle A \rangle_1 \, , \qquad \langle S \rangle_1 \, , \qquad \text{and} \qquad)_1 .$$

Similarly, the righthand side of production 2 has three prefixes encoded by $(_1$, b_1, and $)_2$. Note that the prefix (, encoded by $(_1$, is common to all righthand sides. The consequences of encoding prefixes will become clear as the pushdown machine is described in more detail.

The control of the pushdown machine is specified by two tables. First a conventional control table, to be discussed later, is used to decide whether to shift or reduce. If the selected decision involves a push, the decision only specifies which grammatical symbol should be represented by the new stack symbol. The "push table" of Fig. 11.9 is used to determine which of the stack symbols representing that grammatical symbol should be pushed. The determination is based on both the stack symbol above which the new stack symbol is to be pushed and on the grammatical symbol which the new stack symbol represents. The table of Fig. 11.9 has a row for each stack symbol above which a new stack symbol may be pushed, and a column for each grammatical symbol. The nonblank entries in the table give the symbol to be pushed for the corresponding combination of stack symbol and grammatical symbol. The blank entries represent combinations for which the machine

	a	b	(	)	$\langle S \rangle$	$\langle A \rangle$
a_1			$(_1$			$\langle A \rangle_2$
a_2			$(_1$	$)_4$		
b_1			$(_1$	$)_2$		
$(_1$	a_2	b_1	$(_1$		$\langle S \rangle_2$	$\langle A \rangle_1$
$\langle S \rangle_1$			$(_1$	$)_1$		
$\langle S \rangle_2$	a_1		$(_1$			
$\langle S \rangle_3$			$(_1$			
$\langle A \rangle_1$			$(_1$		$\langle S \rangle_1$	
$\langle A \rangle_2$			$(_1$	$)_3$		
$\triangledown$			$(_1$		$\langle S \rangle_3$	

Figure 11.9

rejects. The table has no rows for stack symbols $)_1$, $)_2$, $)_3$, and $)_4$ because the control never attempts to push a symbol when the top of the stack represents a right parenthesis.

To see that the table of Fig. 11.9 maintains the consistency of the encoded information, consider the column for pushing stack symbols representing a right parenthesis. According to the table , $)_1$ gets pushed if the top stack symbol is $\langle S \rangle_1$, $)_2$ gets pushed if the top stack symbol is b_1, $)_3$ gets pushed if the top is $\langle A \rangle_2$, and $)_4$ gets pushed if the top is a_2. For other top stack symbols, the machine rejects.

First, consider the decision to push $)_1$ when $\langle S \rangle_1$ is the top stack symbol. According to the information encoded in $\langle S \rangle_1$, the top three stack symbols represent ($\langle A \rangle$ $\langle S \rangle$. Because the $)_1$ being pushed represents), the four new top stack symbols represent the concatenation of ($\langle A \rangle$ $\langle S \rangle$ with), namely ($\langle A \rangle$ $\langle S \rangle$) and *this is the encoded string of* $)_1$. In other words, the consistency of the encoded information in the newly pushed $)_1$ is evident from the string encoded in the symbol below and the fact that $)_1$ represents). We cannot push any of the symbols $)_2$, $)_3$, or $)_4$ above $\langle S \rangle_1$ because the string encoded by each of these symbols is inconsistent with the string that would be represented by the resulting stack.

An investigation similar to that of the above paragraph shows that $)_2$, $)_3$, and $)_4$ are pushed in situations where the consistency of the pushed symbol can be verified from the symbol below. Furthermore, in each of these situations, the string encoded in the symbol below rules out the possibility that any other symbol representing) could be used.

Now consider the decision to reject when $\langle A \rangle_1$ is the top stack symbol and right parenthesis is the input symbol. According to the string encoded by $\langle A \rangle_1$ the top two stack symbols represent the string ($\langle A \rangle$. Pushing a symbol representing a right parenthesis would produce a stack with the top three symbols representing ($\langle A \rangle$). The machine is designed so that at any stage in the processing of an acceptable input sequence the concatenation of the string represented by the stack with the string of unprocessed inputs can be derived from $\langle S \rangle$ by a rightmost derivation. There is no way that an $\langle A \rangle$ alone between two matching parentheses can appear in a string derived from $\langle S \rangle$, therefore the input sequence cannot be acceptable and the machine is certainly justified in rejecting. A similar analysis applies to the other top stack symbols for which the machine rejects.

We have seen that for each of the possible top stack symbols, it happens that there is at most one stack symbol (representing a right parenthesis) whose encoded string is consistent with appending a right parenthesis to the string encoded by the top stack symbol. In cases where there is no such stack symbol, it happens that rejection can be justified on the grounds that the string represented by the proposed new stack and unprocessed inputs cannot be derived from $\langle S \rangle$. These "happenings" can be traced back to the fact that the stack symbol set was designed to encode prefixes of righthand sides. If the prefix encoded by the top stack symbol concatenates with right parenthesis to give another prefix, the push table gives the stack symbol which encodes that longer prefix. If the concatenation is not a prefix, an unacceptable combination of inputs has been found between matching parentheses, and the machine safely rejects.

The push-table entries for other grammatical symbols are designed according to similar considerations. If concatenating the grammatical symbol to the prefix encoded in the stack symbol results in another prefix, the stack symbol encoding the new prefix is the symbol pushed. In the case that the grammatical symbol is left parenthesis, it is assumed that the left parenthesis is the beginning of a new righthand side, and the machine pushes $(_1$ which encodes the one symbol string (. If the grammatical symbol cannot be used to continue the prefix encoded in the top stack symbol or to begin a new prefix, the machine rejects on the grounds that the further inputs cannot complete a righthand side and therefore cannot complete an acceptable sequence. An exception occurs with stack symbol $\triangledown$ and grammatical symbol $\langle S \rangle$ since an acceptable sequence (in fact all acceptable sequences) can be generated from a single $\langle S \rangle$. In this case the push table selects $\langle S \rangle_3$, which encodes string $\triangledown$ $\langle S \rangle$.

Figure 11.10 shows the control table of the pushdown machine. The table selects a transition routine for every combination of input and top stack symbol. (We have omitted the word RETAIN from those routines that do not advance the input.)

The word PUSHT appearing in the shift and reduce routines is the name of an operation which uses the push table in Fig. 11.9 to determine which, if any, stack symbol to push. The argument of PUSHT gives the grammatical symbol involved in the table look up; the stack symbol involved comes from the top of the stack. The routines SHIFT, REDUCE(1), REDUCE(2), REDUCE(3), and REDUCE(4) are the same as the routines of the same name used in the previous section, except here PUSHT is used instead of PUSH. The effect of using PUSHT instead of PUSH is that PUSHT includes the extra step of consulting a push table to decide which symbol to push.

	(	a	b	)	⊣
a_1	SHIFT	SHIFT	SHIFT	SHIFT	REJECT
a_2	SHIFT	SHIFT	SHIFT	SHIFT	REJECT
b_1	SHIFT	SHIFT	SHIFT	SHIFT	REJECT
$(_1$	SHIFT	SHIFT	SHIFT	SHIFT	REJECT
$)_1$	REDUCE(1)	REDUCE(1)	REDUCE(1)	REDUCE(1)	REDUCE(1)
$)_2$	REDUCE(2)	REDUCE(2)	REDUCE(2)	REDUCE(2)	REDUCE(2)
$)_3$	REDUCE(3)	REDUCE(3)	REDUCE(3)	REDUCE(3)	REDUCE(3)
$)_4$	REDUCE(4)	REDUCE(4)	REDUCE(4)	REDUCE(4)	REDUCE(4)
$<S>_1$	SHIFT	SHIFT	SHIFT	SHIFT	REJECT
$<S>_2$	SHIFT	SHIFT	SHIFT	SHIFT	REJECT
$<S>_3$	SHIFT	SHIFT	SHIFT	SHIFT	ACCEPT
$<A>_1$	SHIFT	SHIFT	SHIFT	SHIFT	REJECT
$<A>_2$	SHIFT	SHIFT	SHIFT	SHIFT	REJECT
∇	SHIFT	SHIFT	SHIFT	SHIFT	REJECT

Starting stack: ∇

SHIFT: PUSHT(current input), ADVANCE
REDUCE(1):   POP, POP, POP, POP, PUSHT($<S>$)
REDUCE(2):   POP, POP, POP, PUSHT($<S>$)
REDUCE(3):   POP, POP, POP, POP, POP, PUSHT($<A>$)
REDUCE(4):   POP, POP, POP, PUSHT($<A>$)
PUSHT refers to table in Figure 11.9

Figure 11.10

Consider the table entries in row $)_1$ of Fig. 11.10. According to these entries, REDUCE(1) is selected whenever $)_1$ is the top stack symbol, regardless of the current input. REDUCE(1) is a routine specifically designed for production 1. REDUCE(1) removes one symbol from the stack for each of the four symbols in the righthand side of production 1 and then does PUSHT using the lefthand side $\langle S \rangle$ of production 1 as its argument. The appropriateness of calling REDUCE(1) can be verified from the information encoded in $)_1$, because *the encoded information is precisely the righthand side of production 1.* Similarly, stack symbols $)_2$, $)_3$, and $)_4$ have encoded strings which are precisely the righthand sides of productions 2, 3, and 4, and the control table selects corresponding REDUCE routines in each of these other cases. Thus whenever a symbol corresponding to right parenthesis is on top of the stack a REDUCE routine appropriate to the encoded string is called. The immediate decision to call a specific REDUCE routine is in contrast to the situation in the previous section where a stack symbol corresponding to right parenthesis caused routine IDENTIFY1 to be called to decide which REDUCE routine to call.

	Stack	Input	Action
1.	$\triangledown$	$(\,(\,(\,b\,)\,a\,(\,a\,)\,)\,(\,b\,)\,) \dashv$	SHIFT
2.	$\triangledown\,(_1$	$(\,(\,b\,)\,a\,(\,a\,)\,)\,(\,b\,)\,) \dashv$	SHIFT
3.	$\triangledown\,(_1\,(_1$	$(\,b\,)\,a\,(\,a\,)\,)\,(\,b\,)\,) \dashv$	SHIFT
4.	$\triangledown\,(_1\,(_1\,(_1$	$b\,)\,a\,(\,a\,)\,)\,(\,b\,)\,) \dashv$	SHIFT
5.	$\triangledown\,(_1\,(_1\,(_1\,b_1$	$)\,a\,(\,a\,)\,)\,(\,b\,)\,) \dashv$	SHIFT
6.	$\triangledown\,(_1\,(_1\,(_1\,b_1\,)_2$	$a\,(\,a\,)\,)\,(\,b\,)\,) \dashv$	REDUCE(2)
7.	$\triangledown\,(_1\,(_1\,\langle S\rangle_2$	$a\,(\,a\,)\,)\,(\,b\,)\,) \dashv$	SHIFT
8.	$\triangledown\,(_1\,(_1\,\langle S\rangle_2\,a_1$	$(\,a\,)\,)\,(\,b\,)\,) \dashv$	SHIFT
9.	$\triangledown\,(_1\,(_1\,\langle S\rangle_2\,a_1\,(_1$	$a\,)\,)\,(\,b\,)\,) \dashv$	SHIFT
10.	$\triangledown\,(_1\,(_1\,\langle S\rangle_2\,a_1\,(_1\,a_2$	$)\,)\,(\,b\,)\,) \dashv$	SHIFT
11.	$\triangledown\,(_1\,(_1\,\langle S\rangle_2\,a_1\,(_1\,a_2\,)_4$	$)\,(\,b\,)\,) \dashv$	REDUCE(4)
12.	$\triangledown\,(_1\,(_1\,\langle S\rangle_2\,a_1\,\langle A\rangle_2$	$)\,(\,b\,)\,) \dashv$	SHIFT
13.	$\triangledown\,(_1\,(_1\,\langle S\rangle_2\,a_1\,\langle A\rangle_2\,)_3$	$(\,b\,)\,) \dashv$	REDUCE(3)
14.	$\triangledown\,(_1\,\langle A\rangle_1$	$(\,b\,)\,) \dashv$	SHIFT
15.	$\triangledown\,(_1\,\langle A\rangle_1\,(_1$	$b\,)\,) \dashv$	SHIFT
16.	$\triangledown\,(_1\,\langle A\rangle_1\,(_1\,b_1$	$)\,) \dashv$	SHIFT
17.	$\triangledown\,(_1\,\langle A\rangle_1\,(_1\,b_1\,)_2$	$)\dashv$	REDUCE(2)
18.	$\triangledown\,(_1\,\langle A\rangle_1\,\langle S\rangle_1$	$)\dashv$	SHIFT
19.	$\triangledown\,(_1\,\langle A\rangle_1\,\langle S\rangle_1\,)_1$	$\dashv$	REDUCE(1)
20.	$\triangledown\,\langle S\rangle_3$	$\dashv$	ACCEPT

Figure 11.11

1. ∇	$((b)b(a))\dashv$	SHIFT
2. $\nabla\,($	$(b)b(a))\dashv$	SHIFT
3. $\nabla\,((\,$	$b)b(a))\dashv$	SHIFT
4. $\nabla\,((\,b$	$)b(a))\dashv$	SHIFT
5. $\nabla\,((\,b\,)$	$b(a))\dashv$	REDUCE(2)
6. $\nabla\,((\,\langle S\rangle$	$b(a))\dashv$	SHIFT
7. $\nabla\,((\,\langle S\rangle\,b$	$(a))\dashv$	SHIFT
8. $\nabla\,((\,\langle S\rangle\,b\,($	$a))\dashv$	SHIFT
9. $\nabla\,((\,\langle S\rangle\,b\,(\,a$	$))\dashv$	SHIFT
10. $\nabla\,((\,\langle S\rangle\,b\,(\,a\,)$	$)\dashv$	REDUCE(4)
11. $\nabla\,((\,\langle S\rangle\,b\,\langle A\rangle$	$)\dashv$	SHIFT
12. $\nabla\,((\,\langle S\rangle\,b\,\langle A\rangle\,)$	$\dashv$	REJECT

(a)

1. ∇	$((b)b(a))\dashv$	SHIFT
2. $\nabla\,(_1$	$(b)b(a))\dashv$	SHIFT
3. $\nabla\,(_1\,(_1$	$b)b(a))\dashv$	SHIFT
4. $\nabla\,(_1\,(_1\,b_1$	$)b(a))\dashv$	SHIFT
5. $\nabla\,(_1\,(_1\,b_1\,)_2$	$b(a))\dashv$	REDUCE(2)
6. $\nabla\,(_1\,\langle S\rangle_2$	$b(a))\dashv$	REJECT

(b)

Fig. 11.12 (a) Movie for machine of Fig. 11.6 (b) Movie for machine of Fig. 11.10

Looking at the endmarker column of Fig. 11.10, it is evident that acceptance occurs if and only if the stack symbols represent the specific sequence $\nabla\ \langle S\rangle$ which is the sequence encoded in $\langle S\rangle_3$. Here, the machine does in a single step what IDENTIFY2 did in the previous section.

Figure 11.11 shows a stack movie of the pushdown machine accepting:

$$(((\,b\,)\,a\,(\,a\,))(\,b\,))$$

A comparison of Fig. 11.11 with Fig. 11.5 shows the similarity of the approaches of this and the previous section. Figure 11.11 is nothing more than Fig. 11.5 with subscripts added to the stack symbols.

Figure 11.12(a) and (b) show the two machines rejecting the sequence:

$$((\,b\,)\,b\,(\,a\,))$$

The two machines reject at different places in the sequence. The machine of Fig. 11.6 rejects while processing the endmarker when the identify routine finds that there is no production with righthand side ($\langle S \rangle$ b $\langle A \rangle$). The machine of Fig. 11.10 rejects five input symbols earlier, while processing the second b, when the push table detects that b cannot be pushed on top of $\langle S \rangle_2$.

11.5 GRAMMATICAL PRINCIPLES OF BOTTOM-UP PROCESSING

All the bottom-up design methods discussed in this book involve the construction of a pushdown machine from a suitable underlying grammar. The methods all yield pushdown machines which can be interpreted as "using" the underlying grammar, and there is much commonality in the way the grammars are "used." In particular, the machines all use their pushdown stacks in essentially the same way. In this section, we present the grammatical principles behind the use of the pushdown stack and discuss two ways in which the machine can be controlled. The principles and control methods have been illustrated in the previous two sections, but here we separate those features common to all the bottom-up processors to be discussed in this book from those features peculiar to the particular processors of the previous two sections.

One common feature of the bottom-up processors of this book is that stack symbols and stack contents have a grammatical interpretation. Specifically:

> Each stack symbol except the bottommarker is associated with a terminal or nonterminal of the underlying grammar. At each step in the processing, the pushdown stack represents the string obtained by taking the string of stack symbols implied by the top-symbol-on-right convention, deleting ▽, and replacing each remaining stack symbol with its associated grammatical symbol.

The simplest method of establishing a correspondence between stack symbols and grammatical symbols is to design the stack symbol set to be the set of terminals and nonterminals from the grammar. The correspondence in Section 11.3 was obtained in this way. In general, however, there may be several stack symbols corresponding to the same grammatical symbol as in Section 11.4. In Section 11.4, the design was based on encoded prefixes, but there are other ways of designing a many-to-one correspondence between stack and grammatical symbols.

The bottom-up pushdown machines in this book manipulate their stacks and current inputs using shift and reduce operations. By "shift operation" and "reduce operation", we mean:

A *shift operation* is an operation which pushes a symbol corresponding to the current input on the stack and advances the current input.

A *reduce operation* for production p with r symbols in its righthand side is an operation which is only selected when the top r stack symbols represent the righthand side of production p. The reduce operation pops the top r symbols off the stack and pushes a symbol corresponding to the lefthand side of production p.

We commonly use a single shift operation named SHIFT and a reduce operation named REDUCE(p) for each production p. When the machine is designed so that some grammatical symbols have many corresponding stack symbols, the shift and reduce operations choose a specific corresponding symbol to push on the stack. In Section 11.4, the machine used the push table to make this decision.

Because the grammars studied in Chapters 12 and 13 are all unambiguous, we take the liberty in the subsequent discussion of referring to "the" rightmost derivation associated with an acceptable input sequence.

Each stack and input configuration which occurs during bottom-up processing of an acceptable input sequence corresponds to an intermediate string in the rightmost derivation of the input sequence. The correspondence is as follows:

The string represented by the stack symbols concatenated with the unprocessed terminals (including the current input if it is not the endmarker) is an intermediate string in the rightmost derivation of the original input string from the starting symbol.

The bottom-up machine seeks to replace the handle of the represented string by the lefthand nonterminal of the handle production. At each step (except the last) in the processing of an acceptable input string, the machine selects either a shift or one of the reduce operations. If the handle of the represented intermediate string corresponds to the top stack symbols, the machine performs the reduce corresponding to the handle production. If the handle is not on top of the stack, the machine performs a shift. At the last step, when the represented string is the starting symbol, the machine accepts.

For the grammar of Fig. 11.1, the presence of a handle on top of the stack is trivial to detect because each righthand side ends with a right parenthesis. The handle itself begins with the preceding left parenthesis. The identity of the handle production is also trivial to determine because each of the parenthesized righthand sides is different from any of the others.

For other grammars, the decisions are less obvious, and the designer must exploit more subtle properties of the grammar. Chapters 12 and 13 are devoted to the discussion of such properties. For some grammars, there is no way for a pushdown machine to detect or identify handles, and the designer must resort to a different grammar or another processing method.

For any bottom-up machine designed in this book, the sequence of shift and reduce operations performed while processing acceptable input strings can be described by a translation grammar. The input grammar of the translation grammar is the underlying grammar of the machine. The translation grammar has an action symbol {REDUCE(p)} for each production p. This action symbol is inserted at the right end of the righthand side of production p. For the grammar of Fig. 11.1, the translation grammar is the grammar of Fig. 11.13. If each input symbol in an activity sequence is thought of as representing the SHIFT performed when that symbol is the current input, then the activity sequence describes exactly the sequence of shift and reduce operations performed during the processing of the input string. For the sample input sequence

$$(((b) a (a)) (b))$$

analyzed in Figs. 11.5 and 11.11, the corresponding activity sequence using the grammar of Fig. 11.13 is:

$$(((b) \text{ \{REDUCE(2)\} } a (a) \text{ \{REDUCE(4)\} })$$
$$\text{\{REDUCE(3)\} } (b) \text{ \{REDUCE(2)\} }) \text{ \{REDUCE(1)\} }$$

It can be seen that the 19 symbols in this activity sequence match the sequence of 19 shift and reduce operations shown in the two figures. For example, the sixth symbol in the sequence is {REDUCE(2)}, the operation associated with line 6. The seventh symbol is a and the operation associated with line 7 is the SHIFT performed when the corresponding a is the current input. The reason the activity sequences describe the sequence of shift and reduce operations is that each reduce is performed immediately after the corresponding handle is pushed on the stack, which is also immediately after the processing of the rightmost symbol in the righthand side is completed.

In this book, we concentrate on machines which select shift and reduce operations by one of two methods. One method, which we call the "shift-

1. $\langle S \rangle \rightarrow (\langle A \rangle \langle S \rangle)$ {REDUCE(1)}
2. $\langle S \rangle \rightarrow (b)$ {REDUCE(2)}
3. $\langle A \rangle \rightarrow (\langle S \rangle a \langle A \rangle)$ {REDUCE(3)}
4. $\langle A \rangle \rightarrow (a)$ {REDUCE(4)}

Starting symbol: $\langle S \rangle$

Figure 11.13

identify method," is illustrated by the machine of Section 11.3. The other, which we call the "shift-reduce method," is illustrated by the machine of Section 11.4.

In the *shift-identify method,* we use the grammatical symbols as stack symbols. At each step in the processing, on the basis of the top stack symbol and the current input, the machine selects either SHIFT, REJECT, or an identify routine. Each identify routine may look at several of the symbols on top of the stack and on the basis of these symbols perform a reduce operation, ACCEPT, or REJECT. These routines are called identify routines because whenever a handle is on top of the stack, the handle production is identified by one of these routines. Note, however, that in Fig. 11.6, the routine IDENTIFY2 only chooses between ACCEPT and REJECT.

In the *shift-reduce method,* we use many stack symbols for each grammatical symbol. At each step in the processing, the machine uses the top stack symbol and current input to select among SHIFT, ACCEPT, REJECT, and REDUCE(p) for each production p. This selection implies a design in which enough information is encoded into the stack symbols to detect handles and identify handle productions without looking below the top stack symbol. However the encoded information need not be expressible as a "prefix" as was the case in Section 11.4. In the shift-reduce method, the shift and reduce operations must determine which stack symbol to push corresponding to a given grammatical symbol, and this decision is made using a *push table* which specifies which symbol if any to push for a particular combination of grammatical symbol and top stack symbol below the new symbol to be pushed. For certain combinations of top stack symbol and grammatical symbol, the push table may specify that the input string be rejected. Therefore the shift and reduce operations using the shift-reduce method differ from the shift and reduce operations using the shift-identify method in that the former consult a push table and may reject the input sequence.

11.6 POLISH TRANSLATIONS

We now describe how the pushdown recognizers discussed in the previous section can be extended to perform translations. Central to our discussion is the concept of a Polish translation grammar.

> A translation grammar is said to be a *Polish translation grammar* if
> and only if all the action symbols in each righthand side occur to the
> right of all the input and nonterminal symbols.

For example, Fig. 11.14 shows a Polish string translation grammar which has the grammar of Fig. 11.1 as input grammar. The term Polish is used by

1. $\langle S \rangle \rightarrow (\langle A \rangle \langle S \rangle) \{x\}$
2. $\langle S \rangle \rightarrow (b) \{z\}$
3. $\langle A \rangle \rightarrow (\langle S \rangle a \langle A \rangle) \{x\} \{y\}$
4. $\langle A \rangle \rightarrow (a)$

Starting symbol: $\langle S \rangle$

Figure 11.14

analogy with the translation grammar of Section 7.3 for translating the infix form of arithmetic expressions into the Polish form.

Given a Polish translation grammar and given a bottom-up pushdown recognizer which uses the input grammar in the manner described in the last section, the recognizer can easily be modified to perform the translation. The modification is to make each reduce operation perform the actions described by the action symbols in the corresponding production. In the case of Fig. 11.14, the recognizers of Sections 11.3 and 11.4 can be modified to perform the translation simply by having REDUCE(1) output x, REDUCE(2) output z, and REDUCE(3) output xy. Operation REDUCE(4) is not modified since there are no action symbols associated with production 4. The reason the modified machines work is that, as described in the last section, the calling of each REDUCE(p) can be described by appending {REDUCE(p)} to the right end of production p, the same position where the action symbols appear in a Polish translation grammar. Comparing for example Fig. 11.13 and 11.14, we see that {REDUCE(1)} occupies the same position as $\{x\}$, {REDUCE(2)} the same position as $\{z\}$, and {REDUCE(3)} the same position as $\{x\}$ $\{y\}$. Since in the processing of an input sequence, each REDUCE(p) operation is performed at the same time that the actions for production p are to be performed, the REDUCE operation can perform the actions.

In Summary

Given a Polish translation grammar whose input grammar can be used by a pushdown recognizer of the form described in Section 11.5, a pushdown device can be obtained to perform the translation. The pushdown translator is obtained from the recognizer by augmenting the reduce operations.

11.7   S-ATTRIBUTED GRAMMARS

We now describe how the pushdown recognizers discussed in the previous section can be extended to perform attributed translations. Central to our discussion is the concept of an S-attributed grammar.

An attributed translation grammar is called S-attributed if and only if the following three conditions hold:

1. All the attributes of the nonterminals are synthesized.

2. Each rule for a synthesized attribute is independent of the synthesized attributes of the symbol whose attribute is being specified.

3. Each rule for an inherited attribute depends only on attributes of symbols on the righthand side of the production that occur to the left of the symbol whose attribute is being specified.

(In terms of Section 9.2, an attributed grammar is S-attributed if and only if it is L-attributed and all the nonterminal attributes are synthesized.) The letter S in "S-attributed" stands for "synthesized" — a reminder that nonterminal attributes are synthesized.

When we say an attribute "depends only" on a certain set of attributes, we mean that the rule for computing the attribute can be expressed as a function of attributes from the set. This function need not involve all attributes from the set and may, in fact, be independent of all attributes. As an example, Fig. 11.15 shows an S-attributed version of Fig. 11.14. In production 1, the rule for attribute $r2$ "depends only" on attributes q, $r1$, and s, but is expressed as a function of $r1$ alone. Attribute p "depends only" on attributes q, $r1$, s, and $r2$, but is expressed as a function of $r1$ and s. In production 3, attribute v "depends only" on attributes p, $i1$, $q3$, r, s, t, and $i2$, but is expressed as a function involving no attributes. In production 4, attribute q depends only on attribute $r1$, but is expressed in terms of the parameterless function NEW.

Given an S-attributed Polish translation grammar and given a bottom-up pushdown recognizer which uses the input grammar in the manner of

All nonterminal attributes are SYNTHESIZED.
All action symbol attributes are INHERITED.

1. $\langle S \rangle_p \rightarrow (\langle A \rangle_{q,r1} \langle S \rangle_s) \{x_{r2}\}$
   $\qquad r2 \leftarrow r1 \qquad p \leftarrow r1 - s$

2. $\langle S \rangle_{p3} \rightarrow (b_{p1}) \{z_{p2}\}$
   $\qquad (p3, p2) \leftarrow p1$

3. $\langle A \rangle_{u,v} \rightarrow (\langle S \rangle_p \, a_{i1} \langle A \rangle_{q3,r}) \{x_s\} \{y_{t,i2}\}$
   $\qquad s \leftarrow p * r \qquad t \leftarrow s + q3 \qquad i2 \leftarrow i1 \qquad u \leftarrow r + 10 \qquad v \leftarrow 13$

4. $\langle A \rangle_{q,r2} \rightarrow (a_{r1})$
   $\qquad q \leftarrow \text{NEW} \qquad r2 \leftarrow r1$

Starting symbol: $\langle S \rangle$

Figure 11.15

Section 11.5, it is easy to augment the pushdown machine to perform the attributed translation. In the augmented machine each stack symbol consists of a *name part* and an associated set of *fields*. The fields of any symbol on the stack are storage locations which are available for storing and retrieving information during the lifetime of that symbol (i.e., from push to pop). For expository purposes, we imagine a stack symbol with n fields as being represented on the pushdown stack by $n + 1$ cells where the top cell contains the symbol name and the lower cells represent the fields. Figure 11.16 shows such a picture of stack

$$\nabla\ C\ A\ B\ A$$

where A has two fields, B one field, and C no fields.

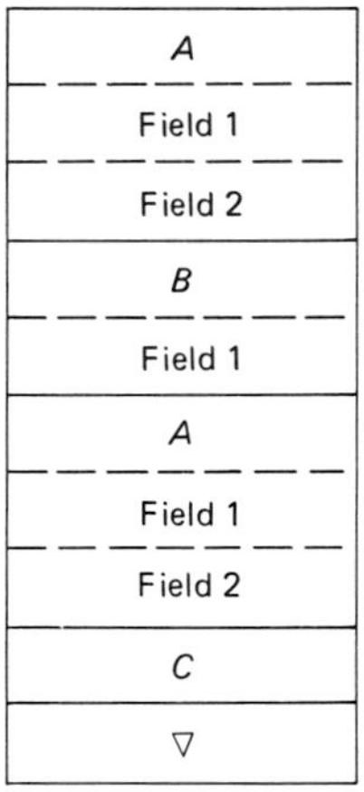

Figure 11.16

In the augmented processor, each stack symbol has an associated field for each attribute of the corresponding grammatical symbol. These fields are filled in with the attribute values at the time the symbol is pushed and remain unchanged during the lifetime of the symbol.

The shift operation is augmented so that the attributes of the current input are placed in the corresponding fields of the stack symbol which the shift operation pushes.

When the reduce operation for production p is selected the top stack symbols represent the righthand side of production p of the input grammar, and the fields contain the grammatical symbol attributes. The reduce operation is augmented to use these attributes to compute all action-symbol attributes associated with the production and all the attributes of the lefthand nonterminal. The action-symbol attributes are used to produce the desired output or perform the associated actions. The lefthand nonterminal attributes are used to fill in the fields of the symbol representing the lefthand nonterminal, which the reduce routine pushes on the stack.

Figure 11.17 shows an example of how an augmented form of the machine of Section 11.4 would perform the transition from line 13 to line 14 in Fig. 11.11. The figure assumes the attributed translation is the one shown in Fig. 11.15 and that previous operations have produced attribute values 2, 5, 3, and 7 as shown in the "before" stack. The transition is performed by an augmented REDUCE(3) operation. It replaces the righthand side of production 3 with the lefthand side and computes attribute values 15 and 13 for the lefthand side and 35, 37, and 3 for the outputs. The attributed outputs are produced and the attributes of the lefthand side are placed in the fields of the new stack symbol $\langle A \rangle_1$.

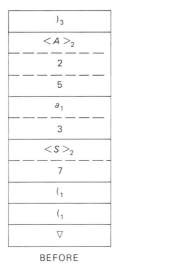
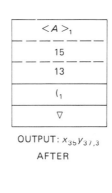

Figure 11.17

In Summary

Given an S-attributed Polish translation grammar whose input grammar can be used by a pushdown recognizer of the form described in Section 11.5, a pushdown device can be designed to perform the translation. The pushdown translator is obtained from the recognizer by adding fields to the stack symbols and augmenting the shift and reduce operations.

PROBLEMS

1. According to the grammar of Fig. 11.1, find the handle, if any, of each of the following strings.

   a) $(\ \langle A \rangle \ \langle S \rangle \ )$

   b) $\langle A \rangle$

   c) $(\ a\ )$

   d) $\langle S \rangle$

   e) $(\ \langle A \rangle \ (\ (\ \langle S \rangle \ a \ \langle A \rangle \ )\ (\ b\ )\ )\ )$

   f) $(\ \langle A \rangle \ (\ (\ a\ )\ \langle S \rangle \ )\ )$

   g) $(\ a\ )\ (\ b\ )$

2. a) Show that the grammar of Fig. 11.1 is not LL(1).

   b) Draw the stack movie as the machine of Section 11.3 processes the sequence:

   $$(\ (\ (\ (\ a\ )\ (\ b\ )\ )\ a\ (\ a\ )\ )\ (\ b\ )\ )$$

   c) Draw the stack movie as the machine of Section 11.4 processes the sequence of Part b).

3. A bottom-up processor for the following grammar

   1. $\langle S \rangle \rightarrow \langle S \rangle \ \langle S \rangle \ a$
   2. $\langle S \rangle \rightarrow \langle S \rangle \ b$
   3. $\langle S \rangle \rightarrow \langle S \rangle \ \langle S \rangle \ \langle S \rangle \ c$
   4. $\langle S \rangle \rightarrow d$

   recognizes the productions in a given sequence in the order:

   $$4,\ 4,\ 4,\ 1,\ 4,\ 4,\ 1,\ 3,\ 2$$

   a) What is that sequence?

   b) In what order would a top-down processor processing the sequence recognize the productions?

4. The following stack movie corresponds to a bottom-up pushdown recognizer. Draw the derivation tree for the input sequence of the movie.

∇	$e\ c\ d\ a\ e\ a\ c\ b\ b \dashv$
$\nabla\ e$	$c\ d\ a\ e\ a\ c\ b\ b \dashv$
$\nabla\ \langle A \rangle$	$c\ d\ a\ e\ a\ c\ b\ b \dashv$
$\nabla\ \langle A \rangle\ c$	$d\ a\ e\ a\ c\ b\ b \dashv$
$\nabla\ \langle A \rangle\ \langle S \rangle$	$d\ a\ e\ a\ c\ b\ b \dashv$
$\nabla\ \langle A \rangle\ \langle S \rangle\ d$	$a\ e\ a\ c\ b\ b \dashv$
$\nabla\ \langle A \rangle$	$a\ e\ a\ c\ b\ b \dashv$
$\nabla\ \langle A \rangle\ a$	$e\ a\ c\ b\ b \dashv$
$\nabla\ \langle A \rangle\ a\ e$	$a\ c\ b\ b \dashv$
$\nabla\ \langle A \rangle\ a\ \langle A \rangle$	$a\ c\ b\ b \dashv$

$$\nabla \langle A \rangle \, a \, \langle A \rangle \, a \qquad\qquad c\,b\,b \dashv$$
$$\nabla \langle A \rangle \, a \, \langle A \rangle \, a\,c \qquad\qquad b\,b \dashv$$
$$\nabla \langle A \rangle \, a \, \langle A \rangle \, a \, \langle S \rangle \qquad\qquad b\,b \dashv$$
$$\nabla \langle A \rangle \, a \, \langle A \rangle \, a \, \langle S \rangle \, b \qquad\qquad b \dashv$$
$$\nabla \langle A \rangle \, a \, \langle S \rangle \qquad\qquad b \dashv$$
$$\nabla \langle A \rangle \, a \, \langle S \rangle \, b \qquad\qquad \dashv$$
$$\nabla \langle S \rangle \qquad\qquad \dashv$$

5. The sentence generated by the following tree is being recognized bottom-up by a pushdown machine. Draw the pruned tree after the machine has made six reductions.

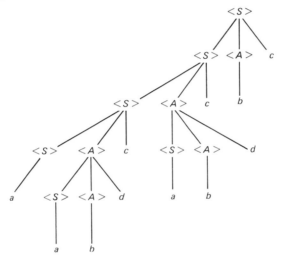

6. A *marked right-parenthesis* grammar is a context-free grammar in which the righthand side of each production ends with a distinct terminal symbol and each of these terminals occurs nowhere else in the grammar.

   Show that a language that has a marked right-parenthesis grammar can be recognized by a shift-identify parser.

7. Which of the entries in the control table of Fig. 11.6 could be changed to REJECT without changing the language recognized by the machine.

8. The following stacks are constructed from the stack alphabet of Fig. 11.8. For which of these stacks is the encoded string of each stack symbol consistent with the string represented by the stack?

   a) ∇

   b) $\nabla \, (_1 \, \langle S \rangle_1 \, a_1 \, \langle A \rangle_2$

   c) $\nabla \, (_1 \, (_1 \, (_1 \, (_1 \, (_1$

   d) $\nabla \, (_1 \, \langle A \rangle_1 \, \langle S \rangle_1 \,)_1$

9. a) Which entries in the push table of Fig. 11.9 could be changed to REJECT without changing the language recognized by the machine?

   b) Which entries in the control table of Fig. 11.10 could be changed to REJECT without changing the language recognized by the machine?

10. A *parenthesis grammar* is a context-free grammar in which the righthand side of each production begins with a left parenthesis and ends with a right parenthesis, and in which no parenthesis occurs elsewhere in the grammar.

   An *invertible grammar* is one in which no two productions have the same righthand side.

   a) Show that any language that has an invertible parenthesis grammar can be recognized by a shift-identify parser.

   b) Show that any language that has a parenthesis grammar can be recognized by a pushdown machine.

11. The following push table was designed for the shift-reduce parser of a parenthesis grammar. (See the previous problem.) Find the grammar.

	a	$,$	$($	$)$	$\langle S \rangle$
$\text{›}1$			$(_1$		$\langle S \rangle_2$
a_1			$(_1$	$)_3$	
$(_1$	a_1		$(_1$		$\langle S \rangle_1$
$\langle S \rangle_1$		$\text{›}1$	$(_1$	$)_1$	
$\langle S \rangle_2$			$(_1$	$)_2$	
$\langle S \rangle_3$			$(_1$		
$\triangledown$			$(_1$		$\langle S \rangle_3$

12. Design a shift-identify parser and a shift-reduce parser for the following grammar with starting symbol $\langle S \rangle$.

$$\langle S \rangle \to a \, \langle S \rangle \, \langle A \rangle \, 1$$
$$\langle S \rangle \to a \, \langle A \rangle \, 1$$
$$\langle S \rangle \to a \, \langle S \rangle \, 0$$
$$\langle A \rangle \to b \, \langle A \rangle \, \langle S \rangle \, 0$$
$$\langle A \rangle \to b \, \langle A \rangle \, \langle A \rangle \, 1$$
$$\langle A \rangle \to a \, b \, 0$$

13. Design a shift-reduce parser for the following grammar.

$$\langle S \rangle \to 1 \, \langle S \rangle \, 1$$
$$\langle S \rangle \to 0 \, \langle S \rangle \, 0$$
$$\langle S \rangle \to 2$$

14. A certain grammar has productions:

   a) $p_1, p_2,$ and p_3, with righthand sides consisting of a single terminal and two nonterminals;

b) p_4, p_5, and p_6, with righthand sides consisting of a single terminal.

When a particular sentence in the language is parsed top-down according to that grammar, the order in which the productions are recognized is

$$P_1 \, P_2 \, P_4 \, P_3 \, P_5 \, P_6 \, P_2 \, P_4 \, P_1 \, P_5 \, P_6$$

If this same sentence is parsed bottom-up according to that grammar, in what order would the productions be recognized?

15. Show that if a grammar is LL(1), a pushdown machine processing top down can input a string generated by the grammar and output the sequence of production numbers in the order they would be recognized by a pushdown machine processing bottom up.

16. Given any unambiguous grammar show how to find a translation grammar which describes the translation of any sentence in the language into a sequence of production names used in its derivation in the order these productions would be recognized by a:

a) top-down parser,

b) bottom-up parser.

17. Consider the following grammar that generates LISP S-expressions in dot notation:

1. $\langle S \rangle \rightarrow (\langle S \rangle . \langle S \rangle)$
2. $\langle S \rangle \rightarrow a$

a) Design a shift-identify parser for this grammar.

b) Design a shift-reduce parser for this grammar.

c) For the parser of Part a), design a set of error messages to be put out by the identify routine when it detects an error.

d) For the parser of Part b), design error messages for the REJECT entries in the push table.

18. Assume that in addition to popping and pushing, a reduce operation can also advance the current input.

a) Modify the machine of Fig. 11.6 so that it never pushes a right parenthesis on the stack.

b) Draw the stack movie as the modified machine processes the input string:

$$(((b) a (a)) (b))$$

19. Show the stack movie as the sequence:

$$((((a) (b)) a (a)) (b))$$

is processed by a shift-reduce processor

a) designed by the methods of Section 11.6, for the Polish translation grammar of Fig. 11.14;

b) designed by the methods of Section 11.7, for the attributed Polish translation grammar of Fig. 11.15. Assume values for input symbol attributes.

20. Consider the following S-attributed translation grammar with starting symbol $\langle S \rangle$. Nonterminal $\langle S \rangle$ has one attribute and nonterminal $\langle A \rangle$ has two.

1. $\langle S \rangle_x \rightarrow (\langle A \rangle_{u,v} \, a_y) \{ d_z \}$
   $\qquad z \leftarrow u * v + y \qquad x \leftarrow 3$

2. $\langle S \rangle_x \rightarrow (b_y \, \langle S \rangle_u) \{ f_v \} \{ d_z \}$
   $\qquad v \leftarrow y \qquad z \leftarrow v - 2 \qquad x \leftarrow u + z$

3. $\langle A \rangle_{x,y} \rightarrow (a_z \, b_u \, \langle S \rangle_v)$
   $\qquad x \leftarrow z + u - v \qquad y \leftarrow u$

4. $\langle A \rangle_{x,y} \rightarrow (\ )$
   $\qquad x \leftarrow 1 \qquad y \leftarrow 2$

a) Design a shift-identify processor for this grammar.

b) Design a shift-reduce processor for this grammar.

21. Consider the following grammar for arithmetic expressions

$$\langle E \rangle \rightarrow (\langle E \rangle + \langle E \rangle)$$
$$\langle E \rangle \rightarrow (\langle E \rangle * \langle E \rangle)$$
$$\langle E \rangle \rightarrow I$$

Assume I is a token whose value part is a pointer to a table entry for an identifier. We wish to translate strings in this language into strings composed of the atoms $\text{ADD}_{p,q,r}$ and $\text{MULT}_{p,q,r}$, where p, q, r are pointers to table entries for the left operand, right operand, and result.

a) Design an S-attributed Polish translation grammar to specify this translation.

b) Design a bottom-up processor to carry out this translation.

22. Consider the following translation grammar with starting symbol $\langle S \rangle$.

1. $\langle S \rangle \rightarrow \langle E \rangle \{ \text{ANSWER} \}$
2. $\langle E \rangle \rightarrow \langle P \rangle$
3. $\langle E \rangle \rightarrow \langle E \rangle + \langle P \rangle$
4. $\langle E \rangle \rightarrow \langle E \rangle - \langle P \rangle$
5. $\langle P \rangle \rightarrow c$
6. $\langle P \rangle \rightarrow (\langle E \rangle)$

a) Assume c is a token representing a constant and has a value part which is the value of the constant. Add attributes to this grammar so that $\{ \text{ANSWER} \}$ has an attribute that is equal to the numerical value of the expression.

b) Design an augmented bottom-up processor for the grammar of Part a).

23. Show that given any translation grammar, there is a Polish translation grammar that defines the same translation.

24. Suppose the input grammar for Problem 7.24 is changed to the following:

1. $\langle \text{conditional statement} \rangle \rightarrow \langle \text{if clause} \rangle \langle \text{unconditional statement} \rangle$
2. $\langle \text{conditional statement} \rangle \rightarrow \langle \text{full conditional} \rangle \langle \text{statement} \rangle$

3. ⟨full conditional⟩ → ⟨if clause⟩ ⟨unconditional statement⟩ **else**

4. ⟨if clause⟩ → **if** ⟨boolean expression⟩ **then**

   a) Design a bottom-up recognizer based on the above grammar.

   b) Add action symbols and attributes to the grammar so as to obtain an S-attributed Polish translation grammar specifying the translation described in Problem 7.24.

   c) Design the augmented processor based on the grammar of Part b).

25. For the grammar of Fig. 11.1 design a bottom-up pushdown machine parser which has the prefix property for errors (Section 8.8). Use a stack alphabet that encodes more information than that of Fig. 11.8.

26. a) Give an example of an ambiguous grammar for which every string has at most one handle.

   b) Give an example of an ambiguous grammar for which every string has at most one handle production.

   c) Show that a grammar is unambiguous if and only if each string has at most one handle and one handle production.

27. Design an S-attributed Polish translation grammar that specifies the translation described in each of the following problems. In each case a different input grammar must be designed.

   a) Problem 7.25

   b) Problem 9.11

   c) Problem 9.27

12
Shift-Identify
Processing

12.1   INTRODUCTION

In the last chapter we discussed two methods of bottom-up parsing, the shift-identify method and the shift-reduce method. In this chapter, we consider a specific kind of pushdown processor that uses the shift-identify method. We refer to these machines as SHIFT-IDENTIFY machines. To be more specific, when we refer to a SHIFT-IDENTIFY machine for a given grammar, we refer to a machine in which:

1. The stack symbols of the machine are the grammatical symbols of the given grammar and the bottommarker.

2. The input symbols of the machine are the terminal symbols of the given grammar and the endmarker.

3. The control of the machine is specified by a SHIFT-IDENTIFY control table which specifies SHIFT, REJECT, or an identify routine for each combination of stack and input symbol.

4. Each identify routine looks at several of the top stack symbols and selects either REDUCE for one of the productions or ACCEPT or REJECT.

5. During the processing of an acceptable input string, the string represented by the stack contents and the unprocessed inputs is an intermediate string in a rightmost derivation of the original input string. The control selects an identify routine whenever the handle of the represented string is on top of the stack or the current input is endmarker; otherwise, the control selects SHIFT.

Throughout this chapter, we assume we are dealing with unambiguous grammars which have no ε-productions. Therefore, we can talk about *the* rightmost derivation. We also assume that dead and unreachable nonterminals have been eliminated from the grammar.

12.2   THE SHIFT-IDENTIFY CONTROL

We are interested in methods for designing a SHIFT-IDENTIFY machine given a particular grammar. It is convenient to think of the design problem as consisting of two parts. The first (considered in this section) is to decide which entries of the SHIFT-IDENTIFY control table are to contain SHIFT, which are to contain identify routines, and which are to contain REJECT. The second part of the design problem, finding suitable identify routines, is discussed in later sections.

Assume now that we have a SHIFT-IDENTIFY machine for a given grammar with starting symbol $\langle S \rangle$. At each step in the processing of a given input sequence by the SHIFT-IDENTIFY machine, exactly one of the four following assertions is true:

1. The input is acceptable and the top of the stack represents the handle of the string represented by the stack and unprocessed inputs.

2. The input is acceptable, the stack is $\nabla \langle S \rangle$, and the current input is the endmarker.

3. The input is acceptable, the current input is not the endmarker, and the top of the stack does not represent the handle of the represented string.

4. The input is not acceptable.

Whenever the machine reaches a configuration described by the first two assertions, it must select an identify routine. This selection is made by the control table, solely on the basis of the top stack symbol and current input symbol. Suppose now that a situation corresponding to assertion 1 or assertion 2 does arise with a given combination of stack symbol and input symbol. Since the machine must select an identify routine in this situation, the control table entry for the given combination of stack symbol and input symbol must be designed to contain an identify routine. In general, for each combination of stack and input symbols occurring in situations described by assertion 1 or 2, the control table must be designed to select an identify routine.

Whenever the machine reaches a configuration described by assertion 3, the machine must select SHIFT. Therefore, the control-table entries for the combinations of stack and input symbols occurring in configurations described by assertion 3 must contain SHIFT.

It might seem that configurations described by situation 4 would imply that certain control-table entries must contain REJECT, but this is not the case. In fact there are no control implications for these configurations because, if an input sequence cannot be derived from $\langle S \rangle$, no combination of shift and reduce operations can convert the initial represented string (the original input string) into the represented string $\langle S \rangle$. Thus, no matter how the control table entries are filled in with SHIFT, REJECT, and identify routines, all unacceptable inputs will be rejected.

To decide which SHIFT-IDENTIFY control-table entries should contain SHIFT and which should contain identify routines, the designer must analyze the grammar to anticipate which table entries could occur in configurations covered by assertions 1 and 2, and which entries could occur in configurations covered by assertion 3. For some grammars, the analysis indicates that a table entry can occur in both a situation described by assertions 1 or 2 and a situation described by assertion 3. In such an event, the above arguments indicate the table entry must contain both SHIFT and an identify routine. In this case, the given grammar cannot be processed by a SHIFT-IDENTIFY control, and the designer must resort to some other grammar or type of machine.

As an aid in the grammatical analysis, we use the concepts of follow and first sets.

Given a context-free grammar with starting symbol $\langle S \rangle$ and grammatical symbol x,

1. we define

   FOLLOW(x)

to be the set of input symbols (possibly including $\dashv$) that can immediately follow an x in an intermediate string derived from $\langle S \rangle \dashv$, and

2. we define

   FIRST(x)

to be the set of those grammatical symbols that occur at the beginning of intermediate strings derived from x.

Except for trivial differences, these are the definitions of FOLLOW and FIRST from Chapter 8 and can be computed if desired by the methods of Section 8.7. The calculations are simplified by the absence of ϵ-productions. In Section 8.6, FIRST is defined for sequences whereas here we are only interested in the FIRST of single symbols. We also include nonterminals in the FIRST sets whereas we were only interested in terminals in Chapter 8.

1. $\langle S \rangle \rightarrow b \langle A \rangle \langle S \rangle \langle B \rangle$
2. $\langle S \rangle \rightarrow b \langle A \rangle$
3. $\langle A \rangle \rightarrow d \langle S \rangle c \, a$
4. $\langle A \rangle \rightarrow e$
5. $\langle B \rangle \rightarrow c \langle A \rangle a$
6. $\langle B \rangle \rightarrow c$

Starting symbol: $\langle S \rangle$

Figure 12.1

$\text{FIRST}(\langle S \rangle) = \{b, \langle S \rangle\}$ $\text{FOLLOW}(\langle S \rangle) = \{c, \dashv\}$
$\text{FIRST}(\langle A \rangle) = \{d, e, \langle A \rangle\}$ $\text{FOLLOW}(\langle A \rangle) = \{a, b, c, \dashv\}$
$\text{FIRST}(\langle B \rangle) = \{c, \langle B \rangle\}$ $\text{FOLLOW}(\langle B \rangle) = \{c, \dashv\}$
$\text{FIRST}(a) = \{a\}$ $\text{FOLLOW}(a) = \{a, b, c, \dashv\}$
$\text{FIRST}(b) = \{b\}$ $\text{FOLLOW}(b) = \{d, e\}$
$\text{FIRST}(c) = \{c\}$ $\text{FOLLOW}(c) = \{a, c, d, e, \dashv\}$
$\text{FIRST}(d) = \{d\}$ $\text{FOLLOW}(d) = \{b\}$
$\text{FIRST}(e) = \{e\}$ $\text{FOLLOW}(e) = \{a, b, c, \dashv\}$

Figure 12.2

The first and follow sets for the symbols in the grammar of Fig. 12.1 are given in Fig. 12.2. The computation of the first sets is trivial because each production begins with a terminal. Note that each grammatical symbol is in its own first set.

The set $\text{FOLLOW}(\langle S \rangle)$ contains the endmarker because $\langle S \rangle$ is followed by $\dashv$ in sequence $\langle S \rangle \dashv$. The set also contains c because c follows the occurrence of $\langle S \rangle$ in production 3. Because of the $\langle S \rangle$ in the righthand side of production 1, the follow set also contains all the terminals in $\text{FIRST}(\langle B \rangle)$, but this set only contains c.

To compute $\text{FOLLOW}(\langle A \rangle)$, observe that $\langle A \rangle$ occurs on the righthand side of productions 1, 2, and 5. The occurrence in production 1 contributes the terminal symbols in $\text{FIRST}(\langle S \rangle)$, namely b. The occurrence in production 2 contributes the input symbols in $\text{FOLLOW}(\langle S \rangle)$, namely c and $\dashv$. The occurrence in production 5 contributes a.

The other follow sets can be computed in a similar manner.

Returning to the question of how the control table requirements can be deduced from a grammar, we consider the problem of designing a SHIFT-IDENTIFY control for the grammar of Fig. 12.1.

Many control-table entries can be filled in just by observing which righthand-side symbols appear exclusively as the rightmost symbol and which appear exclusively in other positions. For example, symbols b, d, and $\langle S \rangle$ do not occur anywhere as the rightmost symbol of a righthand side and thus b, d, $\langle S \rangle$, or ∇ as top stack symbols cannot be the rightmost symbol of a handle. Therefore, when one of these symbols is the top stack symbol, the pushdown machine can safely shift any input (other than endmarker), and the corresponding control-table entries can be designed accordingly.

The symbols a, e, and $\langle B \rangle$ occur exclusively on the extreme right of the production righthand sides; thus an a, e, or $\langle B \rangle$ as top stack symbol can only correspond to the rightmost symbol of a handle. Therefore the pushdown machine can safely call an identify routine when one of these symbols is the top stack symbol, and the corresponding control table can be designed to call identify routines.

Only when $\langle A \rangle$ or c is the top stack symbol is design by these simple considerations not possible. Nonterminal $\langle A \rangle$ occurs once as a rightmost symbol (production 2) and twice in other positions (productions 1 and 5). Terminal c also occurs as a rightmost symbol once and elsewhere twice. To design $\langle A \rangle$ and c rows of the control table, a deeper analysis must be made of configurations which might occur.

Figure 12.3 shows three machine configurations and their corresponding pruned derivation trees in which $\langle A \rangle$ is the top stack symbol. Figure 12.3(c)

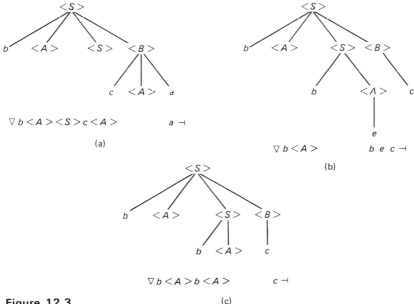

Figure 12.3

shows a situation in which assertion 1 is true and Figs. 12.3(a) and (b) show situations where assertion 3 holds. Figure 12.3(c) demonstrates that the row $\langle A \rangle$ control-table entry for input c must contain an identify routine and Figs. 12.3(a) and (b) demonstrate that the entries for inputs a and b must contain SHIFT. As designers, we want to know if other situations can occur which contradict the table-entry choices for inputs a, b, and c. We also want to know what choices may be mandated for inputs d and e.

First, we seek to find all inputs x such that the control table must have an identify routine for the row $\langle A \rangle$ column x entry. Thus we must find all input symbols x for which a situation corresponding to assertion 1 above can arise with top stack symbol $\langle A \rangle$ and input symbol x. Since the only righthand side occurrence of $\langle A \rangle$ that can end a handle is in production 2, we must find the input symbols that can follow the $\langle A \rangle$ from production 2 in a derivation starting from $\langle S \rangle$ $\dashv$. Because the lefthand side of production 2 is $\langle S \rangle$, *we are equivalently asking for the set of x such that x can follow any occurrence of $\langle S \rangle$ in a derivation.* For if $\langle S \rangle$ can be followed by x, substituting production 2 gives the desired $\langle A \rangle$ followed by x, and if the desired $\langle A \rangle$ is followed by x, the corresponding REDUCE(2) places lefthand side $\langle S \rangle$ next to x. The desired set of input symbols is FOLLOW($\langle S \rangle$). From Fig. 11.2

$$\text{FOLLOW}(\langle S \rangle) = \{c, \dashv\}$$

Thus the only inputs for which an identify routine is required are c and $\dashv$.

Now we seek to find all inputs y such that the control table in row $\langle A \rangle$ column y must contain SHIFT. These are the inputs that can follow occurrences of $\langle A \rangle$ from productions 1 and 5. The occurrence in production 5 can only be followed by an a, namely the a following the $\langle A \rangle$ in production 5. The occurrence of $\langle A \rangle$ in production 1 is followed by an occurrence of $\langle S \rangle$, and so the $\langle A \rangle$ can be followed by the input symbols in FIRST($\langle S \rangle$), namely b. Combining the two cases, we conclude that the only inputs for which SHIFT is required are a and b. We are now certain that the identify and SHIFT requirements do not conflict. We can also conclude that, during the processing of an acceptable input sequence, the row $\langle A \rangle$ entries for inputs d and e will not be used, and these entries may contain either REJECT, SHIFT, or an identify routine.

The above discussion illustrates two principles which we call the "reducing principle" and the "shifting principle." The *reducing principle* can be stated as follows:

Given a grammar, any SHIFT-IDENTIFY control table for the grammar must be designed to select an identify routine for stack symbol A and input symbol x whenever one of the two following conditions hold:

a) there is a nonterminal $\langle L \rangle$ and string α such that

$$\langle L \rangle \rightarrow \alpha\, A$$

is a production in the grammar and

$$x \text{ is in FOLLOW}(\langle L \rangle);$$

b) A is the starting symbol and x the endmarker

Furthermore, the control can be designed so that identify routines are only selected for the above cases.

It is often convenient to think of the reducing principle in terms of a relation REDUCED-BY determined as follows:

If A is a grammatical symbol and x an input symbol, we write

$$A \text{ REDUCED-BY } x$$

if and only if one of the two conditions given above in the reducing principle holds.

The definition of REDUCED-BY gives a method for computing the relation from the grammar using the calculation of FOLLOW as an intermediate step. This method is used below for the current example. A more direct method is presented in Section 12.6.

The *reducing principle* can now be stated more simply as

The SHIFT-IDENTIFY control must be designed to contain an identify routine for all combinations of stack symbol A and input symbol x such that:

$$A \text{ REDUCED-BY } x$$

No other table entries need contain an identify routine.

The *shifting principle* can be stated as follows:

Given a grammar, any SHIFT-IDENTIFY control table for the grammar must be designed to contain SHIFT for stack symbol A and input symbol x whenever one of the two following conditions hold:

a) There is a grammatical symbol B such that there is an occurrence of the string AB in the righthand side of some production and

$$x \text{ is in FIRST}(B);$$

b) A is the bottommarker and x is in FIRST($\langle S \rangle$) where $\langle S \rangle$ is the starting symbol.

Futhermore, the control can be designed so that SHIFT is only selected for the above cases.

It is often convenient to think of the shifting principle in terms of a relation BELOW defined as follows:

If A is a stack symbol and x an input symbol, we write

$$A \text{ BELOW } x$$

if and only if one of the two conditions given above in the shifting principle holds.

The definition of BELOW gives a method of computing the relation from the grammar using the calculation of FIRST as an intermediate step. This method is employed below for the current example. A more direct method is presented in Section 12.6.

The *shifting principle* can be stated more simply as:

The SHIFT-IDENTIFY control must be designed to contain SHIFT for all combinations of stack symbol A and input symbol x such that

$$A \text{ BELOW } x$$

No other table entries need contain SHIFT.

We say that a grammar has *SHIFT-IDENTIFY conflicts* if and only if there is a grammatical symbol A and a terminal symbol x such that both

$$A \text{ REDUCED-BY } x \text{ and } A \text{ BELOW } x.$$

A grammar with SHIFT-IDENTIFY conflicts cannot form the basis of a SHIFT-IDENTIFY machine, because the reducing and shifting principles together imply that the SHIFT-IDENTIFY control-table entry for stack symbol A and input x contains both an identify routine and SHIFT. This violates the requirement that the table specify a unique routine. If the grammar has no SHIFT-IDENTIFY conflicts, the reducing and shifting principles have the following implications for the control-table design:

1. entries for stack symbol A and input x such that A REDUCED-BY x must contain identify routines,

2. entries for stack symbol A and input x such that A BELOW x must contain SHIFT,

3. other entries may contain either REJECT, SHIFT, or identify routines, except that the endmarker must not be shifted.

Returning to the example, we now consider the control-table row for stack symbol c. Production 6 shows c as a rightmost symbol. The control table therefore needs identify routines for inputs in FOLLOW($\langle B \rangle$), namely c and $\dashv$. Production 3 shows an occurrence of c followed by a, so SHIFT is needed for inputs in FIRST(a), namely a itself. Production 5 shows c followed by $\langle A \rangle$, so SHIFT is also required for inputs in FIRST($\langle A \rangle$), namely d and e. We note that those inputs requiring SHIFT are different from those inputs requiring identify routines, so no conflicts arise in the construction for stack symbol c.

A full analysis is now possible for all control-table rows. We observed earlier, for example, that all entries in row $\langle B \rangle$ could be assigned identify routines but now we are able to distinguish between those entries that must contain identify routines and those which could optionally contain REJECT or SHIFT instead. The only inputs x such that

$$\langle B \rangle \text{ REDUCED-BY } x$$

are c and $\dashv$; so only these two table entries in the row must contain identify routines.

Figure 12.4 shows all control table implications for the example. The entries have been filled with SHIFT and IDENTIFY where required and filled with REJECT wherever a choice is permitted. A completed design would require that identify routines be supplied where the table says IDENTIFY.

12.3   SUFFIX-FREE SI GRAMMARS

We now begin our study of identify routines. We assume we have a grammar with no SHIFT-IDENTIFY conflicts since otherwise no SHIFT-IDENTIFY machine exists for the given grammar. The methods of the previous section

	a	b	c	d	e	$\dashv$
$<S>$	REJECT	REJECT	SHIFT	REJECT	REJECT	IDENTIFY
$<A>$	SHIFT	SHIFT	IDENTIFY	REJECT	REJECT	IDENTIFY
$<B>$	REJECT	REJECT	IDENTIFY	REJECT	REJECT	IDENTIFY
a	IDENTIFY	IDENTIFY	IDENTIFY	REJECT	REJECT	IDENTIFY
b	REJECT	REJECT	REJECT	SHIFT	SHIFT	REJECT
c	SHIFT	REJECT	IDENTIFY	SHIFT	SHIFT	IDENTIFY
d	REJECT	SHIFT	REJECT	REJECT	REJECT	REJECT
e	IDENTIFY	IDENTIFY	IDENTIFY	REJECT	REJECT	IDENTIFY
$\triangledown$	REJECT	SHIFT	REJECT	REJECT	REJECT	REJECT

Figure 12.4

specify *when* identify routines are to be called (i.e., for which combination of input and stack symbols); the objective of this and the next two sections is to decide *what* the identify routines should be in detail. From the previous section we know that an identify routine is called during the processing of an acceptable input sequence if and only if some of the top stack symbols represent a handle or (for the final step) if the stack is specifically the string $\nabla \langle S \rangle$.

Now consider a SHIFT-IDENTIFY machine for the grammar of Fig. 12.1. The righthand sides of the productions in this grammar have the property that no righthand side is a suffix of any other righthand side or of $\nabla \langle S \rangle$. Therefore *a string of stack symbols can end with at most one righthand side or* $\nabla \langle S \rangle$. For instance if a string of stack symbols ends with c, only production 6 matches the end of the string, regardless of what stack symbols are below the c. If a stack symbol string ends in $c \langle A \rangle a$, only production 5 matches the end of the string, regardless of the other stack symbols. If a stack symbol string ends in $\nabla \langle S \rangle$, no productions match the end of the string.

When an identify routine is selected during the processing of an acceptable input string, the top of the stack represents a handle or $\nabla \langle S \rangle$. The top of the stack must therefore match the righthand side of the handle production or $\nabla \langle S \rangle$. Because only one righthand side or $\nabla \langle S \rangle$ can be on top of the stack, the very presence of a righthand side on top of the stack indicates that the righthand side is, in fact, the handle. Therefore when an identify routine finds the righthand side of a production p on top of the stack, it must select REDUCE(p). Similarly, the presence of $\nabla \langle S \rangle$ on top of the stack is incompatible with there being a handle on the stack, and the correct action for an identify routine finding $\nabla \langle S \rangle$ on top of the stack is to ACCEPT if the current input is $\dashv$. In short, an identify routine need only ascertain which righthand side (or $\nabla \langle S \rangle$) matches the top of the stack and select the appropriate REDUCE (or ACCEPT).

Thus for the grammar of Fig. 12.1, it is possible to design a SHIFT-IDENTIFY recognizer with only a single identify routine. This routine is used in all control-table entries where an identify routine is required by the control-table analysis of the previous section. The routine simply checks the top several stack symbols to see if they match the righthand side of any of the productions or the string $\nabla \langle S \rangle$. If a match with the righthand side of a production p is found, the routine performs REDUCE(p). If the top two symbols are found to be $\nabla \langle S \rangle$, the routine checks to see if the current input is endmarker and accepts if it is. If none of the above occurs, the routine rejects. Thus the control table design of Fig. 12.4 could be completed with the following single identify routine.

if top of stack is $b \langle A \rangle \langle S \rangle \langle B \rangle$ then REDUCE(1)
  else if top of stack is $b \langle A \rangle$ then REDUCE(2)
  else if top of stack is $d \langle S \rangle c\ a$ then REDUCE(3)
  else if top of stack is e then REDUCE(4)
  else if top of stack is $c \langle A \rangle a$ then REDUCE(5)
  else if top of stack is c then REDUCE(6)
  else if top of stack is $\triangledown \langle S \rangle$ and current input is $\dashv$ then ACCEPT
  else REJECT

This "one-routine" method is not the only method of completing the design and has certain inefficiencies. A more efficient design is shown in Fig. 12.5, where a different identify routine has been supplied for each row of Fig. 12.4 containing an identify entry.

	a	b	c	d	e	$\dashv$
$\langle S \rangle$	REJECT	REJECT	SHIFT	REJECT	REJECT	IDENTIFY1
$\langle A \rangle$	SHIFT	SHIFT	IDENTIFY2	REJECT	REJECT	IDENTIFY2
$\langle B \rangle$	REJECT	REJECT	IDENTIFY3	REJECT	REJECT	IDENTIFY3
a	IDENTIFY4	IDENTIFY4	IDENTIFY4	REJECT	REJECT	IDENTIFY4
b	REJECT	REJECT	REJECT	SHIFT	SHIFT	REJECT
c	SHIFT	REJECT	IDENTIFY5	SHIFT	SHIFT	IDENTIFY5
d	REJECT	SHIFT	REJECT	REJECT	REJECT	REJECT
e	IDENTIFY6	IDENTIFY6	IDENTIFY6	REJECT	REJECT	IDENTIFY6
$\triangledown$	REJECT	SHIFT	REJECT	REJECT	REJECT	REJECT

Starting stack: $\triangledown$

SHIFT: PUSH(current input), ADVANCE

IDENTIFY1: if top of stack is $\triangledown < S >$ then ACCEPT
     else REJECT

IDENTIFY2: if top of stack is $b < A >$ then REDUCE(2)
     else REJECT

IDENTIFY3: if top of stack is $b < A > < S > < B >$ then REDUCE(1)
     else REJECT

IDENTIFY4: if top of stack is $d < S > c\ a$ then REDUCE(3)
     else if top of stack is $c < A > a$ then REDUCE(5)
     else REJECT

IDENTIFY5: REDUCE(6)

IDENTIFY6: REDUCE(4)

Figure 12.5

For example, routine IDENTIFY2 is called only when the top stack symbol is $\langle A \rangle$, and the routine is designed to take advantage of the fact that only the righthand side of production 2 has an $\langle A \rangle$ as rightmost symbol. The routine merely checks to see if the righthand side of production 2 is on top of the stack and reduces or rejects accordingly. IDENTIFY5 is only called when c is on top of the stack and the routine simply does REDUCE(6) since the c on top of the stack constitutes the complete righthand side of production 6. Routine IDENTIFY4 is the only one where a choice of productions is made, a choice between the two productions whose righthand sides end with a. The use of "if" statements in the figure is for convenience of description and is not intended to suggest a preferred implementation.

The above design methods work for a class of grammars which we call "suffix free." A string α is called a *suffix* of string β if β ends with the symbols of α. Note that in particular, every string is a suffix of itself and ϵ is a suffix of every string.

> We say that a grammar is *suffix free* if the righthand side of each production is not a suffix of the righthand side of any other production or a suffix of the string $\nabla \langle S \rangle$. We call a suffix-free grammar without SHIFT-IDENTIFY conflicts a *suffix-free SI grammar*.

As an example, the grammar of Fig. 12.1 is a suffix-free SI grammar.

The importance of suffix-free grammars is that for a SHIFT-IDENTIFY machine, the top of the stack can match the righthand side of at most one production (or $\nabla \langle S \rangle$) if and only if the grammar is suffix free.

In designing a SHIFT-IDENTIFY machine for a suffix-free SI grammar, the methods of the last section can be used to design the control table. Identify routines can then be designed which:

1. perform operation REDUCE(p) whenever the righthand side of p is on top of the stack;

2. accept if and only if the stack $\nabla \langle S \rangle$ (where $\langle S \rangle$ is the starting symbol) and the current input is endmarker.

The SHIFT-IDENTIFY design can always be completed by designing a single identify routine. Alternatively, one may decide to have a separate identify routine for each row, as in Fig. 12.5. A method for performing this second type of design is presented below. Although we say the procedure gives a "one-routine-per-row" design, it may produce two routines in the starting symbol row, one for input endmarker and one for other identify entries.

Given a suffix-free SI grammar, a SHIFT-IDENTIFY recognizer for that grammar can be obtained as follows.

1. Perform the analysis of Section 12.2 and determine which control-table entries are to contain identify routines.

2. For each row of the control table, introduce an identify-routine name to be entered in each entry of that control-table row which requires an identify routine (with the exception of the endmarker entry in the starting symbol row which is treated in step 3). This identify routine considers those right-hand sides whose rightmost symbol is the same as the symbol labeling the row and tries to match these righthand sides with the top stack symbols. If a match is found, the corresponding REDUCE operation is performed. Otherwise, the routine rejects.

3. Introduce an identify routine name to be entered in the control-table entry in the starting-symbol row and endmarker column. This identify routine accepts if the symbol immediately below the starting symbol is the bottommarker. Otherwise the routine proceeds as described in step 2 (and therefore rejects if no righthand sides end with the starting symbol).

We conclude the following:

Any suffix-free SI grammar can be used as the basis of a SHIFT-IDENTIFY recognizer for the language specified by the grammar.

12.4 WEAK-PRECEDENCE GRAMMARS

When a given grammar without SHIFT-IDENTIFY conflicts is not suffix free, a SHIFT-IDENTIFY control for the grammar will sometimes select an identify routine when several righthand sides match the top of the stack. For instance, suppose we are given the grammar of Fig. 12.6 and want to design an identify routine to be selected when the top stack symbol is $\langle T \rangle$. This identify routine must choose among REDUCE(1), REDUCE(2), and RE-JECT.

The righthand side of production 2 is a suffix of the righthand side of production 1. When the top three stack symbols form the string $\langle E \rangle + \langle T \rangle$,

1. $\langle E \rangle \rightarrow \langle E \rangle + \langle T \rangle$
2. $\langle E \rangle \rightarrow \langle T \rangle$
3. $\langle T \rangle \rightarrow \langle T \rangle * \langle P \rangle$
4. $\langle T \rangle \rightarrow \langle P \rangle$
5. $\langle P \rangle \rightarrow (\langle E \rangle)$
6. $\langle P \rangle \rightarrow a$

Starting symbol: $\langle E \rangle$

Figure 12.6

the righthand sides of productions 1 and 2 both match the top of the stack. Conceivably, on some occasions when $\langle E \rangle + \langle T \rangle$ is on top of the stack, production 1 is the handle production, and on other occasions production 2 is the handle production. However, suppose REDUCE(2) were performed when the top of the stack is $\langle E \rangle + \langle T \rangle$. The effect of REDUCE(2) would be to pop the $\langle T \rangle$ off the top of the stack (thereby exposing the $+$ as the top stack symbol) and then to push lefthand side $\langle E \rangle$ on top of the $+$.

The only occurrence of $+$ in the grammar of Fig. 12.6 is in production 1, and this occurrence is followed by the symbol $\langle T \rangle$. Therefore the only symbols that can be pushed on top of $+$ in the processing of an acceptable input string are symbols in FIRST($\langle T \rangle$). Inspecting the grammar, one can compute

$$\text{FIRST}(\langle T \rangle) = \{\langle T \rangle, \langle P \rangle, (, a\}$$

Since $\langle E \rangle$ is not in this set, we know that $\langle E \rangle$ cannot be pushed on top of $+$ during the processing of an acceptable input string and hence, when the top of the stack is $\langle E \rangle + \langle T \rangle$, production 2 is not the handle production. The identify routine can therefore be designed to select REDUCE(1) when the top of the stack is $\langle E \rangle + \langle T \rangle$.

To describe the principle illustrated by the above example, we extend relation BELOW as follows:

If A and x are symbols in some given grammar, we write

$$A \text{ BELOW } x$$

if and only if there is a grammatical symbol B such that string AB appears in the righthand side of some production of the grammar and x is in FIRST(B). If x is a grammatical symbol, we write

$$\nabla \text{ BELOW } x$$

if and only if x is in FIRST($\langle S \rangle$) where $\langle S \rangle$ is the starting symbol.

This definition agrees with that of Section 12.2 except that now nonterminal symbols are also permitted on the right side of BELOW. The "shifting principle" of Section 12.2 can now be generalized to the following *pushing principle:*

Given a SHIFT-IDENTIFY recognizer for a given grammar, and given two stack symbols A and x, there is an acceptable input sequence which causes an x to be pushed immediately above an A if and only if:

$$A \text{ BELOW } x$$

As illustrated in the above discussion of the example, the choice between righthand sides as possible handles can be resolved in favor of the longer righthand side when the relation BELOW can be used to show the impossibility of the shorter righthand side being the handle. The general principle can be stated as follows:

If a given grammar has two productions of the form

$$\langle A \rangle \rightarrow \alpha \; y \; \gamma$$
$$\langle B \rangle \rightarrow \gamma$$

where α and γ are strings and y is a grammatical symbol, and if it is false that y BELOW $\langle B \rangle$, then the second production cannot be the handle production when the righthand side of the first production is on top of the stack. Hence, the identify routines for a SHIFT-IDENTIFY machine based on the given grammar can be designed so that, when both righthand sides are on top of the stack, the reduce operation corresponding to the second production is not performed.

A grammar is known as a "weak-precedence grammar" if it has no SHIFT-IDENTIFY conflicts and if all identification problems resulting from suffixes can be resolved by the above design principle. Specifically,

A grammar is called a *weak-precedence grammar* if and only if the following four conditions hold:

1. The grammar has no SHIFT-IDENTIFY conflicts.

2. There are no two productions with identical righthand sides.

3. For any two productions of the form

$$\langle A \rangle \rightarrow \alpha \; y \; \gamma$$
$$\langle B \rangle \rightarrow \gamma$$

where α and γ are strings and y a grammatical symbol, it is false that
$$y \text{ BELOW } \langle B \rangle.$$

4. It is not true that $\langle S \rangle \overset{+}{\Rightarrow} \langle S \rangle$, where $\langle S \rangle$ is the starting symbol. (This condition is incorporated to exclude a particular kind of grammatical ambiguity not necessarily excluded by the other conditions. We said in Section 12.1 that all grammars dealt with in this chapter are assumed to be unambiguous. With condition 4 included in the definition of weak-precedence grammars, any grammar satisfying the definition is guaranteed to be unambiguous.)

A SHIFT-IDENTIFY machine can be designed for a given weak-precedence grammar in the same manner as for suffix-free SI grammars except that the identify routines must be designed to perform the REDUCE operation corresponding to the longest righthand side on top of the stack. The identify routines can test for the longer righthand side first, so one might write:

> if top of stack is $\langle E \rangle + \langle T \rangle$ then REDUCE(1)
>
> else if top of stack is $\langle T \rangle$ then REDUCE(2)

but it would be incorrect to write:

> if top of stack is $\langle T \rangle$ then REDUCE(2)
>
> else if top of stack is $\langle E \rangle + \langle T \rangle$ then REDUCE(1).

Returning to the example, the FIRST and FOLLOW sets of each non-terminal in Fig. 12.6 are shown in Fig. 12.7. The BELOW relation for the grammar is shown by the matrix in Fig. 12.8. As discussed above, $+$ BELOW $\langle E \rangle$ does not hold so the suffix conflict between productions 1 and 2 can be resolved in favor of the longer production. Similarly, $*$ BELOW $\langle T \rangle$ does not hold so the suffix conflict between productions 3 and 4 can be resolved in favor of the longer production. Since there are no other suffix conflicts and since the grammar has no SHIFT-IDENTIFY conflicts, the grammar is a weak-precedence grammar. Figure 12.9 shows a SHIFT-IDENTIFY machine for this grammar. The machine is designed by the one-identify-routine-per-row method of the previous section. Note that routines IDENTIFY2 and IDENTIFY3 check for the longer righthand side first.

Because the design methods for suffix-free SI grammar generalize to weak-precedence grammars, we conclude

> Any weak-precedence grammar can be used as the basis of a SHIFT-IDENTIFY recognizer for the language specified by the grammar.

$$\text{FIRST}(\langle E \rangle) = \{ (, a, \langle E \rangle, \langle T \rangle, \langle P \rangle \}$$
$$\text{FIRST}(\langle T \rangle) = \{ (, a, \langle T \rangle, \langle P \rangle \}$$
$$\text{FIRST}(\langle P \rangle) = \{ (, a, \langle P \rangle \}$$
$$\text{FOLLOW}(\langle E \rangle) = \{ +,), \dashv \}$$
$$\text{FOLLOW}(\langle T \rangle) = \{ +, *,), \dashv \}$$
$$\text{FOLLOW}(\langle P \rangle) = \{ +, *,), \dashv \}$$

Figure 12.7

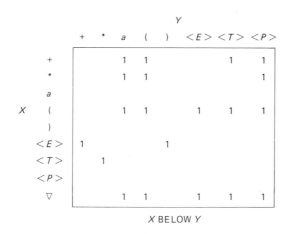

Figure 12.8

	+	*	a	(	)	⊣
<E>	SHIFT	REJECT	REJECT	REJECT	SHIFT	IDENTIFY1
<T>	IDENTIFY2	SHIFT	REJECT	REJECT	IDENTIFY2	IDENTIFY2
<P>	IDENTIFY3	IDENTIFY3	REJECT	REJECT	IDENTIFY3	IDENTIFY3
+	REJECT	REJECT	SHIFT	SHIFT	REJECT	REJECT
*	REJECT	REJECT	SHIFT	SHIFT	REJECT	REJECT
a	IDENTIFY4	IDENTIFY4	REJECT	REJECT	IDENTIFY4	IDENTIFY4
(	REJECT	REJECT	SHIFT	SHIFT	REJECT	REJECT
)	IDENTIFY5	IDENTIFY5	REJECT	REJECT	IDENTIFY5	IDENTIFY5
▽	REJECT	REJECT	SHIFT	SHIFT	REJECT	REJECT

Starting stack: ▽

IDENTIFY1: if top of stack is ▽ <E> then ACCEPT else REJECT

IDENTIFY2: if top of stack is <E>+<T> then REDUCE(1)
            else REDUCE(2)

IDENTIFY3: if top of stack is <T>*<P> then REDUCE(3)
            else REDUCE(4)

IDENTIFY4: REDUCE(6)

IDENTIFY5: if top of stack is (<E>) then REDUCE(5)
            else REJECT

SHIFT: PUSH current input, ADVANCE

Figure 12.9

12.5 SIMPLE MIXED-STRATEGY-PRECEDENCE GRAMMARS

When a given grammar meets all the conditions for being a weak precedence grammar except that several productions have the same righthand side, it might still be possible to process the grammar with a SHIFT-IDENTIFY machine. In this section we investigate the strategy of allowing the machine to look at the stack symbol below a righthand side that is common to more than one production. For instance, suppose we are given the grammar of Fig. 12.10. The first and follow sets for the grammar are shown in Fig. 12.11. The relation BELOW is shown in Fig. 12.12, and the control-table specifications implied by the relations are shown in Fig. 12.13. There are no SHIFT-IDENTIFY conflicts. The grammar is not a weak-precedence grammar because productions 1 and 7 have the same righthand side $\langle B \rangle$ v and because productions 3 and 5 have the same righthand side u. To design identify routines for this grammar, some means must be found for selecting the handle production when the top of the stack is $\langle B \rangle$ v and when the top of the stack is u.

$$1. \ \langle S \rangle \rightarrow \langle B \rangle \ v$$
$$2. \ \langle S \rangle \rightarrow v \langle C \rangle$$
$$3. \ \langle A \rangle \rightarrow u$$
$$4. \ \langle A \rangle \rightarrow v \langle B \rangle \langle S \rangle$$
$$5. \ \langle B \rangle \rightarrow u$$
$$6. \ \langle B \rangle \rightarrow yw$$
$$7. \ \langle C \rangle \rightarrow \langle B \rangle \ v$$
$$8. \ \langle C \rangle \rightarrow y \langle A \rangle \ w$$

Starting symbol: $\langle S \rangle$

Figure 12.10

$\text{FIRST}(\langle S \rangle) = \{\langle S \rangle, \langle B \rangle, u, v, y\}$ $\text{FOLLOW}(\langle S \rangle) = \{w, \dashv\}$

$\text{FIRST}(\langle A \rangle) = \{\langle A \rangle, u, v\}$ $\text{FOLLOW}(\langle A \rangle) = \{w\}$

$\text{FIRST}(\langle B \rangle) = \{\langle B \rangle, u, y\}$ $\text{FOLLOW}(\langle B \rangle) = \{u, v, y\}$

$\text{FIRST}(\langle C \rangle) = \{\langle B \rangle, \langle C \rangle, u, y\}$ $\text{FOLLOW}(\langle C \rangle) = \{w, \dashv\}$

$\text{FIRST}(u) = \{u\}$ $\text{FOLLOW}(u) = \{u, v, w, y\}$

$\text{FIRST}(v) = \{v\}$ $\text{FOLLOW}(v) = \{u, w, y, \dashv\}$

$\text{FIRST}(w) = \{w\}$ $\text{FOLLOW}(w) = \{u, v, w, y, \dashv\}$

$\text{FIRST}(y) = \{y\}$ $\text{FOLLOW}(y) = \{u, v, w\}$

Figure 12.11

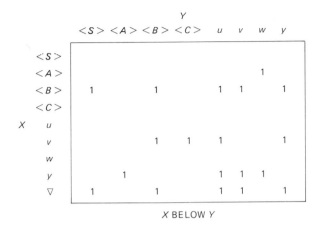

X BELOW Y

Figure 12.12

	u	v	w	y	⊣
<S>	REJECT	REJECT	IDENTIFY	REJECT	IDENTIFY
<A>	REJECT	REJECT	SHIFT	REJECT	REJECT
<B>	SHIFT	SHIFT	REJECT	SHIFT	REJECT
<C>	REJECT	REJECT	IDENTIFY	REJECT	IDENTIFY
u	IDENTIFY	IDENTIFY	IDENTIFY	IDENTIFY	REJECT
v	SHIFT	REJECT	IDENTIFY	SHIFT	IDENTIFY
w	IDENTIFY	IDENTIFY	IDENTIFY	IDENTIFY	IDENTIFY
y	SHIFT	SHIFT	SHIFT	REJECT	REJECT
▽	SHIFT	SHIFT	REJECT	SHIFT	REJECT

Figure 12.13

First, consider the situation when $\langle B \rangle v$ is on top of the stack and the control selects an identify routine. The identify routine must select RE-DUCE(1) if production 1 is the handle production or REDUCE(7) if production 7 is the handle production. We now show how the identify routine can make this decision using the symbol below the $\langle B \rangle v$ on the stack. In particular we show that production 1 can only be the handle production if the symbol below the $\langle B \rangle v$ is $\langle B \rangle$ or $\triangledown$ and production 7 can only be the handle production if the symbol below the $\langle B \rangle v$ is v. Therefore, an identify routine designed to inspect the symbol below righthand side $\langle B \rangle v$ can make a satisfactory choice between REDUCE(1) and REDUCE(7).

To demonstrate that production 1 can only be the handle production if the symbol below $\langle B\rangle v$ is either $\langle B\rangle$ or ∇, consider the effect of operation REDUCE(1). The effect of this operation is to replace the $\langle B\rangle v$ with lefthand side $\langle S\rangle$, thereby pushing $\langle S\rangle$ on the symbol below. By the pushing principle, the only symbols that can appear below $\langle S\rangle$ during the processing of an acceptable input are those stack symbols X such that X BELOW $\langle S\rangle$. The symbols X which satisfy this relation are given in Fig. 12.12 and are $\langle B\rangle$ and ∇. To demonstrate that production 7 can only be the handle if the symbol below is v, observe that the effect of REDUCE(7) is to replace $\langle B\rangle$ v with $\langle C\rangle$ and v is the only stack symbol X to satisfy X BELOW $\langle C\rangle$.

Now consider the case when u is on top of the stack and an identify routine is selected. The lefthand sides of productions 3 and 5 are $\langle A\rangle$ and $\langle B\rangle$, respectively. From Fig. 12.12 we see that the stack symbols that can be

	u	v	w	y	$\dashv$
$\langle S\rangle$			IDENTIFY1		IDENTIFY2
$\langle A\rangle$			SHIFT		
$\langle B\rangle$	SHIFT	SHIFT		SHIFT	
$\langle C\rangle$			IDENTIFY3		IDENTIFY3
u	IDENTIFY4	IDENTIFY4	IDENTIFY4	IDENTIFY4	
v	SHIFT		IDENTIFY5	SHIFT	IDENTIFY5
w	IDENTIFY6	IDENTIFY6	IDENTIFY6	IDENTIFY6	IDENTIFY6
y	SHIFT	SHIFT	SHIFT		
∇	SHIFT	SHIFT		SHIFT	

Starting stack: ∇

IDENTIFY1: if top of stack is $v<B><S>$ then REDUCE(4)
else REJECT

IDENTIFY2: if top of stack is $\nabla <S>$ then ACCEPT
else IDENTIFY1

IDENTIFY3: if top of stack is $v<C>$ then REDUCE(2)
else REJECT

IDENTIFY4: if top of stack is yu then REDUCE(3)
else if top of stack is $<B>u$ or vu or ∇u
then REDUCE(5) else REJECT

IDENTIFY5: if top of stack is $<B><B>v$ or $\nabla<B>v$ then
REDUCE(1) else if top of stack is $v<B>v$ then
REDUCE(7) else REJECT

IDENTIFY6: if top of stack is yw then REDUCE(6)
else if top of stack is $y<A>w$ then REDUCE(8)
else REJECT

SHIFT: PUSH current input, ADVANCE

Figure 12.14

below these nonterminals during the processing of an acceptable input sequence are:

$$y \quad \text{BELOW} \ \langle A \rangle$$
$$\langle B \rangle \ \text{BELOW} \ \langle B \rangle$$
$$v \quad \text{BELOW} \ \langle B \rangle$$
$$\triangledown \ \text{BELOW} \ \langle B \rangle$$

Therefore, if y is below the u, only production 3 can be the handle production and if $\langle B \rangle$, v, or $\triangledown$ is below the u, only production 5 can be the handle production.

A SHIFT-IDENTIFY machine for the example is shown in Fig. 12.14. Note how, in routines IDENTIFY4 and IDENTIFY5, the symbol below the righthand side is included in the test.

The reasoning used in this example is based on the "pushing principle" of the previous section. The pushing principle says that given a stack symbol A and a nonterminal $\langle B \rangle$, there is an acceptable input sequence that causes $\langle B \rangle$ to be pushed on top of A if and only if:

$$A \ \text{BELOW} \ \langle B \rangle$$

Thus if the machine reaches a configuration in which the stack top is $A\beta$ and there is a production in the grammar

$$\langle B \rangle \rightarrow \beta$$

this production cannot be the handle production if A does not satisfy:

$$A \ \text{BELOW} \ \langle B \rangle$$

The general design principle can be stated as follows

If a given grammar has two productions of the form

$$\langle B \rangle \rightarrow \beta$$
$$\langle C \rangle \rightarrow \beta$$

and if for a given stack symbol A

$$A \ \text{BELOW} \ \langle B \rangle$$

but not

$$A \ \text{BELOW} \ \langle C \rangle$$

then the second production cannot be the handle production when $A\beta$ is on top of the stack. Hence, the identify routines for a SHIFT-IDENTIFY machine based on the given grammar can be designed so that when $A\beta$ is on top of the stack, the reduce operation corresponding to the second production is not performed.

A grammar is known as a "simple mixed-strategy-precedence grammar" if it has no SHIFT-IDENTIFY conflicts and all identification problems can be resolved by the methods of this and the previous section. Specifically, a grammar is called a *simple mixed-strategy-precedence grammar* if and only if the following four conditions hold:

1. The grammar has no SHIFT-IDENTIFY conflicts.
2. For any two productions with the same righthand side

$$\langle A \rangle \rightarrow \alpha$$
$$\langle B \rangle \rightarrow \alpha$$

there is no symbol X such that X BELOW $\langle A \rangle$ and X BELOW $\langle B \rangle$.

3. For any two productions of the form

$$\langle A \rangle \rightarrow \alpha y \gamma$$
$$\langle B \rangle \rightarrow \gamma$$

where α and γ are strings and y is a grammatical symbol, it is false that y BELOW $\langle B \rangle$.

4. It is not true that $\langle S \rangle \overset{+}{\Rightarrow} \langle S \rangle$, where $\langle S \rangle$ is the starting symbol.

Conditions 1, 3, and 4 are the same as for weak-precedence grammars; condition 2 is the new condition that holds for identical righthand sides.

A SHIFT-IDENTIFY machine can be designed for a given simple mixed-strategy-precedence grammar in the same manner as for a weak-precedence grammar except that when several productions have the same righthand side the identify routines must look at the stack symbol below the righthand side to select the appropriate reduce operations. Therefore:

> any simple mixed-strategy-precedence grammar can be used as the basis of a SHIFT-IDENTIFY recognizer for the language specified by the grammar.

An important property of simple mixed-strategy-precedence grammars is that they exactly characterize the class of languages that can be recognized by a pushdown machine. (By a pushdown machine we mean here the primitive machine introduced in Chapter 5 as well as all the "extended" pushdown machines which are discussed in other chapters.)

> A language can be recognized by a pushdown machine if and only if it is generated by some simple mixed-strategy-precedence grammar.

One way to prove this statement would be to supply procedures to:

1. given a simple mixed-strategy-precedence grammar, obtain a SHIFT-

IDENTIFY pushdown machine to recognize its language;

2. given a pushdown machine, obtain a simple mixed-strategy-precedence grammar that generates the language recognized by the machine.

The first procedure has been indicated in this section. The second procedure is given in Aho, Denning, and Ullman [1972] and Aho and Ullman [1973a], but is not presented here since it is not needed in compiler design.

The above statement does not imply that the grammar used in the design of a pushdown machine is always a simple mixed-strategy-precedence grammar. It simply says that if a pushdown machine exists for a particular language, then that language has some grammar which is simple mixed-strategy precedence. The statement can be extended to include translations:

> A translation can be performed by a pushdown machine if and only if it can be specified by a Polish-translation grammar for which the input grammar is a simple mixed-strategy-precedence grammar.

Again the methods given in this chapter and Chapter 11 specify a design method for the machine given the grammar and we omit the proof of the converse.

The S-attributed translations introduced in Chapter 11 do not characterize the attributed translations that can be performed by a pushdown machine augmented in the manner described in Chapters 9 and 11. (A characterizing class of attributed translations is given in Lewis, Rosenkrantz, and Stearns [1974] .) However in practice, S-attributed translations whose input grammars are weak-precedence or simple mixed-strategy-precedence are almost always adequate for real design problems.

12.6 COMPUTING BELOW AND REDUCED-BY

The purpose of this section is to present a procedure for computing BELOW and REDUCED-BY. The results of the procedure can then be used to check for SHIFT-IDENTIFY conflicts, design a control, test for weak precedence, test for simple mixed-strategy precedence, and design identify routines for simple mixed-strategy-precedence grammars.

The procedure for computing REDUCED-BY and BELOW is outlined in Fig. 12.15. The procedure makes use of three primitive relations that can be picked directly off the grammar (steps 1, 2, and 3) and relational operations described in Appendix B.

Step 1 is to construct the relation BEGINS-DIRECTLY-WITH described in Section 8.7. In the absence of ϵ-productions,

If A and B are symbols in a given grammar we write

$$A \text{ BEGINS-DIRECTLY-WITH } B$$

if and only if there is a production of the form

$$A \rightarrow B\beta$$

where β is an arbitrary string.

The relation BEGINS-DIRECTLY-WITH for the grammar of Fig. 12.16 is shown in Fig. 12.17(a). It is obtained from the grammar by taking each production and marking the corresponding matrix entry. For example, the lefthand side of production 1 is $\langle S \rangle$ and the righthand side begins with $\langle A \rangle$, so the entry in row $\langle S \rangle$ and column $\langle A \rangle$ is marked with a 1. The matrix cannot have marked entries in the terminal symbol rows since there are no terminal lefthand sides, but these rows are shown in the figure for completeness.

1. Construct the relation BEGINS-DIRECTLY-WITH.
2. Construct the relation IS-DIRECT-END-OF.
3. Construct the relation IS-FOLLOWED-DIRECTLY-BY.
4. Compute relation $\lessdot$ defined by:

    IS-FOLLOWED-DIRECTLY-BY · BEGINS-DIRECTLY-WITH*
5. Compute relation $\gtrdot$ defined by:

    IS-DIRECT-END-OF$^+$ · $\lessdot$
6. Extend $\lessdot$ to BELOW by adding pairs $(\triangledown, X)$ such that

    $\langle S \rangle$ BEGINS-DIRECTLY-WITH* X

    for starting symbol $\langle S \rangle$.
7. Extend $\gtrdot$ to REDUCED-BY by adding pairs $(X, \dashv)$ such that

    X IS-DIRECT-END-OF* $\langle S \rangle$

    for starting symbol $\langle S \rangle$.

Fig. 12.15 Procedure for finding BELOW and REDUCED-BY

1. $\langle S \rangle \rightarrow \langle A \rangle\, z$
2. $\langle S \rangle \rightarrow y\, z$
3. $\langle A \rangle \rightarrow \langle B \rangle\, \langle B \rangle\, \langle S \rangle$
4. $\langle A \rangle \rightarrow d$
5. $\langle B \rangle \rightarrow y\, x\, \langle A \rangle$
6. $\langle B \rangle \rightarrow x\, \langle A \rangle$

Starting symbol: $\langle S \rangle$

Figure 12.16

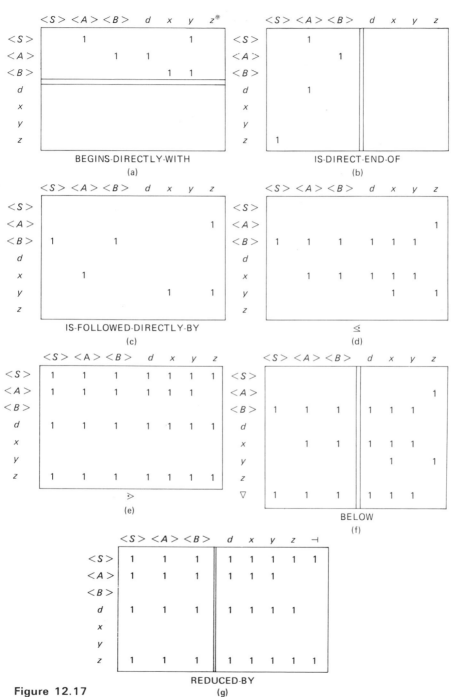

Figure 12.17

Step 2 of the procedure is to construct the relation IS-DIRECT-END-OF described in Section 8.7 In the absence of ϵ-productions:

If A and B are symbols in a given grammar, we write

$$A \text{ IS-DIRECT-END-OF } B$$

if and only if there is a production of the form

$$B \rightarrow \alpha A$$

where α is an arbitrary string.

The relation IS-DIRECT-END-OF for the sample grammar is shown in Fig. 12.17(b). It is obtained from the grammar by taking each production and marking the corresponding matrix entry. For example, the lefthand side of production 1 is $\langle S \rangle$ and the righthand side ends with z, so the entry in row z and column $\langle S \rangle$ is marked with a 1. The matrix cannot have marked entries in terminal symbol columns, however these columns are shown for completeness.

Step 3 of the procedure is to compute the relation IS-FOLLOWED-DIRECTLY-BY described in Section 8.7. In the absence of ϵ-productions:

If A and B are symbols in the given grammar, we write

$$A \text{ IS-FOLLOWED-DIRECTLY-BY } B$$

if and only if there is a production of the form

$$D \rightarrow \alpha A B \gamma$$

where α and γ are arbitrary strings.

The historical name for IS-FOLLOWED-DIRECTLY-BY in the no-ϵ-production case is $\doteq$, which is pronounced "equal precedence," although it is not an equivalence relation. The relation IS-FOLLOWED-DIRECTLY-BY for the sample grammar is shown in Fig. 12.17(c). It is obtained from the grammar by taking each righthand side and marking the matrix for each pair of adjacent symbols. Thus on inspection the righthand side of production 1 yields

$$\langle A \rangle \text{ IS-FOLLOWED-DIRECTLY-BY } z.$$

Production 3 yields

$$\langle B \rangle \text{ IS-FOLLOWED-DIRECTLY-BY } \langle B \rangle$$

and

$$\langle B \rangle \text{ IS-FOLLOWED-DIRECTLY-BY } \langle S \rangle.$$

Step 4 of the procedure is to compute the relation ≤ defined by the product

IS-FOLLOWED-DIRECTLY-BY · BEGINS-DIRECTLY-WITH*

We use the name ≤ because this relation is the union of the relation ≐ and another relation, commonly called <, defined by

IS-FOLLOWED-DIRECTLY-BY · BEGINS-DIRECTLY-WITH$^+$

(note + instead of *). Relation < is called "less-than precedence" although it is not transitive like the arithmetic less-than relation. To compute ≤, we take the reflexive transitive closure of BEGINS-DIRECTLY-WITH and then compute the above product. The result for the sample grammar is shown in Fig. 12.17(d). Note that the reflexive transitive closure of BEGINS-DIRECTLY-WITH describes the FIRST sets; i.e., B is in FIRST(C) if and only if

C BEGINS-DIRECTLY-WITH* B.

The product then pairs each grammatical symbol A with symbols in the FIRST(C) for all C immediately following an occurrence of A in a righthand side. In other words, relation ≤ is relation BELOW without the bottom-marker.

Step 5 of the procedure is to compute the relation > using the product:

IS-DIRECT-END-OF $^+$· ≤

Relation > is commonly called "greater-than-precedence" although the relation is not transitive like the arithmetic greater-than. The result of this calculation for the sample grammar is shown in Fig. 12.17(e). Note that the relation > can be expressed as

IS-DIRECT-END-OF · (IS-DIRECT-END-OF* · ≤)

The parenthesized relation describes the FOLLOW sets except for the end-marker; i.e., grammatical symbol B is in FOLLOW(C) if and only if:

C (IS-DIRECT-END-OF* · ≤) B

The relation > thus pairs each grammatical symbol A with the grammatical symbols in FOLLOW(C), for all nonterminals C having a production ending in A. Therefore, for any grammatical symbol A and terminal symbol x, A REDUCED-BY x if and only if A > x.

At this point in the calculation, relations ≤ and > can be compared to see if there are any SHIFT-IDENTIFY conflicts. The addition of bottom-markers and endmarkers to obtain BELOW and REDUCED-BY does not affect the outcome of the conflict test.

Step 6 of the calculation is to extend $\leq$ to BELOW by finding those X such that

$$\langle S \rangle \text{ BEGINS-DIRECTLY-WITH* } X$$

(where $\langle S \rangle$ is the starting symbol) and marking those X in a bottommarker row appended to the matrix. If the matrix for BEGINS-DIRECTLY-WITH* has been computed as an intermediate calculation in step 4, the $\langle S \rangle$ row of that matrix can be appended to the matrix for $\leq$ as the bottommarker row The result for the example is Fig. 12.17(f). The columns representing non-terminals are not used in the control-table design but are used in checking for weak precedence and in designing identify routines for simple mixed-strategy-precedence grammars.

Step 7 of the calculation is to extend $>$ to REDUCED-BY by finding those X such that

$$X \text{ IS-DIRECT-END-OF* } \langle S \rangle$$

(where $\langle S \rangle$ is the starting symbol) and marking those X in an endmarker column appended to the matrix. The result for the example is shown in Fig. 12.17(g). Technically, the columns corresponding to nonterminals are not included in REDUCED-BY since the second component of a pair in RE-DUCED-BY is supposed to be an input symbol, and these columns may be discarded. Step 7 completes the procedure.

12.7   ERROR PROCESSING IN SHIFT-IDENTIFY PARSING

Compilers often encounter input sequences that are not in the language being recognized. We call these sequences *nonsentences*.

When confronted with a nonsentence, a compiler must detect that an error has occurred, i.e., that the input is a nonsentence. Moreover, the compiler is expected to produce a list of error messages indicating what errors the programmer might have made.

The number and wording of the error messages for a given nonsentence are usually a matter of judgment, and are often debatable. In fact, different compilers for the same programming language often produce different error messages for the same nonsentence.

A pushdown recognizer detects that its input sequence is a nonsentence the first time it encounters a REJECT configuration. At this point the compiler is expected to produce an error message describing what mistake the programmer might have made. Furthermore, the compiler is expected to somehow modify the configuration of the pushdown machine so that the processing of the input sequence can be continued and, if appropriate, additional messages can be produced. This modification process is termed *error recovery*.

There are two types of situations in which a SHIFT-IDENTIFY machine will reject an input string: a) by using a control-table entry containing REJECT, or b) by using an identify routine that selects REJECT. For REJECT entries in the control table, the error message is customarily based only on the top stack symbol and the current input. The key fact about control-table REJECT entries is that they occur in situations where there is no intermediate string in a rightmost derivation in which the grammatical symbol represented by the top stack symbol is followed by the current input. Thus a conceivable format for the error message is

 FOLLOWS _____

where the first dash contains the name of the input symbol and the second dash contains the name of the top stack symbol (suitably paraphrased to be intelligible to the user).

For REJECT situations in IDENTIFY routines there is no obvious format for error messages. The key fact about identify-routine rejections is that they occur in situations where the top stack symbol and current input indicate that a handle should be on top of the stack but no handle has been found. For a suffix-free SI grammar or weak-precedence grammar, there is no righthand side on top of the stack. For a simple mixed-strategy-precedence grammar, there is either no righthand side on top of the stack or there is a righthand side but the preceding symbol on the stack is not BELOW any corresponding lefthand nonterminal.

One approach to producing an error message is to inspect the stack to determine the shortest sequence of top stack symbols that is neither the suffix of any righthand side nor a righthand side preceded by a symbol that is BELOW a corresponding lefthand side. The error message is then some statement that this sequence of symbols followed by the current input is not an acceptable combination of symbols.

As an example, suppose a grammar has the production

$$\langle S \rangle \to \text{IF } \langle B \rangle \text{ THEN } \langle S1 \rangle \text{ ELSE } \langle S1 \rangle$$

Also suppose statements of this type are always followed by a semicolon, and this is the only production whose last two symbols are:

$$\text{ELSE } \langle S1 \rangle$$

Now suppose that at some point in the processing of an invalid input string, the top of the stack is

$$\text{IF } \langle B \rangle \text{ THEN } \langle S1 \rangle \text{ ELSE } \langle S1 \rangle \text{ ELSE } \langle S1 \rangle$$

and the current input is a semicolon. In this configuration, the control will select an identify routine. The identify routine will determine that the top stack symbols do not form a handle and that the top four stack symbols

$$\text{ELSE} \langle S1 \rangle \text{ ELSE } \langle S1 \rangle$$

form the smallest sequence that is not the suffix of any righthand side. The processor could then insert these four symbols and the current input into the standard message:

$$\text{CONSTRUCTION} \underline{\hspace{1.5cm}} \text{NOT PERMITTED}$$

to obtain:

CONSTRUCTION ELSE STATEMENT ELSE STATEMENT; NOT PERMITTED

If the error were considered very common, the construction could be detected as a special case, and the processor might produce the tailored error message:

TWO CONSECUTIVE ELSE CLAUSES

As a more complete example, consider the following grammar with starting symbol $\langle S \rangle$, which was used as an example of error processing in Section 8.8.

1. $\langle S \rangle \rightarrow a$
2. $\langle S \rangle \rightarrow (\langle S \rangle \langle R \rangle$
3. $\langle R \rangle \rightarrow , \langle S \rangle \langle R \rangle$
4. $\langle R \rangle \rightarrow)$

The grammar generates LISP-like expressions, such as

$$a$$

$$(a, (a, a))$$

$$((a, (a, a), (a, a)), a)$$

The grammar is a suffix-free SI grammar. Fig. 12.18 shows the SHIFT-IDENTIFY machine with each REJECT situation labeled with a different letter. Situations a through q correspond to REJECT entries in the control table and situations r and s correspond to REJECT in identify routines.

An appropriate set of error messages is shown in Fig. 12.19. In situations e, f, h, i, j, k, m, and n, both input and stack symbols are terminals and the error messages are in the suggested format. The format is changed only slightly for configurations g and l where the input symbol is the endmarker, and for configurations o and p where the stack symbol is the bottommarker.

	a	$($	$)$	$,$	$\dashv$
$<S>$	REJECT a	REJECT b	SHIFT	SHIFT	IDENTIFY1
$<R>$	REJECT c	REJECT d	IDENTIFY2	IDENTIFY2	IDENTIFY2
$($	SHIFT	SHIFT	REJECT e	REJECT f	REJECT g
$)$	REJECT h	REJECT i	IDENTIFY3	IDENTIFY3	IDENTIFY3
$,$	SHIFT	SHIFT	REJECT j	REJECT k	REJECT ℓ
a	REJECT m	REJECT n	IDENTIFY4	IDENTIFY4	IDENTIFY4
$\triangledown$	SHIFT	SHIFT	REJECT o	REJECT p	REJECT q

IDENTIFY1: if top of stack is $\triangledown <S>$ then ACCEPT
       else REJECT r

IDENTIFY2: if top of stack is $(<S><R>$ then
          REDUCE(2)
       else if top of stack is $,<S><R>$ then
          REDUCE(3)
       else REJECT s

IDENTIFY3: REDUCE(4)

IDENTIFY4: REDUCE(1)

REDUCE(1): POP, PUSH($<S>$)

REDUCE(2): POP, POP, POP, PUSH($<S>$)

REDUCE(3): POP, POP, POP, PUSH($<R>$)

REDUCE(4): POP, PUSH($<R>$)

Figure 12.18

a, b, c, d :   Not needed (see text)

e, f, h, i, j, k, m, n : "(input symbol)
         FOLLOWS (stack symbol)"

g, ℓ : "S-EXPRESSION INCOMPLETE"

o, p : "(input symbol) AT BEGINNING
      OF S-EXPRESSION"

q : "S-EXPRESSION MISSING"

r : "MISSING RIGHT PARENTHESIS"

s : "UNMATCHED PARENTHESIS"

Figure 12.19

Configuration q where the input string is the null string receives a special message.

No error message is specified for situations a, b, c, and d because those table entries can never be reached even for nonsentences. For example, consider situation a with $\langle S \rangle$ as top stack symbol and a as input symbol. Since $\langle S \rangle$ is a nonterminal, it cannot be pushed on the stack by a SHIFT. It can only be pushed on the stack by REDUCE(1) or REDUCE (2), both of which can only be selected by identify routines. Since the control-table column for input a does not even contain any identify routines, there is no way $\langle S \rangle$ can be pushed on the stack when a is the current input. Hence situation a cannot be reached. Similar considerations apply to situations b, c, and d.

Messages for error situations in IDENTIFY routines are often more meaningful if designed on an individual basis rather than using a standard format. Situation r occurs when the current input is the endmarker and the top stack symbol is $\langle S \rangle$, but the stack is not $\nabla \langle S \rangle$. We first note that a stack symbol below an occurrence of $\langle S \rangle$ on the stack must have the property that some input symbol in FIRST($\langle S \rangle$) can be shifted above it. FIRST($\langle S \rangle$) consists of a and left parenthesis. From the control table we see that these input symbols can only be shifted on top of comma, left parenthesis, or bottommarker. Hence we conclude that only comma or left parenthesis can be under $\langle S \rangle$ in situation r. In either case, it appears that a right parenthesis is missing and so we select the message to that effect given in Fig. 12.19.

We can make a similar analysis for situation s. Since FIRST($\langle R \rangle$) is comma and right parenthesis, and these symbols can only be shifted on top of $\langle S \rangle$, we conclude that when IDENTIFY2 is called the top two stack symbols are $\langle S \rangle \langle R \rangle$. By the same reasoning, the only symbols that can be under $\langle S \rangle$ are comma, left parenthesis, or bottommarker. Since comma or left parenthesis is acceptable in IDENTIFY2, we conclude that in situation s the entire stack is:

$$\nabla \; \langle S \rangle \; \langle R \rangle$$

Since every sequence derived from $\langle R \rangle$ contains one more right parenthesis than left parenthesis, the right parenthesis ending the $\langle R \rangle$ on top of the stack has no matching left parenthesis; so we select the message given in Fig. 12.19.

At this point, the error messages listed in Fig. 12.19 must remain tentative until after the error-recovery routines are designed, since these routines might change the above analysis.

Now we consider the problem of error recovery. Our approach is to design error-recovery routines which adjust the input and stack, and then continue processing as if no error had occurred. If the pushdown machine subsequently encounters another REJECT entry, it then adds that entry's error message to the list of error messages produced thus far and uses that entry's recovery procedure. We hope that any error message produced after the recovery represents additional mistakes that the programmer would like called to his attention. There is a risk that the compiler might later generate bogus error messages which annoy the programmer because they do not seem to correspond to additional mistakes in the program. Any attempt at error recovery therefore represents a compromise between the desire to detect as many errors as possible and the desire to avoid bogus messages.

First, we consider an approach to error recovery that might be characterized as being "local" in nature. The idea is to fill in each of the REJECT entries with ordinary stack and input operations. If a particular error is detected, first the error message is produced, then the indicated stack and input operations are performed and then the usual processing is resumed. The designer selects the operations for each error entry individually based on his intuition as to what the error might be and how the stack and input might best be adjusted to resume the processing.

Figure 12.20 shows a reasonable set of local error-recovery routines for the machines of Fig. 12.18. Note that routines are specified for situations a, b,

a, b: PUSH(,) RETAIN

c, d: IDENTIFY2

e, f, j, k: PRINT(Message from Fig. 12.19)
                      PUSH(a)
                      RETAIN

g, l, q: PRINT(Message from Fig. 12.19)
              EXIT

h, i: PRINT(Message from Fig. 12.19)
         IDENTIFY3

m, n: PRINT(Message from Fig. 12.19)
         IDENTIFY4

o, p: PRINT(Message from Fig. 12.19)
         ADVANCE

r: PRINT(Message from Fig. 12.19)
    PUSH( ))
    RETAIN

s: PRINT(Message from Fig. 12.19)
    POP
    RETAIN

Figure 12.20

$$\nabla \qquad\qquad\qquad\qquad (\,a\,,\,,\,a \dashv$$
$$\nabla \,(\qquad\qquad\qquad\qquad a\,,\,,\,a \dashv$$
$$\nabla \,(\,a \qquad\qquad\qquad\qquad ,\,,\,a \dashv$$
$$\nabla \,(\,\langle S \rangle \qquad\qquad\qquad ,\,,\,a \dashv$$
$$\nabla \,(\,\langle S \rangle\,, \qquad\qquad\qquad ,\,a \dashv$$
PRINT("COMMA FOLLOWS COMMA")
$$\nabla \,(\,\langle S \rangle\,,\,a \qquad\qquad ,\,a \dashv$$
$$\nabla \,(\,\langle S \rangle\,,\,\langle S \rangle \qquad\qquad ,\,a \dashv$$
$$\nabla \,(\,\langle S \rangle\,,\,\langle S \rangle\,, \qquad\qquad a \dashv$$
$$\nabla \,(\,\langle S \rangle\,,\,\langle S \rangle\,,\,a \qquad\qquad \dashv$$
$$\nabla \,(\,\langle S \rangle\,,\,\langle S \rangle\,,\,\langle S \rangle \qquad \dashv$$
PRINT("MISSING RIGHT PARENTHESIS")
$$\nabla \,(\,\langle S \rangle\,,\,\langle S \rangle\,,\,\langle S \rangle\,) \qquad \dashv$$
$$\nabla \,(\,\langle S \rangle\,,\,\langle S \rangle\,,\,\langle S \rangle \,\langle R \rangle \qquad \dashv$$
$$\nabla \,(\,\langle S \rangle\,,\,\langle S \rangle \,\langle R \rangle \qquad \dashv$$
$$\nabla \,(\,\langle S \rangle \,\langle R \rangle \qquad \dashv$$
$$\nabla \,\langle S \rangle \qquad\qquad\qquad \dashv$$

EXIT

Figure 12.21

c, and d which are now reachable as part of the recovery from situations m, n, h, and i. Note also that the analysis behind the error messages of Fig. 12.19 is still valid.

Figure 12.21 shows a stack movie of this machine processing the sequence:

$$(\,a\,,\,,\,a$$

This figure can be compared with Fig. 8.29(a) which showed this same sequence processed by the machine of Fig. 8.28.

We now discuss an approach to error recovery that might be characterized as being "global." This second approach might be used when the designer has insufficient confidence in the accuracy of any local recovery routines or when memory limitations do not allow individual recovery routines for each error entry.

The basic idea is to scan ahead in the input sequence until one of a set of "trustworthy" input symbols is found. The error recovery then depends on that symbol and the top stack symbol. Two types of trustworthy symbols can be considered.

1. **Ending Symbols**   An ending symbol is one which the designer has reasonable confidence marks the end of the righthand side of some production such that the symbol at the beginning of the righthand side is on the stack. The ending symbol can be either the last terminal symbol generated by the righthand side or the first symbol after the end of the righthand side. Typical ending symbols in a block-structured language are END and semicolon.

During error recovery, the input string is scanned until an ending symbol is found. Then the stack is popped until a matching stack symbol is found which the designer feels begins the righthand side whose end is marked by the ending symbol. This stack symbol is then replaced by a nonterminal that the designer feels is the lefthand side of the production whose beginning and end have been found. Normal processing is resumed using as input the first symbol after the end of the production.

2. **First Symbols**   A first symbol is one which the designer has reasonable confidence starts a production that the designer wants checked for additional errors. In many block-structured languages the reserved word BEGIN can be used as a first symbol.

During error recovery, when a first symbol is encountered in a scan of the input string, the stack operations

$$\text{PUSH}(\{\text{ERROR}\}), \text{SHIFT}$$

are performed and then normal processing resumes. Later in the processing, when {ERROR} reaches the top of the stack it is popped off and the error-recovery routine resumes scanning for another ending or first symbol.

It should be emphasized that the sets of ending and first symbols must be considered together. For example, suppose that for some block-structured language, the designer wishes to use END and semicolon as ending symbols. It would be incorrect to scan over a BEGIN in search of these symbols, since the compiler would then have an incorrect analysis of the block structure. Thus BEGIN must be used as a first symbol.

12.8   MINI-BASIC SYNTAX BOX

In this section, we design a MINI-BASIC syntax box based on an S-attributed Polish translation grammar whose input grammar is a simple mixed-strategy-precedence grammar. The job of the syntax box is to input a token string produced by the lexical box of Chapter 4 and produce as output an atom string which will be used as input to the code generator described in Chapter 14. Another syntax box with the identical input-output relation was designed in Chapter 10 using top-down methods.

We begin by discussing the simple mixed-strategy-precedence grammar

Program Structure

1. ⟨program⟩ → ⟨statement list⟩ END
2. ⟨statement list⟩ → ⟨statement list⟩ ⟨statement⟩ LINE
3. ⟨statement list⟩ → LINE

Null Statement

4. ⟨statement list⟩ → ⟨statement list⟩ LINE

Assignment Statement

5. ⟨statement⟩ → ASSIGN ⟨expression⟩

GOTO Statement

6. ⟨statement⟩ → GOTO

IF Statement

7. ⟨statement⟩ → IF ⟨expression⟩ RELATIONAL OPERATOR
                     ⟨expression⟩ ⟨if jump⟩
8. ⟨if jump⟩ → GOTO

GOSUB Statement

9. ⟨statement⟩ → GOSUB

RETURN Statement

10. ⟨statement⟩ → RETURN

FOR Statement

11. ⟨statement⟩ → ⟨for statement⟩ ⟨statement list⟩ NEXT

Fig. 12.22 Simple Mixed-Strategy-Precedence Grammar for MINI-BASIC Syntax
Box

underlying the translation. The grammar is shown in Fig. 12.22 and can be
compared with the MINI-BASIC grammar given in Section 6.15.

The terminal set of the grammar is the set of tokens listed in Fig. 4.1
except that here the five arithmetic operators are represented as five tokens
instead of as previously represented in Fig. 4.1 as a single token with five
possible value parts. It may be helpful to recall the actual character strings
corresponding to each token. For instance, the token ASSIGN corresponds
to the word LET followed by a variable followed by =, and the token LINE
corresponds to the line number at the beginning of a line.

Observe that production 11 generates both the FOR statement and the
matching NEXT statement. The productions for the FOR statement are
designed so that when action symbols are subsequently inserted to obtain a
translation grammar, the translation grammar will be Polish.

It is readily verified that the grammar of Fig. 12.22 is in fact a simple
mixed-strategy-precedence grammar.

12. ⟨for statement⟩ → ⟨for clause⟩ ⟨to clause⟩ STEP ⟨expression⟩
13. ⟨for statement⟩ → ⟨for clause⟩ ⟨to clause⟩
14. ⟨for clause⟩ → FOR ⟨expression⟩
15. ⟨to clause⟩ → TO ⟨expression⟩

REM Statement

16. ⟨statement⟩ → COMMENT

Expressions

17. ⟨expression⟩ → ⟨expression⟩ + ⟨term⟩
18. ⟨expression⟩ → ⟨expression⟩ − ⟨term⟩
19. ⟨expression⟩ → + ⟨term⟩
20. ⟨expression⟩ → − ⟨term⟩
21. ⟨expression⟩ → ⟨term⟩
22. ⟨term⟩ → ⟨term⟩ * ⟨factor⟩
23. ⟨term⟩ → ⟨term⟩ / ⟨factor⟩
24. ⟨term⟩ → ⟨factor⟩
25. ⟨factor⟩ → ⟨factor⟩ ↑ ⟨primary⟩
26. ⟨factor⟩ → ⟨primary⟩
27. ⟨primary⟩ → (⟨expression⟩)
28. ⟨primary⟩ → OPERAND

Starting symbol: ⟨program⟩

Figure 12.22 (continued)

Now we are ready to specify the atom set and the translation grammar. The complete atom set with description of all the attributes was shown in Fig. 10.2 as a part of the syntax-box design given in Chapter 10. The text accompanying that figure describes the intended use of each atom. Although the timing for producing each atom is described in terms of the grammar in Chapter 10, the reader should be able to understand the atom set from that description.

Figure 12.23 shows the Polish translation grammar and Fig. 12.24 shows the S-attributed translation grammar. The purpose of most of the nonterminal attributes should be obvious. The only nonterminal with more than one attribute is ⟨for statement⟩. Its first attribute is a pointer to the table entry of the FOR variable; its second attribute is a pointer to the table entry for the value by which the FOR variable should be incremented; its third and fourth attributes are pointers to the table entries for the two labels involved in the loop; its fifth attribute contains the line number on which the

Program Structure

1. ⟨program⟩ → ⟨statement list⟩ END
2. ⟨statement list⟩ → ⟨statement list⟩ ⟨statement⟩
                        LINE {LINEN} {SET LINE NUMBER}
3. ⟨statement list⟩ → LINE {LINEN} {SET LINE NUMBER}

Null Statement

4. ⟨statement list⟩ → ⟨statement list⟩ LINE {LINEN} {SET LINE NUMBER}

Assignment Statement

5. ⟨statement⟩ → ASSIGN ⟨expression⟩ {ASSIGN}

GOTO Statement

6. ⟨statement⟩ → GOTO {JUMP}

IF Statement

7. ⟨statement⟩ → IF ⟨expression⟩ RELATIONAL OPERATOR ⟨expression⟩
                     ⟨if jump⟩ {CONDJUMP}
8. ⟨if jump⟩ → GOTO

GOSUB Statement

9. ⟨statement⟩ → GOSUB {JUMPSAVE}

RETURN Statement

10. ⟨statement⟩ → RETURN {RETURNJUMP}

FOR Statement

11. ⟨statement⟩ → ⟨for statement⟩ ⟨statement list⟩ NEXT {CHECK} {INCR}
                      {JUMP} {LABEL}

Fig. 12.23 Polish Translation Grammar for MINI-BASIC Syntax Box

All Action Symbol Attributes are INHERITED
Description of Action Routine {SET LINE NUMBER}$_p$
LINE NUMBER ← p
Description of Action Routine {CHECK}$_{p,w,y}$
IF $p \neq w$ THEN print warning message

Program Structure

1. ⟨program⟩ → ⟨statement list⟩ END
2. ⟨statement list⟩ → ⟨statement list⟩ ⟨statement⟩ LINE$_{p1}$ {LINEN$_{p2}$} {SET
                        LINE NUMBER}$_{p3}$
     $(p2, p3) \leftarrow p1$
3. ⟨statement list⟩ → LINE$_{p1}$ {LINEN$_{p2}$} {SET LINE NUMBER}$_{p3}$
     $(p2, p3) \leftarrow p1$

Fig. 12.24 S-Attributed Grammar for MINI-BASIC Syntax Box

12. $\langle$for statement$\rangle \rightarrow \langle$for clause$\rangle$ $\langle$to clause$\rangle$ STEP $\langle$expression$\rangle$ {SAVE}
    {LABEL} {TEST}
13. $\langle$for statement$\rangle \rightarrow \langle$for clause$\rangle$ $\langle$to clause$\rangle$ {SAVE} {LABEL} {TEST}
14. $\langle$for clause$\rangle \rightarrow$ FOR $\langle$expression$\rangle$ {ASSIGN}
15. $\langle$to clause$\rangle \rightarrow$ TO $\langle$expression$\rangle$ {SAVE}

REM Statement
16. $\langle$statement$\rangle \rightarrow$ COMMENT

Expressions
17. $\langle$expression$\rangle \rightarrow \langle$expression$\rangle$ + $\langle$term$\rangle$ {ADD}
18. $\langle$expression$\rangle \rightarrow \langle$expression$\rangle$ − $\langle$term$\rangle$ {SUBT}
19. $\langle$expression$\rangle \rightarrow$ + $\langle$term$\rangle$ {PLUS}
20. $\langle$expression$\rangle \rightarrow$ − $\langle$term$\rangle$ {NEG}
21. $\langle$expression$\rangle \rightarrow \langle$term$\rangle$
22. $\langle$term$\rangle \rightarrow \langle$term$\rangle$ * $\langle$factor$\rangle$ {MULT}
23. $\langle$term$\rangle \rightarrow \langle$term$\rangle$ / $\langle$factor$\rangle$ {DIV}
24. $\langle$term$\rangle \rightarrow \langle$factor$\rangle$
25. $\langle$factor$\rangle \rightarrow \langle$factor$\rangle$ ↑ $\langle$primary$\rangle$ {EXP}
26. $\langle$factor$\rangle \rightarrow \langle$primary$\rangle$
27. $\langle$primary$\rangle \rightarrow$ ($\langle$expression$\rangle$)
28. $\langle$primary$\rangle \rightarrow$ OPERAND
Starting symbol: $\langle$program$\rangle$

Figure 12.23 (continued)

Null Statement
4. $\langle$statement list$\rangle \rightarrow \langle$statement list$\rangle$ LINE$_{p1}$ {LINEN$_{p2}$} {SET LINE
    NUMBER}$_{p3}$

    $(p2, p3) \leftarrow p1$

Assignment Statement
5. $\langle$statement$\rangle \rightarrow$ ASSIGN$_{p1}$ $\langle$expression$\rangle_{q1}$ {ASSIGN$_{p2,q2}$}
    $p2 \leftarrow p1$ $q2 \leftarrow q1$

GOTO Statement
6. $\langle$statement$\rangle \rightarrow$ GOTO$_{p1}$ {JUMP$_{p2}$}
    $p2 \leftarrow p1$

Figure 12.24 (continued)

IF Statement

7. $\langle$statement$\rangle \rightarrow$ IF $\langle$expression$\rangle_{p1}$ RELATIONAL OPERATOR$_{r1}$ $\langle$expression$\rangle_{q1}$ $\langle$ifjump$\rangle_{s1}$ {CONDJUMP$_{p2,q2,r2,s2}$}

$\qquad p2 \leftarrow p1 \qquad q2 \leftarrow q1 \qquad r2 \leftarrow r1 \qquad s2 \leftarrow s1$

8. $\langle$if jump$\rangle_{s2} \rightarrow$ GOTO$_{s1}$

$\qquad s2 \leftarrow s1$

GOSUB Statement

9. $\langle$statement$\rangle \rightarrow$ GOSUB$_{p1}$ {JUMPSAVE}$_{p2}$

$\qquad p2 \leftarrow p1$

RETURN Statement

10. $\langle$statement$\rangle \rightarrow$ RETURN {RETURNJUMP}

FOR Statement

11. $\langle$statement$\rangle \rightarrow \langle$for statement$\rangle_{p1,t1,u1,v1,y1}$ $\langle$statement list$\rangle$ NEXT$_{w1}$
$\qquad\qquad$ {CHECK}$_{p2,w2,y2}$ {INCR$_{p3,t2}$} {JUMP$_{u2}$} {LABEL$_{v2}$}

$\qquad (p2, p3) \leftarrow p1 \qquad w2 \leftarrow w1 \qquad y2 \leftarrow y1$

$\qquad t2 \leftarrow t1 \qquad u2 \leftarrow u1 \qquad v2 \leftarrow v1$

12. $\langle$for statement$\rangle_{p3,t3,u2,v2,y} \rightarrow \langle$for clause$\rangle_{p1}$ $\langle$to clause$\rangle_{s1}$ STEP $\langle$expression$\rangle_{r1}$
$\qquad\qquad$ {SAVE$_{r2,t1}$} {LABEL$_{u1}$} {TEST$_{p2,s2,t2,v1}$}

$\qquad (t1, t2, t3) \leftarrow$ NEWTSR

$\qquad (u1, u2) \leftarrow$ NEWTL $\qquad\qquad s2 \leftarrow s1$

$\qquad (v1, v2) \leftarrow$ NEWTL $\qquad\qquad y \leftarrow$ LINE NUMBER

$\qquad (p2, p3) \leftarrow p1 \qquad\qquad\quad x2 \leftarrow x1$

13. $\langle$for statement$\rangle_{p3,t3,u2,v2,y} \rightarrow \langle$for clause$\rangle_{p1}$ $\langle$to clause$\rangle_{s1}$ {SAVE$_{x,t1}$} {LA-
$\qquad\qquad$ BEL$_{u1}$} {TEST$_{p2,s2,t2,v1}$}

$\qquad (t1, t2, t3) \leftarrow$ NEWTSR

$\qquad (u1, u2) \leftarrow$ NEWTL $\qquad\qquad s2 \leftarrow s1$

$\qquad (v1, v2) \leftarrow$ NEWTL $\qquad\qquad y \leftarrow$ LINE NUMBER

$\qquad (p2, p3) \leftarrow p1$

$\qquad x \leftarrow$ pointer to a table entry for the constant 1

14. $\langle$for clause$\rangle_{p3} \rightarrow$ FOR$_{p1}$ $\langle$expression$\rangle_{q1}$ {ASSIGN$_{p2,q2}$}

$\qquad (p2, p3) \leftarrow p1 \qquad q2 \leftarrow q1$

Figure 12.24 (continued)

FOR statement appears. This fifth attribute is used by action routine {CHECK} as part of its warning message in case the matching NEXT statement does not refer to the same variable.

In designing the attributed grammar we have assumed the existence of three table-entry-allocating procedures: NEWTR, NEWTSR, and NEWTL.

15. $\langle$to clause$\rangle_{s2} \rightarrow$ TO $\langle$expression$\rangle_{r1}$ $\{SAVE_{r2,s1}\}$

   $r2 \leftarrow r1$ $(s1, s2) \leftarrow$ NEWTSR

REM Statement

16. $\langle$statement$\rangle \rightarrow$ COMMENT

Expressions

17. $\langle$expression$\rangle_{r2} \rightarrow \langle$expression$\rangle_{p1} + \langle$term$\rangle_{q1}$ $\{ADD_{p2,q2,r1}\}$

   $(r1, r2) \leftarrow$ NEWTR $p2 \leftarrow p1$ $q2 \leftarrow q1$

18. $\langle$expression$\rangle_{r2} \rightarrow \langle$expression$\rangle_{p1} - \langle$term$\rangle_{q1}$ $\{SUBT_{p2,q2,r1}\}$

   $(r1, r2) \leftarrow$ NEWTR $p2 \leftarrow p1$ $q2 \leftarrow q1$

19. $\langle$expression$\rangle_{r2} \rightarrow + \langle$term$\rangle_{p1}$ $\{PLUS_{p2,r1}\}$

   $(r1, r2) \leftarrow$ NEWTR $p2 \leftarrow p1$

20. $\langle$expression$\rangle_{r2} \rightarrow - \langle$term$\rangle_{p1}$ $\{NEG_{p2,r1}\}$

   $(r1, r2) \leftarrow$ NEWTR $p2 \leftarrow p1$

21. $\langle$expression$\rangle_{r2} \rightarrow \langle$term$\rangle_{r1}$

   $r2 \leftarrow r1$

22. $\langle$term$\rangle_{r2} \rightarrow \langle$term$\rangle_{p1} * \langle$factor$\rangle_{q1}$ $\{MULT_{p2,q2,r1}\}$

   $(r1, r2) \leftarrow$ NEWTR $p2 \leftarrow p1$ $q2 \leftarrow q1$

23. $\langle$term$\rangle_{r2} \rightarrow \langle$term$\rangle_{p1} / \langle$factor$\rangle_{q1}$ $\{DIV_{p2,q2,r1}\}$

   $(r1, r2) \leftarrow$ NEWTR $p2 \leftarrow p1$ $q2 \leftarrow q1$

24. $\langle$term$\rangle_{r2} \rightarrow \langle$factor$\rangle_{r1}$

   $r2 \leftarrow r1$

25. $\langle$factor$\rangle_{r2} \rightarrow \langle$factor$\rangle_{p1} \uparrow \langle$primary$\rangle_{q1}$ $\{EXP_{p2,q2,r1}\}$

   $(r1, r2) \leftarrow$ NEWTR $p2 \leftarrow p1$ $q2 \leftarrow q1$

26. $\langle$factor$\rangle_{r2} \rightarrow \langle$primary$\rangle_{r1}$

   $r2 \leftarrow r1$

27. $\langle$primary$\rangle_{r2} \rightarrow (\langle$expression$\rangle_{r1})$

   $r2 \leftarrow r1$

28. $\langle$primary$\rangle_{r2} \rightarrow$ OPERAND$_{r1}$

   $r2 \leftarrow r1$

Starting symbol: $\langle$program$\rangle$

Figure 12.24 (continued)

NEWTR returns a pointer to a new table entry for a partial result; NEWTSR returns a pointer to a new table entry for the result of a SAVE atom; and NEWTL returns a pointer to a new table entry for a label. As we shall see in Chapter 14, each of these types of table entries has certain fields needed by the code generator. Some of these fields are to be initialized by NEWTR,

NEWTSR, or NEWTL when the entries are allocated, however, we will defer discussion of this initialization until Chapter 14. Here we need only know that NEWTR, NEWTSR, and NEWTL return appropriate pointers.

In production 13 we assume the ability to obtain a pointer to a previously prepared table entry for the constant 1.

Now we are ready to describe the pushdown processor. Figure 12.25 shows the stack alphabet including the fields of all the stack symbols.

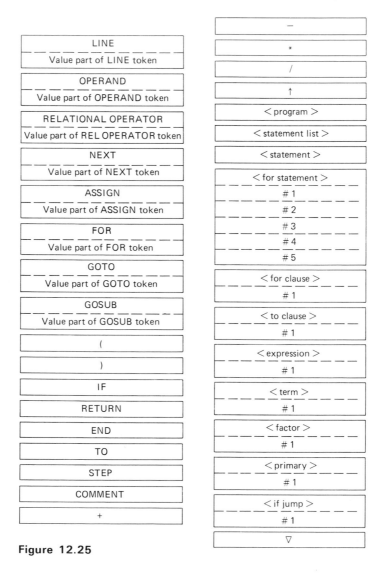

Figure 12.25

	LINE	OPERAND	REL OPERATOR	NEXT	ASSIGN	FOR	GOTO	GOSUB	LEFT PAREN	RIGHT PAREN	IF	RETURN	END	TC	STEP	COMMENT	+	−	*	/	↑	ERROR	ENDMARKER
LINE	1	α	α	1	1	1	1	1	α	α	1	1	1	α	α	1	α	α	α	α	α	γ	β
OPERAND	2	α	2	α	α	α	2	α	α	2	α	α	α	2	2	α	2	2	2	2	2	γ	β
REL OPERATOR	α	S	α	α	α	α	α	α	S	α	α	α	α	α	α	α	S	S	α	α	α	γ	β
NEXT	3	α	α	α	α	α	α	α	α	α	α	α	α	α	α	α	α	α	α	α	α	γ	β
ASSIGN	α	S	α	α	α	α	α	α	S	α	α	α	α	α	α	α	S	S	α	α	α	γ	β
FOR	α	S	α	α	α	α	α	α	S	α	α	α	α	α	α	α	S	S	α	α	α	γ	β
GOTO	4	α	α	α	α	α	α	α	α	α	α	α	α	α	α	α	α	α	α	α	α	γ	β
GOSUB	5	α	α	α	α	α	α	α	α	α	α	α	α	α	α	α	α	α	α	α	α	γ	β
LEFT PAREN	α	S	α	α	α	α	α	α	S	α	α	α	α	α	α	α	S	S	α	α	α	γ	β
RIGHT PAREN	6	α	6	α	α	α	6	α	α	6	α	α	α	6	6	α	6	6	6	6	6	γ	β
IF	α	S	α	α	α	α	α	α	S	α	α	α	α	α	α	α	S	S	α	α	α	γ	β
RETURN	7	α	α	α	α	α	α	α	α	α	α	α	α	α	α	α	α	α	α	α	α	γ	β
END	α	α	α	α	α	α	α	α	α	α	α	α	α	α	α	α	α	α	α	α	α	γ	8
TO	α	S	α	α	α	α	α	α	S	α	α	α	α	α	α	α	S	S	α	α	α	γ	β
STEP	α	S	α	α	α	α	α	α	S	α	α	α	α	α	α	α	S	S	α	α	α	γ	β
COMMENT	9	α	α	α	α	α	α	α	α	α	α	α	α	α	α	α	α	α	α	α	α	γ	β
+	α	S	α	α	α	α	α	α	S	α	α	α	α	α	α	α	α	α	α	α	α	γ	β
−	α	S	α	α	α	α	α	α	S	α	α	α	α	α	α	α	α	α	α	α	α	γ	β
*	α	S	α	α	α	α	α	α	S	α	α	α	α	α	α	α	α	α	α	α	α	γ	β
/	α	S	α	α	α	α	α	α	S	α	α	α	α	α	α	α	α	α	α	α	α	γ	β
↑	α	S	α	α	α	α	α	α	S	α	α	α	α	α	α	α	α	α	α	α	α	γ	β
< program >	ρ	ρ	ρ	ρ	ρ	ρ	ρ	ρ	ρ	ρ	ρ	ρ	ρ	ρ	ρ	ρ	ρ	ρ	ρ	ρ	ρ	ρ	10
< statement list >	S	ρ	ρ	S	S	S	S	S	ρ	ρ	S	S	S	ρ	ρ	S	ρ	ρ	ρ	ρ	ρ	ρ	ρ
< statement >	S	ρ	ρ	ρ	ρ	ρ	ρ	ρ	ρ	ρ	ρ	ρ	ρ	θ	θ	ρ	ρ	ρ	ρ	ρ	ρ	ρ	ρ
< for statement >	S	ρ	ρ	ρ	ρ	ρ	ρ	ρ	ρ	ρ	ρ	ρ	ρ	λ	μ	ρ	ρ	ρ	ρ	ρ	ρ	ρ	ρ
< for clause >	ν	ρ	ρ	ρ	ρ	ρ	ρ	ρ	ρ	ρ	ρ	ρ	ρ	S	ξ	ρ	ρ	ρ	ρ	ρ	ρ	ρ	ρ
< to clause >	11	ρ	ρ	ρ	ρ	μ	μ	μ	μ	ρ	ρ	ρ	ρ	π	S	ρ	ρ	ρ	ρ	ρ	ρ	ρ	ρ
< expression >	12	ρ	S	ρ	ρ	ρ	S	ρ	ρ	S	ρ	ρ	ρ	12	12	ρ	S	S	ρ	ρ	ρ	ρ	ρ
< term >	13	ρ	13	ρ	ρ	ρ	13	ρ	ρ	13	ρ	ρ	ρ	13	13	ρ	13	13	S	S	ρ	ρ	ρ
< factor >	14	ρ	14	ρ	ρ	ρ	14	ρ	ρ	14	ρ	ρ	ρ	14	14	ρ	14	14	14	14	S	ρ	ρ
< primary >	15	ρ	15	ρ	ρ	ρ	15	ρ	ρ	15	ρ	ρ	ρ	15	15	ρ	15	15	15	15	15	ρ	ρ
< if jump >	16	ρ	ρ	ρ	ρ	ρ	ρ	ρ	ρ	ρ	ρ	ρ	ρ	ρ	ρ	ρ	ρ	ρ	ρ	ρ	ρ	ρ	ρ
▽	S	δ	δ	δ	δ	δ	δ	δ	δ	δ	δ	δ	δ	δ	δ	δ	δ	δ	δ	δ	δ	γ	ζ

Figure 12.26

Figure 12.26 shows the control table. Entries labeled *S* correspond to SHIFT. Numbered entries correspond to identify routines. A separate identify routine is specified for each row. Entries labeled with Greek letters correspond to error situations.

The identify routines and error entries are described in Fig. 12.27. Figure 12.28 shows the REDUCE routines and Fig. 12.29 describes the routine ERROR. The REDUCE routines generate the appropriate atoms using a routine PRODUCEATOM which produces its parameter as an atom.

The routine ERROR described in Fig. 12.29 is called when an error is detected. The routine has a string as a parameter and this string is printed as an error message together with the line number obtained from the variable

1: if top of stack is ⟨statement list⟩ ⟨statement⟩ LINE then REDUCE(2)

    else if top of stack is ⟨statement list⟩ LINE then REDUCE(4) else RE-
DUCE(3)

2: REDUCE(28)

3: if top of stack is ⟨for statement⟩ ⟨statement list⟩ NEXT then REDUCE(11)

    else ERROR (NEXT STATEMENT NOT MATCHED WITH FOR
STATEMENT)

4: if top of stack is ⟨statement list⟩ GOTO then REDUCE(6)

    else if top of stack is ⟨expression⟩ GOTO then REDUCE(8)

    else ERROR(COMPILER ERROR)

5: REDUCE(9)

6: if top of stack is (⟨expression⟩) then REDUCE(27)

    else ERROR(UNMATCHED RIGHT PARENTHESIS)

7: REDUCE(10)

8: if top of stack is ⟨statement list⟩ END then REDUCE (1)

    else ERROR(COMPILER ERROR)

9: REDUCE(16)

10: if top of stack is ∇ ⟨program⟩ then PRODUCEATOM(FINIS)

    else ERROR(FOR STATEMENTS INCORRECTLY NESTED – MISS-
ING NEXT)

11: if top of stack is ⟨for clause⟩ ⟨to clause⟩ then REDUCE(13)

    else ERROR(COMPILER ERROR)

12: if top of stack is ASSIGN ⟨expression⟩ then REDUCE(5)

    else if top of stack is ⟨for clause⟩ ⟨to clause⟩ STEP ⟨expression⟩ then
REDUCE(12)

    else if top of stack is FOR ⟨expression⟩ then REDUCE(14)

    else if top of stack is TO ⟨expression⟩ then REDUCE(15)

    else if top of stack is (⟨expression⟩ then ERROR(UNMATCHED LEFT
PARENTHESIS)

    else ERROR(CONSTRUCTION $(second stack symbol from top) $(top
stack symbol) $(input) NOT ALLOWED)

Figure 12.27

13: if top of stack is ⟨expression⟩ + ⟨term⟩ then REDUCE(17)
      else if top of stack is ⟨expression⟩ − ⟨term⟩ then REDUCE(18)
      else if top of stack is + ⟨term⟩ then REDUCE(19)
      else if top of stack is − ⟨term⟩ then REDUCE(20)
      else REDUCE(21)
14: if top of stack is ⟨term⟩ * ⟨factor⟩ then REDUCE(22)
      else if top of stack is ⟨term⟩ / ⟨factor⟩ then REDUCE(23)
      else REDUCE(24)
15: if top of stack is ⟨factor⟩ ↑ ⟨primary⟩ then REDUCE(25)
      else REDUCE(26)
16: if top of stack is IF ⟨expression⟩ RELATIONAL OPERATOR ⟨expression⟩
         ⟨if jump⟩ then REDUCE(7)
      else if top of stack is RELATIONAL OPERATOR ⟨expression⟩ ⟨if jump⟩
        then ERROR(RELATION MISPLACED)
      else ERROR(CONSTRUCTION \$(top three stack symbols) NOT AL-
        LOWED)

α: ERROR(\$(input) FOLLOWS \$(top stack symbol))
β: ERROR(MISSING END STATEMENT)
γ: ERROR( )
δ: ERROR(INITIAL LINE NUMBER MISSING)
ζ: ERROR(NO PROGRAM)
θ: ERROR(\$(input) OCCURS IN ASSIGNMENT STATEMENT)
λ: ERROR(TWO TO CLAUSES IN FOR STATEMENT)
μ: ERROR(TWO STEP CLAUSES IN FOR STATEMENT)
ν: ERROR(FOR STATEMENT INCOMPLETE)
ξ: ERROR(MISSING OR MISPLACED TO CLAUSE IN FOR STATEMENT)
π: ERROR(TWO CONSECUTIVE TO CLAUSES)
ρ: ERROR(COMPILER ERROR)

Figure 12.27 (continued)

REDUCE(1): POP, POP, PUSH($\langle$program$\rangle$)
REDUCE(2): $p \leftarrow$ field of stack symbol LINE
    PRODUCEATOM(LINEN$_p$)
    LINE NUMBER $\leftarrow p$
    POP, POP, POP, PUSH($\langle$statement list$\rangle$)
REDUCE(3): $p \leftarrow$ field of stack symbol LINE
    PRODUCEATOM(LINEN$_p$)
    LINE NUMBER $\leftarrow p$
    POP, PUSH($\langle$statement list$\rangle$)
REDUCE(4): $p \leftarrow$ field of stack symbol LINE
    PRODUCEATOM(LINEN$_p$)
    LINE NUMBER $\leftarrow p$
    POP, POP, PUSH($\langle$statement list$\rangle$)
REDUCE(5): $p \leftarrow$ field of stack symbol ASSIGN
        $q \leftarrow$ field of stack symbol $\langle$expression$\rangle$
    PRODUCEATOM(ASSIGN$_{p,q}$)
    POP, POP, PUSH($\langle$statement$\rangle$)
REDUCE(6): $p \leftarrow$ field of stack symbol GOTO
    PRODUCEATOM(JUMP$_p$)
    POP, PUSH($\langle$statement$\rangle$)
REDUCE(7): $p \leftarrow$ field of lower stack symbol $\langle$expression$\rangle$
        $q \leftarrow$ field of higher stack symbol $\langle$expression$\rangle$
        $r \leftarrow$ field of stack symbol RELATIONAL OPERATOR
        $s \leftarrow$ field of stack symbol $\langle$if jump$\rangle$
    PRODUCEATOM(CONDJUMP$_{p,q,r,s}$)
    POP, POP, POP, POP, POP, PUSH($\langle$statement$\rangle$)
REDUCE(8): $s \leftarrow$ field of stack symbol GOTO
    POP, PUSH($\langle$if jump$\rangle_s$)
REDUCE(9): $p \leftarrow$ field of stack symbol GOSUB
    PRODUCEATOM(JUMPSAVE$_p$)
    POP, PUSH($\langle$statement$\rangle$)
REDUCE(10): PRODUCEATOM(RETURNJUMP)
    POP, PUSH($\langle$statement$\rangle$)

Figure 12.28

REDUCE(11): $p \leftarrow$ first field of stack symbol ⟨for statement⟩

$\qquad$ $t \leftarrow$ second field of stack symbol ⟨for statement⟩

$\qquad$ $u \leftarrow$ third field of stack symbol ⟨for statement⟩

$\qquad$ $v \leftarrow$ fourth field of stack symbol ⟨for statement⟩

$\qquad$ $y \leftarrow$ fifth field of stack symbol ⟨for statement⟩

$\qquad$ $w \leftarrow$ field of stack symbol NEXT

$\quad$ if $(p \neq w)$ then PRINT(NEXT VARIABLE DIFFERS FROM FOR VARI-
ABLE ON LINE \$$(y)$ – ASSUMED FOR VARIABLE INTENDED)

$\quad$ PRODUCEATOM(INCR$_{p,t,}$)

$\quad$ PRODUCEATOM(JUMP$_u$)

$\quad$ PRODUCEATOM(LABEL$_v$)

$\quad$ POP, POP, POP, PUSH(⟨statement⟩)

REDUCE(12): $p \leftarrow$ field of stack symbol ⟨for clause⟩

$\qquad$ $s \leftarrow$ field of stack symbol ⟨to clause⟩

$\qquad$ $x \leftarrow$ field of stack symbol ⟨expression⟩

$\qquad$ $t \leftarrow$ NEWTSR

$\qquad$ $u \leftarrow$ NEWTL

$\qquad$ $v \leftarrow$ NEWTL

$\qquad$ $y \leftarrow$ LINE NUMBER

$\quad$ PRODUCEATOM(SAVE$_{x,t}$)

$\quad$ PRODUCEATOM(LABEL$_u$)

$\quad$ PRODUCEATOM(TEST$_{p,s,t,v}$)

$\quad$ POP, POP, POP, POP, PUSH(⟨for statement⟩$_{p,t,u,v,y}$)

REDUCE(13): $p \leftarrow$ field of stack symbol ⟨for clause⟩

$\qquad$ $s \leftarrow$ field of stack symbol ⟨to clause⟩

$\qquad$ $t \leftarrow$ NEWTSR

$\qquad$ $u \leftarrow$ NEWTL

$\qquad$ $v \leftarrow$ NEWTL

$\qquad$ $y \leftarrow$ LINE NUMBER

$\qquad$ $x \leftarrow$ pointer to table entry for constant 1

$\quad$ PRODUCEATOM(SAVE$_{x,t}$)

$\quad$ PRODUCEATOM(LABEL$_u$)

$\quad$ PRODUCEATOM(TEST$_{p,s,t,v}$)

Figure 12.28 (continued)

POP, POP, PUSH($\langle$for statement$\rangle_{p,t,u,v,y}$)
REDUCE(14): $p \leftarrow$ field of stack symbol FOR
$q \leftarrow$ field of stack symbol $\langle$expression$\rangle$
PRODUCEATOM(ASSIGN$_{p,q}$)
POP, POP, PUSH($\langle$for clause$\rangle_p$)
REDUCE(15): $r \leftarrow$ field of stack symbol $\langle$expression$\rangle$
$s \leftarrow$ NEWTSR
PRODUCEATOM(SAVE$_{r,s}$)
POP, POP, PUSH($\langle$to clause$\rangle_s$)
REDUCE(16): POP, PUSH($\langle$statement$\rangle$)
REDUCE(17): $p \leftarrow$ field of stack symbol $\langle$expression$\rangle$
$q \leftarrow$ field of stack symbol $\langle$term$\rangle$
$r \leftarrow$ NEWTR
PRODUCEATOM(ADD$_{p,q,r}$)
POP, POP, POP, PUSH($\langle$expression$\rangle_r$)
REDUCE(18): $p \leftarrow$ field of stack symbol $\langle$expression$\rangle$
$q \leftarrow$ field of stack symbol $\langle$term$\rangle$
$r \leftarrow$ NEWTR
PRODUCEATOM(SUBT$_{p,q,r}$)
POP, POP, POP, PUSH($\langle$expression$\rangle_r$)
REDUCE(19): $p \leftarrow$ field of stack symbol $\langle$term$\rangle$
$r \leftarrow$ NEWTR
PRODUCEATOM(PLUS$_{p,r}$)
POP, POP, PUSH($\langle$expression$\rangle_r$)
REDUCE(20): $p \leftarrow$ field of stack symbol$\langle$term$\rangle$
$r \leftarrow$ NEWTR
PRODUCEATOM(NEG$_{p,r}$)

Figure 12.28 (continued)

LINE NUMBER. Thus if error β occurred at line 100, the message would be:

100: MISSING END STATEMENT

We assume the capability of inserting particular pieces of information into the error message. In particular when $(input), $(top stack symbol), $(second stack symbol from top), or $(top three stack symbols) appear in an error message, they are replaced by the corresponding symbol or symbols.

POP, POP, PUSH($\langle$expression$\rangle_r$)

REDUCE(21): $r \leftarrow$ field of stack symbol $\langle$term$\rangle$

    POP, PUSH($\langle$expression$\rangle_r$)

REDUCE(22): $p \leftarrow$ field of stack symbol $\langle$term$\rangle$

            $q \leftarrow$ field of stack symbol $\langle$factor$\rangle$

            $r \leftarrow$ NEWTR

    PRODUCEATOM(MULT$_{p,q,r}$)

    POP, POP, POP, PUSH($\langle$term$\rangle_r$)

REDUCE(23): $p \leftarrow$ field of stack symbol $\langle$term$\rangle$

            $q \leftarrow$ field of stack symbol $\langle$factor$\rangle$

            $r \leftarrow$ NEWTR

    PRODUCEATOM(DIV$_{p,q,r}$)

    POP, POP, POP, PUSH($\langle$term$\rangle_r$)

REDUCE(24): $r \leftarrow$ field of stack symbol $\langle$factor$\rangle$

    POP, PUSH($\langle$term$\rangle_r$)

REDUCE(25): $p \leftarrow$ field of stack symbol $\langle$factor$\rangle$

            $q \leftarrow$ field of stack symbol $\langle$primary$\rangle$

            $r \leftarrow$ NEWTR

    PRODUCEATOM(EXP$_{p,q,r}$)

    POP, POP, POP, PUSH($\langle$factor$\rangle_r$)

REDUCE(26): $r \leftarrow$ field of stack symbol $\langle$primary$\rangle$

    POP, PUSH($\langle$factor$\rangle_r$)

REDUCE(27): $r \leftarrow$ field of stack symbol $\langle$expression$\rangle$

    POP, POP, POP, PUSH($\langle$primary$\rangle_r$)

REDUCE(28): $r \leftarrow$ field of stack symbol OPERAND

    POP, PUSH($\langle$primary$\rangle_r$)

Figure 12.28 (continued)

Thus if error α occurs at line 20 with stack symbol IF and input TO, the message is

20: TO FOLLOWS IF

When the symbol is RELATIONAL OPERATOR, the name of the operator is used. When the symbol is OPERAND, either the word CONSTANT or the particular variable involved is used. Also, in the warning message produced in REDUCE(11) we have assumed the ability to insert a line number into the message.

The error message

COMPILER ERROR

is used in those situations that a detailed analysis of the grammar shows should never occur, even in processing an incorrect input string. For example, consider identify-routine 8, where END is the top stack symbol. From the control table we see that END can only be placed on the stack by being shifted above top stack symbol ⟨statement list⟩. Therefore an occurrence of END on the stack has an occurrence of ⟨statement list⟩ below it. Thus, in identify-routine 8 the top two stack symbols should always be ⟨statement list⟩ END, and ERROR should never be called.

The error-recovery procedure uses the strategy of skipping to the next line. The reason for making a special case of the FOR statements is to attempt to avoid bogus error messages about unmatched FOR and NEXT statements. Note that when the error recovery involves pushing ⟨for statement⟩ on the stack, the fifth field is filled in with the current line number for possible usage in a subsequent error message.

The debugging program given in Fig. 10.8 for the syntax box designed in Chapter 10 can also be used as a debugging program for the present design. It visits all the nonerror entries in the control table and all the nonerror branches of the IDENTIFY and REDUCE routines.

Print error message.
Set error flag to indicate an error has occurred.
Scan input string, including current token, until LINE or ⊣ is found.
If token is ⊣, end compilation.

Otherwise, POP stack until one of the symbols in the table below is the top stack symbol and take the indicated action.

Stack Symbol	Action
FOR or ⟨for clause⟩	POP
	PUSH(⟨for statement⟩$_{p,t,u,v,y}$)
	$\quad p \leftarrow$ field of FOR or ⟨for clause⟩
	$\quad t \leftarrow$ NEWTSR
	$\quad u \leftarrow$ NEWTL
	$\quad v \leftarrow$ NEWTL
	$\quad y \leftarrow$ LINE NUMBER
⟨for statement⟩	NONE
⟨statement list⟩	NONE
▽	PUSH(⟨statement list⟩)

Fig. 12.29 Description of Routine ERROR

12.9   REFERENCES

Historically, shift-identify parsing was developed in terms of the concept of "precedence." The initial formulation of precedence methods and the definitions of several classes of grammars that can be parsed using these methods is covered in Floyd [1963], Pair [1964], and Wirth and Weber [1966]. Weak-precedence grammars are defined in Ichbiah and Morse [1970]. Simple mixed-strategy-precedence grammars are introduced in Aho, Denning, and Ullman [1972], and are a special case of the mixed-strategy-precedence grammars of McKeeman, Horning, and Wortman [1970]. The properties of classes of precedence grammars are studied in Fischer [1969] Graham [1970], Learner and Lim [1970], McAfee and Presser [1972], and Gray and Harrison [1972, 1973]. The various classes of precedence grammars are extensively studied in Aho and Ullman [1972a, 1973a].

Error recovery for shift-identify parsing is discussed in Wirth [1968].

PROBLEMS

1. Find two grammars that generate different languages but have the same SHIFT-IDENTIFY control table (without conflicts).

2. Find a grammar with starting symbol $\langle S \rangle$ for which the following is a SHIFT-IDENTIFY control table

	0	1	$\dashv$
$\langle S \rangle$	REJECT	SHIFT	IDENTIFY
$\langle A \rangle$	SHIFT	IDENTIFY	IDENTIFY
0	IDENTIFY	IDENTIFY	IDENTIFY
1	SHIFT	SHIFT	REJECT
$\triangledown$	SHIFT	REJECT	REJECT

3. Show whether each of the following statements is true or false. If a statement is false, give a counterexample.

   a) Let A be a stack symbol and X an input symbol. Then

$$A \text{ BELOW } X$$

   if and only if

$$X \text{ is in FOLLOW}(A).$$

   b) Every language generated by a grammar with no shift-identify conflicts is also generated by some grammar with shift-identify conflicts.

   c) Suppose there is a production

$$\langle L \rangle \rightarrow \alpha A$$

   for string α and symbol A. If $\langle L \rangle$ REDUCED-BY X, then A REDUCED-BY X.

d) If A BELOW B and B BELOW C, then A BELOW C.

4. Design a weak-precedence processor for the following grammar with starting symbol $\langle S \rangle$:

$$\langle S \rangle \rightarrow \langle S \rangle \langle A \rangle$$
$$\langle S \rangle \rightarrow \langle A \rangle$$
$$\langle A \rangle \rightarrow 1 \langle S \rangle 0$$
$$\langle A \rangle \rightarrow 1 0$$

5. For each of the following languages, find a weak-precedence grammar and design the corresponding pushdown recognizer.

a) $\{1^n \, 0^n\}$ $n > 0$

b) $\{w \, m \, w^r\}$ w in $(0 + 1)^*$

c) $\{1^n \, a \, 0^n\} \cup \{1^n \, b \, 0^{2n}\}$ $n > 0$

6. Show that every regular set not containing ϵ has a weak-precedence grammar.

7. Find a weak-precedence grammar for Boolean expressions in ALGOL. Do not carry the derivation below the level of $\langle$unsigned number$\rangle$, $\langle$variable$\rangle$, or $\langle$function designator$\rangle$.

8. Why does it not make sense to define a class of grammars analogous to weak precedence such that if two potential handles are on the stack, the shorter one is always the correct handle?

9. Using your favorite language write a program to implement the processor of Fig. 12.5.

10. Show that the following grammar is not a simple mixed-strategy-precedence grammar.

$$\langle S \rangle \rightarrow 1 \langle S \rangle 0$$
$$\langle S \rangle \rightarrow 0 \langle S \rangle 1$$
$$\langle S \rangle \rightarrow 1 0$$

11. Design a simple mixed-strategy-precedence processor for the following grammar (Aho, Denning, and Ullman [1972]):

$$\langle S \rangle \rightarrow a \langle A \rangle$$
$$\langle S \rangle \rightarrow b \langle B \rangle$$
$$\langle A \rangle \rightarrow \langle C \rangle \langle A \rangle 1$$
$$\langle A \rangle \rightarrow \langle C \rangle 1$$
$$\langle B \rangle \rightarrow \langle D \rangle \langle B \rangle \langle E \rangle 1$$
$$\langle B \rangle \rightarrow \langle D \rangle \langle E \rangle 1$$
$$\langle C \rangle \rightarrow 0$$
$$\langle D \rangle \rightarrow 0$$
$$\langle E \rangle \rightarrow 1$$

12. Design a simple mixed-strategy-precedence grammar and the corresponding processor for the language

$$\{a\ 0^n\ 1^n\} \cup \{b\ 0^n\ 1^{2n}\} \qquad n > 0$$

13. For the following ALGOL-like grammar with starting symbol ⟨program⟩:

    1. ⟨program⟩ → ⟨block⟩

    2. ⟨program⟩ → ⟨compound statement⟩

    3. ⟨block⟩ → ⟨block head⟩ ; ⟨compound tail⟩

    4. ⟨block head⟩ → **begin** d

    5. ⟨block head⟩ → ⟨block head⟩; d

    6. ⟨compound tail⟩ → s **end**

    7. ⟨compound tail⟩ → s ; ⟨compound tail⟩

    8. ⟨compound statement⟩ → **begin** ⟨compound tail⟩

  a) Show that the grammar is weak precedence.

  b) Design the weak-precedence parser.

  c) Design an appropriate set of error messages.

  d) Design local error-recovery routines.

  e) Design global error-recovery routines.

14. a) Design a weak-precedence grammar for S-expressions in LISP.

  b) Design the corresponding processor.

  c) Design error messages and error-recovery routines.

15. Design the error processing for the weak-precedence arithmetic-expression processor of Fig. 12.9. Specify the error messages and the error-recovery methods.

16. For each of the following machines, design a debugging sequence (or sequences) that visits all the nonerror configurations.

  a) Fig. 12.5

  b) Fig. 12.9

  c) Fig. 12.14

17. For each REJECT situation in Fig. 12.18, find the shortest input sequence that reaches that situation.

18. Find three error sequences for which the local error-recovery procedures of Fig. 12.20 do a bad job. Describe what went wrong.

19. Restate the definition of weak-precedence grammars using the relations $<$, $\leq$, $\doteq$, $>$ defined in Section 12.6.

20. a) Find a grammar with no SHIFT-IDENTIFY conflicts for the language:

$$\{w\ w^r\} \qquad w\ \text{in}\ (0 + 1)^+$$

  b) Show why this language cannot be recognized by a pushdown machine.

21. Using your favorite language, write a program which will test a given grammar

to see if it is weak precedence and, if it is, will output a weak-precedence-parsing program for that grammar.

22. Using your favorite language, write a program to which you can input a grammar and which will output either a SHIFT-IDENTIFY table or the set of SHIFT-IDENTIFY conflicts.

23. For some grammars that have no SHIFT-IDENTIFY conflicts, but are not simple mixed-strategy-precedence grammars, identify routines can be designed that use the current input in selecting the handle production.

   a) For the following grammar, design a SHIFT-IDENTIFY machine using this capability.

$$\langle S \rangle \rightarrow \langle A \rangle \, c$$
$$\langle S \rangle \rightarrow \langle B \rangle \, d$$
$$\langle A \rangle \rightarrow a$$
$$\langle B \rangle \rightarrow a$$

Starting symbol: $\langle S \rangle$

   b) Formulate the above capability as a design principle.

24. Show that every context-free language has a grammar with no SHIFT-IDENTIFY conflicts (Answer in Appendix C).

25. Find the atom string output of the MINI-BASIC syntax box design of Section 12.8 for the debugging program of Fig. 10.8.

26. Show why each of the entries mark ρ in Fig. 12.26 cannot be reached even for nonsentences.

27. List the error messages that would be produced by the MINI-BASIC syntax box design of Section 12.8 for the following input sequence.

```
10 END
20 FOR A = 1 STEP 1 TO 2
30 FOR B = 2
40 LET Y = (B + (C * D)
50 NEXT A
60 IF A > B > C LET X = 6
70 GOSUB 65
80 GOTO 80
80 IF A = B GOSUB 80
```

28. a) Show that, in the MINI-BASIC grammar of Fig. 12.22, if production 7 is changed to

   7′ $\langle$statement$\rangle \rightarrow$ IF $\langle$expression$\rangle$ RELATIONAL OPERATOR $\langle$expression$\rangle$ GOTO

   and production 8 is deleted, the resulting grammar is weak precedence.

b) Design the corresponding weak-precedence parser.

c) Suppose a MINI-BASIC program which contains the incorrect statement

$$100 \text{ IF } 1 < X < 2 \text{ GOTO } 10$$

but is otherwise correct is input to that processor. Show that, no matter where the incorrect statement occurs in the program, the processor does not detect the error until it is processing the final END statement.

29. Design a more-sophisticated error-recovery procedure than that used in Section 12.8.

30. Find an incorrect MINI-BASIC program for which the error messages produced by the syntax box design of Section 12.8 are misleading.

31. a) Assuming the MINI-BASIC lexical box of Chapter 4 is working correctly, determine which error entries in the transition table of Fig. 12.26 can never be reached.

b) Find a small set of MINI-BASIC programs that exercises all the reachable error transitions.

c) Based on the results of Part a, design an improved set of error messages.

32. a) Using your favorite language, implement the MINI-BASIC syntax box design of Section 12.8.

b) Debug your program using the program of Fig. 10.8. Check to see that the output is correct for this program.

33. Show that the MINI-BASIC grammar given in Fig. 12.22 is a simple mixed-strategy-precedence grammar.

34. Rewrite productions 11 through 15 in Fig. 12.24 so that FOR/NEXT constructions generate atoms suitable for generating code to implement the run-time flow chart of Fig. 10.18 (instead of that of Fig. 10.3a).

35. Show that whenever identify-routine 12 in Fig. 12.27 is selected, and the top two stack symbols are STEP ⟨expression⟩, the preceding two stack symbols are ⟨for clause⟩ ⟨to clause⟩.

36. Rewrite the identify routines of Fig. 12.27 to take advantage of the fact that not all sequences of stack symbols can be pushed on the stack. For instance, identify-routine 8 can be changed to REDUCE(1) and the first line of identify routine 14 can be changed to

if top of stack is * ⟨factor⟩ then REDUCE(22)

37. Find an S-attributed Polish translation grammar with a weak-precedence input grammar that specifies the processing performed by the MINI-BASIC lexical box of Chapter 4.

38. Find an incorrect MINI-BASIC program for which the processor of Chapter 10 detects the error earlier in the program than does the processor of Section 12.8.

39. Consider the following grammar with starting symbol ⟨body⟩ (Morse and Harris, unpublished).

1. ⟨body⟩ → DECLARATION ; ⟨body⟩
2. ⟨body⟩ → ⟨statement list⟩
3. ⟨statement list⟩ → ⟨statement list⟩; STATEMENT
4. ⟨statement list⟩ → STATEMENT

a) Show that this grammar is not weak precedence.

b) Show that it is still possible to design a SHIFT-IDENTIFY processor for this grammar since, whenever the righthand sides of both productions 3 and 4 are on top of the stack, it is always true that production 3 is the handle.

40. A grammar is said to be a *simple precedence grammar* (Wirth and Weber [1966]) if there are no grammatical symbols A and B such that two or more of the following relations hold (the relations are defined in Section 12.6):

$$A \lessdot B$$

$$A \doteq B$$

$$A \gtrdot B$$

A grammar is said to be *uniquely invertible* if no two productions have the same righthand side.

a) Show that every uniquely invertible simple-precedence grammar is a weak-precedence grammar.

b) Show that a language has a simple-precedence grammar if and only if it has a weak-precedence grammar (Aho, Denning, and Ullman [1972]).

41. The size of a SHIFT-IDENTIFY machine can sometimes be reduced by the use of precedence functions (Aho and Ullman [1973a]). For stack symbol x, let $f(x)$ be an associated integer and for input symbol y, let $g(y)$ be an associated integer. Note that since a terminal symbol z is both a stack symbol and input symbol, it has two associated integers $f(z)$ and $g(z)$. Suppose that for stack symbol x and input symbol y, whenever x BELOW y, it is the case that $f(x) < g(y)$. Suppose also that whenever x REDUCED-BY y, it is the case that $f(x) > g(y)$. Then the control table of the machine can be replaced with tables for the precedence functions f and g.

a) Find precedence functions for the control table of Fig. 12.9.

b) Find precedence functions for the control table of Fig. 12.4.

c) Find precedence functions for the control table of Fig. 12.13.

d) Show that the following grammar is a suffix-free SI grammar but that it is impossible to describe its control table with precedence functions.

$$⟨S⟩ → ⟨A⟩ \ a$$
$$⟨S⟩ → ⟨B⟩ \ b$$
$$⟨A⟩ → ba$$
$$⟨B⟩ → ab$$

Starting symbol: ⟨S⟩

e) Find precedence functions for the control table of Fig. 12.26. Design error messages for the resulting processor.

f) Describe a general procedure which, given a SHIFT-IDENTIFY control table, will determine whether or not precedence functions exist and, if they do, will find appropriate precedence functions.

42. a) An operator grammar is one with no ϵ-productions and no occurrence of two adjacent nonterminals on the righthand side of a production. Show that an intermediate string derived from the starting symbol of an operator grammar cannot have two adjacent nonterminals.

b) Given an operator grammar with starting symbol $\langle S \rangle$, define TFOLLOW(X) as the set of input symbols that can either immediately follow an X or immediately follow a nonterminal that immediately follows an X in an intermediate string derived from $\langle S \rangle \dashv$. Define TFIRST(X) as the set of input symbols that occur as the first terminal symbol in an intermediate string derived from X. Compute the TFOLLOW and TFIRST sets for the following grammar:

$$\langle S \rangle \rightarrow a$$
$$\langle S \rangle \rightarrow (\langle S \rangle)$$
$$\langle S \rangle \rightarrow (\langle A \rangle)$$
$$\langle A \rangle \rightarrow \langle S \rangle, \langle S \rangle$$
$$\langle A \rangle \rightarrow \langle S \rangle, \langle A \rangle$$

Starting symbol: $\langle S \rangle$

c) For some operator grammars, a parsing method can be used where the decision to shift or identify is based on the topmost stack symbol that is not a nonterminal and on the current input. Formulate a reducing principle and a shifting principle, similar to those stated in Section 12.2, for the control table of such a parser. This parsing method is a variant of operator-precedence parsing (Floyd [1963]).

d) Use the principles of Part c) to design a machine for the grammar of Part b).

e) Use the above principles to design a recognizer for the grammar of Fig. 12.6. Assume the recognizer need only produce a "sparse" parse (Gray and Harrison [1972, 1973]), where a single stack symbol represents nonterminals $\langle E \rangle$, $\langle T \rangle$, and $\langle F \rangle$, and where productions 2 and 4 are not recognized.

43. Suppose that the control table for a simple mixed-strategy-precedence grammar is filled in with SHIFT and IDENTIFY only when required by the shifting and reducing principles.

a) Show how to test the grammar to determine which REJECT entries in the control table will never be accessed, even for nonsentences.

b) Show how to test the grammar to determine which identify routines need not check for errors.

13
Shift-Reduce
Processing

13.1 INTRODUCTION

In this chapter we consider SHIFT-REDUCE processing. Recall from Chapter 11 that in SHIFT-REDUCE processing the stack symbols are not just the grammatical symbols but can encode additional information that allows the machine to eliminate the IDENTIFY step and perform reductions directly using only the information in the top stack symbol and the current input. For this reason, when compared with SHIFT-IDENTIFY processors SHIFT-REDUCE processors generally require less time to process a given input string but require more storage space. Furthermore, the SHIFT-REDUCE processors presented in this chapter have a particular property (discussed in Section 13.7) that usually allows better error messages and error-recovery methods than those for SHIFT-IDENTIFY processors.

SHIFT-REDUCE methods and SHIFT-IDENTIFY methods are applicable to exactly the same class of languages; i.e., if a language can be recognized by a machine of one type, then it can also be recognized by a machine of the other type. However the set of grammars that can be processed by the SHIFT-IDENTIFY methods presented in this book are properly contained in the set of grammars that can be processed by the SHIFT-REDUCE methods presented in this book.

13.2 AN EXAMPLE

We first consider the problem of processing the grammar of Fig. 13.1 in a bottom-up manner. This grammar is not a simple mixed-strategy-precedence grammar because there is a shift-identify conflict with stack symbol $\langle A \rangle$ and input b.

1. $\langle S \rangle \rightarrow a \langle A \rangle b$
2. $\langle S \rangle \rightarrow c$
3. $\langle A \rangle \rightarrow b \langle S \rangle$
4. $\langle A \rangle \rightarrow \langle B \rangle b$
5. $\langle B \rangle \rightarrow a \langle A \rangle$
6. $\langle B \rangle \rightarrow c$

Starting symbol: $\langle S \rangle$

Figure 13.1

Looking more closely at the situation of stack symbol $\langle A \rangle$ and input b, we could choose between shift and identify or even shift and reduce if we could ascertain whether the stack symbol $\langle A \rangle$ represents the $\langle A \rangle$ from the righthand side of production 1 or the $\langle A \rangle$ in the righthand side of production 5. If the $\langle A \rangle$ represents the $\langle A \rangle$ in the righthand side of production 1 the top of the stack is not a handle and the proper pushdown action is to push b. If the $\langle A \rangle$ represents the $\langle A \rangle$ in the righthand side of production 5, there is a handle on top of the stack and the handle production is production 5. The correct pushdown operation is therefore REDUCE(5).

Our plan in this chapter is to design SHIFT-REDUCE pushdown machines whose stack symbols are based on entities like "the $\langle A \rangle$ in the righthand side of production 1" and "the $\langle A \rangle$ from production 5." To facilitate discussion, we refer to such entities as "grammatical occurrences." Specifically,

> a *grammatical occurrence* (except for the starting occurrence defined below) is specified by a production name and a position number. The position gives the location of a symbol in the righthand side of the given production, counting the leftmost symbol as the first symbol.

The $\langle A \rangle$ in the righthand side of production 1 is specified by production 1 and position 2 or simply $(1, 2)$. The c from production 6 is given by pair $(6, 1)$.

In a bottom-up processor for the grammar of Fig. 13.1, a stack symbol representing nonterminal $\langle S \rangle$ might correspond to the occurrence of $\langle S \rangle$ in production 3, in which case the appropriate pushdown operation is REDUCE(3). However the stack symbol might instead correspond to the $\langle S \rangle$ which begins the derivation of the original input sequence, in which case the processor should accept if the current input is endmarker. To associate a grammatical occurrence with this second case, we adopt the convention that

> every grammar has a grammatical occurrence known as the *starting occurrence* which is specified by the starting symbol.

It is often convenient to use a notation for occurrences that emphasizes the grammatical symbol of which a particular grammatical occurrence is an occurrence. One such notation is to represent a grammatical occurrence by a grammatical symbol with two subscripts giving production name and position number. Under this convention, grammatical occurrence (1, 2) from Fig. 13.1 would be written $\langle A \rangle_{1,2}$, because the second symbol of the right-hand side of production 1 is $\langle A \rangle$. Similarly we would write $\langle B \rangle_{4,1}$ instead of (4, 1). The name $\langle A \rangle_{1,2}$ has an advantage over (1, 2) in that one can see from the name $\langle A \rangle_{1,2}$ that an occurrence of $\langle A \rangle$ is indicated.

It frequently happens that knowing the grammatical symbol and the production name is sufficient to identify a grammatical occurrence. This happens whenever there is only one occurrence of the given grammatical symbol in the righthand side of the given production. In such cases, the subscript notation can be shortened by eliminating the position subscript. In the current example, name $\langle A \rangle_{1,2}$ can be shortened to $\langle A \rangle_1$ because there is only one occurrence of $\langle A \rangle$ in the righthand side of production 1, namely the second symbol. We also employ the single subscript $_0$ to indicate the starting occurrence.

Given a derivation tree, there is a straightforward way of associating nodes with grammatical occurrences. The root node is associated with the starting occurrence and every other node is associated in the obvious way with a corresponding grammatical occurrence in the righthand side of the production used to place the node on the tree. For example, Fig. 13.2(a)

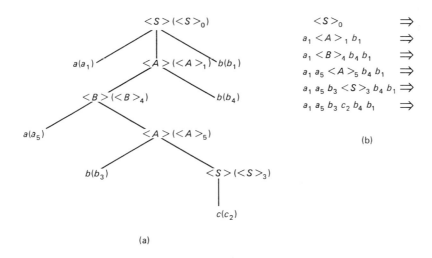

(a)

$$
\begin{array}{ll}
\langle S \rangle_0 & \Rightarrow \\
a_1\ \langle A \rangle_1\ b_1 & \Rightarrow \\
a_1\ \langle B \rangle_4\ b_4\ b_1 & \Rightarrow \\
a_1\ a_5\ \langle A \rangle_5\ b_4\ b_1 & \Rightarrow \\
a_1\ a_5\ b_3\ \langle S \rangle_3\ b_4\ b_1 \Rightarrow \\
a_1\ a_5\ b_3\ c_2\ b_4\ b_1 & \Rightarrow
\end{array}
$$

(b)

Figure 13.2

shows the derivation tree for *aabcbb* using the grammar of Fig. 13.1. The grammatical occurrence associated with each node is shown in parentheses.

Similarly, given a derivation, a grammatical occurrence can be associated with each symbol in each intermediate string of the derivation. Figure 13.2(b) shows the rightmost derivation of *aabcbb*, where, for convenience, we write the names of the grammatical occurrences rather than the names of the grammatical symbols.

We now show how the idea of grammatical occurrences can be used in a SHIFT-REDUCE processor. Figure 13.3 shows a SHIFT-REDUCE recognizer for the grammar in Fig. 13.1. Part a) gives the push table (with the blank entries understood to contain REJECT) and part b) gives the control table. The machine uses the grammatical occurrences of the grammar as stack symbols. The notation of the figure is the single subscript notation in which the subscript is the production number. Each REDUCE routine is assumed to consist of a number of POP's equal to the length of the righthand side of the corresponding production, followed by a PUSHT of the lefthand side nonterminal, as described in Chapter 11. For instance, REDUCE(1) is

	a	b	c	$<S>$	$<A>$	$<B>$
∇	a_1		c_2	$<S>_0$		
$<S>_0$						
a_1	a_5	b_3	c_6		$<A>_1$	$<B>_4$
$<A>_1$		b_1				
b_1						
c_2						
b_3	a_1		c_2	$<S>_3$		
$<S>_3$						
$<B>_4$		b_4				
b_4						
a_5	a_5	b_3	c_6		$<A>_5$	$<B>_4$
$<A>_5$						
c_6						

Push table

(a)

Figure 13.3

equivalent to

$$\text{POP, POP, POP, PUSHT}(\langle S \rangle)$$

The grammatical symbol represented by each stack symbol is the grammatical symbol corresponding to the occurrence; e.g. the grammatical symbol represented by $\langle A \rangle_1$ is simply $\langle A \rangle$. The information encoded in each stack symbol is the specification of a particular occurrence of the represented grammatical symbol. Since the machine is a bottom-up recognizer, during the processing of an acceptable input string, the string represented by the stack concatenated with the unprocessed terminals is an intermediate string in the rightmost derivation of the original input string. The machine is designed so that

for any acceptable input, the symbols on the stack are the grammatical occurrences associated with the represented intermediate string.

To illustrate this feature, Fig. 13.4 shows a stack movie of the machine accepting *aabcbb*, the input string corresponding to Fig. 13.2. The movie

	a	b	c	$\dashv$
∇	SHIFT	SHIFT	SHIFT	REJECT
$\langle S \rangle_0$	REJECT	REJECT	REJECT	ACCEPT
a_1	SHIFT	SHIFT	SHIFT	REJECT
$\langle A \rangle_1$	SHIFT	SHIFT	SHIFT	REJECT
b_1	REDUCE(1)	REDUCE(1)	REDUCE(1)	REDUCE(1)
c_2	REDUCE(2)	REDUCE(2)	REDUCE(2)	REDUCE(2)
b_3	SHIFT	SHIFT	SHIFT	REJECT
$\langle S \rangle_3$	REDUCE(3)	REDUCE(3)	REDUCE(3)	REDUCE(3)
$\langle B \rangle_4$	SHIFT	SHIFT	SHIFT	REJECT
b_4	REDUCE(4)	REDUCE(4)	REDUCE(4)	REDUCE(4)
a_5	SHIFT	SHIFT	SHIFT	REJECT
$\langle A \rangle_5$	REDUCE(5)	REDUCE(5)	REDUCE(5)	REDUCE(5)
c_6	REDUCE(6)	REDUCE(6)	REDUCE(6)	REDUCE(6)

Control table

(b)

Figure 13.3 (continued)

1. $\triangledown$	$a\ a\ b\ c\ b\ b \dashv$	SHIFT
2. $\triangledown\ a_1$	$a\ b\ c\ b\ b \dashv$	SHIFT
3. $\triangledown\ a_1\ a_5$	$b\ c\ b\ b \dashv$	SHIFT
4. $\triangledown\ a_1\ a_5\ b_3$	$c\ b\ b \dashv$	SHIFT
5. $\triangledown\ a_1\ a_5\ b_3\ c_2$	$b\ b \dashv$	REDUCE(2)
6. $\triangledown\ a_1\ a_5\ b_3\ \langle S \rangle_3$	$b\ b \dashv$	REDUCE(3)
7. $\triangledown\ a_1\ a_5\ \langle A \rangle_5$	$b\ b \dashv$	REDUCE(5)
8. $\triangledown\ a_1\ \langle B \rangle_4$	$b\ b \dashv$	SHIFT
9. $\triangledown\ a_1\ \langle B \rangle_4\ b_4$	$b \dashv$	REDUCE(4)
10. $\triangledown\ a_1\ \langle A \rangle_1$	$b \dashv$	SHIFT
11. $\triangledown\ a_1\ \langle A \rangle_1\ b_1$	$\dashv$	REDUCE(1)
12. $\triangledown\ \langle S \rangle_0$	$\dashv$	ACCEPT

Figure 13.4

may be compared with Fig. 13.2 to verify the correspondence. For example, the a_1 in the stack movie is seen to correspond to the node labeled with grammatical occurrence a_1 in Fig. 13.2(a), and to the a_1 in the intermediate strings of Fig. 13.2(b).

Consider line 1 of Fig. 13.4, with top stack symbol $\triangledown$ and input symbol a. Since the top stack symbol is $\triangledown$, the first input symbol must begin a string derivable from $\langle S \rangle$. From the two productions for $\langle S \rangle$, we see that the first input symbol must correspond to one of the two occurrences a_1 or c_2. Therefore the input symbol a must correspond to occurrence a_1 and, in particular, does not correspond to occurrence a_5. The push-table entry for row $\triangledown$ and column a in fact specifies that stack symbol a_1 be pushed.

Now consider line 2 of Fig. 13.4, with top stack symbol a_1 and input symbol a. Since a_1 is not the rightmost occurrence in production 1, the top of the stack does not represent a handle. From the grammar, we see that the occurrence of a_1 must be followed by a portion of the input string generated from occurrence $\langle A \rangle_1$. The string generated from $\langle A \rangle_1$ can begin with either occurrence b_3 or occurrence $\langle B \rangle_4$. The string generated from $\langle B \rangle_4$ can begin with either a_5 or c_6. Therefore the input symbol a corresponds to occurrence a_5, not to occurrence a_1. The push table entry for row a_1 and column a, in fact, specifies that stack symbol a_5 be pushed.

In line 3 of Fig. 13.4, the top stack symbol is a_5 and the input symbol is b. From the grammar, we see that occurrence a_5 must be followed by occurrence $\langle A \rangle_5$, which can generate a string beginning with either b_3 or $\langle B \rangle_4$, which in turn can generate a string beginning with either a_5 or c_6. We conclude that the input symbol b corresponds to occurrence b_3 and not to occurrences b_1 or b_4.

In line 4, the top stack symbol is b_3 and the input symbol is c. From the grammar, occurrence b_3 must be followed by occurrence $\langle S \rangle_3$, which can generate a string beginning with either a_1 or c_2. Therefore the input symbol c corresponds to occurrence c_2.

In line 5, the top stack symbol is c_2 and the input symbol is b. Since c_2 is the rightmost occurrence in its production, the presence of stack symbol c_2 on top of the stack indicates that there is a handle on top of the stack and that the handle production is production 2. The machine performs REDUCE(2), which pops c_2 off the stack and replaces it with a stack symbol representing grammatical symbol $\langle S \rangle$, the lefthand side of production 2. The stack symbol below the handle is b_3. From the grammar, we see that occurrence b_3 must be followed by occurrence $\langle S \rangle_3$, and cannot be followed by occurrence $\langle S \rangle_0$. Therefore the pushed stack symbol, representing grammatical symbol $\langle S \rangle$ must be $\langle S \rangle_3$. In fact, the push-table entry for row b_3 and column $\langle S \rangle$ specifies that stack symbol $\langle S \rangle_3$ be pushed.

In line 6, the top stack symbol is $\langle S \rangle_3$ and the input symbol is b. Since $\langle S \rangle_3$ is the rightmost occurrence in its production, there is a handle on top of the stack and the handle production is production 3. The machine performs REDUCE(3), which pops the top two symbols off the stack and replaces them with a stack symbol representing $\langle A \rangle$. The stack symbol below the handle is a_5. An analysis shows that the only occurrence of $\langle A \rangle$ that can follow a_5 is $\langle A \rangle_5$, not $\langle A \rangle_1$. Therefore $\langle A \rangle_5$ is pushed above a_5.

The stack movie continues in a similar manner. Finally, in step 12 the top stack symbol is $\langle S \rangle_0$ and the input symbol is $\dashv$. Since the top stack symbol is $\langle S \rangle_0$, the represented grammatical string is $\langle S \rangle$. Therefore in this configuration the machine does ACCEPT.

Having demonstrated how this machine recognizes a particular input sequence, we now discuss how the machine can be designed. The design methods of Chapter 12 were based on the relation BELOW which describes the grammatical symbols that can be represented by adjacent stack symbols during the processing of an acceptable input. In this chapter, the design procedures are based on considerations of which grammatical occurrences can be represented by adjacent stack symbols during the processing of an acceptable input. We express the new design procedures in terms of a relation on grammatical occurrences we call OBELOW. As the name suggest, OBELOW can be thought of as BELOW defined for occurrences.

Before defining OBELOW, we present a variation of FIRST which we call OFIRST.

If X_i is a grammatical occurrence of symbol X and Y_j is a grammatical occurrence of symbol Y, we write

$$X_i \text{ in OFIRST}(Y_j)$$

if and only if either

a) X_i is Y_j itself, or

b) X_i begins an intermediate string derived from Y without using ϵ-productions.

When we say in condition 2 that "X_i begins an intermediate string derived from Y," we mean symbolically that

$$Y \overset{*}{\Rightarrow} \langle L \rangle\ \beta \Rightarrow X\ \alpha\ \beta$$

for some $\langle L \rangle$, β and α such that X_i is the leftmost occurrence in the right-hand side of production:

$$\langle L \rangle \rightarrow X\ \alpha$$

Since the grammar of Fig. 13.1 has no ϵ-productions, the need for the second clause in condition 2 does not arise in this example. The clause is included in the definition for use in later sections where ϵ-productions are considered.

Given the generalization of FIRST to OFIRST, we now generalize BELOW (given in Section 12.4) to OBELOW as follows:

If A is a grammatical occurrence or the bottommarker and Y_j is a grammatical occurrence, we write

$$A \text{ OBELOW } Y_j$$

if and only if one of the following two conditions holds:

a) there is a grammatical occurrence Z_i immediately following occurrence A in the righthand side of some production, and

$$Y_j \text{ is in OFIRST}(Z_i); \text{ or}$$

b) A is the bottommarker and

$$Y_j \text{ is in OFIRST}(\langle S \rangle_0)$$

where $\langle S \rangle_0$ is the starting occurrence.

Returning to the example of Fig. 13.1, it can be calculated that

$$\text{OFIRST}(\langle A \rangle_1) = \{a_5, b_3, c_6, \langle A \rangle_1, \langle B \rangle_4\},$$

and therefore

$a_1 \text{ OBELOW } a_5,$ $a_1 \text{ OBELOW } b_3,$ $a_1 \text{ OBELOW } c_6,$

$a_1 \text{ OBELOW } \langle A \rangle_1,$ $a_1 \text{ OBELOW } \langle B \rangle_4.$

The OBELOW matrix for the given grammar is given in Fig. 13.5.

The push table of Fig. 13.3(a) is designed to push a symbol if and only if the top stack symbol and the newly pushed symbol satisfy relation

OBELOW. Because of this, the push table and the matrix can be viewed as representing the same information. For example, the matrix indicates

$$a_1 \text{ OBELOW } \langle A\rangle_1$$

and the push table says that $\langle A\rangle_1$ is the $\langle A\rangle$ to be pushed on top of a_1. Generally, each row of the push table has one nonblank entry for each nonblank entry in the relation matrix. The occurrence names in the push-table row are the matrix column names which have a 1 in the corresponding matrix row. Thus the push table can be viewed as a representation of the relation OBELOW.

The push table of Fig. 13.3(a) also has an interpretation as the specification of a certain finite-state "handle detector." This handle detector is shown in Fig. 13.6. The states of the handle detector are the stack symbols of Fig. 13.3(a), i.e., the grammatical occurrences and the bottommarker. The input set of the handle detector consists of the grammatical symbols and a new symbol named TOP. Symbol TOP is to be used as an endmarker for the handle detector. We use TOP instead of $\dashv$ so that handle-detector input sequences will not be confused with pushdown-machine input sequences.

The transitions in the columns labeled with grammatical symbols are identical to the entries in the push table of Fig. 11.3(a). The transitions in the

	$\langle S\rangle_0$	a_1	$\langle A\rangle_1$	b_1	c_2	b_3	$\langle S\rangle_3$	$\langle B\rangle_4$	b_4	a_5	$\langle A\rangle_5$	c_6
▽	1	1			1							
$\langle S\rangle_0$												
a_1			1			1		1		1		1
$\langle A\rangle_1$					1							
b_1												
c_2												
b_3		1			1		1					
$\langle S\rangle_3$												
$\langle B\rangle_4$									1			
b_4												
a_5					1			1		1	1	1
$\langle A\rangle_5$												
c_6												

Figure 13.5 OBELOW

	a	b	c	$\langle S \rangle$	$\langle A \rangle$	$\langle B \rangle$	TOP
$\triangledown$	a_1		c_2	$\langle S \rangle_0$			NOT YET
$\langle S \rangle_0$							STARTING
a_1	a_5	b_3	c_6		$\langle A \rangle_1$	$\langle B \rangle_4$	NOT YET
$\langle A \rangle_1$		b_1					NOT YET
b_1							PROD(1)
c_2							PROD(2)
b_3	a_1		c_2	$\langle S \rangle_3$			NOT YET
$\langle S \rangle_3$							PROD(3)
$\langle B \rangle_4$		b_4					NOT YET
b_4							PROD(4)
a_5	a_5	b_3	c_6		$\langle A \rangle_5$	$\langle B \rangle_4$	NOT YET
$\langle A \rangle_5$							PROD(5)
c_6							PROD(6)

Figure 13.6

column for symbol TOP are exits. For each state corresponding to a rightmost grammatical occurrence in a production, the exit in the TOP column is the name of that production; for the state corresponding to the starting occurrence, the exit is "STARTING"; for all other states the exit is "NOT YET."

We say that a string of grammatical symbols, α, *ends in a handle* if and only if there is a string of terminal symbols β such that $\alpha \beta$ is an intermediate string in a rightmost derivation from the starting nonterminal, and this intermediate string has a handle which occurs at the end of α. We call the machine of Fig. 13.6 a "handle detector" because when presented with α followed by TOP, it determines whether α ends in a handle and, if so, what the handle production is. For instance, when the handle detector is presented with the string

$$a\ a\ b\ \langle S \rangle\ \text{TOP}$$

the handle detector performs the transitions

$$\triangledown \xrightarrow{a} a_1 \xrightarrow{a} a_5 \xrightarrow{b} b_3 \xrightarrow{\langle S \rangle} \langle S \rangle_3 \xrightarrow{\text{TOP}} \text{PROD(3)}$$

The exit PROD(3) indicates that

$$a \; a \; b \; \langle S \rangle$$

ends in a handle and that production 3 is the handle production.

In addition to detecting handles, the handle detector also checks for the specific input string:

$$\langle S \rangle \; \text{TOP}$$

In this case, the intermediate string is the starting intermediate string, and the handle detector notes this fact by taking exit "STARTING."

To illustrate the use of exit NOT YET, consider the input string:

$$a \; \langle B \rangle \; \text{TOP}$$

When presented with this input, the handle detector performs the transitions:

$$\nabla \xrightarrow{a} a_1 \xrightarrow{\langle B \rangle} \langle B \rangle_4 \xrightarrow{\text{TOP}} \text{NOT YET}$$

The string $a \langle B \rangle$ does not end in a handle, but if we append terminal string b to $a \langle B \rangle$, the resulting string

$$a \; \langle B \rangle \; b$$

has handle $\langle B \rangle \; b$.

In general, if the handle detector takes exit NOT YET when presented with input string

$$\alpha \; \text{TOP}$$

this indicates there is a terminal string β such that $\alpha\beta$ has a handle, and the handle involves some symbols in β.

To illustrate the use of exit REJECT, consider the input string:

$$a \; \langle S \rangle \; c \; \text{TOP}$$

When presented with this input, the handle detector performs the transitions

$$\nabla \xrightarrow{a} a_1 \xrightarrow{\langle S \rangle} \text{REJECT}$$

Inspection of the grammar indicates that occurrence a_1 cannot be followed by any occurrence of $\langle S \rangle$, and that therefore $a \; \langle S \rangle \; c$ cannot begin any intermediate string in a rightmost derivation.

In general, when the handle detector rejects input string

$$\alpha \; \text{TOP}$$

this indicates that α does not end in a handle and that there is no terminal string β such that $\alpha\beta$ has a handle involving symbols from β.

Now we illustrate the close relationship between the handle detector and the pushdown machine. Suppose we are told that while processing some input sequence, the pushdown machine enters a configuration with a stack representing grammatical string

$$a \; a \; b \; \langle S \rangle$$

but we are not told which grammatical occurrences are on the stack. Because the accumulation of stack symbols and the transitions of the handle detector are both controlled by the same table, the handle detector can be used to reconstruct the pushdown configuration. To do this, we append symbol TOP to the end of the grammatical string and present it to the handle detector obtaining the transition sequence:

$$\nabla \xrightarrow{\;a\;} a_1 \xrightarrow{\;a\;} a_5 \xrightarrow{\;b\;} b_3 \xrightarrow{\langle S \rangle} \langle S \rangle_3 \xrightarrow{\text{TOP}} \text{PROD}(3)$$

The state sequence

$$\nabla \; a_1 \; a_5 \; b_3 \; \langle S \rangle_3$$

is the stack of the pushdown configuration (line 6 of Fig. 13.4) and the exit PROD(3) tells us that the handle of production 3 is on top of the stack. The exit confirms that the pushdown operation REDUCE(3) is appropriate for the reconstructed stack.

In general, if α is a string represented by a pushdown stack obtained while processing some pushdown machine input, and input sequence

$$\alpha \; \text{TOP}$$

is presented to the handle detector, the state sequence will match the stack from which α was obtained and the exit will confirm the appropriateness of the next machine operation. A PROD(i) confirms a REDUCE(i); a NOT YET confirms a SHIFT (if the next input is not ⊣); and STARTING confirms ACCEPT (if the next input is ⊣). Exit REJECT is taken if and only if α does not come from a stack in the first place.

Altogether, we have three interpretations for Fig. 13.3(a), the push-table interpretation, the relation interpretation, and the finite-state handle-detector interpretation.

13.3   ANOTHER EXAMPLE

Suppose we are asked to find a SHIFT-REDUCE processor for the grammar of Fig. 13.7. The discussion of the previous section suggests we start by finding the relation OBELOW for the grammatical occurrences. This relation is shown in Fig. 13.8. Note that since the righthand side of production 1 has two occurrences of $\langle A \rangle$, we describe these occurrences in double subscript notation as $\langle A \rangle_{1,1}$ and $\langle A \rangle_{1,2}$. All other occurrences are written in the usual single subscript notation, with the subscript giving the production number.

As suggested by the previous section, we now represent the relation OBELOW by a table in which the columns are labeled with grammatical symbols and the table entries say which grammatical occurrence of the grammatical symbol has matrix entry one in Fig. 13.8. The resulting table is shown in Fig. 13.9(a). The table exhibits a complication not found in the example of the previous section. Some of the table entries contain more than one grammatical occurrence. One such entry is the entry for row $\langle A \rangle_4$ and column c which contains the two grammatical occurrences c_2 and c_5. The entry indicates that both:

$$\langle A \rangle_4 \text{ OBELOW } c_2 \text{ and } \langle A \rangle_4 \text{ OBELOW } c_5$$

Because of the entries with more than one grammatical occurrence, the table of Fig. 13.9(a) cannot be used as a push table for a pushdown machine whose stack symbols are the grammatical occurrences. A push-table entry must specify a single stack symbol or REJECT.

The previous section also suggests the possibility that the table of Fig. 13.9(a) obtained from OBELOW can be regarded (when augmented with a TOP column) as the transition table of a finite-state "handle detector," where the row labels are the states of the machine. Since some of the entries in Fig. 13.9(a) contain more than one row label, Fig. 13.9(a) must be interpreted as a *nondeterministic* transition table. In Fig. 13.9(b) we add a TOP column to Fig. 13.9(a) in accordance with the principles of the previous section. Those rows representing rightmost occurrences contain the name of the corresponding production, the row for the starting occurrence contains STARTING, and the other rows contain NOT YET. The nondeterministic machine of Fig. 13.9(b) has the property that, when presented with input string

$$\alpha \text{ TOP}$$

where α is a string of grammatical symbols, there exists a sequence of transitions leading to exit PROD(i) if and only if α ends in a handle and production i is the handle production.

In Fig. 13.10(a) we show a deterministic handle detector obtained by making the machine of Fig. 13.9(b) deterministic. Blank entries in Fig. 13.10(a) are interpreted as reject exits rather than as transitions to a state representing the empty set.

There are six rows of Fig. 13.10(a) which represent several grammatical occurrences. For five of these rows (all except $\{\langle S \rangle_0, \langle S \rangle_7\}$), the TOP entry in Fig. 13.9(b) for each of the grammatical occurrences in the row is NOT YET. Therefore exit NOT YET is appropriate independent of which grammatical occurrence might actually be represented by the grammatical symbol that caused the handle detector to enter a state labeling the row.

1. $\langle S \rangle \rightarrow \langle A \rangle \langle A \rangle \, d$
2. $\langle S \rangle \rightarrow c \, \langle A \rangle \, d$
3. $\langle S \rangle \rightarrow b$
4. $\langle A \rangle \rightarrow \langle A \rangle \langle S \rangle \, c$
5. $\langle A \rangle \rightarrow c \, d$
6. $\langle A \rangle \rightarrow a$
7. $\langle A \rangle \rightarrow \langle S \rangle \, b$

Starting symbol: $\langle S \rangle$

Figure 13.7

For the row $\{\langle S \rangle_0, \langle S \rangle_7\}$, the TOP entries in Fig. 13.9(b) for $\langle S \rangle_0$ and $\langle S \rangle_7$ are STARTING and NOT YET. The handle detector of Fig. 13.10(a) can be regarded as having a special exit named:

STARTING, NOT YET

Suppose the machine takes this exit when presented with input string

α TOP

Then, since the nondeterministic handle detector of Fig. 13.9(b) has a sequence of transitions for α TOP which result in exit STARTING, the string α must consist of just the starting symbol $\langle S \rangle$. Furthermore since the machine of Fig. 13.9(b) has a (different) sequence of transitions for α TOP which result in exit NOT YET, there is some terminal string that can be appended to $\langle S \rangle$ such that the resulting string has a handle. Thus exit STARTING, NOT YET of Fig. 13.10(a) indicates that the machine has encountered the intermediate string consisting of the starting symbol

$\langle S \rangle$

that this intermediate string does not end in a handle, and that there is some continuation of terminal symbols which would end in a handle.

Observe that the grammatical occurrences represented by each state in Fig. 13.10(a) are all occurrences of the same grammatical symbol. Thus for example, the grammatical occurrences in state $\{\langle A \rangle_{1,1}, \langle A \rangle_{1,2}, \langle A \rangle_4\}$ are all occurrences of grammatical symbol $\langle A \rangle$. It is not surprising that this is true, because the method of making machines deterministic can only place two states in the same set when there is an input column that has transitions to both states. Each input column of Fig. 13.9 has transitions only to grammatical occurrences of the grammatical symbol at the top of the column (i.e., the input symbol). The fact that each state of the deterministic machine contains only occurrences of a single symbol makes it possible to rename the

	b_7	$<S>_7$	a_6	d_5	c_5	c_4	$<S>_4$	$<A>_4$	b_3	d_2	$<A>_2$	c_2	d_1	$<A>_{1,2}$	$<A>_{1,1}$	$<S>_0$
$\triangledown$																1
$<S>_0$		1	1		1			1	1			1		1	1	
$<A>_{1,1}$		1	1		1			1	1			1				
$<A>_{1,2}$													1			
d_1		1	1		1			1	1			1				
c_2											1					
$<A>_2$										1						
d_2																
b_3						1										
$<A>_4$		1	1		1		1	1	1			1				
$<S>_4$				1												
c_4																
c_5																
d_5																
a_6																
$<S>_7$	1															
b_7																

Fig. 13.8 OBELOW for the grammar of Fig. 13.7

	$\langle S \rangle$	$\langle A \rangle$	a	b	c	d
$\triangledown$	$\langle S \rangle_0, \langle S \rangle_7$	$\langle A \rangle_{1,1}, \langle A \rangle_4$	a_6	b_3	c_2, c_5	
$\langle S \rangle_0$						
$\langle A \rangle_{1,1}$	$\langle S \rangle_7$	$\langle A \rangle_{1,1}, \langle A \rangle_{1,2}, \langle A \rangle_4$	a_6	b_3	c_2, c_5	
$\langle A \rangle_{1,2}$						d_1
d_1						
c_2	$\langle S \rangle_7$	$\langle A \rangle_{1,1}, \langle A \rangle_2, \langle A \rangle_4$	a_6	b_3	c_2, c_5	
$\langle A \rangle_2$						d_2
d_2						
b_3						
$\langle A \rangle_4$	$\langle S \rangle_4, \langle S \rangle_7$	$\langle A \rangle_{1,1}, \langle A \rangle_4$	a_6	b_3	c_2, c_5	
$\langle S \rangle_4$					c_4	
c_4						
c_5						d_5
d_5						
a_6						
$\langle S \rangle_7$				b_7		
b_7						

(a)

Figure 13.9

states in such a way that each name is a subscripted grammatical symbol and the grammatical symbol in each name matches the grammatical symbol of the occurrences. Figure 13.10(b) shows the handle detector renamed in this way.

Those states representing a single grammatical occurrence are renamed with the occurrence name. Thus $\{d_1\}$ is renamed d_1 and so forth. The states representing many occurrences, namely $\{\langle S \rangle_0, \langle S \rangle_7\}$, $\{\langle S \rangle_4, \langle S \rangle_7\}$, $\{\langle A \rangle_{1,1}, \langle A \rangle_4\}$, $\{\langle A \rangle_{1,1}, \langle A \rangle_{1,2}, \langle A \rangle_4\}$, $\{\langle A \rangle_{1,1}, \langle A \rangle_2, \langle A \rangle_4\}$, and $\{c_2, c_5\}$ are renamed $\langle S \rangle_x$, $\langle S \rangle_y$, $\langle A \rangle_x$, $\langle A \rangle_y$, $\langle A \rangle_z$, and c_x respectively.

Figure 13.11 shows a SHIFT-REDUCE recognizer for the given grammar. This machine can be thought of as having been obtained from the handle detector of Fig. 13.10(b). The stack symbols of the SHIFT-REDUCE machine are the states of the deterministic handle detector, the push table is the handle-detector control table without the TOP column, and the SHIFT-

	$<S>$	$<A>$	a	b	c	d	TOP
$\triangledown$	$<S>_0, <S>_7$	$<A>_{1,1}, <A>_4$	a_6	b_3	c_2, c_5		NOT YET
$<S>_0$							STARTING
$<A>_{1,1}$	$<S>_7$	$<A>_{1,1}, <A>_{1,2}, <A>_4$	a_6	b_3	c_2, c_5		NOT YET
$<A>_{1,2}$						d_1	NOT YET
d_1							PROD(1)
c_2	$<S>_7$	$<A>_{1,1}, <A>_2, <A>_4$	a_6	b_3	c_2, c_5		NOT YET
$<A>_2$						d_2	NOT YET
d_2							PROD(2)
b_3							PROD(3)
$<A>_4$	$<S>_4, <S>_7$	$<A>_{1,1}, <A>_4$	a_6	b_3	c_2, c_5		NOT YET
$<S>_4$					c_4		NOT YET
c_4							PROD(4)
c_5						d_5	NOT YET
d_5							PROD(5)
a_6							PROD(6)
$<S>_7$				b_7			NOT YET
b_7							PROD(7)

(b)

Figure 13.9 (continued)

REDUCE control table makes the decisions implied by the TOP column in the handle detector.

The entries in the SHIFT-REDUCE control table are actions suggested by the TOP column of the handle detector. Whenever the machine of Fig. 13.11 pushes a symbol on the stack, this symbol is identical to the state the handle detector of Fig. 13.10(b) would be in if it were presented with the grammatical string represented by the stack. Whenever the top stack symbol of the pushdown machine is identical to a state of Fig. 13.10(b) for which the TOP entry is PROD(i), the represented grammatical string ends in a handle and production i is the handle production. Therefore the control table row for that stack symbol is filled in with REDUCE(i). For those stack symbols having NOT YET in the TOP entry of the handle detector, the SHIFT-REDUCE control table has SHIFT for all inputs except endmarker, which has REJECT. The SHIFT is appropriate because the fact that the TOP exit is

	$\langle S \rangle$	$\langle A \rangle$	a	b	c	d	TOP
$\{\nabla\}$	$\{\langle S \rangle_0, \langle S \rangle_7\}$	$\{\langle A \rangle_{1,1}, \langle A \rangle_4\}$	$\{a_6\}$	$\{b_3\}$	$\{c_2, c_5\}$		NOT YET
$\{\langle S \rangle_0, \langle S \rangle_7\}$		$\{\langle A \rangle_{1,1}, \langle A \rangle_{1,2}, \langle A \rangle_4\}$		$\{b_7\}$			STARTING, NOT YET
$\{\langle A \rangle_{1,1}, \langle A \rangle_4\}$	$\{\langle S \rangle_4, \langle S \rangle_7\}$	$\{\langle A \rangle_{1,1}, \langle A \rangle_{1,2}, \langle A \rangle_4\}$	$\{a_6\}$	$\{b_3\}$	$\{c_2, c_5\}$		NOT YET
$\{\langle A \rangle_{1,1}, \langle A \rangle_{1,2}, \langle A \rangle_4\}$	$\{\langle S \rangle_4, \langle S \rangle_7\}$	$\{\langle A \rangle_{1,1}, \langle A \rangle_{1,2}, \langle A \rangle_4\}$	$\{a_6\}$	$\{b_3\}$	$\{c_2, c_5\}$	$\{d_1\}$	NOT YET
$\{d_1\}$							PROD(1)
$\{c_2, c_5\}$	$\{\langle S \rangle_7\}$	$\{\langle A \rangle_{1,1}, \langle A \rangle_2, \langle A \rangle_4\}$	$\{a_6\}$	$\{b_3\}$	$\{c_2, c_5\}$	$\{d_5\}$	NOT YET
$\{\langle A \rangle_{1,1}, \langle A \rangle_2, \langle A \rangle_4\}$	$\{\langle S \rangle_4, \langle S \rangle_7\}$	$\{\langle A \rangle_{1,1}, \langle A \rangle_{1,2}, \langle A \rangle_4\}$	$\{a_6\}$	$\{b_3\}$	$\{c_2, c_5\}$	$\{d_2\}$	NOT YET
$\{d_2\}$							PROD(2)
$\{b_3\}$							PROD(3)
$\{\langle S \rangle_4, \langle S \rangle_7\}$				$\{b_7\}$	$\{c_4\}$		NOT YET
$\{c_4\}$							PROD(4)
$\{d_5\}$							PROD(5)
$\{a_6\}$				$\{b_7\}$			PROD(6)
$\{\langle S \rangle_7\}$							NOT YET
$\{b_7\}$							PROD(7)

(a)

Figure 13.10

	$\langle S \rangle$	$\langle A \rangle$	a	b	c	d	TOP
$\triangledown$							NOT YET
$\langle S \rangle_x$	$\langle S \rangle_x$	$\langle A \rangle_x$	a_6	b_3	c_x		STARTING, NOT YET
$\langle A \rangle_x$				b_7			NOT YET
$\langle A \rangle_y$	$\langle S \rangle_y$	$\langle A \rangle_y$	a_6	b_3	c_x		NOT YET
d_1	$\langle S \rangle_y.$	$\langle A \rangle_y$	a_6	b_3	c_x	d_1	PROD(1)
c_x							NOT YET
$\langle A \rangle_z$	$\langle S \rangle_7$	$\langle A \rangle_z$	a_6	b_3	c_x	d_5	NOT YET
d_2	$\langle S \rangle_y$	$\langle A \rangle_y$	a_6	b_3	c_x	d_2	PROD(2)
b_3							PROD(3)
$\langle S \rangle_y$				b_7	c_4		NOT YET
c_4							PROD(4)
d_5							PROD(5)
a_6							PROD(6)
$\langle S \rangle_7$				b_7			NOT YET
b_7							PROD(7)

(b)

Figure 13.10 (continued)

	$\langle S \rangle$	$\langle A \rangle$	a	b	c	d
$\triangledown$	$\langle S \rangle_x$	$\langle A \rangle_x$	a_6	b_3	c_x	
$\langle S \rangle_x$				b_7		
$\langle A \rangle_x$	$\langle S \rangle_y$	$\langle A \rangle_y$	a_6	b_3	c_x	
$\langle A \rangle_y$	$\langle S \rangle_y$	$\langle A \rangle_y$	a_6	b_3	c_x	d_1
d_1						
c_x	$\langle S \rangle_7$	$\langle A \rangle_z$	a_6	b_3	c_x	d_5
$\langle A \rangle_z$	$\langle S \rangle_y$	$\langle A \rangle_y$	a_6	b_3	c_x	d_2
d_2						
b_3						
$\langle S \rangle_y$				b_7	c_4	
c_4						
d_5						
a_6						
$\langle S \rangle_7$				b_7		
b_7						

(a)

Fig. 13.11 (a) Push table (b) Control table.

NOT YET indicates that the represented grammatical string does not end in a handle, but would if extended by the addition of suitable terminal symbols. The one REJECT entry is required to conform to the rule that our machines are not to advance beyond the endmarker.

For stack symbol $\langle S \rangle_x$, which has a TOP entry of STARTING, NOT YET in the handle detector, the control table has SHIFT for all inputs except endmarker, which has ACCEPT. The ACCEPT in the endmarker column is appropriate because the represented grammatical string is the starting intermediate string $\langle S \rangle$, and it generates the entire terminal sequence. ACCEPT is inappropriate for the other columns, because for these columns the represented intermediate string $\langle S \rangle$ only generates a portion of the terminal sequence. However SHIFT is appropriate for these columns because the represented intermediate string does not end in a handle (although it would end in a handle if extended by the addition of suitable terminal symbols).

Since we have shown that each possible move of the machine is appropriate, it should be evident that the machine is a SHIFT-REDUCE recognizer for the given grammar.

	a	b	c	d	⊣
▽	SHIFT	SHIFT	SHIFT	SHIFT	REJECT
$<S>_x$	SHIFT	SHIFT	SHIFT	SHIFT	ACCEPT
$<A>_x$	SHIFT	SHIFT	SHIFT	SHIFT	REJECT
$<A>_y$	SHIFT	SHIFT	SHIFT	SHIFT	REJECT
d_1	REDUCE(1)	REDUCE(1)	REDUCE(1)	REDUCE(1)	REDUCE(1)
c_x	SHIFT	SHIFT	SHIFT	SHIFT	REJECT
$<A>_z$	SHIFT	SHIFT	SHIFT	SHIFT	REJECT
d_2	REDUCE(2)	REDUCE(2)	REDUCE(2)	REDUCE(2)	REDUCE(2)
b_3	REDUCE(3)	REDUCE(3)	REDUCE(3)	REDUCE(3)	REDUCE(3)
$<S>_y$	SHIFT	SHIFT	SHIFT	SHIFT	REJECT
c_4	REDUCE(4)	REDUCE(4)	REDUCE(4)	REDUCE(4)	REDUCE(4)
d_5	REDUCE(5)	REDUCE(5)	REDUCE(5)	REDUCE(5)	REDUCE(5)
a_6	REDUCE(6)	REDUCE(6)	REDUCE(6)	REDUCE(6)	REDUCE(6)
$<S>_7$	SHIFT	SHIFT	SHIFT	SHIFT	REJECT
b_7	REDUCE(7)	REDUCE(7)	REDUCE(7)	REDUCE(7)	REDUCE(7)

(b)

Figure 13.11 (continued)

In the previous section, we considered a pushdown machine in which the stack symbols could be interpreted as either grammatical occurrences or handle-detector states because the set of states and occurrences were the same. In the example of this section, we find that handle-detector states correspond to sets of grammatical occurrences and the pushdown recognizer uses these states, not the occurrences, as the stack symbols. The reason that the handle detector states become the dominant stack symbol interpretation is that it is the deterministic handle detector state which permits a decision among shift and reduce operations.

13.4 LR(0) GRAMMARS

In the previous section, we took the grammar of Fig. 13.7 and through a series of informal steps (Figs. 13.8 through 13.10) arrived at the pushdown recognizer of Fig. 13.11 in which the stack symbols could be regarded as "handle-detector" states. In this section, we present a formal procedure describing how such a construction can be performed in general circumstances. This procedure is only applicable to grammars with no ε-rules, and the class of grammars for which the procedure succeeds is known as "the class of LR(0) grammars with no ε-rules."

For any given grammar with no ε-rules, the following procedure either constructs a SHIFT-REDUCE recognizer or asserts that the grammar is not LR(0):

1. Compute the relation OBELOW for the given grammar.

2. Construct a nondeterministic table in which there is a row for the bottommarker and for each grammatical occurrence, and a column for each grammatical symbol. The entry for each row A_i and column B contains all the grammatical occurrences B_j of grammatical symbol B such that

$$A_i \text{ OBELOW } B_j$$

3. Make the table from step 2 deterministic by treating it as a nondeterministic finite-state transition table with starting state bottommarker.

4. The states obtained from step 3 (except the state corresponding to the empty set) are to be used as stack symbols. The transition table is used as the push table (with transitions to the state corresponding to the empty set treated as REJECT entries).

5. The SHIFT-REDUCE control table is filled in on a row-by-row basis according to the set of grammatical occurrences corresponding to the stack symbol (state) labeling the row.

    a) If the set contains the starting occurrence as its only element, the endmarker entry is ACCEPT and the other entries in the row are REJECT.

    b) If the set contains a single grammatical occurrence and that occurrence is the rightmost occurrence in a production p, then all entries in the row are REDUCE(p).

    c) If the stack symbol is the bottommarker or if all grammatical occurrences in the set represented by the stack symbol are from right-hand-side positions which are not the rightmost position, the endmarker entry is REJECT and all other entries are SHIFT.

    d) If the set contains the starting occurrence plus at least one additional occurrence which is not a rightmost occurrence, but no occurrence which is a rightmost occurrence, the endmarker entry is ACCEPT and all other entries are SHIFT.

If some set of grammatical occurrences is found not covered by a, b, c or d, then the grammar is not LR(0) and no machine is produced.

The procedure fails to produce a SHIFT-REDUCE recognizer only when the deterministic table produced in step 3 has a state containing both a rightmost occurrence and some additional occurrence.

The name "LR(0) grammar" is intended to indicate that the machine begins scanning on the _L_eft, it identifies a production when it gets to the _R_ightmost symbol derived from that production, and each handle can be detected without looking at any (i.e., looking at *zero*) input symbols beyond the last input symbol derived from the handle. Any grammar for which the above design procedure results in a machine has this property since, when a handle is on top of the stack, the machine calls the same REDUCE routine no matter what the current input symbol is. Thus the machine is not "looking at" the input symbol beyond the handle. Conversely it is also a fact that for any grammar without ϵ-rules having the above property, the design procedure results in a machine. We do not attempt to give the rather complex justification of this fact.

The push tables produced by the above procedure generally contain rows consisting entirely of REJECT entries. Figure 13.3(a) has seven such rows including rows $\langle S \rangle_0$ and b_1. Figure 13.11(a) also has seven of these rows. A totally blank push-table row indicates that the machine is forbidden to push any symbols on top of the given stack symbol. By the nature of the construction, these are rows whose stack symbols represent a rightmost occurrence or the starting occurrence. By construction of the SHIFT-REDUCE control table, the control does not even attempt to push a symbol onto one of these symbols. Therefore there are no circumstances under which the SHIFT-REDUCE machine will look up information in these rows of the push table, and there is no reason to include these rows in the push table. Thus we can add the following step to the procedure:

6. Delete rows from the push table that only have REJECT entries.

In subsequent sections, we present methods of improving step 5 of the procedure so that pushdown machines can be designed for certain grammars which are not LR(0). We also investigate improvements to accommodate ϵ-productions.

13.5   SLR(1) GRAMMARS

In this section, we revise step 5 of the procedure of the last section in order to accommodate certain grammars which are not LR(0). As an example we consider the old friend in Fig. 13.12. Applying step 1 of the procedure in Section 13.4 to this grammar gives the OBELOW table of Fig. 13.13(a). Applying step 2 gives the nondeterministic table of Fig. 13.13(b). Applying step 3 gives the deterministic table in Fig. 13.14(a). For convenience, we rename the states to obtain Fig. 13.14(b). In this second figure, certain subscripts have been dropped where there is only one grammatical occurrence of a grammatical symbol (e.g., $+_1$ is the only occurrence of $+$) and $\{\langle E\rangle_0, \langle E\rangle_1\}$, $\{\langle E\rangle_1, \langle E\rangle_6\}$, $\{\langle T\rangle_2, \langle T\rangle_3\}$, and $\{\langle T\rangle_1, \langle T\rangle_3\}$ have been renamed respectively $\langle E\rangle_x$, $\langle E\rangle_y$, $\langle T\rangle_x$, and $\langle T\rangle_y$. The table in Fig. 13.14(b) is to be used as the push table in accordance with step 4.

At step 5, we find that the grammar is not LR(0) because stack symbols $\langle T\rangle_x$ and $\langle T\rangle_y$ are not covered by parts a), b), c), and d) of the rule. Symbol $\langle T\rangle_x$ is not covered because the corresponding occurrence set is $\{\langle T\rangle_2, \langle T\rangle_3\}$ which contains rightmost occurrence $\langle T\rangle_2$ and is not a one element set. A similar remark holds for $\langle T\rangle_y$. Therefore step 5 of the procedure would fail to produce control-table entries for rows $\langle T\rangle_x$ and $\langle T\rangle_y$. However, we show below that, with some additional analysis, it is possible to find suitable control-table entries for these rows. The analysis considers each entry in the row as a separate problem and makes use of the particular current input symbol associated with that entry. Therefore, the resulting machine "looks at" the input symbol in making a choice between SHIFT and REDUCE.

Consider for example the control-table entry for stack symbol $\langle T\rangle_x$ and input $+$. The fact that the occurrence set represented by $\langle T\rangle_x$ contains rightmost occurrence $\langle T\rangle_2$ suggests that REDUCE(2) might be an appropriate action, and the fact that $\langle T\rangle_3$ is contained in the occurrence set suggests that SHIFT might be appropriate. However, shifting input symbol $+$ cannot possibly lead to acceptance, because the push table calls for rejection whenever a $+$ is proposed to be pushed on a $\langle T\rangle_x$. Therefore, only the action REDUCE(2) is appropriate for acceptable input strings and the control-table entry can accordingly be REDUCE(2).

Again consider stack symbol $\langle T\rangle_x$, this time with input $*$. Now the push table indicates that shifting $*$ can be appropriate for acceptable input strings. Furthermore, we can show that in this case REDUCE(2) is inappropriate. Assuming the input acceptable, selecting REDUCE(2) would cause a stack symbol representing $\langle E\rangle$ to be pushed on the stack, $\langle E\rangle$ being the lefthand side of production 2. The current input would remain $*$ so the stack concat-

    1. $\langle E\rangle \to \langle E\rangle + \langle T\rangle$
    2. $\langle E\rangle \to \langle T\rangle$
    3. $\langle T\rangle \to \langle T\rangle * \langle P\rangle$
    4. $\langle T\rangle \to \langle P\rangle$
    5. $\langle P\rangle \to a$
    6. $\langle P\rangle \to (\,\langle E\rangle\,)$
    Starting symbol: $\langle E\rangle$

Figure 13.12

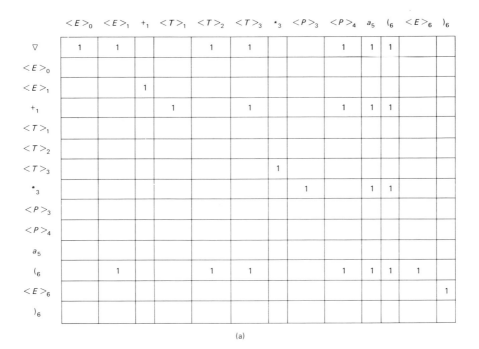

(a)

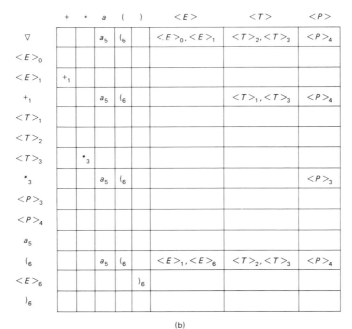

(b)

Figure 13.13

	+	*	a	(	)	$<E>$	$<T>$	$<P>$
▽			$\{a_5\}$	$\{(_6\}$		$\{<E>_0,<E>_1\}$	$\{<T>_2,<T>_3\}$	$\{<P>_4\}$
$\{a_5\}$								
$\{(_6\}$			$\{a_5\}$	$\{(_6\}$		$\{<E>_1,<E>_6\}$	$\{<T>_2,<T>_3\}$	$\{<P>_4\}$
$\{<E>_0,<E>_1\}$	$\{+_1\}$							
$\{<T>_2,<T>_3\}$		$\{*_3\}$						
$\{<P>_4\}$								
$\{<E>_1,<E>_6\}$	$\{+_1\}$				$\{)_6\}$			
$\{+_1\}$			$\{a_5\}$	$\{(_6\}$			$\{<T>_1,<T>_3\}$	$\{<P>_4\}$
$\{*_3\}$			$\{a_5\}$	$\{(_6\}$				$\{<P>_3\}$
$\{)_6\}$								
$\{<T>_1,<T>_3\}$		$\{*_3\}$						
$\{<P>_3\}$								

(a)

	+	*	a	(	)	$<E>$	$<T>$	$<P>$
▽			a	(		$<E>_x$	$<T>_x$	$<P>_4$
a								
(			a	(		$<E>_y$	$<T>_x$	$<P>_4$
$<E>_x$	+							
$<T>_x$		*						
$<P>_4$								
$<E>_y$	+				)			
+			a	(			$<T>_y$	$<P>_4$
*			a	(				$<P>_3$
)								
$<T>_y$		*						
$<P>_3$								

(b)

Figure 13.14

enated with the remaining inputs would represent some intermediate string in which an occurrence of $\langle E \rangle$ is immediately followed by $*$. However, it is easily computed that $*$ is not in FOLLOW($\langle E \rangle$) and hence no such intermediate string exists. Accordingly, action REDUCE(2) is ruled out and the control-table entry can be filled in with SHIFT.

The principles illustrated in the above discussion can be used to revise rule 5 of the LR(0) test and design procedure of the previous section. Grammars which satisfy the revised rule are commonly called "SLR(1) grammars without ϵ-productions." In the next section, we discuss the treatment of ϵ-productions. The new step 5 is the following:

5. Given a stack symbol representing the bottommarker or a set of grammatical occurrences Q and given an input z, fill in the corresponding SHIFT-REDUCE control-table entry as follows:

a) If Q contains the starting occurrence and z is the endmarker, make the entry ACCEPT.

b) If the input z is not the endmarker and the push table has a nonREJECT entry for the given stack symbol and input, make the entry SHIFT.

c) If Q contains the rightmost occurrence of production p and z is in FOLLOW($\langle L \rangle$) where $\langle L \rangle$ is the lefthand side of p, make the entry REDUCE(p).

	$+$	$*$	a	$($	$)$	$\dashv$
$\triangledown$			SHIFT	SHIFT		
a	REDUCE(5)	REDUCE(5)			REDUCE(5)	REDUCE(5)
$($			SHIFT	SHIFT		
$\langle E \rangle_x$	SHIFT					ACCEPT
$\langle T \rangle_x$	REDUCE(2)	SHIFT			REDUCE(2)	REDUCE(2)
$\langle P \rangle_4$	REDUCE(4)	REDUCE(4)			REDUCE(4)	REDUCE(4)
$\langle E \rangle_y$	SHIFT				SHIFT	
$+$			SHIFT	SHIFT		
$*$			SHIFT	SHIFT		
$)$	REDUCE(6)	REDUCE(6)			REDUCE(6)	REDUCE(6)
$\langle T \rangle_y$	REDUCE(1)	SHIFT			REDUCE(1)	REDUCE(1)
$\langle P \rangle_3$	REDUCE(3)	REDUCE(3)			REDUCE(3)	REDUCE(3)

Blank entries are REJECT

Figure 13.15

When a), b), and c) above impose conflicting requirements on the design, the grammar is not SLR(1). Those entries on which no requirements are placed can be made REJECT.

The 1 in SLR(1) refers to the fact that one input beyond a handle is being looked at and S stands for "simple" in contrast to a more complicated class of grammars called LR(1).

For the sample grammar, the appropriate FOLLOW sets are:

$$\text{FOLLOW}(\langle E \rangle) = \{+,), \dashv\}$$
$$\text{FOLLOW}(\langle T \rangle) = \{*, +,), \dashv\}$$
$$\text{FOLLOW}(\langle P \rangle) = \{*, +,), \dashv\}$$

The SHIFT-REDUCE control table obtained from the new procedure is shown in Fig. 13.15. Figure 13.15 together with the push table of Fig. 13.14(b) constitutes the complete design.

As was the case with LR(0) grammars, the nature of the design procedure prevents the SHIFT-REDUCE machine from ever looking up an entry in the push table in a row which has only reject entries. Thus the suggested step 6 of discarding blank push table rows also can be applied here. Thus in Fig. 13.14(b), rows a, $\langle P \rangle_4$,), and $\langle P \rangle_3$ can be dropped.

13.6 EPSILON PRODUCTIONS

We now consider the problem of designing a SHIFT-REDUCE machine when the given grammar has ϵ-productions. To begin, we consider the grammar of Fig. 13.16 with ϵ-productions 2 and 6. One string generated from this grammar is *daa* whose derivation tree is shown in Fig. 13.17.

The design problem for grammars with ϵ-productions is essentially the previous design problem with one added complication: namely deciding when the handle of an ϵ-production is on top of the stack. At every step in the processing, the top of the stack matches the righthand side of each ϵ-pro-

1. $\langle S \rangle \rightarrow d \langle A \rangle a$
2. $\langle S \rangle \rightarrow \epsilon$
3. $\langle A \rangle \rightarrow a \langle S \rangle \langle B \rangle$
4. $\langle A \rangle \rightarrow d \langle S \rangle c$
5. $\langle B \rangle \rightarrow b$
6. $\langle B \rangle \rightarrow \epsilon$
Starting symbol: $\langle S \rangle$

Figure 13.16

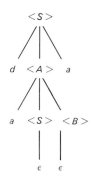

Figure 13.17

duction p, and so each control table entry must be regarded as a candidate for REDUCE(p) until the designer can find reasons to the contrary.

To illustrate the operation of a SHIFT-REDUCE machine in the ϵ-production case, we show a stack movie in Fig. 13.18(a) of input sequence *daa* being processed. The movie is only approximate in that the stack symbols are shown as grammatical symbols and are not the stack symbols of the fully designed machine. However, the detail is sufficient to see the effect of REDUCE(2) and REDUCE(6) applied at steps 3 and 4. In each of the eight configurations, the top zero symbols match the righthand side of productions 2 and 6, but the SHIFT-REDUCE control must be designed so as to recognize that the top null sequence is a handle only in lines 3 and 4.

The rightmost derivation corresponding to the stack movie is shown in Fig. 13.18(b). Each line of the stack movie corresponds to a represented intermediate string of the derivation, and this correspondence is indicated by labeling each intermediate string with the numbers of the corresponding stack movie lines. The handle of each intermediate string is underlined. Note that for the last two intermediate strings, the handle is the null sequence. In the stack movie, REDUCE(2) or REDUCE(6) is performed only when the handle of the represented intermediate string is the null string, and the stack contains the portion of the intermediate string ending in the handle.

The SLR(1) design procedure for the ϵ-production case begins with the same first four steps as in the previous case. These steps completely ignore the ϵ-production, and produce the same result as for the same grammar with

1.	∇	$d\ a\ a\ \dashv$	SHIFT
2.	$\nabla\ d$	$a\ a\ \dashv$	SHIFT
3.	$\nabla\ d\ a$	$a\ \dashv$	REDUCE(2)
4.	$\nabla\ d\ a\ <S>$	$a\ \dashv$	REDUCE(6)
5.	$\nabla\ d\ a\ <S><B>$	$a\ \dashv$	REDUCE(3)
6.	$\nabla\ d\ <A>$	$a\ \dashv$	SHIFT
7.	$\nabla\ d\ <A>\ a$	$\dashv$	REDUCE(1)
8.	$\nabla\ <S>$	$\dashv$	ACCEPT

(a)

8.	$<S>$	$\Rightarrow$
6, 7.	$d\ \underline{<A>}\ a$	$\Rightarrow$
5.	$d\ a\ \underline{<S><B>}\ a$	$\Rightarrow$
4.	$d\ a\ <S>\ \_\ a$	$\Rightarrow$
1, 2, 3.	$d\ a\ \_\ a$	

(b)

Figure 13.18

ϵ-productions deleted. This happens because adding or deleting ϵ-productions from a grammar does not add or delete grammatical occurrences and does not affect the relation OBELOW. All the modifications to the procedure are modifications to step 5 and these modifications are in the form of additions.

To bring our example up to the critical point, we apply the first four steps of the procedure. Figure 13.19 shows the relation OBELOW from step 1 and Fig. 13.20 shows the table from step 2. This table is in fact deterministic so it also represents the result of step 3 and is to be used as the push table.

The construction of the control table is based on an expanded version of the rule 5 given in the previous section. The expanded rule includes parts a, b, c of the previous section and says which entries should be ACCEPT, SHIFT, and REDUCE(p) for non-ϵ-productions. A new part is to be added stating which entries should have REDUCE(p) for ϵ-productions. The procedure succeeds and the grammar is SLR(1) if the four parts do not impose conflicting requirements on a given control-table entry.

The basic idea behind the new part is similar to those behind the preceding parts. We use various relations to show that certain control-table entries cannot possibly be REDUCE(p) for an ϵ-production and hope that this reasoning is sufficient to prevent conflicting ways of filling in an entry.

	$<S>_0$	d_1	$<A>_1$	a_1	a_3	$<S>_3$	$<B>_3$	d_4	$<S>_4$	c_4	b_5
∇	1	1									
$<S>_0$											
d_1			1		1			1			
$<A>_1$				1							
a_1											
a_3		1				1					
$<S>_3$							1				1
$<B>_3$											
d_4		1							1		
$<S>_4$										1	
c_4											
b_5											

OBELOW

Figure 13.19

	$\langle S \rangle$	$\langle A \rangle$	$\langle B \rangle$	a	b	c	d
∇	$\langle S \rangle_0$						d_1
$\langle S \rangle_0$							
d_1		$\langle A \rangle_1$		a_3			d_4
$\langle A \rangle_1$				a_1			
a_1							
a_3	$\langle S \rangle_3$						d_1
$\langle S \rangle_3$			$\langle B \rangle_3$		b_5		
$\langle B \rangle_3$							
d_4	$\langle S \rangle_4$						d_1
$\langle S \rangle_4$						c_4	
c_4							
b_5							

Push table

Figure 13.20

We first consider production 6. The action REDUCE(6) does not pop any stack symbols because the righthand side of production 6 has length zero. The only effect is to push some stack symbol representing $\langle B \rangle$, the lefthand side of production 6. The stack symbol pushed is determined by the push-table entry in column $\langle B \rangle$ and the row corresponding to the same stack symbol used by the control table in selecting REDUCE(6). Since the only nonREJECT entry in column $\langle B \rangle$ of the PUSH table is in the $\langle S \rangle_3$ row, we know that $\langle S \rangle_3$ is the only stack symbol on top of which a stack symbol representing $\langle B \rangle$ can be pushed. Hence in the control table, REDUCE(6) can only be appropriate in the $\langle S \rangle_3$ row.

Now consider the control-table entry for row $\langle S \rangle_3$ and column b. The effect of selecting REDUCE(6) would be for a stack symbol representing $\langle B \rangle$ to be pushed on the stack. The current input would remain b so the stack concatenated with the remaining inputs would represent some intermediate string in which an occurrence of $\langle B \rangle$ is immediately followed by b. However, it is easily computed that b is not in FOLLOW($\langle B \rangle$); hence no such intermediate string exists in a derivation of an acceptable input sequence. Accordingly, REDUCE(6) is inappropriate for the control-table entry under consideration.

For reference we show the follow sets in Fig. 13.21. FOLLOW is some-times tricky to compute when there are ϵ-productions and the procedure of Section 8.7 should be used if it is difficult to compute by inspection.

Referring to Fig. 13.21, we see that FOLLOW($\langle B \rangle$) only contains a. Hence REDUCE(6) can only be appropriate in the a column of the control table.

$$\text{FOLLOW}(\langle S \rangle) = \{a, b, c, \dashv\}$$
$$\text{FOLLOW}(\langle A \rangle) = \{a\}$$
$$\text{FOLLOW}(\langle B \rangle) = \{a\}$$

Figure 13.21

We conclude therefore that REDUCE(6) is only appropriate for the control-table entry in row $\langle S \rangle_3$ and column a. A check of parts a, b, and c of rule 5 indicates that no other action is appropriate for this entry. Therefore the grammar has no conflicts involving REDUCE(6).

We now consider the problem of REDUCE(2). Again the first consid-eration is to put REDUCE(2) only in rows where the top stack symbol and lefthand side (in this case $\langle S \rangle$) have a nonREJECT push table entry. There-fore, REDUCE(2) will only be put in rows ∇, a_3, and d_4. The second consideration is to only put REDUCE(2) in columns where the input symbol is in FOLLOW of the lefthand side (in this case $\langle S \rangle$). Therefore, RE-DUCE(2) will only be put in columns a, b, c, and $\dashv$. Combining both considerations, we put REDUCE(2) in the intersection of rows ∇, a_3, d_4, and columns a, b, c, and $\dashv$.

Adding the control table entries obtained from parts a), b), and c) of rule 5, we end up with the control table of Fig. 13.22. Since there are no conflicts in the table, the given grammar is SLR(1).

Summarizing the points illustrated above as a general principle:

For a given stack symbol, given input, and ϵ-production p with lefthand side $\langle L \rangle$, we make the SHIFT-REDUCE control-table entry REDUCE(p) only if the given input is in FOLLOW($\langle L \rangle$) and the push table has a nonREJECT entry for the given stack symbol row and $\langle L \rangle$ column.

The effect of REDUCE(p) on the string represented by the stack concat-enated with the remaining inputs is to insert $\langle L \rangle$ immediately after the portion of the string represented by the stack. The first condition of the above principle says that $\langle L \rangle$ followed by the current input symbol must

	a	b	c	d	$\dashv$
$\triangledown$	REDUCE(2)	REDUCE(2)	REDUCE(2)	SHIFT	REDUCE(2)
$<S>_0$					ACCEPT
d_1	SHIFT			SHIFT	
$<A>_1$	SHIFT				
a_1	REDUCE(1)	REDUCE(1)	REDUCE(1)		REDUCE(1)
a_3	REDUCE(2)	REDUCE(2)	REDUCE(2)	SHIFT	REDUCE(2)
$<S>_3$	REDUCE(6)	SHIFT			
$<B>_3$	REDUCE(3)				
d_4	REDUCE(2)	REDUCE(2)	REDUCE(2)	SHIFT	REDUCE(2)
$<S>_4$			SHIFT		
c_4	REDUCE(4)				
b_5	REDUCE(5)				

Figure 13.22

appear in some intermediate string generated by the grammar. The second condition says that the string represented by the stack concatenated with $\langle L \rangle$ must either end in a handle or have some continuation which ends in a handle.

We now put all the pieces together into a complete SLR(1) test and design procedure:

1. Compute the relation OBELOW for the given grammar. (The ϵ-productions have no part in this calculation.)

2. Contruct a nondeterministic table in which there is a row for the bottommarker and for each grammatical occurrence, and a column for each grammatical symbol. The entry for each row A_i and column B contains all of the grammatical occurrences B_j of grammatical symbol B such that:

$$A_i \text{ OBELOW } B_j$$

3. Make the table from step 2 deterministic by treating it as a nondeterministic finite-state control table with bottommarker as the starting state.

4. The states obtained from step 3 are to be used as stack symbols (except the state corresponding to the empty set). The transition table is used as the

push table (with transitions to the state corresponding to the empty set treated as REJECT entries).

5. Given a stack symbol representing the bottommarker or a set of grammatical occurrences Q and given an input z, fill in the corresponding SHIFT-REDUCE control table entry as follows:

   a) If Q contains the starting occurrence, and z is the endmarker, make the entry ACCEPT.

   b) If the input z is not the endmarker, and the push table has a nonREJECT entry for the given stack symbol and input, make the entry SHIFT.

   c) If Q contains the rightmost occurrence of production p, and z is in FOLLOW($\langle L \rangle$) where $\langle L \rangle$ is the lefthand side of p, make the entry REDUCE(p). (Section 8.7 can be used to compute FOLLOW.)

   d) If p is an ϵ-production with lefthand side $\langle L \rangle$, z is in FOLLOW($\langle L \rangle$), and the push table has a nonREJECT entry for the given stack symbol row and $\langle L \rangle$ column, make the entry REDUCE(p).

   When a), b), c), and d) above impose conflicting requirements on the design, the grammar is not SLR(1). Those entries on which no requirements are placed can be made REJECT.

6. Delete any push-table rows which contain only REJECT entries.

The optimization represented by step 6 works because the revised step 5, like those which preceded it, prevents the SHIFT-IDENTIFY machine from ever referencing push-table rows which have only REJECT entries.

13.7   ERROR PROCESSING IN SHIFT-REDUCE PARSING

Error processing in SHIFT-REDUCE parsing is quite similar to that for SHIFT-IDENTIFY parsing discussed in Section 12.7. However, the SHIFT REDUCE parsers described in this chapter have a special property, not shared by SHIFT-IDENTIFY parsers, that usually allows more meaningful error messages to be produced and better error-recovery procedures to be designed. Given a pushdown recognizer and a nonsentence, we refer to a symbol of that nonsentence as the *offending symbol* if it is the current input when the recognizer rejects. A pushdown recognizer is said to have the *prefix property* if, for all nonsentences, the sequence of symbols to the left of the offending symbol is the prefix of some acceptable input string. In other words, a recognizer has the prefix property if the offending symbol is the first input inconsistent with the hypothesis that the input sequence is going to be acceptable. A pushdown recognizer with the prefix property thus detects an

error at the earliest possible input. The machines defined in this chapter all
have the prefix property because the push table is based on the handle
detector for the grammar and at each step in the processing before the input
sequence is rejected, the string represented by the stack either ends in a
handle, or has some continuation that ends in a handle. If an attempt is
made to push a stack symbol such that the represented string does not have
this property, the push table rejects.

A SHIFT-REDUCE machine can reject an input sequence by accessing
a reject entry in either its control table or its push table. In either case, an
appropriate form of the error message might be

$$\text{``\underline{\hspace{2em}} FOLLOWS \underline{\hspace{2em}}''}$$

where the first dash is filled in with a paraphrased version of the column
symbol and the second dash with a paraphrased version of the row symbol
corresponding to the reject entry.

Since the stack symbols represent occurrences and not just grammatical
symbols, it may be difficult to design paraphrased descriptions that are
understandable to the programmer. Yet it may be important to accurately
describe occurrences since a given input may be allowable after one occurrence of a particular grammatical symbol and not allowable after another
occurrence of the same symbol. Unless the error message accurately describes the second occurrence, the programmer may find the message un-
enlightening.

It can be demonstrated that recognizers designed by the SLR(1)
methods of Sections 13.5 and 13.6 have the property that REJECT entries in
the push table are never accessed, even for nonsentences. A consequence of
this fact is that machines constructed by the SLR(1) methods do not require
error messages for push-table entries.

As an example of error-message design, we return to the S-expression
grammar that appeared in Sections 12.7 and 8.8.

1. $\langle S \rangle \rightarrow a$
2. $\langle S \rangle \rightarrow (\langle S \rangle \langle R \rangle$
3. $\langle R \rangle \rightarrow , \langle S \rangle \langle R \rangle$
4. $\langle R \rangle \rightarrow)$

Figure 13.23 shows the control and push tables for an SLR(1) parser for the
grammar. The REJECT entries in these tables have been labeled, and an
appropriate set of error messages is given in Fig. 13.24.

The messages in the rows corresponding to terminals all follow the
standard format except for those in the endmarker column which are slight

	a	,	(	)	⊣
a	REJECT a	REDUCE(1)	REJECT b	REDUCE(1)	REDUCE(1)
,	SHIFT	REJECT c	SHIFT	REJECT d	REJECT e
(	SHIFT	REJECT f	SHIFT	REJECT g	REJECT h
)	REJECT i	REDUCE(4)	REJECT j	REDUCE(4)	REDUCE(4)
$\langle S \rangle_0$	REJECT k	REJECT ℓ	REJECT m	REJECT n	ACCEPT
$\langle S \rangle_2$	REJECT o	SHIFT	REJECT p	SHIFT	REJECT q
$\langle S \rangle_3$	REJECT r	SHIFT	REJECT s	SHIFT	REJECT t
$\langle R \rangle_2$	REJECT u	REDUCE(2)	REJECT v	REDUCE(2)	REDUCE(2)
$\langle R \rangle_3$	REJECT w	REDUCE(3)	REJECT x	REDUCE(3)	REDUCE(3)
∇	SHIFT	REJECT y	SHIFT	REJECT z	REJECT zz

Control table
(a)

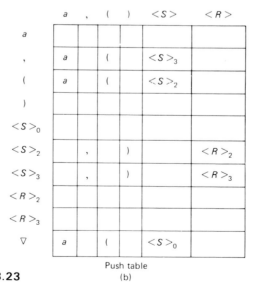

	a	,	(	)	$\langle S \rangle$	$\langle R \rangle$
a						
,	a		(		$\langle S \rangle_3$	
(	a		(		$\langle S \rangle_2$	
)						
$\langle S \rangle_0$						
$\langle S \rangle_2$		,		)		$\langle R \rangle_2$
$\langle S \rangle_3$		,		)		$\langle R \rangle_3$
$\langle R \rangle_2$						
$\langle R \rangle_3$						
∇	a		(		$\langle S \rangle_0$	

Push table
(b)

Figure 13.23

perturbations of the standard format. The entries in the bottommarker row are also quite similar to the standard format.

In the rows corresponding to nonterminals, the entries in the a and $($ columns are not reachable even for nonsentences. For example,

$$\text{REJECT } r$$

in the $\langle S \rangle_3$ row and a column is not reachable because $\langle S \rangle_3$ is only the top stack symbol immediately after REDUCE(1) or REDUCE(2) is performed and neither of these reductions is performed with a as the input symbol. The remaining entries in the nonterminal rows, l, n, q, and t are individually designed based on an interpretation of the occurrence specified by the row. For example, the message for entry l is based on the fact that the top stack symbol represents the starting occurrence.

> a, b, c, d, f, g, i, j: "(input symbol) FOLLOWS (stack symbol)"
> e, h: "S-EXPRESSION INCOMPLETE"
> l: "COMMA AFTER COMPLETE S-EXPRESSION"
> n: "EXTRA RIGHT PARENTHESIS"
> q, t: "MISSING RIGHT PARENTHESIS"
> y, z: "(input symbol) AT BEGINNING OF S-EXPRESSION"
> zz: "S-EXPRESSION MISSING"
> $k, m, o, p, r, s, u, v, w, x$: Not Needed (See text)

Figure 13.24

Error recovery methods for SHIFT-REDUCE parsing are similar to those for SHIFT-IDENTIFY parsing. Figure 13.25 shows a reasonable set of local error-recovery routines for the machine of Fig. 13.23. Note that the recovery routine for entries a and b makes entries k, m, o, p, r and s reachable. Similarly, the recovery routine for entries i and j makes entries u, v, w, and x reachable. However, no new error messages are needed for these situations. Figure 13.26 shows a stack movie of this machine processing the sequence

$$(a , , a$$

This figure can be compared with Figs. 8.29(a) and 12.21 which show this same sequence processed by other machines.

$a, b:$ PRINT(Message from Fig. 13.24)
REDUCE(1)
RETAIN

$c, d, f, g:$ PRINT(Message from Fig. 13.24)
PUSH(a)
RETAIN

$e, h, k, l, m, n, q, t, zz:$ PRINT(Message from Fig. 13.24)
EXIT

$i, j:$ PRINT(Message from Fig. 13.24)
REDUCE(4)
RETAIN

$o, p, r, s:$ PUSH(,)
RETAIN

$u, v:$ REDUCE(2)
RETAIN

$w, x:$ REDUCE(3)
RETAIN

$y, z:$ PRINT(Message from Fig. 13.24)
ADVANCE

Figure 13.25

∇ $(a , , a \dashv$
$\nabla \,($ $a , , a \dashv$
$\nabla \,(\, a$ $, , a \dashv$
$\nabla \,(\, \langle S \rangle_2$ $, , a \dashv$
$\nabla \,(\, \langle S \rangle_2 ,$ $, a \dashv$

PRINT ("COMMA FOLLOWS COMMA")

$\nabla \,(\, \langle S \rangle_2 , a$ $, a \dashv$
$\nabla \,(\, \langle S \rangle_2 , \langle S \rangle_3$ $, a \dashv$
$\nabla \,(\, \langle S \rangle_2 , \langle S \rangle_3 ,$ $a \dashv$
$\nabla \,(\, \langle S \rangle_2 , \langle S \rangle_3 , a$ $\dashv$
$\nabla \,(\, \langle S \rangle_2 , \langle S \rangle_3 , \langle S \rangle_3$ $\dashv$

PRINT ("MISSING RIGHT PARENTHESIS")
EXIT

Figure 13.26

13.8   REFERENCES

The SLR(1) grammars are properly contained within a class of grammars called the LR(1) grammars, which are those grammars that can be recognized by SHIFT-REDUCE methods with a lookahead of 1. In fact, for each integer $k \geq 0$, there is a class of grammars called the LR(k) grammars which are those grammars that can be recognized by SHIFT-REDUCE methods with a lookahead of k.

LR(k) grammars were introduced in Knuth [1965]. There are many variants of the definition, as discussed in Geller and Harrison [1973]. A major variation (which is used in Aho and Ullman [1972a]) of the definition of LR(0) grammars given in Section 13.4 requires that no state of the deterministic handle detector contain both the starting occurrence and some other occurrence.

Aho and Ullman [1972a, 1973a] discuss most aspects of LR(k) grammars, including their own earlier work on improving the size and speed of LR(k) parsers (e.g., Aho and Ullman [1972b]). DeRemer [1971] introduced SLR grammars. Other relevant papers are Korenjak [1969], DeRemer [1969], Pager [1970, 1973], Aho and Johnson [1974], Hayashi [1971], and Kemp [1973]. An alternative approach to SHIFT-REDUCE parsing, based on the concept of strict deterministic grammars, is introduced in Harrison and Havel [1972, 1973, 1974].

PROBLEMS

1. Draw the stack movie as the machine of Fig. 13.3 processes the sequence:

$$a\ b\ a\ c\ b\ b\ b$$

2. Find all the entries in the push table and control table of Fig. 13.3 that are actually reached by:

  a) acceptable sequences

  b) unacceptable sequences

3. For the following grammar with starting symbol $\langle S \rangle$

  1. $\langle S \rangle \rightarrow a$

  2. $\langle S \rangle \rightarrow (\ \langle S \rangle\ \langle R \rangle$

  3. $\langle R \rangle \rightarrow ,\ \langle S \rangle\ \langle R \rangle$

  4. $\langle R \rangle \rightarrow)$

    a) Compute OFIRST for each occurrence

    b) Compute OBELOW

    c) Design an LR(0) recognizer

4. Construct an LR(0) recognizer for each of the following grammars:

a) 1. $\langle S \rangle \rightarrow a \langle S \rangle b$
   2. $\langle S \rangle \rightarrow a \langle S \rangle c$
   3. $\langle S \rangle \rightarrow a b$

b) 1. $\langle S \rangle \rightarrow c \langle A \rangle$
   2. $\langle S \rangle \rightarrow c c \langle B \rangle$
   3. $\langle A \rangle \rightarrow c \langle A \rangle$
   4. $\langle A \rangle \rightarrow a$
   5. $\langle B \rangle \rightarrow c c \langle B \rangle$
   6. $\langle B \rangle \rightarrow b$

c) 1. $\langle S \rangle \rightarrow a \langle S \rangle \langle S \rangle b$
   2. $\langle S \rangle \rightarrow a \langle S \rangle \langle S \rangle \langle S \rangle$
   3. $\langle S \rangle \rightarrow c$

5. A certain grammar has the deterministic handle detector shown in Fig. 13.27. Each state of the handle detector consists of a set of occurrences, where each occurrence consists of a grammatical symbol labeled with the production in which it occurs. Find the grammar from which the table was designed.

	a	b	c	$<S>$	$<A>$
$\triangledown$		$\{b_1\}$		$\{<S>_0\}$	
$\{a_2, a_3\}$	$\{a_2, a_3\}$	$\{b_2\}$	$\{c_4\}$		$\{<A>_3\}$
$\{b_1\}$	$\{a_2, a_3\}$		$\{c_4\}$		$\{<A>_1\}$
$\{b_2\}$	$\{a_2, a_3\}$		$\{c_4\}$		$\{<A>_2\}$
$\{b_3\}$					
$\{c_4\}$					
$\{<S>_0\}$					
$\{<A>_1\}$					
$\{<A>_2\}$					
$\{<A>_3\}$		$\{b_3\}$			

Figure 13.27

6. For each of the following languages find one LR(0) grammar and the corresponding pushdown recognizer.

a) $\{1^n a \, 0^n\} \cup \{1^n b \, 0^{2n}\}$ $n \geq 0$
b) $\{a \, 1^n \, 0^n\} \cup \{b \, 1^n \, 0^{2n}\}$ $n > 0$
c) $\{1^n \, 0^m\}$ $0 < n < m$
d) $\{w \, n \, w^r\}$ w in $(0 + 1)^*$

7. Design an SLR(1) processor for each of the languages in the previous problem.

8. Show that the following grammar is not SLR(1).

$$\langle S \rangle \rightarrow 1 \langle S \rangle 0$$
$$\langle S \rangle \rightarrow 0 \langle S \rangle 1$$
$$\langle S \rangle \rightarrow 1 0$$

9. Determine which, if any, of the following grammars are SLR(1). In each case the starting symbol is $\langle S \rangle$.

a) $\langle S \rangle \rightarrow \langle L \rangle = R$
$\langle S \rangle \rightarrow \langle R \rangle$
$\langle L \rangle \rightarrow * \langle R \rangle$
$\langle L \rangle \rightarrow a$
$\langle R \rangle \rightarrow \langle L \rangle$

b) $\langle S \rangle \rightarrow a \langle A \rangle d$
$\langle S \rangle \rightarrow b \langle A \rangle c$
$\langle S \rangle \rightarrow a e c$
$\langle S \rangle \rightarrow b e d$
$\langle A \rangle \rightarrow e$

10. Design an SLR(1) processor for each of the following grammars:

a) Fig. 12.1

b) Fig. 12.10

11. Design an SLR(1) parser for the grammar of Fig. 13.7. Compare with the LR(0) parser for that grammar given in Fig. 13.11(b).

12. Describe how the SLR(1) parser of Section 13.5 can be implemented using a single table to control the pushdown machine. The columns are the grammatical symbols plus the endmarker; the rows are the stack symbols. Demonstrate your method on the arithmetic expression grammar of Fig. 13.12.

13. Show that SLR(1) machines designed according to Section 13.5 never cycle.

14. Draw the stack movie and list all the error messages that would be put out by the machine of Fig. 13.23 for the input sequence

$$, a , a a (a , , ( ) a , , ,$$

15. Find three sequences for which the local error-recovery procedure of the machine of Fig. 13.23 does a poor job. Describe what went wrong.

16. Change the error-recovery routine for k, l, m, and n in Fig. 13.25 so that an attempt is made to discover errors in the remaining unprocessed input symbols.

17. For each of the following machines, design a debugging sequence (or sequences) that visits all the nonerror transitions in the control and push tables.

a) Fig. 13.14 and 13.15

b) Fig. 13.20 and 13.22

c) Fig. 13.23

   d) Fig. 13.11. How do you define a debugging sequence for an LR(0) machine?

18. Design the error processing for the SLR(1) arithmetic expression processor of Figs. 13.14 and 13.15. Specify the error messages and the error recovery methods.

19. For the following ALGOL-like grammar with starting symbol ⟨program⟩:

   1. ⟨program⟩ → ⟨block⟩

   2. ⟨program⟩ → ⟨compound statement⟩

   3. ⟨block⟩ → ⟨block head⟩ ; ⟨compound tail⟩

   4. ⟨block head⟩ → **begin** d

   5. ⟨block head⟩ → ⟨block head⟩ ; d

   6. ⟨compound tail⟩ → S **end**

   7. ⟨compound tail⟩ → S ; ⟨compound tail⟩

   8. ⟨compound statement⟩ → **begin** ⟨compound tail⟩

   a) Show that the grammar is SLR(1).

   b) Design the SLR(1) recognizer.

   c) Design an appropriate set of error messages.

   d) Design local error-recovery routines.

   e) Design global error-recovery routines.

20. Show that every simple mixed-strategy precedence grammar is also an SLR(1) grammar.

21. For each of the translations described in Problem 5.13a) and b):

   a) design a string translation grammar for which the input grammar is SLR(1);

   b) design the corresponding processor.

22. Design an SLR(1) processor for the MINI-BASIC syntax box using the weak-precedence grammar of Fig. 12.22.

23. Show that for any primitive pushdown machine, the set of possible stack contents (i.e., the set consisting of every sequence that can be on the stack at some point in the processing of some input sequence) is a regular language.

24. a) Design an SLR(1) grammar for S-Expressions in LISP.

   b) Design the corresponding processor.

   c) Design error messages and error-recovery routines.

25. For each REJECT entry in Fig. 13.23a:

   a) find the shortest input sequence, if any, that reaches that entry;

   b) for each sequence found in a), delete the offending symbol and find the shortest sequence that can be concatenated with the prefix sequence to form a correct sentence.

26. Find an SLR(1) grammar for each of the following constructions in ALGOL. Do not carry the derivation below the level of ⟨unsigned number⟩, ⟨variable⟩, ⟨function designator⟩ or ⟨statement⟩.

   a) Arithmetic expressions

   b) Boolean expressions

   c) Array declarations

   d) Switch declarations

   e) **for** statements

27. Design an SLR(1) processor for the following grammar with starting symbol ⟨S⟩:

   ⟨S⟩ → a ⟨A⟩
   ⟨S⟩ → b ⟨B⟩
   ⟨A⟩ → 1 ⟨A⟩ 0
   ⟨A⟩ → ϵ
   ⟨B⟩ → 1 ⟨B⟩ 0 0
   ⟨B⟩ → ϵ

28. Design an SLR(1) processor for the following grammar with starting symbol ⟨program⟩:

   ⟨program⟩ → **begin** ⟨declaration list⟩ ⟨statement list⟩ **end**
   ⟨declaration list⟩ → ⟨declaration list⟩ d ;
   ⟨declaration list⟩ → ϵ
   ⟨statement list⟩ → ⟨statement list⟩ ; ⟨statement⟩
   ⟨statement list⟩ → ⟨statement⟩
   ⟨statement⟩ → s
   ⟨statement⟩ → ϵ

29. Consider the following ambiguous translation grammar for arithmetic expressions:

   ⟨E⟩ → ⟨E⟩ + ⟨E⟩ {+}
   ⟨E⟩ → ⟨E⟩ * ⟨E⟩ {*}
   ⟨E⟩ → a {a}

   Attempt to design an SLR(1) processor for this grammar. Wherever the final tables have more than one entry, select the "correct" one so as to achieve the desired translation. Compare the final processor with that of Fig. 13.14 and 13.15. (For a discussion of this approach, see Aho, Johnson, and Ullman [1973]).

30. Show that for an LR(0) language, if there exist terminal strings x, y and z such that x, xz and y are all in the language, then yz is also in the language (Geller and Harrison [1973].

31. Show that a grammar with no ϵ-productions is LL(1) if and only if the finite-state handle detector formed directly from the relation OBELOW is deterministic.

32. Find grammars which satisfy each of the following conditions.

   a) Weak precedence but not LR(0).

   b) LR(0) but not simple mixed strategy precedence.

   c) LR(0) but not LL(1).

33. Prove that SLR(1) recognizers have the property that all the REJECT entries in the push table are unreachable, even for nonsentences.

14

A Code Generator
for the
MINI-BASIC
Compiler

14.1 INTRODUCTION

In this chapter we present a design of a MINI-BASIC code generator. This
code generator completes the MINI-BASIC compiler and gives an indication of how a more complicated code generator might be structured. Also, in
Section 14.9 we present a solution to an important compilation problem
which does not arise in MINI-BASIC, namely the processing of declarations
in block-structured languages.

14.2 THE COMPILER ENVIRONMENT
AND THE TARGET MACHINE

Many of the details of a code generator are dependent on the environment in
which the compiler operates and on the machine for which it is producing
code. We make the following assumptions (most of which simplify the design).

1. The compilation is entirely in main memory. As the code generator
produces instructions and constants, they are put in the main-memory locations at which they will reside at execution time; they remain in these locations during the remainder of the compilation. (Alternatives to this assumption include buffering the instructions and utilizing a loader.)

2. All the arithmetic operations at execution time are in floating-point, and
the machine has only one floating-point arithmetic register.

3. The machine has the usual set of instructions for loading, storing, performing arithmetic operations (including reverse substract and reverse di-

vide instructions), and doing comparisons and transfers. Exponentiation is carried out by a subroutine. The specific instructions assumed will be discussed as they are needed.

4. We assume there are four index registers for indirect addressing or passing parameters to run-time routines.

14.3   THE SIMULATION OF RUN TIME

Consider the expression

$$(A + B) + (X + Y)$$

An obvious way to compute this expression in machine language is to:

1. load A into the arithmetic register;
2. add B to the arithmetic register;
3. store result $A + B$ in a temporary location;
4. load X into the arithmetic register;
5. add Y to the arithmetic register;
6. add temporary result $A + B$ to the $X + Y$ in the arithmetic register.

Each of the three additions is preceded by a different string of loads and stores.

1. The first addition is preceded by a load instruction to get one of its operands into the arithmetic register.

2. The second addition is preceded by both a store and a load. The store is required to save the contents of the arithmetic register which would otherwise be destroyed by the evaluation of $X + Y$. The load is required to get an operand into place.

3. The third addition is not preceded by any stores or loads. No load is required because one operand, namely $X + Y$, is already in the arithmetic register. No store is required because the previous contents of the arithmetic register are of no subsequent value.

To generate code similar to that described above, our code generator maintains certain information about what will happen at run time when the code it generates is executed. In particular, as the code for each atom is being generated by the code generator, information is maintained as to where the operands will be found and where the results will be placed when this code is being executed at run time. In this way loads and stores can be generated as appropriate to the run-time situation. The bookkeeping required to keep this information is referred to as the "run-time simulation." The details of this simulation are discussed in subsequent sections.

Our efforts to eliminate unnecessary loads and stores can be thought of as an elementary form of optimization. The use of run-time simulation is an optimization technique used in many optimizing compilers, but with much more elaborate bookkeeping. A more primitive MINI-BASIC code generator would dispense with the run-time simulation and generate a load, add, store for each addition.

14.4 MEMORY LAYOUT

Our first step in the design of the code generator is to determine how the memory of the computer will be organized at the run time of the compiled program. The proposed memory layout is shown in Fig. 14.1. The PROGRAM area contains the instructions in the object program. The SUBROUTINE STACK is used to store the return address of subroutine calls (the bottom cell of the stack is initialized with the address of a run-time error routine). The SAVED RESULTS area is used to store the results of SAVE operations in FOR statements. The CONSTANTS and VARIABLES areas are used to store the values of constants and variables respectively.

The TEMPORARY RESULTS area is used to save partial results. As discussed in Section 14.3, only certain partial results require saving; other partial results can spend their brief lifetime in the arithmetic register. For each partial result requiring a temporary location, the code generator assigns one. To conserve space, the code generator assigns locations in such a way that two partial results may share a location if the two results do not need to be saved at the same time during program execution.

The actual assignment of temporary locations to partial results is carried out in such a way that the results are stored as in a run-time stack with the most recently saved values on top. This assignment is possible because the most recently saved result is always needed before any of the other saved

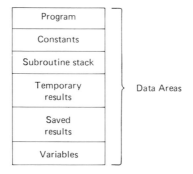

Figure 14.1

Compile-time variables

Name	Initialized to
INSTCOUNTER	Run-time location of first instruction
TEMPCOUNTER	Run-time location of first temporary
CONSTCOUNTER	Run-time location of first constant
SAVECOUNTER	Run-time location of first saved variable

Compile-time constants

Name	Value
INSTLIM	Maximum location for instructions + 1
TEMPLIM	Maximum location for temporaries + 1
TEMPSTART	Run-time location of first temporary
CONSTLIM	Maximum location for constants + 1
SAVELIM	Maximum location for saved variables + 1
SUBSTKLIM	Maximum location for subroutine stack + 1

Figure 14.2

results. We emphasize that the run-time stacking is not accomplished by run time push and pop operations, but is accomplished by each store and load instruction referencing the specific "stack" location where the data is to be stored. The only thing resembling a pushdown simulator is a compile-time variable giving the location of the last saved result. This variable behaves like a top of stack pointer, although the actual stacking of information is not done until run time.

Figure 14.2 shows various compile-time variables and constants involved in keeping track of the run-time storage allocation. Each of these compile-time variables is used to keep track of the next available location in the corresponding run-time storage area.

14.5 TABLE ENTRIES

The code generator uses table entries to keep track of information about the parameters of the atoms. Each table entry has a MODE field, which indicates the kind of item described by the entry, as well as one or two other fields. The MODE field contains one of the following five values: CONSTANT, VARIABLE, PARTIAL RESULT, SAVED RESULT, or LABEL. Each kind of table entry is described below:

1. CONSTANT. The table entry consists of a MODE field and a VALUE field. The value field is filled in by the lexical box and contains the value of the constant.

2. VARIABLE. The table entry consists of a MODE field and an AD-DRESS field. The ADDRESS field contains the preassigned (by the compiler designer) run-time address of the variable.

3. PARTIAL RESULT. The table entry consists of a MODE field and an ADDRESS field. The ADDRESS field contains information for the run-time simulation and may change during the compilation. At any point in the compilation between the creation of a partial result and its use, the AD-DRESS field indicates where the partial result will be residing at run time at the corresponding point in the program execution. A zero in the AD-DRESS field indicates that at run time the partial result is in the arithmetic register. A nonzero ADDRESS field indicates that at run time the partial result is in main memory, in the address contained in the ADDRESS field. An entry corresponding to a particular partial result is first accessed by the code generator at the point in the compilation when code is generated to compute the partial result. Since the partial result is computed in the arithmetic register, the ADDRESS field of the entry is set to zero at this time. If it later becomes necessary to generate code to store the partial result in main memory, the ADDRESS field is changed to the address of the main-memory location. Still later when code is generated to use the partial result, the ADDRESS field is used to obtain the location of the partial result. After the partial result has been used, the table entry will never be accessed again, and the ADDRESS field becomes irrelevant. The routines that modify the AD-DRESS field for partial results are described in the next two sections.

4. SAVED RESULT. The table entry consists of a MODE field and an ADDRESS field. The entry is used to store information about the result of a SAVE atom. The ADDRESS field contains the run-time address where the saved result is to be stored. The ADDRESS field is filled in by a call in the code generator to a function named NEWSAVED. NEWSAVED returns the current value of SAVECOUNTER. It also increments SAVECOUNTER and compares the new value with SAVELIM.

5. LABEL. The table entry consists of a MODE field, a STATUS field, and an ADDRESS field. Each line number and each label created by the syntax box for the FOR statement has such an entry. The STATUS field can contain one of two values: OWED or ASSIGNED. The ADDRESS field can contain either zero or a run-time address in the PROGRAM area. Both these fields may be modified during compilation and are discussed further in the next section.

The MODE field is filled in when a table entry is first created, but in certain cases is changed by the code generator. To accommodate this change, PARTIAL RESULT and SAVED RESULT entries are assumed to be laid out in such a way that they can be transformed into an entry with a VALUE field. This requirement can be met by making each entry large enough to contain a MODE field, an ADDRESS field, and a VALUE field; or by using table entry formats where the same field can serve as either an ADDRESS field or a VALUE field.

14.6   THE GEN ROUTINE

We assume the code generator contains a routine named GEN that constructs the binary representation of the generated instruction. GEN is called with two parameters: the operation code (say, ADD) of the generated instruction and a pointer to the table entry corresponding to the address field of the generated instruction.

For instance if we wanted to generate an instruction to subtract the value of variable A from the arithmetic register, we would write

$$\text{GEN (SUBT, } p)$$

where p is a pointer to the table entry for variable A.

For convenience, when a generated instruction involves an index register or special addressing mode (such as "indirect"), this information is included in the first parameter of GEN. In a more complex code generator, this information is likely to be supplied to a GEN-like routine as additional parameters. Routine GEN takes the following actions:

1. The bits corresponding to the first parameter of GEN are obtained.

2. The bits corresponding to the second parameter of GEN are obtained (as described below).

3. The bits composing the generated instruction are placed in the location corresponding to the current value of INSTCOUNTER.

4. INSTCOUNTER is incremented and compared with INSTLIM.

The actions taken by GEN in obtaining the bits corresponding to the second parameter depend on the mode of that table entry, as follows:

VARIABLE, SAVED RESULT.   The bits used are those contained in the ADDRESS field of the table entry.

CONSTANT.   GEN stores the value of the constant (obtained from the VALUE field of the table entry) in the memory location whose address is the current value of the compile-time variable CONSTCOUNTER. In addition, this address is used in the generated instruction. GEN also increments CONSTCOUNTER and compares the new value with CONSTLIM.

PARTIAL RESULT.   GEN is called with a partial-result entry as a parameter in order to generate either a STORE instruction (which moves the partial result from the register to the TEMPORARY RESULTS stack) or an instruction that uses a partial result residing in the TEMPORARY RESULTS stack.

GEN checks whether the ADDRESS field is zero. A zero ADDRESS field indicates that at run time the partial result is in the arithmetic register. The only instruction that can be generated in this case is a store into temporary. GEN allocates the next available TEMPORARY RESULTS cell by storing the current value of TEMPCOUNTER in the ADDRESS field of the table entry and by using this value as part of the generated STORE instruction. GEN also increments TEMPCOUNTER and compares the new value with TEMPLIM.

When the ADDRESS field is nonzero, the instruction to be generated involves using the temporary result which is currently on top of the temporary stack. GEN de-allocates the run-time TEMPORARY RESULTS cell by using the contents of the ADDRESS field in the generated instruction and by decrementing TEMPCOUNTER.

LABEL.   Whenever a LABEL entry is created by the lexical box or syntax box, the STATUS field is initialized with OWED and the ADDRESS field with zero. When the code generator encounters the LINEN or LABEL atom whose value part is a pointer to that table entry, the STATUS field is changed to ASSIGNED and the current value of INSTCOUNTER is put in the ADDRESS field.

GEN is called with a label entry as a parameter when some sort of transfer instruction to that label is to be generated. GEN first checks whether the STATUS field is ASSIGNED. If so, the label occurs in the program prior to the transfer instruction, and GEN uses the ADDRESS field in the generated instruction.

When the STATUS field contains OWED, a transfer instruction must be generated to a label whose address has not yet been assigned. This case is called a *forward reference* to the label, and is a problem faced by all compilers.

We solve this problem by preparing a linked list of all the generated instructions involving a forward reference to the same label and pointing the ADDRESS field of the table entry for the label to the head of the list. Specifically, when the STATUS field of the label entry is OWED, GEN puts the value of the entry's ADDRESS field in the generated instruction, and then puts the address of this generated instruction in the ADDRESS field of the label entry. Thus the new forward reference is added to the head of the list, and the ADDRESS field contains a pointer to the enlarged linked list. Subsequently, when the LINEN or LABEL atom is encountered, the address of the label (obtained from INSTCOUNTER) is placed in each of the generated instructions involving a forward reference. We assume that a procedure named FLUSH(p) places the address of the label in each instruction on the linked list.

It is possible for a line number to be referenced, as in

GOTO 390

but never to appear at the beginning of a line. To account for this case, when the compilation is completed, a check is made that the STATUS field of each line-number entry is ASSIGNED. An error message is printed for any line-number entry whose STATUS is OWED.

14.7   THE REGISTER MANAGER

As part of the run-time simulation we require that, at each point in the compilation, the code generator knows the corresponding run-time contents of the arithmetic register. The register manager is that portion of the code generator responsible for keeping track of the contents of the arithmetic register. The register manager is also used to generate instructions to save the contents of the arithmetic register (and update the appropriate table entry) when the contents correspond to a partial result that must be saved.

The register manager has a compile-time variable named REG, which contains information about the current status of the arithmetic register. If the register is unoccupied, the value of REG is zero. If the register is occupied, REG contains a pointer to the table entry for the partial result currently in the register.

The code generator communicates with the register manager using the following routines:

USED.   This routine tells the register manager that the contents of the register is being used for the last time and that the register has thereby become devoid of any useful information. The routine notes this fact by setting REG equal to zero. Since each partial result is used only once, each use is a "last-time" use and USED should be called. If the use involves an arithmetic operation, a call on some other procedure is required to inform the register manager of the new contents.

CLEAR.   This routine tells the register manager that the register is needed for some operation, but that operation does not involve the current contents of the register. Thus if the register contains some partial result, instructions must be produced to save that partial result in a temporary location. CLEAR does nothing if REG is zero. If REG is nonzero, CLEAR calls GEN via

GEN(STORE,REG)

and then sets REG to zero.

LINK(*P*).   This routine tells the register manager that the partial result corresponding to table entry *P* has just been computed in the arithmetic register. The routine sets REG to *P* and initializes the ADDRESS field of *P* to zero.

14.8   ROUTINES FOR THE ATOMS

The set of atoms was previously listed in Fig. 10.2. There is an initial transfer vector in the code generator that uses the name of the input atom to transfer to a routine that processes that atom and generates any necessary instructions. If the error flag has been set, the code generator ends the compilation on encountering atom FINIS, and immediately returns to the syntax box on encountering other atoms. The routines for the atoms when the error flag has not been set are listed below.

FINIS

> For each line number table entry whose STATUS field contains OWED: **call** ERROR("UNDEFINED LINE NUMBER");
>
> generate whatever code is needed to end run-time program; end compilation and initiate run of compiled program if error flag has not been set.

LINEN *P*; LABEL *P*

> **if** STATUS(*P*) = OWED **then call** FLUSH(*P*)
>
> **let** STATUS(*P*) = ASSIGNED
>
> **let** ADDRESS(*P*) = INSTCOUNTER

ASSIGN *P*, *Q*

> **if** ADDRESS(*Q*) = 0 **then**
>
> > **begin**
> >
> > **comment** *Q* IN REGISTER
> >
> > **call** USED
> >
> > **call** GEN(STORE,*P*)
> >
> > **end**
>
> **else begin**
>
> > **comment** *Q* IN MEMORY
> >
> > **call** GEN(LOAD,*Q*)
> >
> > **call** GEN(STORE,*P*)
> >
> > **end**

JUMP *P*

> **call** GEN(TRANSFER, *P*)

JUMPSAVE *P*

We assume the existence of a run-time stack in which we keep the return addresses of subroutine calls and an index register XREGSUBSTK that points to the top of that stack. We wish to generate an instruction to store the new return address on this stack. But, first, instructions are generated to check that the subroutine stack does not overflow.

We assume the target machine has a COMPARE instruction which compares the contents of the arithmetic register with the memory location addressed in the instruction, setting certain indicators according to the comparison. We also assume there is a conditional transfer instruction for each possible outcome of the COMPARE instruction. Also, we assume the second parameter in the first three calls on GEN is in a suitable form for GEN.

call GEN(COMPARE.XREGSUBSTK, SUBSTKLIM)

call GEN(TRA.ON.GREATER.OR.EQUAL, OVERFLOW.LABEL)

call GEN(STORE.IN.LOCATION.POINTED.TO.BY.XREG-SUBSTK, INSTCOUNTER + 3)

call GEN(INCREMENT.XREGSUBSTK.BY.1, −)

call GEN(TRANSFER, *P*)

Several of the above instructions might be performed by a single instruction on some target computers.

RETURNJUMP

call GEN(DECREMENT.XREGSUBSTK.BY.1, −)

call GEN(TRANSFER.TO.ADDRESS.POINTED.TO.BY.XREG-SUBSTK, −)

CONDJUMP *P, Q, N, L*

Figure 14.3 gives the RELOPNAME and REVRELOPNAME tables for the operation code of the conditional transfer instruction appropriate for each

OP	RELOPNAME	REVRELOPNAME
=	TRA.ON.ZERO	TRA.ON.ZERO
≠	TRA.ON.NOT.ZERO	TRA.ON.NOT.ZERO
<	TRA.ON.LESS	TRA.ON.GREATER
≤	TRA.ON.LESS.OR.EQUAL	TRA.ON.GREATER.OR.EQUAL
>	TRA.ON.GREATER	TRA.ON.LESS
≥	TRA.ON.GREATER.OR.EQUAL	TRA.ON.LESS.OR.EQUAL

Fig. 14.3 RELOPNAME and REVRELOPNAME Tables

relational operator. To perform a conditional transfer one of the operands must be in the register. If the left operand is in the register, the operation code for the instruction to be generated is obtained from the relational operator using the RELOPNAME table. If the right operand is in the register, the operation code is obtained from the relational operator using the REVRELOPNAME table.

> **if** ADDRESS(P) $= 0$ **then**
> > **begin**
> > **comment** P IN REGISTER
> > **call** USED
> > **call** GEN(COMPARE, Q)
> > **call** GEN(RELOPNAME(N), L)
> > **end**
>
> **else if** ADDRESS(Q) $= 0$ **then**
> > **begin**
> > **comment** Q IN REGISTER
> > **call** USED
> > **call** GEN(COMPARE, P)
> > **call** GEN(REVRELOPNAME(N), L)
> > **end**
>
> > **else begin**
> > **comment** P AND Q IN MEMORY
> > **call** GEN(LOAD, P)
> > **call** GEN(COMPARE, Q)
> > **call** GEN(RELOPNAME(N), L)
> > **end**

SAVE P, R
> **if** MODE(P) $=$ CONSTANT **then**
> > **begin**
> > **comment** NO SAVE INSTRUCTIONS REQUIRED
> > **let** MODE(R) $=$ CONSTANT
> > **let** VALUE(R) $=$ VALUE(P)
> > **end**

>   **else begin**
>   **let** ADDRESS(R) = NEWSAVED
>   **if** ADDRESS(P) = 0 **then call** USED
>   **else call** GEN(LOAD, P)
>   **call** GEN(STORE, R)
>   **end**

TEST P, Q, R, L

The code generator first checks whether the step is a constant. If so, its sign can be determined at compile time, and the generated code need not test the sign at run time. Otherwise, the generated code does test the sign and corresponds to the flow chart of Fig. 14.4. We assume the target machine has an instruction SET.INDICATORS which sets the indicators according to a comparison of the contents of the memory location addressed in the instruction with zero.

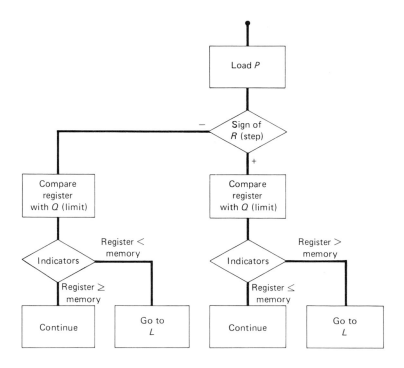

Figure 14.4

if MODE(R) = CONSTANT **then**

       begin

       call GEN(LOAD, P)

       call GEN(COMPARE, Q)

       if value of constant ≥ 0

             then call GEN(TRA.ON.GREATER, L)

             else call GEN(TRA.ON.LESS, L)

       end

    else begin

       call GEN(LOAD, P)

       call GEN(SET.INDICATORS, R)

       call GEN(TRA.ON.GREATER, INSTCOUNTER + 4)

       call GEN(COMPARE, Q)

       call GEN(TRA.ON.LESS, L)

       call GEN(TRANSFER, INSTCOUNTER + 3)

       call GEN(COMPARE, Q)

       call GEN(TRA.ON.GREATER, L)

       end

INCR P, Q

Instructions must be generated to increment P by Q. Both operands are known to be in memory, but the addition requires the arithmetic register.

       call GEN(LOAD, Q)

       call GEN(ADD, P)

       call GEN(STORE, P)

ADD P, Q, R;   SUBT P, Q, R;   MULT P, Q, R;   DIV P, Q, R

These atoms are all treated in the same manner. To perform the operation corresponding to any of these atoms, one operand must be in the register. If both operands are in memory, instructions are generated to load the left operand into the register.

    With one operand in the register and the other in memory, an instruction is generated to perform the mathematical operation corresponding to the atom. If the left operand is in the register, the operation code of this instruction is obtained from the atom name using the OPNAME table of Fig. 14.5; if the right operand is in the register, the operation code is obtained from the

OPERATOR	OPNAME	REVOPNAME
ADD	ADD	ADD
SUBT	SUBT	REVERSE.SUBT
MULT	MULT	MULT
DIV	DIV	REVERSE.DIV

Fig. 14.5 OPNAME and REVOPNAME Tables for Arithmetic Operators

atom using the REVOPNAME table in the same figure. Thus for the atom SUBT, either operation SUBT or REVERSE.SUBT is selected, depending on which operand is in the register. The instruction REVERSE.SUBT subtracts the contents of the register from the contents of the memory location, placing the result in the register.

> **if** ADDRESS(P) $= 0$ **then**
> > **begin**
> > **comment** P IN REGISTER
> > **call** USED
> > **call** GEN(OPNAME(ATOM), Q)
> > **end**
> **else if** ADDRESS(Q) $= 0$ **then**
> > **begin**
> > **comment** Q IN REGISTER
> > **call** USED
> > **call** GEN(REVOPNAME(ATOM), P)
> > **end**
> > **else begin**
> > **comment** P AND Q IN MEMORY
> > **call** CLEAR
> > **call** GEN(LOAD, P)
> > **call** GEN(OPNAME(ATOM), Q)
> > **end**
> **call** LINK(R)

EXP P, Q, R

Code is generated to call an exponentiation routine. Two index registers, XREG1 and XREG2 are loaded with the addresses of the two operands and a transfer and link (which stores the return address in XREGLK) is made to the routine. The exponentiation routine returns its value in the arithmetic register.

> **call** CLEAR
> **call** GEN(LOAD.ADDRESS.INTO.XREG2, Q)
> **call** GEN(LOAD.ADDRESS.INTO.XREG1, P)
> **call** GEN(TRANSFER.AND.LINK.VIA.
>   XREGLK, EXPONENTIATION.ROUTINE)
> **call** LINK(R)

PLUS P, Q

No code needs to be generated for this atom. However, the table entry for Q must be properly filled in and linked to the register manager if appropriate.

> **let** MODE(Q) = MODE(P)
> **if** MODE(P) = CONSTANT **then** **let** VALUE(Q) = VALUE(P)
> > **else** **begin**
> > > **let** ADDRESS(Q) = ADDRESS(P)
> > > **if** ADDRESS(Q) = 0 **then** LINK(Q)
> > > **end**

NEG P, Q

We assume an instruction NEG which negates the contents of the arithmetic register, and LOADNEG which loads the negative of the contents of a memory location into the register.

> **if** ADDRESS(P) = 0 **then**
> > **begin**
> > **comment** P IN REGISTER
> > **call** USED
> > **call** LINK(Q)
> > **call** GEN(NEG, $-$)
> > **end**
> > **else** **begin**
> > **comment** P IN MEMORY
> > **call** CLEAR
> > **call** LINK(Q)
> > **call** GEN(LOADNEG, P)
> > **end**

```
010 REM PROGRAM TO DEBUG CODE GENERATOR
020 LET A1 = 3 * 4 * 2
030 LET B = + A1 * 6/7
040 LET C = A1 + B * 9.6
050 LET D = A1 - 7.2 * C
060 LET E = A1 * (C + D)
070 LET F = (C * A)/(E - C)
080 LET G = - E * F
090 LET H = -(F ↑ G) + A1
100 LET J = A1 * B * (C ↑ D * (E - F) + G/H) - 3E4
110 IF A1 = B GOTO 200
120 IF H + B <> C GOTO 100
130 IF D + E < G GOTO 200
140 IF H <= E GOTO 120
150 IF A1 * B > 10 GOTO 200
160 IF 9.6 >= 32 GOTO 300
170 IF A1 = 3 + B GOTO 200
180 IF B + 2 <> G - 1 GOTO 200
190 IF C < 5 * J GOTO 170
200 IF D - E <= B * C + D GOTO 240
210 IF H + J > B/C GOTO 120
220 IF F >= A1 ↑ 3 GOTO 120
230 GOSUB 250
240 GOTO 400
250 FOR H = 1 TO 100 STEP 10
260 FOR I = A1 TO C + D STEP B
270 LET A1 = 10 + H + I
280 NEXT I
290 NEXT H
300 FOR K = 100 TO 0 STEP - 1
310 LET W = A1 * B + C + K
320 NEXT K
330 LET V = + (C + D) - E
340 FOR K = A1 + B TO 1000 + B
350 FOR Z = 1 TO 10 STEP C + D
360 LET J = K + Z + J
370 NEXT Z
380 NEXT K
390 RETURN
400 END
```

Figure 14.6

This completes the set of routines. A test program that visits each part of the code generator is shown in Fig. 14.6.

14.9   PROCESSING DECLARATIONS IN BLOCK-STRUCTURED LANGUAGES

In block structured languages, such as ALGOL and PL/I, a program can contain several declarations for the same identifier. Each time that identifier occurs in the program, the compiler must determine which declaration (if any) to associate with that occurrence. In this section, we describe one method of accomplishing this association.

We assume that the compiler consists of two passes. The first pass contains the lexical and syntax boxes; the second pass contains the code generator.

The lexical box replaces all occurrences in the program of a particular identifier with a token whose value part is an integer associated with that identifier. Note that all occurrences of the same identifier are represented by tokens with the same value part.

When the syntax box encounters a declaration, it creates a table entry corresponding to that declaration, and places the information contained in the declaration (such as type, number of dimensions of an array, etc.) into the table entry. When the syntax box encounters an occurrence of an identifier other than a declaration, it produces a translation into atoms using the same value part for the identifier as is used in the token. For instance, the assignment statement:

$$CORDELIA := GONERIL + REGAN$$

might be translated into the token string:

$$IDENTIFIER_6 := IDENTIFIER_9 + IDENTIFIER_{62}$$

and then into the atom string:

$$ADD_{9,62,500} \qquad ASSIGN_{6,500}$$

Now consider the processing of the atom string by the code generator. Assume for convenience that the set of value parts for the identifiers in the program are consecutive integers. Then the code generator will maintain a one-dimensional array with an element for each identifier. Each array element will be a pointer to the table entry corresponding to the currently visible declaration for the associated identifier. Thus, to process the atom $ADD_{9,62,500}$ the code generator uses the 9th and 62nd elements of the array

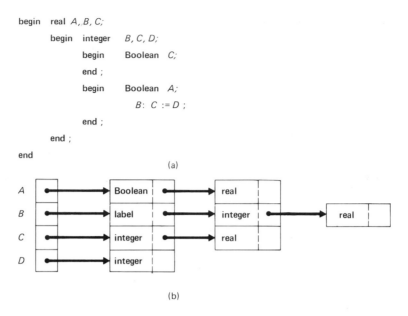

```
begin   real A, B, C;
          begin   integer   B, C, D;
                   begin      Boolean   C;
                   end ;
                   begin      Boolean   A;
                              B: C := D ;
                   end ;
          end ;
   end
```

(a)

(b)

Figure 14.7

to obtain the table entries corresponding to the currently visible declarations for the identifiers involved.

The code generator can maintain the array by having, for each identifier, a pushdown stack of table entries for that identifier, with the array always containing a pointer to the top entry on the stack. The basic plan for updating the set of pushdown stacks is that when the code generator encounters the beginning of a block containing a declaration for a particular identifier, the table entry corresponding to that declaration is pushed on top of the stack for that identifier (and also becomes the entry pointed to by the array). When that block ends, the table entry is popped off the stack. As an example consider the program of Fig. 14.7(a). Assume that each table entry on a stack contains a pointer to the entry below it on the stack. Then at the time the code generator is processing the assignment statement in the program of Fig. 14.7(a), the array and pushdown stacks have the form shown in Fig. 14.7(b).

Our method of keeping track of when to update the stacks involves making a linked list of all the table entries associated with a particular block. The attributed production for a block might be

$$\langle \text{statement} \rangle \rightarrow \textbf{begin} \quad \{ \text{BEGINBLOCK}_p \} \quad \langle \text{blockbody} \rangle_p$$
$$\textbf{end} \; \{ \text{ENDBLOCK}_p \}$$
$$p \leftarrow \text{NEWTABLEENTRYFORABLOCK}$$

The table entry p corresponding to the block will contain a pointer to a linked list of table entries for declarations occurring in the block. Whenever the syntax box creates a table entry for a new declaration, this new table entry is added to the linked list for the current block.

During the second pass, when the code generator encounters the atom BEGINBLOCK, it pushes each of the table entries corresponding to declarations occurring in that block on top of the appropriate stack. When the code generator encounters the atom ENDBLOCK, each of the table entries on the linked list for the block is popped off the appropriate stack.

This completes the description of the method. The total time required for this method is proportional to the number of occurrences of identifiers in the program. One final note is that the array elements for built-in procedures, such as SIN, can be initialized to point to pre-allocated table entries describing these procedures, and that the other array elements can be initialized to a special table entry saying "NO VISIBLE DECLARATION."

14.10   REFERENCES

For a discussion of several useful techniques in code generation, see Gries [1971]. The method of Section 14.9 is similar in its principles to one described in Naur [1964]. Some of the other aspects of the MINI-BASIC code generator are modeled on a particular code generator designed by W. W. Stone.

PROBLEMS

1. What is the code that would be generated by each of the following MINI-BASIC programs?

   a) 10   LET I = (6 + 7) * 5 + 7

      20   IF I > 12 + 6 GOTO 50

      30   LET X = (7 + 1) * (I + 2)

      50   END

   b) 10   FOR X1 = 1 TO −5 + 10

      20   FOR X2 = 1 TO 12

      30   LET X3 = X1 + X2

      40   NEXT X2

      60   NEXT X1

      70   END

2. Describe how the code generator can be expanded to allow operands of different types (integer and floating point). Assume each symbol table entry has a TYPE field indicating the type.

3. a) Devise a better implementation of the FOR statements in which the sign of the step is only computed once rather than each time around the loop.

   b) Assume the machine has an instruction ADD.1.TO.STORE and use this instruction when possible in the compiled code.

4. Show how the expansion of CONDJUMP could be optimized by checking at compile time if one of the operands is the constant 0.

5. Show how the expansions of the binary and unary operators can be optimized by checking the mode of the operands and, if they are both constants, performing the operations at compile time.

6. Assume that MINI-BASIC has the restriction (as in FORTRAN) that the controlled variable cannot be changed in a FOR loop. Design an implementation for the FOR statement that takes advantage of this restriction. Assume the machine has a number of index registers.

7. Redesign the routines for SUBT and DIV assuming that the machine does not have reverse subtract and reverse divide instructions.

8. Describe in words how this code generator organization could be extended to deal with subscripted variables.

9. Describe how the MINI-BASIC compiler could be modified so that when the same constant occurs more than once in a program, only one run-time location is allocated to that constant.

10. Show that using a stack for temporary results would be inadequate for PL/1. (Hint: Look at multiple assignment statements with subscripted variables.)

11. a) Assume that the computer for which MINI-BASIC object code is being generated has two floating-point registers. Describe how the table entries and the register manager can be modified so that the code generator can generate code that takes advantage of both registers. Describe in detail how the code generator expands the ASSIGN and ADD atoms.

    b) Repeat part a) for the case when the target computer has N registers, where N is a parameter of the code generator.

12. Modify the method of Section 14.9, so that if a block contains more than one declaration for the same identifier, this error is detected.

13. In the ALGOL 60 program

    begin integer procedure F ; $F := 1$;

    $\qquad F := 2$

    end

    the first assignment statement is valid, but the second contains an error. Describe how the methods of Section 14.9 can be extended to detect this type of error.

14. In ALGOL 60 (see Section 5.2.4.2 of Naur, et al. [1963]), an identifier which appears in the expression for a subscript bound of an array declaration cannot itself be declared in the same block as the array declaration. Thus the occurrence of an identifier in an array bound is not only a use of the identifier, but also an

"anti-declaration" of the identifier for the block in which the array declaration appears. Describe how the method of Section 14.9 can be extended to detect this type of error.

15. Develop a method which, given an occurrence of a qualified name in COBOL, checks that the qualified name is unambiguous and finds the structure member being referred to. (A method is described in Knuth [1968b].)

15

A Survey of
Object-Code
Optimization

15.1   INTRODUCTION

In this chapter we briefly discuss a number of transformations that can be
performed on programs to increase the efficiency of the object code. These
transformations are commonly called "optimizations," although "improvements" is a more appropriate word. The transformations can be done in
various boxes of a compiler, but the more complicated ones are generally
done by a separate optimization box between the syntax box and the code
generator. We only discuss the transformations themselves, and not the
processing techniques necessary to determine when the transformations are
applicable and to actually perform them.

We illustrate the transformations with examples written in MINI-
BASIC, extended by the inclusion of one- and two-dimensional arrays.

15.2   REGISTER ALLOCATION

One aspect of conventional computer architecture which is a major consideration in the generation of efficient object code is the availability of only
a limited number of high-speed registers in addition to a larger amount of
main memory. Instructions involving main memory may be slower and may
require more space for their specification than those involving registers.
Therefore it is desirable to use the registers as efficiently as possible. Register
allocation is the determination of what the contents of each register should
be at each point in the program execution. Registers can be used to hold
variables, partial results, and information (such as return addresses and
pointers to areas of main memory) involved in the run-time implementation
of the language.

A frequently used technique is to allocate a register, instead of a main-memory location, to a variable either for the entire program or a portion of the program. Even for a variable that has been allocated a main memory location, when that variable is assigned a new value which has been computed in a register, the compiler may not immediately generate an instruction to store the contents of the register into the main-memory location corresponding to the variable. The compiler temporarily uses the register rather than the main-memory location as the carrier of the variable's value.

Similar ideas are used in the assignment of registers for partial results, array indices, return addresses for procedure calls, etc. Each of these items can be assigned to a register or to main memory for all or part of its life. The use of registers for storing partial results was discussed briefly in Chapter 14 and is considered again in Section 15.5.

15.3   ONE-ATOM OPTIMIZATIONS

Some simple kinds of optimizations can be performed by inspecting the parameters of each atom for special cases and then generating tailored code when a special case is detected. For instance, the operands of the atom ADD can be inspected to determine if one of them is the constant zero. In this case, no code need be generated. Also, when both operands are constants, the addition can be performed at compile time instead of run time and no code need be generated.

Another example of a special case occurs in exponentiation when the second parameter of the EXP atom is some small constant. For instance, for $A \uparrow 2$, the compiler can generate code corresponding to $A * A$ instead of generating code to call some general exponentiation routine.

Sometimes a computer has certain instructions that can only be used in special cases. For example, suppose the computer has an instruction STOREZERO which stores the constant zero into a memory location. Then for the atom

$$\text{ASSIGN}_{p,q}$$

which is supposed to generate code to store the value corresponding to its second parameter in the address corresponding to its first parameter, the compiler can generate STOREZERO when the second parameter is the constant zero.

15.4   OPTIMIZATIONS OVER A WINDOW OF ATOMS

Sometimes there are possible optimizations that can be detected by inspecting some fixed number of consecutive atoms, called a "window." For instance, suppose a grammar has the production:

⟨statement⟩ → IF ⟨Boolean expression⟩ THEN ⟨statement⟩

In the attributed translation grammar for the syntax box, this production might become

$\langle$statement$\rangle \rightarrow$ IF $\langle$Boolean expression$\rangle_{R1}$ THEN $\{$JUMPFALSE$_{R2,L1}\}$

                 $\langle$statement$\rangle$ $\{$LABEL$_{L2}\}$

                 $(L1, L2) \leftarrow$ NEWTL $R2 \leftarrow R1$

where $R1$ is a synthesized attribute and NEWTL returns a pointer to a new table entry for a label. When THEN is followed by a goto statement, a typical atom string corresponding to the conditional statement might be

$$\text{JUMPFALSE}(39, 62) \qquad \text{JUMP}(92) \qquad \text{LABEL}(62)$$

This atom string can be replaced by the more efficient atom string

$$\text{JUMPTRUE}(39, 92)$$

The compiler can detect this situation by looking for an occurrence of

$$\text{JUMPFALSE} \qquad \text{JUMP} \qquad \text{LABEL}$$

where the second parameter of JUMPFALSE and the parameter of LABEL are the same.

15.5   OPTIMIZATIONS WITHIN A STATEMENT

We now consider some transformations that can involve an unbounded number of consecutive atoms, but are involved in a single statement.

Rearranging Expressions

More efficient code for the evaluation of an expression can often be produced if the operations occurring in the expression are evaluated in a different order than in the atom string corresponding to a Polish translation of the original expression. For instance, suppose there is no reverse subtract instruction and only one register is available for evaluating the expression

$$A * B - C * D$$

If the operations involved are carried out in the Polish order, the object code has eight instructions

LOAD	A
MULT	B
STORE	TEMP1
LOAD	C
MULT	D
STORE	TEMP2
LOAD	TEMP1
SUBT	TEMP2

However, if the expression can be reordered so that $C * D$ is evaluated before $A * B$, the following six-instruction object code can be generated.

```
LOAD      C
MULT      D
STORE     TEMP1
LOAD      A
MULT      B
SUBT      TEMP1
```

For a machine with a fixed number of registers, sometimes rearranging the expression will permit its evaluation without any storage of partial results in main memory. For example, suppose there are two registers available, and the expression to be evaluated is

$$A * B + (C + D) * (E + F)$$

Evaluating the expression in Polish order produces the following nine instructions (where the operation code for each instruction is assumed to include the number of the register involved).

```
LOAD1     A
MULT1     B
LOAD2     C
ADD2      D
STORE1    TEMP
LOAD1     E
ADD1      F
MULT1     REGISTER2
ADD1      TEMP
```

However, the expression can be rearranged to produce the following eight instructions.

```
LOAD1     C
ADD1      D
LOAD2     E
ADD2      F
MULT1     REGISTER2
LOAD2     A
MULT2     B
ADD1      REGISTER2
```

Routine Calls

Frequently, reductions can be made in the execution time of routines and functions called within a statement. The compiler can check the parameters, and if they fall within various special categories, can generate code which calls a specialized version of the routine that executes more rapidly than a general version handling all possible parameters.

Sometimes code to perform the routine is generated directly in-line, thereby saving the overhead of calling a routine.

Combining Transfers

Occasionally, a program contains a transfer or conditional transfer to a label, and the first atom after the label is a transfer to some second label. In this case, the first transfer can be changed to go directly to the second label. An example of this situation occurs in the ALGOL statement

$$\textbf{if } X > Y \quad \textbf{then } Z := Q \quad \textbf{else go to } L$$

The conditional transfer based on whether X is greater than Y can go directly to the label L, and no code need be generated for **go to** L.

15.6 OPTIMIZATIONS OVER SEVERAL STATEMENTS

We now discuss some program transformations which can be done within a single statement, but which in general are done over several statements. Performing these optimizations may involve a complex analysis of the program.

Common Subexpressions

A "common subexpression" is a subexpression that occurs more than once in the program but for which code can be generated that only evaluates the subexpression once. For instance, in the expression

$$(A + B) * C + D/(A + B)$$

the addition $A + B$ need only be performed once.

Common subexpressions occur quite frequently in the evaluation of the addresses of subscripted variables. For instance in the statement

$$\text{LET } A(I, J) = A(I, J) + B(I, J)$$

the address of $A(I, J)$ need only be computed once. Furthermore if A and B have the same dimensions, there may be a common subexpression in the computation of the addresses of $A(I, J)$ and $B(I, J)$.

A particular occurrence of a subexpression need not be recomputed if it is already computed in all program execution paths leading to the occurrence. For instance, consider a program with the following statements

```
40  LET X = A * B + C
50  GOTO  100
          .
          .
          .
90  LET W = A * B — E
100  LET Z = 3 — A * B
```

If there is no other transfer of control to line 100, then every time line 100 is executed, the value of $A * B$ will have been previously computed (at line 40 or line 90) and $A * B$ need not be recomputed.

Constant Propagation

Operations involving constants can be performed at compile time instead of at run time. Sometimes the operations can be "propagated" over several statements. For instance, in the sequence of statements

```
10  LET A = 1
20  LET B = 2
30  LET C = A + B
```

the addition in the third statement can be done at compile time, and the statement can effectively be replaced by

```
30  LET C = 3
```

One use of constant propagation is in the computation of the addresses of subscripted variables when the subscript values can be determined at compile time.

15.7 OPTIMIZATIONS OVER LOOPS

There are certain improvements which are specifically aimed at making loops more efficient.

Code Motion

Sometimes generated code can be moved out of a loop and executed prior to the loop. Therefore instead of being executed once each time around the loop, the code is executed once for the entire loop execution. For instance, if a statement inside a loop involves the subexpression $A * B$, and neither A

nor *B* are changed during execution of the loop, the product can be computed once before entering the loop, and this result used during the loop.

The opportunities for this type of improvement frequently occur in the computation of the addresses of subscripted variables. For example, if the subscripted variable $A(I, J)$ appears in a loop for which I is the loop variable, there may be a subexpression involving J and a constant that can be moved outside the loop.

In the literature of code optimization, code that can be moved outside a loop is frequently called "invariant" in that loop.

Loop Fusion

Sometimes two loops can be combined into a single loop, thereby reducing the number of test and increment instructions executed. For instance the MINI-BASIC statements:

```
100    FOR I = 1 TO 100
110    LET A(I) = 0
120    NEXT I
130    FOR J = 1 TO 100
140    LET B(J) = 3 * C(J)
150    NEXT J
```

can be combined into the single loop:

```
100    FOR K = 1 TO 100
110    LET A(K) = 0
120    LET B(K) = 3 * C(K)
130    NEXT K
```

Unswitching

Sometimes one loop can be split into two loops of which only one need be executed. For instance the loop:

```
300    FOR I = 1 TO 100
310    IF X > Y  GOTO 340
320    LET A(I) = B(I) + X
330    GOTO 350
340    LET A(I) = B(I) - Y
350    NEXT I
```

can be converted into:

```
300     IF X > Y  GOTO 350
310     FOR I = 1 TO 100
320     LET A(I) = B(I) + X
330     NEXT I
340     GOTO 380
350     FOR I = 1 TO 100
360     LET A(I) = B(I) − Y
370     NEXT I
380
```

In the transformed program the conditional statement is only executed once whereas in the original program it was executed 100 times.

Strength Reduction

Strength reduction involves replacing one operation by another which is executed more rapidly. For instance the loop:

```
100     FOR I = 1 TO 100
110     LET Q(I) = I * 5
120     NEXT I
```

can be changed to:

```
100     LET J = 5
110     FOR I = 1 TO 100
120     LET Q(I) = J
130     LET J = J + 5
140     NEXT I
```

The multiplication $I * 5$ in the original loop is replaced by the faster addition $J + 5$.

Loop Unrolling

Loop unrolling involves reducing the number of executions of a loop by performing the computations corresponding to two (or more) executions of the loop in each single execution. For example the loop:

```
100     FOR I = 1 TO 100 STEP 1
110     LET A(I) = B(I) * C(I)
120     NEXT I
```

can be transformed into the loop:

```
100    FOR I = 1 TO 99 STEP 2
110    LET A(I) = B(I) * C(I)
120    LET A(I + 1) = B(I + 1) * C(I + 1)
130    NEXT I
```

This transformation reduces from one hundred to fifty the number of times the controlled variable *I* is tested to determine if the loop is over. Furthermore, on a machine with parallelism, it might be possible to execute the two new assignment statements in the same amount of time it takes to execute the original assignment statement.

Array Linearization

Array linearization involves generating code as if an *n*-dimensional array were one dimensional. For example, the double loop

```
100    FOR I = 1 TO 20
110    FOR J = 1 TO 20
120    LET A(I, J) = 0
130    NEXT J
140    NEXT I
```

zeros out the four hundred elements of the two-dimensional array *A*. The same effect is achieved by the following loop, which treats *A* as though it is a one dimensional array with four hundred elements:

```
100    FOR I = 1 TO 400
110    LET A(I) = 0
120    NEXT I
```

15.8   MISCELLANEOUS

There are a number of additional techniques which at first glance seem aimed at correcting foolish programming, but which may become significant after other techniques have transformed the program.

Removal of Useless Statements

A statement is called useless if there is no way to transfer control to that statement. In addition, an assignment is called useless if the value assigned to a variable is not used prior to the next assignment to that same variable. Useless statements and assignments can be deleted from a program.

Peephole Optimization

Sometimes a scan of the generated instructions indicates an instruction that can be deleted. For instance, if two consecutive instructions are

STORE A

LOAD A

and there is no transfer of control to the LOAD instruction, then the LOAD instruction can be deleted.

15.9 REFERENCES

Much of this chapter is based on Allen and Cocke [1972]. For a further discussion of object code optimization, including methods for performing various optimization transformations, see Aho and Ullman [1973a], Cocke and Schwartz [1970], and Allen [1969].

Appendix A
MINI-BASIC
Language Manual

A.1   GENERAL FORM OF A MINI-BASIC PROGRAM

A MINI-BASIC program is a sequence of lines each of which begins with a number. These numbers are called *line numbers* and are used to identify the lines. The remainder of each line excluding the line number is called a *statement*. Line numbers also serve to specify the order in which the statements are executed. Normally, statements are executed in numerical order of their line numbers unless a transfer of control is specified by a GOTO Statement, an IF Statement, a FOR Statement, a NEXT Statement, a GOSUB Statement, or a RETURN Statement.

Spaces have no significance and are ignored by the compiler. However, spaces can be added where desired for clarity.

Example:

```
10   LET X = 12
20   IF X > 10 GOTO 30
30   END
```

A.2   NUMBERS

A number may be written in either of two forms:

a) a sequence of decimal digits with or without a decimal point optionally preceded by a sign, such as:

$$3.4712$$
$$-1235$$
$$2.$$

b) a sequence of decimal digits with or without a decimal point optionally preceded by a sign followed by the symbol E followed by a
sequence of decimal digits optionally preceded by a sign, such as:

$$1234E-11$$

$$12.34E-9$$

$$.00000001234E0$$

which all represent the same number.

A.3 VARIABLES

A variable is denoted by a single letter or a single letter followed by a single
digit.

Examples:

$$X$$

$$Y1$$

$$Z9$$

$$Q0$$

A.4 ARITHMETIC EXPRESSIONS

Arithmetic expressions are formulas for computing a value. They are made
up using *numbers*, *variables*, and the five arithmetic operators.

+ Addition
− Subtraction
* Multiplication
/ Division
↑ Exponentiation

as well as the left and right parentheses.

Any meaningful formula made from these symbols is acceptable except
that when the + and − are used as unary operators they must appear only
at the beginning of an expression or immediately after a left parenthesis.
Thus, two operators can never be adjacent.

Examples of unary operators:

$$-A * B$$

$$-(A * B)$$

$$C * (-A * B)$$

Examples of general expressions:

$$A1 + B * (C + D \uparrow (C + E))$$

$$A1 + 3.14159/4 * (C + 12)$$

The order in which operations are performed is normally from left to right except that

1. Operations within parentheses are carried out before the parenthesized quantity is used in further computations.

2. Exponentiations are done before multiplications and divisions which in turn are done before additions or subtractions.

Example

The order of operations is indicated below the following expression:

$$A + (B/(C + D)) * F \uparrow G \uparrow (H + B) + C$$
$$7 \quad 2 \quad 1 \quad \quad 6 \quad 3 \quad 5 \quad 4 \quad 8$$

A.5 STATEMENTS

The following are the allowable types of statements.

a) Assignment Statement

The general form of an Assignment statement is

LET ⟨variable⟩ = ⟨arithmetic expression⟩

The value of the arithmetic expression is computed and assigned to the variable.

Example

LET X1 = Y1 + 12.6 * Z + X1

b) GOTO Statement

The general form of a GOTO statement is

GOTO ⟨line number⟩

Control is transferred to the statement with the specified line number.

Example

GOTO 75

c) Conditional Statement

The general form of a Conditional Statement is:

      IF ⟨arithmetic expression⟩ ⟨relational operator⟩
      ⟨arithmetic expression⟩ GOTO ⟨line number⟩

where the relational operators are

$=$	equal
$<>$	not equal
$<$	less than
$<=$	less than or equal
$>$	greater than
$>=$	greater than or equal

If the relation holds between the values of the two arithmetic expressions, control is transferred to the specified line number. Otherwise, control passes to the next statement in sequence.

Examples

      IF X > Y GOTO 12
      IF Z + (X * Y) = X1 + 12 GOTO 75

d) FOR Statement and NEXT Statement

FOR and NEXT statements are used to set up program loops.

There are two general forms of FOR Statements:

      FOR ⟨variable⟩ = ⟨arithmetic expression 1⟩ TO
      ⟨arithmetic expression 2⟩ STEP ⟨arithmetic expression 3⟩

      FOR ⟨variable⟩ = ⟨arithmetic expression 1⟩ TO
      ⟨arithmetic expression 2⟩

The second form is interpreted in the same way as the first except that the step size (arithmetic expression 3) is assumed equal to 1. The FOR statement forms the entrance of a program loop that continues through any number of subsequent statements until a NEXT statement to close the loop is reached. The general form of a NEXT statement is

              NEXT ⟨variable⟩

where the variable must be the same as the variable of the FOR statement.

Example

```
FOR X = 1 TO 100 STEP 5
    LET W = X + Y + Z
    LET Z = X * Y
NEXT X
```

Informally, the statements in the loop between the FOR statement and the NEXT statements are executed over and over again a
number of times as specified by the FOR statement. Each time
around the loop the value of the variable is incremented by the step
and compared with the final value to determine whether to enter the
loop again or to terminate the FOR statement.

Specifically, the execution of the FOR Statement is as follows:

i) Arithmetic expression 1 (the *initial value*), arithmetic expression
2 (the *final value*), and arithmetic expression 3 (the *step size*) are all
computed.

ii) The *initial value* is assigned to the variable.

iii) A test is made, depending on the value of the *step size*.

• If the *step size* is greater than or equal to zero, and the value of the
variable is less than or equal to the *final value*, control passes to the
statement following the FOR statement (i.c., the loop is entered).
Otherwise, control passes to the statement following the associated
NEXT (i.e., the loop is not entered and the FOR statement is completed.)

• If the *step size* is negative, and the value of the variable is greater
than or equal to the *final value*, control passes to the statement following the FOR statement (i.e., the loop is entered). Otherwise, control passes to the statement following the associated NEXT (i.e., the
loop is not entered and the FOR statement is completed).

iv) If the loop is entered, the statements between the FOR statement
and the associated NEXT are executed.

v) When NEXT is reached, the value of the *step size* is added to the
current value of the variable and the result assigned to the variable.
The procedure then continues at step iii). Note the *initial value, final
value*, and *step size* are computed only once, at the beginning, not
every time around the loop. However, the value of the controlled

variable can be changed by the statements within the loop and the latest value is always used for the incrementing and testing steps.

It is allowable to have loops within loops, but they must be properly nested.

Example

```
┌   FOR X = 1 TO N
│   ...
│ ┌ FOR Y = 1 TO N
│ │ ...
│ └ NEXT  Y
│   ...
└   NEXT X
```

e) GOSUB and RETURN Statements

Subroutines can be defined and called using the GOSUB and RE-TURN statements. The general form of a GOSUB statement is:

GOSUB ⟨line number⟩

Control is transferred to the specified line number and the subsequent statements are executed until a RETURN statement is reached. The general form of a RETURN statement is:

RETURN

Control is transferred to the line number immediately after the last GOSUB statement executed.

More than one RETURN statement can exist in one subroutine. However, subroutines can be left only by a RETURN statement. Using a GOTO statement or an IF statement to leave a subroutine will not work properly.

A GOSUB statement can be used within a subroutine to call still another subroutine. However, such a GOSUB cannot refer to a subroutine already entered. (Recursion is not allowed.)

f) END Statement

Every program must have a single END statement — the last (highest-numbered) statement in the program. The general form of an END statement is

END

g) REM Statement

Comments can be added to a program using the REM statement, the general form of which is

REM ⟨any sequence of characters⟩

The compiler ignores the remainder of the line after the line number. However, the line number of a REM statement can be used in GOTO, IF, and GOSUB statements.

Appendix B
Relations

B.1 INTRODUCTION

Suppose we are given a set of integers, say $\{1, 2, 3, 4\}$, and we want to describe the ordering relation $<$ as it applies to this set. One way to do this would be by giving the set of all ordered pairs (m, n) such that $m < n$. Specifically, the relation would be described by the set

$$\{(1, 2), (1, 3), (1, 4), (2, 3), (2, 4), (3, 4)\}.$$

From this description, we can determine that the relationship $1 < 4$ holds because pair $(1, 4)$ is in this set and that relationship $3 < 2$ does not hold because pair $(3, 2)$ is not in the set. For mathematical purposes, it is convenient to say that this set of pairs *is* the relation $<$ for the set $\{1, 2, 3, 4\}$.

As a second example of the relation concept, consider the graph shown in Fig. B.1. It shows a set of five nodes with certain pairs of nodes connected by arrows. We want to describe a relation called POINTS-AT such that the relation

$$x \text{ POINTS-AT } y$$

holds for two nodes x and y if and only if there is an arrow from node x to node y in the graph. This relation POINTS-AT is described by the following set of ordered pairs:

$$\{(a, b), (b, c), (d, b), (d, d), (e, a), (e, c)\}.$$

Thus we say that relationships

$$a \text{ POINTS-AT } b \qquad \text{and} \qquad d \text{ POINTS-AT } d$$

577

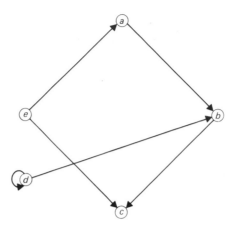

Figure B.1

hold whereas relationships

c POINTS-AT *a*   and   *c* POINTS-AT *b*

do not hold. Again for mathematical purposes, we say that the relation POINTS-AT *is* the set of ordered pairs.

The general mathematical concept of a relation is defined as follows:

> Given a set *S*, a *relation R* on the set *S* is a set of ordered pairs of elements from *S*. If *s* and *t* are in *S*, we say that relationship *s R t* holds if and only if the pair (*s, t*) is in the set *R* of ordered pairs.

B.2 REPRESENTING RELATIONS ON FINITE SETS

One way of representing a relation on a finite set is simply to list all the ordered pairs in the relation. This method has already been employed in the previous section to present the two examples. In this section, we introduce two alternate methods which we call the "graph method" and the "matrix method."

Graph method.   In this method, a relation on set *S* is represented by a graph in which there is one node for each element in *S* and an arrow from node *s* to node *t* if and only if the ordered pair (*s, t*) is in the set of ordered pairs which define the relation. The graph method has, in fact, already been illustrated in the previous section where the relation POINTS-AT was first described by the graph in Fig. B.1. Now we observe that the graph is, in effect, a representation of the set and vice versa. Applying the graph method to the example of the relation $<$ on the set $\{1, 2, 3, 4\}$, the result is the graph of Fig. B.2 where an arrow has been drawn from node m to node n if and only if $m < n$.

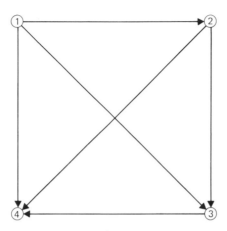

Figure B.2

Matrix method.   In this method, a relation on set S is represented by a matrix in which each element of S is associated with one of the rows and one of the columns. If s and t are elements of S, then the matrix entry for row s and column t is assigned value 1 if the ordered pair (s, t) is in the defining set and is assigned value 0 if the pair (s, t) is not in the defining set. The matrix for the relation $<$ on $\{1, 2, 3, 4\}$ is shown in Fig. B.3. The matrix is simply a table which shows for every combination of row and column whether or not the relation holds for the corresponding pair. Thus the 1 in row 2 and column 3 indicates that relation $2 < 3$ holds and the 0 in row 4 and column 3 indicates that $4 < 3$ does not hold. The matrix for the relation POINTS-AT is shown in Fig. B.4.

	1	2	3	4
1	0	1	1	1
2	0	0	1	1
3	0	0	0	1
4	0	0	0	0

Matrix for $<$

Figure B.3

	a	b	c	d	e
a	0	1	0	0	0
b	0	0	1	0	0
c	0	0	0	0	0
d	0	1	0	1	0
e	1	0	1	0	0

Matrix for POINTS-AT

Figure B.4

B.3   THE PRODUCT OF RELATIONS

It sometimes happens that one interesting relation can be defined in terms of two other relations. For example, if S is a set of people for which the relations SPOUSE-OF and MOTHER-OF have been defined, a relation MOTHER-IN-LAW-OF might be defined as follows:

Relationship

$$a \text{ MOTHER-IN-LAW-OF } b$$

holds if and only if there is a c such that

$$a \text{ MOTHER-OF } c \quad \text{and} \quad c \text{ SPOUSE-OF } b.$$

In this case, we would say that the relation MOTHER-IN-LAW-OF is the product of the relations MOTHER-OF and SPOUSE-OF. The concept of a product is defined as follows:

Given relations P and Q, their *product* is the relation consisting of all pairs (a, b) for which there is a c such that

$$aPc \quad \text{and} \quad cQb.$$

We use the operator $\cdot$ to indicate the product of two relations, and write the product as $P \cdot Q$.

The principle application of the product-relation concept is in certain computational problems in which we want to construct some relation $R = P \cdot Q$ by first constructing relations P and Q and then constructing the product.

Suppose we have graph representations of two relations P and Q on some set S and we want to construct a graph representing the product relation $P \cdot Q$. We begin by constructing a graph showing the set of nodes S

without any arrows. Then we inspect the nodes of P and Q and add arrows to the new graph, as required by the definition. Suppose, for example, that we are given the graphs shown in Figs. B.5(a) and B.5(b). Looking at the node v for P and Q, we see that zPv and vQw. We therefore draw an arrow from node z to node w in the new graph. Repeating this process for all nodes, we get the graph for $P \cdot Q$ shown in Fig. B.5(c). Once an arrow has been drawn from node a to node b, no further arrows are drawn from a to b even though the corresponding relation is implied by other combinations from P and Q. For example, the relationship $yP \cdot Qv$ is implied both by the relationships yPy and yQv and by the relationships yPz and zQv, but the arrow from y to v in the product-relation graph is only drawn once.

When the relations P and Q are represented by the matrix method, the matrix for $P \cdot Q$ can be constructed by finding each row i and column j for which the P matrix entry is 1 and then inspecting the row j of the Q matrix to find those k such that jQk. Having thus determined that iPj and jQk, a 1 is placed in the (i, k) entry of the $P \cdot Q$ matrix.

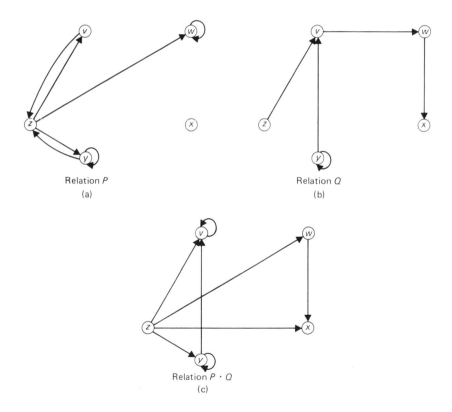

Relation P

(a)

Relation Q

(b)

Relation $P \cdot Q$

(c)

Fig. B.5 (a) Relation P (b) Relation Q (c) Relation $P \cdot Q$

A BASIC program to compute the product of two relations is shown in Fig. B.6. It assumes that the matrices for P and Q are stored in arrays named A and B, respectively, and that the product matrix is to be constructed in an array C that has been initialized to have all entries equal to zero.

```
10   REM COMPUTES PRODUCT OF RELATIONS IN A AND B, BOTH N
15   REM BY N MATRICES.
20   REM ASSUMES MATRIX C IS N BY N AND INITIALIZED TO ZERO
30   FOR J = 1 TO N STEP 1
40   FOR I = 1 TO N STEP 1
50   IF A(I,J) = 0 GOTO 120
60   REM DO LOOP TO INSPECT ROW J OF B MATRIX IF AND ONLY IF
65   REM A(I,J) = 1
70   FOR K = 1 TO N STEP 1
80   IF B(J,K) = 0 GOTO 110
90   REM ASSIGNMENT IF AND ONLY IF A(I,J) = B(J,K) = 1
100  LET C(I,K) = 1
110  NEXT K
120  NEXT I
130  NEXT J
140  END
```

Fig. B.6 BASIC Program for Computing Product of Relations

B.4   TRANSITIVE CLOSURE

It sometimes happens that an interesting relation can be defined in terms of a repeated application of some other relation. For example, if S is a set for which the relation PARENT-OF has been defined, a relation ANCESTOR-OF might be defined as follows:

Relationship

$$a \text{ ANCESTOR-OF } b$$

holds if and only if there is a sequence $c_1, \ldots, c_n$ such that

$$a = c_1, \qquad b = c_n \qquad \text{and} \qquad c_i \text{ PARENT-OF } c_{i+1}$$

for all i such that $1 \leq i < n$.

For instance if $c_1 =$ Abraham, $c_2 =$ Isaac, $c_3 =$ Jacob, and $c_4 =$ Joseph, we have

> Abraham PARENT-OF Isaac
>
> Isaac PARENT-OF Jacob
>
> Jacob PARENT-OF Joseph

and can include that

> Abraham ANCESTOR-OF Joseph

The relation ANCESTOR-OF is called the transitive closure of the relation PARENT-OF. The concept of transitive closure can be defined as follows.

Given a relation Q, the *transitive closure* of Q is the relation consisting of all pairs (a, b) for which there is a sequence

$$c_1, \ldots, c_n$$

for some $n > 1$ such that

$$a = c_1, \qquad b = c_n \qquad \text{and} \qquad c_i \, Q \, c_{i+1}$$

for all i satisfying $1 \leq i < n$. We use the superscript "+" to indicate the transitive closure, writing it as Q^+.

The principle application of the transitive closure concept is for certain computational problems in which we want to construct some relation $R = Q^+$ by first constructing relation Q and then constructing its transitive closure.

The concept of transitive closure has a concrete interpretation in terms of the graph representation of relations. Suppose we have a graph representation of a relation Q. Then

$$a \, Q^+ b$$

if and only if the graph for Q has a chain of arrows going from a to b.

Suppose we want to construct the graph representing Q^+. We begin the construction by making a copy of the graph for Q. Then we look for combinations of three nodes a, b, c such that there are arrows from a to b and b to c. For each such combination, we add an arrow from a to c if there is not already such an arrow. When no further arrows can be added by this means, every pair of nodes which is connected by a chain is also connected by an arrow. Therefore the construction is complete and the resulting graph is the graph for Q^+.

In order to systematically carry out the process of adding arrows, we consider the nodes one at a time. For each path of length two passing through the node under consideration, we want to ensure that there is an arrow from the start node to the end node of the path. To do this, we draw arrows from the nodes which point at the node under consideration to nodes pointed at by the node under consideration, except that we do not duplicate arrows previously drawn. For example, suppose we wish to compute the relation POINTS-AT + where POINTS-AT is the relation defined by the graph in Fig. B.1. Starting with the graph of Fig. B.1 and inspecting node *a* we see an arrow from *e* to *a* and an arrow from *a* to *b*. Hence we add an arrow from *e* to *b* and the result is Fig. B.7(a). Node *b* has three arrows coming in, namely from *a, d,* and *e,* and an arrow going out to node *c,* so arrows must be included from *a* to *c,* from *d* to *c,* and from *e* to *c.* Since there is already an

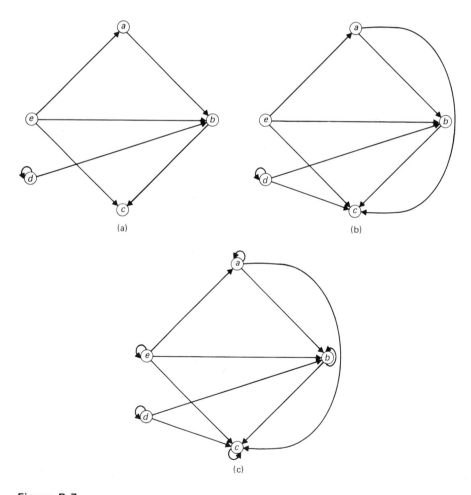

(a)

(b)

(c)

Figure B.7

arrow from e to c, the only arrows to be added are those from a to c and d to c; the result is Fig. B.7(b). Node c has no arrows leaving so no new arrows are required. Node d has no arrows entering except the one from d itself and arrows which connect a node to itself cannot imply any new arrows. Hence no new arrows are implied by node d. Similarly, node e has no arrows entering so no new arrows are required. Figure B.7(b) shows the resulting graph after each node has been inspected once.

It might appear that the set of nodes would have to be inspected over again in case arrows added subsequent to the inspection of a given node might imply some new arrows upon reinspection of that node. However, a theorem due to Warshall [1962] assures us that this is not the case and that even if new arrows have been drawn to or from a given node subsequent to its inspection, reinspection can not imply any arrows not already drawn. Thus one inspection of each node suffices and the result in Fig. B.7(b) is in fact the relation POINTS-AT$^+$.

When the relation Q is represented by a matrix, a matrix for Q is converted to a matrix for Q^+ by changing certain 0's in the matrix to 1's. The general principle is to imitate the technique discussed above of considering the nodes of the graph one at a time. Suppose we are considering node j. In terms of the graph, we want to ensure that if there is an arrow from i to j and an arrow from j to k, there is an arrow from i to k. An arrow in the graph from node i to node j corresponds to the matrix entry for row i and column j being a 1. An arrow in the graph from node j to node k corresponds to the matrix entry for row j and column k being a 1. Ensuring that there is an arrow from node i to node k corresponds to setting the matrix entry for row i and column k equal to 1. Therefore, if there is a 1 in the entry for row i and column j (corresponding to an arrow from i to j), then for each k such that there is a 1 in row j and column k (corresponding to an arrow from j to k) we will set the entry for row i and column k equal to 1 (corresponding to an arrow from i to k). When all values of j have been considered, the resulting matrix is the matrix for Q^+.

A BASIC program to compute the transitive closure of a relation represented by a matrix is shown in Fig. B.8. It assumes that the matrix of the relation is given in an array A and it computes its result in A. The algorithm is commonly known as Warshall's algorithm (Warshall [1962].)

Mathematically a relation R is called *transitive* if aRb and bRc implies aRc, i.e., if whenever the pairs (a, b) and (b, c) are in the relation, then so is the pair (a, c). The $<$ relation is transitive but the POINTS-AT relation is not.

For any relation Q, the relation Q^+ is always a transitive relation. It is termed the "transitive closure" because it can be thought of as the set of pairs obtained from Q by adding the minimum number of pairs necessary to achieve a transitive relation.

```
10   REM COMPUTES TRANSITIVE CLOSURE OF RELATION IN
15   REM N BY N MATRIX A
20   REM COMPUTES RESULT IN MATRIX A.
30   FOR J = 1 TO N STEP 1
40   FOR I = 1 TO N STEP 1
50   IF A(I,J) = 0 GOTO 120
60   REM DO LOOP TO INSPECT ROW J IF AND ONLY IF A(I,J) = 1
70   FOR K = 1 TO N STEP 1
80   IF A(J,K) = 0 GOTO 110
90   REM ASSIGNMENT IF AND ONLY IF A(I,J) AND A(J,K) EQUAL 1
100  LET A(I,K) = 1
110  NEXT K
120  NEXT I
130  NEXT J
140  END
```

Fig. B.8 BASIC Program for Computing Transitive Closure of a Relation

B.5   REFLEXIVE TRANSITIVE CLOSURE

The transitive closure of a relation R defined in the last section is simply the relation obtained by chaining together elements related by R. It often happens that we also wish to think of each element as being "chained" to itself. In that case, we add pairs of the form (a, a) to the transitive closure and obtain the set known as the "reflexive transitive closure." This concept may be defined as follows:

> Given a relation Q, the *reflexive transitive closure* of Q is the relation consisting of all pairs (a, b) such that either
>
> $$a \ Q^+ \ b \qquad \text{or} \qquad a = b.$$

We use the superscript "*" to indicate the reflexive transitive closure, writing it as Q^*.

Given a graph representing Q^+, a graph representing Q^* is constructed by adding arrows so that each node points to itself. For instance, from the graph of Fig. B.7(b) for the transitive closure of the relation POINTS-AT the graph in Fig. B.7(c) is obtained showing the reflexive transitive closure.

Given a matrix representing Q^+, a matrix for Q^* is obtained simply by entering a 1 in each of the row-i, column-i entries in the matrix (i.e., entering a 1 for each entry on the main diagonal of the matrix).

The BASIC program given in Fig. B.8 for computing the transitive closure of a relation expressed as a matrix can be changed to compute the reflexive transitive closure by adding the single statement:

$$125 \quad \text{LET A(J,J)} = 1$$

Mathematically, a relation R on a set S is called *reflexive* if and only if aRa for all a in S. Relation R^* is called the reflexive transitive closure because it can be obtained from the set of pairs R by adding the minimum number of pairs necessary to achieve a relation that is both reflexive and transitive.

PROBLEMS

1. Two computer scientists enter a bar. One computer scientist is the father of the other computer scientist's son. How are the two computer scientists related?

2. Give a name to each of the following products of relations defined on the set of all males.

   a) (FIRST-COUSIN-OF) · (SON-OF)

   b) (FATHER-OF) · (FIRST-COUSIN-OF)

   c) (SON-OF) · (BROTHER-OF) · (FATHER-OF)

3. A relation R on the set $\{1, 2, 3, 4\}$ consists of the following set of pairs

$$(1, 2), (2, 3), (3, 4), (4, 1)$$

   a) Draw the graphs for R, $R \cdot R$, $R \cdot R \cdot R$, and $R \cdot R \cdot R \cdot R$.

   b) Which of these four graphs represent transitive relations.

   c) Which of these four graphs represent reflexive transitive relations.

4. Which of the following relations on the set of all females is transitive.

   a. SISTER-OF

   b. MOTHER-OF

   c. COUSIN-OF

   d. OLDER-THAN

   e. THE-SAME-AGE-AS

   f. THE-SAME-AGE-OR-OLDER-THAN

   g. HAS-THE-SAME-HALF-SISTER-AS

5. Relations P and Q on the set $\{1, 2, 3, 4\}$ are represented by the following two matrices.

$$
\begin{bmatrix}
1 & 0 & 0 & 1 \\
1 & 0 & 1 & 1 \\
0 & 1 & 0 & 0 \\
0 & 0 & 1 & 0
\end{bmatrix},
\begin{bmatrix}
0 & 1 & 0 & 1 \\
1 & 0 & 0 & 0 \\
0 & 0 & 0 & 1 \\
0 & 1 & 0 & 0
\end{bmatrix}
$$

a) List the pairs that constitute P and Q.

b) Draw the graphs for P and Q.

c) From the matrices for P and Q, find the matrix for $P \cdot Q$.

d) From the graphs for P and Q, find the graph for $Q \cdot P$.

e) From the matrix for P, find the matrix for P^+.

f) From the graph for Q, find the graph for Q^*.

g) Find the graph for $(Q \cdot P)^* \cdot (P \cdot Q)^+$.

6. a) Show that the product operation on relations is associative, i.e., that

$$P \cdot (Q \cdot R) = (P \cdot Q) \cdot R$$

where P, Q, and R are relations.

b) Show that the product operation is not commutative, i.e.,

$$P \cdot Q \neq Q \cdot P.$$

c) Give examples of particular relations P and Q such that $P \cdot Q$ does equal $Q \cdot P$.

7. a) Define the reflexive closure of a relation.

b) Give a BASIC program for computing the reflexive closure of a relation expressed as a matrix.

8. Describe a test for determining whether or not a relation R is transitive.

9. a) Show that a relation R is transitive if and only if all the pairs in $R \cdot R$ are also in R.

b) Give an example of a transitive relation R for which R contains at least one pair that is not in $R \cdot R$.

10. Consider the following relation, R, between states in a finite-state machine:

sRt if and only if there is some input symbol that will cause a transition from state s to state t.

a) Express the relation R for the finite-state machine of Fig. 2.15(a) as a matrix.

b) Using the transitive closure of R, define a procedure for determining the extraneous states of a finite-state machine.

c) Demonstrate your procedure on the machine of Fig. 2.15(a).

11. Define powers of relations as follows

$$R^1 = R$$
$$R^2 = R \cdot R$$
$$R^3 = R \cdot R \cdot R, \text{ etc.}$$

with R^0 defined to be the identity relation ($\bar{a}R^0a$ for each a). Further define the union of two relations to be those ordered pairs that are in either or both relations. Denote the union of P and Q as $P + Q$. Show that

a) $R^+ = R + R^2 + R^3 + \cdots$

b) $R^* = R^0 + R + R^2 + R^3 + \cdots$

c) If R is a relation on a set with n elements, then:

$$R^+ = R + R^2 + R^3 + \cdots + R^n$$

d) If R is a relation on a set with n elements, then:

$$R^* = R^0 + R + R^2 + R^3 + \cdots + R^{n-1}$$

12. Suppose P and Q are two relations expressed as matrices M_P and M_Q respectively. Show that

$$P \cdot Q = M_P \cdot M_Q$$

where $M_P \cdot M_Q$ is the ordinary matrix product using the Boolean operations AND and OR instead of the arithmetic MULTIPLY and ADD operations.

13. A certain relation among n objects can be expressed as a matrix consisting of all 1's above the main diagonal and all zeros elsewhere. Show that the relation is transitive for all n.

14. State and prove Warshall's theorem as described informally in Section B.4.

Appendix C
Grammatical
Transformations

C.1 INTRODUCTION

Many of the design procedures in this book require that the given context-free grammar have certain properties (e.g., be LL(1) or SHIFT-IDENTIFY consistent). Frequently the grammar obtained from the language manual or by some other means does not possess the required property. In this appendix, we present a number of transformation methods that can be used to rewrite a given grammar to obtain a new grammar that generates the same language but has certain of these desired properties. Sections C.2 through C.7 contain transformations pertinent to obtaining top-down parsable grammars and Sections C.8 through C.10 contain transformations for bottom-up parsing. Throughout this appendix, we assume all productions involving extraneous symbols have been deleted.

These transformations are not guaranteed to rewrite any arbitrary grammar into a top-down or bottom-up parsable grammar, since some context-free languages have no grammars that can be parsed top down or bottom up by a pushdown machine. However, it is our experience that for most real programming languages, the syntax-box design can be based on any one of the following grammar types: q-grammars, LL(1), weak precedence, simple mixed-strategy precedence, SLR(1). Furthermore, it is our experience that the transformations presented in this appendix are usually adequate to rewrite a programming language grammar into any one of the required types.

C.2 TOP-DOWN PROCESSING OF LISTS

Many programming languages contain constructions involving lists of entities such as variables, parameters, dimensions, and statements. These constructions occur so frequently that a designer desiring to express a language

591

	No Punctuation	Punctuated with Comma
Null list not permitted	I. $<L> \rightarrow \quad a<R>$ $<R> \rightarrow \quad a<R>$ $<R> \rightarrow \quad \epsilon$	II. $<L> \rightarrow \quad a<R>$ $<R> \rightarrow \quad , a<R>$ $<R> \rightarrow \quad \epsilon$
Null list permitted	III. $<L> \rightarrow \quad \epsilon$ $<L> \rightarrow \quad a<R>$ $<R> \rightarrow \quad a<R>$ $<R> \rightarrow \quad \epsilon$ or III′. $<L> \rightarrow \quad \epsilon$ $<L> \rightarrow \quad a<L>$	IV. $<L> \rightarrow \quad \epsilon$ $<L> \rightarrow \quad a<R>$ $<R> \rightarrow \quad , a<R>$ $<R> \rightarrow \quad \epsilon$

Fig. C.1. Grammars that generate lists from $<L>$

with an LL(1) grammar usually has to include suitable list-generating productions. To aid in designing list-generating productions, we present five
LL(1) grammars for lists in Fig. C.1. This figure can be used as a table of
standard list grammars.

Grammar I shows a grammar for generating a list of one or more a's.
Nonterminal $\langle L \rangle$ generates the list itself and $\langle R \rangle$ can be thought of as
generating the list "remainder" after the initial a.

Grammar II shows a grammar for generating a list of one or more a's
separated by commas.

Grammar III shows a grammar for generating a list of zero or more a's.
Grammar III′ is an alternate grammar for this language. Grammar III′ is
simpler but is sometimes unsuitable for translation purposes.

Grammar IV is for generating a list of zero or more a's separated by
commas. This grammar can be thought of as the master prototype since a
grammar without punctuation (i.e., III) is obtained from IV by deleting the
comma; a grammar forbidding the zero-length list (i.e., II) is obtained by
deleting the epsilon production for $\langle L \rangle$; grammar I is obtained by making
both changes.

In each of the grammars, the list "remainder" generated from $\langle R \rangle$ is
itself a list of zero or more items. In grammar II, for example, $\langle R \rangle$ generates
a list of zero or more occurrences of $,a$. In each grammar, the productions for
$\langle R \rangle$ are patterned after grammar III′ which gives the simplest way of generating a list of zero or more items. Thus, in a sense, grammar III′ is the basic
list grammar and the others are merely more elaborate grammars which

Action symbol attributes INHERITED

1. $\langle L \rangle \rightarrow \{NULL\}$
2. $\langle L \rangle \rightarrow a_{I1} \{FIRST_{I2}\} \langle R \rangle$
   $I2 \leftarrow I1$
3. $\langle R \rangle \rightarrow , a_{I1} \{NEXT_{I2}\} \langle R \rangle$
   $I2 \leftarrow I1$
4. $\langle R \rangle \rightarrow \{TERMINATE\}$

(a)

1. $\langle L \rangle \rightarrow \{NULL\}$
2. $\langle L \rangle \rightarrow \{INITIALIZE\} \; a \; \langle R \rangle$
3. $\langle R \rangle \rightarrow \{NEXT\}, a \; \langle R \rangle$
4. $\langle R \rangle \rightarrow \{LAST\}$

(b)

Action symbol attributes INHERITED

1. $\langle L \rangle \rightarrow \{NULL\}$
2. $\langle L \rangle \rightarrow a_{I1} \langle R \rangle \{TERMINATE_{I2}\}$
   $I2 \leftarrow I1$
3. $\langle R \rangle \rightarrow , a_{I1} \langle R \rangle \{NEXT_{I2}\}$
   $I2 \leftarrow I1$
4. $\langle R \rangle \rightarrow \{INITIATE\}$

(c)

Figure C.2

incorporate lists of zero or more items. From this point of view, grammar II is described as generating an *a* followed by a list of zero or more ,*a*'s.

There are a number of ways action symbols and attributes can be added to the grammars of Fig. C.1. We continue our discussion by adding to grammar IV since it serves as a "master prototype." Figure C.2 shows three ways of adding actions and attributes to this grammar.

One activity sequence produced by the grammar of Fig. C.2(a) is

$$a_1 \{FIRST_1\}, a_2 \{NEXT_2\}, a_3 \{NEXT_3\} \{TERMINATE\}$$

The *a*'s occur in the action-symbol sequence in the same order as they occur on the input symbol list.

One activity sequence produced by the grammar of Fig. C.2(b) is

$$\{INITIALIZE\} \; a \; \{NEXT\}, a \; \{NEXT\}, a \; \{LAST\}$$

Action $\{NEXT\}$ follows each occurrence of *a* except the last which is followed by $\{LAST\}$.

The grammar of Fig. C.2(b) has the advantage that the action symbols are at the left end of their productions and do not require the creation of stack symbols. The grammar has the disadvantage that attributes of the a's cannot be passed to the succeeding action symbol without introducing an inherited attribute for $\langle R \rangle$.

One activity sequence produced by the grammar of Fig. C.2(c) is

$$a_1, a_2, a_3 \ \{\text{INITIATE}\} \ \{\text{NEXT}_3\} \ \{\text{NEXT}_2\} \ \{\text{TERMINATE}_1\}$$

The a's occur in the action-symbol sequence in the reverse order of their occurrence on the input-symbol list.

C.3   LEFT FACTORING

Suppose a grammar contains the two productions

$$\langle S \rangle \rightarrow \text{IF} \ \langle B \rangle \ \text{THEN} \ \langle S1 \rangle$$
$$\langle S \rangle \rightarrow \text{IF} \ \langle B \rangle \ \text{THEN} \ \langle S1 \rangle \ \text{ELSE} \ \langle S \rangle$$

The grammar cannot be LL(1) because both the sample productions have IF in their selection sets. Whenever two productions with the same lefthand side have righthand sides beginning with the same symbol or symbols, and these common symbols generate at least one nonnull terminal string, the selection sets contain common symbols and the grammar is not LL(1).

In designing an LL(1) grammar, it is important that language constructs with a similar beginning be generated from a common production. For the example discussed above, a common beginning could be achieved by replacing the two given productions by the following three productions:

$$\langle S \rangle \rightarrow \text{IF} \ \langle B \rangle \ \text{THEN} \ \langle S1 \rangle \ \langle \text{something} \rangle$$
$$\langle \text{something} \rangle \rightarrow \text{ELSE} \ \langle S \rangle$$
$$\langle \text{something} \rangle \rightarrow \epsilon$$

where $\langle \text{something} \rangle$ is a new nonterminal not appearing elsewhere in the grammar. These three productions are said to have been obtained from the original two by "left factoring," since the common left portion of the righthand sides have been "factored" into a single production.

The principle of left factoring can be stated in symbolic terms as follows:

If a grammar contains n productions

$$\langle A \rangle \rightarrow \alpha \ \beta_1$$

$$.$$
$$.$$
$$.$$

$$\langle A \rangle \rightarrow \alpha \ \beta_n$$

where $\langle A \rangle$ is a nonterminal and α and β_i for $1 \le i \le n$ are sequences of nonterminals and terminals, then these productions can be replaced by the $n + 1$ productions

$$\langle A \rangle \rightarrow \alpha \, \langle \text{new} \rangle$$
$$\langle \text{new} \rangle \rightarrow \beta_1$$

.

.

.

$$\langle \text{new} \rangle \rightarrow \beta_n$$

where $\langle \text{new} \rangle$ is a nonterminal symbol not in the original grammar. The grammar obtained by making this replacement generates the same language as the original and is said to have been obtained by *left factoring*.

Left factoring can also be applied to string translation grammars. For example, the two productions

$\langle S \rangle \rightarrow$ IF $\langle B \rangle$ {JUMPF} THEN $\langle S1 \rangle$ {LABEL}

$\langle S \rangle \rightarrow$ IF $\langle B \rangle$ {JUMPF} THEN $\langle S1 \rangle$ {JUMP} {LABEL} ELSE $\langle S \rangle$ {LABEL}

can be left factored into

$\langle S \rangle \rightarrow$ IF $\langle B \rangle$ {JUMPF} THEN $\langle S1 \rangle$ $\langle$else clause$\rangle$

$\langle$else clause$\rangle \rightarrow$ {LABEL}

$\langle$else clause$\rangle \rightarrow$ {JUMP} {LABEL} ELSE $\langle S \rangle$ {LABEL}

C.4 CORNER SUBSTITUTION

Consider a given grammatical occurrence of a nonterminal on the righthand side of a production. Every time that production is used in a derivation, the occurrence must subsequently be replaced by the righthand side of some production for that nonterminal.

It is possible to modify the given grammar so that the step of replacing the occurrence is eliminated. The modification is called "substitution" and is described symbolically as follows:

If a grammar contains n productions

$$\langle A \rangle \rightarrow \alpha_1$$

$$.$$

$$.$$

$$.$$

$$\langle A \rangle \rightarrow \alpha_n$$

with lefthand side $\langle A \rangle$ (and no others), and if the grammar has a given production of the form

$$\langle B \rangle \rightarrow \beta \langle A \rangle \gamma$$

for some nonterminal $\langle B \rangle$ and some sequences of nonterminals and terminals β and γ, then the given production can be replaced by the n productions:

$$\langle B \rangle \rightarrow \beta \alpha_1 \gamma$$

$$.$$

$$.$$

$$.$$

$$\langle B \rangle \rightarrow \beta \alpha_n \gamma$$

The grammar obtained by this replacement generates the same language as the original and is said to have been obtained by *substitution* for the occurrence of $\langle A \rangle$ in the given production.

For any grammatical production, we refer to the leftmost occurrence (if any) in its righthand side as the *corner* of the production. An ϵ-production has no corner. If a substitution is made for the corner of a given production, we call the substitution a *corner substitution*. Corner substitution is a basic technique for obtaining and improving LL(1) grammars.

To illustrate how corner substitution can be used in obtaining LL(1) grammars, consider the following grammar with starting symbol $\langle A \rangle$:

1. $\langle A \rangle \rightarrow a$
2. $\langle A \rangle \rightarrow \langle B \rangle c$
3. $\langle B \rangle \rightarrow a \langle A \rangle$
4. $\langle B \rangle \rightarrow b \langle B \rangle$

This grammar is not LL(1) because the selection sets of productions 1 and 2 both contain a. Substituting for the corner of production 2 (i.e., the $\langle B \rangle$ in the righthand side of production 2), we obtain the grammar

   1. $\langle A \rangle \rightarrow a$
2a. $\langle A \rangle \rightarrow a \langle A \rangle c$
2b. $\langle A \rangle \rightarrow b \langle B \rangle c$
   3. $\langle B \rangle \rightarrow a \langle A \rangle$
   4. $\langle B \rangle \rightarrow b \langle B \rangle$

where production 2 is now replaced by two productions, one for each production with lefthand side $\langle B \rangle$.

The new grammar is not LL(1) because productions 1 and 2a both have
a in their selection sets. It was of course expected that one of the replacement
productions would generate a sequence beginning with a since the original
production generated such a sequence. The important feature of the new
grammar is that the conflicting productions both begin with a and can be left
factored. After performing left factoring, the grammar does become LL(1).

Corner substitution is also useful in changing LL(1) grammars into q-
grammars. For example, consider the following LL(1) grammar with starting
symbol $\langle S \rangle$:

1. $\langle S \rangle \rightarrow c \langle S \rangle$
2. $\langle S \rangle \rightarrow \langle A \rangle c$
3. $\langle A \rangle \rightarrow a \langle S \rangle$
4. $\langle A \rangle \rightarrow b$

This grammar is not a q-grammar because the corner of production 2 is a
nonterminal. Substituting for this corner gives the grammar

   1. $\langle S \rangle \rightarrow c \langle S \rangle$
2a. $\langle S \rangle \rightarrow a \langle S \rangle c$
2b. $\langle S \rangle \rightarrow b c$

Since the substitution removes the occurrence of $\langle A \rangle$ in production 2 from
the grammar, productions 3 and 4 become unreachable and are dropped.
The new grammar is a q-grammar.

Corner substitution preserves the LL(1) property and can always be used
to make an LL(1) grammar into a q-grammar. The general principle is as
follows:

> If an LL(1) grammar is modified by corner substitution, the result-
> ing grammar is itself LL(1).

If an LL(1) grammar is repeatedly modified by corner substitution until all corners are terminals, then the resulting grammar is a *q*-grammar.

The advantage of modifying an LL(1) grammar by corner substitution is that the pushdown machine for the new grammar can parse in fewer steps. The disadvantage is that the resulting grammar usually has more productions and the corresponding machine is larger.

C.5   SINGLETON SUBSTITUTION

When attempting to achieve an LL(1) grammar, it is normally counter-productive to substitute for occurrences which are not corners. The reason for this is that such substitutions normally replace one production with several productions having the same corner and the common corner causes selection set conflicts. A notable exception is the case where there is only one production with a given lefthand side. A production which is the only pro-duction with a given lefthand side is called a *singleton.*

The important property of a singleton production is that, if its lefthand side occurs in the righthand side of production p, substituting for that occur-rence simply results in replacing production p by one other production. Thus occurrences of the lefthand side may be repeatedly substituted without in-creasing the number of productions.

Consider for example the following grammar with starting symbol $\langle S \rangle$:

1. $\langle S \rangle \rightarrow a \langle A \rangle \langle A \rangle$
2. $\langle S \rangle \rightarrow b \langle A \rangle$
3. $\langle S \rangle \rightarrow c$
4. $\langle A \rangle \rightarrow a \langle S \rangle b$

In this example, production 4 is the only production with lefthand side $\langle A \rangle$. Substituting for the $\langle A \rangle$ in production 2 results in the replacement of pro-duction 2 by the one production

$$\langle S \rangle \rightarrow b \, a \langle S \rangle b$$

By further substituting for the occurrences of $\langle A \rangle$ in production 1, one obtains the grammar

1. $\langle S \rangle \rightarrow a \, a \langle S \rangle b \, a \langle S \rangle b$
2. $\langle S \rangle \rightarrow b \, a \langle S \rangle b$
3. $\langle S \rangle \rightarrow c$

where production 4 has been dropped because it is unreachable. This new grammar is simpler than the old in that it has fewer productions and fewer nonterminals; it is more complex in that more symbol occurrences are required to represent the righthand sides. Both grammars are q-grammars.

We use the term *singleton substitution* to refer to substitution for occurrences of nonterminals which are the lefthand side of singleton productions.

An important property of singleton substitution is that each new production has the same selection set as the production it replaces, so singleton substitution preserves the LL(1) property. As in the example, singleton substitution can be repeated until all righthand occurrences of a lefthand side are eliminated. The singleton can then be discarded unless its lefthand side is the starting symbol. The discarded production is said to be eliminated by singleton substitution. The resulting grammar is LL(1) if the original is, and the corresponding machine has fewer stack symbols.

One unimportant exception to the above discussion is the case where the righthand side of the singleton production contains the lefthand side as in the production

$$\langle L \rangle \rightarrow a \, \langle L \rangle \, b$$

In such a case, the lefthand symbol is dead and the production disappears under elimination of extraneous symbols.

C.6   LEFT RECURSION

A *nonterminal* is called *left recursive* if a string beginning with that nonterminal can be derived from that nonterminal itself by applying one or more productions. A *production* is called *left recursive* if it can be used as the first step in such a derivation. Symbolically, nonterminal $\langle A \rangle$ is left recursive if and only if there is a string β such that

$$\langle A \rangle \overset{+}{\Rightarrow} \langle A \rangle \, \beta$$

and production

$$\langle A \rangle \Rightarrow \alpha$$

is left recursive if and only if there is a β such that

$$\alpha \overset{*}{\Rightarrow} \langle A \rangle \, \beta$$

A production is called *self left recursive* if its corner and lefthand side are the same. Such a production must also be left recursive because the righthand side is itself a string beginning with the lefthand side and the required derivation is achieved in zero steps. Self left recursion is illustrated by production 1 in Fig. C.3 which has $\langle S \rangle$ as its corner and lefthand side. The other production in this grammar is not left recursive.

1. $\langle S \rangle \rightarrow \langle S \rangle\ a$
2. $\langle S \rangle \rightarrow b$

Starting symbol: $\langle S \rangle$

Figure C.3

1. $\langle A \rangle \rightarrow a\ \langle B \rangle$
2. $\langle A \rangle \rightarrow \langle B \rangle\ b$
3. $\langle B \rangle \rightarrow \langle A \rangle\ c$
4. $\langle B \rangle \rightarrow d$

Starting symbol: $\langle A \rangle$

Figure C.4

An example of left recursion without self left recursion is illustrated by the grammar of Fig. C.4. Here nonterminals $\langle A \rangle$ and $\langle B \rangle$ are left recursive as evidenced by the derivations

$$\langle A \rangle \Rightarrow \langle B \rangle\ b \Rightarrow \langle A \rangle\ c\ b$$
$$\langle B \rangle \Rightarrow \langle A \rangle\ c \Rightarrow \langle B \rangle\ b\ c$$

These derivations begin with productions 2 and 3 respectively which are therefore also left recursive productions. The left recursiveness is demonstrated by the relations

$$\langle B \rangle\ b \overset{*}{\Rightarrow} \langle A \rangle\ c\ b \qquad \text{and} \qquad \langle A \rangle\ c \overset{*}{\Rightarrow} \langle B \rangle\ b\ c$$

Productions 1 and 4 are not left recursive.

A grammar with a left recursive nonterminal cannot be LL(1). The central idea of the proof of this statement is that the selection set of any left recursive production with lefthand side $\langle X \rangle$ must contain FIRST($\langle X \rangle$) itself, and thereby it conflicts with the selection sets of all other productions with lefthand side $\langle X \rangle$. In the case of Fig. C.4, the selection set conflict between production 1 and left recursive production 2 is demonstrated by

$$\text{SELECT}(1) = \text{FIRST}(a\ \langle B \rangle) = \{a\}$$
$$\text{SELECT}(2) = \text{FIRST}(\langle B \rangle\ b) = \{a, d\}$$

A grammar with left recursion can always be rewritten as a grammar without left recursion. The general techniques for doing this are somewhat complex, but there is one special case in which rewriting the grammar is very straightforward. This is the case in which each left recursive production is self left recursive. Fortunately, this case applies to most practical programming language applications.

The basic idea for treating this case is to think of a recursive nonterminal as generating some string followed by a list of zero or more items. In Fig. C.3 for example we think of $\langle S \rangle$ as generating a b followed by a list of zero or more a's. The natural top-down method of expressing this thought is with the productions

$$\langle A \rangle \rightarrow b \langle \text{list} \rangle$$
$$\langle \text{list} \rangle \rightarrow a \langle \text{list} \rangle$$
$$\langle \text{list} \rangle \rightarrow \epsilon$$

where the productions with lefthand side $\langle \text{list} \rangle$ are patterned after grammar III' from Fig. C.1.

The above idea generalizes to other grammars by the following transformation for eliminating self left recursion:

Suppose that nonterminal $\langle A \rangle$ has m self left recursive productions

$$\langle A \rangle \rightarrow \langle A \rangle \, \alpha_i \qquad \text{for} \qquad 1 \leq i \leq m$$

and n productions

$$\langle A \rangle \rightarrow \beta_j \qquad \text{for} \qquad 1 \leq j \leq n$$

which are not self left recursive. Then replace these productions with the productions

$$\langle A \rangle \rightarrow \beta_j \langle \text{list } A \rangle \qquad \text{for} \qquad 1 \leq j \leq n$$
$$\langle \text{list } A \rangle \rightarrow \alpha_i \langle \text{list } A \rangle \qquad \text{for} \qquad 1 \leq i \leq m$$
$$\langle \text{list } A \rangle \rightarrow \epsilon$$

where $\langle \text{list } A \rangle$ is a new nonterminal.

The new productions are interpreted as saying that an $\langle A \rangle$ generates one of the β_j's followed by a list of zero or more α_i's.

With the exception of certain ambiguous grammars:

If a given grammar is such that all left recursive productions are self left recursive, then an equivalent grammar without left recursion can be obtained by applying the above transformation to all left recursive nonterminals.

When used in conjunction with corner substitution, the above transformation rule can be used to eliminate left recursion even when some left recursive productions are not self left recursive. Taking Fig. C.4 as an example, left recursion can be eliminated by first substituting for the corner of production 2 and then applying the transformation to nonterminal $\langle A \rangle$.

1. $\langle A \rangle \rightarrow a \langle B \rangle$ 1. $\langle A \rangle \rightarrow a \langle B \rangle \langle \text{list} \rangle$

2.4. $\langle A \rangle \rightarrow d \, b$ 2.4. $\langle A \rangle \rightarrow d \, b \langle \text{list} \rangle$

2.3. $\langle A \rangle \rightarrow \langle A \rangle c \, b$ 2.3. $\langle \text{list} \rangle \rightarrow c \, b \langle \text{list} \rangle$

3. $\langle B \rangle \rightarrow \langle A \rangle c$ x. $\langle \text{list} \rangle \rightarrow \epsilon$

4. $\langle B \rangle \rightarrow d$ 3. $\langle B \rangle \rightarrow \langle A \rangle c$

              4. $\langle B \rangle \rightarrow d$

(a)   (b)

Figure C.5

Substituting for the corner of production 2 results in the grammar of Fig. C.5(a) where production 2.4 is the result of substituting production 4 into the corner of production 2, and production 2.3 is the result of substituting production 3. Eliminating self left recursion for nonterminal $\langle A \rangle$ results in the grammar of Fig. C.5(b). This grammar has no left recursion.

C.7   GOAL-CORNER TRANSFORMATION

Given a non-LL(1) grammar for a practical programming language, the methods of Sections C.2 through C.6 are usually adequate to rewrite the grammar so that it is LL(1). However situations sometimes arise for which a more powerful technique is needed. In this section we present one such technique that we have found useful — the "goal-corner transformation."

In almost all cases of practical interest, this transformation eliminates all left recursion even when that recursion is not self left recursion. In addition, this transformation can be easily used in a computer program to transform grammars.

First consider the illustrative grammar

1. $\langle D \rangle \rightarrow \langle E \rangle c$
2. $\langle E \rangle \rightarrow \langle E \rangle a$
3. $\langle E \rangle \rightarrow b$

with starting symbol $\langle D \rangle$. A sample derivation in this grammar is:

$$\langle D \rangle \Rightarrow \langle E \rangle c \Rightarrow \langle E \rangle a c \Rightarrow \langle E \rangle a a c \Rightarrow \langle E \rangle a a a c \Rightarrow b a a a c$$

Since a terminal string derived from a $\langle D \rangle$ always begins with a b, we introduce a new nonterminal to generate the rest of a $\langle D \rangle$ after the b. We name this new nonterminal $\langle D, E \rangle$ to indicate that it generates strings that can be appended to an example of an $\langle E \rangle$ (e.g., b is an example of an $\langle E \rangle$) to produce an example of a $\langle D \rangle$. We create the new production

$$\langle D \rangle \rightarrow b \langle D, E \rangle$$

to indicate that an example of a $\langle D \rangle$ consists of a b followed by a string (generated from $\langle D, E \rangle$) which when appended to an example of an $\langle E \rangle$ produces an example of a $\langle D \rangle$.

From production 2, we know that an a can be appended to any given example of an $\langle E \rangle$ to produce a longer example of an $\langle E \rangle$. Suppose some string α is generated from $\langle D, E \rangle$. Then α appended to the longer example of an $\langle E \rangle$ produces an example of a $\langle D \rangle$. But then $a\alpha$ is a string which can be appended to the given example of an $\langle E \rangle$ to produce an example of a $\langle D \rangle$. Therefore $a\alpha$ should be in the language generated from $\langle D, E \rangle$. Summarizing: a string which can be appended to an example of an $\langle E \rangle$ to produce an example of a $\langle D \rangle$ can consist of an a followed by some string generated from $\langle D, E \rangle$. We therefore create the new production

$$\langle D, E \rangle \rightarrow a \langle D, E \rangle$$

From production 1, c can be appended to an example of an $\langle E \rangle$ to produce an example of a $\langle D \rangle$. We therefore can create the new production

$$\langle D, E \rangle \rightarrow c$$

The complete new grammar is

$$\langle D \rangle \rightarrow b \langle D, E \rangle$$
$$\langle D, E \rangle \rightarrow a \langle D, E \rangle$$
$$\langle D, E \rangle \rightarrow c$$

This grammar has no left recursion, and is in fact LL(1). The grammar is a slightly simplified version of the one which would be produced by the goal-corner transformation, but illustrates the general principles involved.

To perform the goal-corner transformation, we make a distinction between "corner" productions and "noncorner" productions.

A production whose righthand side has a nonterminal as its leftmost symbol is called a *corner production* and all other productions are called *noncorner productions*.

In the grammar of Fig. C.4, productions 2 and 3 are corner productions and productions 1 and 4 are noncorner productions.

A key concept behind the goal-corner transformation is that of a "corner derivation."

A leftmost derivation $\langle G \rangle \overset{*}{\Rightarrow}_L \alpha$ is called a *corner derivation* if and only if the last production applied is a noncorner production and all the others are corner productions.

For the grammar of Fig. C.4, the leftmost derivation (where the production numbers are written above the arrow)

$$\langle A \rangle \overset{2}{\Rightarrow}_L \langle B \rangle \, b \overset{3}{\Rightarrow}_L \langle A \rangle \, c \, b \overset{1}{\Rightarrow}_L a \langle B \rangle \, c \, b$$

is a corner derivation because the last production applied is noncorner production 1 and the other productions applied are corner productions. Another example of a corner derivation is

$$\langle B \rangle \overset{4}{\Rightarrow}_L d$$

since the last production applied is noncorner production 4 and the others (zero in number) are all corner productions.

The statement of the goal-corner transformation makes the following distinction based on corner derivations:

> A production p is called *relevant for* nonterminal $\langle G \rangle$ if and only if it can be used in some corner derivation beginning with $\langle G \rangle$. All other productions are called *irrelevant for* nonterminal $\langle G \rangle$. A nonterminal $\langle A \rangle$ is called an *extended corner* of $\langle G \rangle$ if and only if $\langle A \rangle$ is the lefthand side of a production relevant for $\langle G \rangle$.

In the example of Fig. C.4, all productions are relevant for both $\langle A \rangle$ and $\langle B \rangle$. We illustrate the irrelevant case later. The term "extended corner of $\langle G \rangle$" is used because $\langle A \rangle$ is an extended corner of $\langle G \rangle$ if and only if there is a sequence of grammatical symbols α such that $\langle A \rangle \, \alpha$ can be obtained from $\langle G \rangle$ by a leftmost derivation using zero or more corner productions.

The basic idea of the goal-corner transformation is to provide an alternate method of performing corner derivations. We present the transformation, interpret its steps, and then show alternative corner derivations for the example.

Given a context-free grammar for a given language, a new grammar for the language can be obtained by the following procedure, which we call the goal-corner transformation:

1. Select a nonterminal $\langle G \rangle$ from the given grammar. Nonterminal $\langle G \rangle$ is called the *goal* for this iteration of steps 2 and 3.

2. For each nonterminal $\langle C \rangle$ which is a generalized corner of $\langle G \rangle$, add a new nonterminal $\langle G, C \rangle$ to the set of nonterminals.

3. Construct a *replacement production* set for $\langle G \rangle$ as follows:

    a) For each relevant corner production in the original grammar

    $$\langle C \rangle \rightarrow \langle D \rangle \, \alpha$$

    place the production

    $$\langle G, D \rangle \rightarrow \alpha \, \langle G, C \rangle$$

    in the replacement set for $\langle G \rangle$.

    b) For each relevant noncorner production in the original grammar

    $$\langle C \rangle \rightarrow \beta$$

place the production

$$\langle G \rangle \rightarrow \beta \langle G, C \rangle$$

in the replacement set for $\langle G \rangle$.

c) Place the production

$$\langle G, G \rangle \rightarrow \epsilon$$

in the replacement set for $\langle G \rangle$.

4. Repeat steps 1 through 3 for each possible choice of goal $\langle G \rangle$ from the original grammar. Discard the old productions and combine the replacement sets to obtain a new set of productions. The starting symbol is the same for both grammars.

An interpretation of a new nonterminal $\langle G, C \rangle$ introduced in step 2 is that it generates an example of a string that can be appended to an example of a $\langle C \rangle$ to produce an example of a $\langle G \rangle$. More formally, $\langle G, C \rangle$ generates the set of terminal strings x such that

$$\langle G \rangle \overset{*}{\Rightarrow}_R \langle C \rangle \, x$$

Under this interpretation, the replacement production of step 3b says that an example of a $\langle G \rangle$ can consist of a string generated from β (i.e., an example of a $\langle C \rangle$) followed by a string generated from $\langle G, C \rangle$ (i.e., a string that can be appended to an example of a $\langle C \rangle$ to produce an example of a $\langle G \rangle$). The replacement production of step 3a says that a string that can be appended to an example of a $\langle D \rangle$ to produce an example of a $\langle G \rangle$ can itself consist of a string generated from α (i.e., a string which appended to an example of a $\langle D \rangle$ produces an example of a $\langle C \rangle$) followed by a string which appended to an example of a $\langle C \rangle$ produces an example of a $\langle G \rangle$. The replacement production of step 3c says that the null string can be appended to an example of a $\langle G \rangle$ to produce an example of a $\langle G \rangle$.

In Fig. C.6, we show the transformed version of Fig. C.4. The production numbers in Fig. C.6 were obtained by combining the productions numbers with goal names. Thus production 2A was obtained by transforming production 2 for goal $\langle A \rangle$ as required by step 3a of the procedure. Productions 5A and 5B are ϵ-productions introduced by step 3c of the procedure and do not correspond to productions of the original grammar. The new grammar is LL(1) and could be compacted somewhat by singleton substitution.

We previously showed how $a \, \langle B \rangle \, c \, b$ could be obtained from $\langle A \rangle$ in the old grammar by a corner derivation. In the new grammar, $a \, \langle B \rangle \, c \, b$ is obtained through a sequence of rightmost substitutions namely

$$\langle A \rangle \overset{1A}{\Longrightarrow}_R a \, \langle B \rangle \, \langle A, A \rangle \overset{3A}{\Longrightarrow}_R a \, \langle B \rangle \, c \, \langle A, B \rangle \overset{2A}{\Longrightarrow}_R$$

$$a \, \langle B \rangle \, c \, b \, \langle A, A \rangle \overset{5A}{\Longrightarrow}_R a \, \langle B \rangle \, c \, b$$

1A. $\langle A \rangle \rightarrow a \langle B \rangle \langle A, A \rangle$

2A. $\langle A, B \rangle \rightarrow b \langle A, A \rangle$

3A. $\langle A, A \rangle \rightarrow c \langle A, B \rangle$

4A. $\langle A \rangle \rightarrow d \langle A, B \rangle$

5A. $\langle A, A \rangle \rightarrow \epsilon$

1B. $\langle B \rangle \rightarrow a \langle B \rangle \langle B, A \rangle$

2B. $\langle B, B \rangle \rightarrow b \langle B, A \rangle$

3B. $\langle B, A \rangle \rightarrow c \langle B, B \rangle$

4B. $\langle B \rangle \rightarrow d \langle B, B \rangle$

5B. $\langle B, B \rangle \rightarrow \epsilon$

Starting symbol: $\langle A \rangle$

Figure C.6

Now consider the sequence of productions used in the old and new derivations of $a \langle B \rangle c b$ from $\langle A \rangle$. The productions appearing in the original corner derivation (i.e., 2, 3, and 1) have transformed versions (i.e., 2A, 3A, and 1A) appearing in the new sequence. Furthermore, the new productions occur in reverse order of the original and are followed by one of the new ϵ-productions created under rule 3c. This reversal is typical of the general case which is as follows:

> Suppose string α is generated from $\langle G \rangle$ by a leftmost derivation that applies zero or more corner productions $p_1 \cdots p_n$ in that order and then applies noncorner production q. Let $\bar{p}_1, \cdots, \bar{p}_n$ and $\bar{q}$ be the transformed versions of these productions obtained by applying rules 3a and 3b with goal $\langle G \rangle$ and let $\bar{e}$ be the production $\langle G, G \rangle \rightarrow \epsilon$ called for by rule 3c. Then α can be generated from $\langle G \rangle$ in the new grammar through the rightmost derivation that applies production sequence $\bar{q}, \bar{p}_n, \cdots, \bar{p}_1, \bar{e}$.

The case of zero corner productions can be illustrated with the example of deriving d from $\langle B \rangle$. In the new grammar:

$$\langle B \rangle \overset{4\text{B}}{\underset{R}{\Longrightarrow}} d \langle B, B \rangle \overset{5\text{B}}{\underset{R}{\Longrightarrow}} d$$

In Fig. C.7(a), we show the derivation tree of $adcb$ using the grammar of Fig. C.4. The tree has two nonterminal nodes not representing corners, namely the starting node and the $\langle B \rangle$ immediately above terminal d. The starting node can be regarded as the root of a corner derivation of $a \langle B \rangle c b$ from $\langle A \rangle$ and the $\langle B \rangle$ can be regarded as the root of a corner derivation of d.

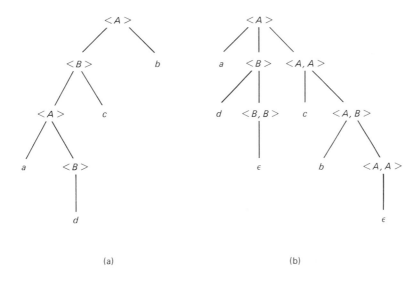

(a)   (b)

Figure C.7

Figure C.7(b) shows a derivation of the same terminal sequence in the transformed grammar. Again the tree shows a derivation of $a \langle B \rangle c b$ from $\langle A \rangle$ and a derivation of d from $\langle B \rangle$, but these derivations are carried out in the transformed way.

In Fig. C.8, we provide another illustrative example. The extended corners of $\langle A \rangle$ are $\langle A \rangle$, $\langle B \rangle$, and $\langle C \rangle$. All productions are relevant for $\langle A \rangle$ except for 8 and 9. Nonterminal $\langle B \rangle$ has extended corners $\langle B \rangle$ and $\langle C \rangle$ and has relevant productions 3, 4, 5, 6, and 7. Nonterminal $\langle C \rangle$ has only itself as extended corner, and productions 6 and 7 are the only relevant productions. Similarly, $\langle D \rangle$ has only itself as extended corner, and only 8 and 9 are relevant.

Extended corners are easy to compute by the transitive-closure method of Appendix B. The relation IS-EXTENDED-CORNER-OF is the reflexive transitive closure of the relation IS-CORNER-OF where

$$\langle X \rangle \text{ IS-CORNER-OF } \langle Y \rangle$$

if and only if

$$\langle Y \rangle \rightarrow \langle X \rangle \, \alpha$$

is a production of the grammar for some α.

In Fig. C.8(b), we show the transformed grammar for Fig. C.8(a). Three of the ϵ-productions introduced by step 3c of the procedure are singleton productions, namely 10A, 10C, and 10D.

1. $\langle A \rangle \rightarrow \langle B \rangle\, a$
2. $\langle A \rangle \rightarrow a$
3. $\langle B \rangle \rightarrow \langle B \rangle\, b$
4. $\langle B \rangle \rightarrow \langle C \rangle$
5. $\langle B \rangle \rightarrow b\, c$

6. $\langle C \rangle \rightarrow a\, c\, \langle A \rangle$
7. $\langle C \rangle \rightarrow b\, \langle D \rangle$
8. $\langle D \rangle \rightarrow d\, \langle B \rangle\, a$
9. $\langle D \rangle \rightarrow \epsilon$

Starting symbol: $\langle A \rangle$

(a)

1A. $\langle A, B \rangle \rightarrow a\, \langle A, A \rangle$
2A. $\langle A \rangle \rightarrow a\, \langle A, A \rangle$
3A. $\langle A, B \rangle \rightarrow b\, \langle A, B \rangle$
4A. $\langle A, C \rangle \rightarrow \langle A, B \rangle$
5A. $\langle A \rangle \rightarrow b\, c\, \langle A, B \rangle$
6A. $\langle A \rangle \rightarrow a\, c\, \langle A \rangle\, \langle A, C \rangle$
7A. $\langle A \rangle \rightarrow b\, \langle D \rangle\, \langle A, C \rangle$
10A. $\langle A, A \rangle \rightarrow \epsilon$
8D. $\langle D \rangle \rightarrow d\, \langle B \rangle\, a\, \langle D, D \rangle$
9D. $\langle D \rangle \rightarrow \langle D, D \rangle$
10D. $\langle D, D \rangle \rightarrow \epsilon$

3B. $\langle B, B \rangle \rightarrow b\, \langle B, B \rangle$
4B. $\langle B, C \rangle \rightarrow \langle B, B \rangle$
5B. $\langle B \rangle \rightarrow b\, c\, \langle B, B \rangle$
6B. $\langle B \rangle \rightarrow a\, c\, \langle A \rangle\, \langle B, C \rangle$
7B. $\langle B \rangle \rightarrow b\, \langle D \rangle\, \langle B, C \rangle$
10B. $\langle B, B \rangle \rightarrow \epsilon$
6C. $\langle C \rangle \rightarrow a\, c\, \langle A \rangle\, \langle C, C \rangle$
7C. $\langle C \rangle \rightarrow b\, \langle D \rangle\, \langle C, C \rangle$
10C. $\langle C, C \rangle \rightarrow \epsilon$

Starting symbol: $\langle A \rangle$

(b)

Figure C.8

When the singletons 10A, 10C, and 10D of the example are eliminated by substitution, productions 2A, 6C, 7C, 8D, and 9D are restored to their untransformed forms. Also, nonterminals $\langle C \rangle$ and $\langle C, C \rangle$ are unreachable, so productions 6C, 7C, and 10C can be discarded.

The grammar of Fig. C.8(b) is not LL(1) but can be made LL(1) by left factoring productions 2A and 6A, 5A and 7A, and 5B and 7B.

C.8　ELIMINATING ϵ-PRODUCTIONS

The SHIFT-IDENTIFY methods of Chapter 12 can only be applied to grammars that contain no ϵ-productions. However this restriction is not critical in the sense that if we are given a grammar with ϵ-productions, it can always be rewritten without ϵ-productions. The rewritten grammar generates the same language as the original grammar except that, if the original language contains the null sequence, the language generated by the new grammar will not. A grammar without ε-productions cannot generate the null sequence.

To illustrate the technique in its simplest form, we show how to eliminate the ε-production for ⟨A⟩ from the grammar of Fig. C.9(a). Imagine that there are two kinds of nonterminal ⟨A⟩, a nonterminal ⟨A_{YES}⟩ to which the ε-production is always applied and a nonterminal ⟨A_{NO}⟩ to which the ε-production is never applied. Replacing the one kind of ⟨A⟩ with two kinds results in the grammar of Fig. C.9(b). Notice that production 1 has been converted into two productions, one containing ⟨A_{NO}⟩ on the right and one containing ⟨A_{YES}⟩. The lefthand side of production 4 has been made ⟨A_{YES}⟩ because it is used when applying the ε-production, and the lefthand side of production 3 has been made ⟨A_{NO}⟩ because it is used when not applying the ε-production.

The ε-production in Fig. C.9(b) is a singleton production since it is by construction the only production with lefthand side ⟨A_{YES}⟩. (The non-ε-productions for ⟨A⟩ all have lefthand side ⟨A_{NO}⟩.) This production can be eliminated by the method of Section C.5 to obtain Fig. C.9(c). Since name ⟨A_{YES}⟩ is no longer around, we replace ⟨A_{NO}⟩ by the old name ⟨A⟩ and obtain Fig. C.9(d). Figure C.9(d) thus generates the same language as Fig. C.9(a), but the symbols ⟨A⟩ do not. They differ in that the ⟨A⟩ of Fig. C.9(a) can generate ε, but the ⟨A⟩ in Fig. C.9(d) cannot.

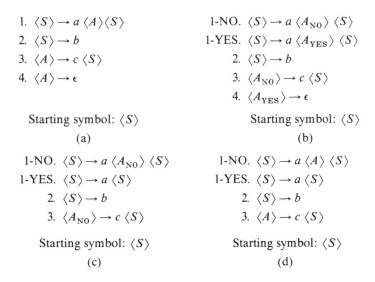

1. ⟨S⟩ → a ⟨A⟩⟨S⟩
2. ⟨S⟩ → b
3. ⟨A⟩ → c ⟨S⟩
4. ⟨A⟩ → ε

Starting symbol: ⟨S⟩

(a)

1-NO. ⟨S⟩ → a ⟨A_{NO}⟩ ⟨S⟩
1-YES. ⟨S⟩ → a ⟨A_{YES}⟩ ⟨S⟩
2. ⟨S⟩ → b
3. ⟨A_{NO}⟩ → c ⟨S⟩
4. ⟨A_{YES}⟩ → ε

Starting symbol: ⟨S⟩

(b)

1-NO. ⟨S⟩ → a ⟨A_{NO}⟩ ⟨S⟩
1-YES. ⟨S⟩ → a ⟨S⟩
2. ⟨S⟩ → b
3. ⟨A_{NO}⟩ → c ⟨S⟩

Starting symbol: ⟨S⟩

(c)

1-NO. ⟨S⟩ → a ⟨A⟩ ⟨S⟩
1-YES. ⟨S⟩ → a ⟨S⟩
2. ⟨S⟩ → b
3. ⟨A⟩ → c ⟨S⟩

Starting symbol: ⟨S⟩

(d)

Figure C.9

Now disregard $\langle A_{\text{YES}} \rangle$ and $\langle A_{\text{NO}} \rangle$ and consider as a single step how Fig. C.9(d) was obtained from Fig. C.9(a). Production 1 was divided into two productions obtained by substituting and not substituting the production $\langle A \rangle \rightarrow \epsilon$ into the righthand occurrence of $\langle A \rangle$, and the ϵ-production was discarded.

The idea of substituting and not substituting ϵ for a given nonterminal becomes slightly more complicated if a righthand side has several occurrences of a nonterminal. Suppose for example that production 1 in the previous example (Fig. C.9a) was

$$\langle S \rangle \rightarrow a \langle A \rangle \langle S \rangle \langle A \rangle$$

This production would have to be separated into four cases. In terms of $\langle A_{\text{YES}} \rangle$ and $\langle A_{\text{NO}} \rangle$, the cases would be

$$\langle S \rangle \rightarrow a \langle A_{\text{NO}} \rangle \langle S \rangle \langle A_{\text{NO}} \rangle$$
$$\langle S \rangle \rightarrow a \langle A_{\text{YES}} \rangle \langle S \rangle \langle A_{\text{NO}} \rangle$$
$$\langle S \rangle \rightarrow a \langle A_{\text{NO}} \rangle \langle S \rangle \langle A_{\text{YES}} \rangle$$
$$\langle S \rangle \rightarrow a \langle A_{\text{YES}} \rangle \langle S \rangle \langle A_{\text{YES}} \rangle$$

The actual transformed productions would be

$$\langle S \rangle \rightarrow a \langle A \rangle \langle S \rangle \langle A \rangle$$
$$\langle S \rangle \rightarrow a \langle S \rangle \langle A \rangle$$
$$\langle S \rangle \rightarrow a \langle A \rangle \langle S \rangle$$
$$\langle S \rangle \rightarrow a \langle S \rangle$$

The transformed productions are achieved by substituting or not substituting $\langle A \rangle \rightarrow \epsilon$ *in all combinations.*

As another example suppose a grammar has two nonterminals, $\langle A \rangle$ and $\langle B \rangle$, each of which can generate the null string. Suppose the production under consideration is

$$\langle S \rangle \rightarrow a \langle A \rangle \langle S \rangle \langle B \rangle$$

By substituting ϵ for $\langle A \rangle$ and $\langle B \rangle$ in all combinations, this production can be transformed into the four productions

$$\langle S \rangle \rightarrow a \langle A \rangle \langle S \rangle \langle B \rangle$$
$$\langle S \rangle \rightarrow a \langle S \rangle \langle B \rangle$$
$$\langle S \rangle \rightarrow a \langle A \rangle \langle S \rangle$$
$$\langle S \rangle \rightarrow a \langle S \rangle$$

We now present the ideas discussed above as a general procedure for eliminating ϵ-productions.

1. Determine which nonterminals can generate the null string. These non-terminals are called *nullable,* and a procedure for finding them is given in Section 8.7.

2. Replace each production whose righthand side contains at least one nullable nonterminal by a set of new productions. If the righthand side contains k occurrences ($k \geq 1$) of nullable nonterminals, the replacement set consists of the 2^k productions corresponding to all possible ways of deleting or retaining each of the k occurrences.

3. Delete all ϵ-productions (including any introduced in step 2).

Note that in certain ambiguous cases, step 2 may produce less than 2^k distinct productions. For example, production

$$\langle S \rangle \rightarrow a \langle A \rangle \langle A \rangle$$

is replaced by three instead of four productions, namely

$$\langle S \rangle \rightarrow a \langle A \rangle \langle A \rangle \qquad \langle S \rangle \rightarrow a \langle A \rangle \qquad \langle S \rangle \leftarrow a$$

The production $\langle S \rangle \rightarrow a \langle A \rangle$ is obtained both by deleting the first $\langle A \rangle$ and by deleting the second.

Finally, note that if the starting symbol is nullable, the language generated by the new grammar will differ from the old in that it will not contain the null sequence.

C.9   MAKING TRANSLATIONS POLISH

Suppose we wish to implement the translation specified by the production

$$\langle \text{statement} \rangle \rightarrow \text{IF } \langle \text{Boolean expression} \rangle \text{ \{JUMPF\} THEN } \langle \text{statement} \rangle$$
$$\text{\{LABEL\}}$$

and we are using a bottom up implementation method that only allows Polish translation. We solve this problem by replacing the one production with two productions in such a way that {JUMPF} is at the extreme right of one production and {LABEL} is at the extreme right of the other. The replacement productions are obtained by introducing a new nonterminal $\langle$if clause$\rangle$ to generate the string IF $\langle$Boolean expression$\rangle$ {JUMPF} and replacing the occurrence of this string in the given production by the new nonterminal. The replacement productions are:

$$\langle \text{statement} \rangle \rightarrow \langle \text{if clause} \rangle \text{ THEN } \langle \text{statement} \rangle \text{ \{LABEL\}}$$
$$\langle \text{if clause} \rangle \rightarrow \text{IF } \langle \text{Boolean expression} \rangle \text{ \{JUMPF \}}$$

In general, if we have a production of the form

$$\langle L \rangle \rightarrow \alpha \ \{ A \} \ \beta$$

where α and β are strings of grammatical symbols, a new nonterminal $\langle \text{new} \rangle$ can be invented and the production replaced by the two productions

$$\langle L \rangle \rightarrow \langle \text{new} \rangle \, \beta$$
$$\langle \text{new} \rangle \rightarrow \alpha \, \{A\}$$

The result is that action symbol $\{A\}$ has been placed in a rightmost position and the number of action symbols violating the Polish condition has been reduced.

By repeating the above technique on a production by production basis, it is always possible to rewrite a translation grammar as a Polish translation grammar. Furthermore if the given translation grammar does not have any action symbols at the left end of productions, the rewriting can be accomplished without adding ϵ-productions.

C.10   MAKING A GRAMMAR SHIFT-IDENTIFY CONSISTENT

We now give a method whereby any context-free grammar without ϵ-productions can be rewritten as a SHIFT-IDENTIFY-consistent grammar. As an example, consider the following grammar with starting nonterminal $\langle S \rangle$:

1. $\langle S \rangle \rightarrow c \, \langle A \rangle \, a$
2. $\langle A \rangle \rightarrow c \, \langle B \rangle$
3. $\langle A \rangle \rightarrow d \, \langle B \rangle \, a$
4. $\langle B \rangle \rightarrow d \, \langle S \rangle \, e \, \langle B \rangle \, f$
5. $\langle B \rangle \rightarrow g$

There is a SHIFT-IDENTIFY conflict for stack symbol $\langle B \rangle$ and input symbol a because when $\langle B \rangle$ is the top stack symbol and a the input symbol, we do not know whether the $\langle B \rangle$ is from production 3 in which case we should SHIFT, or from production 2, in which case we should IDENTIFY (and perform REDUCE(2)). Our plan is to introduce a new nonterminal $\langle \hat{B} \rangle$ with a singleton production

$$\langle \hat{B} \rangle \rightarrow \langle B \rangle$$

and to replace all occurrences of $\langle B \rangle$ in production righthand sides other than at the extreme right end with $\langle \hat{B} \rangle$. The new productions are

1. $\langle S \rangle \rightarrow c \, \langle A \rangle \, a$
2. $\langle A \rangle \rightarrow c \, \langle B \rangle$
3. $\langle A \rangle \rightarrow d \, \langle \hat{B} \rangle \, a$
4. $\langle B \rangle \rightarrow d \, \langle S \rangle \, e \, \langle \hat{B} \rangle \, f$
5. $\langle B \rangle \rightarrow g$
6. $\langle \hat{B} \rangle \rightarrow \langle B \rangle$

In the new grammar $\langle B \rangle$ only occurs at the extreme right end of productions and hence cannot be BELOW any terminal. Similarly $\langle \hat{B} \rangle$ only occurs at positions other than the extreme right end of productions and hence cannot be REDUCED-BY any terminal. The new grammar is easily seen to be SHIFT-IDENTIFY consistent.

The technique illustrated above is perfectly general and can be used repeatedly to individually eliminate all conflicts.

The general procedure is:

For each grammatical symbol A (nonterminal or terminal) for which there is a SHIFT-IDENTIFY conflict, i.e., there is a terminal Z such that

$$A \text{ REDUCED-BY } Z$$

and

$$A \text{ BELOW } Z$$

introduce a new nonterminal $\langle \hat{A} \rangle$ with a singleton production

$$\langle \hat{A} \rangle \rightarrow A$$

and replace A by $\langle \hat{A} \rangle$ in all righthand side occurrences of A other than at the extreme right end of a production.

Given an input grammar for which it is desired to design a SHIFT-IDENTIFY processor, we recommend that the methods of Sections C.8 through C.10 be applied in the following order.

1. Remove ϵ-productions, if any, using the method of Section C.8.

2. Insert action symbols so that no action symbol is at the extreme left end of a production.

3. Rewrite the translation grammar as a Polish-translation grammar using the methods of Section C.9.

4. Rewrite the translation grammar as a SHIFT-IDENTIFY-consistent grammar using the methods of Section C.10.

We note that making the grammar SHIFT-IDENTIFY consistent in step 4 does not destroy the property of a translation being Polish since the rewriting method of step 4 does not affect the extreme right end of productions.

Using these methods, any context-free grammar can be rewritten as a SHIFT-IDENTIFY-consistent grammar. However there is no guarantee that the resulting grammar will satisfy any of the other properties required for SHIFT-IDENTIFY parsing (e.g., be a weak-precedence grammar or a simple-mixed-strategy precedence grammar).

C.11   REFERENCES

Conversion of grammars to LL(1) form is discussed in Foster [1968] and Stearns [1971]. That left recursion can be eliminated follows from a result of Greibach [1965] to the effect that every grammar whose language does not contain the null string can be rewritten so that the righthand side of every production begins with a terminal symbol. The method of Section C.6 is discussed in Kurki-Suonio [1966]. The goal-corner transformation and similar techniques are discussed in Rosenkrantz [1967], Foster [1968], Griffiths and Petrick [1968], and Wood [1969c]. The class of grammars that can be converted to LL(1) form by the goal-corner transformation is discussed in Rosenkrantz and Lewis [1970]. A more general method of transforming grammars into LL(1) form is discussed in Hammer [1974].

A method for eliminating ϵ-productions was introduced by Bar-Hillel, Perles, and Shamir [1961]. Methods for making grammars SHIFT-IDEN-TIFY consistent are described in Fisher [1969], Learner and Lim [1970], Graham [1971], and McAfee and Presser [1972]. Lomet [1973] describes a method for eliminating left recursion from LR grammars. A variety of grammatical transformation techniques are described in Graham [1974].

PROBLEMS

1. Add attributes to the grammar of Fig. C.2(b) so that the grammar is L-attributed and generates the activity sequence

    $$\{\text{INITIALIZE}\} \ a_1 \ \{\text{NEXT}_1\}, \ a_2 \ \{\text{NEXT}_2\}, \ a_3 \ \{\text{LAST}_3\}$$

2. a) Add attributes to the grammar of Fig. C.2(a) so that the result is L-attributed and {TERMINATE} has an attribute whose value is the number of a's in the list.

    b) Add attributes to the grammar of Fig. C.2(c) so that the result is L-attributed and {INITIATE} has an attribute whose value is the number of a's in the list.

    c) Add attributes to the grammar of Fig. C.2(c) so that the result is L-attributed and {TERMINATE} has an attribute whose value is the number of a's in the list.

3. If a grammar has no extraneous symbols, can a singleton production be left recursive?

4. Prove that a grammar with a left recursive nonterminal cannot be LL(1) (assuming no extraneous symbols).

5. Using the methods of Section C.2 through C.6 rewrite the following grammar with starting symbol $\langle E \rangle$ as an LL(1) grammar

    $$\langle E \rangle \rightarrow \langle E \rangle + \langle T \rangle$$

$$\langle E \rangle \rightarrow \langle T \rangle$$
$$\langle T \rangle \rightarrow \langle T \rangle * \langle P \rangle$$
$$\langle T \rangle \rightarrow \langle P \rangle$$
$$\langle P \rangle \rightarrow (\langle E \rangle)$$
$$\langle P \rangle \rightarrow a$$

6. Rewrite the following fragment of the ALGOL 60 grammar with starting symbol $\langle$identifier$\rangle$ as an LL(1) grammar.

$$\langle \text{identifier} \rangle \rightarrow \langle \text{letter} \rangle$$
$$\langle \text{identifier} \rangle \rightarrow \langle \text{identifier} \rangle \langle \text{letter} \rangle$$
$$\langle \text{identifier} \rangle \rightarrow \langle \text{identifier} \rangle \langle \text{digit} \rangle$$
$$\langle \text{digit} \rangle \rightarrow 0 \mid 1 \mid 2 \mid \cdots \mid 9$$
$$\langle \text{letter} \rangle \rightarrow a \mid b \mid c \mid \cdots \mid z$$

7. Rewrite the following fragment of the ALGOL 60 grammar with starting symbol $\langle$program$\rangle$ as an LL(1) grammar. Do not give productions for $\langle$statement$\rangle$, $\langle$declaration$\rangle$, or $\langle$label$\rangle$.

$$\langle \text{program} \rangle \rightarrow \langle \text{block} \rangle$$
$$\langle \text{program} \rangle \rightarrow \langle \text{compound statement} \rangle$$
$$\langle \text{block} \rangle \rightarrow \langle \text{unlabelled block} \rangle$$
$$\langle \text{block} \rangle \rightarrow \langle \text{label} \rangle : \langle \text{block} \rangle$$
$$\langle \text{compound statement} \rangle \rightarrow \langle \text{unlabelled compound} \rangle$$
$$\langle \text{compound statement} \rangle \rightarrow \langle \text{label} \rangle : \langle \text{compound statement} \rangle$$
$$\langle \text{unlabelled block} \rangle \rightarrow \langle \text{block head} \rangle ; \langle \text{compound tail} \rangle$$
$$\langle \text{unlabelled compound} \rangle \rightarrow \textbf{begin} \langle \text{compound tail} \rangle$$
$$\langle \text{block head} \rangle \rightarrow \textbf{begin} \langle \text{declaration} \rangle$$
$$\langle \text{block head} \rangle \rightarrow \langle \text{block head} \rangle ; \langle \text{declaration} \rangle$$
$$\langle \text{compound tail} \rangle \rightarrow \langle \text{statement} \rangle \ \textbf{end}$$
$$\langle \text{compound tail} \rangle \rightarrow \langle \text{statement} \rangle ; \langle \text{compound tail} \rangle$$

8. Apply the goal-corner transformation to the grammars of each of the following problems. In each case, determine whether or not the resulting grammar is LL(1).

a) Problem C.5

b) Problem C.6

c) Problem C.7

9. Find a left recursive grammar for which the resultant grammar after applying the goal-corner transformation is also left recursive.

10. Show that when the goal-corner transformation is applied to an LL(1) grammar, the resulting grammar is LL(1).

11. Rewrite the following grammar so as to eliminate ϵ-productions.

$$\langle A \rangle \rightarrow \langle A \rangle \langle A \rangle \langle A \rangle$$
$$\langle A \rangle \rightarrow a$$
$$\langle A \rangle \rightarrow \epsilon$$

12. Rewrite the following grammar so as to eliminate ϵ-productions.

$$\langle S \rangle \rightarrow a \langle B \rangle \langle D \rangle$$
$$\langle S \rangle \rightarrow \langle A \rangle \langle B \rangle$$
$$\langle S \rangle \rightarrow \langle D \rangle \langle A \rangle \langle C \rangle$$
$$\langle S \rangle \rightarrow b$$
$$\langle A \rangle \rightarrow \langle S \rangle \langle C \rangle \langle B \rangle$$
$$\langle A \rangle \rightarrow \langle S \rangle \langle A \rangle \langle B \rangle \langle C \rangle$$
$$\langle A \rangle \rightarrow \langle C \rangle b \langle D \rangle$$
$$\langle A \rangle \rightarrow c$$
$$\langle A \rangle \rightarrow \epsilon$$
$$\langle B \rangle \rightarrow c \langle D \rangle$$
$$\langle B \rangle \rightarrow d$$
$$\langle B \rangle \rightarrow \epsilon$$
$$\langle C \rangle \rightarrow \langle A \rangle \langle D \rangle \langle C \rangle$$
$$\langle C \rangle \rightarrow c$$
$$\langle D \rangle \rightarrow \langle S \rangle a \langle C \rangle$$
$$\langle D \rangle \rightarrow \langle S \rangle \langle C \rangle$$
$$\langle D \rangle \rightarrow f g$$

13. Rewrite the following attributed productions into an S-attributed Polish translation:

$\langle \text{Boolean expression} \rangle_p$ SYNTHESIZED p

All action symbol attributes are INHERITED.

$\langle S \rangle \rightarrow$ **if** $\langle B \rangle_{p1}$ $\{\text{JUMPF}\}_{p2,q1}$ **then** $\langle S1 \rangle$ $\{\text{JUMP}\}_{r1}$ $\{\text{LABEL}\}_{q2}$
$$\text{else } \langle S \rangle \; \{\text{LABEL}\}_{r2}$$
$$p2 \leftarrow p1$$
$$(q2, q1) \leftarrow \text{NEWT}$$
$$(r2, r1) \leftarrow \text{NEWT}$$

$\langle S \rangle \rightarrow$ **if** $\langle B \rangle_{p1}$ $\{\text{JUMPF}\}_{p2,q1}$ **then** $\langle S1 \rangle$ $\{\text{LABEL}\}_{q2}$
$$p2 \leftarrow p1$$
$$(q2, q1) \leftarrow \text{NEWT}$$

14. a) Rewrite the following grammar to eliminate SHIFT-IDENTIFY conflicts:

$$\langle S \rangle \rightarrow 1 \langle S \rangle 1$$
$$\langle S \rangle \rightarrow 0 \langle S \rangle 0$$
$$\langle S \rangle \rightarrow 0 \, 0$$
$$\langle S \rangle \rightarrow 1 \, 1$$

b) Can the resulting grammar be parsed by a pushdown machine?

15. Rewrite the following grammar with starting symbol ⟨statement list⟩ so as to make it SHIFT-IDENTIFY consistent. The new grammar need not generate ϵ.

1. ⟨statement list⟩ → ⟨statement list⟩ ; ⟨statement⟩
2. ⟨statement list⟩ → ϵ
3. ⟨statement⟩ → IF ⟨Boolean expression⟩ THEN ⟨statement⟩
4. ⟨statement⟩ → DO ⟨statement⟩ WHILE ⟨Boolean expression⟩
5. ⟨statement⟩ → FOR VARIABLE = ⟨expression⟩ DO ⟨statement⟩ THEN
   STEP ⟨expression⟩ UNTIL ⟨expression⟩
6. ⟨statement⟩ → FOR VARIABLE = ⟨expression⟩ DO ⟨statement⟩
7. ⟨statement⟩ → s
8. ⟨Boolean expression⟩ → b
9. ⟨expression⟩ → e

16. Describe how to simplify the general procedure of Section C.10 for eliminating SHIFT-IDENTIFY conflicts so that A is replaced by $\langle \hat{A} \rangle$ only where absolutely necessary.

17. For each of the following forms, show that every grammar whose language does not contain the null string can be rewritten so that the righthand side of each production

a) is either a single terminal symbol or two nonterminal symbols (Chomsky [1959]);

b) begins with a terminal symbol (Greibach [1965]);

c) both begins with and ends with a terminal symbol (Rosenkrantz [1967]);

d) is no longer than three symbols and begins with a terminal symbol (Greibach [1965]);

e) does not contain two consecutive nonterminals (Greibach [1965]).

Bibliography

Abramson, H., *Theory and Application of a Bottom-up Syntax-directed Translator,* New York: Academic Press, 1973.

Aho, A. V., "Indexed grammars—an extension of context-free grammars," *JACM,* Vol. 15, No. 4, Oct. 1968, pp. 647–671.

Aho, A. V., P. J. Denning, and J. D. Ullman, "Weak and mixed strategy precedence parsing," *JACM,* Vol. 19, No. 2, Apr. 1972, pp. 225–243.

Aho, A. V., J. E. Hopcroft, and J. D. Ullman, "Time and tape complexity of pushdown automaton languages," *Information and Control,* Vol. 13, No. 3, 1968, pp. 186–206.

Aho, A. V., and S. C. Johnson, "LR parsing," *Computing Surveys,* Vol. 6, No. 2, June 1974, pp. 99–124.

Aho, A. V., S. C. Johnson, and J. D. Ullman, "Deterministic parsing of ambiguous grammars," *Conf. Rec ACM Symposium on Principles of Programming Languages,* Boston, Mass., Oct. 1973, pp. 1–21.

Aho, A. V., and T. G. Peterson, "A minimum distance error-correcting parser for context-free languages," *SIAM J. Computing,* Vol. 1, No. 4, Dec. 1972, pp. 305–312.

Aho, A. V., and J. D. Ullman [1969a], "Syntax directed translations and the pushdown assembler," *J. Computer and System Sciences,* Vol. 3, No. 1, Feb. 1969, pp. 37–56.

Aho, A. V., and J. D. Ullman [1969b], "Properties of syntax directed translations, *J. Computer and System Sciences,* Vol. 3, No. 3, Aug. 1969, pp. 319–334.

Aho, A. V., and J. D. Ullman, "Translations on a context-free grammar," *Information and Control,* Vol. 19, No. 5, 1971, pp. 439–475.

Aho, A. V., and J. D. Ullman [1972a, 1973a], *The Theory of Parsing, Translation, and Compiling,* Englewood Cliffs, N.J.: Prentice-Hall, Vol. I, 1972, Vol. II, 1973.

Aho, A. V., and J. D. Ullman, [1972b], "Optimization of LR(k) parsers," *J. Computer and System Sciences,* Vol. 6, No. 6, Dec. 1972, pp. 573–602.

Aho, A. V., and J. D. Ullman [1972c], "Linear precedence functions for weak precedence grammars," *International J. Computer Mathematics,* Vol. 3, No. 4, Dec. 1972, pp. 149–155.

Aho, A. V., and J. D. Ullman [1973b], "A technique for speeding up LR(k) parsers," *SIAM J. Computing,* Vol. 2, No. 2, June 1973, pp. 106–127.

Aho, A. V., and J. D. Ullman [1973c], "Error detection in precedence parsers," *Mathematical Systems Theory,* Vol. 7, No. 2, June 1973, pp. 97–113.

Allen, F. E., "Program optimization," (in) *Annual Review in Automatic Programming,* Vol. 5, Elmsford, N.Y.: Pergamon Press, 1969, pp. 239–307.

Allen F. E., and J. Cocke, "A catalogue of optimizing transformations," (in) *Design and Optimization of Compilers,* (ed.), R. Rustin, Englewood Cliffs, N.J.: Prentice-Hall; 1972, pp. 1–30.

Alpiar, R., "Double syntax oriented processing," *Computer J.,* Vol. 14, No. 1, Feb. 1971, pp. 25–37.

Anderson, T., J. Eve, and J. J. Horning, "Efficient LR(1) parsers," *Acta Informatica,* Vol. 2, 1973, pp. 12–39.

Arbib, M. A., *Theories of Abstract Automata,* Englewood Cliffs, N.J.: Prentice-Hall, 1970.

Arden, B. W., B. A. Galler, and R. M. Graham, "An algorithm for translating Boolean expressions," *JACM,* Vol. 9, No. 2, Apr. 1962, pp. 222–239.

Backes, S., "Top-down syntax analysis and Floyd-Evans production language," *Proc. of the IFIP Congress,* 1971.

Backus, J. W., "The syntax and semantics of the proposed international algebraic language of the Zurich ACM-GAMM Conference," *Proc. Internat. Conf. on Information Processing,* UNESCO, 1959, pp. 125–132.

Backus, J. W., et al., "The FORTRAN automatic coding system," *Proc. Western Joint Computer Conf.,* Vol. 11, Los Angeles, 1957, pp. 188–198. Reprinted in Rosen [1967].

Bar-Hillel, Y., M. Perles, and E. Shamir, "On formal properties of simple phrase structure grammars," *Zeitschrift für Phonetik, Sprachwissenschaft und Kommunikationsforschung,* Vol. 14, No. 2, 1961, pp. 143–172; also in Y. Bar-Hillel, *Language and Information,* Reading, Mass.: Addison-Wesley, 1964, pp. 116–150.

Barnett, M. P., and R. P. Futrelle, "Syntactic analysis by digital computer," *CACM,* Vol. 5, No. 10, Oct. 1962, pp. 515–526.

Batson, A., "The organization of symbol tables," *CACM,* Vol. 8, No. 2, Feb. 1965, pp. 111–112.

Bauer, F. L., and K. Samelson, "Sequentialle formelübersetzung," *Elektronische Rechenanlagen,* 1959, pp. 176–182.

Bauer, F. L., and K. Samelson, "Sequential formula translation," *CACM,* Vol. 3, No. 2, Feb. 1960, pp. 76–83. Reprinted in Rosen [1967] and Pollack [1972].

Bays, C., "The reallocation of hash-coded tables," *CACM,* Vol. 16, No. 1, Jan. 1973, pp. 11–14.

Bays, C., "A note on when to chain overflow items within a direct access table," *CACM,* Vol. 16, No. 1, Jan. 1973, pp. 46–47.

Bell, J. R., "A new method for determining linear precedence functions for precedence grammars," *CACM,* Vol. 12, No. 10, Oct. 1969, pp. 567–569.

Bell, J. R., "The quadratic quotient method: a hash coding eliminating secondary clustering," *CACM,* Vol. 13, No. 2, Feb. 1970, pp. 107–109.

Bell, J. R., and C. H. Kaman, "The linear quotient hash code, *CACM,* Vol. 13, No. 11, Nov. 1970, pp. 675–677.

Booth, T. L., *Sequential Machines and Automata Theory,* New York: John Wiley & Sons, 1967.

Brent, R. P., "Reducing the retrieval time of scatter storage techniques," *CACM,* Vol. 16, No. 2, Feb. 1973, pp. 105–109.

Brooker, R. A., I. R. MacCallum, D. Morris, and J. S. Rohl, "The compiler compiler," (in) *Annual Review in Automatic Programming,* Vol. 3, (ed.) R. Goodman, N.Y. and London: Pergamon Press, 1963, pp. 229–271.

Brooker, R. A., and D. Morris, "An assembly program for a phrase structure language," *Computer J.,* Vol. 3, Oct. 1960, pp. 168–174.

Brooker, R. A., and D. Morris, "A general translation program for phrase structure languages," *JACM,* Vol. 9, No. 1, Jan. 1962, pp. 1–10.

Brooker, R. A., D. Morris, and J. S. Rohl, "Experience with the compiler–compiler," *Computer J.,* Vol. 9, No. 4, Feb. 1967, pp. 345–349.

Burge, W. H., "The evaluation, classification and interpretation of expressions," *Proc. 19th National ACM Conf.,* New York, 1964.

Cantor, D. G. "On the ambiguity problem of Backus Systems," *JACM,* Vol. 9, No. 10, Oct. 1962, pp. 477–479.

Chartres, B. A., and J. J. Florentin, "A universal syntax-directed top-down analyzer," *JACM,* Vol. 15, No. 3, July 1968, pp. 447–463.

Cheatham, T. E., Jr., *The Theory and Construction of Compilers,* Wakefield, Mass.: Computer Associates, 1967.

Cheatham, T., and K. Sattley, "Syntax directed compiling," *Proc. AFIPS 1964 Spring Joint Computer Conf.,* Vol. 25, Baltimore, Md.: Spartan Books, pp. 31–57. Reprinted in Rosen [1967].

Chomsky, N., "Three models for the description of language," *IRE Trans. on Information Theory,* Vol. IT-2, No. 3, 1956, pp. 113–124.

Chomsky, N., *Syntactic Structures,* The Hague, Netherlands: Mouton & Co., 1957.

Chomsky, N., "On certain formal properties of grammars," *Information and Control,* Vol. 2, No. 2, June 1959, pp. 137–167.

Chomsky, N., "Context-free grammars and pushdown storage," *M.I.T. Res. Lab. Electron. Quart. Prog. Rept. No. 65,* 1962, pp. 187–194.

Chomsky, N., "Formal properties of grammars," (in) *Handbook of Mathematical Psychology, Vol. 11,* (eds.) R. D. Luce, R. R. Bush, and E. Galanter, New York: Wiley, 1963, pp. 323–418.

Chomsky, N., and G. A. Miller, "Finite state languages," *Information and Control,* Vol. 1, No. 2, May 1958, pp. 91–112.

Chomsky, N., and M. P. Schützenberger, "The algebraic theory of context-free languages," (in) P. Braffert and D. Hirschberg (eds.), *Computer Programming and Formal Systems,* Amsterdam: North Holland, 1963, pp. 118–161.

Cocke, J., and J. T. Schwartz, *Programming Languages and Their Compilers: Preliminary Notes,* New York: Courant Institute of Mathematical Sciences, 1970.

Cohen, D. J., and C. C. Gotlieb, "A list structure form of grammars for syntactic analysis," *Computing Surveys,* Vol. 2, No. 1, Mar. 1970, pp. 65–82.

Colmerauer, A., "Total precedence relations," *JACM,* Vol. 17, No. 1, Jan. 1970, pp. 14–30.

Conway, M. E., "Design of a separable transition-diagram compiler," *CACM,* Vol. 6, No. 7, July 1963, pp. 396–408.

Conway, R. W., and T. R. Wilcox, "Design and implementation of a diagnostic compiler for PL/I," *CACM,* Vol. 16, No. 3, March 1973, pp. 169–179.

Crowe, D., "Generating parsers for affix grammars," *CACM,* Vol. 15, No. 8, Aug. 1972, pp. 728–734.

Culik, K., "Well-translatable grammars and ALGOL-like languages," (in) T. B. Steel, Jr. (ed.), *Formal Language Description Languages for Computer Programming,* Amsterdam: North Holland, 1966, pp. 76–85.

Culik, K., II, "Contribution to deterministic top-down analysis of context-free languages," *Kybernetika,* Vol. 5, No. 4, 1968, pp. 422–431.

Culik, K., II, "*n*-ary grammars and the description of mapping of languages," *Kybernetika,* Vol. 6, 1970, pp. 99–117.

Culik, K., II, and R. Cohen, "LR-regular grammars—an extension of LR(*k*) grammars," *J. Computer and System Sciences,* Vol. 7, No. 1, Feb. 1973, pp. 66–96.

Culik, K., II, and C. J. W. Morey, "Formal schemes for language translations," *Intern. J. Computer Math.,* Section A., Vol. 3, 1971, pp. 17–48.

Davis, M., *Computability and Unsolvability,* New York: McGraw-Hill, 1958.

Day, A. C., "The use of symbol-state tables," *Computer J.,* Vol. 13, No. 4, Nov. 1970, pp. 332–339.

de la Briandais, R., "File searching using variable length keys," *Proc. Western Joint Computer Conference,* 1959, pp. 295–298.

De Remer, F. L., "Generating parsers for BNF grammars," *Proc. AFIPS 1969 Spring Joint Computer Conf.,* Vol. 34, Montvale, N.J.: AFIPS Press, pp. 793–799.

De Remer, F. L., "Simple LR(*k*) grammars," *CACM,* Vol. 14, No. 7, July 1971, pp. 453–460.

Domolki, B., "An algorithm for syntactic analysis," *Computational Linguistics,* Vol. 3, 1964, pp. 29–46.

Domolki, B., "Algorithms for the recognition of properties of sequences of symbols," *Zhurnal Vychislitel'noi Matematiki i matematicheskoi Fiziki,* Vol. 5, No. 1, 1965, pp. 77–97. Translation in *USSR Computational and Mathematical Physics,* Vol. 5, No. 1, Oxford: Pergamon Press, 1967, pp. 101–130.

Domolki, B., "A universal compiler system based on production rules," *BIT,* Vol. 8, No. 4, Oct. 1968, pp. 262–275.

Donovan, J. J., and H. F. Ledgard, "A formal system for the specification of the syntax and translation of computer languages," *Proc. AFIPS 1967 Fall Joint Computer Conf.,* Vol. 31, Washington, D.C.: Thompson Books, pp. 553–569.

Earley, J., "An efficient context-free parsing algorithm," *CACM,* Vol. 13, No. 2, Feb. 1970, pp. 94–102.

Eickel, J., M. Paul, F. L. Bauer, and K. Samelson, "A syntax controlled generator of formal language processors," *CACM,* Vol. 6, No. 8, Aug. 1963, pp. 451–455.

Ershov, A. P., *Programming Programme for the BESM Computer.* Translated by M. Nadler. New York: Pergamon Press, 1959.

Evans, A., "An ALGOL 60 compiler," *Proc. 18th Natl. ACM Conf.,* Denver, 1962. Also in R. Goodman (ed.), *Annual Review in Automatic Programming,* Vol. 4. New York and London: Pergamon Press, 1964, pp. 87–124. Reprinted in Pollack [1972].

Evey, R. J., "Application of pushdown-store machines," *Proc. AFIPS 1963 Fall Joint Computer Conf.,* Vol. 24, New York: Spartan Books, pp. 215–227.

Evey, R. J., "The theory and application of pushdown store machines," *Mathematical Linguistics and Automatic Translation,* Harvard Univ. Computation Lab. Rept. NSF-10, May, 1963.

Feldman, J. A., "A formal semantics for computer languages and its application in a compiler–compiler," *CACM,* Vol. 9, No. 1, Jan. 1966, pp. 3–9. Reprinted in Pollack [1972].

Feldman, J. A., and D. Gries, "Translator writing systems," *CACM,* Vol. 11, No. 2, Feb. 1968, pp. 77–113.

Fischer, M. J., "Some properties of precedence languages," *Conference Record of ACM Symposium on Theory of Computing,* Marina del Rey, Calif., May 1969, pp. 181–190.

Fischer, P. C., "On computability by certain classes of restricted Turing machines," *IEEE Proceedings Fourth Annual Symposium on Switching Circuit Theory and Logical Design,* Chicago, Ill., 1963, pp. 23–32.

Floyd, R. W., "A descriptive language for symbol manipulation," *JACM,* Vol. 8, No. 4, Oct. 1961, pp. 579–584.

Floyd, R. W., "Syntactic analysis and operator precedence," *JACM,* Vol. 10, No. 3, July 1963, pp. 316–333. Reprinted in Pollack [1972].

Floyd, R. W. [1964a], "Bounded context syntactic analysis," *CACM,* Vol. 7, No. 2, Feb. 1964, pp. 62–67.

Floyd, R. W. [1964b], "The syntax of programming languages—a survey," *IEEE Trans. on Electronic Computers,* Vol. EC-13, No. 4, Aug. 1964, pp. 346–353. Reprinted in Rosen [1967] and Pollack [1972].

Floyd, R. W., "Nondeterministic algorithms," *JACM,* Vol. 14, No. 4, Oct. 1967, pp. 636–644.

Foster, C. C., "Information storage and retrieval using AVL trees," *Proc. 20th Natl. ACM Conf.,* 1965, pp. 192–205.

Foster, C. C., "A generalization of AVL trees," *CACM,* Vol. 16, No. 8, Aug. 1973, pp. 513–517.

Foster, J. M., "A syntax improving program," *Computer J.,* Vol. 11, No. 1, May 1968, pp. 31–34.

Foster, J. M., *Automatic Syntactic Analysis,* New York: American Elsevier Publ. Co., 1970.

Fredkin, E., "Trie memory," *CACM,* Vol. 3, No. 9, Sept. 1960, pp. 490–499.

Freeman, D. N. "Error correction in CORC—the Cornell computing language," *Proc. AFIPS 1964 Fall Joint Computer Conf.,* Vol. 26, Spartan, New York, pp. 15–34. Reprinted in Pollack [1972].

Gauthier, R., and S. Ponto, *Designing Systems Programs,* Englewood Cliffs, N.J.: Prentice-Hall, 1970.

Geller, M. M., and M. A. Harrison, "Characterizations of LR(0) languages," *IEEE Conference Record of 14th Annual Symposium on Switching and Automata Theory,* Oct. 1973, pp. 103–108.

Gilbert, P., "On the syntax of algorithmic languages," *JACM,* Vol. 13, No. 1, Jan. 1966, pp. 90–107.

Gill, A., *Introduction to the Theory of Finite-state Machines,* New York: McGraw-Hill, 1962.

Ginsburg, S., *An Introduction to Mathematical Machine Theory,* Reading, Mass.: Addison-Wesley, 1962.

Ginsburg, S., *The Mathematical Theory of Context-Free Languages,* New York: McGraw-Hill, 1966.

Ginsburg, S., and S. A. Greibach, "Deterministic context-free languages," *Information and Control,* Vol. 9, No. 6, Dec. 1966, pp. 620–648.

Ginsburg, S., and G. F. Rose, "Preservation of languages by transducers," *Information and Control,* Vol. 9, No. 2, Apr. 1966, pp. 153–176.

Ginsburg, S., and G. F. Rose, "A note on preservation of languages by transducers," *Information and Control,* Vol. 12, Nos. 5 and 6, May–June 1968, pp. 549–552.

Ginsburg, S., and J. Ullian, "Ambiguity in context free languages, *JACM,* Vol. 13, No. 1, Jan. 1966, pp. 62–89.

Glass, R. J., "An elementary discussion of compiler/interpreter writing," *Computing Surveys,* Vol. 1, No. 1, Mar. 1969, pp. 55–77.

Graham, R. M., "Bounded context translation," *Proc. AFIPS 1964 Spring Joint Computer Conf.*, Vol. 25, Baltimore, Md.: Spartan Books, pp. 17–29. Reprinted in Rosen [1967].

Graham, S. L., "Extended precedence languages, bounded right context languages and deterministic languages," *IEEE Conf. Record of 1970 11th Annual Symposium on Switching and Automata Theory,* pp. 175–180.

Graham, S. L., "Precedence languages and bounded right context languages," Ph. D. Thesis, Stanford Univ., 1971.

Graham, S. L., "On bounded right context languages and grammars," *SIAM J. Computing,* Vol. 3, No. 3, Sept. 1974, pp. 224–254.

Graham, S. L., and S. P. Rhodes, "Practical syntactic error recovery in compilers," *Conf. Rec. ACM Symposium on Principles of Programming Languages,* Boston, Mass., Oct. 1973, pp. 52–58.

Grau, A. A."Recursive processes and ALGOL translation," *CACM,* Vol. 4, No. 1, Jan. 1961, pp. 10–15.

Grau, A. A., U. Hill, and H. Lungmaack, *Translation of ALGOL 60,* New York: Springer-Verlag, 1967.

Gray, J. N., and M. A. Harrison, "On the covering and reduction problems for context-free grammars," *JACM,* Vol. 19, No. 4, Oct. 1972, pp. 675–698.

Gray, J. N., and M. A. Harrison, "Canonical precedence schemes," *JACM,* Vol. 20, No. 2, Apr. 1973, pp. 214–234.

Greibach, S. A., "A new normal-form theorem for context-free phrase structure grammars," *JACM,* Vol. 12, No. 1, Jan. 1965, pp. 42–52.

Gries, D., "Use of transition matrices in compiling," *CACM,* Vol. 11, No. 1, Jan. 1968, pp. 26–34. Reprinted in Pollack [1972].

Gries, D., *Compiler Construction for Digital Computers,* New York: Wiley, 1971.

Gries, D., M. Paul, and H. R. Wiehle, "Some techniques used in the ALCOR ILLINOIS 7090," *CACM,* Vol. 8, No. 8, Aug. 1965, pp. 496–500. Reprinted in Pollack [1972].

Griffiths, T. V., and S. R. Petrick, "On the relative efficiencies of context-free grammar recognizers," *CACM,* Vol. 8, No. 5, May 1965, pp. 289–300.

Griffiths, T. V., and S. R. Petrick, "Top-down versus bottom-up analysis," *IFIP Congress,* 1968, Software I, Booklet B, pp. 80–85.

Gross, M., and A. Lentin, *Introduction to Formal Grammars,* New York: Springer-Verlag, 1970.

Halstead, M. H., *Machine-independent Computer Programming,* New York: Spartan Books, 1962.

Hammer, M. H., "A new grammatical transformation into LL(k) form," *Proc. Sixth Annual ACM Symp. on Theory of Computing,* 1974, pp. 266–275.

Harrison, M. A. *Introduction to Switching and Automata Theory,* New York: McGraw-Hill, 1965.

Harrison, M. A., and I. M. Havel, "Real-time strict deterministic languages," *SIAM J. Computing,* Vol. 1, No. 4, Dec. 1972, pp. 333–349.

Harrison, M. A., and I. M. Havel, "Strict deterministic grammars," *J. Computer and System Sciences,* Vol. 7, No. 3, June 1973, pp. 237–277.

Harrison, M. A., and I. M. Havel, "On the parsing of deterministic languages," *JACM,* Vol. 21, No. 4, Oct. 1974, pp. 525–548.

Hartmanis, J., and R. E. Stearns, *Algebraic Structure Theory of Sequential Machines,* Englewood Cliffs, N.J.: Prentice-Hall, 1966.

Hayashi, K., "On the construction of LR(k) parsers," *Proc. ACM Annual Conf.,* 1971, N.Y., pp. 538–553.

Hays, D., "Automatic language – data processing," (in) *Computer Applications in the Behavioral Sciences,* (ed.) H. Borko, Englewood Cliffs, N.J.: Prentice-Hall, 1962, pp. 394–421.

Hennie, F. C., *Finite-state Models for Logical Machines,* New York: Wiley, 1968.

Hext, J. B., and P. S. Roberts, "Syntax analysis by Domolki's algorithm," *Computer J.,* Vol. 13, No. 3, Aug. 1970, pp. 263–271.

Hibbard, T. N., "Some combinatorial properties of certain trees with applications to searching and sorting," *JACM,* Vol. 9, No. 1, Jan. 1962, pp. 13–28.

Hopcroft, J. E., "An $n \log n$ algorithm for minimizing states in a finite automaton," (in) *Theory of Machines and Computations,* (eds.) Kohavi and A. Paz, New York: Academic Press, 1972, pp. 189–196.

Hopcroft, J. E., and J. D. Ullman, *Formal Languages and their Relation to Automata,* Reading, Mass.: Addison-Wesley, 1969.

Hopgood, F. R. A., "A solution to the table overflow problem for hash tables," *Computer Bulletin,* Vol. 11, No. 4, Mar. 1968, pp. 297–300.

Hopgood, F. R. A, *Compiling Techniques,* New York: American Elsevier, 1969.

Horwitz, L. P., R. M. Karp, R. E. Miller, and S. Winograd, "Index register allocation," *JACM,* Vol. 13, No. 1, Jan. 1966, pp. 43–61.

Huffman, D. A. "The synthesis of sequential switching circuits," *J. Franklin Inst.,* Vol. 257, Nos. 3 and 4, Mar.–Apr. 1954, pp. 161–190, 275–303. Reprinted in Moore [1964].

Hunt, H. B., III, T. G. Szymanski, and J. D. Ullman, "Operations on sparse relations and efficient algorithms for grammar problems," *IEEE Conference Record of Fifteenth Annual Symposium on Switching and Automata Theory,* Oct. 1974, pp. 127–132.

Ichbiah, J. D. and S. P. Morse, "A technique for generating almost optimal Floyd–Evans productions for precedence grammars," *CACM,* Vol. 13, No. 8, Aug. 1970, pp. 501–508.

Ingerman, P. Z., *A Syntax Oriented Translator,* New York: Academic Press, 1966.

Irons, E. T., "A syntax directed compiler for ALGOL 60," *CACM,* Vol. 4, No. 1, Jan. 1961, pp. 51–55. Reprinted in Rosen [1967].

Irons, E. T. [1963a], "The structure and use of the syntax-directed compiler," (in) *Annual Review in Automatic Programming,* Vol. 3, (ed.) R. Goodman, New York and London: Pergamon Press, 1963, pp. 207–227. Reprinted in Pollack [1972].

Irons, E. T. [1963b], "An error-correcting parse algorithm," *CACM,* Vol. 6, No. 11, Nov. 1963, pp. 669–673. Reprinted in Pollack [1972].

Irons, E. T., "Structural connections in formal languages," *CACM,* Vol. 7, No. 2, Feb. 1964, pp. 67–71.

James E. B., and D. P. Partridge, "Adaptive correction of program statements," *CACM,* Vol. 16, No. 1, Jan. 1973, pp. 27–37.

Johnson, L. R., "Indirect chaining method for addressing on secondary keys," *CACM,* Vol. 4, No. 5, May 1961, pp. 218–222.

Johnson, W. L., et al., "Automatic generation of efficient lexical processors using finite state techniques," *CACM,* Vol. 11, No. 12, Dec. 1968, pp. 805–813.

Kaminger, F. P., "Generation, recognition, and parsing of context-free languages by means of recursive graphs," *Computing,* Vol. 11, No. 1, 1973, pp. 87–96.

Kanner, H., P. Kosinski, and C. L. Robinson, "The structure of yet another ALGOL compiler," *CACM,* Vol. 8, No. 7, July 1965, pp. 427–438. Reprinted in Rosen [1967].

Kasami, T., and K. Torii, "A syntax-analysis procedure for unambiguous context-free grammars," *JACM,* Vol. 16, No. 3, July 1969, pp. 423–431.

Kemp, R., "An estimation of the set of states of the minimal LR(0)-acceptor," (in) *Automata, Languages, and Programming,* (ed.) M. Nivat, Amsterdam: North Holland, 1973, pp. 563–574.

Knuth, D. E., "A history of writing compilers," *Computers and Automation,* Vol. 11, No. 12, Dec. 1962, pp. 8–14. Reprinted in Pollack [1972].

Knuth, D. E., "On the translation of languages from left to right," *Information and Control,* Vol. 8, No. 6, Dec. 1965, pp. 607–639.

Knuth, D. E. [1968a], "Semantics of context-free languages," *Math. Systems Theory,* Vol. 2, No. 2, June 1968, pp. 127–145.

Knuth, D. E. [1968b], *The Art of Computer Programming, Volume I: Fundamental Algorithms,* Reading, Mass.: Addison-Wesley, 1968.

Knuth, D. E., "Top-down syntax analysis," *Acta Informatica,* Vol. 1, No. 2, 1971, pp. 79–110.

Knuth, D. E., *The Art of Computer Programming, Volume III: Sorting and Searching,* Reading, Mass.: Addison-Wesley, 1973.

Korenjak, A. J., "A practical method for constructing LR(k) processors," *CACM,* Vol. 12, No. 11, Nov. 1969, pp. 613–623. Reprinted in Pollack [1972].

Korenjak, A. J., and J. E. Hopcroft, "Simple deterministic languages," *IEEE Conference Record of Seventh Annual Symposium on Switching and Automata Theory,* Berkeley, Calif., Oct. 1966, pp. 36–46.

Kuno, S., "The augmented predictive analyzer for context-free languages—its relative efficiency," *CACM,* Vol. 9, No. 11, Nov. 1966, pp. 810–823.

Kuno, S., and A. G. Oettinger, "Multiple-path syntactic analyzer," (in) *Information Processing 62,* (ed.) C. M. Popplewell, Amsterdam: North-Holland, 1963, pp. 306–311.

Kurki-Suonio, R., "On top-to-bottom recognition and left recursion," *CACM,* Vol. 9, No. 7, July 1966, pp. 527–529.

Kurki-Suonio, R., "Notes on top down languages," *BIT,* Vol. 9, No. 3, 1969, pp. 225–238.

LaLonde, W. R., E. S. Lee, and J. J. Horning, "An LALR(k) parser generator," *Proc. IFIP Congress,* 1971, TA-3, Amsterdam: North Holland, pp. 153–157.

Landweber, P. S., "Decision problems of phrase structure grammars," *IEEE Trans. on Electronic Computers,* Vol. EC-13, No. 4, Aug. 1964, pp. 354–362.

Learner, A., and A. L. Lim, "A note on transforming context-free grammars to Wirth–Weber precedence form," *Computer J.,* Vol. 13, No. 2, May 1970, pp. 142–144.

Ledley, R. S., and J. B. Wilson, "Language translation through syntactic analysis," *CACM,* Vol. 5, No. 3, Mar. 1962, pp. 145–155.

Lee, J. A. N., *Anatomy of a Compiler,* 2nd edition, New York: Van Nostrand, 1974.

Lewis, P. M., II, and D. J. Rosenkrantz, "An ALGOL compiler designed using automata theory," *Proc. Symposium on Computers and Automata,* Microwave Research Institute Symposia Series, Vol. 21, Polytechnic Institute of Brooklyn, N.Y., 1971, pp. 75–88.

Lewis, P. M., II, D. J. Rosenkrantz, and R. E. Stearns, "Attributed translations," *J. Computer and System Sciences,* Vol. 9, No. 3, Dec. 1974, pp. 279–307.

Lewis, P. M., II, and R. E. Stearns, "Syntax-directed transduction," *JACM,* Vol. 15, No. 3, July 1968, pp. 465–488.

Lewis, P. M., II, R. E. Stearns, and J. Hartmanis, "Memory bounds for recognition of context-free and context-sensitive languages," *IEEE Conference Record on Switching Circuit Theory and Logical Design,* Ann Arbor, Mich., Oct. 1965, pp. 191–202.

Lietzke, M. P., "A method of syntax-checking ALGOL 60," *CACM,* Vol. 7, No. 8, Aug. 1964, pp. 475–478.

Liu, C. L., G. D. Chang, and R. E. Marks, "The design and implementation of a table driven compiler system," *Proc. AFIPS 1967 Spring Joint Computer Conf.,* Vol. 30, Washington, D.C.: Thompson Books, pp. 691–697.

Loeckx, J., "An algorithm for the construction of bounded-context parsers," *CACM,* Vol. 13, No. 5, May 1970, pp. 297–307.

Lomet, D. B., "A formalization of transition diagram systems," *JACM,* Vol. 20, No. 2, Apr. 1973, pp. 235–257.

Luccio, F., "Weighted increment linear search for scatter tables," *CACM,* Vol. 15, No. 12, Dec. 1972, pp. 1045–1047.

Lum, V. Y., "General performance analysis of key-to-address transformation methods using an abstract file system," *CACM,* Vol. 16, No. 10, Oct. 1973, pp. 603–612.

Lum, V. Y., P. S. T. Yuen, and M. Dodd, "Key-to-address transform techniques: a fundamental performance study on large existing formatted files," *CACM,* Vol. 14, No. 4, Apr. 1971, pp. 228–239.

Lyon, G., "Syntax-directed least-errors analysis for context-free languages: a practical approach," *CACM,* Vol. 17, No. 1, Jan. 1974, pp. 3–14.

Martin, D. F., "Boolean matrix methods for detection of simple precedence grammars," *CACM,* Vol. 11, No. 10, Oct. 1968, pp. 685–687.

Martin, D. F., "A Boolean matrix method for the computation of linear precedence functions," *CACM,* Vol. 15, No. 6, June 1972, pp. 448–454.

Martin, W. A., and D. N. Ness, "Optimizing binary trees grown with a sorting algorithm," *CACM,* Vol. 15, No. 2, Feb. 1972, pp. 88–93.

Maurer, W. D., "An improved hash code for scatter storage," *CACM,* Vol. 11, No. 1, Jan. 1968, pp. 35–38.

McAfee, J., and L. Presser, "An algorithm for the design of simple precedence grammars," *JACM,* Vol. 19, No. 3, July 1972, pp. 385–395.

McClure, R. M., "TMG–a syntax directed compiler," *Proc. 20th Natl. ACM Conf.,* 1965, New York, pp. 262–274.

McIlroy, M. D., "A variant method of file searching," *CACM,* Vol. 6, No. 3, Mar. 1963, p. 101.

McKeeman, W. M., J. J. Horning, and D. B. Wortman, *A Compiler Generator,* Englewood Cliffs, N.J.: Prentice-Hall, 1970.

McNaughton, R., "Parenthesis grammars," *JACM,* Vol. 14, No. 3, July 1967, pp. 490–500.

Mealy, G. H., "A method for synthesizing sequential circuits," *Bell Syst. Tech. J.,* Vol. 34, No. 5, Sept. 1955, pp. 1045–1079.

Mickunas, M. D., and V. B. Schneider, "A parser-generating system for constructing compressed compilers," *CACM,* Vol. 16, No. 11, Nov. 1973, pp. 669–676.

Minsky, M., *Computation: Finite and Infinite Machines,* Englewood Cliffs, N.J.: Prentice-Hall, 1967.

Moore, E. F., "Gedanken-experiments on sequential machines," (in) *Automata Studies,* Princeton, N.J.: Princeton University Press, 1956, pp. 129–153.

Moore, E. F., (ed.), *Sequential Machines: Selected Papers,* Reading, Mass.: Addison-Wesley, 1964.

Morgan, H. L., "Spelling correction in systems programs," *CACM,* Vol. 13, No. 2, Feb. 1970, pp. 90–94.

Morris, R., "Scatter storage techniques," *CACM,* Vol. 11, No. 1, Jan. 1968, pp. 38–43.

Moulton, P. G., and M. E. Muller, "DITRAN–a compiler emphasizing diagnostics," *CACM,* Vol. 10, No. 1, Jan. 1967, pp. 45–52.

Nakata, I., "On compiling algorithms for arithmetic expressions," *CACM,* Vol. 10, No. 8, Aug. 1967, pp. 492–494.

Naur, P., "The design of the GIER ALGOL compiler," (in) (ed.) R. Goodman, *Annual Review in Automatic Programming,* Vol. 4, New York and London: Pergamon Press, 1964, pp. 49–85.

Naur, P., et al., "Report on the algorithmic language ALGOL 60," *CACM,* Vol. 3, No. 5, May 1960, pp. 299–314; also in *Numerische Mathematik,* Vol. 2, Mar. 1960, pp.106–136.

Naur, P., et al., "Revised report on the algorithmic language ALGOL 60," *CACM,* Vol. 6, No. 1, Jan. 1963, pp. 1–17; also in *Computer J.,* Vol. 5, No. 4, Jan. 1963, pp. 349–367 and in *Numerische Mathematik,* Vol. 4, No. 5, Mar. 1963, pp. 420–452.

Nievergelt, J., "Binary search trees and file organizations," *Computing Surveys,* Vol. 6, No. 3, Sept. 1974, pp. 195–207.

Oettinger, A. G., "Automatic syntactic analysis and the pushdown store," *Proc. Symp. Applied Math,* 12, 1961, American Mathematical Society, Providence, Rhode Island.

Pager, D., "A solution to an open problem by Knuth," *Information and Control,* Vol. 17, No. 5, Dec. 1970, pp. 462–473.

Pager, D., "The lane tracing algorithm for constructing LR(k) parsers," *Conf. Rec. ACM Symposium on Theory of Computing,* Austin, Texas, May 1973, pp. 172–181.

Pair, C., "Trees, pushdown stores and compilation," *RFTI—Chiffres,* Vol. 7, No. 3, 1964, pp. 199–216.

Parikh, R. J., "On context-free languages," *JACM,* Vol. 13, No. 4, Oct. 1966, pp. 570–581.

Paull, M., "Bilateral descriptions of syntactic mappings," *First Annual Princeton Conference on Information Sciences and Systems,* 1967, pp. 76–81.

Paull, M. C., and S. H. Unger, "Structural equivalence of context-free grammars," *J. Computer and System Sciences,* Vol. 2, No. 4, Dec. 1968, pp. 427–468.

Peterson, W. W., "Addressing for random access storage," *IBM J. Res. Develop.,* Vol. 1, No. 2, Apr. 1957, pp. 130–146.

Petrone, L., "Syntactic mappings of context-free languages," *Proc. IFIP Congress,* 1965, Vol. 2, pp. 590–591.

Pollack, B. W. (ed.), *Compiler Techniques,* Philadelphia: Auerbach Publishers, 1972.

Price, C. E., "Table lookup techniques," *Computing Surveys,* Vol. 3, No. 2, June 1971, pp. 49–65.

Rabin, M., and D. Scott, "Finite automata and their decision problems," *IBM J. Res. Develop.,* Vol. 3, No. 2, Apr. 1959, pp. 114–125. Reprinted in Moore [1964].

Radke, C. E., "The use of quadratic residue research," *CACM,* Vol. 13, No. 2, Feb. 1970, pp. 103–105.

Randell, B., and L. J. Russell, *ALGOL 60 Implementation,* London: Academic Press, 1964.

Redziejowski, R. R., "On arithmetic expressions and trees," *CACM,* Vol. 12, No. 2, Feb. 1969, pp. 81–84.

Reynolds, J. C., "An introduction to the COGENT programming language," *Proc. 20th Natl. ACM Conf.,* 1965, New York, pp. 422–436.

Rosen, S., (ed.), *Programming Systems and Languages,* New York: McGraw-Hill, 1967.

Rosen, S., "A compiler-building system developed by Brooker and Morris," *CACM,* Vol. 7, No. 7, July 1964, pp. 403–414. Reprinted in Rosen [1967] and in Pollack [1972].

Rosenkrantz, D. J., "Matrix equations and normal forms for context-free grammars," *JACM,* Vol. 14, No. 3, July 1967, pp. 501–507.

Rosenkrantz, D. J., "Programmed grammars and classes of formal languages," *JACM,* Vol. 16, No. 1, Jan. 1969, pp. 107–131.

Rosenkrantz, D. J., and P. M. Lewis, II, "Deterministic left corner parsing," *IEEE Conf. Record of 1970 Eleventh Annual Symposium Switching and Automata Theory,* pp. 139–152.

Rosenkrantz, D. J., and R. E. Stearns, "Properties of deterministic top-down grammars," *Information and Control,* Vol. 17, No. 3, Oct. 1970, pp. 226–256.

Ross, D. T., "On context and ambiguity in parsing," *CACM,* Vol. 7, No. 2, Feb. 1964, pp. 131–133.

Ross, D. T., and J. E. Rodriguez, "Theoretical foundations of the computer aided design system," *Proc. AFIPS 1963 Spring Joint Computer Conf.,* Vol. 23, Baltimore, Md.: Spartan Books, pp. 305–322.

Salomaa, A., *Theory of Automata,* Elmsford, N.Y.: Pergamon, 1969.

Schaefer, M., *A Mathematical Theory of Global Program Optimization,* Englewood Cliffs, N.J.: Prentice-Hall, 1973.

Schay, G., and W. G. Spruth, "Analysis of a file addressing method," *CACM,* Vol. 4, No. 5, May 1961, pp. 218–222.

Schkolnick, M., "The equivalence of reducing transition languages and deterministic languages," *CACM,* Vol. 17, No. 9, Sept. 1974, pp. 517–519.

Schneider, F. W., and G. D. Johnson, "META-3; a syntax directed compiler writing compiler to generate efficient code," *Proc. 19th National ACM Conf.,* 1964, New York.

Schneider, V., "Syntax-checking and parsing of context-free languages by push-down-store automata," *Proc. AFIPS 1967 Spring Joint Computer Conf.,* Vol. 30, Washington, D.C.: Thompson Books, pp. 685–690.

Schneider, V., "A system for designing fast programming language translators," *Proc. AFIPS 1969 Spring Joint Computer Conf.,* Vol. 34, Montvale, N.J.: AFIPS Press, pp. 777–792.

Schorre, D. V., "META-II: a syntax-oriented compiler writing language," *Proc. 19th Natl. ACM Conf.,* 1964, New York.

Schützenberger, M. P., "On context-free languages and pushdown automata," *Information and Control,* Vol. 6, No. 3, Sept. 1963, pp. 246–264.

Scidmore, A. K., and B. L. Weinberg, "Storage and search properties of a tree-organized memory system," *CACM,* Vol. 6, No. 1, Jan. 1963, pp. 28–31.

Sethi, R., and J. D. Ullman, "The generation of optimal code for arithmetic expressions," *JACM,* Vol. 17, No. 4, Oct. 1970, pp. 715–728. Reprinted in Pollack [1972].

Severance, D. G., "Identifier search: a survey and generalized model," *Computing Surveys,* Vol. 6, No. 3, Sept. 1974, pp. 175–194.

Simpson, H. R., "A compact form of one-track syntax analyzer," *Computer J.,* Vol. 12, No. 1, Aug. 1969, pp. 233–243.

Stearns, R. E., "A regularity test for pushdown machines," *Information and Control,* Vol. 11, No. 3, Sept. 1967, pp. 323–340.

Stearns, R. E., "Deterministic top-down parsing," *Proc. Fifth Annual Princeton Conf. on Information Sciences and Systems,* 1971, pp. 182–188.

Stearns, R. E., and P. M. Lewis, II, "Property grammars and table machines," *Information and Control,* Vol. 14, No. 6, June 1969, pp. 524–549.

Sussenguth, E. H., Jr., "Use of tree structures for processing files," *CACM,* Vol. 6, No. 5, May 1963, pp. 272–279.

Tainiter, M., "Addressing for random-access storage with multiple bucket capacities," *JACM,* Vol. 10, No. 3, July 1963, pp. 307–315.

Terrine, G., "Coordinate grammars and parsers," *Computer J.,* Vol. 16, No. 3, Aug. 1973, pp. 232–244.

Thompson, K., "Regular expression search algorithm," *CACM,* Vol. 11, No. 6, June 1968, pp. 419–422.

Ullman, J. D., "A note on hashing functions," *JACM,* Vol. 19, No. 3, July 1972, pp. 569–575.

Unger, S. H., "A global parser for context-free phrase structure grammars," *CACM,* Vol. 11, No. 4, Apr. 1968, pp. 240–247.

Vere, S., "Translation equation," *CACM,* Vol. 13, No. 2, Feb. 1970, pp. 83–89.

Warshall, S., "A theorem on Boolean matrices," *JACM,* Vol. 9, No. 1, Jan. 1962, pp. 11–12.

Warshall, S., and R. M. Shapiro, "A general purpose table-driven compiler," *Proc. AFIPS 1964 Spring Joint Computer Conf.,* Vol. 25, Baltimore, Md.: Spartan Books, pp. 59–65. Reprinted in Rosen [1967].

Wegner, P., *Programming Languages, Information Structures and Machine Organization,* New York: McGraw-Hill, 1968.

Weingarten, F. W., *Translation of Computer Languages,* San Francisco, Calif.: Holden-Day, 1973.

Wirth, N., "PL360, a programming language for the 360 computers," *JACM,* Vol. 15, No. 1, Jan. 1968, pp. 37–74.

Wirth, N., and H. Weber, "EULER: a generalization of ALGOL, and its formal definition: Part I," *CACM,* Vol. 9, No. 1, Jan. 1966, pp. 13–23.

Wise, D. S., "Generalized overlap resolvable grammars and their parsers," *J. Computer and System Sciences,* Vol. 6, No. 6, Dec. 1972, pp. 538–572.

Wood, D. [1969a], "A note on top-down deterministic languages," *BIT,* Vol. 9, No. 4, 1969, pp. 387–399.

Wood, D. [1969b], "The theory of left factored languages: Part I," *Computer J.,* Vol. 12, No. 4, Nov. 1969, pp. 349–356.

Wood, D. [1969c], "The normal form theorem—another proof," *Computer J.,* Vol. 12, No. 2, May 1969, pp. 139–147.

Younger, D. H., "Recognition and parsing of context-free languages in time n^3," *Information and Control,* Vol. 10, No. 2, Feb. 1967, pp. 189–208.

ABOUT THE AUTHORS

Philip M. Lewis II, Daniel J. Rosenkrantz, and Richard E. Stearns are members of the Mathematics and Software Design Program at the General Electric Corporate Research and Development Center in Schenectady, New York.

Since 1966 they have been doing joint research in automata theory, formal languages, and computational complexity as they relate to compiler design theory. This research has led to ten technical papers. During this time they also designed an ALGOL compiler and the lexical and syntax portions of a FORTRAN compiler. The ALGOL compiler is now offered as one of the services on the General Electric commercial time-sharing system and the FORTRAN compiler is now the standard FORTRAN compiler on the Honeywell 6000.

Philip M. Lewis II received his B.S. from the Rensselaer Polytechnic Institute in 1952 and his S.M. and Sc.D. from the Massachusetts Institute of Technology in 1954 and 1956, respectively.

Dr. Lewis is currently the Manager of the Mathematics and Software Design Program at GE and Adjunct Professor at Rensselaer Polytechnic Institute and State University of New York at Albany. He joined GE in

1959 after three years on the faculty at MIT. While at GE he has done research in such areas as pattern recognition, threshold logic, and the theory of algorithms, in addition to the areas cited earlier. Dr. Lewis has published about twenty-five papers. He is coauthor with C. L. Coates of the book *Threshold Logic* published by John Wiley in 1967.

He has served as Managing Editor of the SIAM Journal on Computing and Chairman of the I.E.E.E. Computer Society Technical Committee on Mathematical Foundations of Computing. He is a member of the Association for Computing Machinery, the I.E.E.E. Computer Society, Sigma Xi, Tau Beta Pi, and Eta Kappa Nu.

Daniel J. Rosenkrantz received his B.S., M.S., and Ph.D. from Columbia University in 1963, 1964, and 1967, respectively.

Dr. Rosenkrantz is currently an information scientist at General Electric and an adjunct faculty member at the State University of New York at Albany. He joined General Electric in Schenectady in 1967, after a year at Bell Telephone Laboratories in Murray Hill, New Jersey. In addition to the research cited above, he has done research in computational complexity, the theory of algorithms, software engineering, and database systems. Dr. Rosenkrantz has published about a dozen papers.

He has served on the program committees of several technical symposia, and done refereeing and reviewing. He is a member of the Association for Computing Machinery, Sigma Xi, Tau Beta Pi, and Eta Kappa Nu.

Richard E. Stearns received his B.S. from Carleton College in 1958 and his Ph.D. in Mathematics from Princeton University in 1961.

Dr. Stearns has been working as a research mathematician at General Electric in Schenectady since 1961. In the spring of 1975, he was visiting professor at the Hebrew University in Jerusalem. In 1970, he taught a compiler course at Union College in Schenectady, N.Y. In addition to the research cited above, he has done research on the structure of sequential machines, computational complexity, the theory of games, and the theory of algorithms.

Dr. Stearns has published about twenty-five papers. He is coauthor with Juris Hartmanis of the book *Algebraic Structure Theory of Sequential Machines* published by Prentice-Hall in 1966.

Dr. Stearns serves as an editor of the SIAM Journal on Computing and a reviewer for Mathematical Reviews. From 1973 to 1975, he was on the executive committee for the ACM special-interest group on Automata and Computing Theory. Dr. Stearns is a member of the Association for Computing Machinery, the American Mathematical Society, and the Mathematical Association of America.

Index

DATE DUE

MAY 3 1995			
GAYLORD			PRINTED IN U.S.A.